TABLE OF CONTENTS

CHAPTER 145: WAR IN THE BALTIC (21)   5

CHAPTER 146: WAR IN THE BALTIC (22)   31

CHAPTER 147: WAR IN THE BALTIC (23)   49

CHAPTER 148: WAR IN THE BALTIC (24)   71

CHAPTER 149: WAR IN THE BALTIC (25)   97

CHAPTER 150: WAR IN THE BALTIC (26)   123

CHAPTER 151: WAR IN THE BALTIC (27)   151

CHAPTER 152: WAR IN THE BALTIC (28)   171

CHAPTER 153: WAR IN THE BALTIC (29)   197

CHAPTER 154: WAR IN THE BALTIC (30)   219

CHAPTER 155: WAR IN THE BALTIC (31)   231

CHAPTER 156: WAR IN THE BALTIC (32)   257

CHAPTER 157: WAR IN THE BALTIC (33)   283

CHAPTER 158: WAR IN THE BALTIC (34)   305

CHAPTER 159: WAR IN THE BALTIC (35)   327

CHAPTER 160: WAR IN THE BALTIC (36)   357

TRANSLATION NOTES   385

BONUS ANIME ART   386

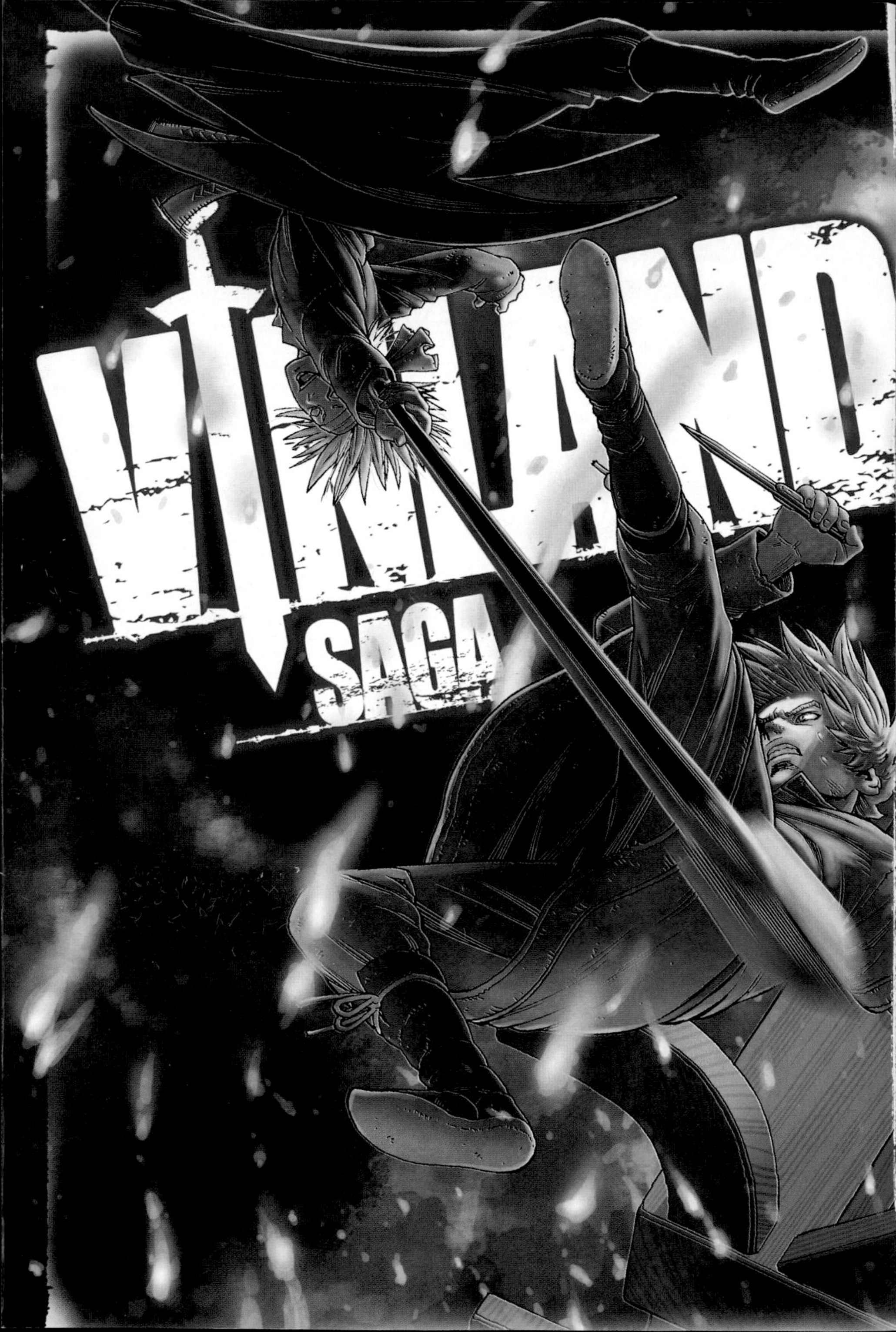
VINLAND
SAGA

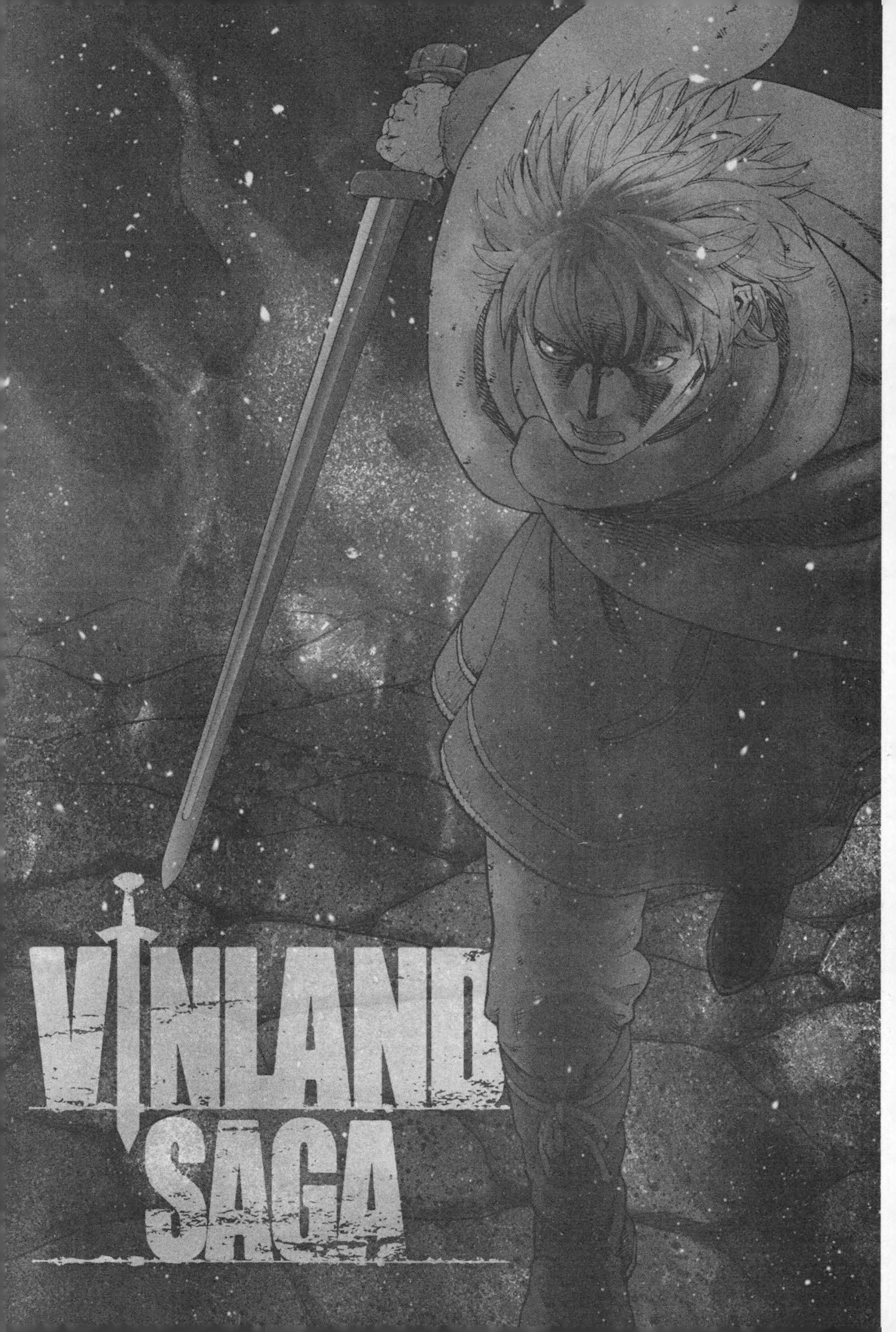
VINLAND
SAGA

CHAPTER 145: WAR IN THE BALTIC (21)

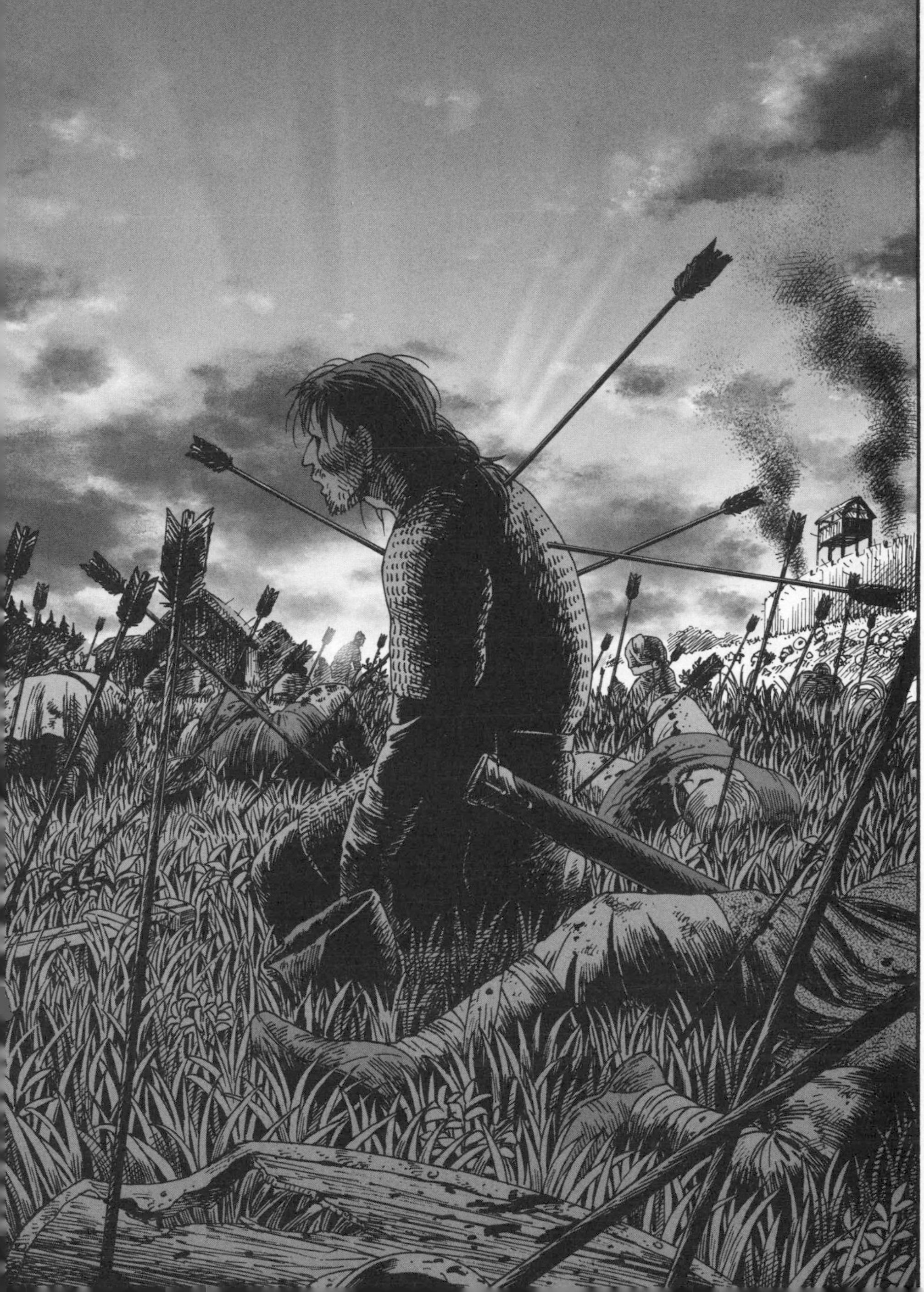

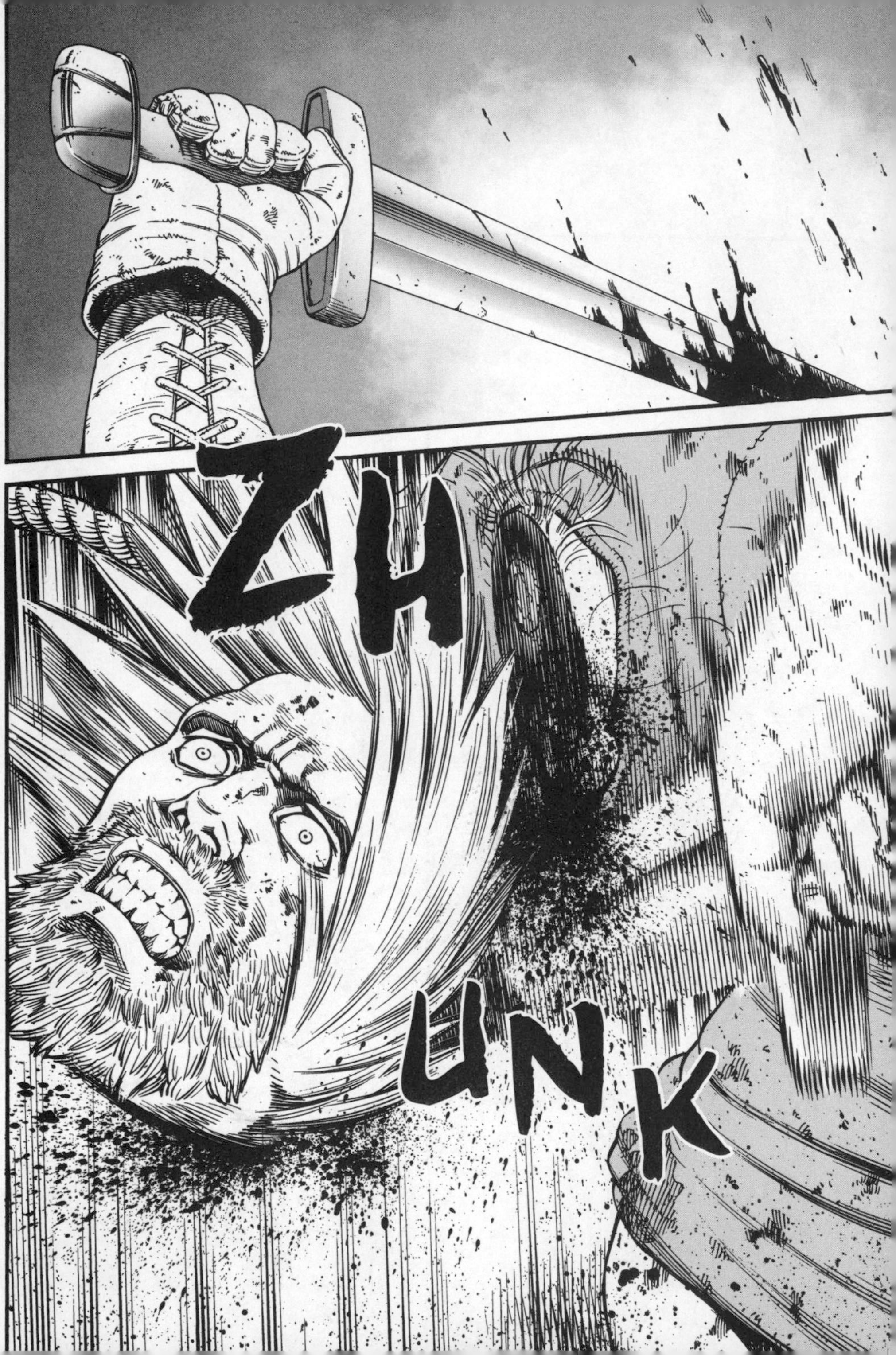
ZHUNK

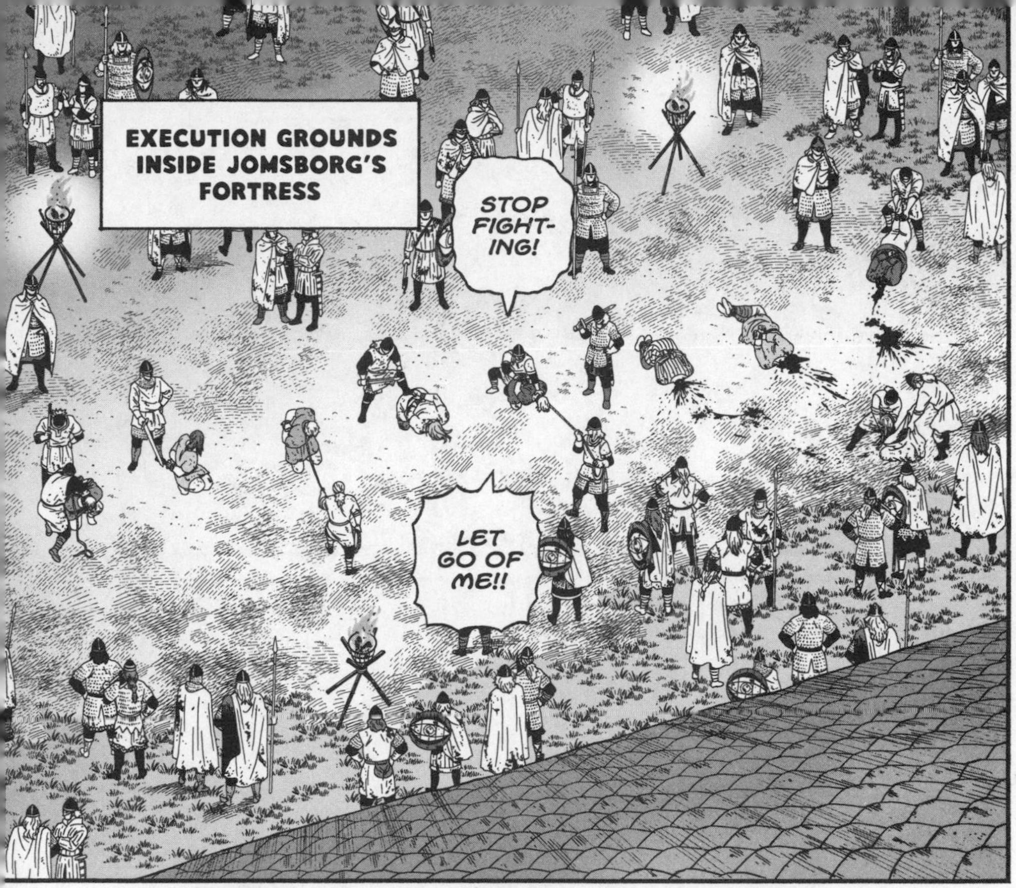
EXECUTION GROUNDS INSIDE JOMSBORG'S FORTRESS
STOP FIGHT-ING!
LET GO OF ME!!

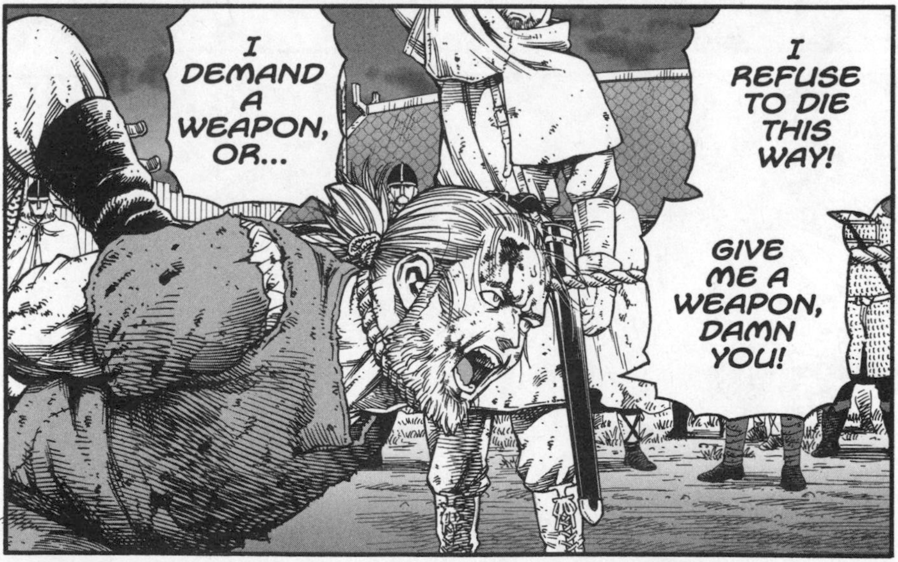
I DEMAND A WEAPON, OR...
I REFUSE TO DIE THIS WAY!
GIVE ME A WEAPON, DAMN YOU!

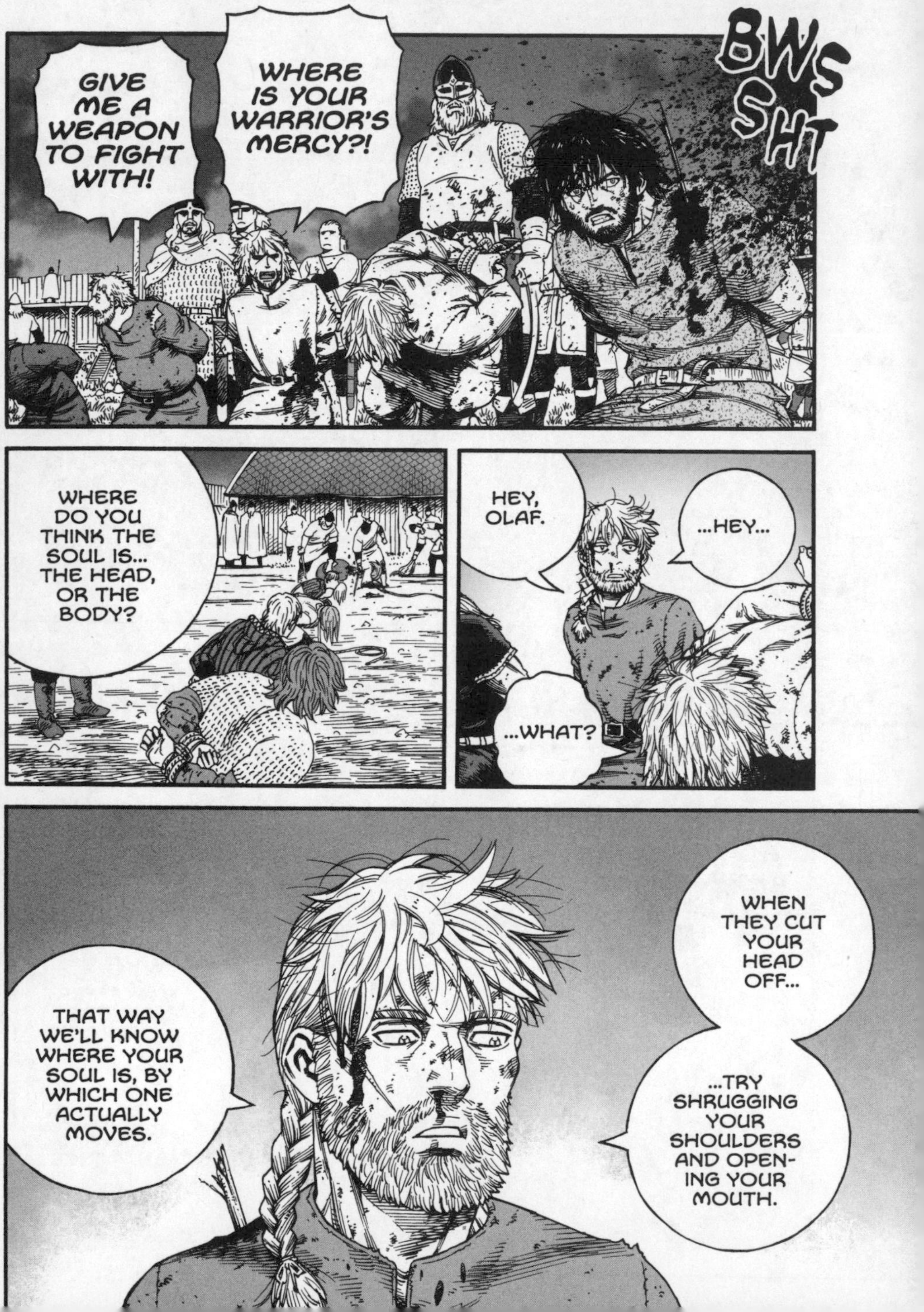
BWS SHT
WHERE IS YOUR WARRIOR'S MERCY?!
GIVE ME A WEAPON TO FIGHT WITH!
HEY, OLAF.
...HEY...
...WHAT?
WHERE DO YOU THINK THE SOUL IS... THE HEAD, OR THE BODY?
WHEN THEY CUT YOUR HEAD OFF...
...TRY SHRUGGING YOUR SHOULDERS AND OPEN-ING YOUR MOUTH.
THAT WAY WE'LL KNOW WHERE YOUR SOUL IS, BY WHICH ONE ACTUALLY MOVES.

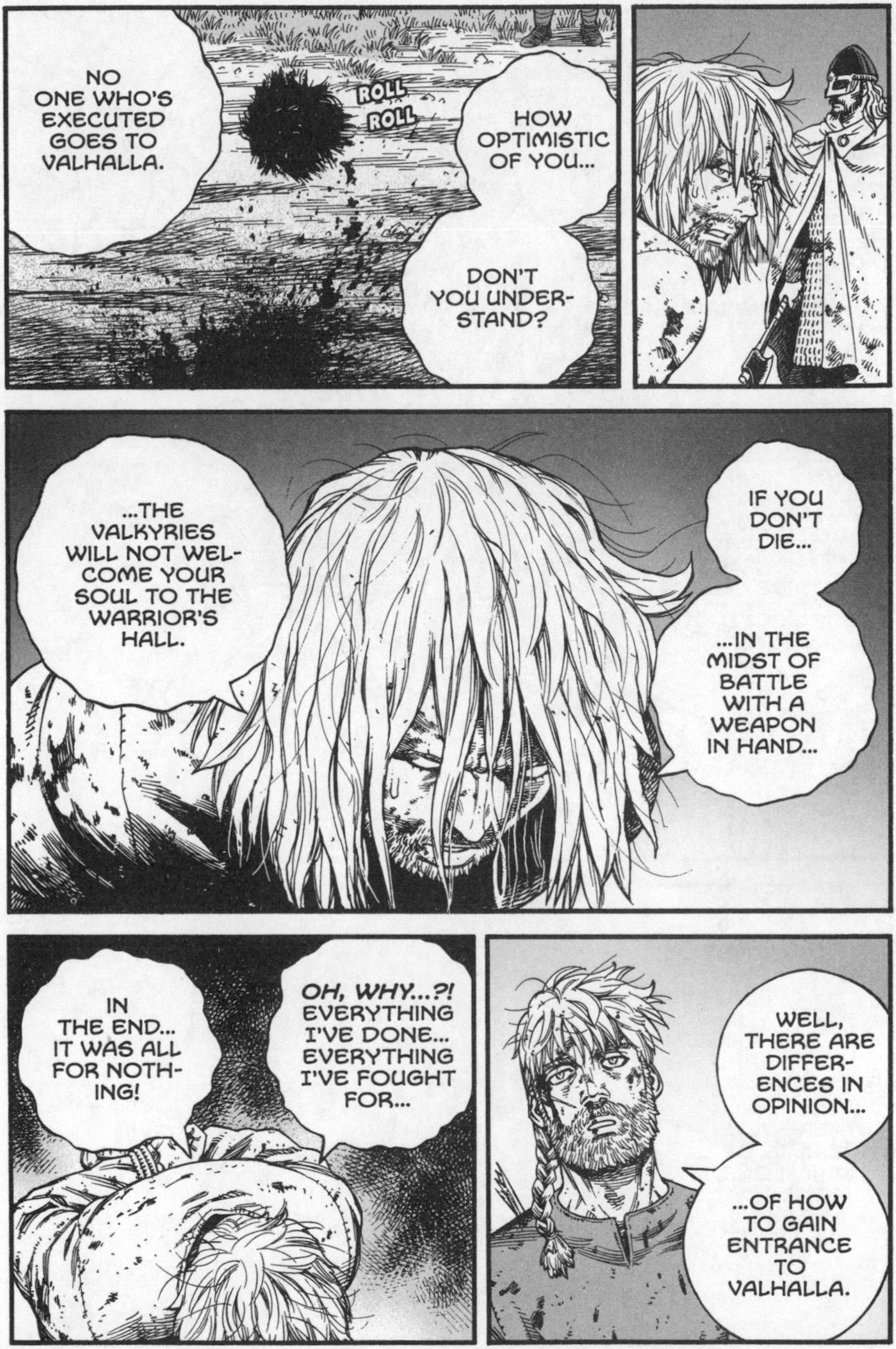
HOW OPTIMISTIC OF YOU...
DON'T YOU UNDERSTAND?
ROLL
ROLL
NO ONE WHO'S EXECUTED GOES TO VALHALLA.
IF YOU DON'T DIE...
...IN THE MIDST OF BATTLE WITH A WEAPON IN HAND...
...THE VALKYRIES WILL NOT WELCOME YOUR SOUL TO THE WARRIOR'S HALL.
WELL, THERE ARE DIFFERENCES IN OPINION...
...OF HOW TO GAIN ENTRANCE TO VALHALLA.
OH, WHY...?! EVERYTHING I'VE DONE... EVERYTHING I'VE FOUGHT FOR...
IN THE END... IT WAS ALL FOR NOTHING!

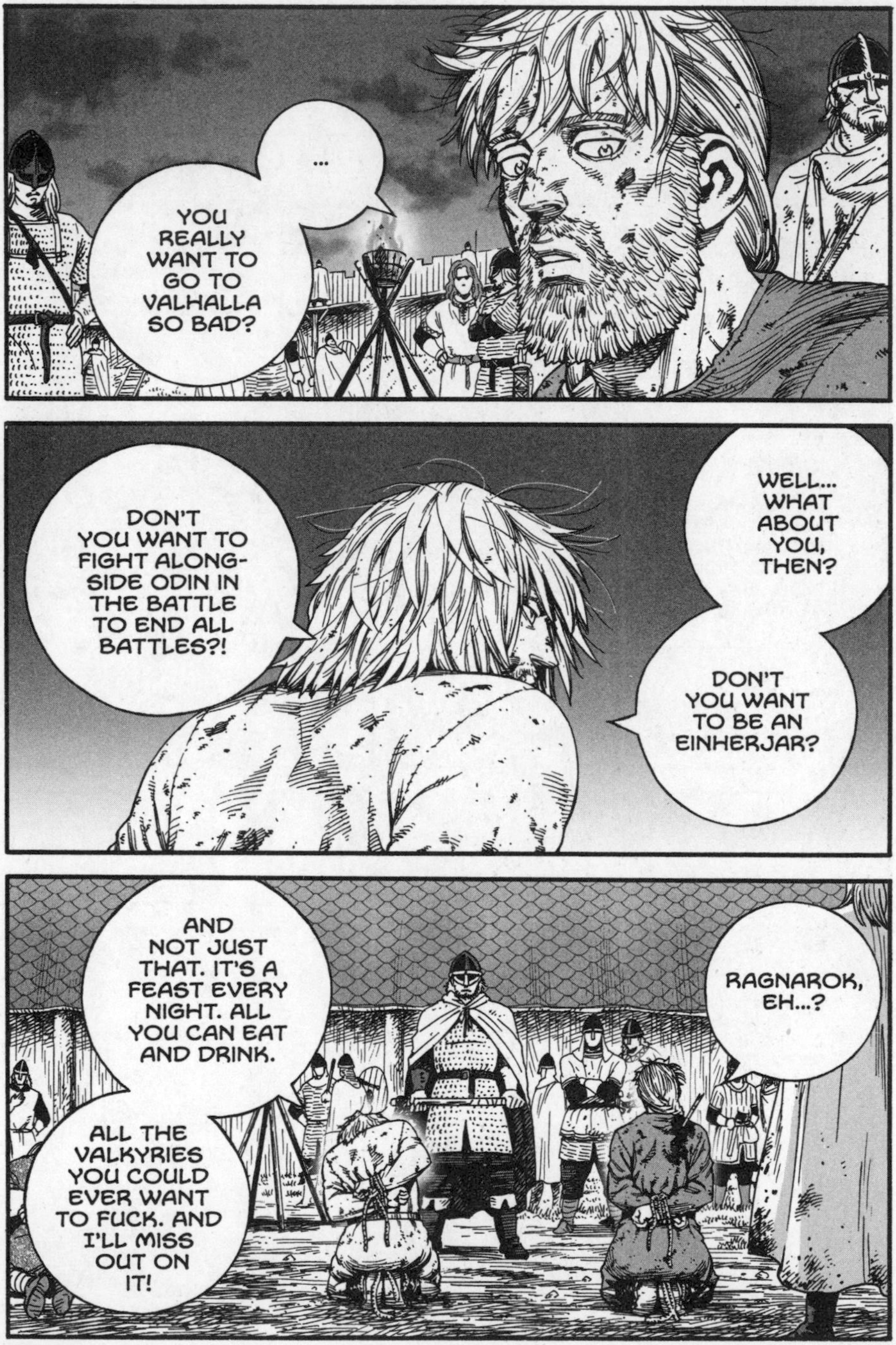
...
YOU REALLY WANT TO GO TO VALHALLA SO BAD?
WELL... WHAT ABOUT YOU, THEN?
DON'T YOU WANT TO BE AN EINHERJAR?
DON'T YOU WANT TO FIGHT ALONG-SIDE ODIN IN THE BATTLE TO END ALL BATTLES?!
RAGNAROK, EH...?
AND NOT JUST THAT. IT'S A FEAST EVERY NIGHT. ALL YOU CAN EAT AND DRINK.
ALL THE VALKYRIES YOU COULD EVER WANT TO FUCK. AND I'LL MISS OUT ON IT!

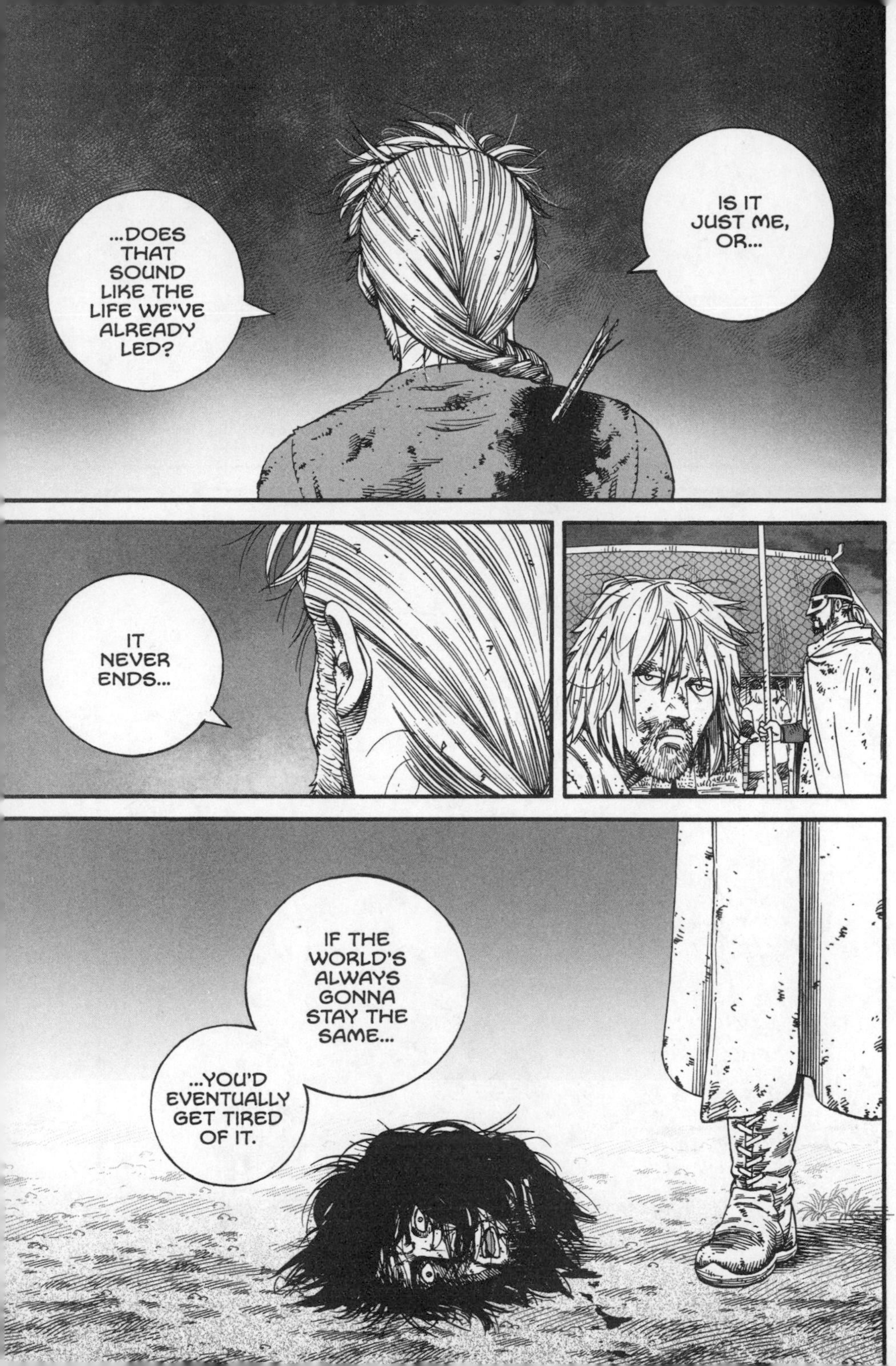
IS IT JUST ME, OR...
...DOES THAT SOUND LIKE THE LIFE WE'VE ALREADY LED?
IT NEVER ENDS...
IF THE WORLD'S ALWAYS GONNA STAY THE SAME...
...YOU'D EVENTUALLY GET TIRED OF IT.

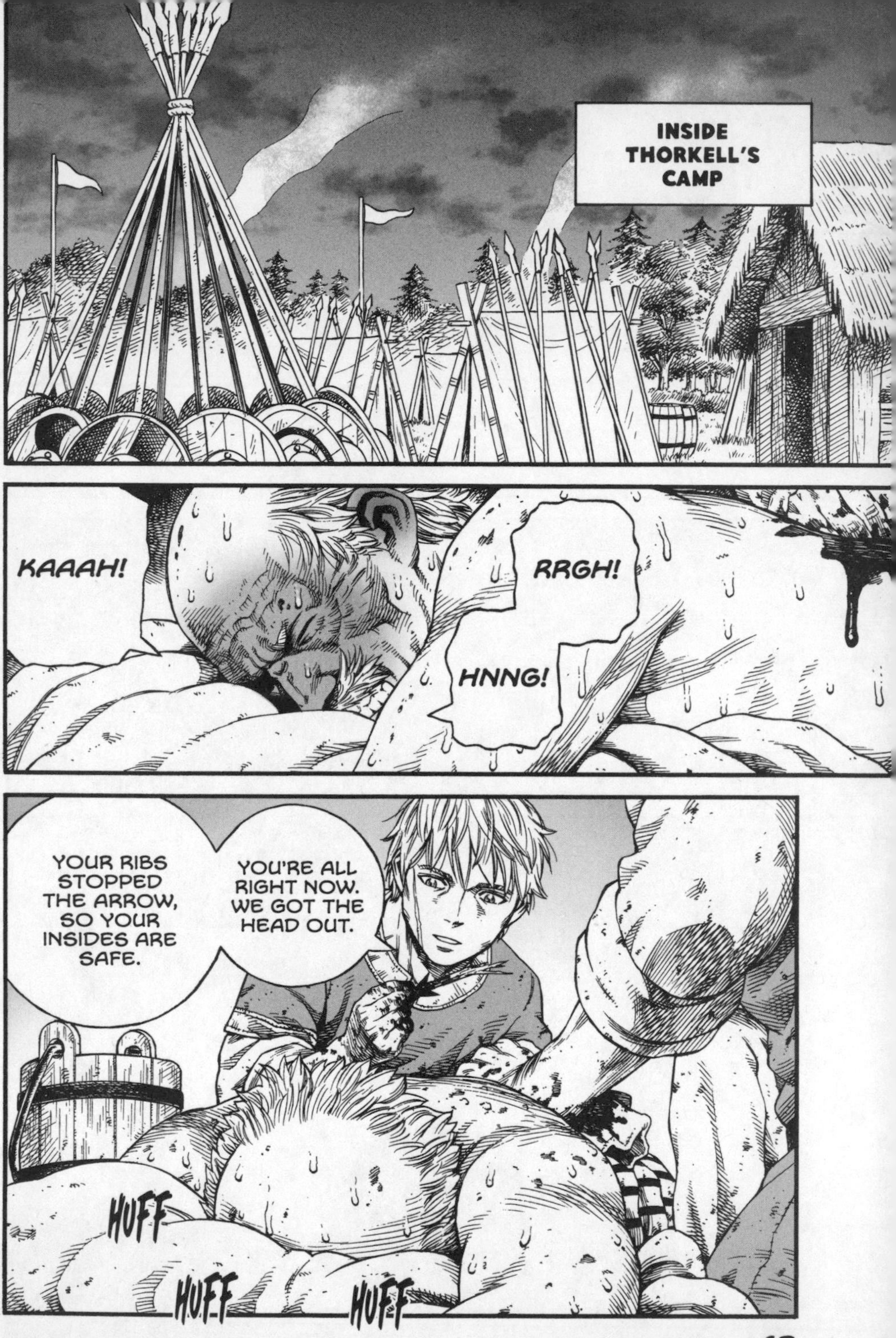
INSIDE THORKELL'S CAMP
RRGH!
HNNG!
KAAAH!
YOU'RE ALL RIGHT NOW. WE GOT THE HEAD OUT.
YOUR RIBS STOPPED THE ARROW, SO YOUR INSIDES ARE SAFE.
HUFF
HUFF
HUFF

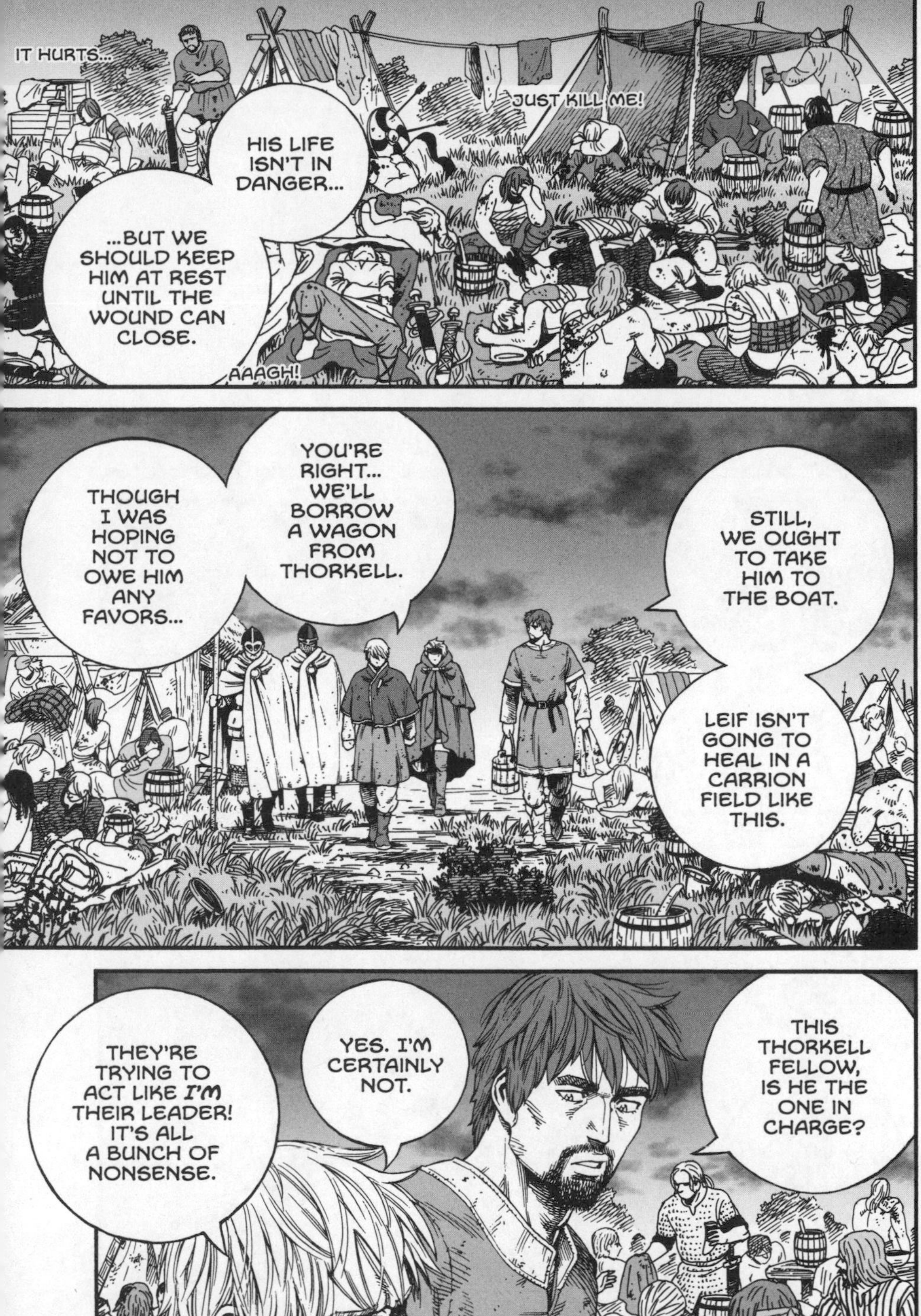
JUST KILL ME!
HIS LIFE ISN'T IN DANGER...
IT HURTS...
...BUT WE SHOULD KEEP HIM AT REST UNTIL THE WOUND CAN CLOSE.
AAAGH!
STILL, WE OUGHT TO TAKE HIM TO THE BOAT.
LEIF ISN'T GOING TO HEAL IN A CARRION FIELD LIKE THIS.
YOU'RE RIGHT... WE'LL BORROW A WAGON FROM THORKELL.
THOUGH I WAS HOPING NOT TO OWE HIM ANY FAVORS...
THIS THORKELL FELLOW, IS HE THE ONE IN CHARGE?
YES. I'M CERTAINLY NOT.
THEY'RE TRYING TO ACT LIKE *I'M* THEIR LEADER! IT'S ALL A BUNCH OF NONSENSE.

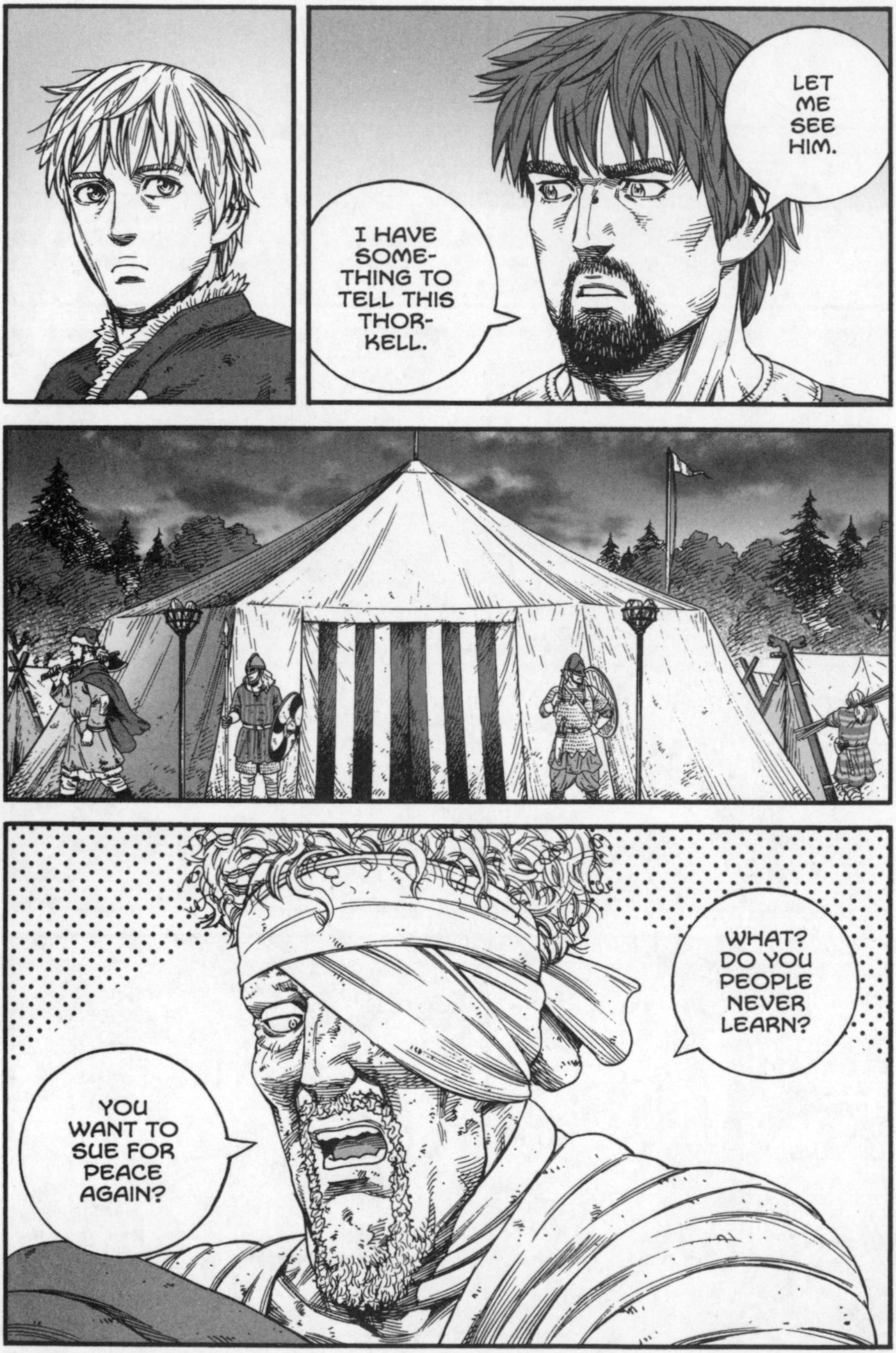
LET ME SEE HIM.
I HAVE SOME-THING TO TELL THIS THOR-KELL.
WHAT? DO YOU PEOPLE NEVER LEARN?
YOU WANT TO SUE FOR PEACE AGAIN?

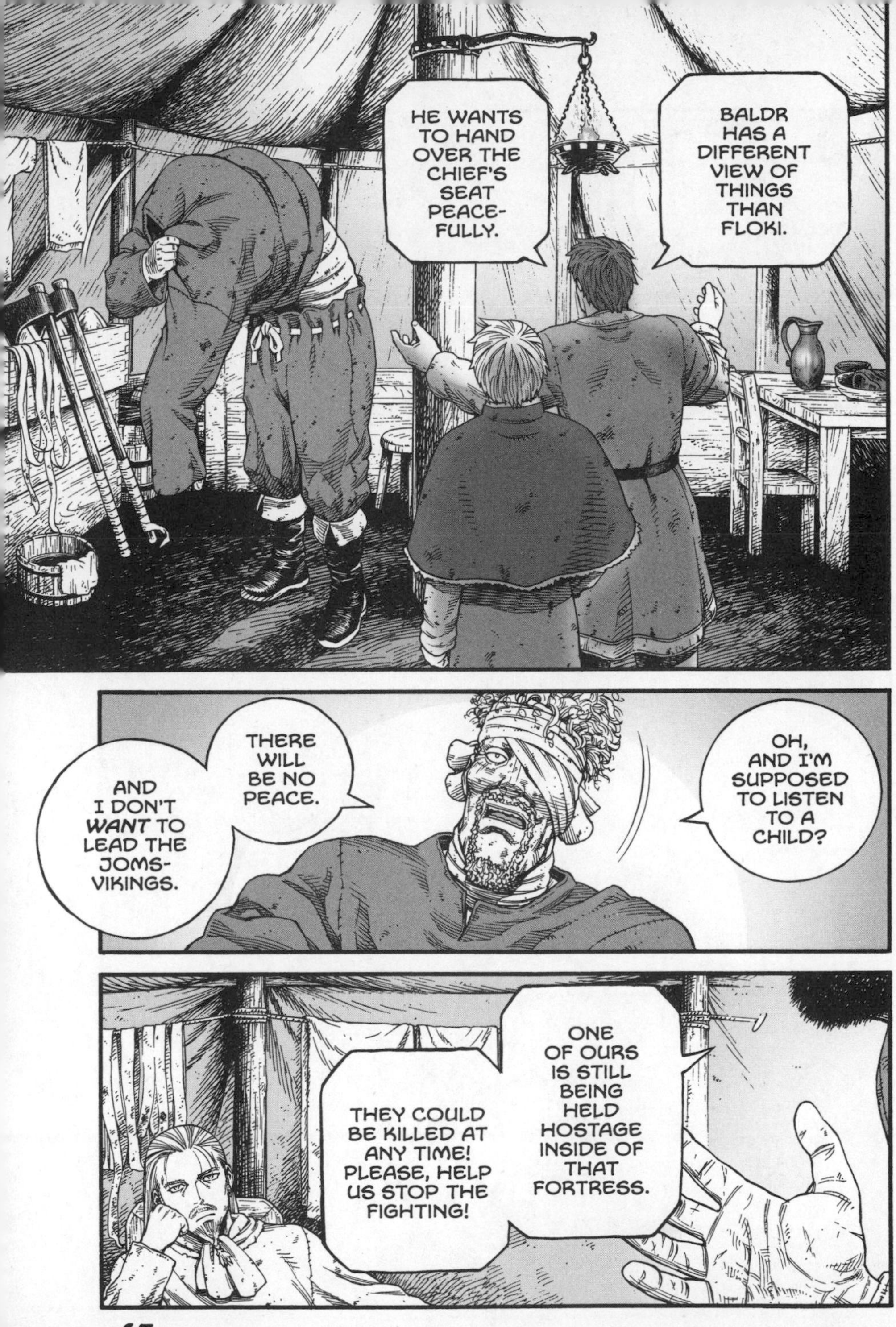
BALDR HAS A DIFFERENT VIEW OF THINGS THAN FLOKI.
HE WANTS TO HAND OVER THE CHIEF'S SEAT PEACE-FULLY.
OH, AND I'M SUPPOSED TO LISTEN TO A CHILD?
THERE WILL BE NO PEACE.
AND I DON'T *WANT* TO LEAD THE JOMS-VIKINGS.
ONE OF OURS IS STILL BEING HELD HOSTAGE INSIDE OF THAT FORTRESS.
THEY COULD BE KILLED AT ANY TIME! PLEASE, HELP US STOP THE FIGHTING!

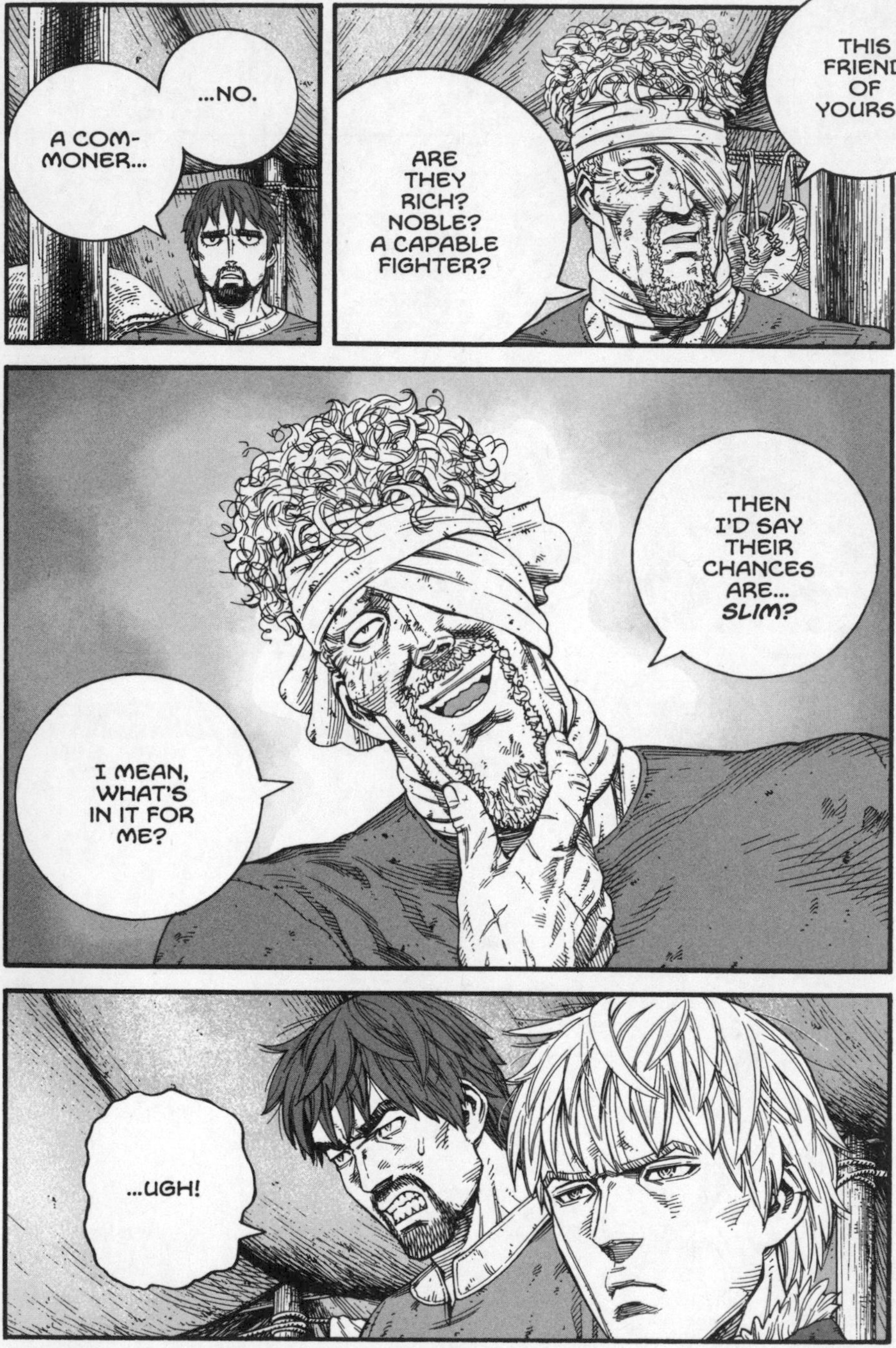
THIS FRIEND OF YOURS...
ARE THEY RICH? NOBLE? A CAPABLE FIGHTER?
...NO.
A COM-MONER...
THEN I'D SAY THEIR CHANCES ARE... *SLIM?*
I MEAN, WHAT'S IN IT FOR ME?
...UGH!

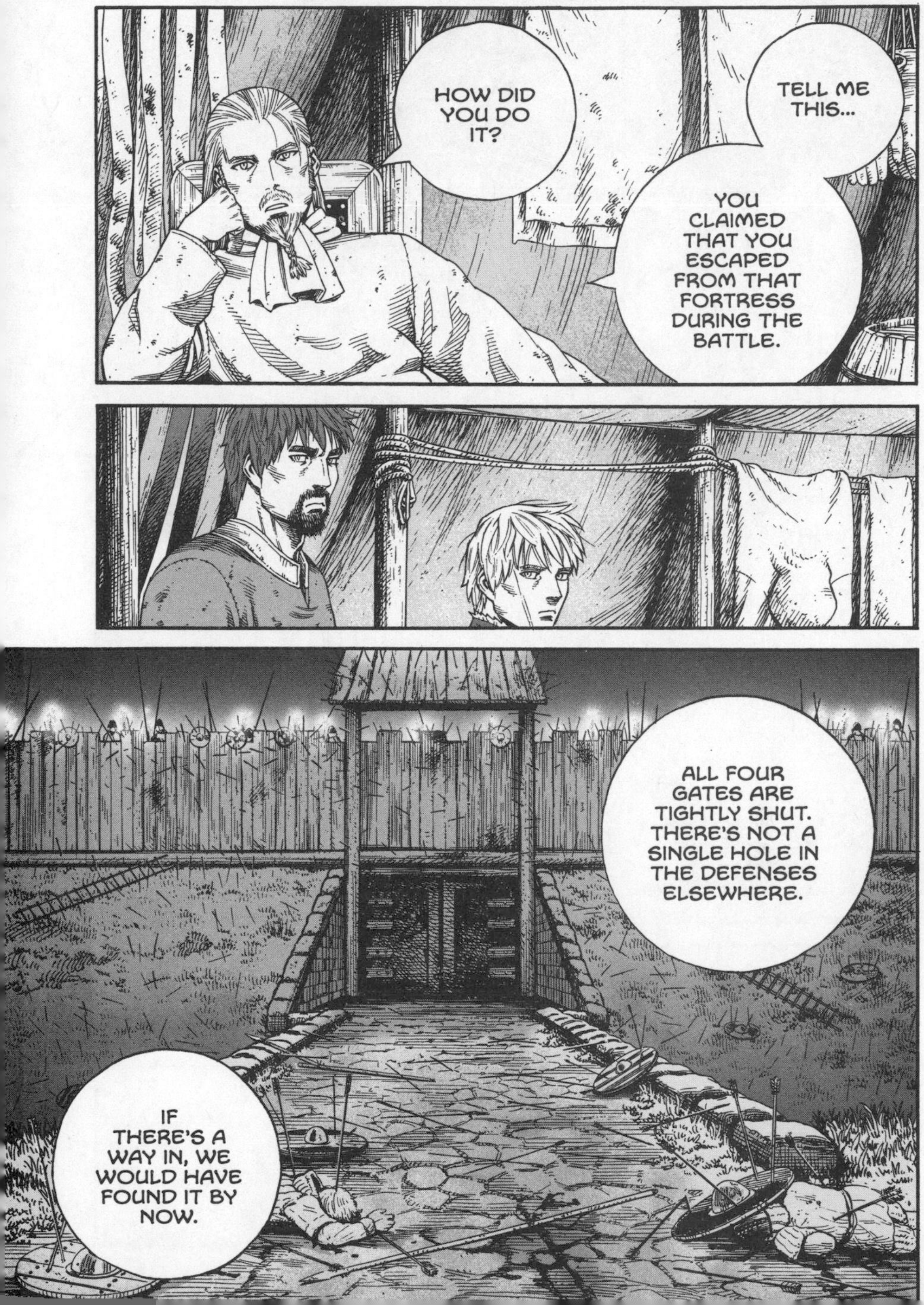
TELL ME THIS...
YOU CLAIMED THAT YOU ESCAPED FROM THAT FORTRESS DURING THE BATTLE.
HOW DID YOU DO IT?
ALL FOUR GATES ARE TIGHTLY SHUT. THERE'S NOT A SINGLE HOLE IN THE DEFENSES ELSEWHERE.
IF THERE'S A WAY IN, WE WOULD HAVE FOUND IT BY NOW.

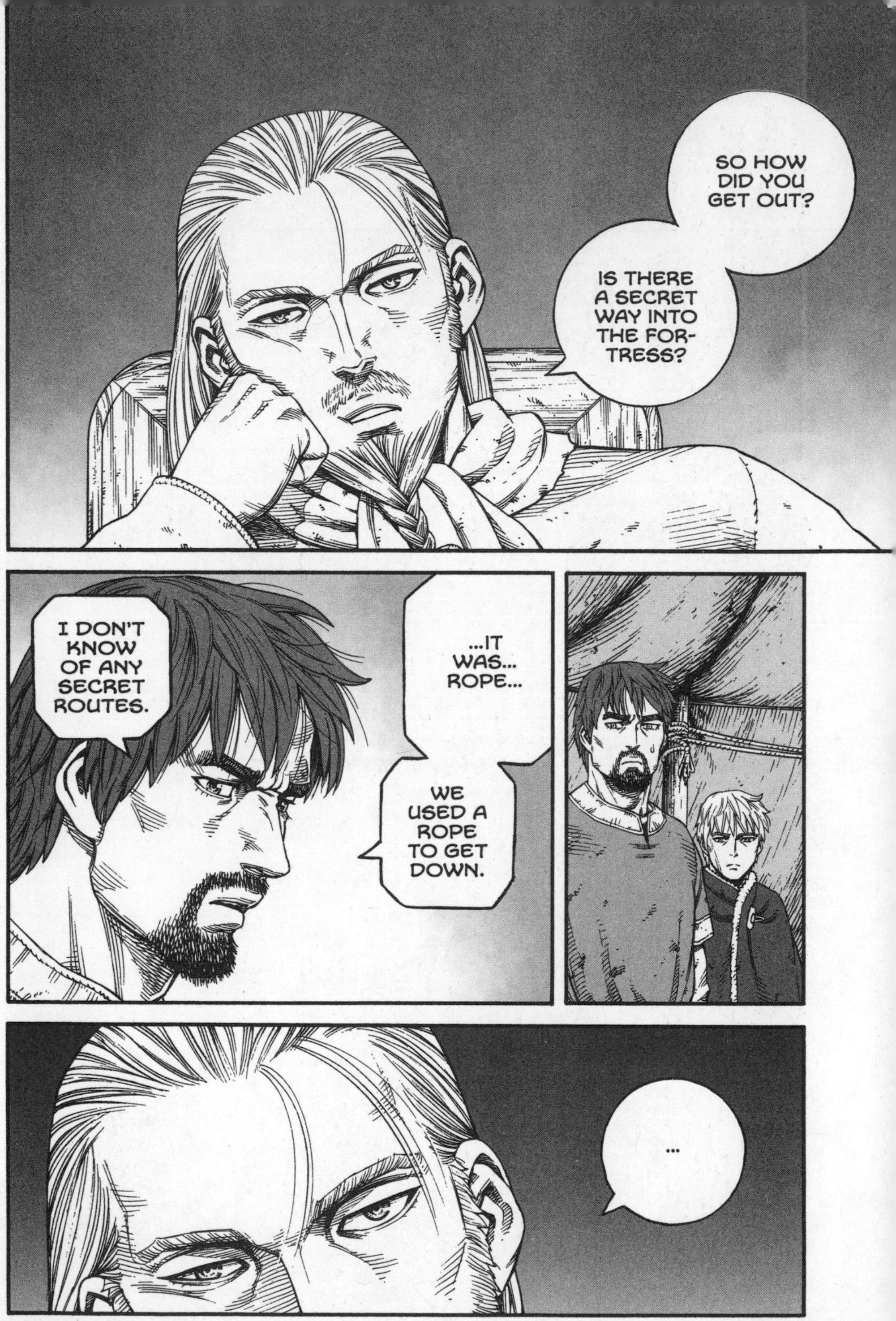
SO HOW DID YOU GET OUT?
IS THERE A SECRET WAY INTO THE FOR-TRESS?
I DON'T KNOW OF ANY SECRET ROUTES.
...IT WAS... ROPE...
WE USED A ROPE TO GET DOWN.
...

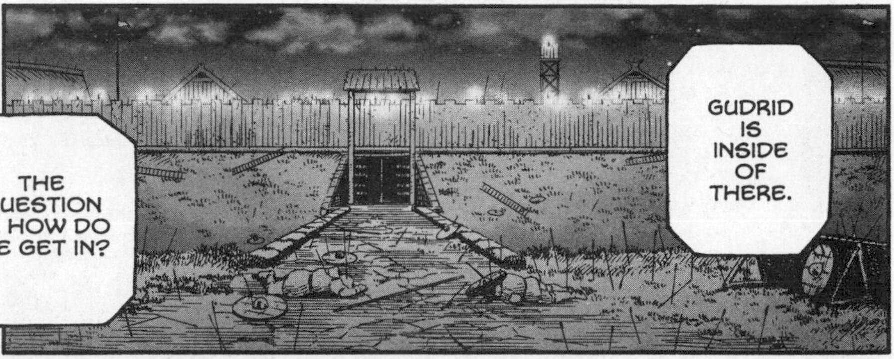
GUDRID IS INSIDE OF THERE.
THE QUESTION IS, HOW DO WE GET IN?

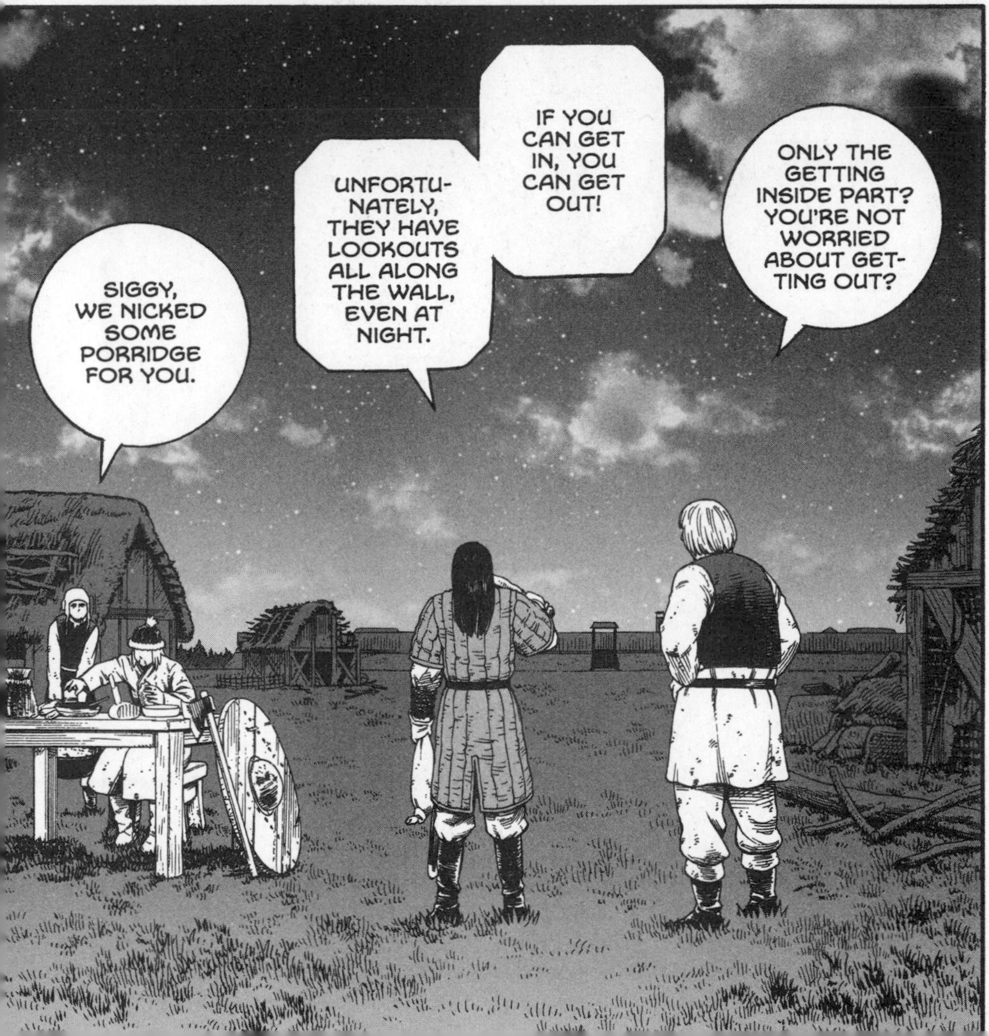
ONLY THE GETTING INSIDE PART? YOU'RE NOT WORRIED ABOUT GET-TING OUT?
IF YOU CAN GET IN, YOU CAN GET OUT!
UNFORTU-NATELY, THEY HAVE LOOKOUTS ALL ALONG THE WALL, EVEN AT NIGHT.
SIGGY, WE NICKED SOME PORRIDGE FOR YOU.

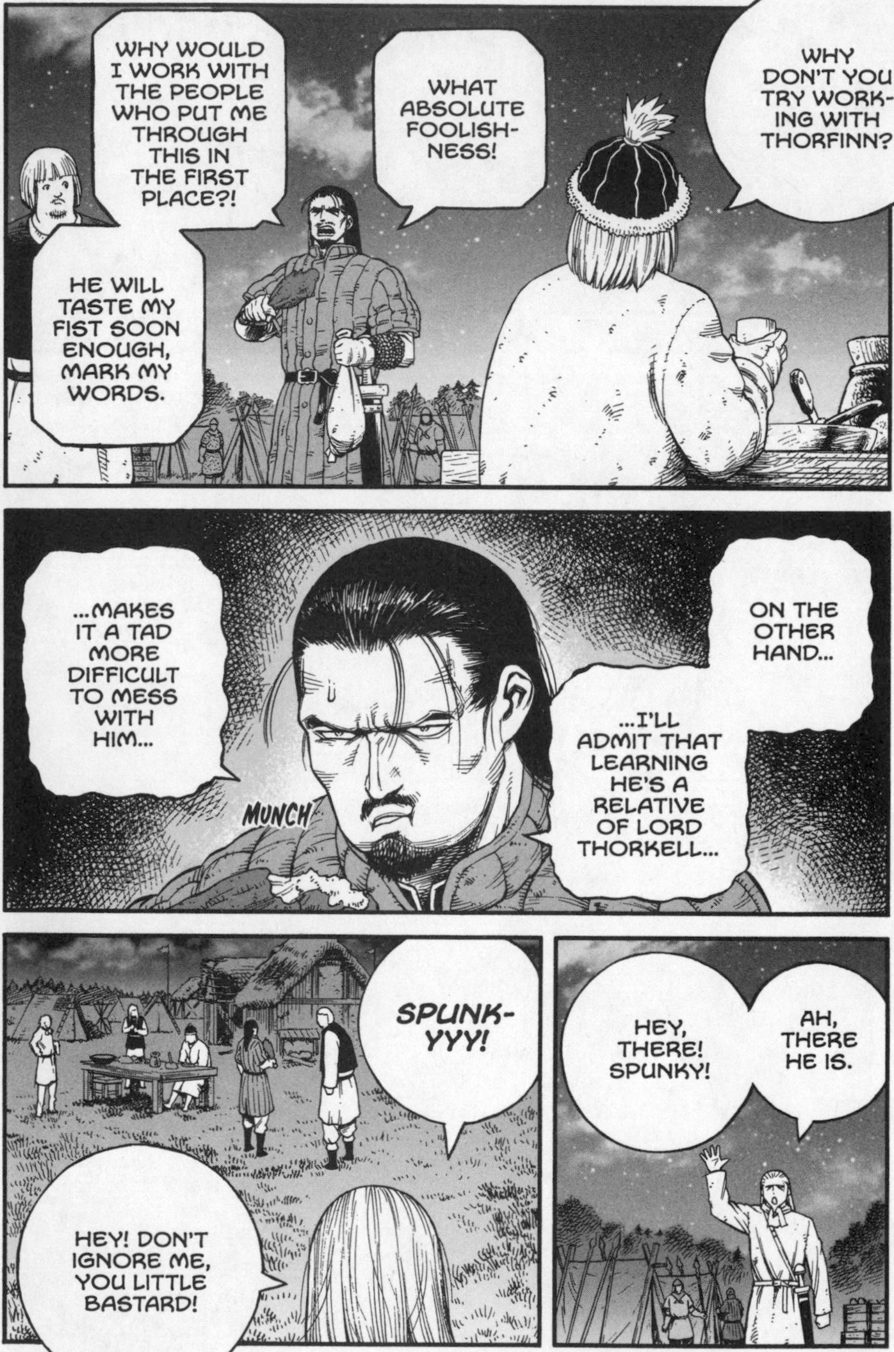
WHY DON'T YOU TRY WORK-ING WITH THORFINN?
WHAT ABSOLUTE FOOLISH-NESS!
WHY WOULD I WORK WITH THE PEOPLE WHO PUT ME THROUGH THIS IN THE FIRST PLACE?!
HE WILL TASTE MY FIST SOON ENOUGH, MARK MY WORDS.
ON THE OTHER HAND...
...I'LL ADMIT THAT LEARNING HE'S A RELATIVE OF LORD THORKELL...
MUNCH
...MAKES IT A TAD MORE DIFFICULT TO MESS WITH HIM...
AH, THERE HE IS.
HEY, THERE! SPUNKY!
SPUNK-YYY!
HEY! DON'T IGNORE ME, YOU LITTLE BASTARD!

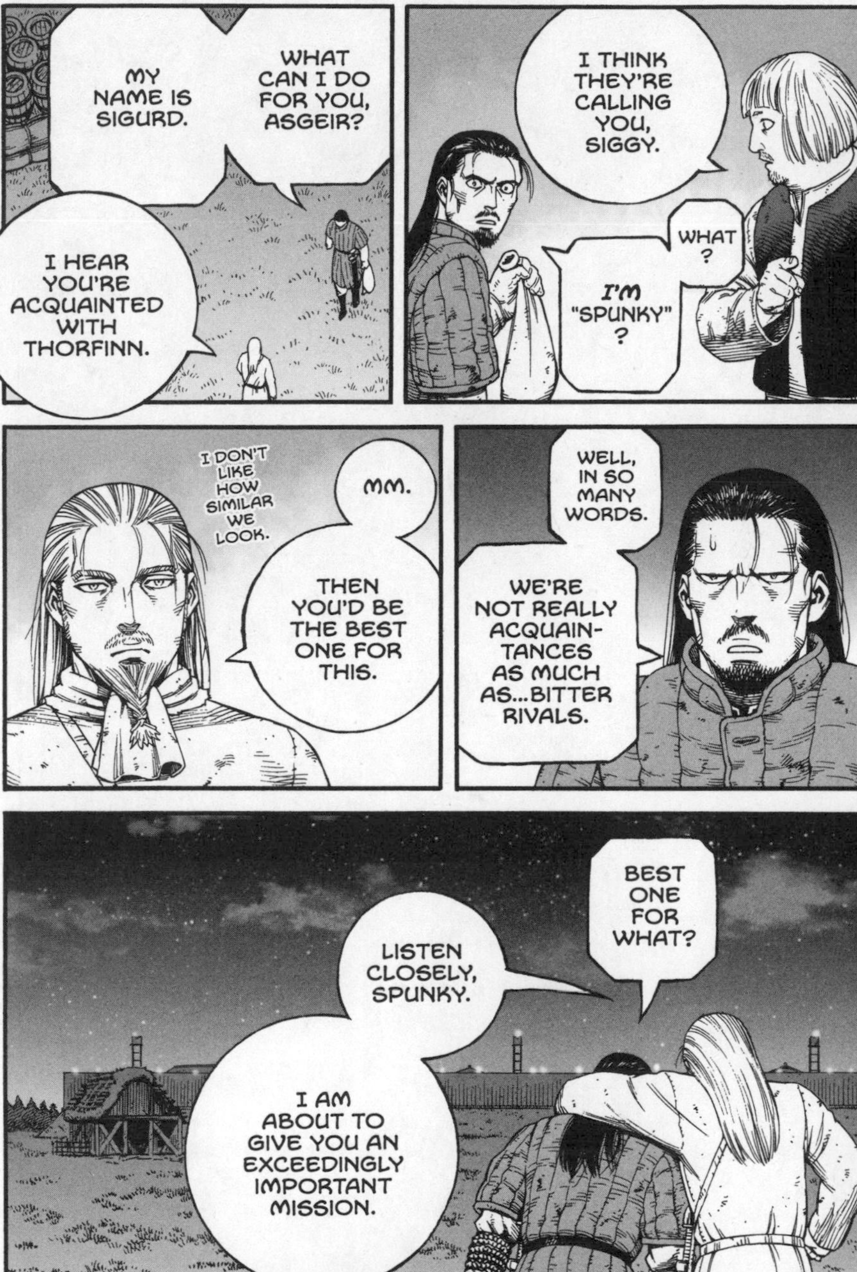
I THINK THEY'RE CALLING YOU, SIGGY.
WHAT?
I'M "SPUNKY"?
WHAT CAN I DO FOR YOU, ASGEIR?
MY NAME IS SIGURD.
I HEAR YOU'RE ACQUAINTED WITH THORFINN.
WELL, IN SO MANY WORDS.
WE'RE NOT REALLY ACQUAIN-TANCES AS MUCH AS...BITTER RIVALS.
MM.
THEN YOU'D BE THE BEST ONE FOR THIS.
I DON'T LIKE HOW SIMILAR WE LOOK.
BEST ONE FOR WHAT?
LISTEN CLOSELY, SPUNKY.
I AM ABOUT TO GIVE YOU AN EXCEEDINGLY IMPORTANT MISSION.

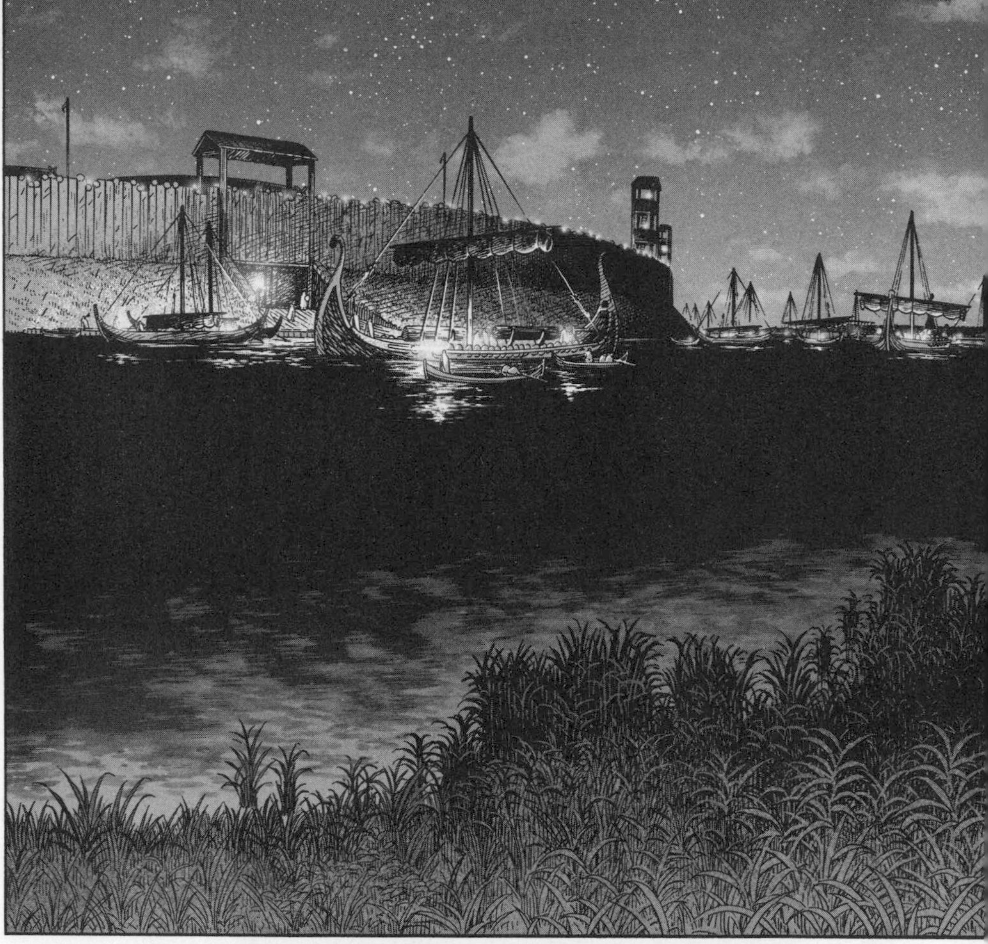

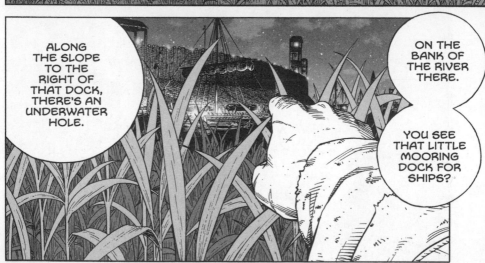

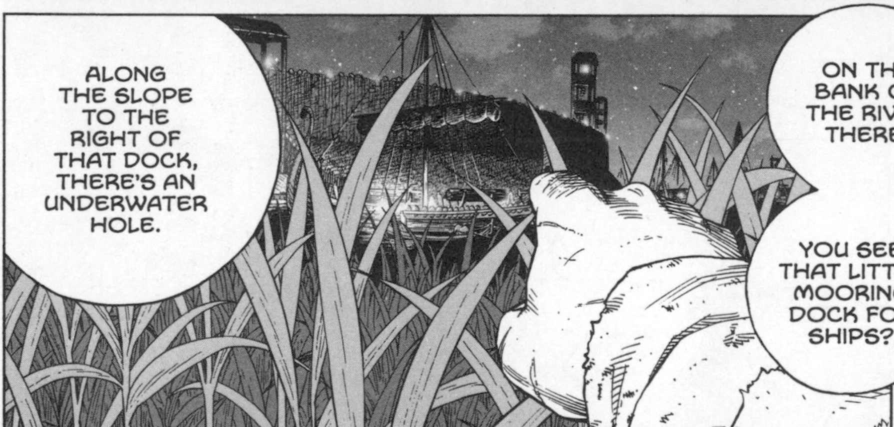
ON THE BANK OF THE RIVER THERE.
YOU SEE THAT LITTLE MOORING DOCK FOR SHIPS?
ALONG THE SLOPE TO THE RIGHT OF THAT DOCK, THERE'S AN UNDERWATER HOLE.

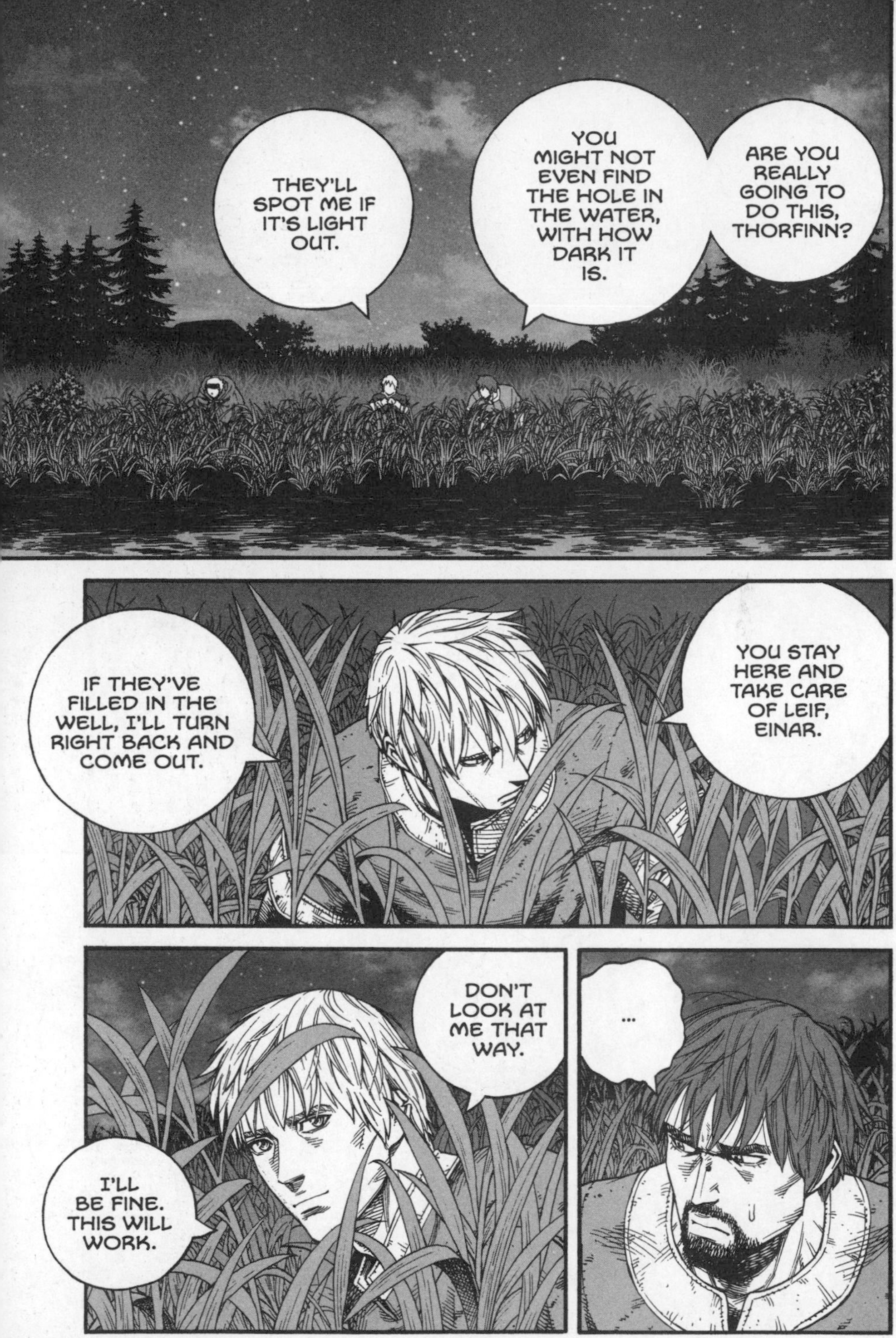
ARE YOU REALLY GOING TO DO THIS, THORFINN?
YOU MIGHT NOT EVEN FIND THE HOLE IN THE WATER, WITH HOW DARK IT IS.
THEY'LL SPOT ME IF IT'S LIGHT OUT.
YOU STAY HERE AND TAKE CARE OF LEIF, EINAR.
IF THEY'VE FILLED IN THE WELL, I'LL TURN RIGHT BACK AND COME OUT.
...
DON'T LOOK AT ME THAT WAY.
I'LL BE FINE. THIS WILL WORK.

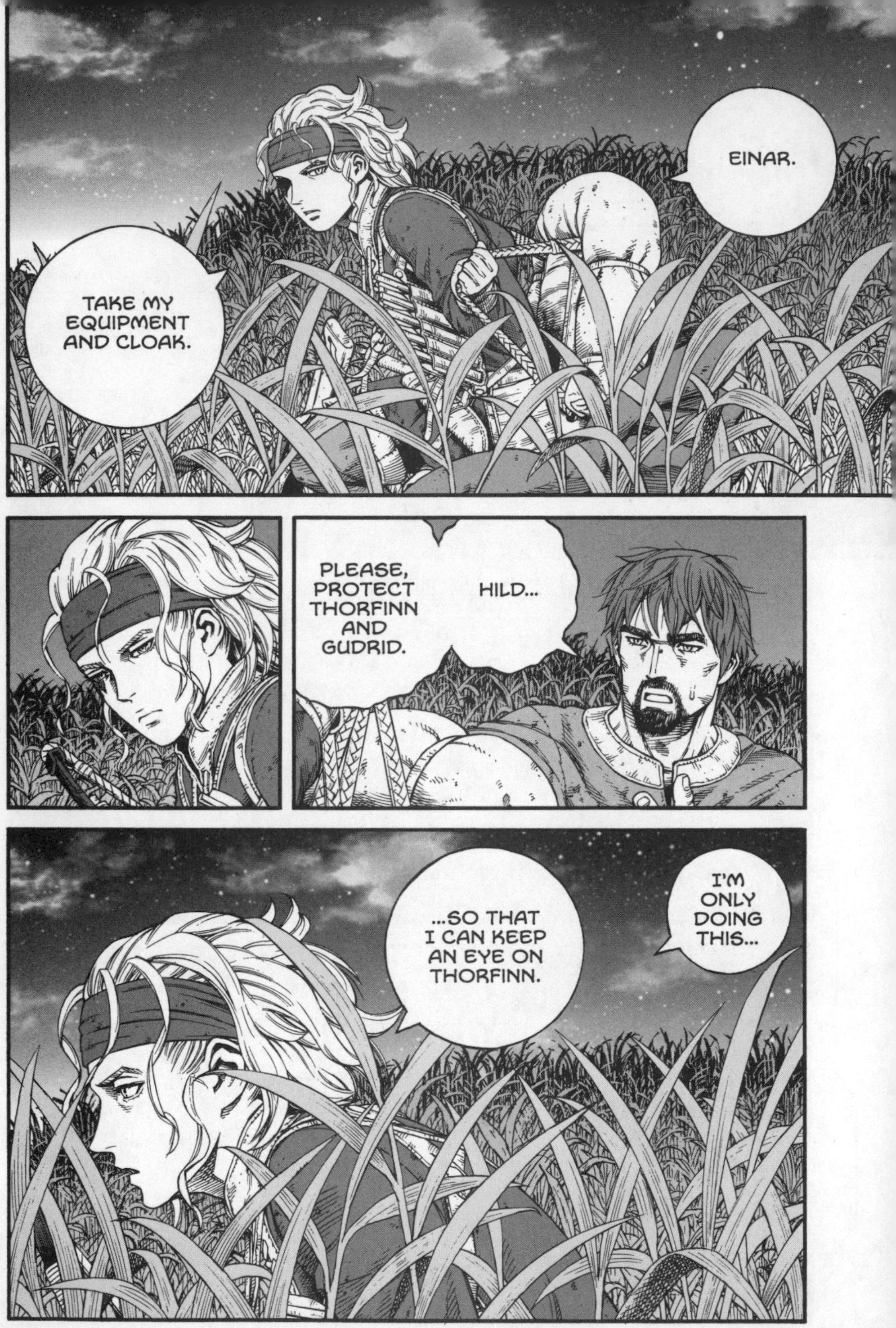
EINAR.
TAKE MY EQUIPMENT AND CLOAK.
HILD...
PLEASE, PROTECT THORFINN AND GUDRID.
I'M ONLY DOING THIS...
...SO THAT I CAN KEEP AN EYE ON THORFINN.

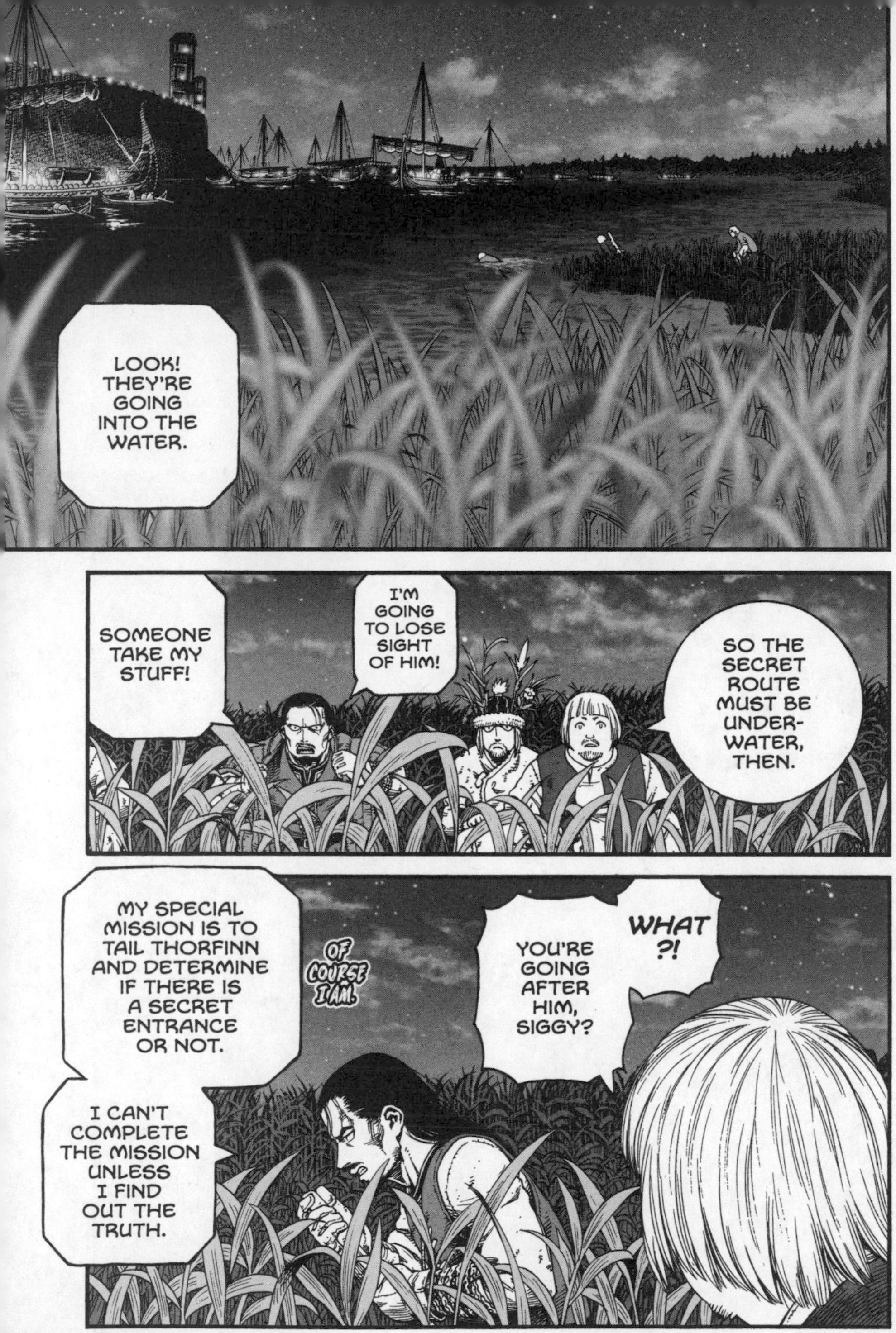
LOOK! THEY'RE GOING INTO THE WATER.
SO THE SECRET ROUTE MUST BE UNDER-WATER, THEN.
I'M GOING TO LOSE SIGHT OF HIM!
SOMEONE TAKE MY STUFF!
WHAT ?!
YOU'RE GOING AFTER HIM, SIGGY?
OF COURSE I AM.
MY SPECIAL MISSION IS TO TAIL THORFINN AND DETERMINE IF THERE IS A SECRET ENTRANCE OR NOT.
I CAN'T COMPLETE THE MISSION UNLESS I FIND OUT THE TRUTH.

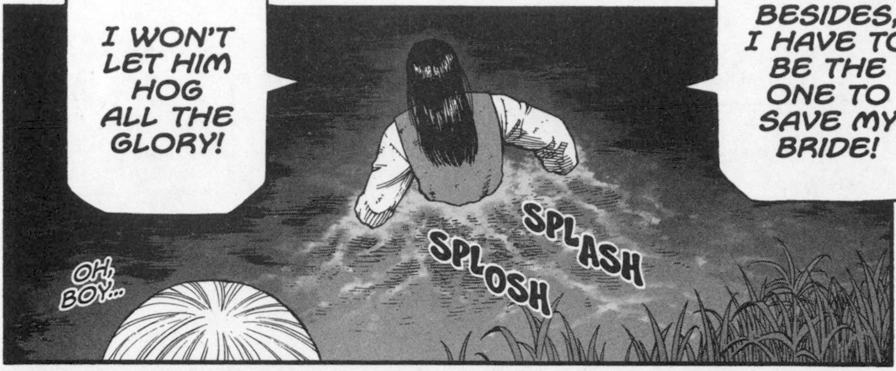
I WON'T LET HIM HOG ALL THE GLORY!
BESIDES, I HAVE TO BE THE ONE TO SAVE MY BRIDE!
SPLASH
SPLOSH
OH, BOY...
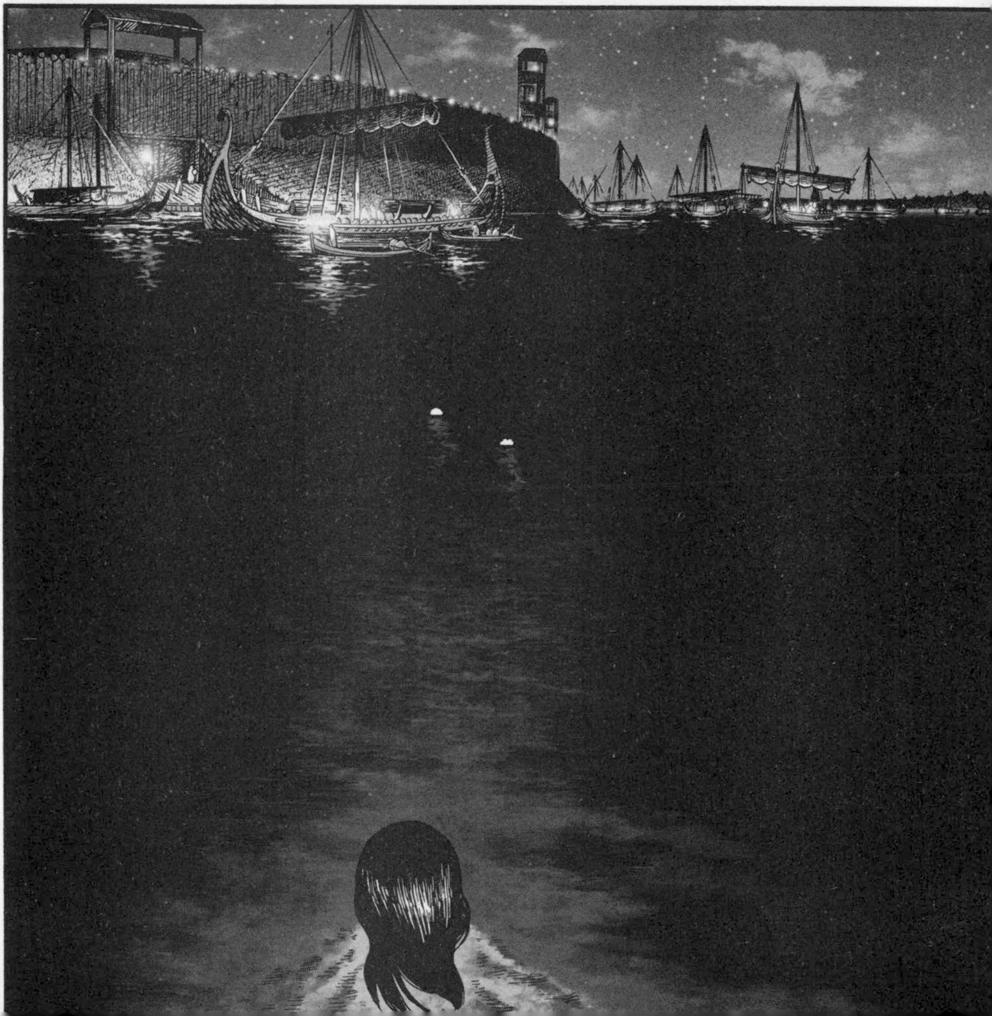

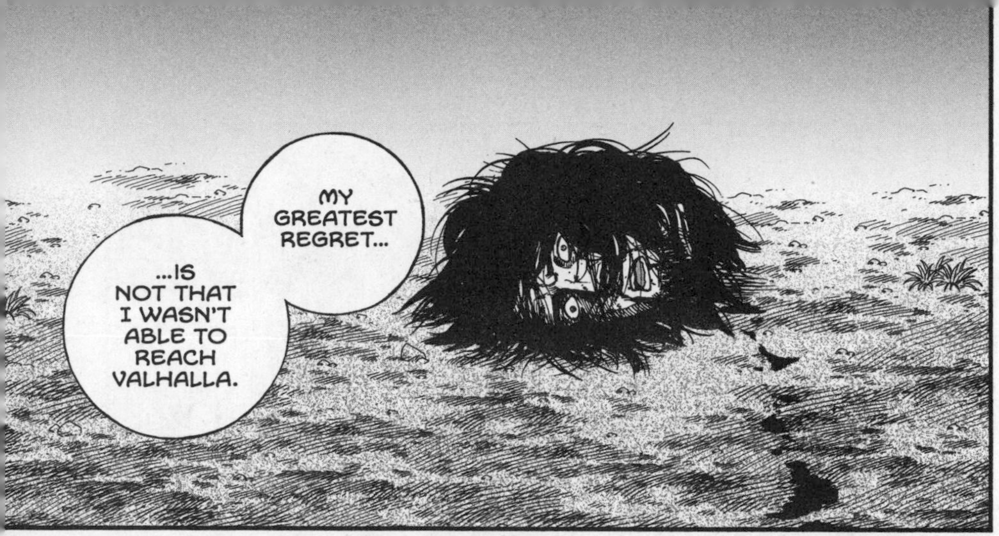
MY GREATEST REGRET...
...IS NOT THAT I WASN'T ABLE TO REACH VALHALLA.
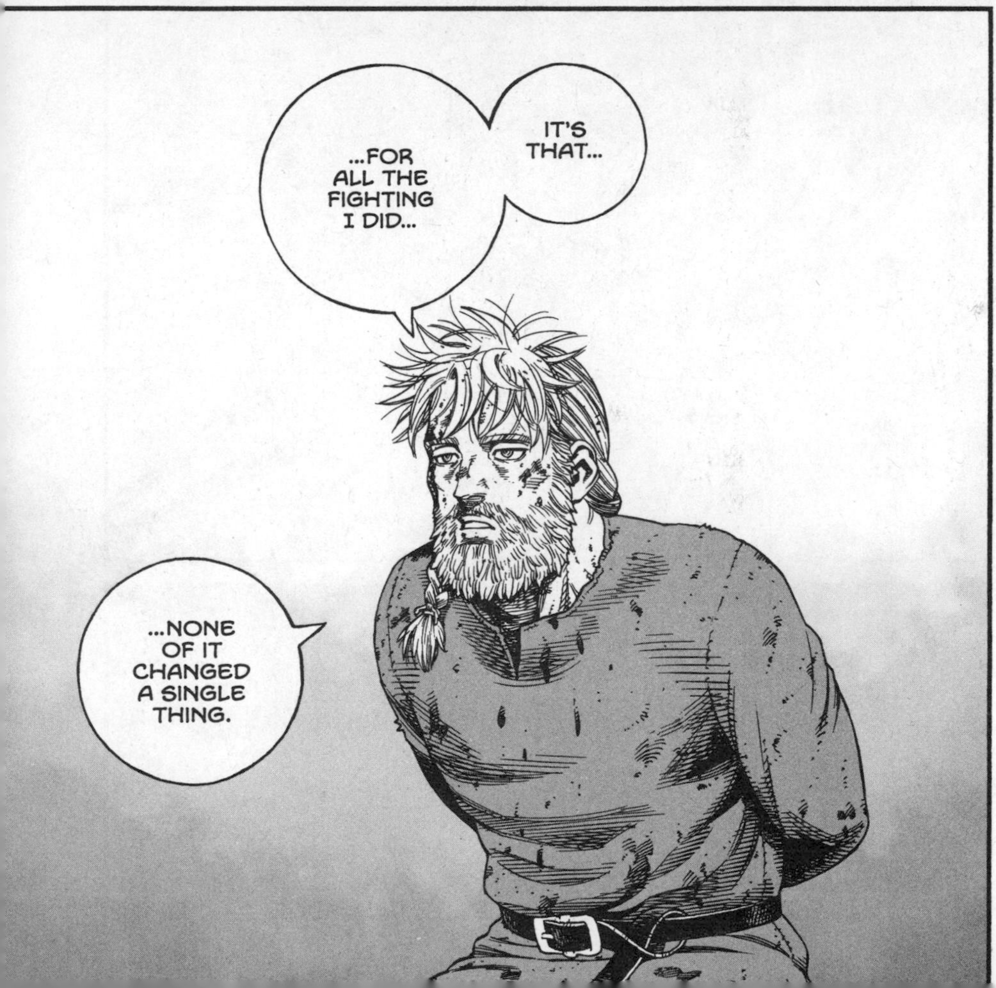
IT'S THAT...
...FOR ALL THE FIGHTING I DID...
...NONE OF IT CHANGED A SINGLE THING.

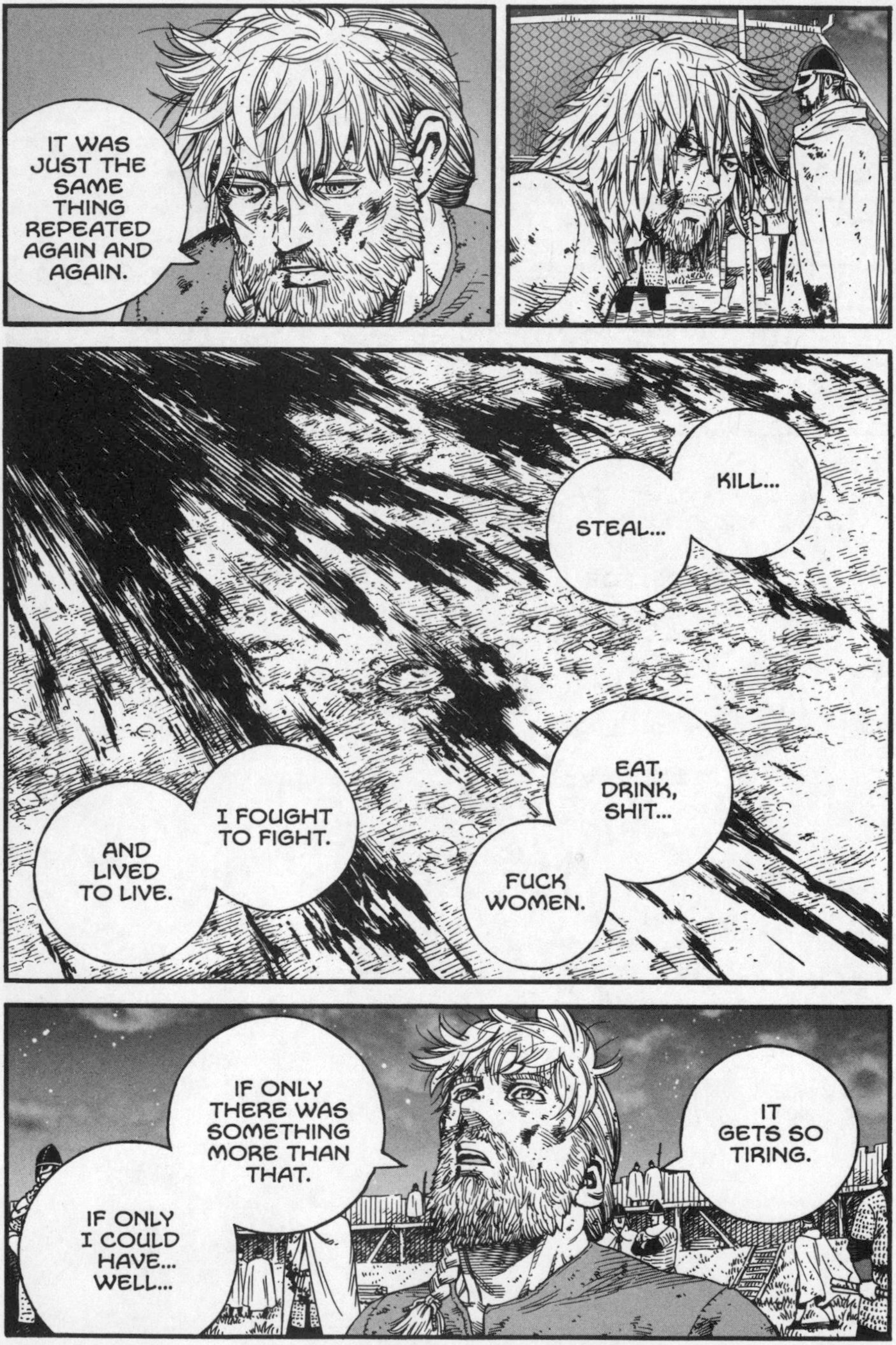
IT WAS JUST THE SAME THING REPEATED AGAIN AND AGAIN.
KILL...
STEAL...
EAT, DRINK, SHIT...
FUCK WOMEN.
I FOUGHT TO FIGHT.
AND LIVED TO LIVE.
IT GETS SO TIRING.
IF ONLY THERE WAS SOMETHING MORE THAN THAT.
IF ONLY I COULD HAVE... WELL...

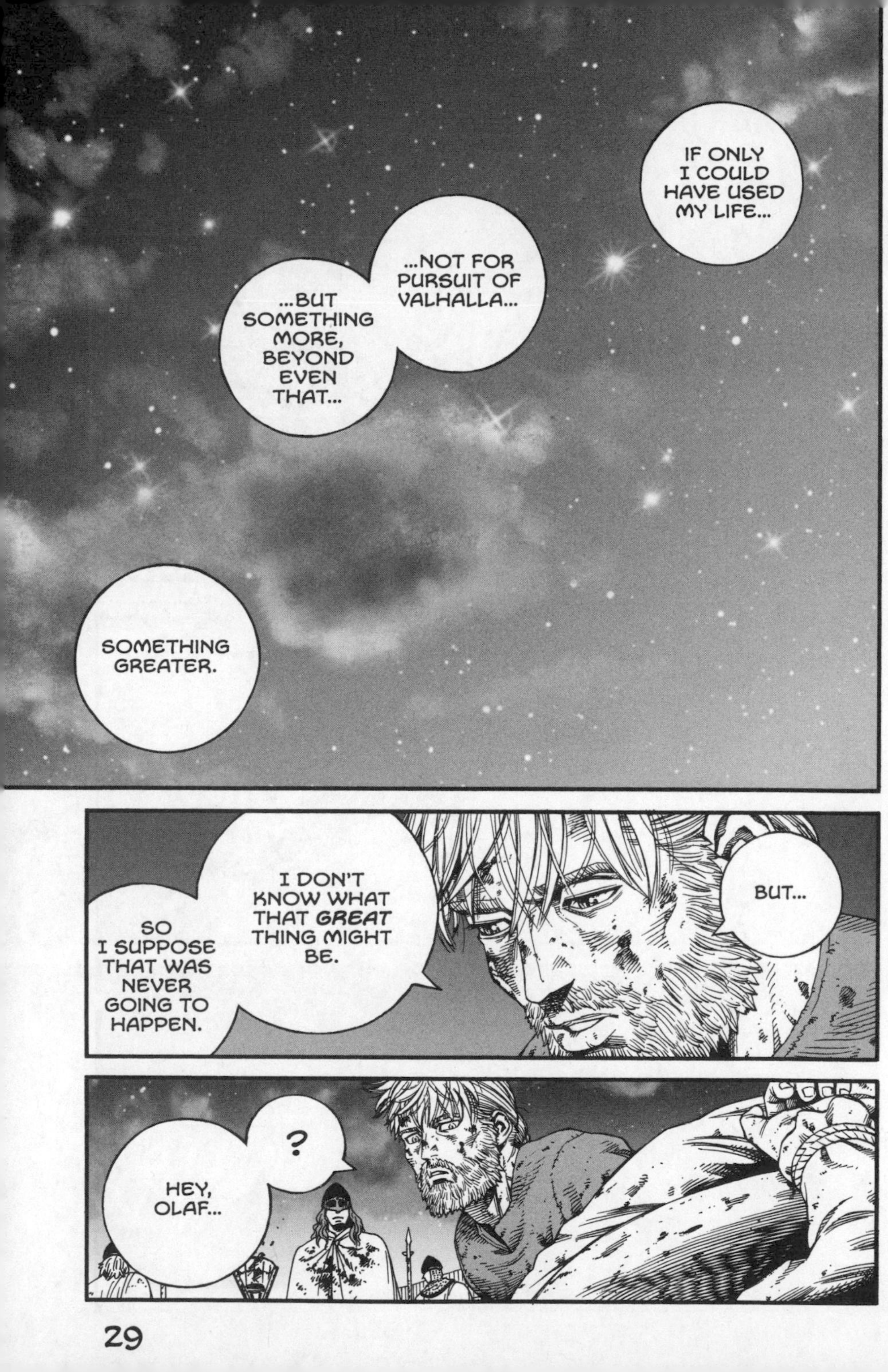
IF ONLY I COULD HAVE USED MY LIFE...
...NOT FOR PURSUIT OF VALHALLA...
...BUT SOMETHING MORE, BEYOND EVEN THAT...
SOMETHING GREATER.
BUT...
I DON'T KNOW WHAT THAT *GREAT* THING MIGHT BE.
SO I SUPPOSE THAT WAS NEVER GOING TO HAPPEN.
?
HEY, OLAF...

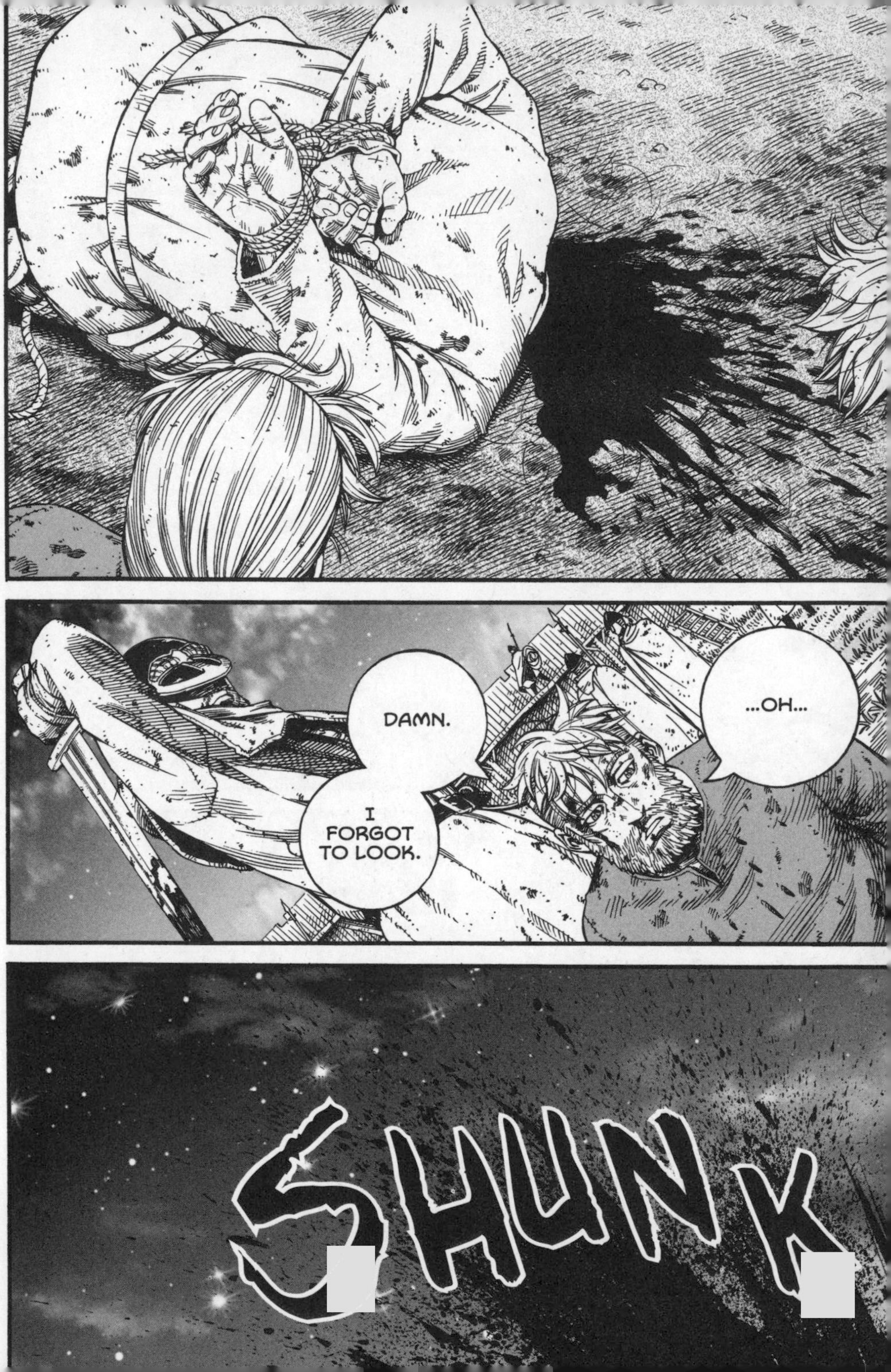
...OH...
DAMN.
I FORGOT TO LOOK.
SHUNK

CHAPTER 145 - END

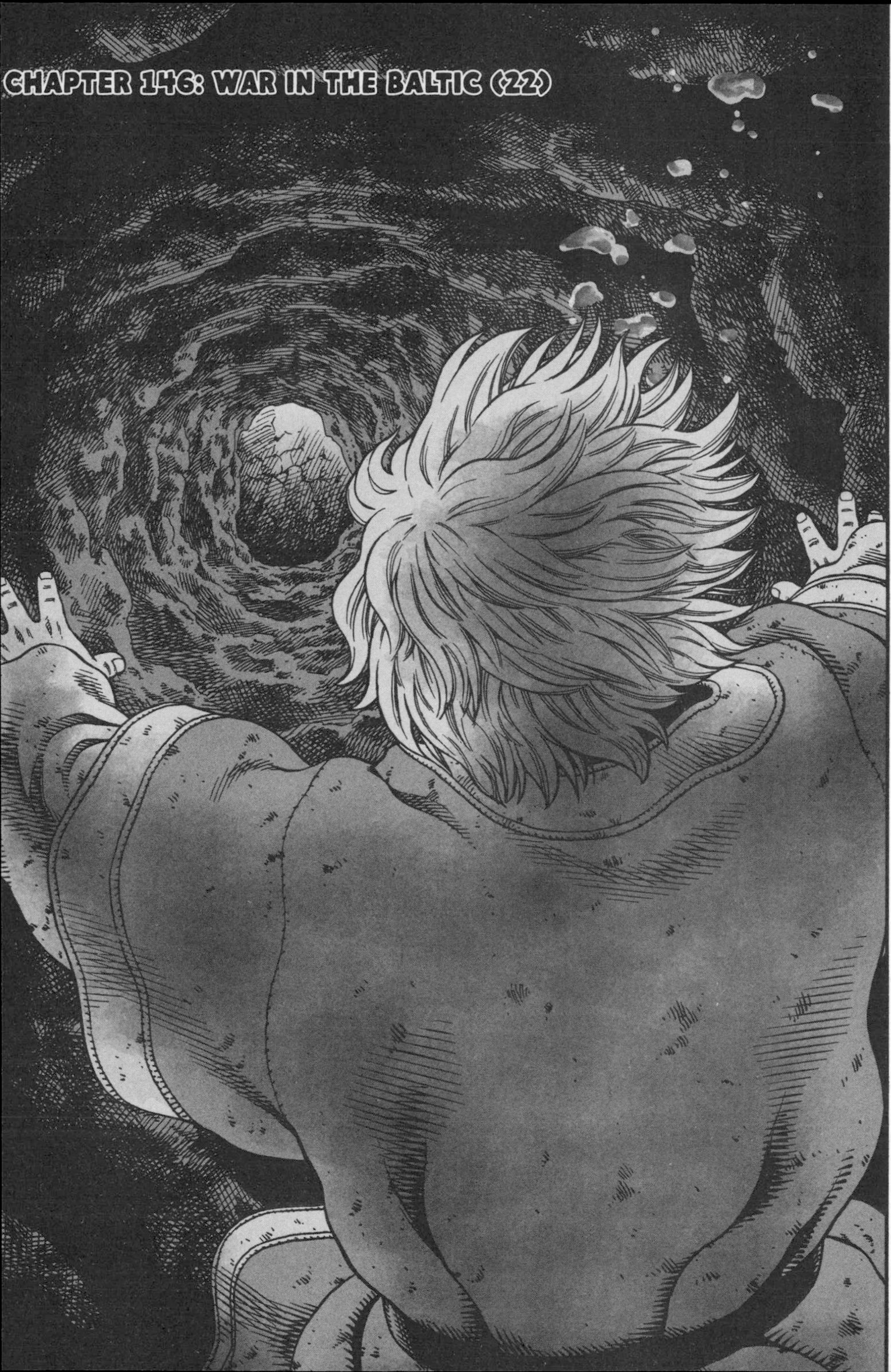
CHAPTER 146: WAR IN THE BALTIC (22)

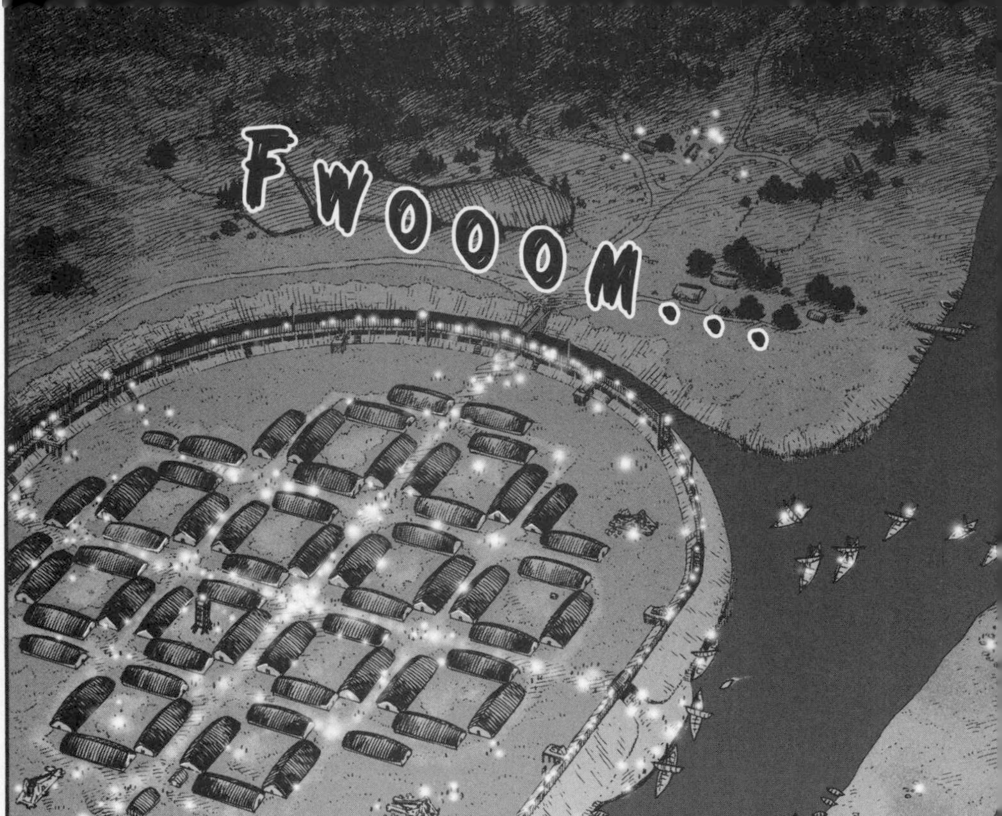
FWOOOM...

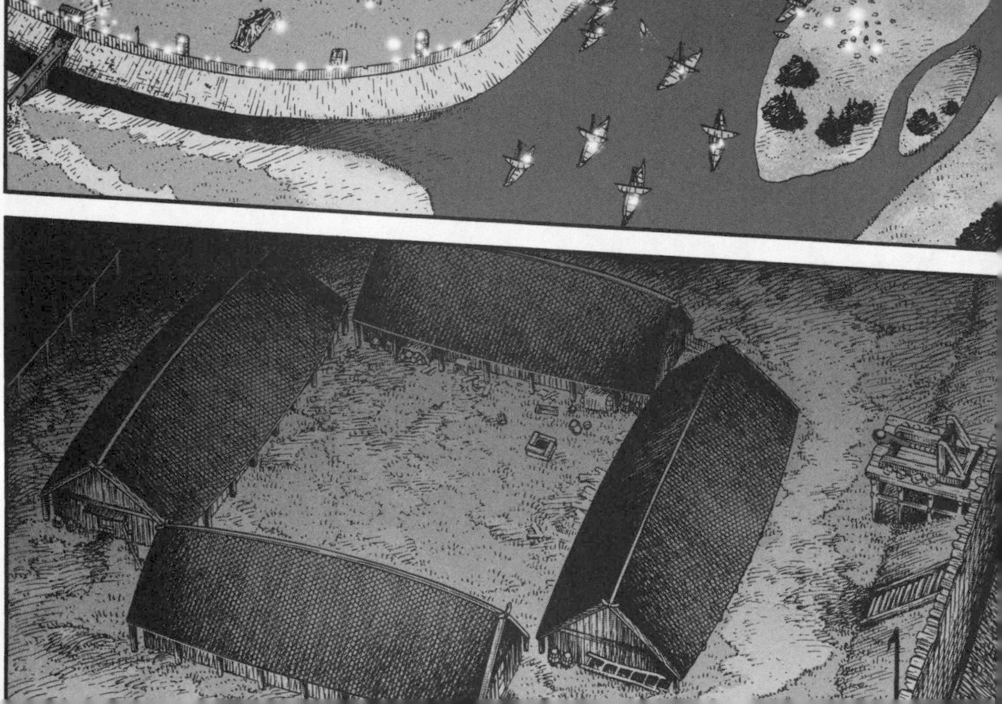

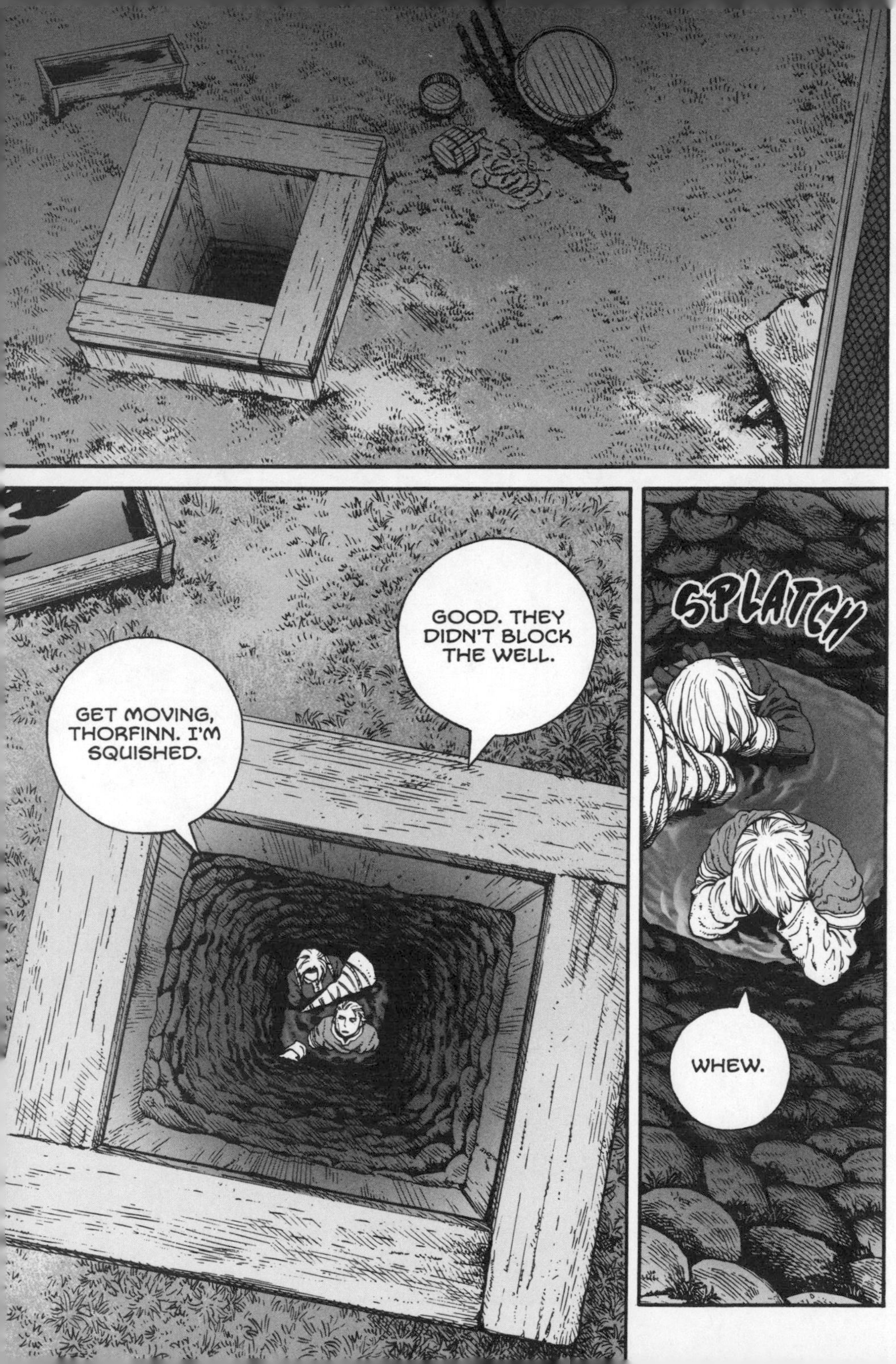
SPLATCH
WHEW.
GOOD. THEY DIDN'T BLOCK THE WELL.
GET MOVING, THORFINN. I'M SQUISHED.

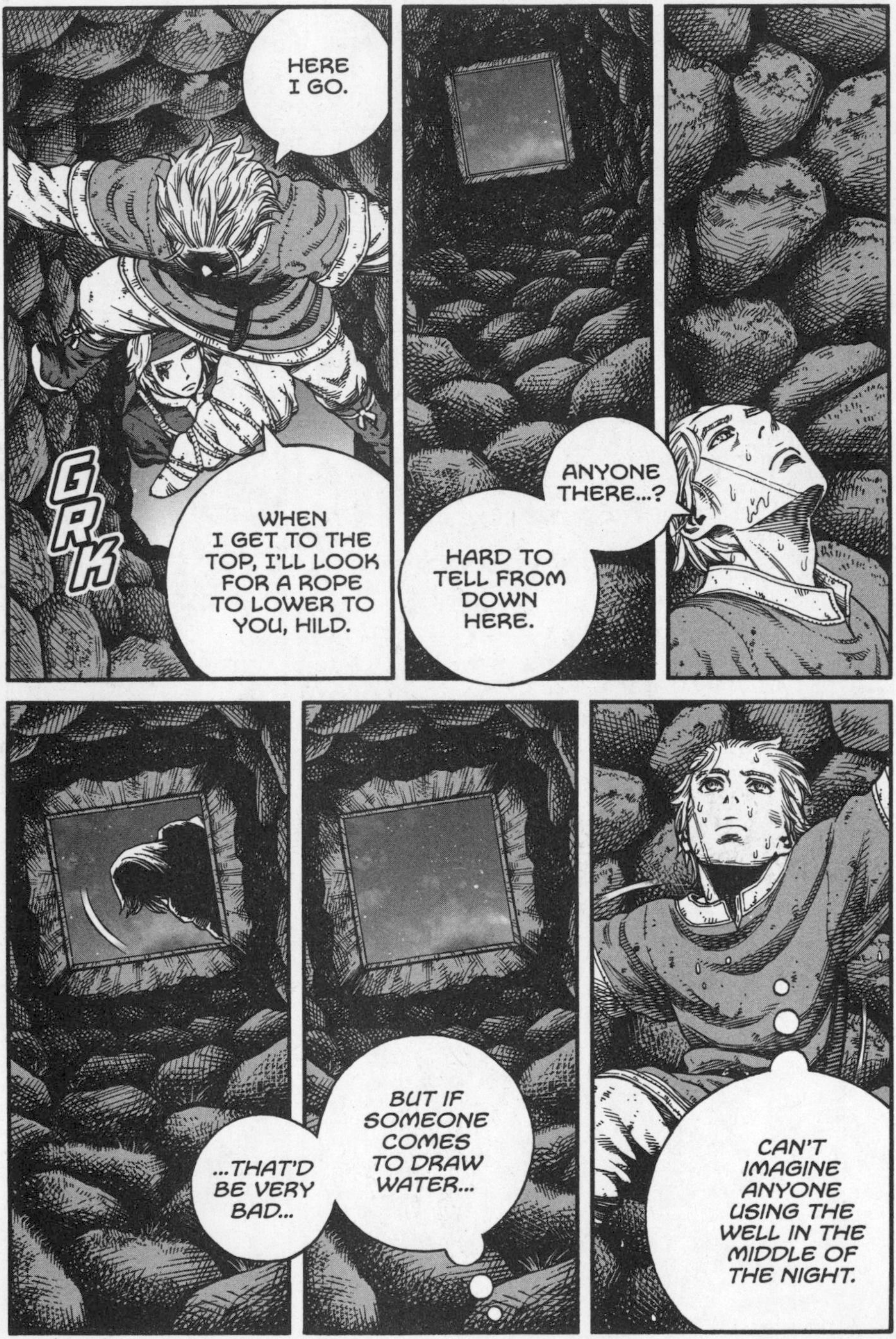
ANYONE THERE...?
HARD TO TELL FROM DOWN HERE.
HERE I GO.
WHEN I GET TO THE TOP, I'LL LOOK FOR A ROPE TO LOWER TO YOU, HILD.
GRK
CAN'T IMAGINE ANYONE USING THE WELL IN THE MIDDLE OF THE NIGHT.
BUT IF SOMEONE COMES TO DRAW WATER...
...THAT'D BE VERY BAD...

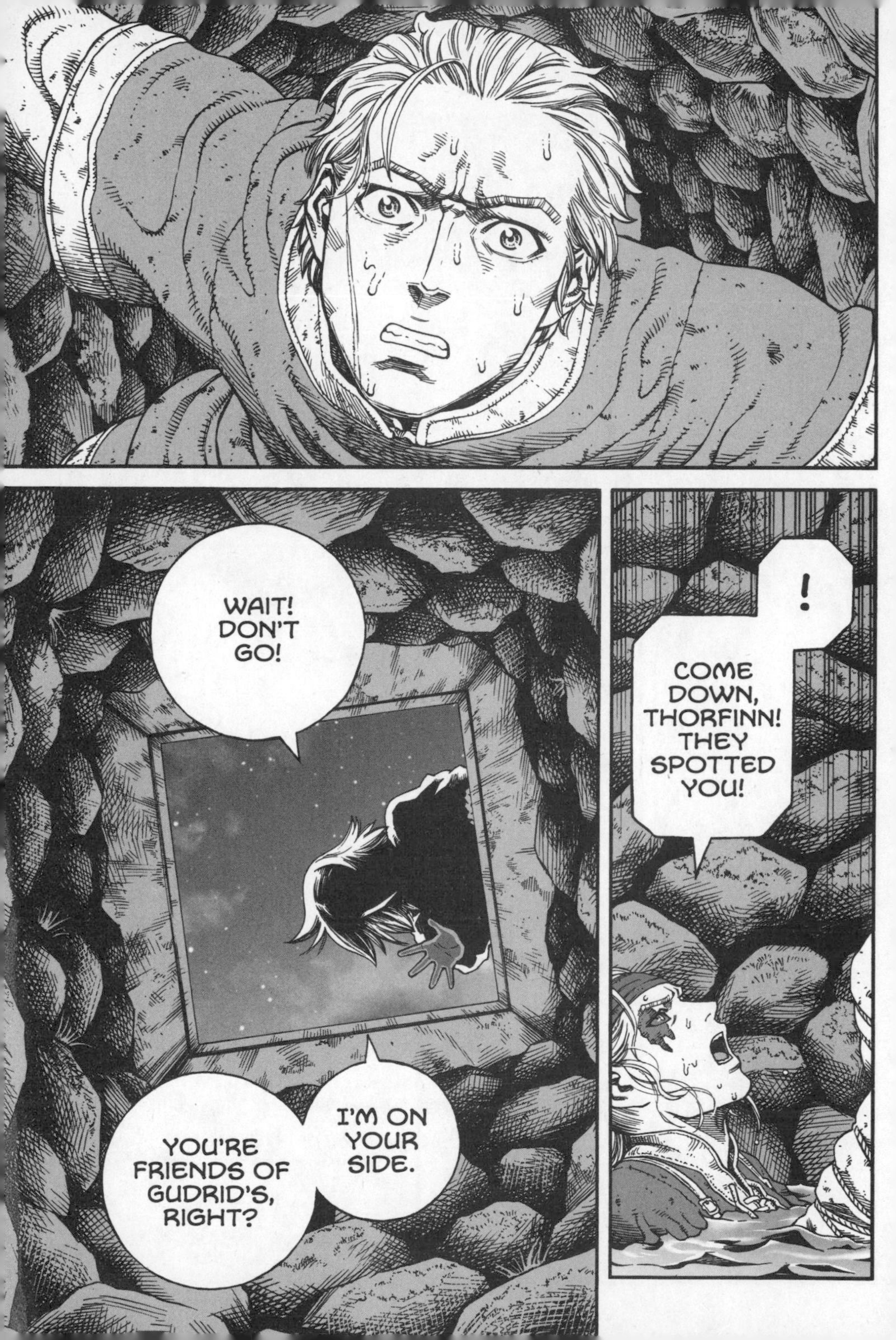
!
COME DOWN, THORFINN! THEY SPOTTED YOU!
WAIT! DON'T GO!
I'M ON YOUR SIDE.
YOU'RE FRIENDS OF GUDRID'S, RIGHT?

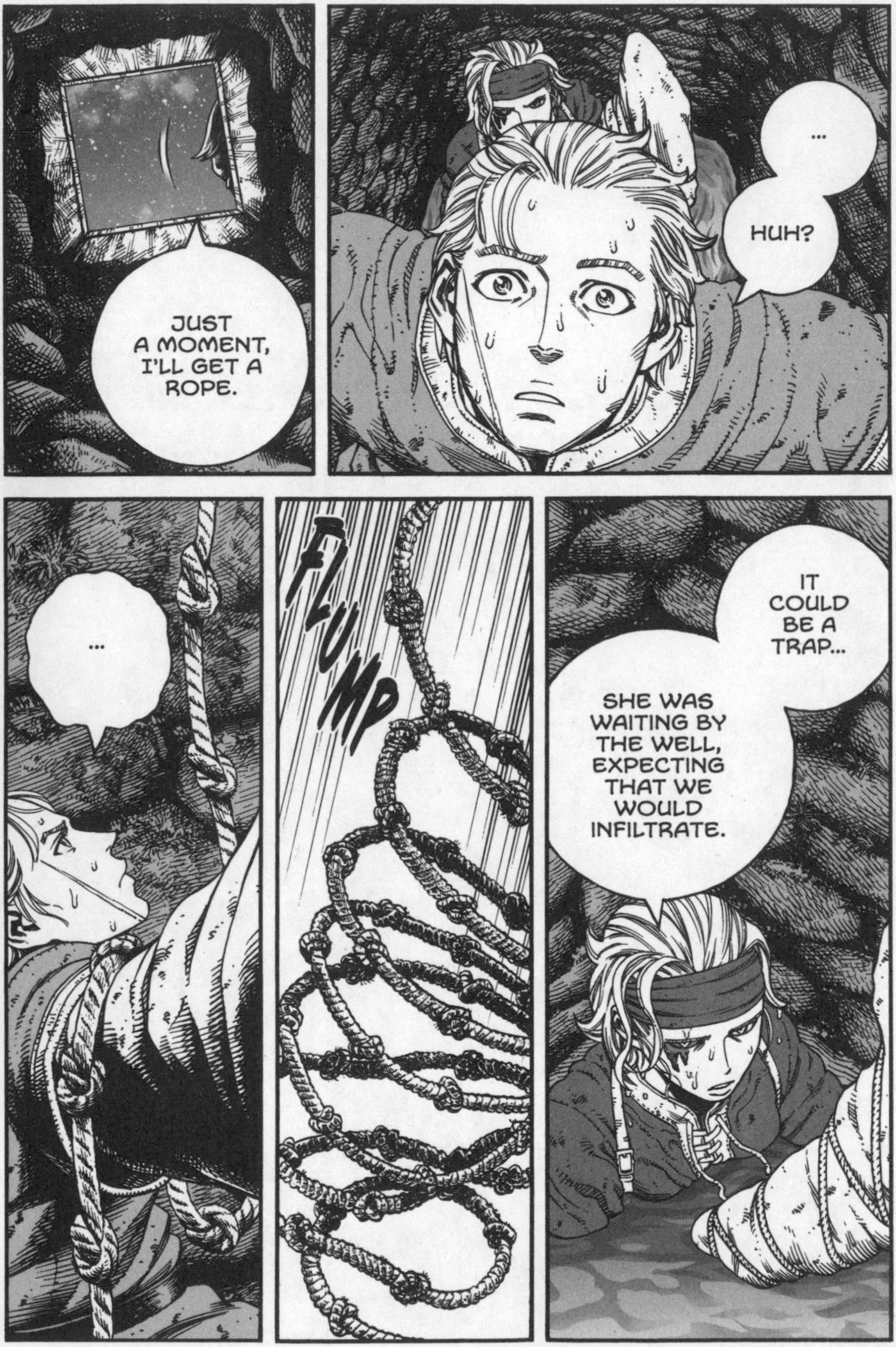
JUST A MOMENT, I'LL GET A ROPE.
...
HUH?
...
FLUMP
IT COULD BE A TRAP...
SHE WAS WAITING BY THE WELL, EXPECTING THAT WE WOULD INFILTRATE.

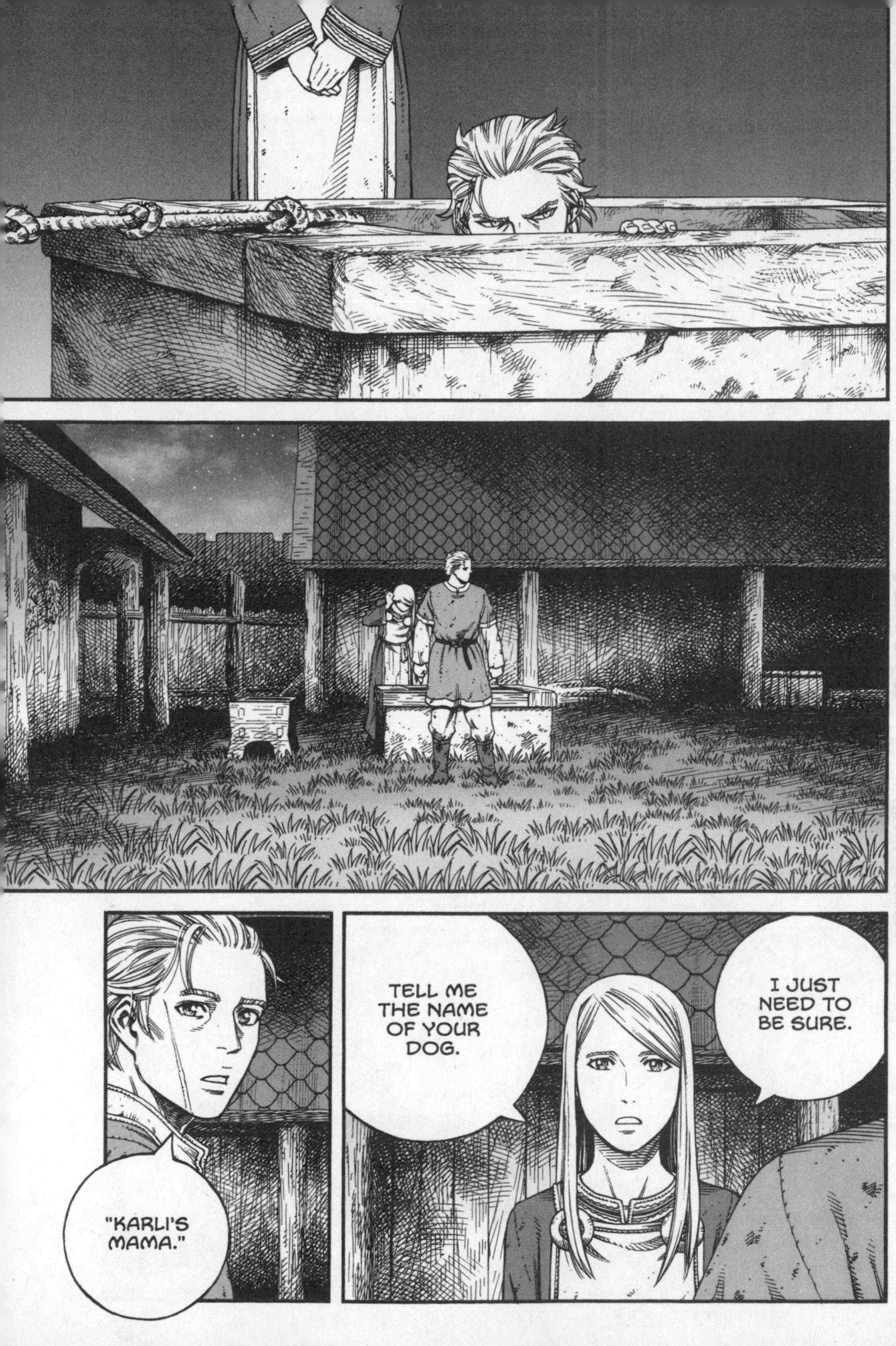
I JUST NEED TO BE SURE.
TELL ME THE NAME OF YOUR DOG.
"KARLI'S MAMA."

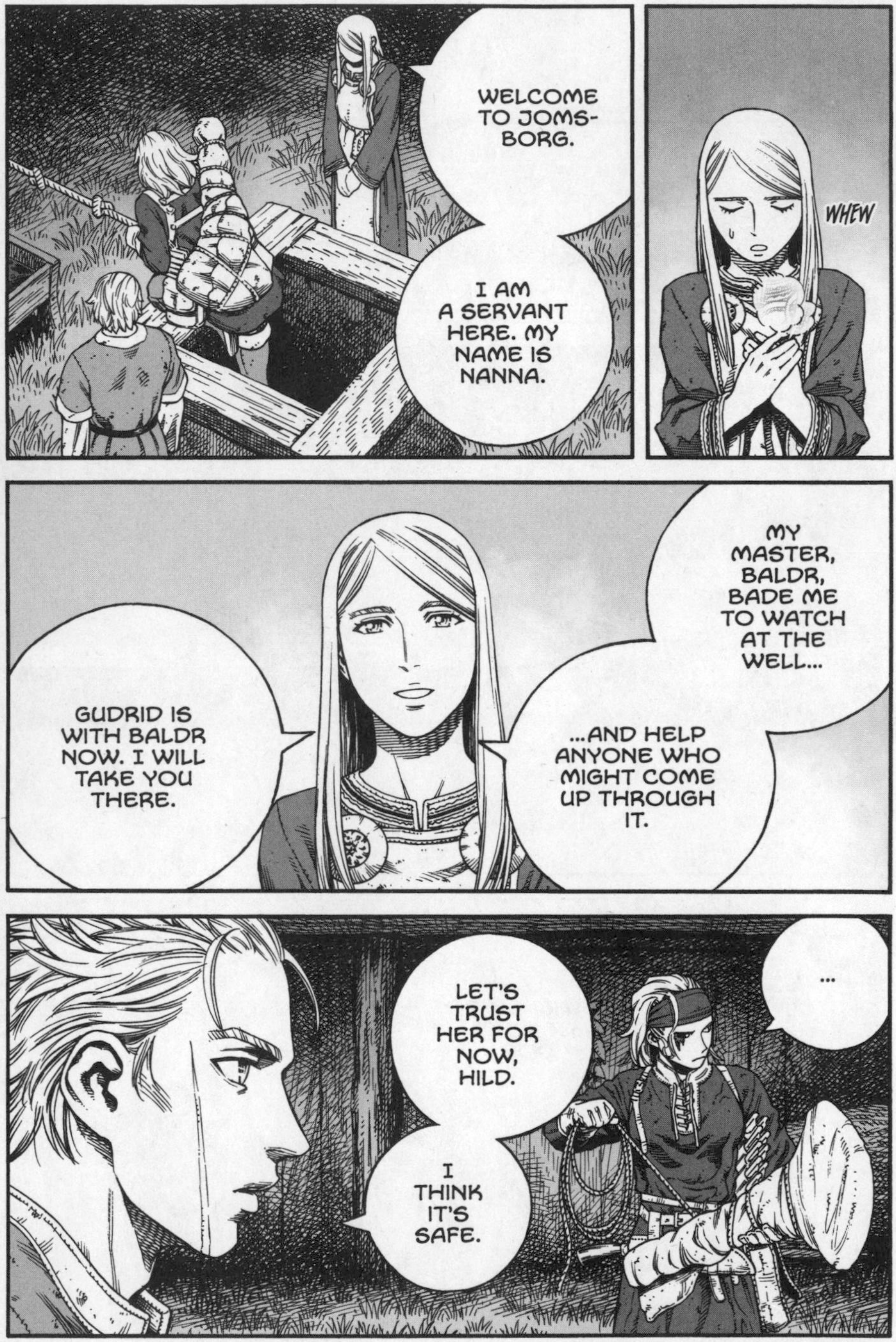
WHEW
WELCOME TO JOMSBORG.
I AM A SERVANT HERE. MY NAME IS NANNA.
MY MASTER, BALDR, BADE ME TO WATCH AT THE WELL...
...AND HELP ANYONE WHO MIGHT COME UP THROUGH IT.
GUDRID IS WITH BALDR NOW. I WILL TAKE YOU THERE.
...
LET'S TRUST HER FOR NOW, HILD.
I THINK IT'S SAFE.

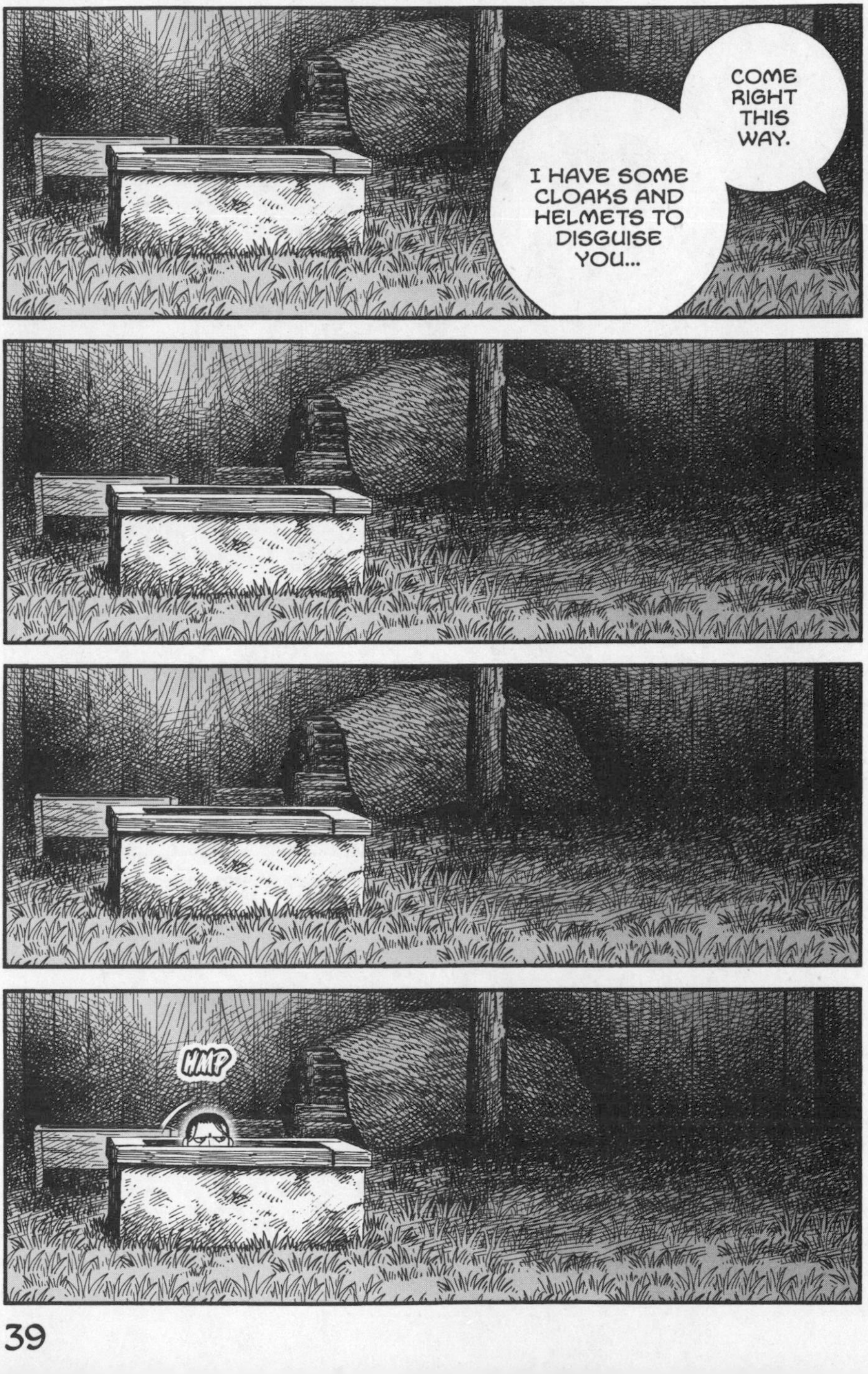
COME RIGHT THIS WAY.
I HAVE SOME CLOAKS AND HELMETS TO DISGUISE YOU...
HMP

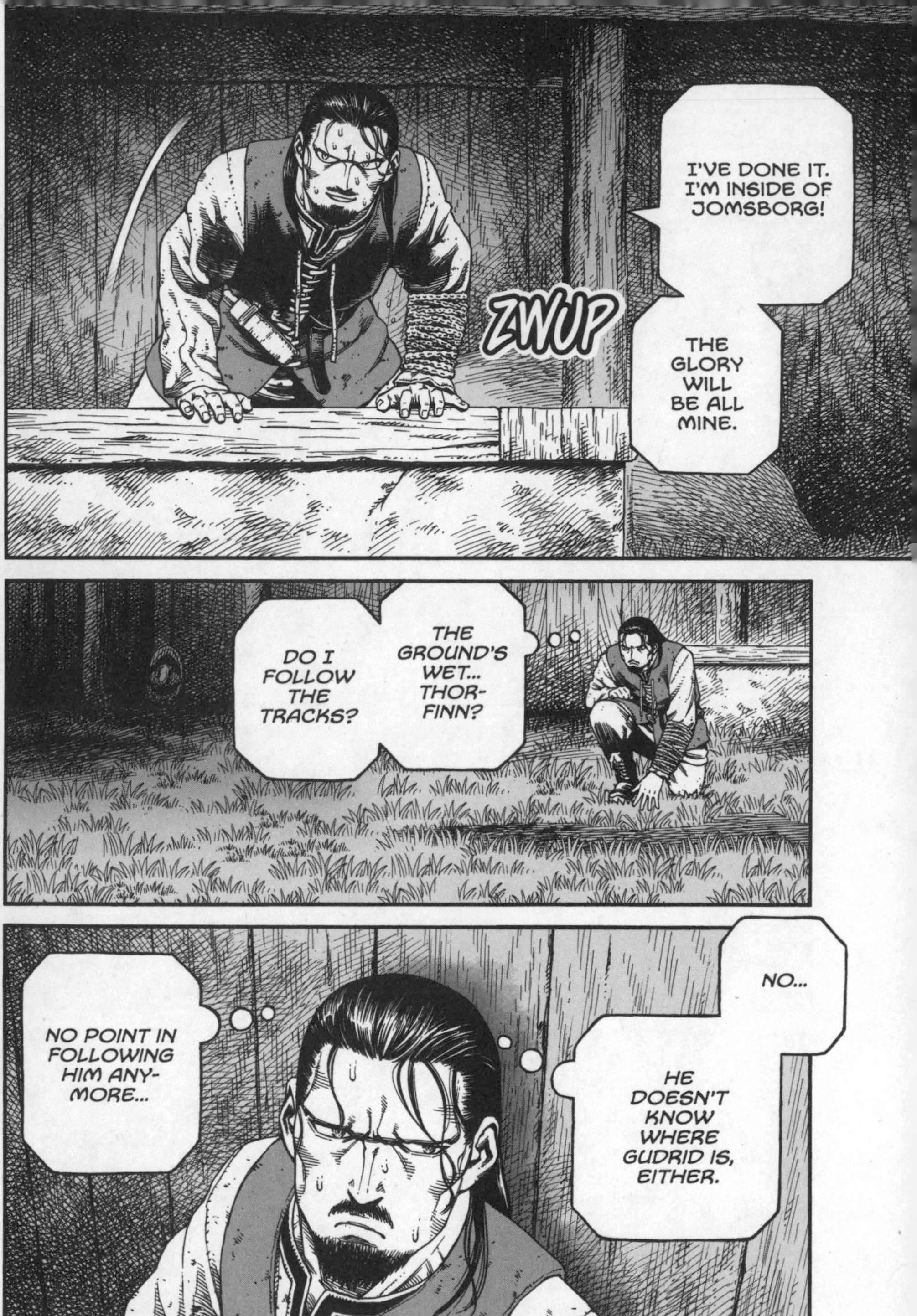
I'VE DONE IT. I'M INSIDE OF JOMSBORG!
THE GLORY WILL BE ALL MINE.
ZWUP
THE GROUND'S WET... THOR-FINN?
DO I FOLLOW THE TRACKS?
NO...
HE DOESN'T KNOW WHERE GUDRID IS, EITHER.
NO POINT IN FOLLOWING HIM ANY-MORE...

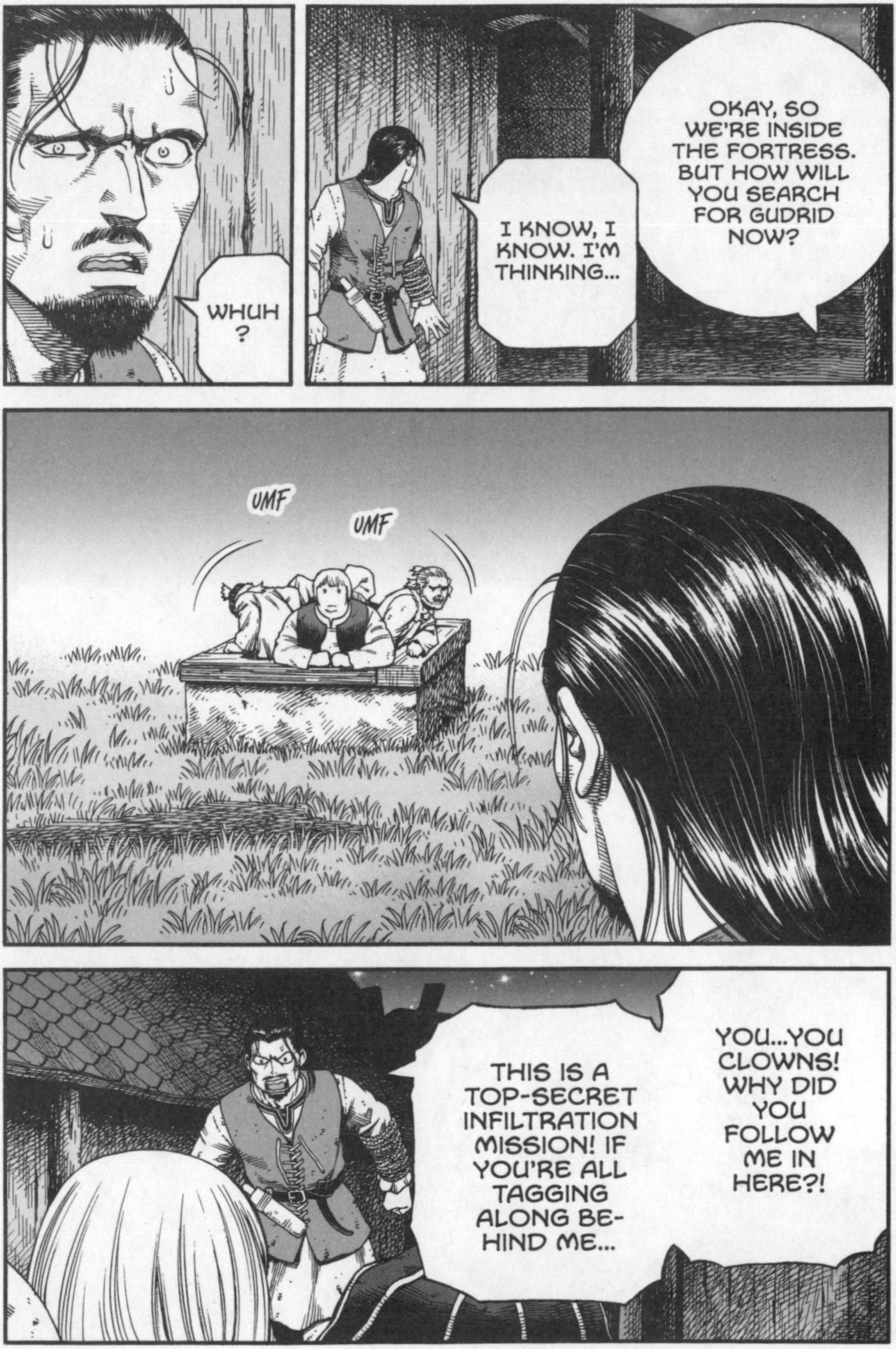
OKAY, SO WE'RE INSIDE THE FORTRESS. BUT HOW WILL YOU SEARCH FOR GUDRID NOW?
I KNOW, I KNOW. I'M THINKING...
WHUH?
UMF
UMF
YOU...YOU CLOWNS! WHY DID YOU FOLLOW ME IN HERE?!
THIS IS A TOP-SECRET INFILTRATION MISSION! IF YOU'RE ALL TAGGING ALONG BE-HIND ME...

DON'T PUSH!
IT'S TIGHT!
YEOW!
YOU MEAN... WE SHOULDN'T HAVE COME?
NO, YOU SHOULDN'T HAVE!
AND WHY ARE ALL FOUR OF YOU TRYING TO GET OUT OF THAT CRAMPED WELL AT ONCE?! USE YOUR BRAINS!
YOU SHOULD'VE TOLD US!
I DID TELL YOU!
I'M THE ONLY ONE WHO'S GOING INTO BATTLE!
LOOK, JUST GET BACK IN THE WELL!
C'MON! BACK IN YOU GO!
YOU'RE SCRAPING ME!
GYAAAA
OW! OW! OW!
THAT HURTS, THAT HURTS, THAT HURTS!!
WAIT, WAIT, NO, STOP, DON'T PUSH! YOU'RE PINCHING THE FLESH! YOU'RE PINCHING!!
STOP SHOUTING!!

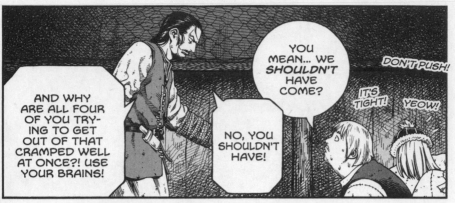

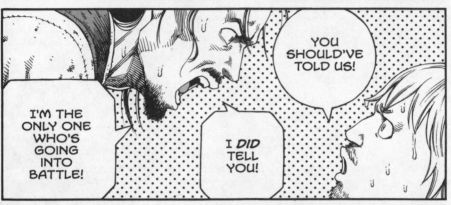

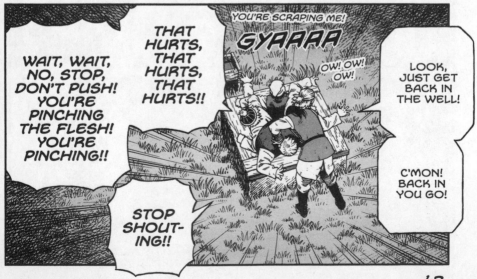

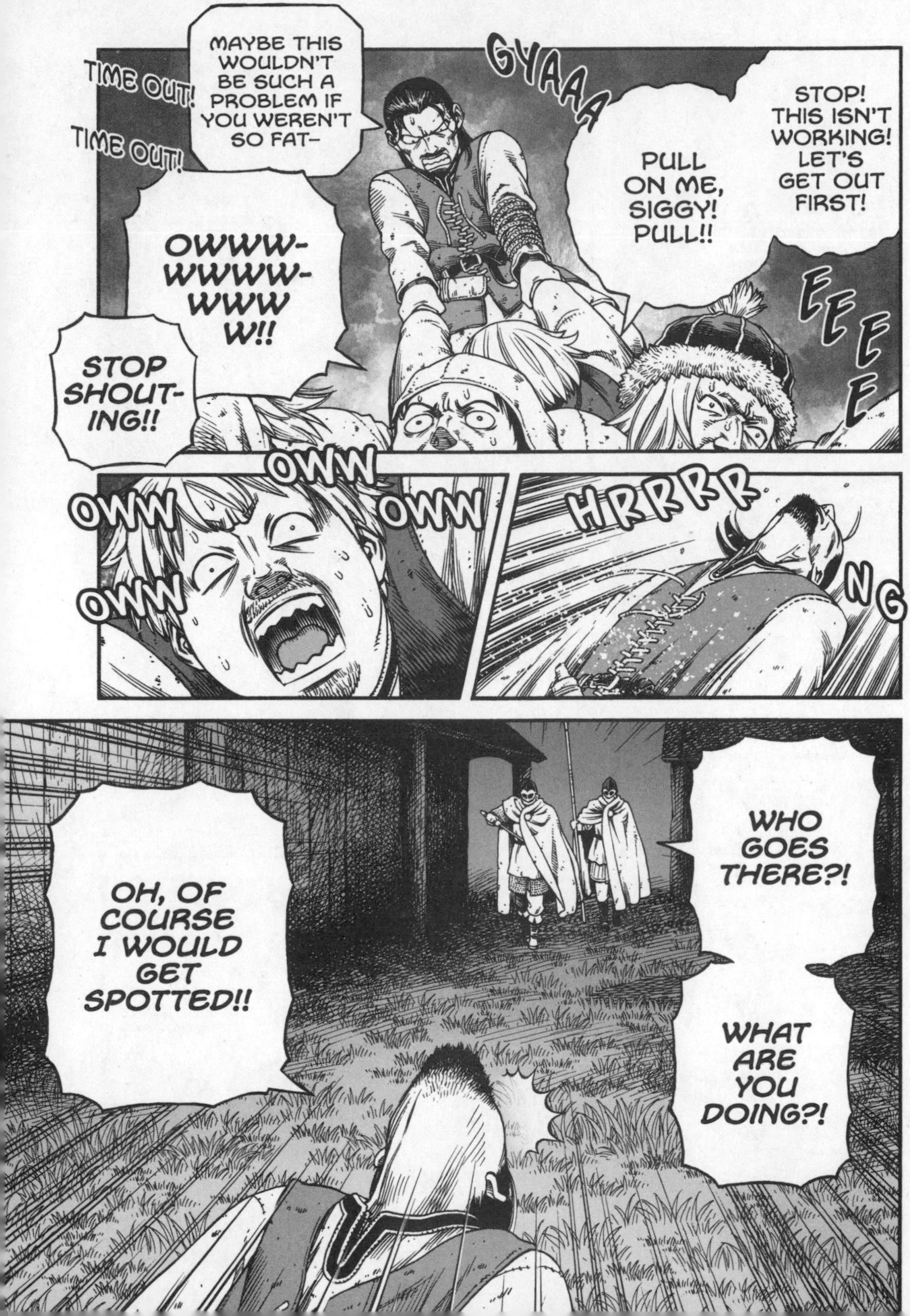
STOP! THIS ISN'T WORKING! LET'S GET OUT FIRST!
GYAAA
PULL ON ME, SIGGY! PULL!!
MAYBE THIS WOULDN'T BE SUCH A PROBLEM IF YOU WEREN'T SO FAT–
TIME OUT!
TIME OUT!
EEEE
OWWW-WWWW-WWWW W!!
STOP SHOUT-ING!!
HRRRRNG
OWW
OWW
OWW
OWW
WHO GOES THERE?!
WHAT ARE YOU DOING?!
OH, OF COURSE I WOULD GET SPOTTED!!

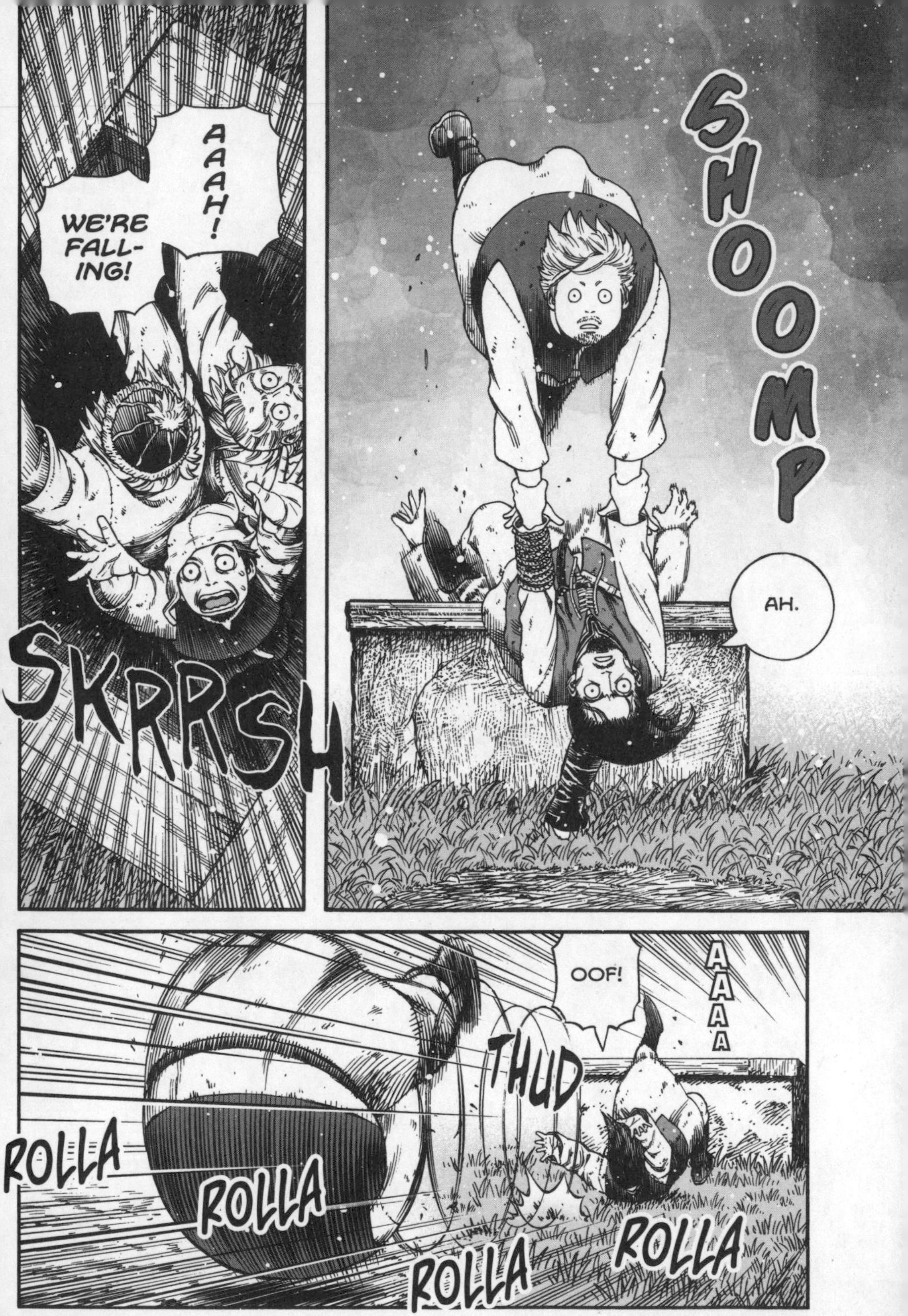
SHOOMP
AH.
AAAAH!
WE'RE FALL-ING!
SKRRSH
AAAA
OOF!
THUD
ROLLA
ROLLA
ROLLA
ROLLA

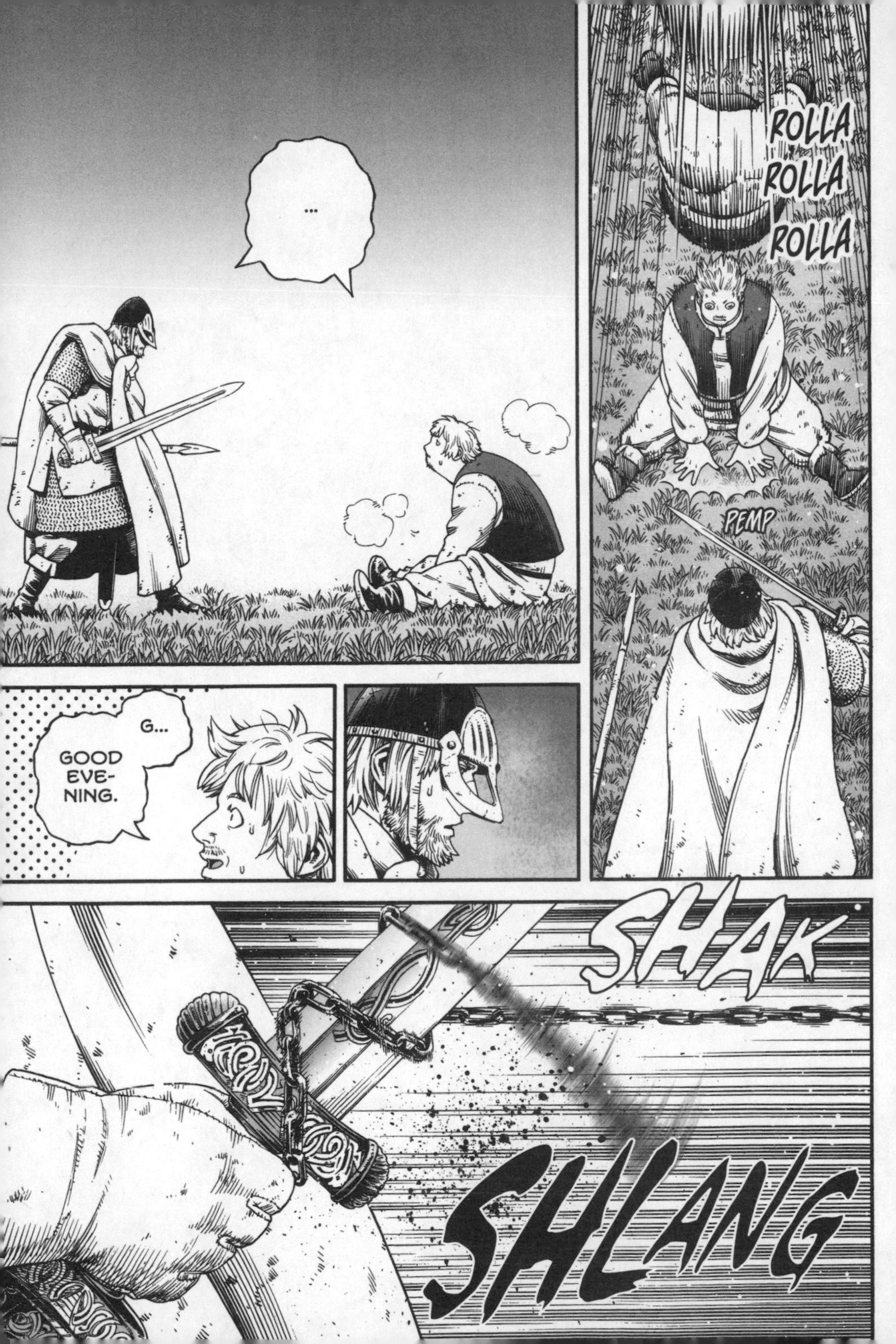
ROLLA ROLLA ROLLA
PEMP
...
G... GOOD EVE-NING.
SHAK
SHLANG

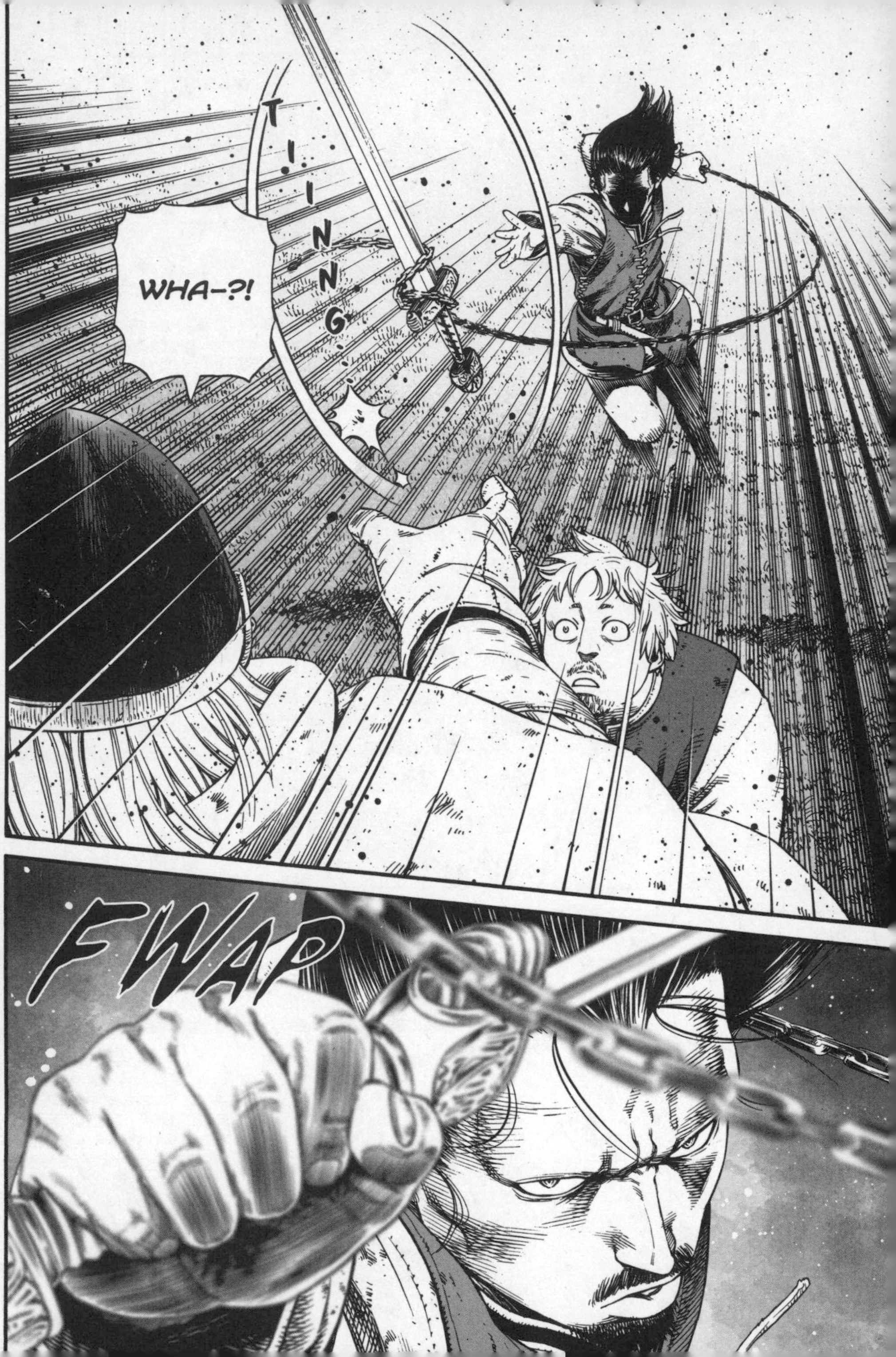
TIINNG
WHA-?!
FWAP

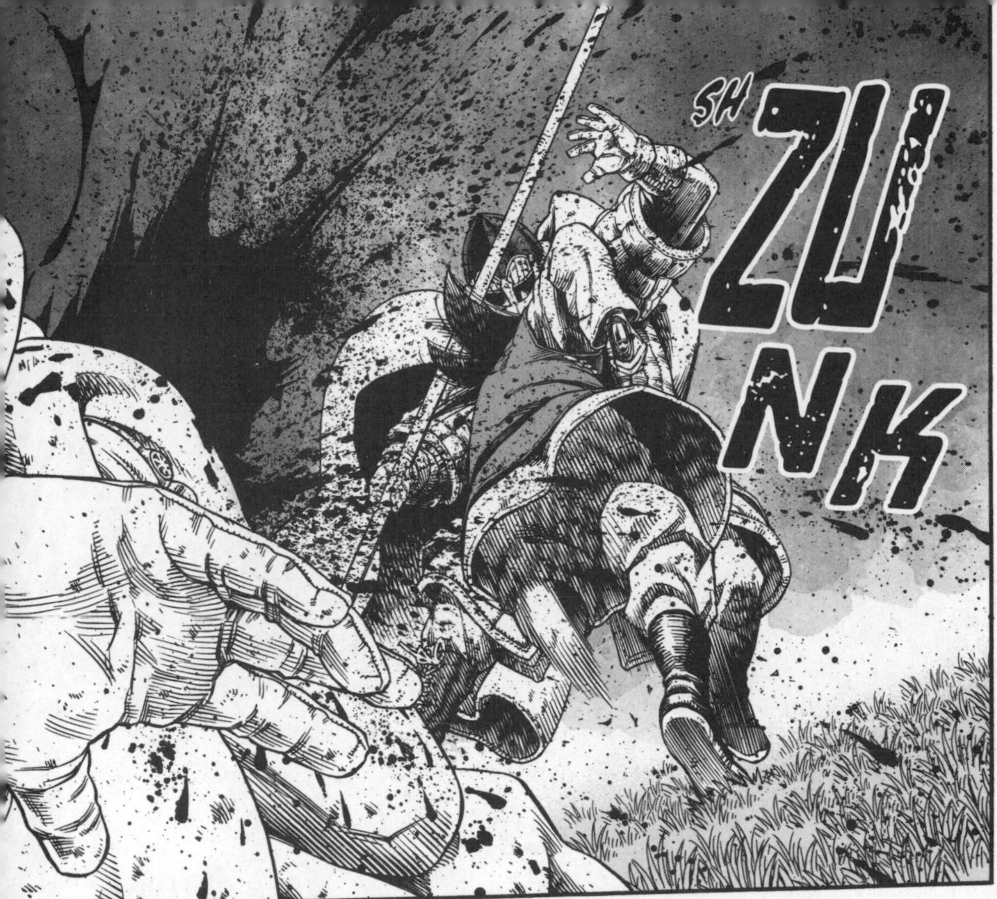
SHZUNK
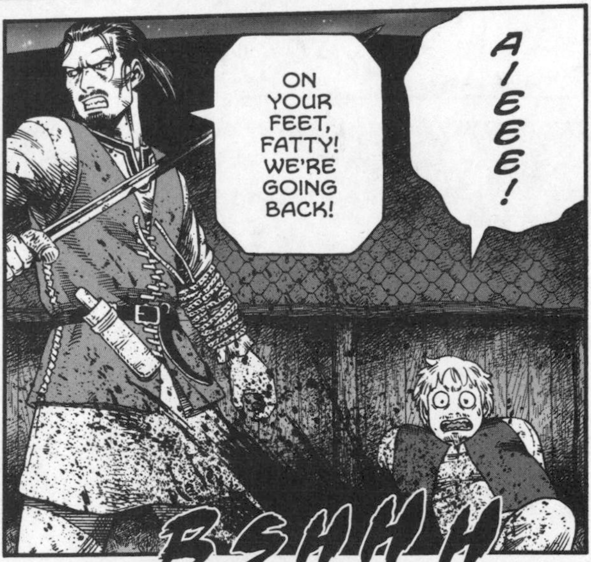
AIEEE!
ON YOUR FEET, FATTY! WE'RE GOING BACK!
BSHHH
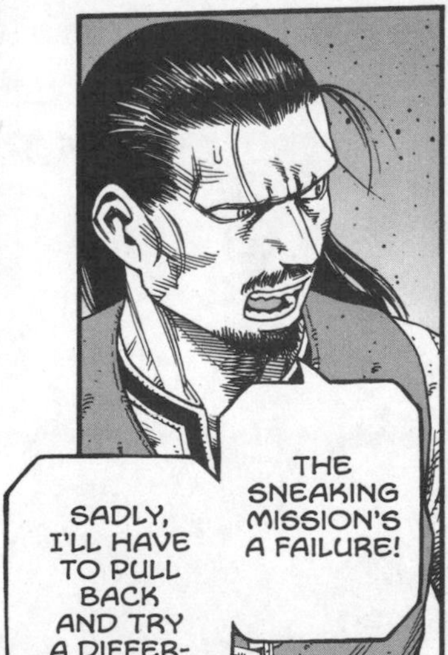
THE SNEAKING MISSION'S A FAILURE!
SADLY, I'LL HAVE TO PULL BACK AND TRY A DIFFERENT...

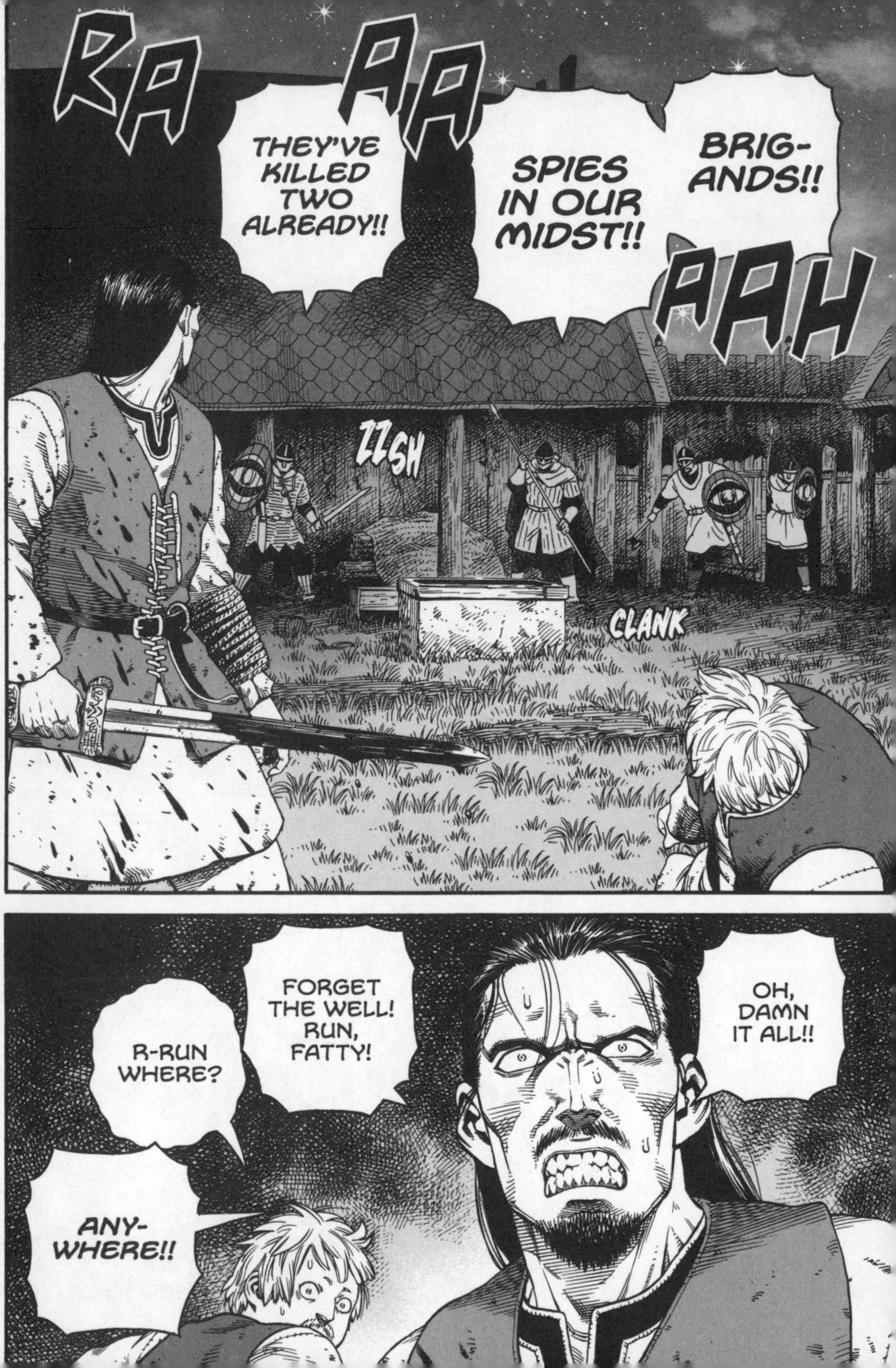
RA AA AAH
BRIG-ANDS!!
SPIES IN OUR MIDST!!
THEY'VE KILLED TWO ALREADY!!
ZZSH
CLANK
OH, DAMN IT ALL!!
FORGET THE WELL! RUN, FATTY!
R-RUN WHERE?
ANY-WHERE!!

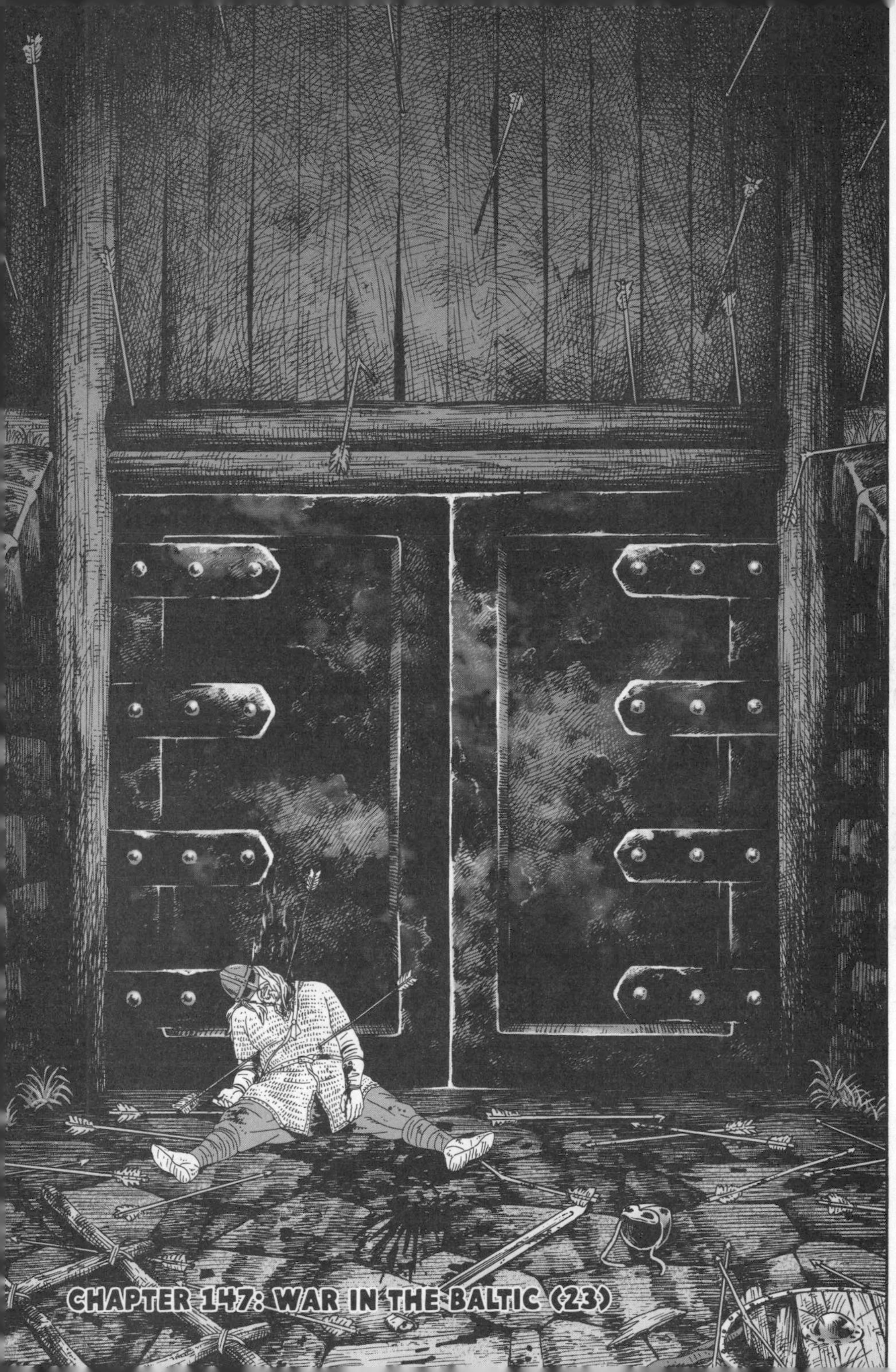
CHAPTER 147: WAR IN THE BALTIC (23)

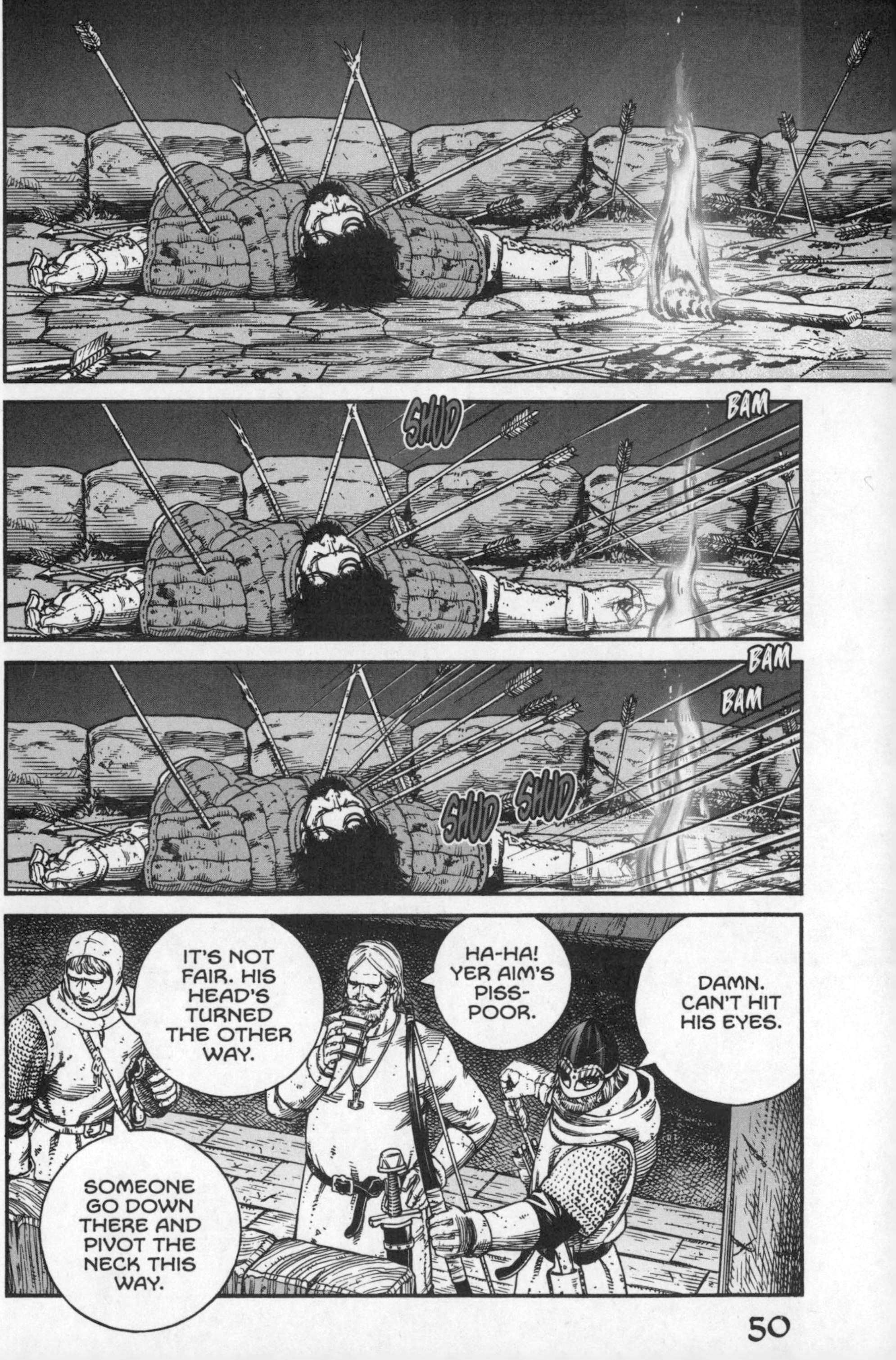
BAM
SHUD
BAM
BAM
SHUD
SHUD
DAMN. CAN'T HIT HIS EYES.
HA-HA! YER AIM'S PISS-POOR.
IT'S NOT FAIR. HIS HEAD'S TURNED THE OTHER WAY.
SOMEONE GO DOWN THERE AND PIVOT THE NECK THIS WAY.

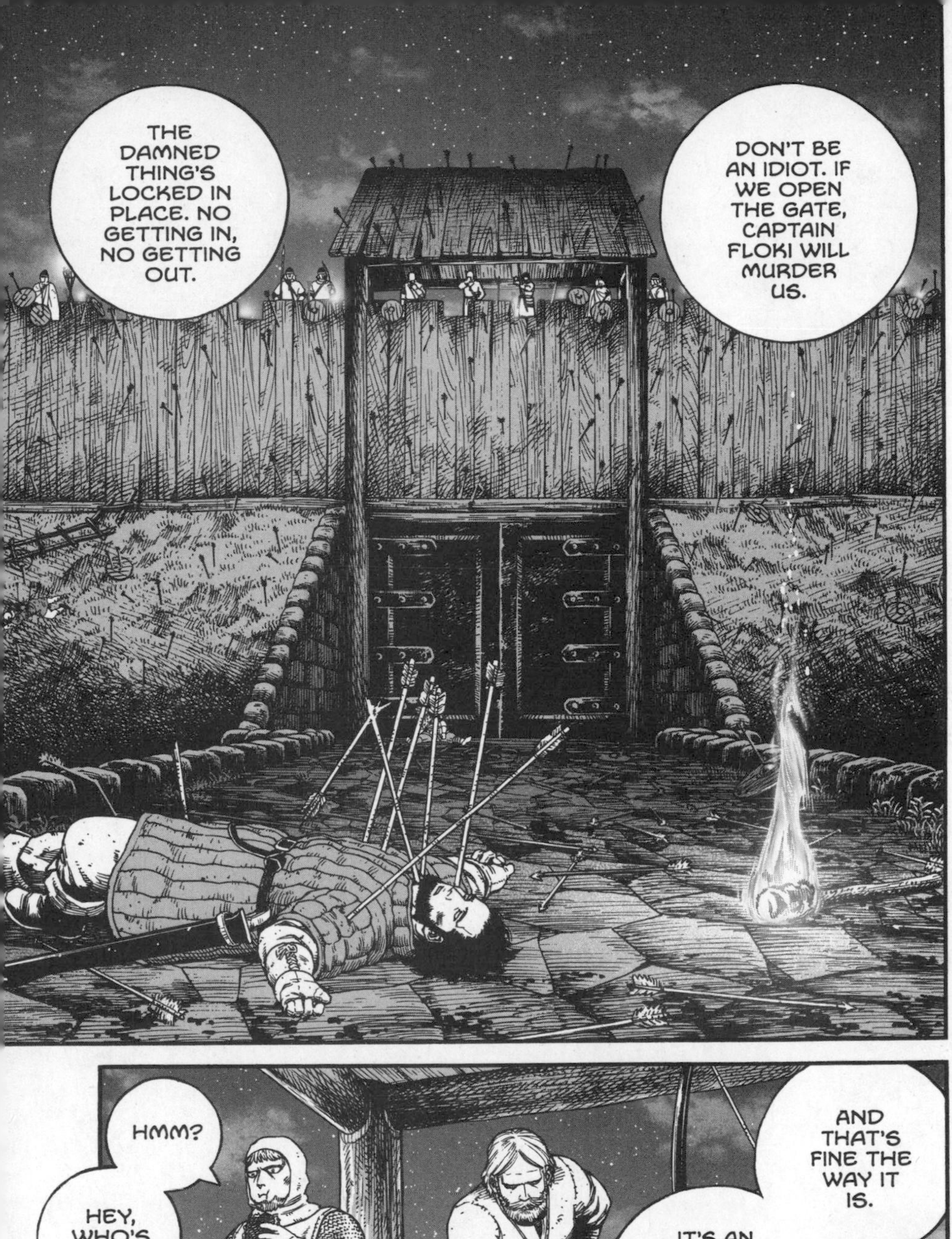
DON'T BE AN IDIOT. IF WE OPEN THE GATE, CAPTAIN FLOKI WILL MURDER US.
THE DAMNED THING'S LOCKED IN PLACE. NO GETTING IN, NO GETTING OUT.

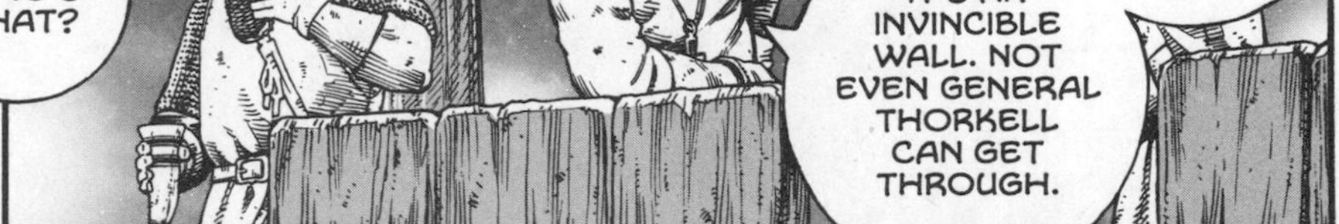
AND THAT'S FINE THE WAY IT IS.
IT'S AN INVINCIBLE WALL. NOT EVEN GENERAL THORKELL CAN GET THROUGH.
HMM?
HEY, WHO'S THAT?

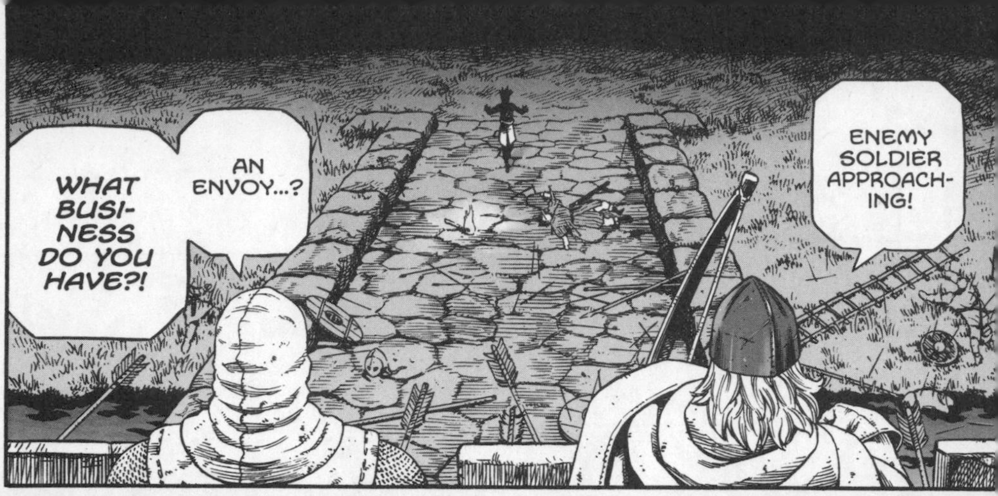
ENEMY SOLDIER APPROACHING!
AN ENVOY...?
WHAT BUSINESS DO YOU HAVE?!

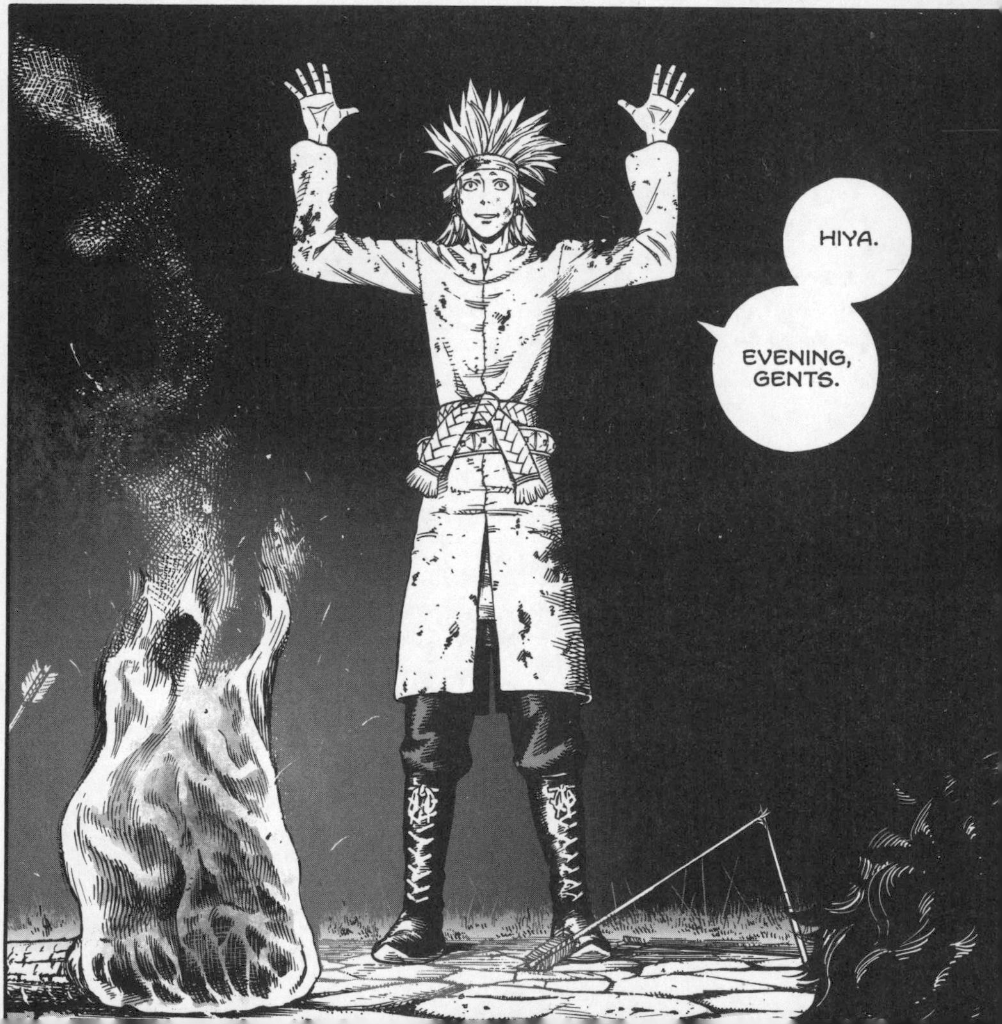
HIYA.
EVENING, GENTS.

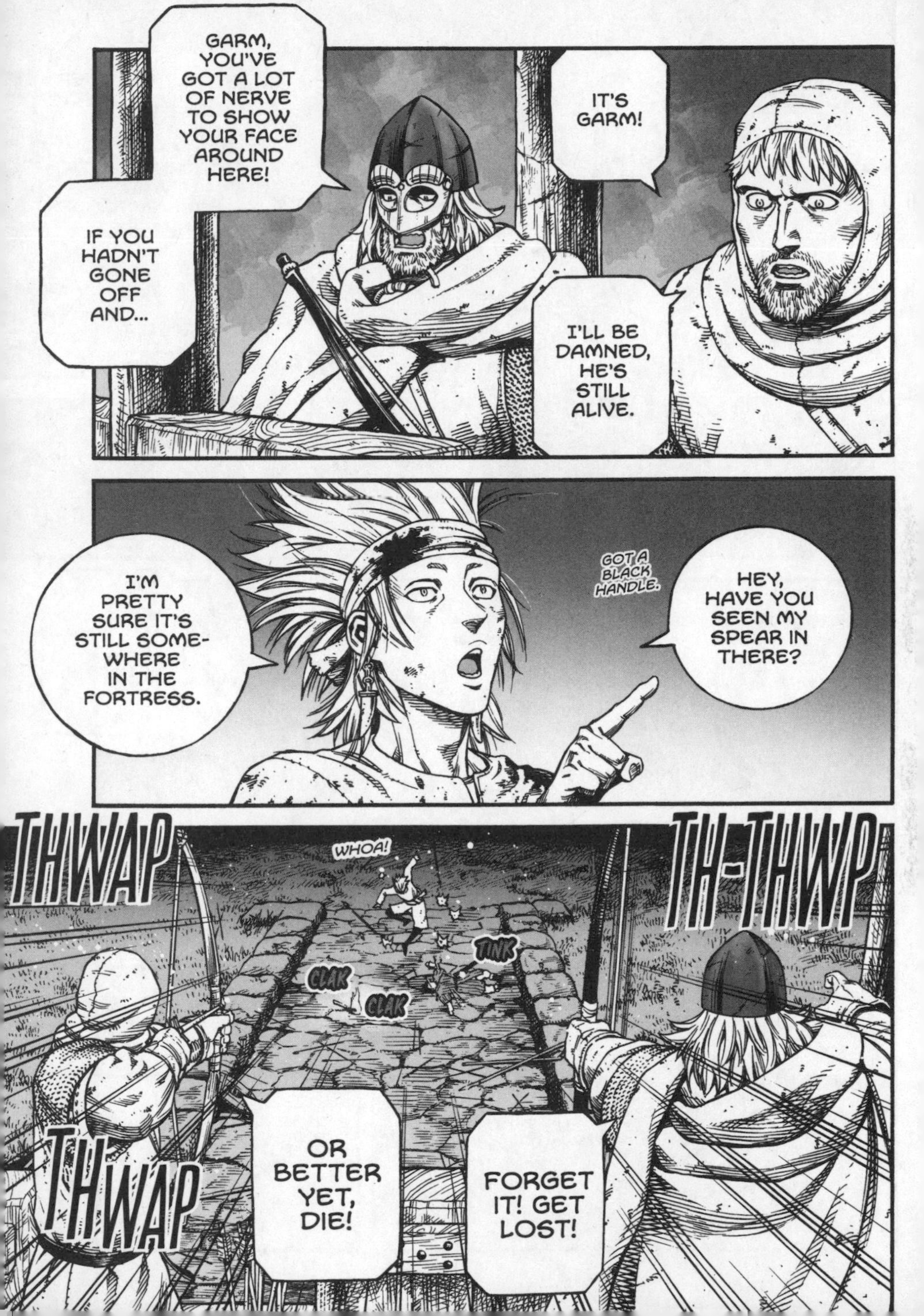
IT'S GARM!
I'LL BE DAMNED, HE'S STILL ALIVE.
GARM, YOU'VE GOT A LOT OF NERVE TO SHOW YOUR FACE AROUND HERE!
IF YOU HADN'T GONE OFF AND...
HEY, HAVE YOU SEEN MY SPEAR IN THERE?
GOT A BLACK HANDLE.
I'M PRETTY SURE IT'S STILL SOME-WHERE IN THE FORTRESS.
TH-THWP
THWAP
WHOA!
TINK
CLAK
CLAK
FORGET IT! GET LOST!
OR BETTER YET, DIE!
THWAP

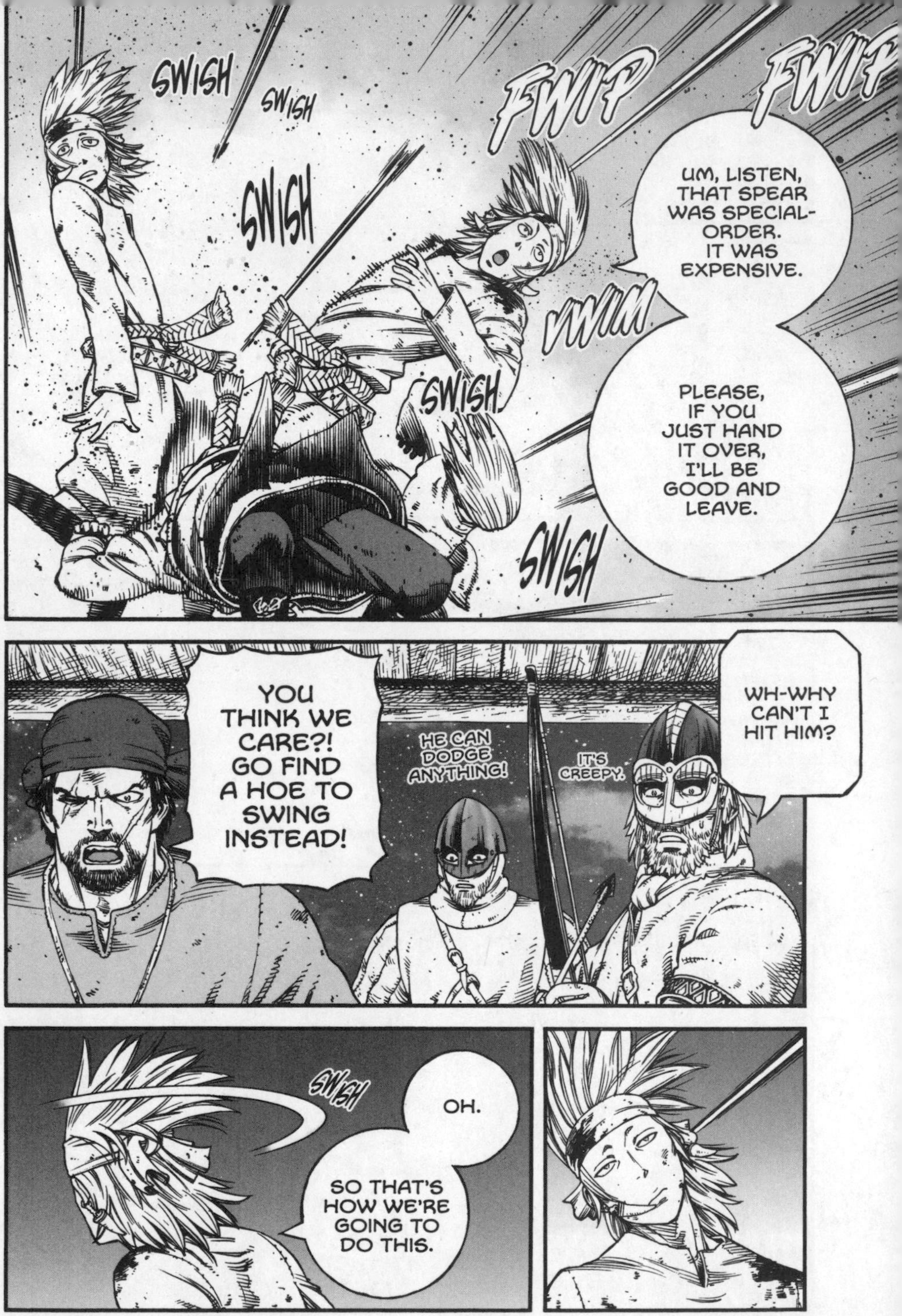
FWIP
FWIP
UM, LISTEN, THAT SPEAR WAS SPECIAL-ORDER. IT WAS EXPENSIVE.
VWIM
PLEASE, IF YOU JUST HAND IT OVER, I'LL BE GOOD AND LEAVE.
SWISH
SWISH
SWISH
SWISH
SWISH
WH-WHY CAN'T I HIT HIM?
IT'S CREEPY.
HE CAN DODGE ANYTHING!
YOU THINK WE CARE?! GO FIND A HOE TO SWING INSTEAD!
SWISH
OH.
SO THAT'S HOW WE'RE GOING TO DO THIS.

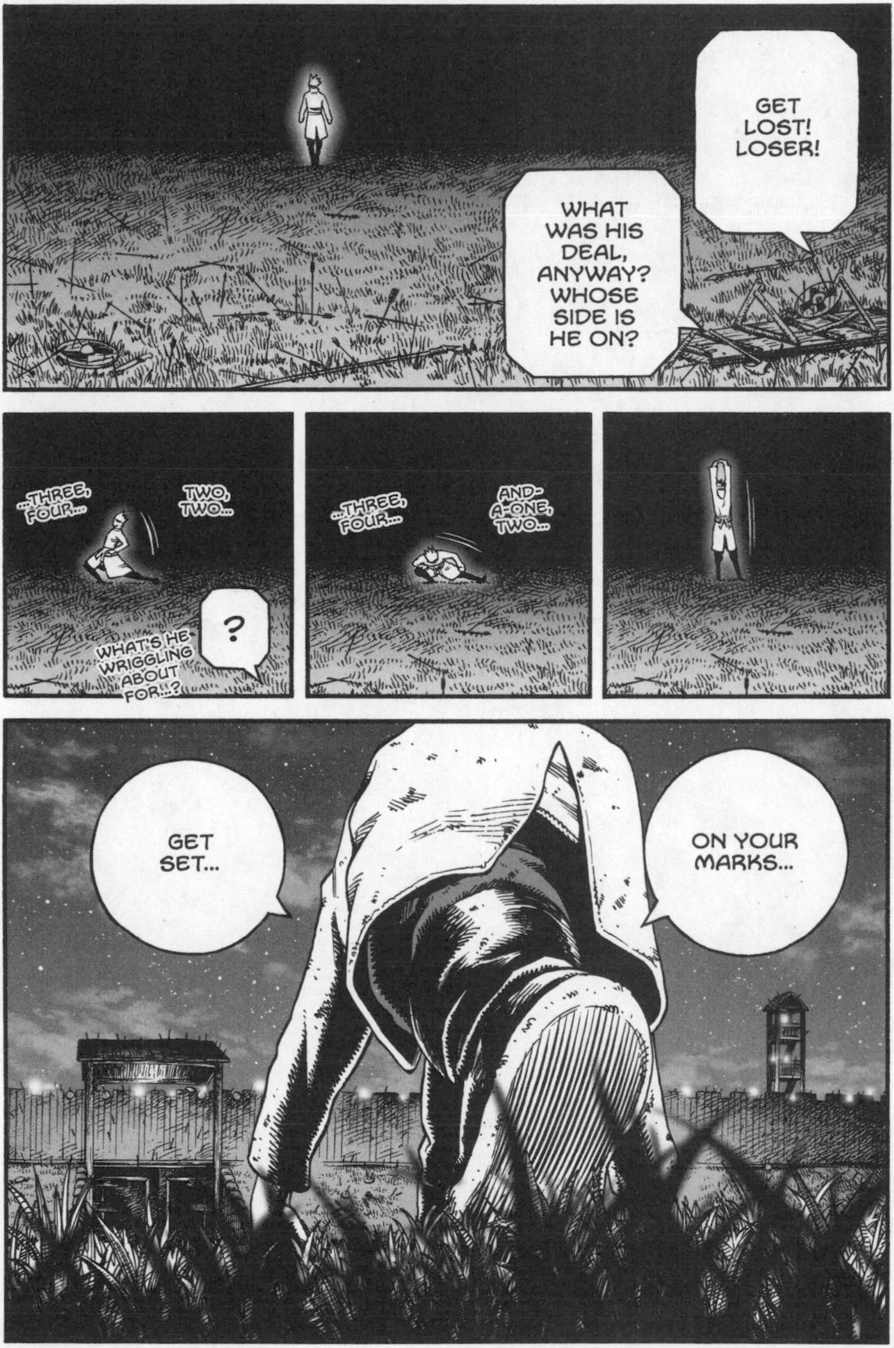
GET LOST! LOSER!
WHAT WAS HIS DEAL, ANYWAY? WHOSE SIDE IS HE ON?
AND-A-ONE, TWO...
...THREE, FOUR...
TWO, TWO...
...THREE, FOUR...
?
WHAT'S HE WRIGGLING ABOUT FOR...?
ON YOUR MARKS...
GET SET...

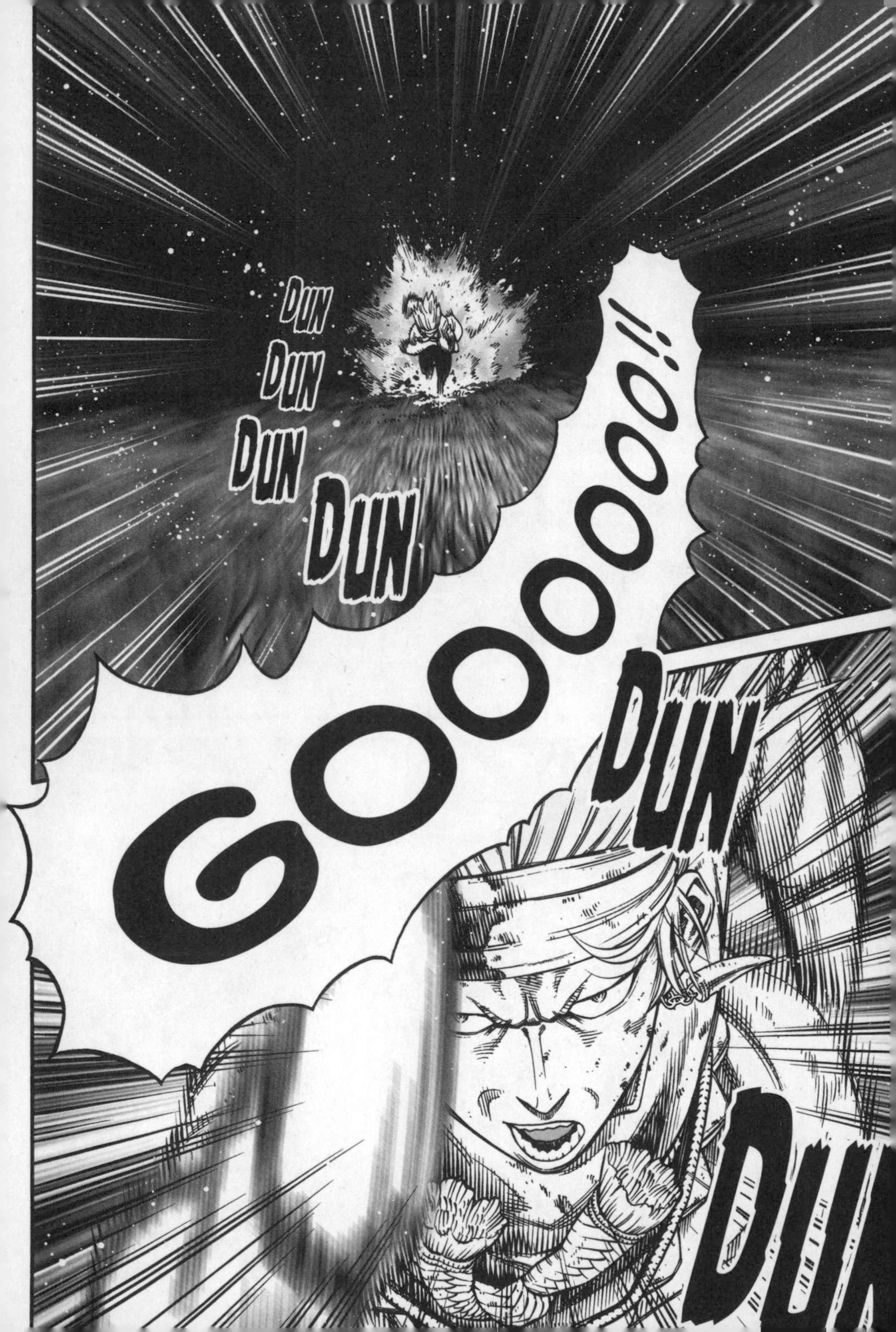
DUN
DUN
DUN
DUN
GOOOOOOO!!
DUN
DUN

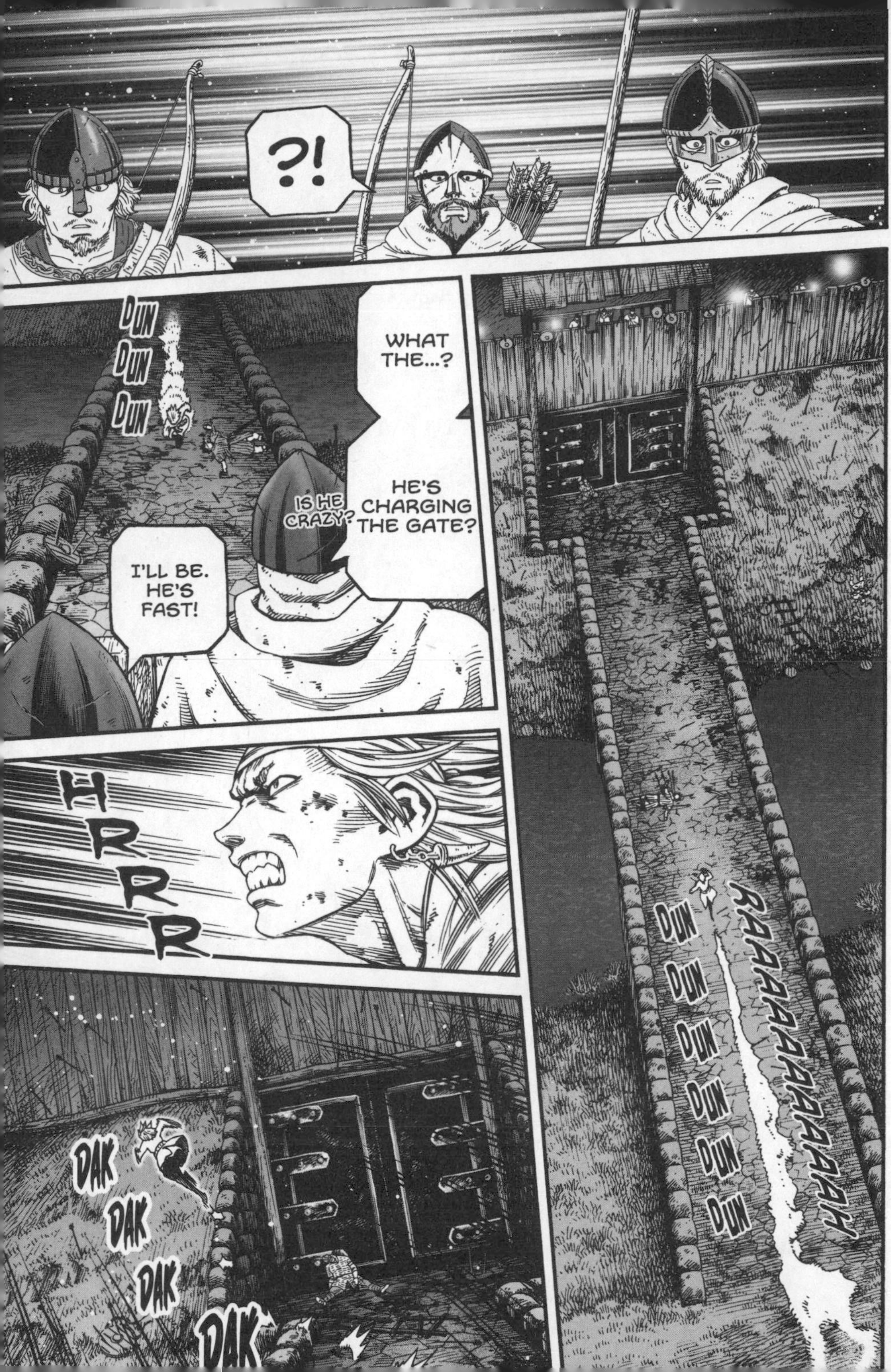
?!
RAAAAAAAAAAAH
DUN DUN DUN DUN DUN DUN
WHAT THE...?
HE'S CHARGING THE GATE?
IS HE CRAZY?
DUN DUN DUN
I'LL BE. HE'S FAST!
HRRR
DAK DAK DAK DAK

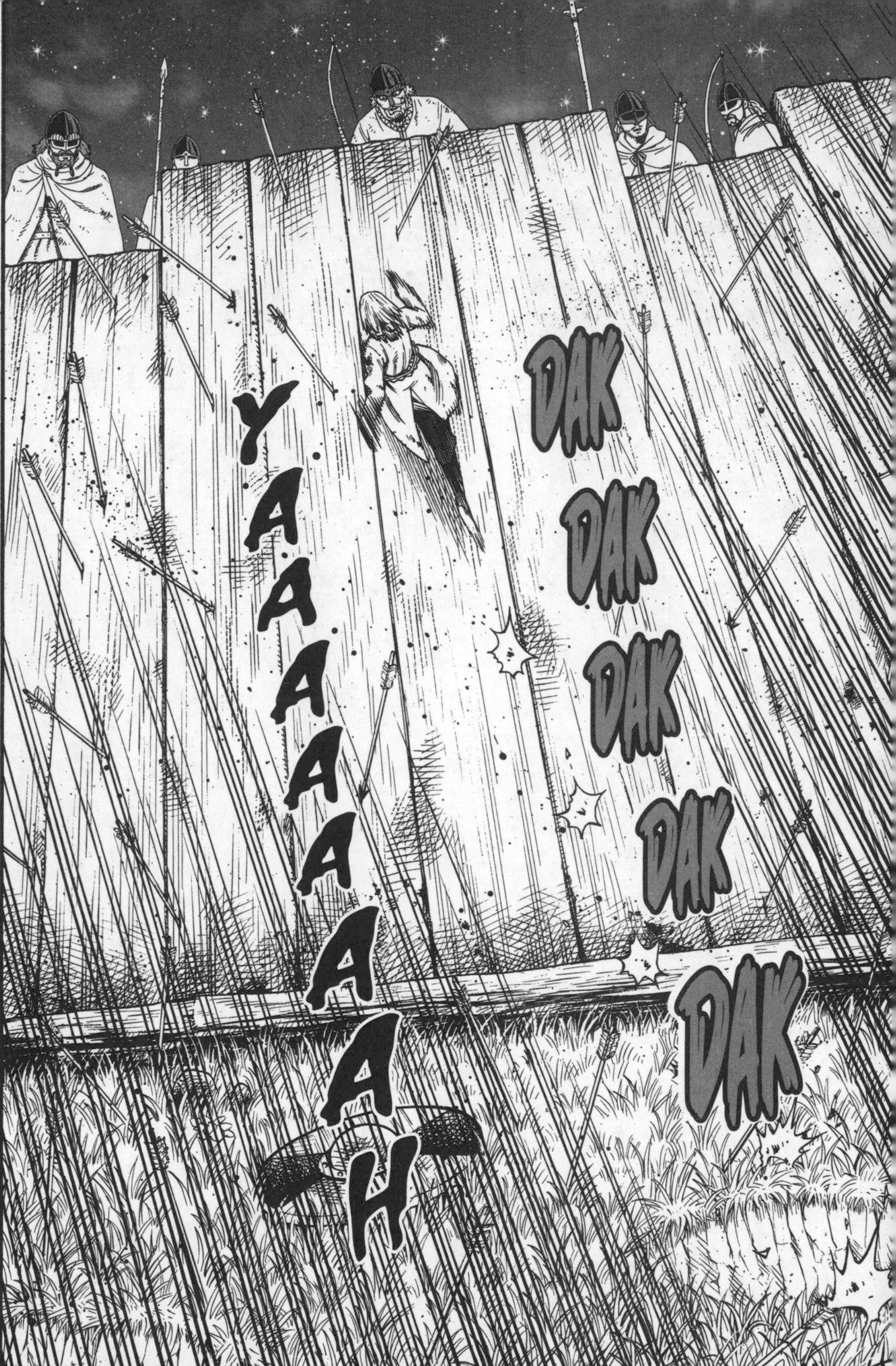

DAK DAK DAK DAK DAK
YAAAAAAAAH

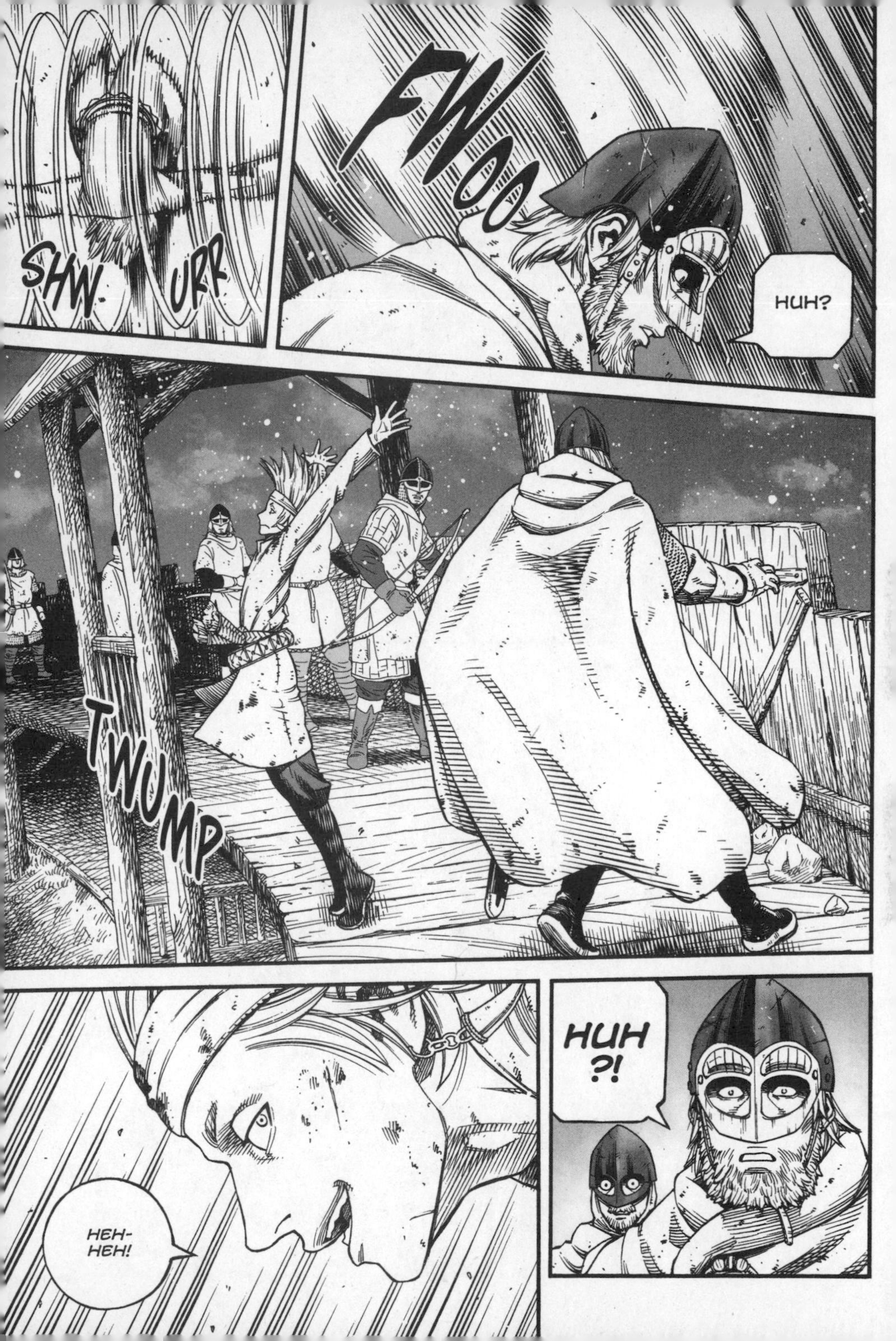
FWOO
HUH?
SHW URR
TWUMP
HUH ?!
HEH-HEH!

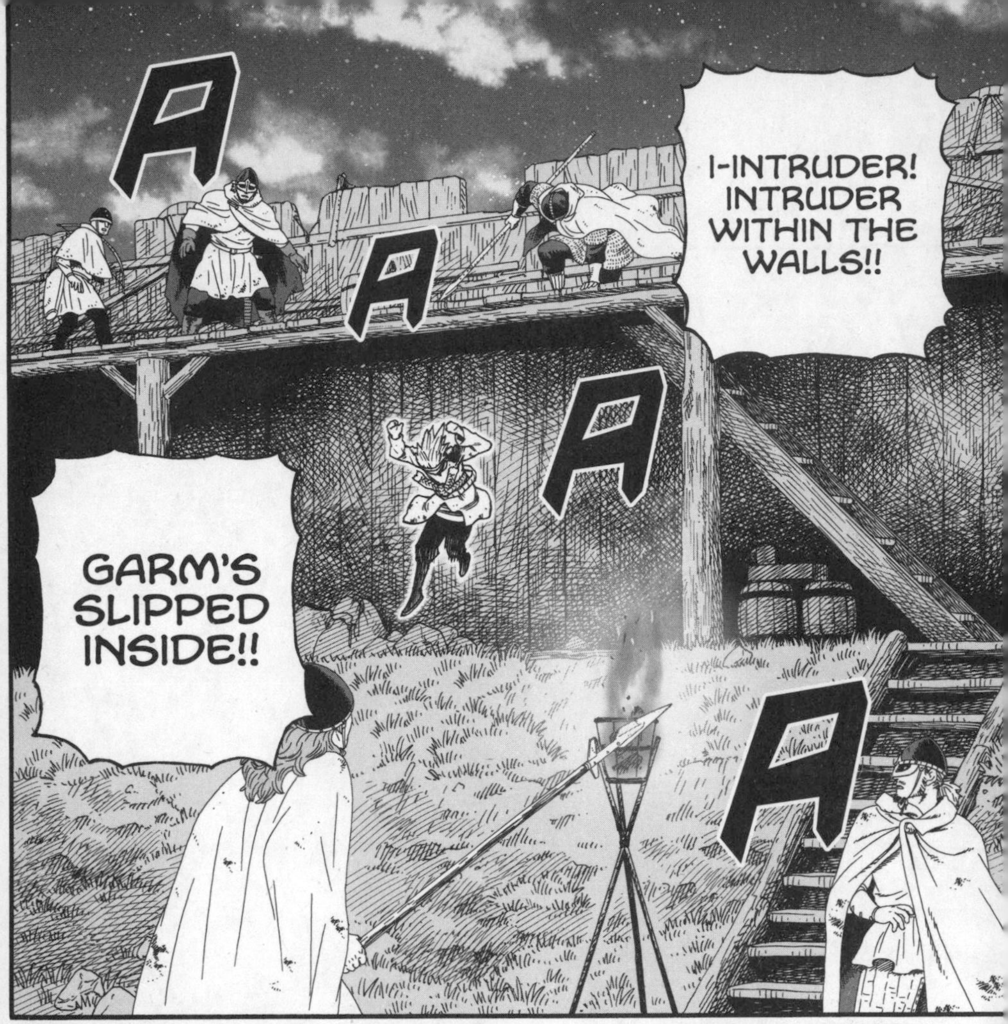
I-INTRUDER! INTRUDER WITHIN THE WALLS!!
AAAAA
GARM'S SLIPPED INSIDE!!
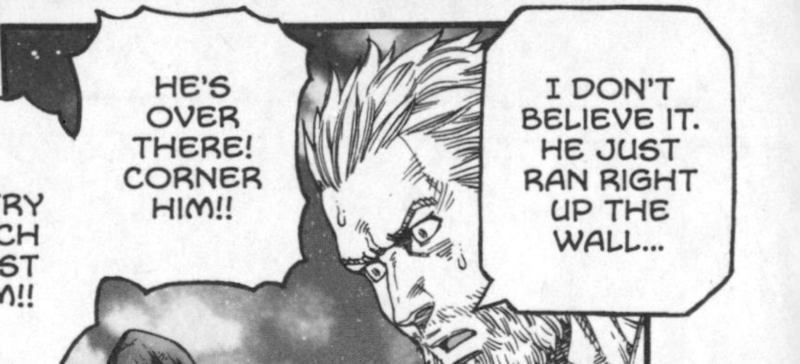
I DON'T BELIEVE IT. HE JUST RAN RIGHT UP THE WALL...
HE'S OVER THERE! CORNER HIM!!
DON'T TRY TO CATCH HIM, JUST KILL HIM!!
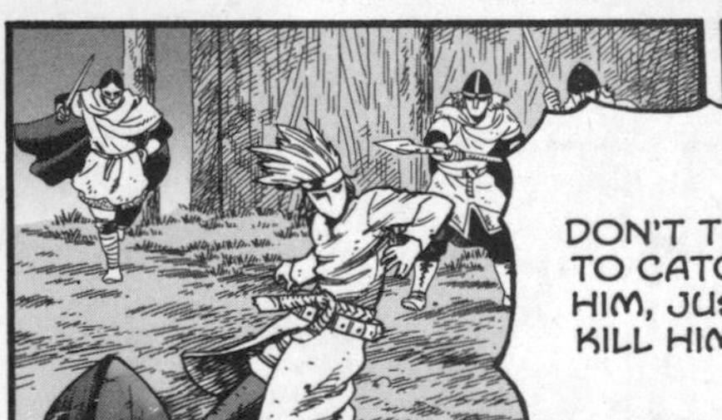

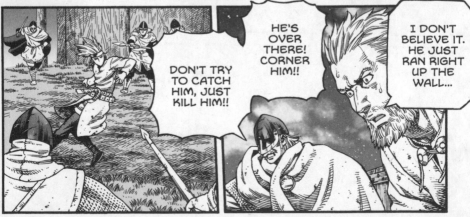

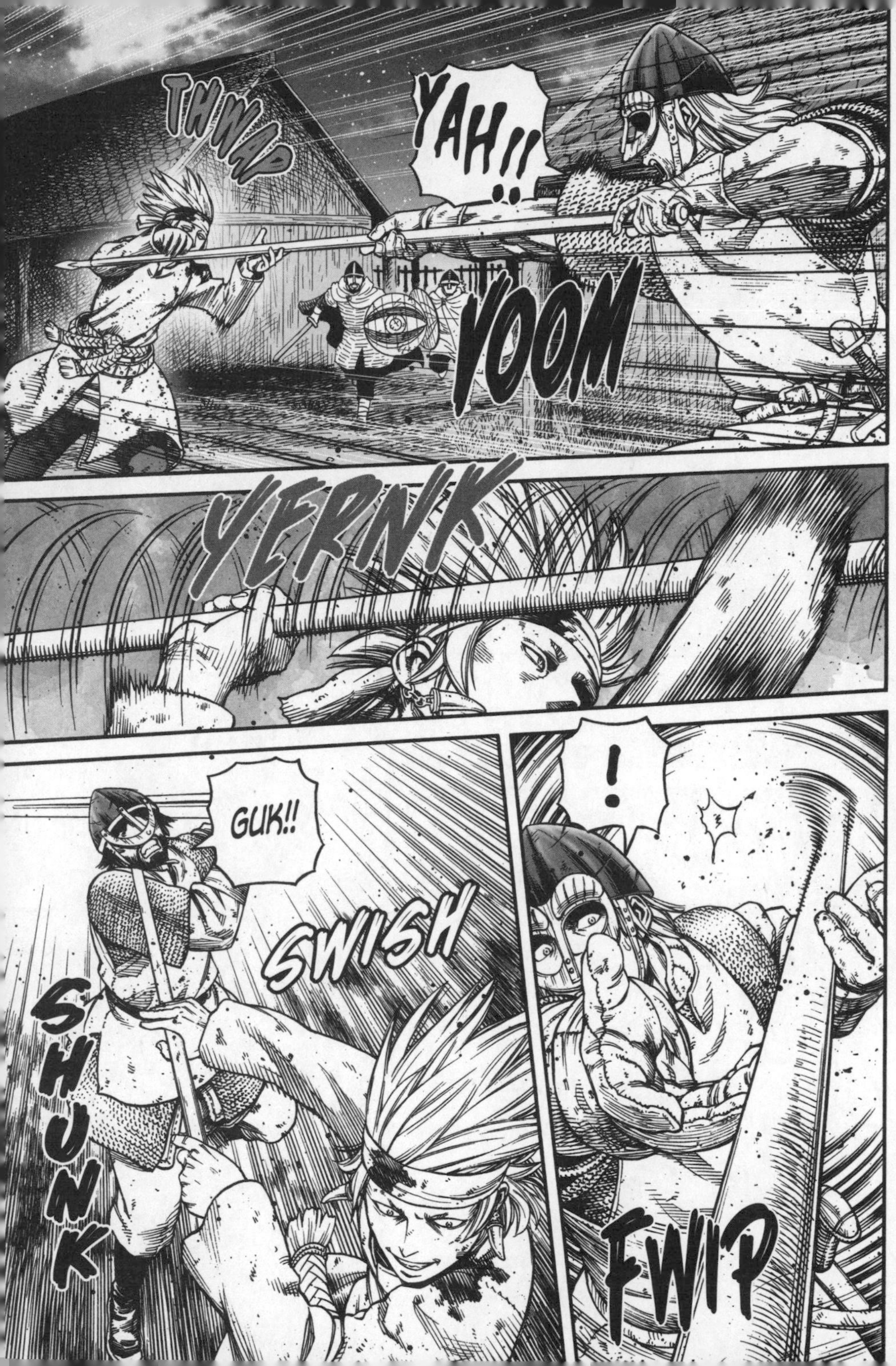
YAH!!
THWAP
VOOM
YERNK
!
FWIP
GUK!!
SWISH
SHUNK

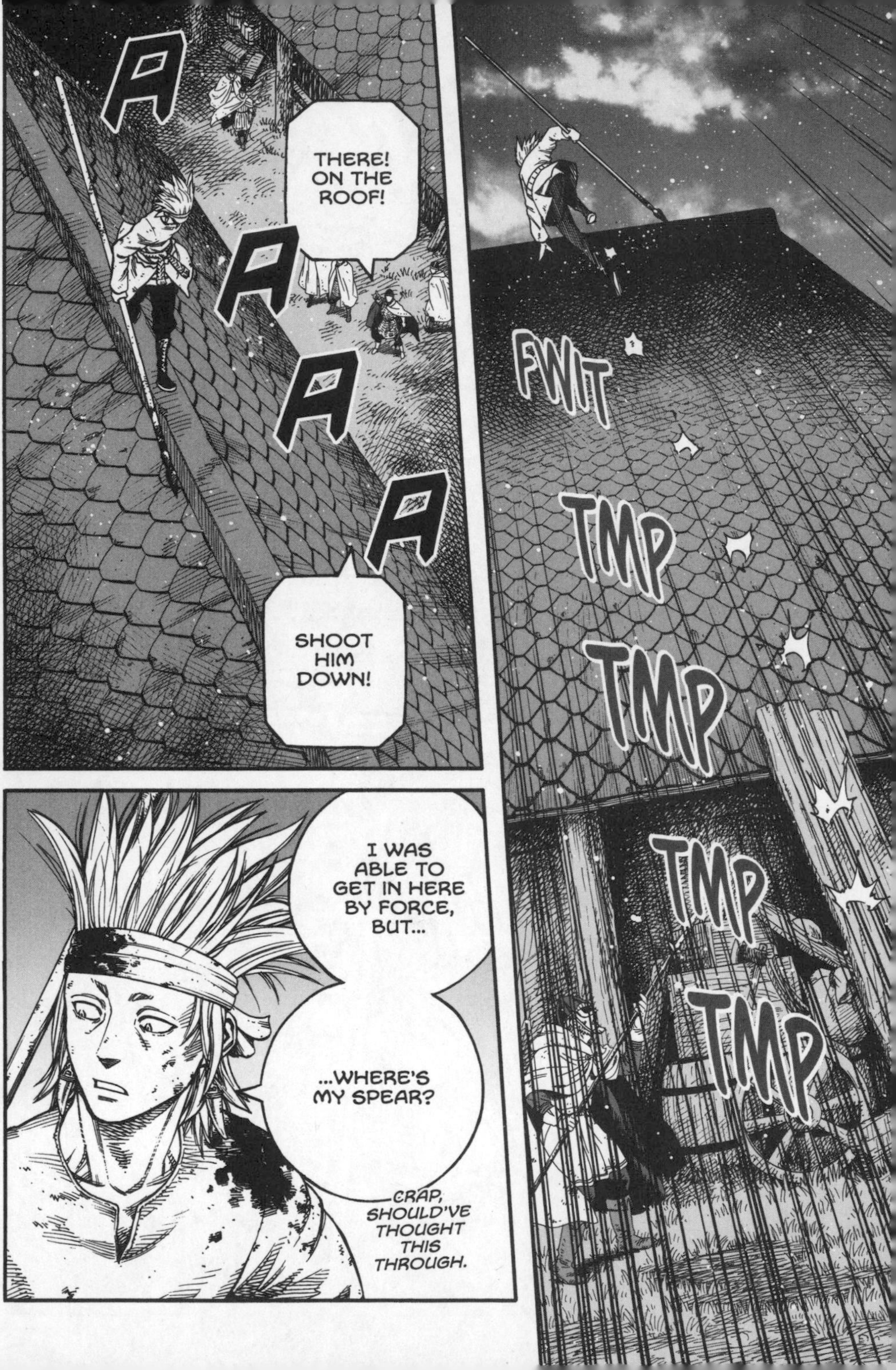

FWIT
TMP
TMP
TMP
TMP
AAAA
THERE! ON THE ROOF!
SHOOT HIM DOWN!
I WAS ABLE TO GET IN HERE BY FORCE, BUT...
...WHERE'S MY SPEAR?
CRAP, SHOULD'VE THOUGHT THIS THROUGH.

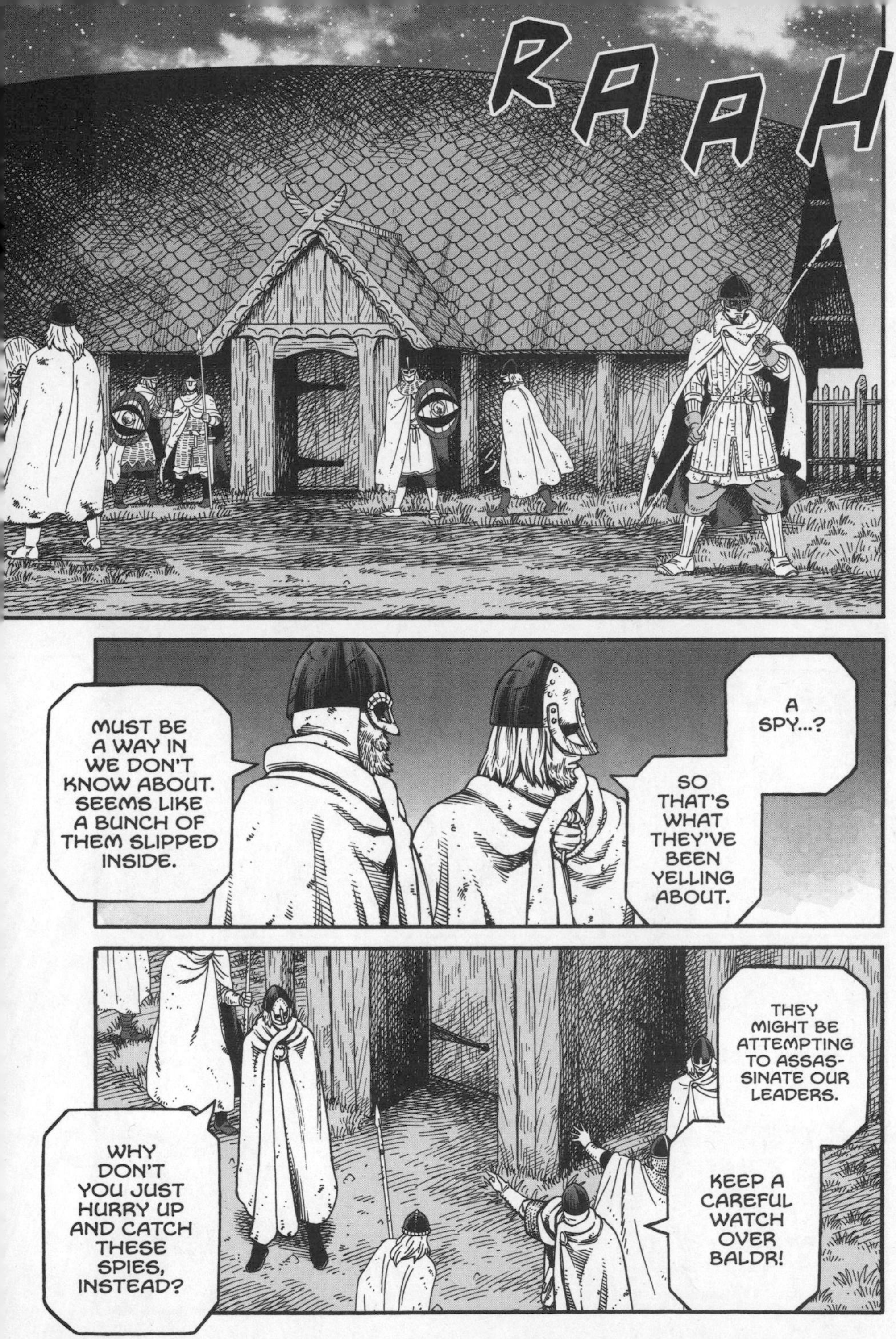
RAAH
A SPY...?
SO THAT'S WHAT THEY'VE BEEN YELLING ABOUT.
MUST BE A WAY IN WE DON'T KNOW ABOUT. SEEMS LIKE A BUNCH OF THEM SLIPPED INSIDE.
THEY MIGHT BE ATTEMPTING TO ASSAS-SINATE OUR LEADERS.
KEEP A CAREFUL WATCH OVER BALDR!
WHY DON'T YOU JUST HURRY UP AND CATCH THESE SPIES, INSTEAD?

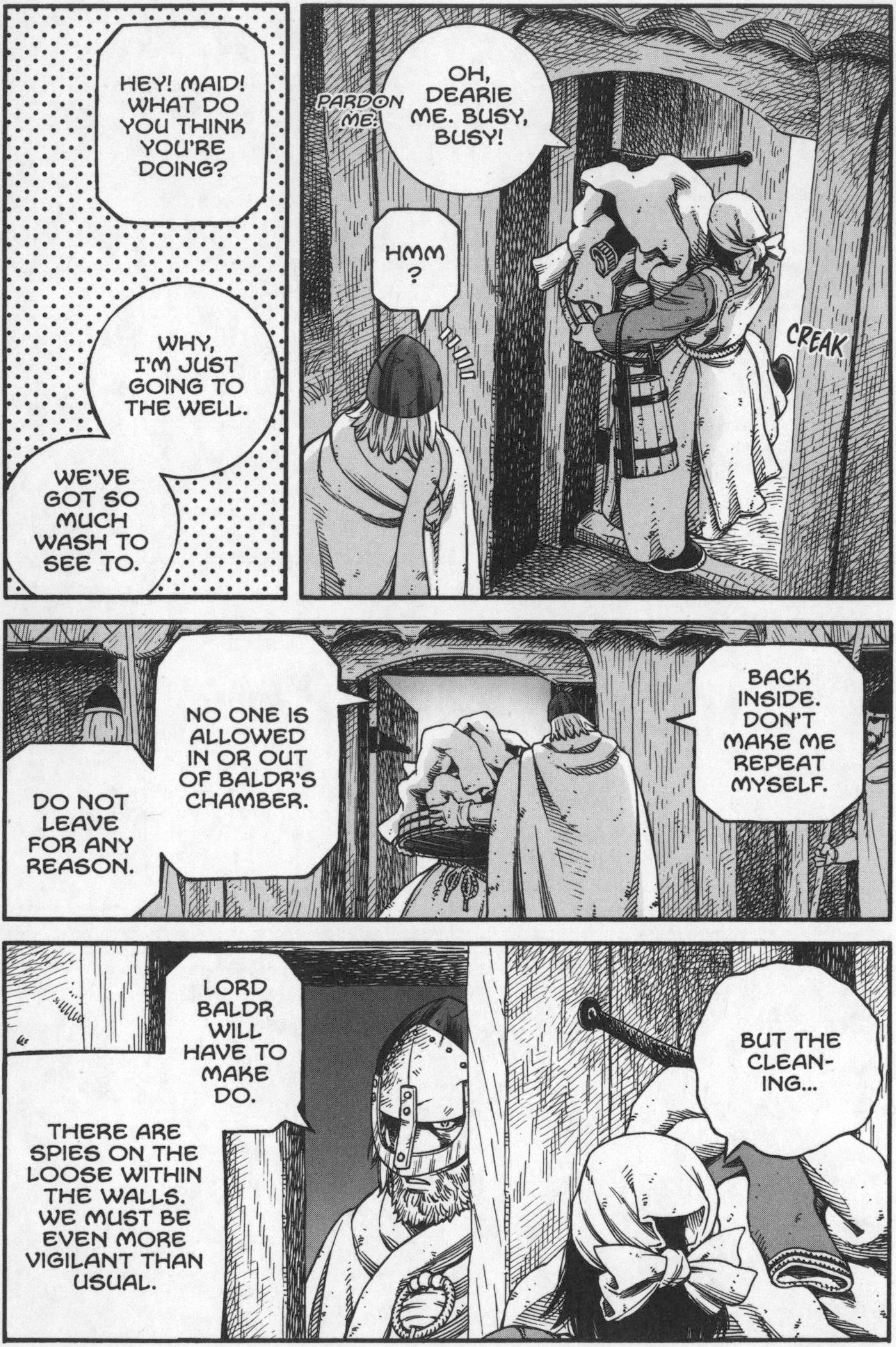
PARDON ME.
OH, DEARIE ME. BUSY, BUSY!
HMM?
CREAK
HEY! MAID! WHAT DO YOU THINK YOU'RE DOING?
WHY, I'M JUST GOING TO THE WELL.
WE'VE GOT SO MUCH WASH TO SEE TO.
BACK INSIDE. DON'T MAKE ME REPEAT MYSELF.
NO ONE IS ALLOWED IN OR OUT OF BALDR'S CHAMBER.
DO NOT LEAVE FOR ANY REASON.
BUT THE CLEAN-ING...
LORD BALDR WILL HAVE TO MAKE DO.
THERE ARE SPIES ON THE LOOSE WITHIN THE WALLS. WE MUST BE EVEN MORE VIGILANT THAN USUAL.

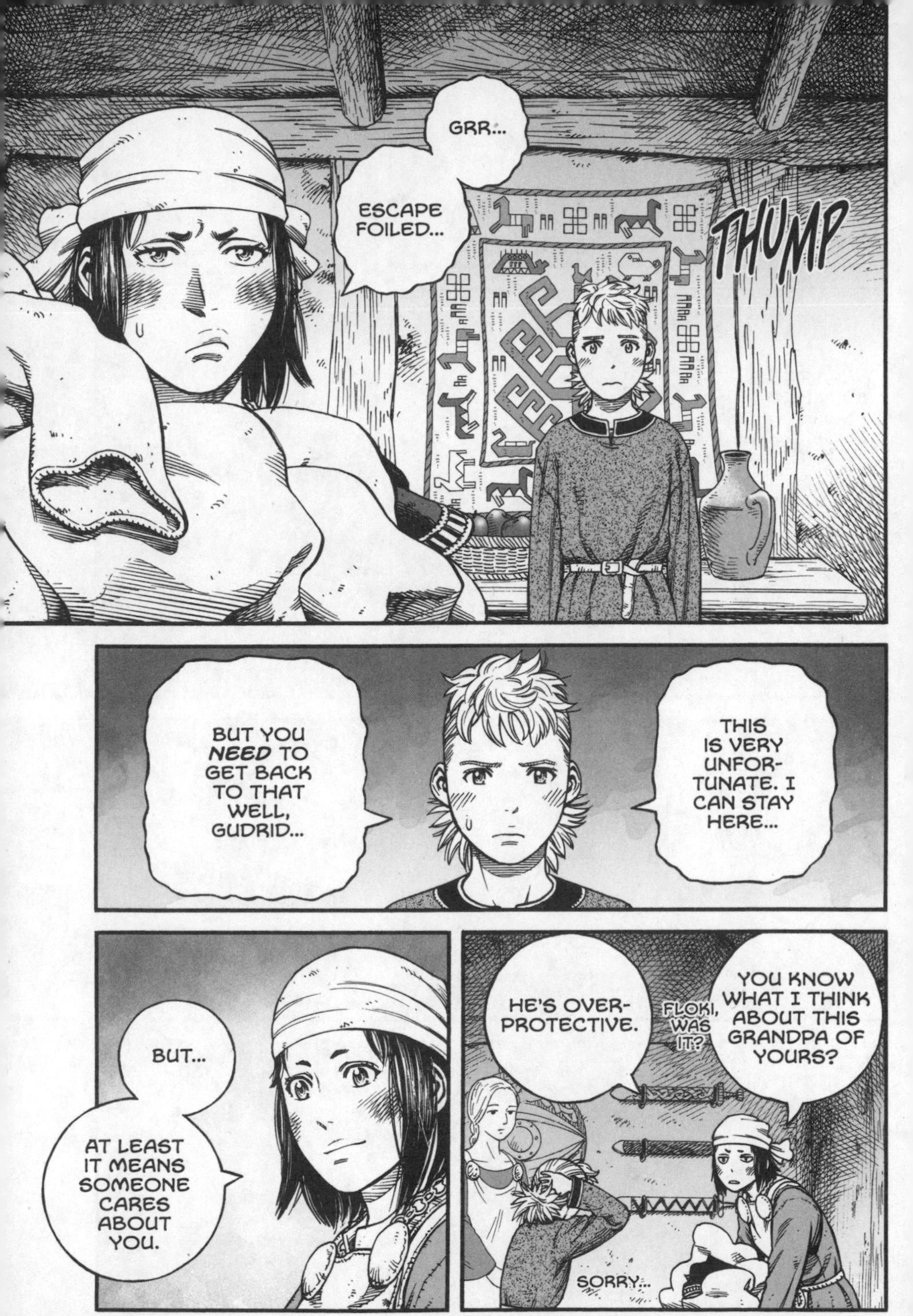
THUMP
GRR...
ESCAPE FOILED...
THIS IS VERY UNFOR-TUNATE. I CAN STAY HERE...
BUT YOU *NEED* TO GET BACK TO THAT WELL, GUDRID...
YOU KNOW WHAT I THINK ABOUT THIS GRANDPA OF YOURS?
FLOKI, WAS IT?
HE'S OVER-PROTECTIVE.
SORRY...
BUT...
AT LEAST IT MEANS SOMEONE CARES ABOUT YOU.

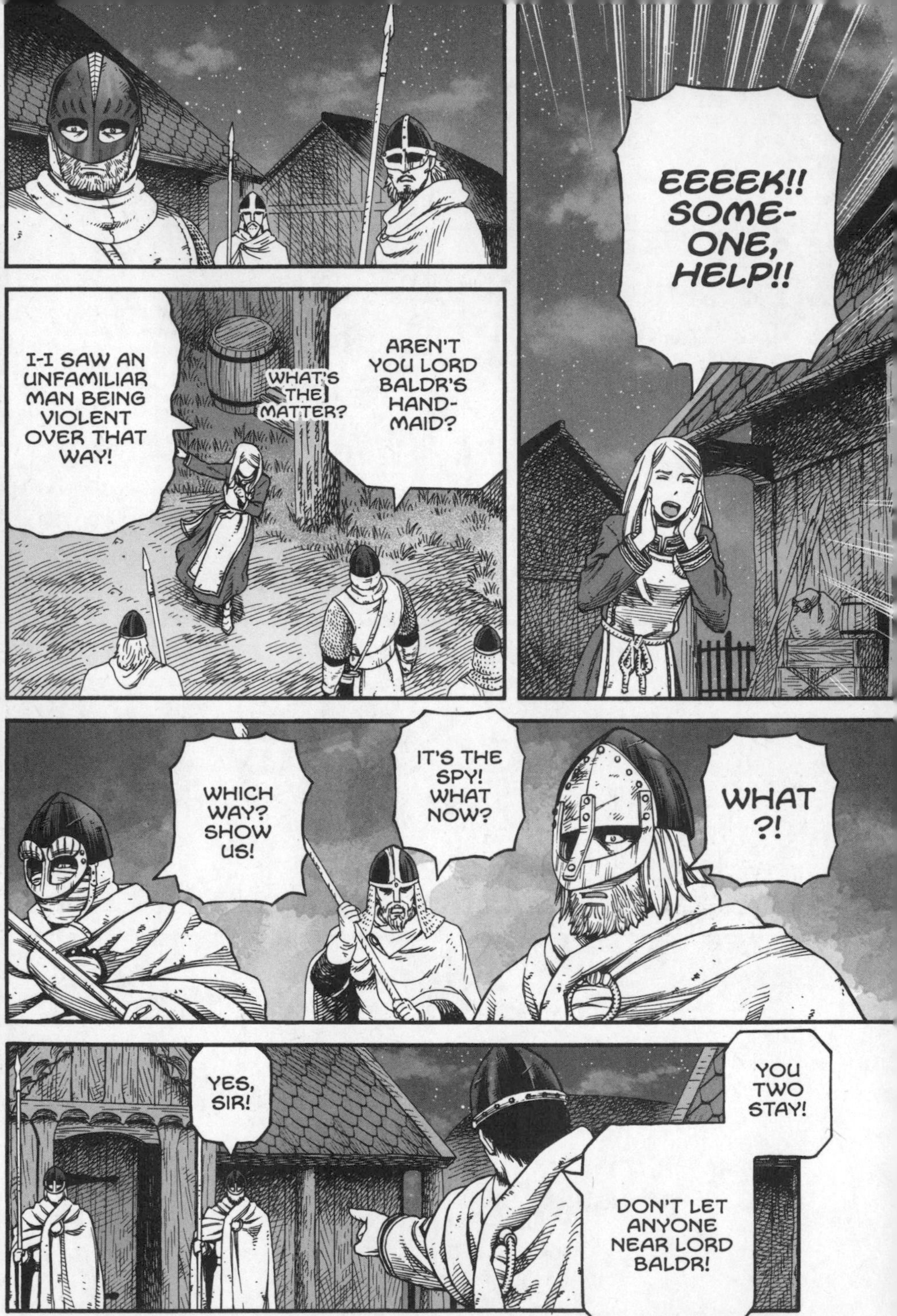
EEEEK!! SOME-ONE, HELP!!
AREN'T YOU LORD BALDR'S HAND-MAID?
WHAT'S THE MATTER?
I-I SAW AN UNFAMILIAR MAN BEING VIOLENT OVER THAT WAY!
WHAT?!
IT'S THE SPY! WHAT NOW?
WHICH WAY? SHOW US!
YOU TWO STAY!
DON'T LET ANYONE NEAR LORD BALDR!
YES, SIR!

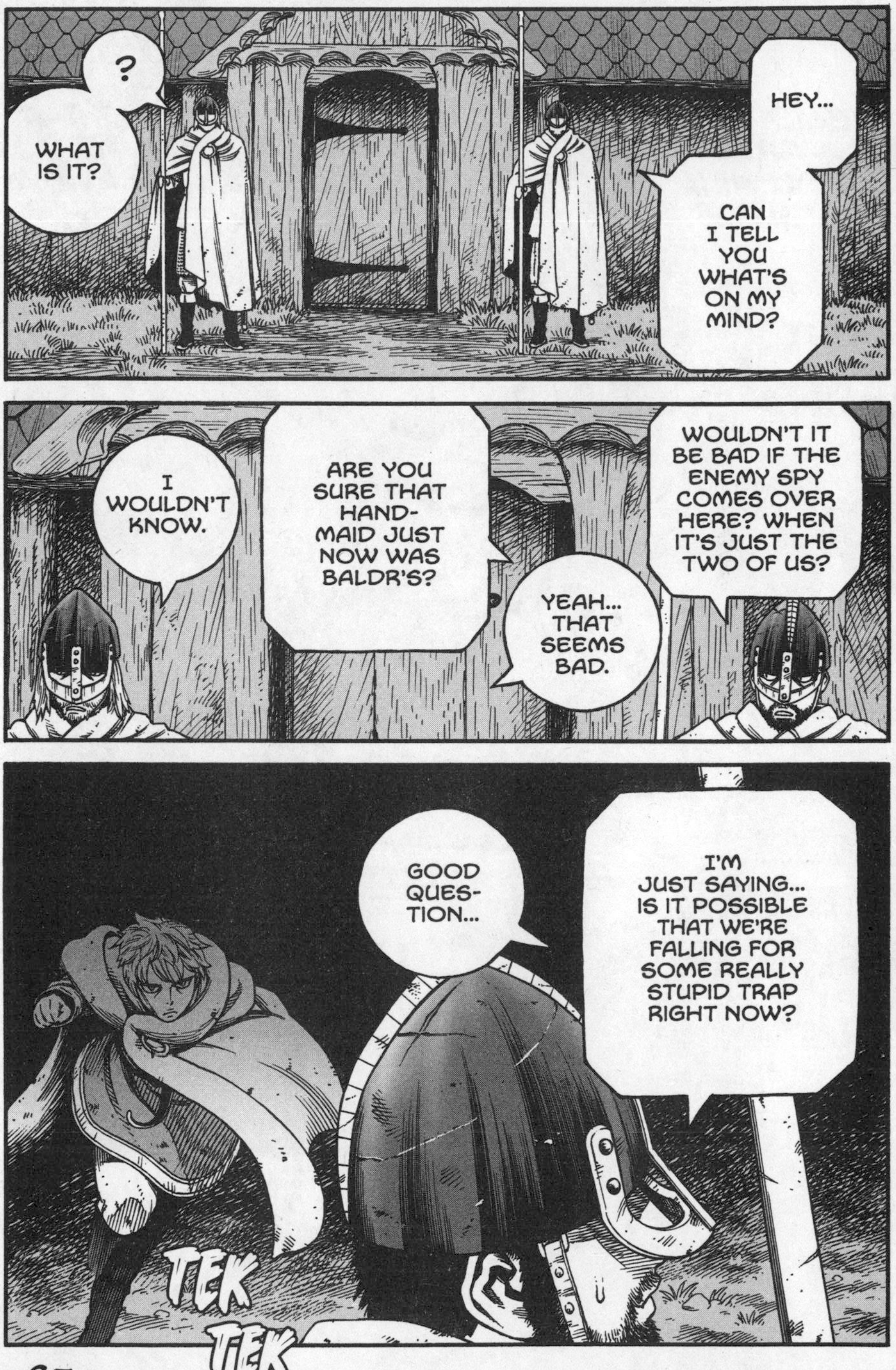
HEY...
CAN I TELL YOU WHAT'S ON MY MIND?
?
WHAT IS IT?
WOULDN'T IT BE BAD IF THE ENEMY SPY COMES OVER HERE? WHEN IT'S JUST THE TWO OF US?
YEAH... THAT SEEMS BAD.
ARE YOU SURE THAT HAND-MAID JUST NOW WAS BALDR'S?
I WOULDN'T KNOW.
I'M JUST SAYING... IS IT POSSIBLE THAT WE'RE FALLING FOR SOME REALLY STUPID TRAP RIGHT NOW?
GOOD QUES-TION...
TEK
TEK

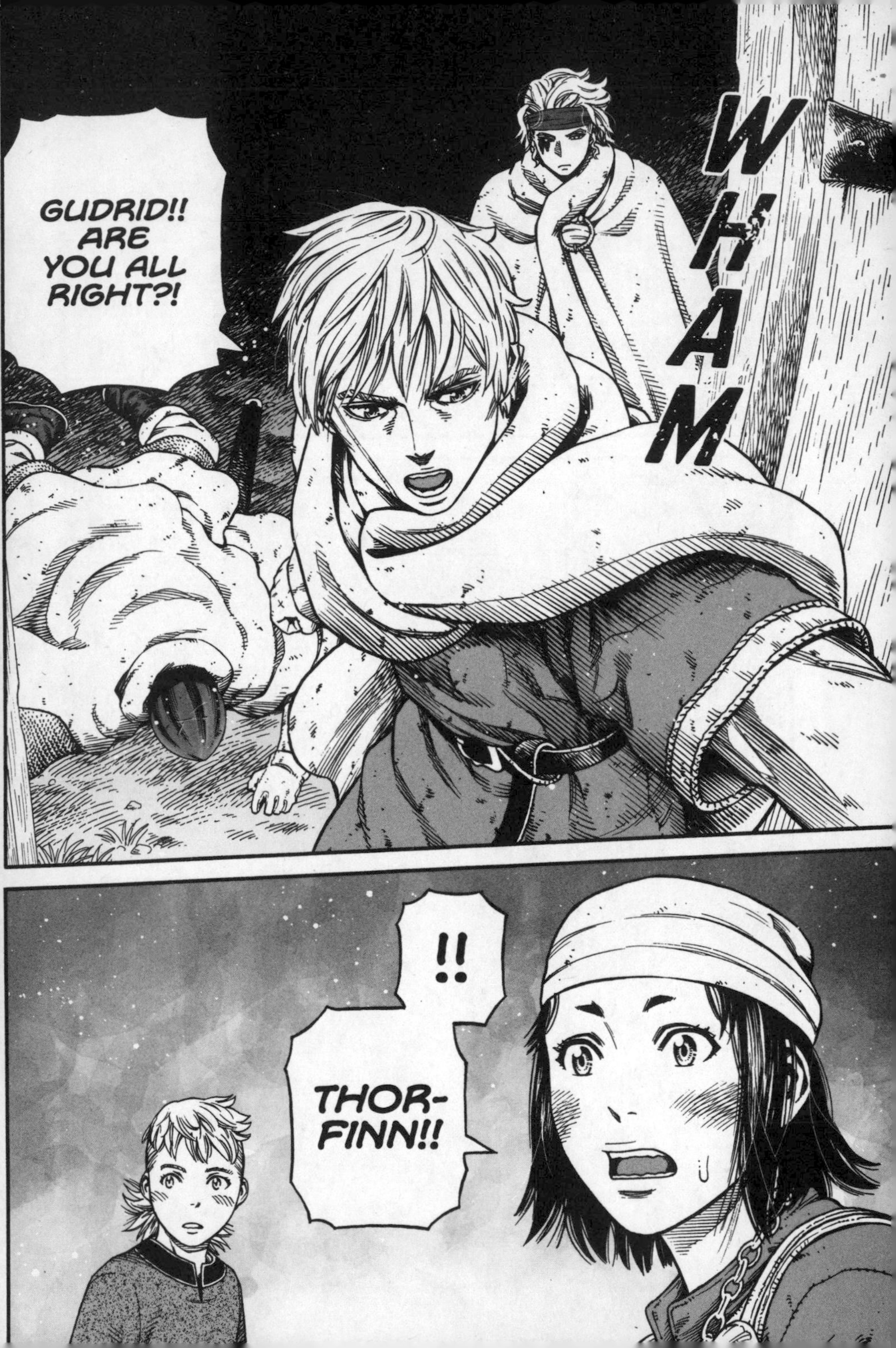
WHAM
GUDRID!! ARE YOU ALL RIGHT?!
!!
THOR-FINN!!

VINLAND SAGA

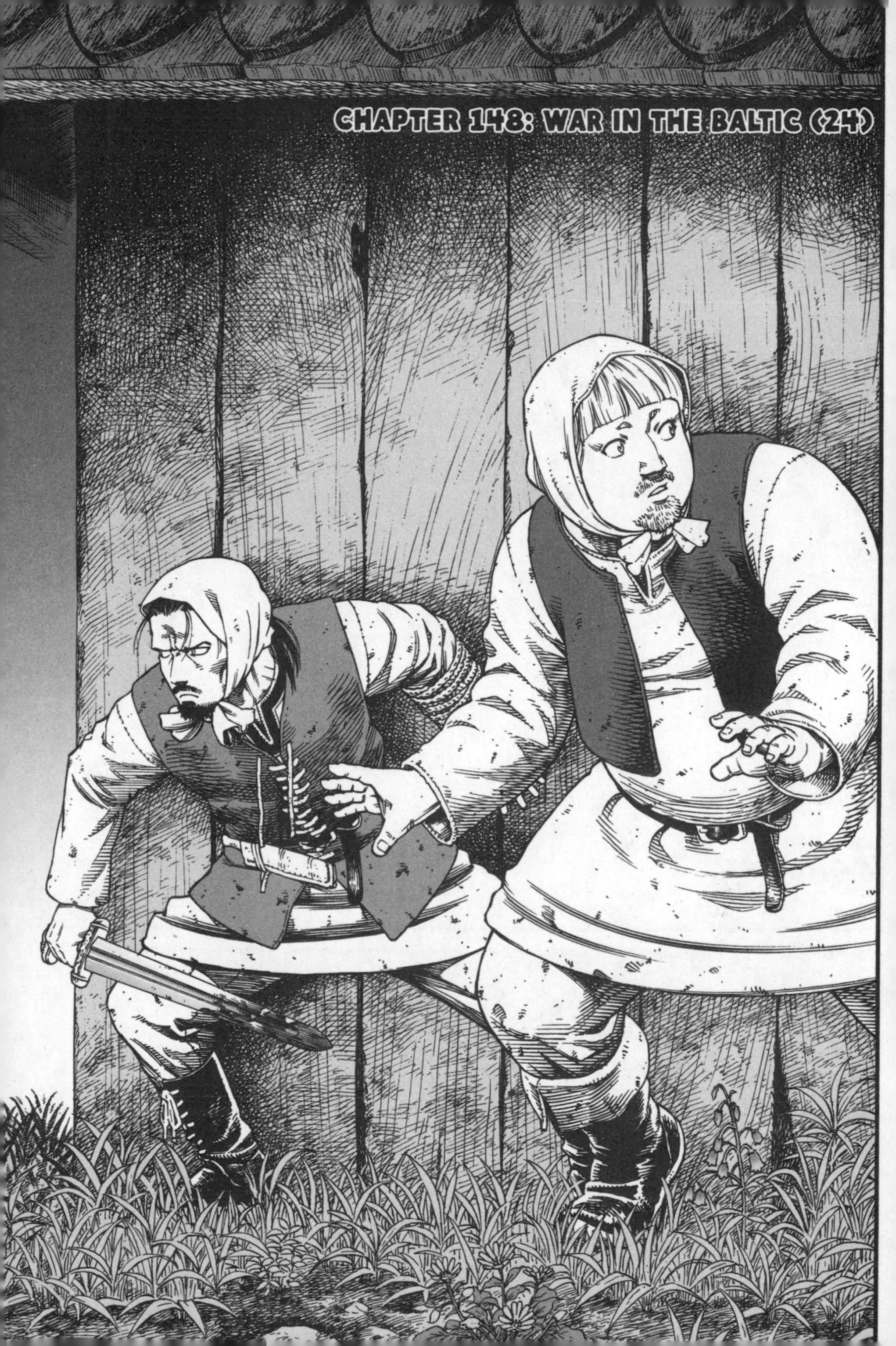
CHAPTER 148: WAR IN THE BALTIC (24)

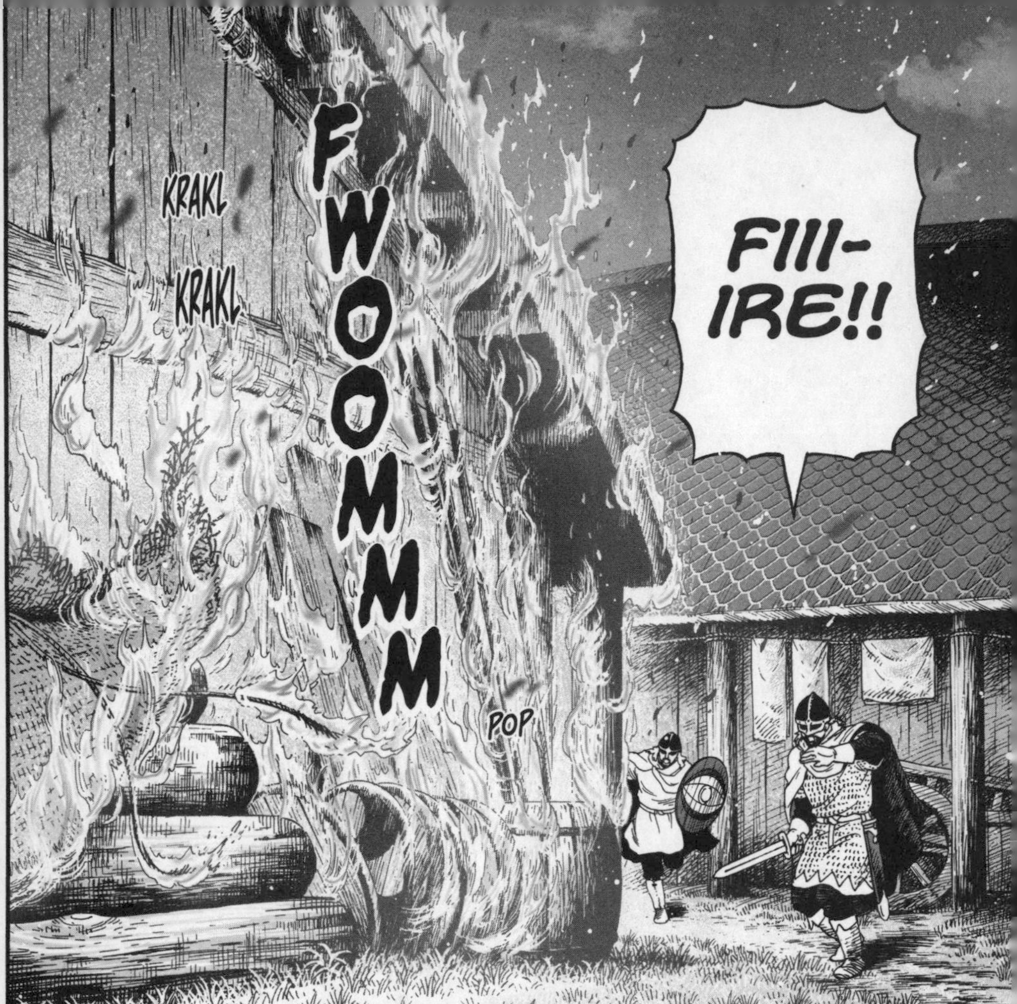
FIII-
IRE!!
FWOOMMM
KRAKL
KRAKL
POP

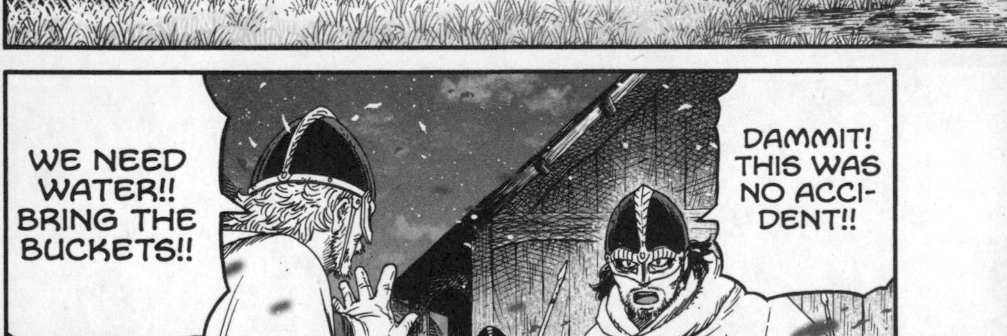
DAMMIT! THIS WAS NO ACCI- DENT!!
WE NEED WATER!! BRING THE BUCKETS!!

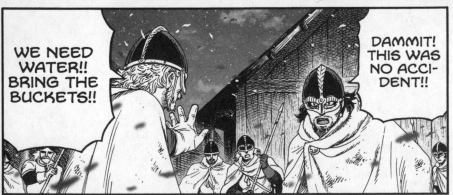

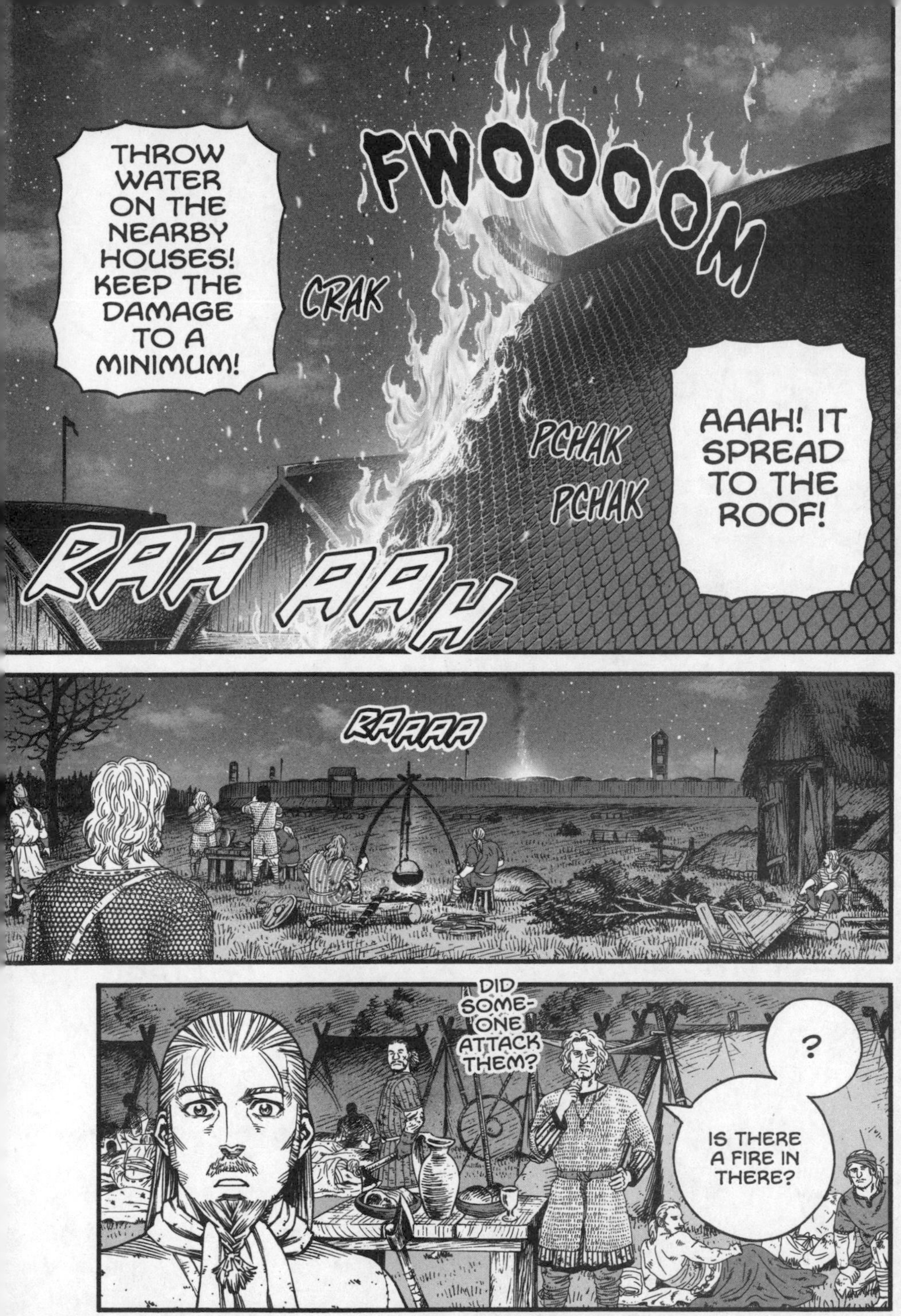
FWOOOOM
AAAH! IT SPREAD TO THE ROOF!
THROW WATER ON THE NEARBY HOUSES! KEEP THE DAMAGE TO A MINIMUM!
CRAK
PCHAK
PCHAK
RAAAAAH
RAAAAA
?
IS THERE A FIRE IN THERE?
DID SOME-ONE ATTACK THEM?

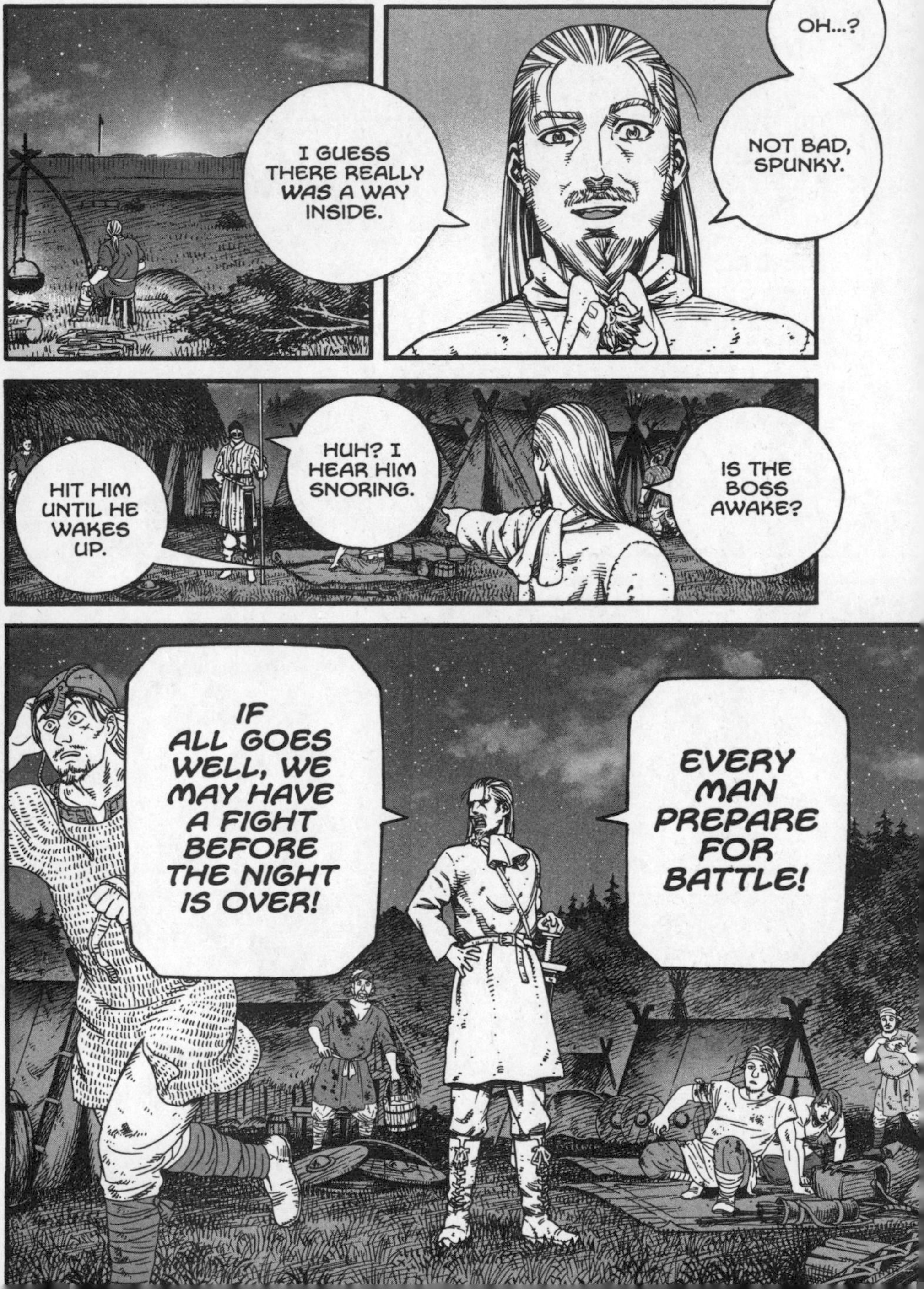
OH...?
NOT BAD, SPUNKY.
I GUESS THERE REALLY WAS A WAY INSIDE.
IS THE BOSS AWAKE?
HUH? I HEAR HIM SNORING.
HIT HIM UNTIL HE WAKES UP.
EVERY MAN PREPARE FOR BATTLE!
IF ALL GOES WELL, WE MAY HAVE A FIGHT BEFORE THE NIGHT IS OVER!

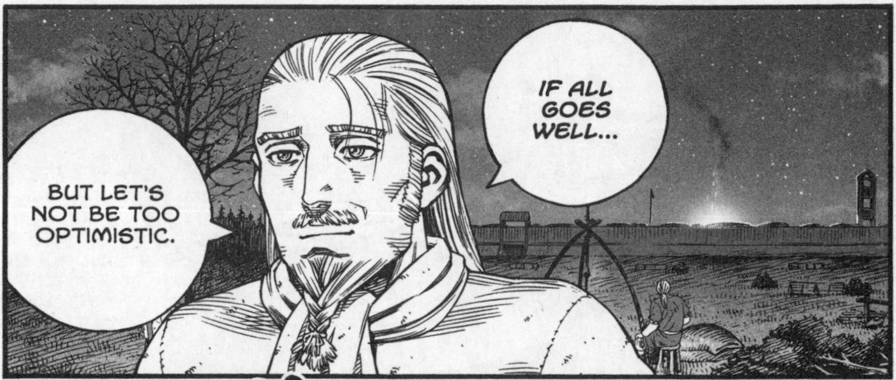
IF ALL GOES WELL...
BUT LET'S NOT BE TOO OPTIMISTIC.
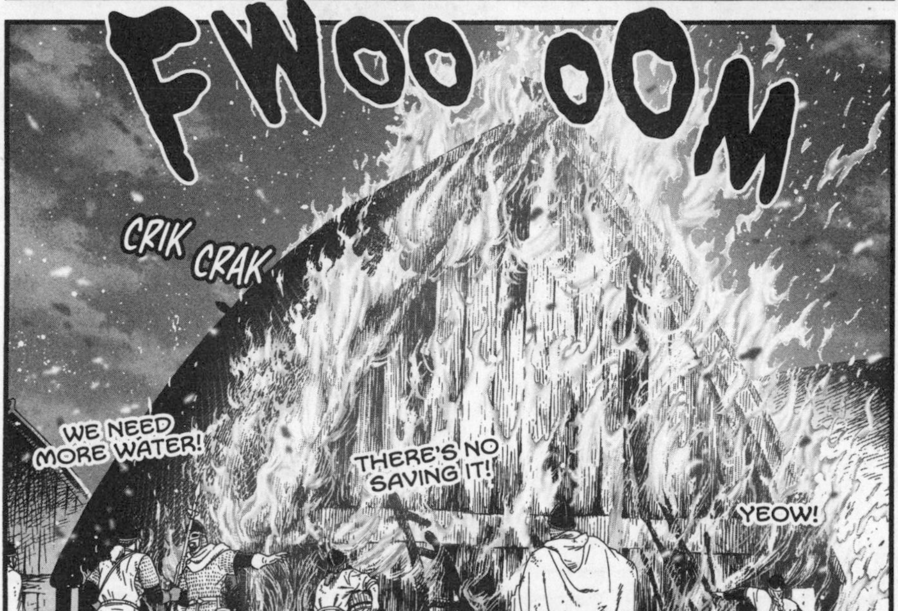
FWOO OOM
CRIK CRAK
YEOW!
THERE'S NO SAVING IT!
WE NEED MORE WATER!
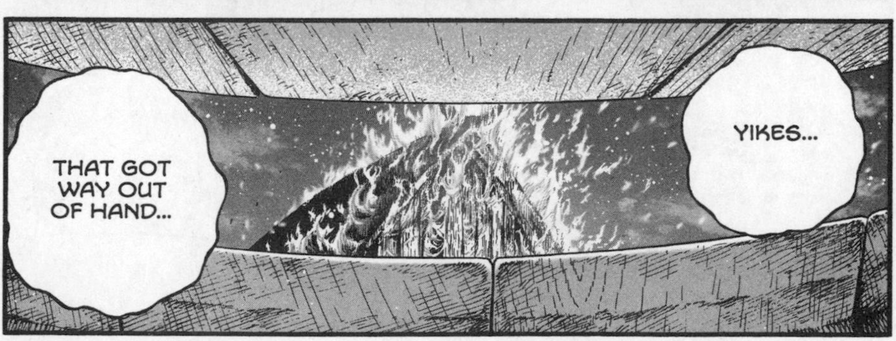
YIKES...
THAT GOT WAY OUT OF HAND...

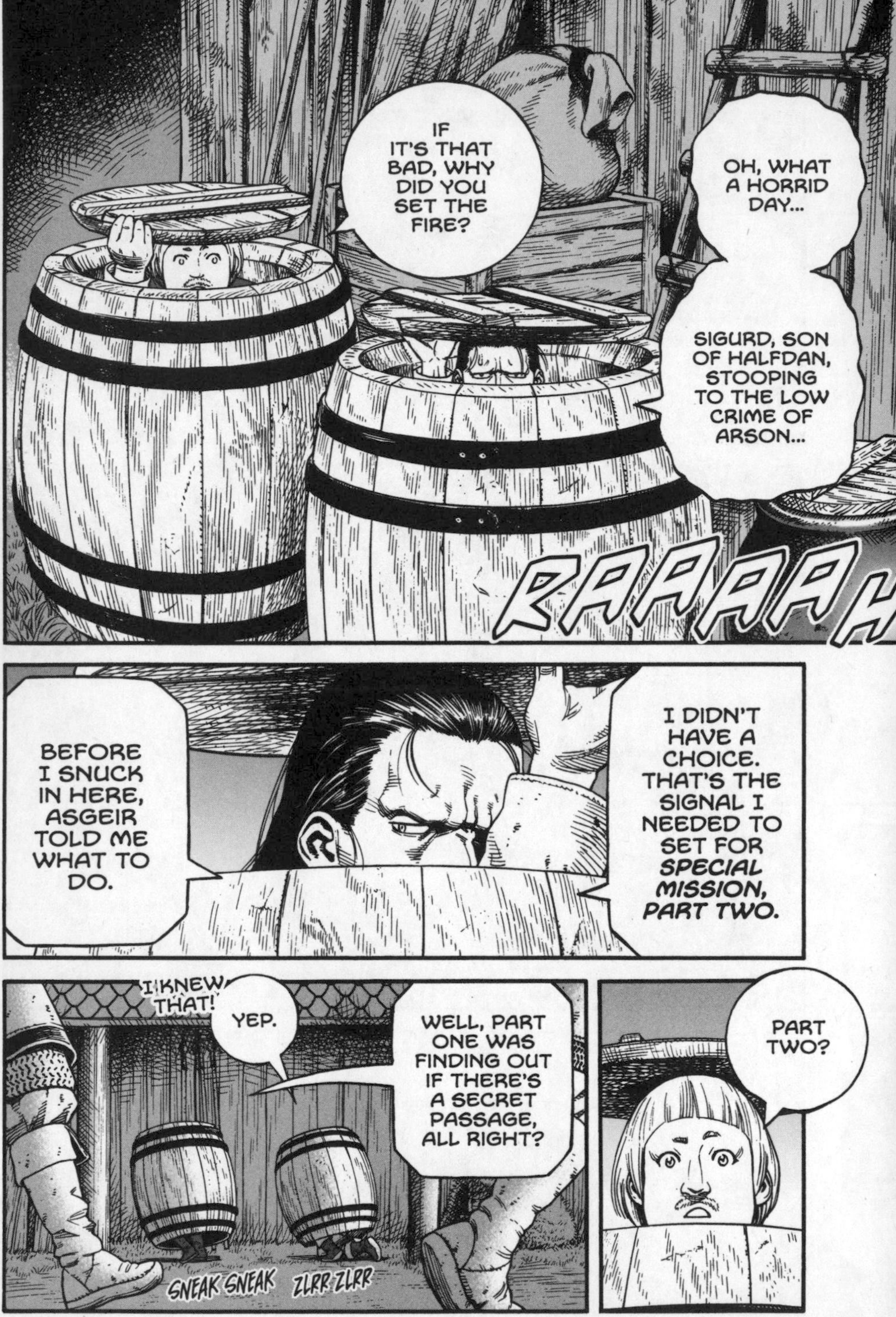
OH, WHAT A HORRID DAY...
SIGURD, SON OF HALFDAN, STOOPING TO THE LOW CRIME OF ARSON...
IF IT'S THAT BAD, WHY DID YOU SET THE FIRE?
RAAAAAH
I DIDN'T HAVE A CHOICE. THAT'S THE SIGNAL I NEEDED TO SET FOR *SPECIAL MISSION, PART TWO.*
BEFORE I SNUCK IN HERE, ASGEIR TOLD ME WHAT TO DO.
PART TWO?
WELL, PART ONE WAS FINDING OUT IF THERE'S A SECRET PASSAGE, ALL RIGHT?
YEP.
I KNEW THAT!
SNEAK SNEAK
ZLRR ZLRR

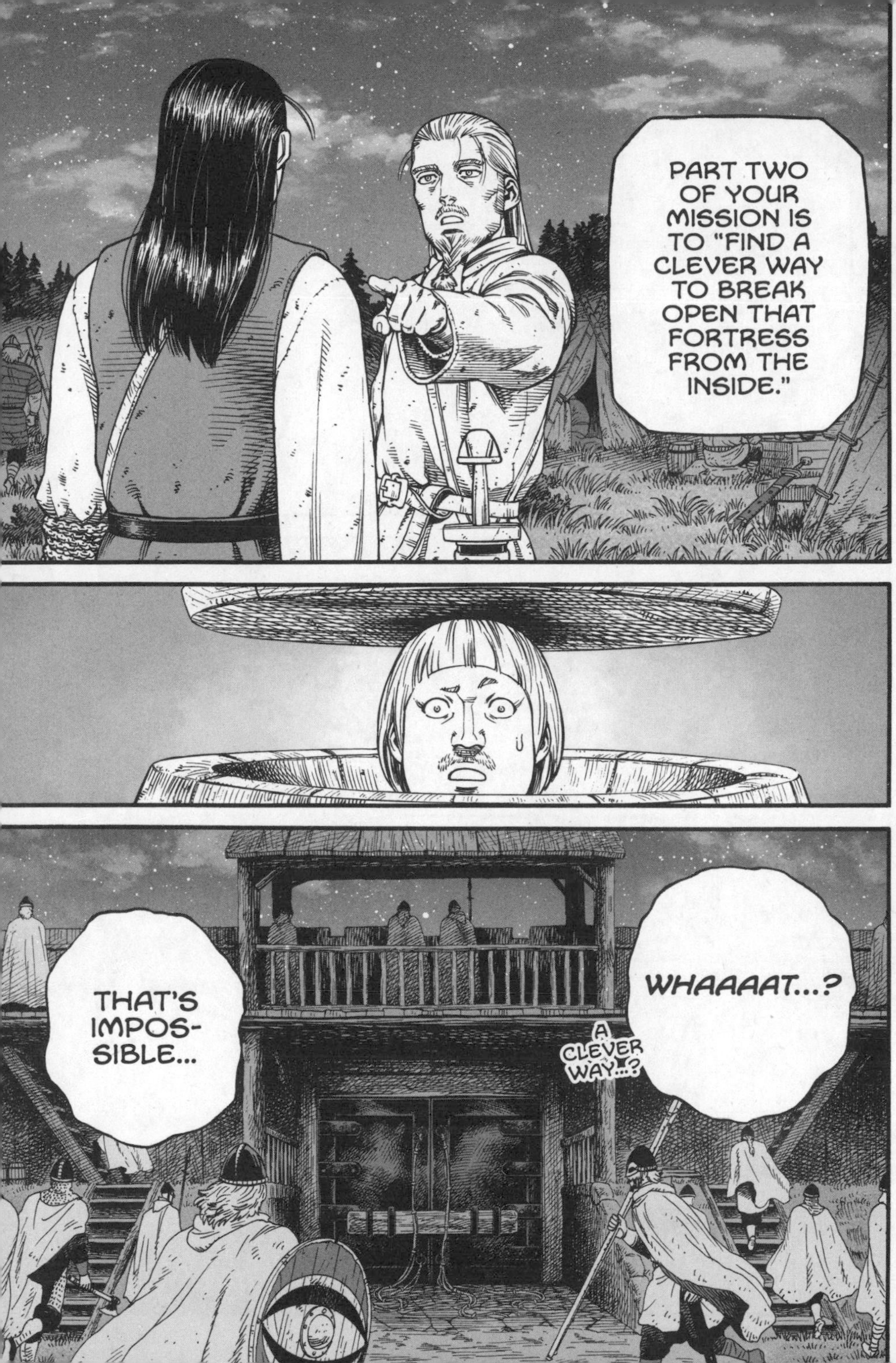
PART TWO OF YOUR MISSION IS TO "FIND A CLEVER WAY TO BREAK OPEN THAT FORTRESS FROM THE INSIDE."
WHAAAAT...?
A CLEVER WAY...?
THAT'S IMPOSSIBLE...

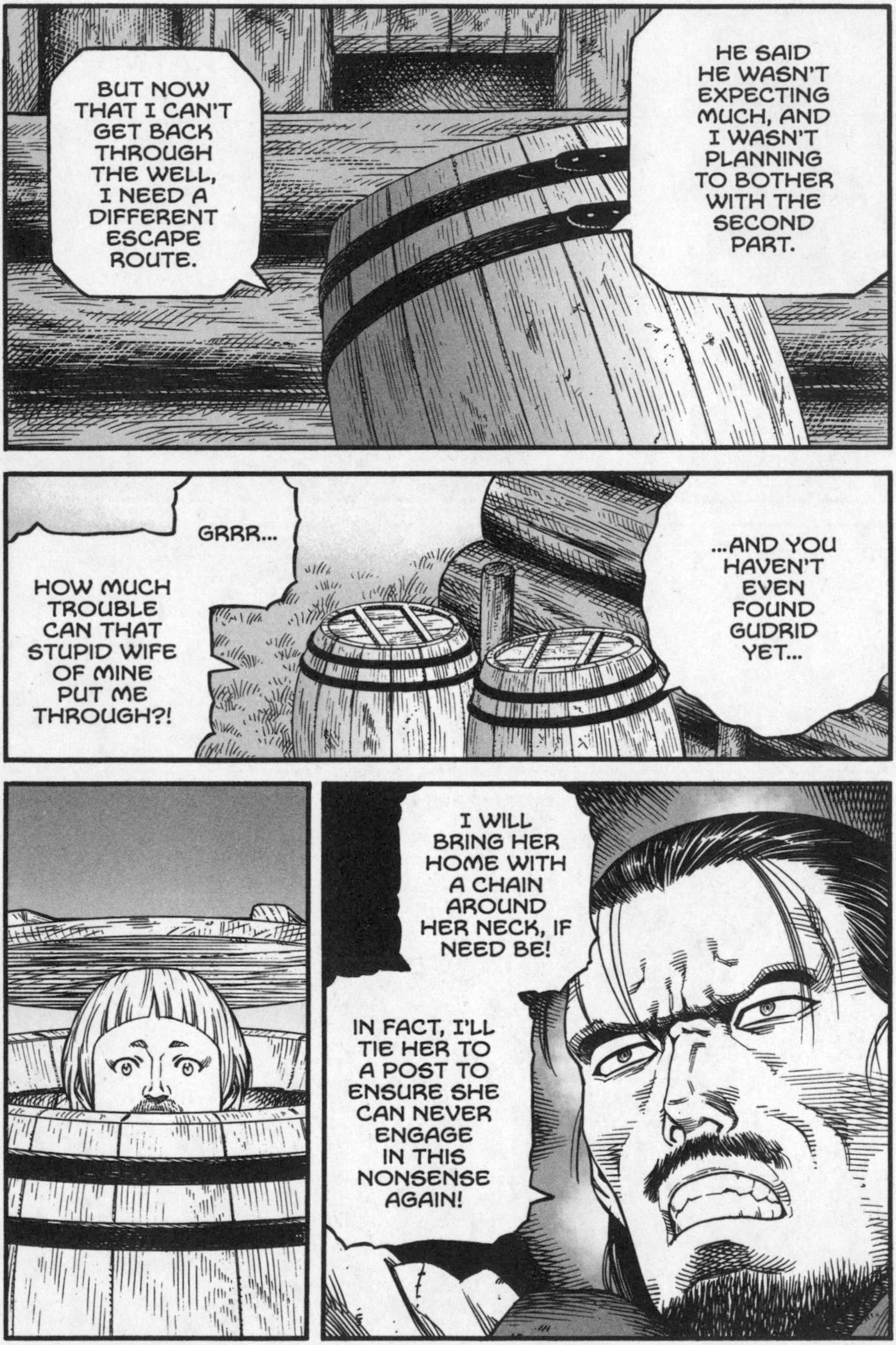
HE SAID HE WASN'T EXPECTING MUCH, AND I WASN'T PLANNING TO BOTHER WITH THE SECOND PART.
BUT NOW THAT I CAN'T GET BACK THROUGH THE WELL, I NEED A DIFFERENT ESCAPE ROUTE.
...AND YOU HAVEN'T EVEN FOUND GUDRID YET...
GRRR...
HOW MUCH TROUBLE CAN THAT STUPID WIFE OF MINE PUT ME THROUGH?!
I WILL BRING HER HOME WITH A CHAIN AROUND HER NECK, IF NEED BE!
IN FACT, I'LL TIE HER TO A POST TO ENSURE SHE CAN NEVER ENGAGE IN THIS NONSENSE AGAIN!

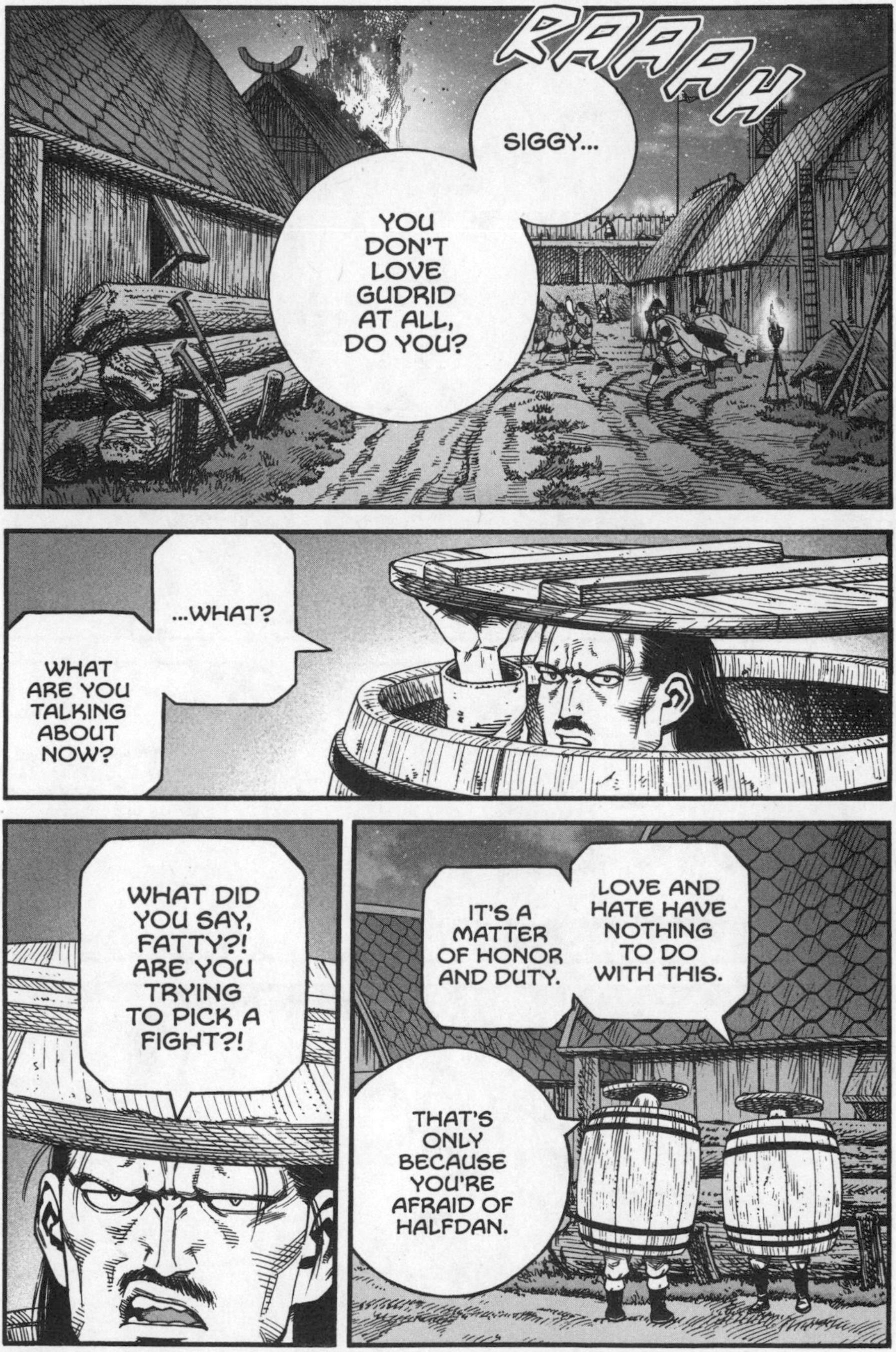
RAAAH
SIGGY...
YOU DON'T LOVE GUDRID AT ALL, DO YOU?
...WHAT?
WHAT ARE YOU TALKING ABOUT NOW?
LOVE AND HATE HAVE NOTHING TO DO WITH THIS.
IT'S A MATTER OF HONOR AND DUTY.
THAT'S ONLY BECAUSE YOU'RE AFRAID OF HALFDAN.
WHAT DID YOU SAY, FATTY?! ARE YOU TRYING TO PICK A FIGHT?!

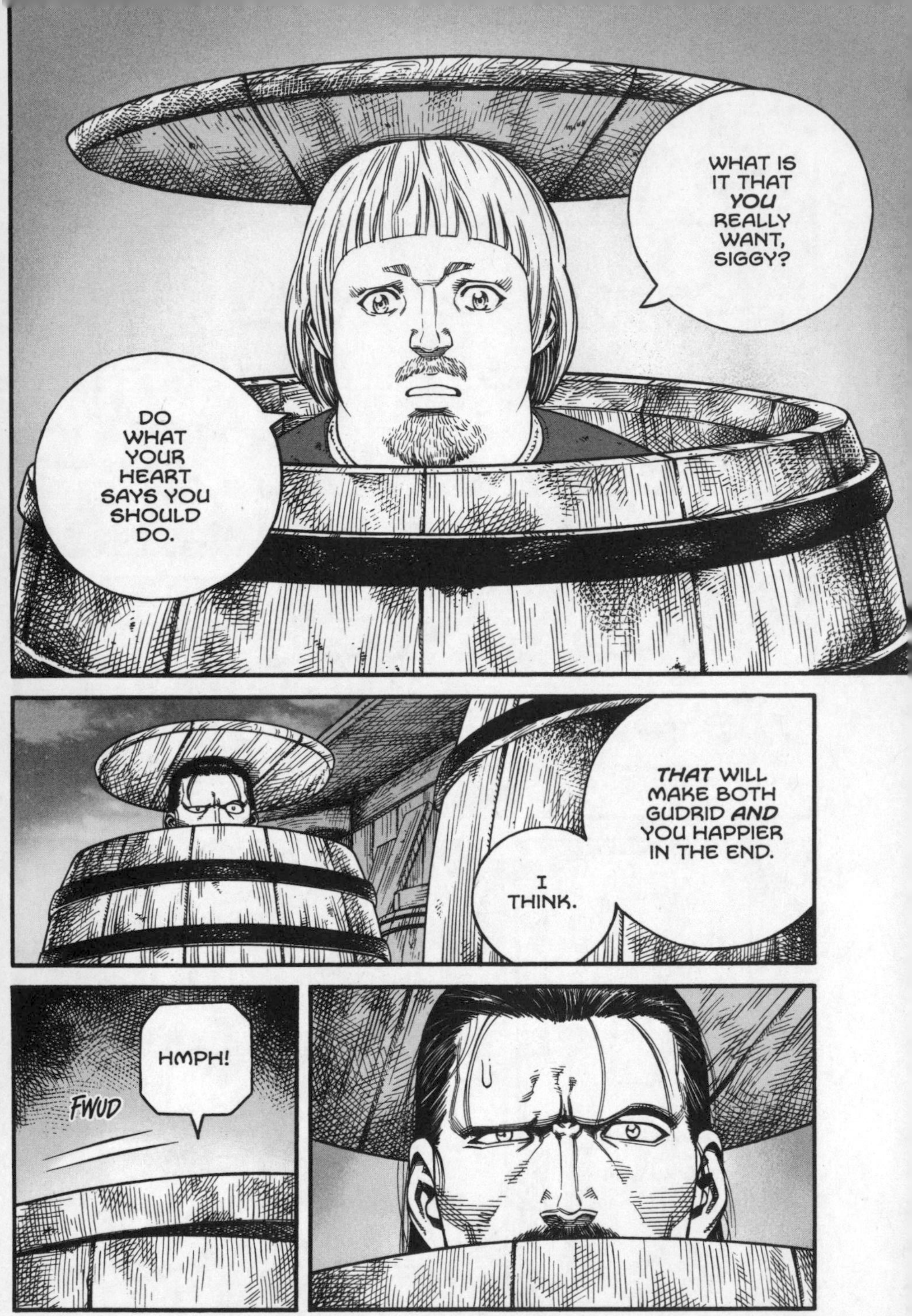
WHAT IS IT THAT YOU REALLY WANT, SIGGY?
DO WHAT YOUR HEART SAYS YOU SHOULD DO.
THAT WILL MAKE BOTH GUDRID AND YOU HAPPIER IN THE END.
I THINK.
HMPH!
FWUD

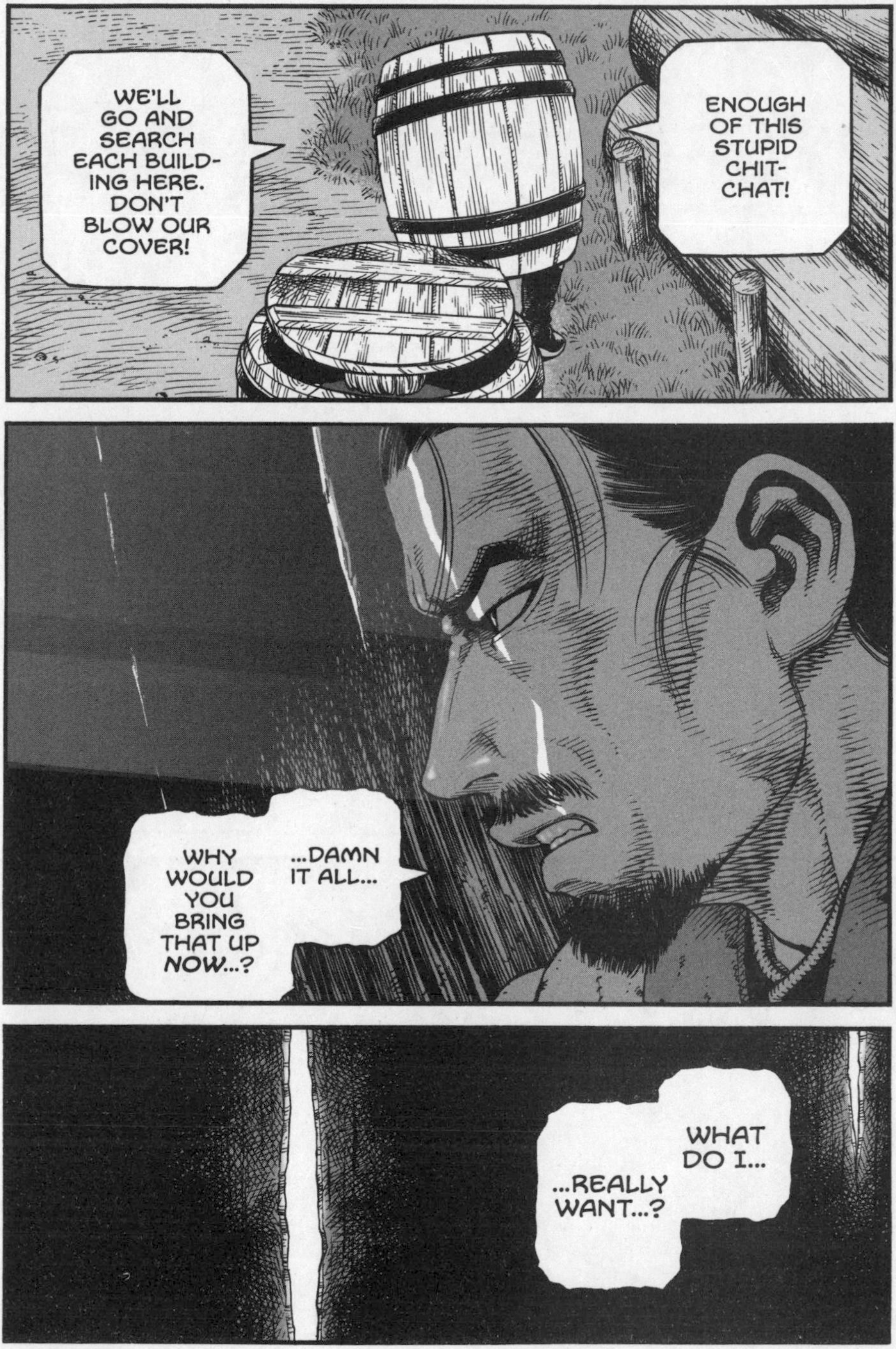
ENOUGH OF THIS STUPID CHIT-CHAT!
WE'LL GO AND SEARCH EACH BUILDING HERE. DON'T BLOW OUR COVER!
...DAMN IT ALL...
WHY WOULD YOU BRING THAT UP NOW...?
WHAT DO I...
...REALLY WANT...?

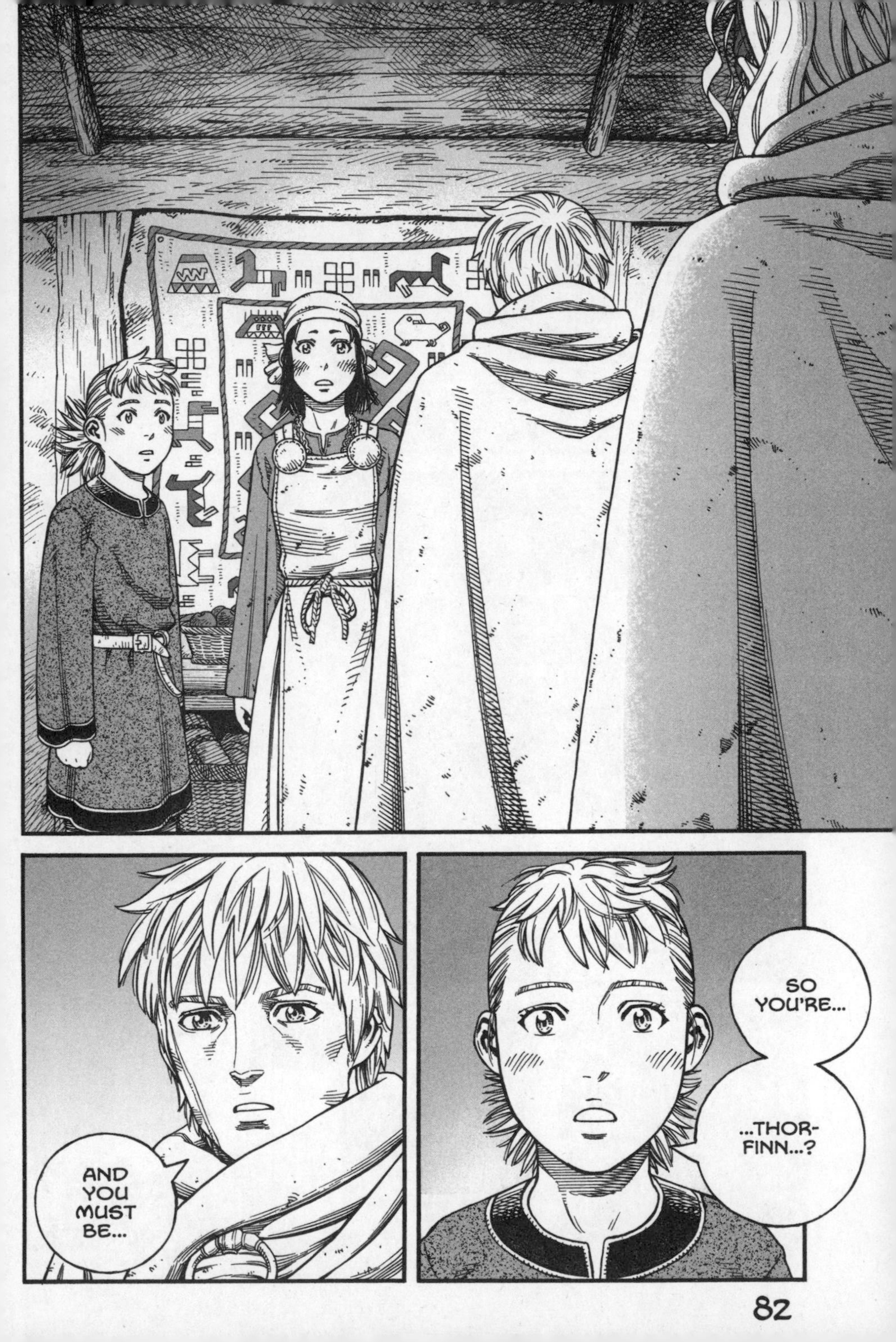
SO YOU'RE...
...THOR-FINN...?
AND YOU MUST BE...

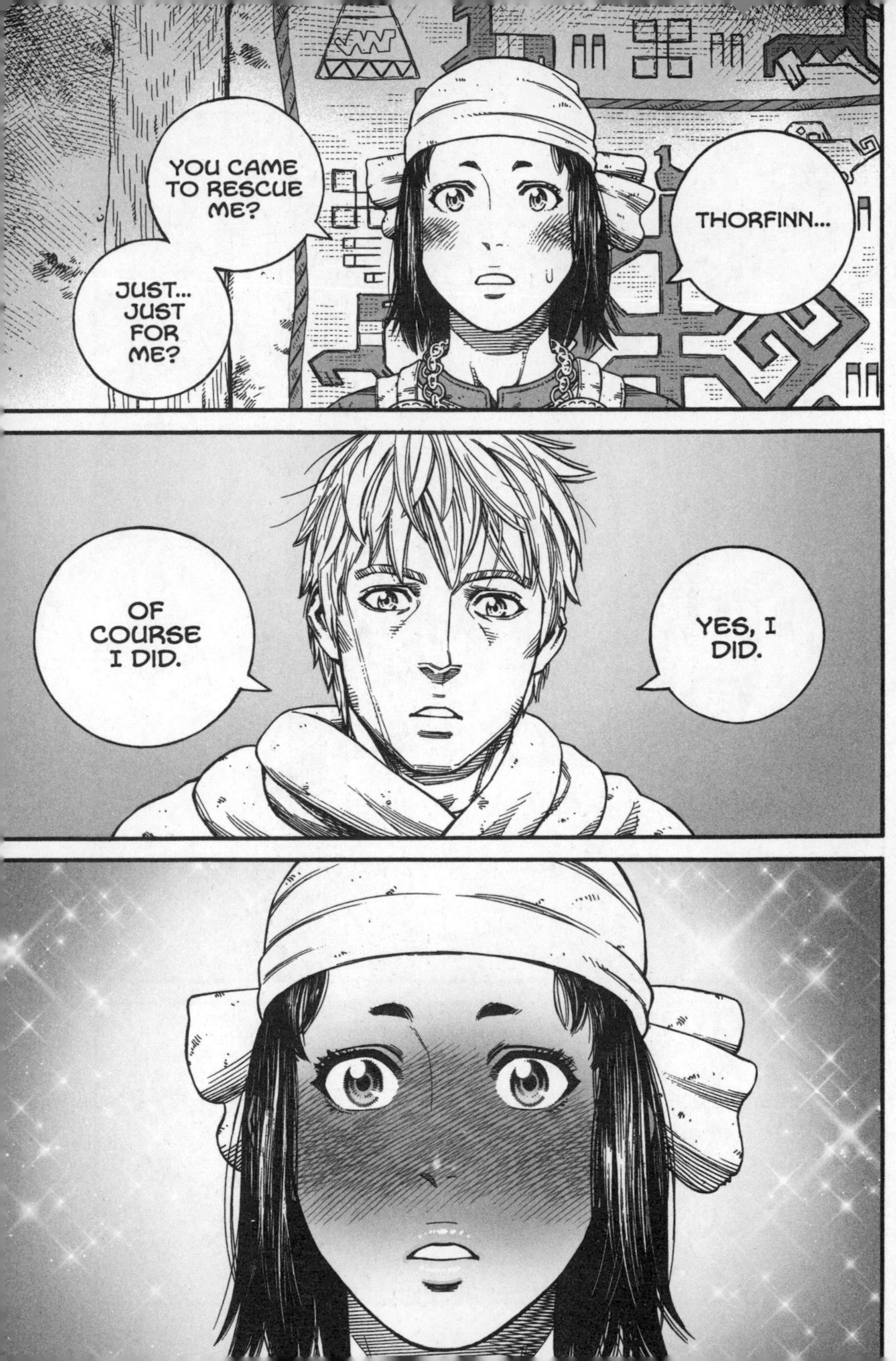
THORFINN...
YOU CAME TO RESCUE ME?
JUST... JUST FOR ME?
YES, I DID.
OF COURSE I DID.

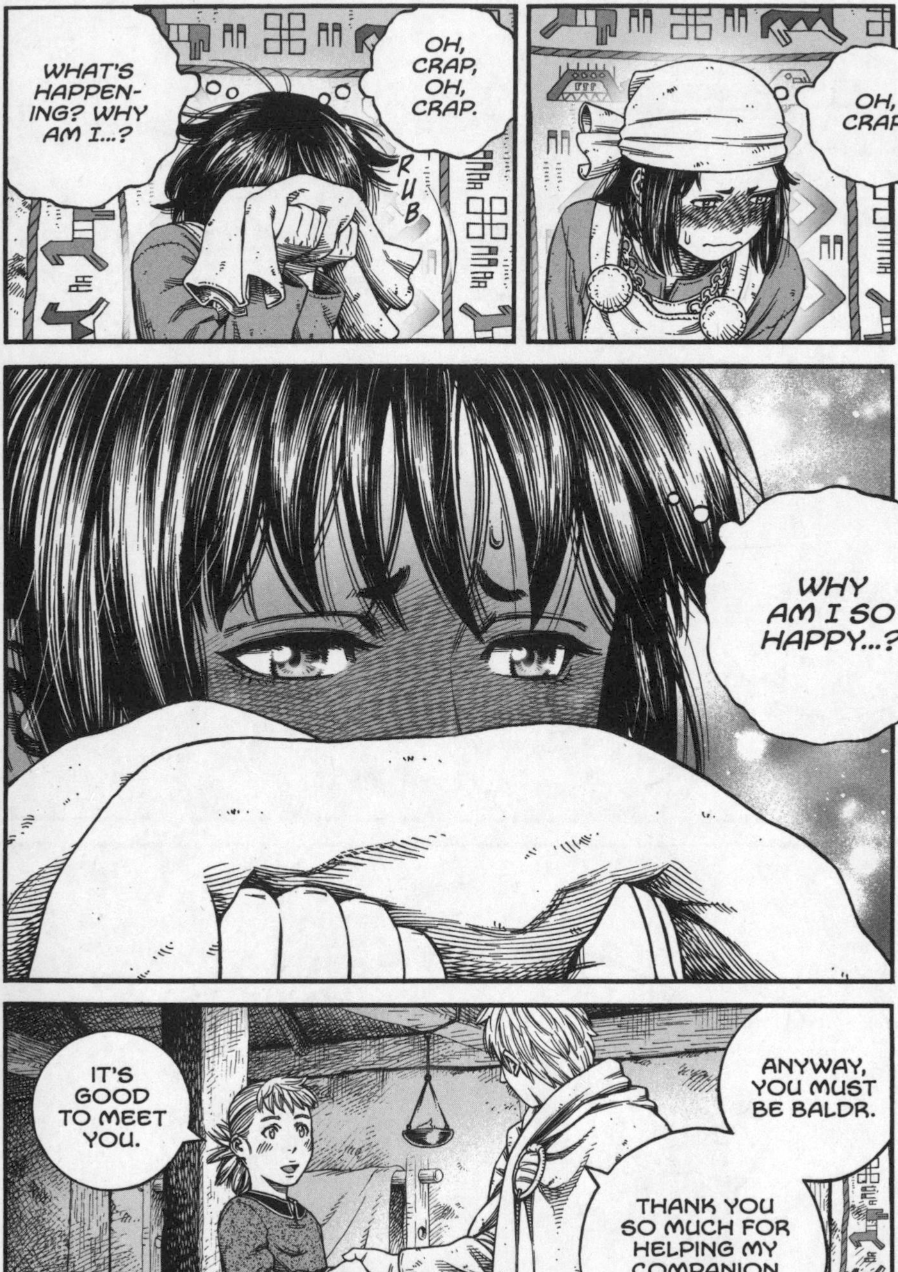
OH, CRAP.
OH, CRAP, OH, CRAP.
RUB
WHAT'S HAPPEN-ING? WHY AM I...?
WHY AM I SO HAPPY...?
ANYWAY, YOU MUST BE BALDR.
THANK YOU SO MUCH FOR HELPING MY COMPANION HERE.
IT'S GOOD TO MEET YOU.

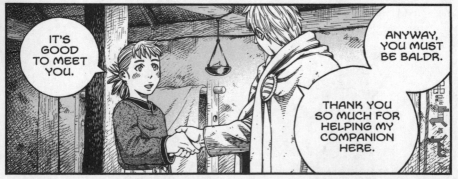

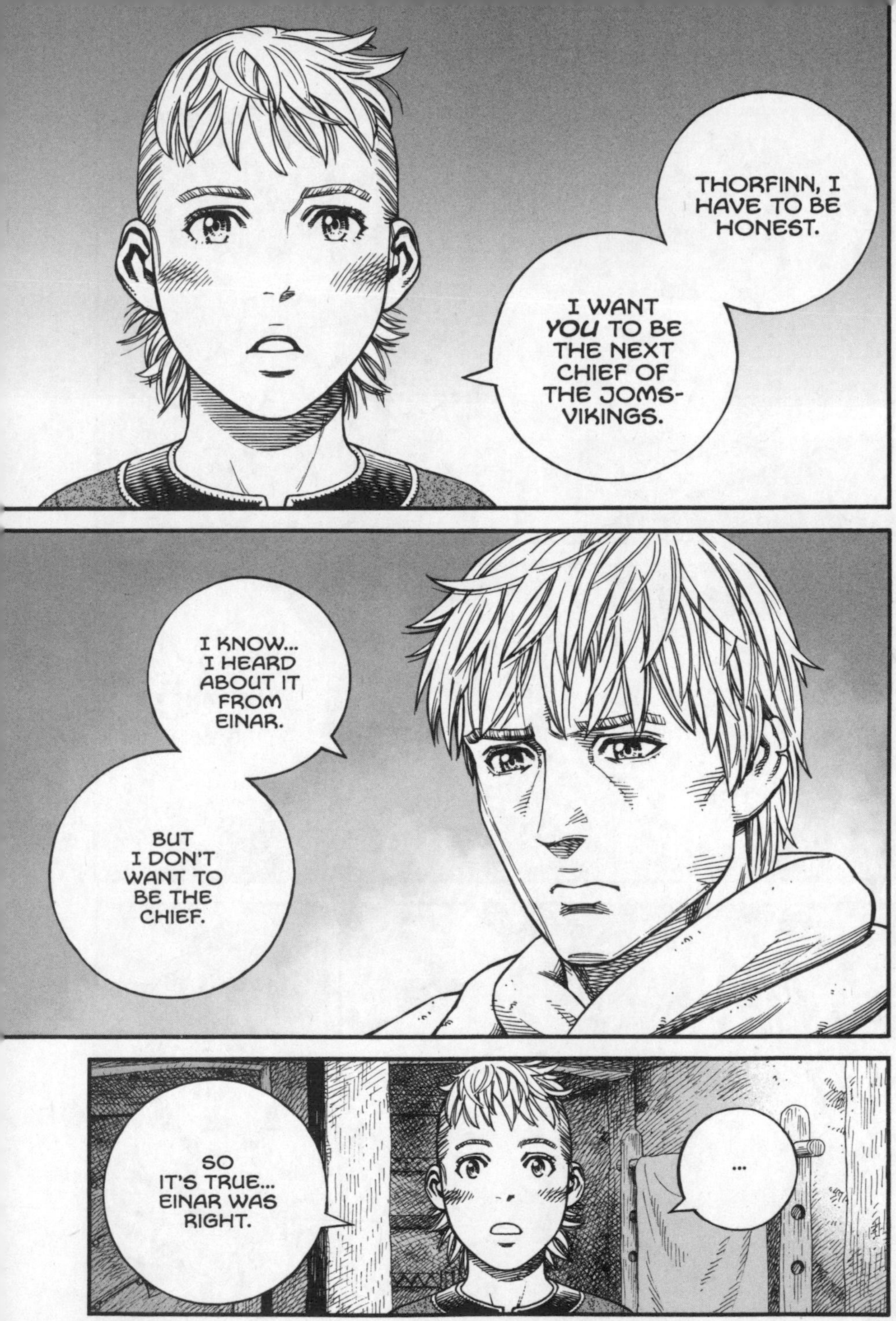
THORFINN, I HAVE TO BE HONEST.
I WANT *YOU* TO BE THE NEXT CHIEF OF THE JOMS-VIKINGS.
I KNOW... I HEARD ABOUT IT FROM EINAR.
BUT I DON'T WANT TO BE THE CHIEF.
...
SO IT'S TRUE... EINAR WAS RIGHT.

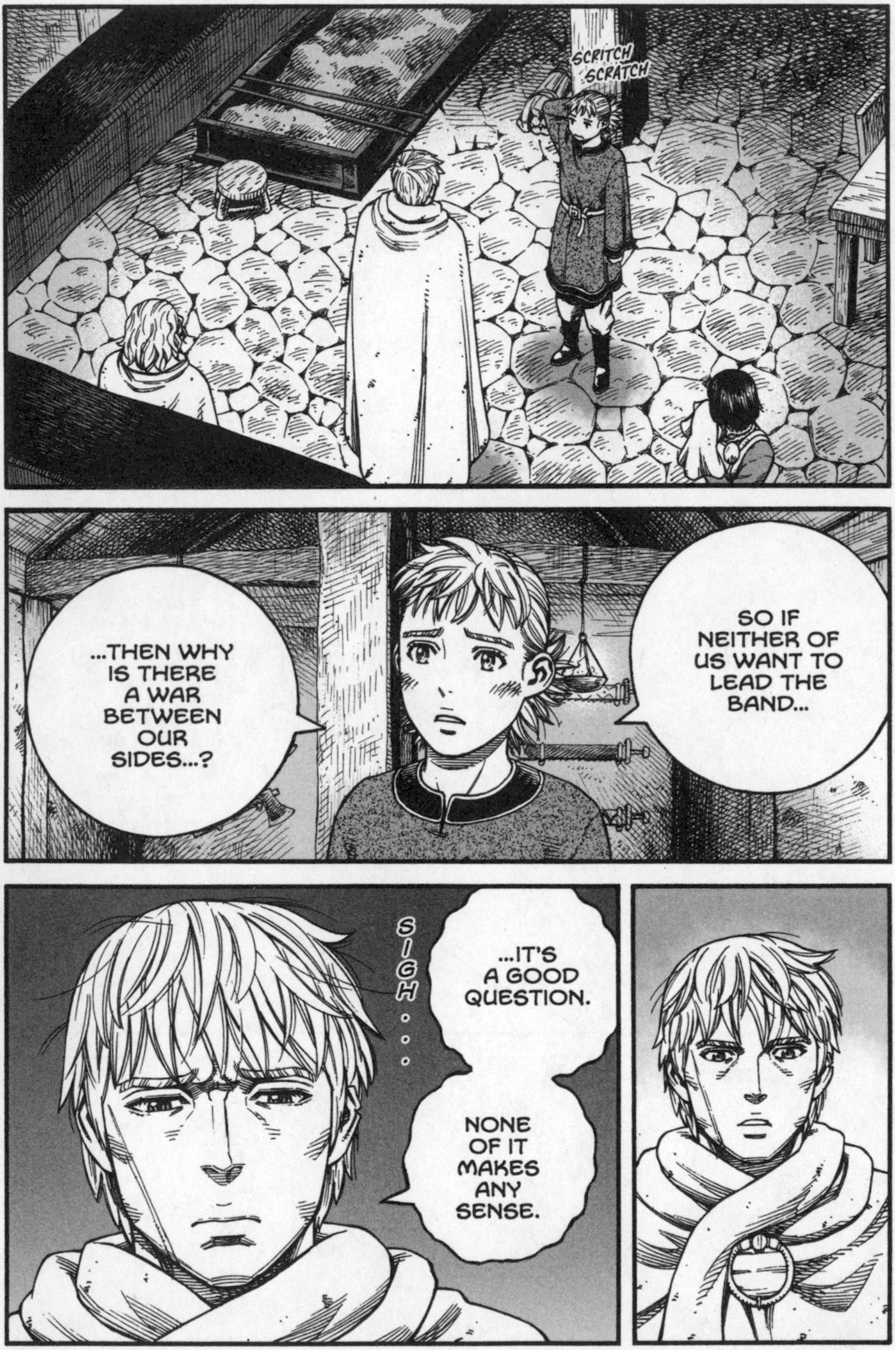
SCRITCH SCRATCH
SO IF NEITHER OF US WANT TO LEAD THE BAND...
...THEN WHY IS THERE A WAR BETWEEN OUR SIDES...?
SIGH...
...IT'S A GOOD QUESTION.
NONE OF IT MAKES ANY SENSE.

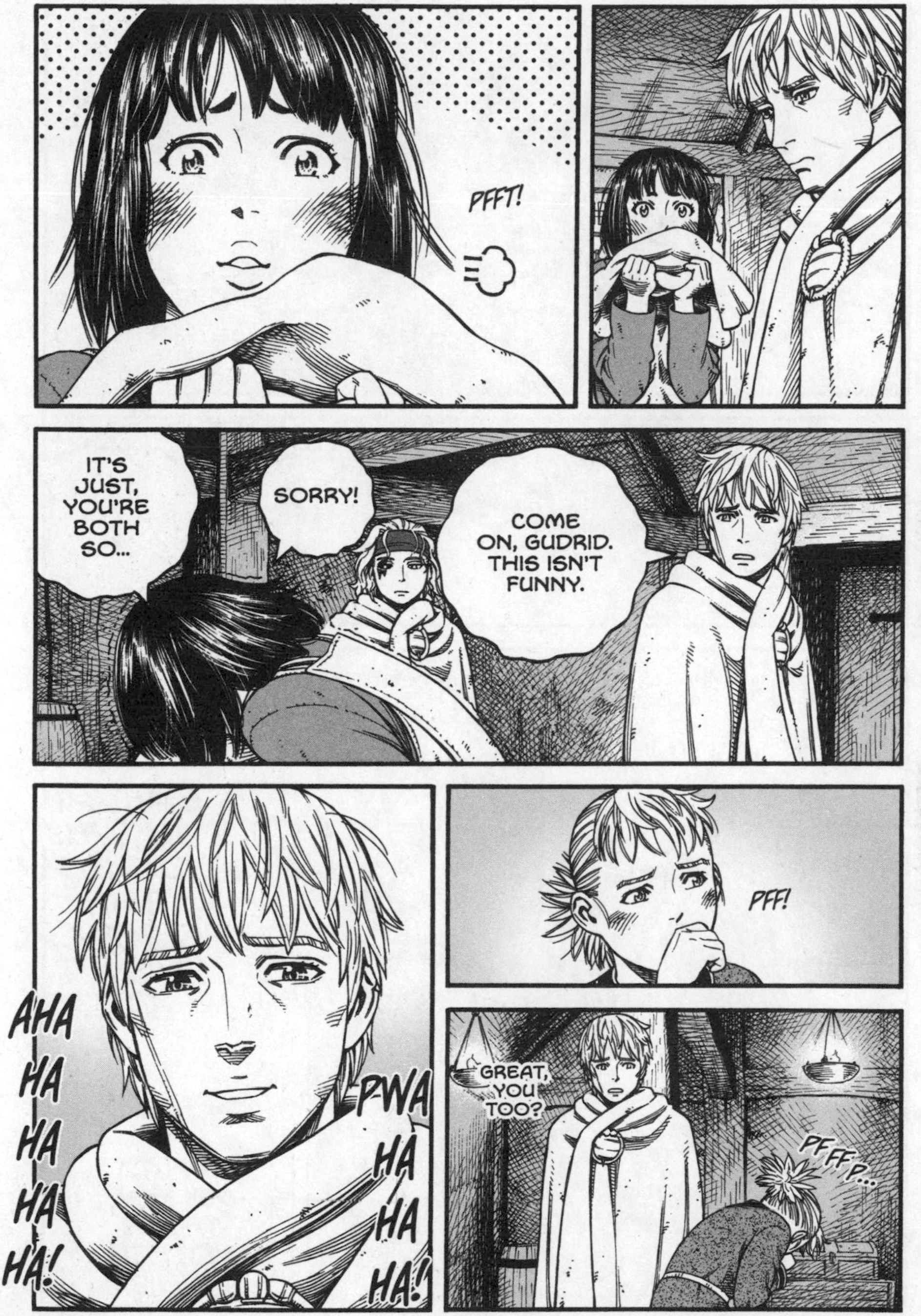
PFFT!
COME ON, GUDRID. THIS ISN'T FUNNY.
SORRY!
IT'S JUST, YOU'RE BOTH SO...
PFF!
PFFFP...
GREAT, YOU TOO?
PWA HA HA HA!
AHA HA HA HA HA HA!

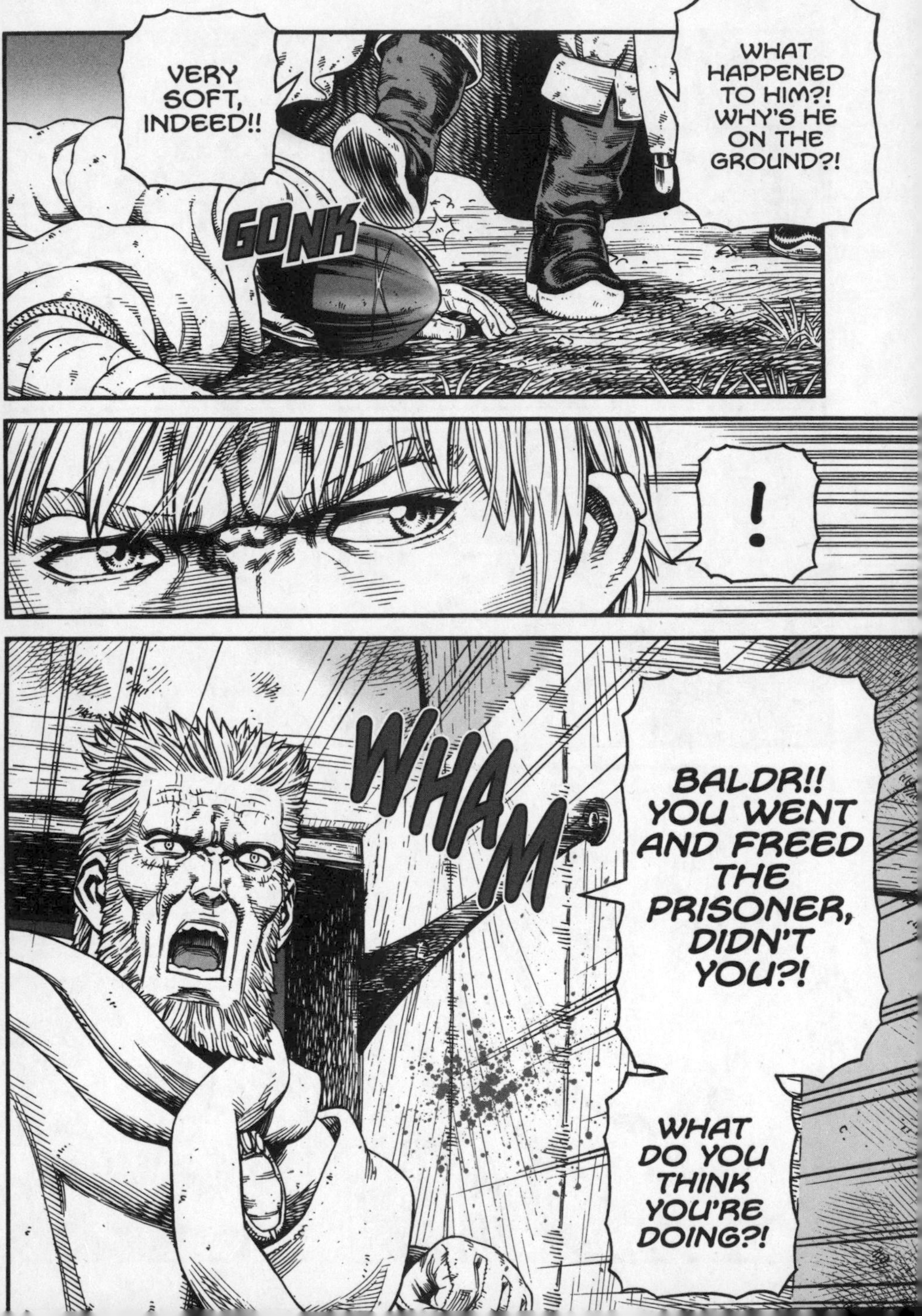
WHAT HAPPENED TO HIM?! WHY'S HE ON THE GROUND?!
VERY SOFT, INDEED!!
GONK
!
WHAM
BALDR!! YOU WENT AND FREED THE PRISONER, DIDN'T YOU?!
WHAT DO YOU THINK YOU'RE DOING?!

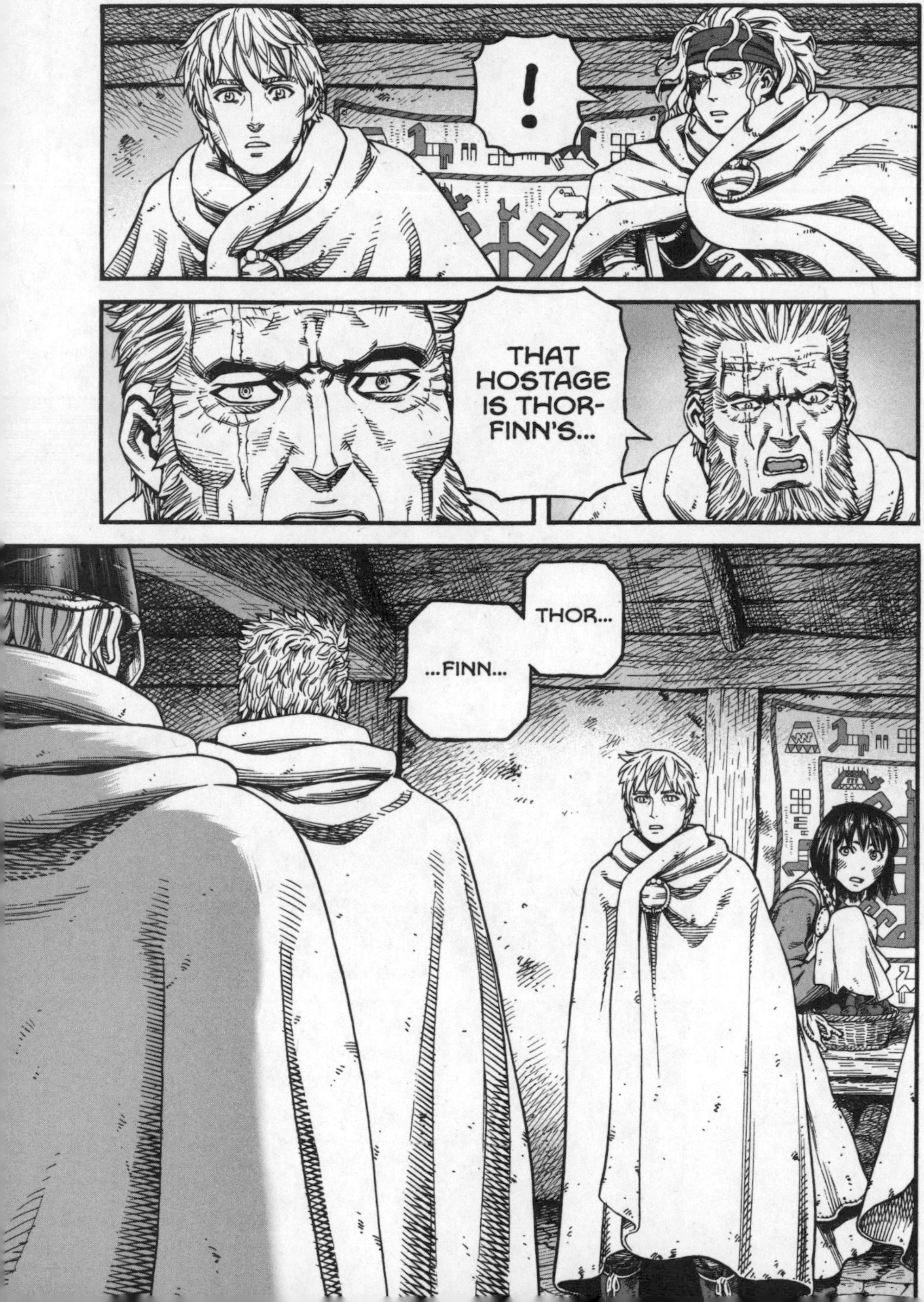
!
THAT HOSTAGE IS THOR-FINN'S...
THOR...
...FINN...

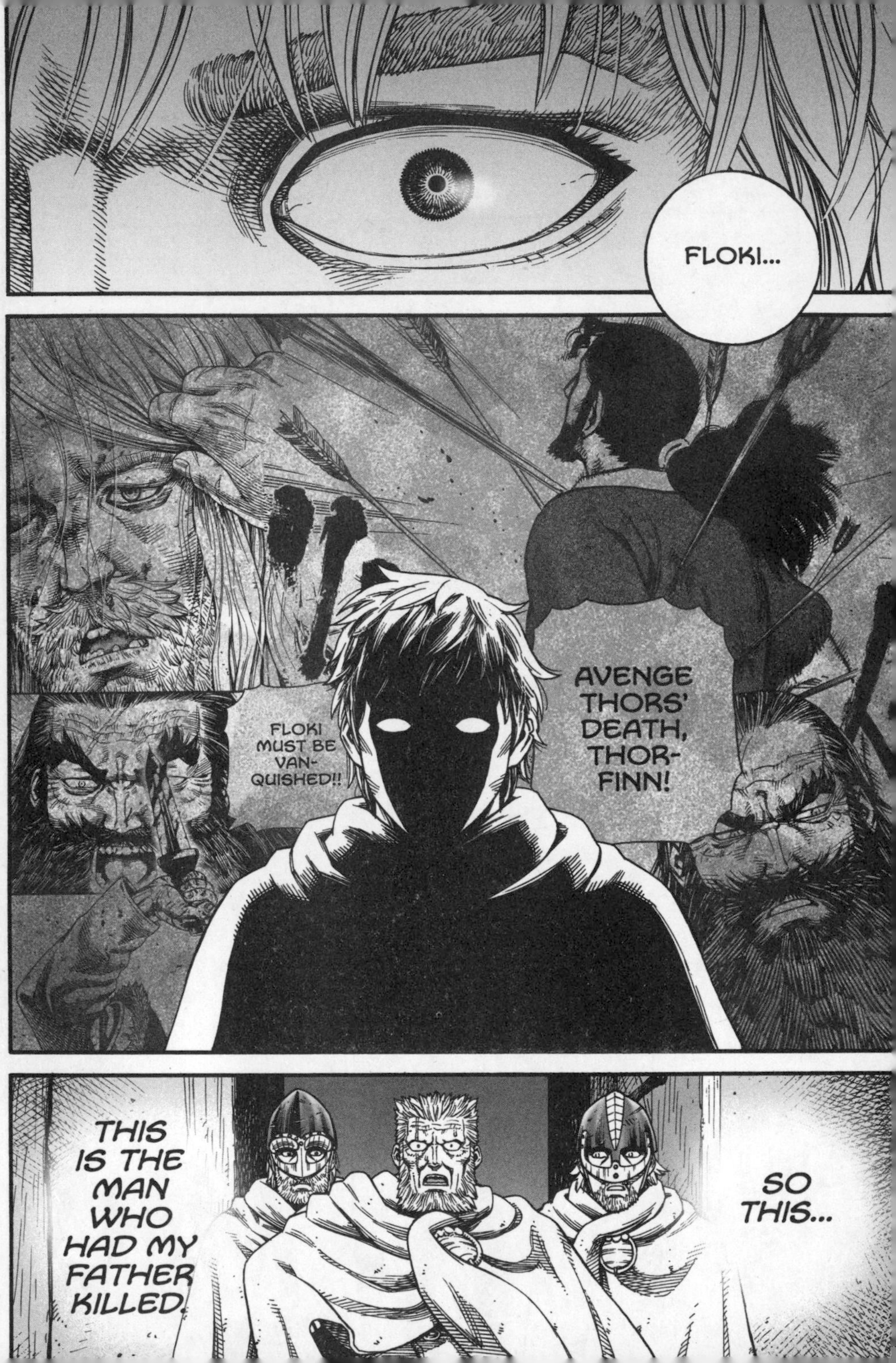
FLOKI...
AVENGE THORS' DEATH, THOR-FINN!
FLOKI MUST BE VAN-QUISHED!!
SO THIS...
THIS IS THE MAN WHO HAD MY FATHER KILLED.

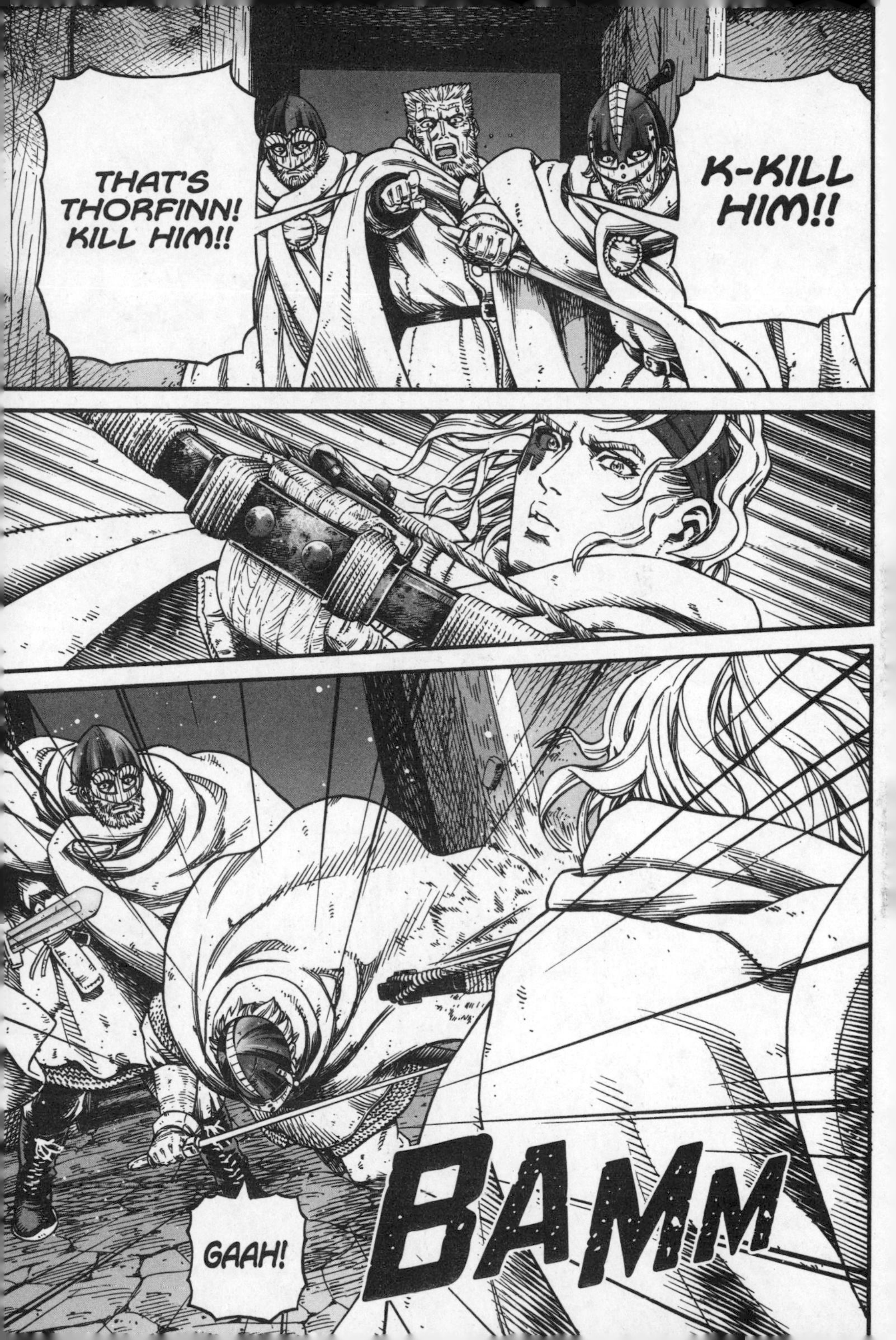
THAT'S THORFINN! KILL HIM!!
K-KILL HIM!!
GAAH!
BAMM

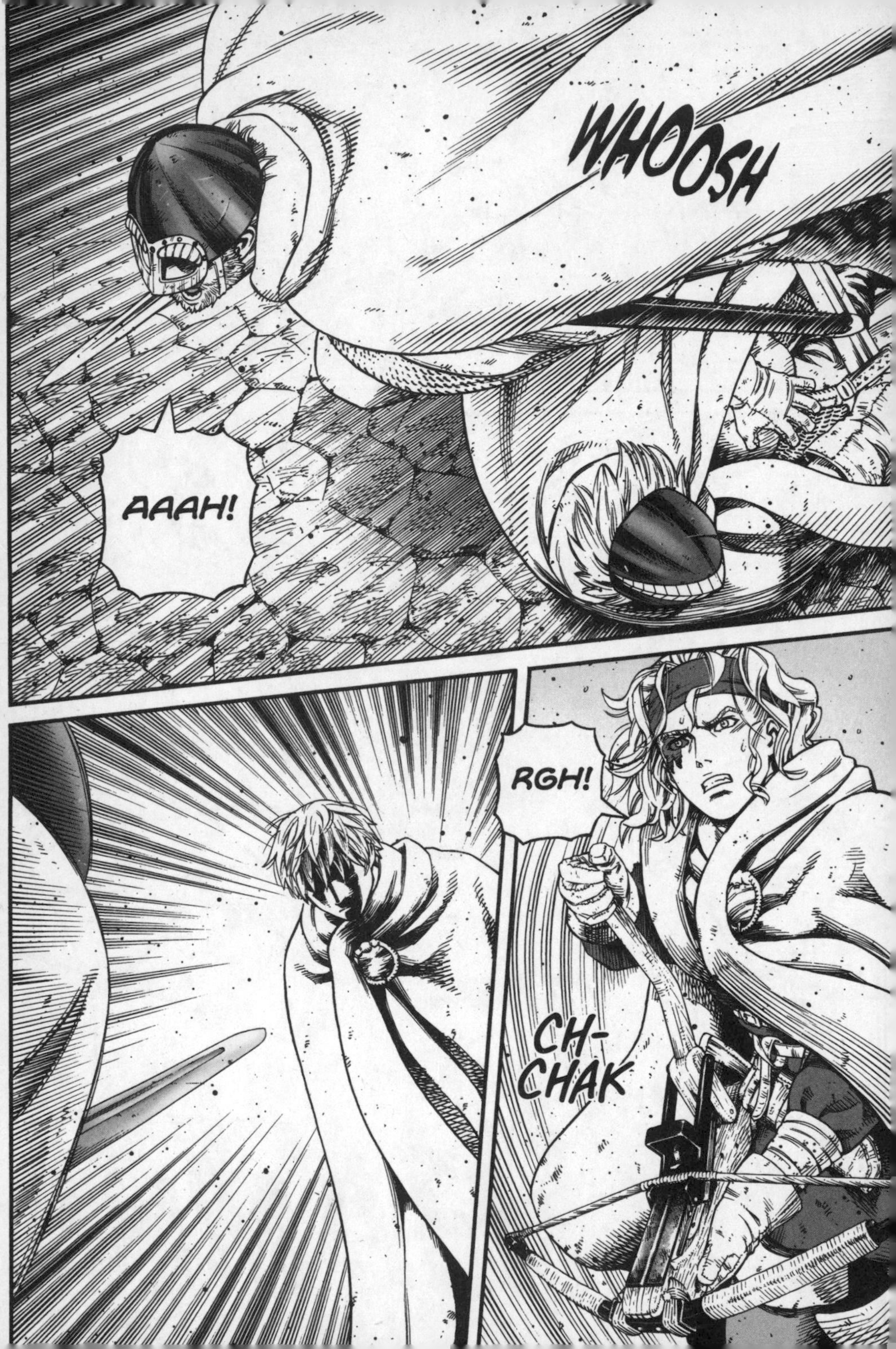
WHOOSH
AAAH!
RGH!
CH-
CHAK

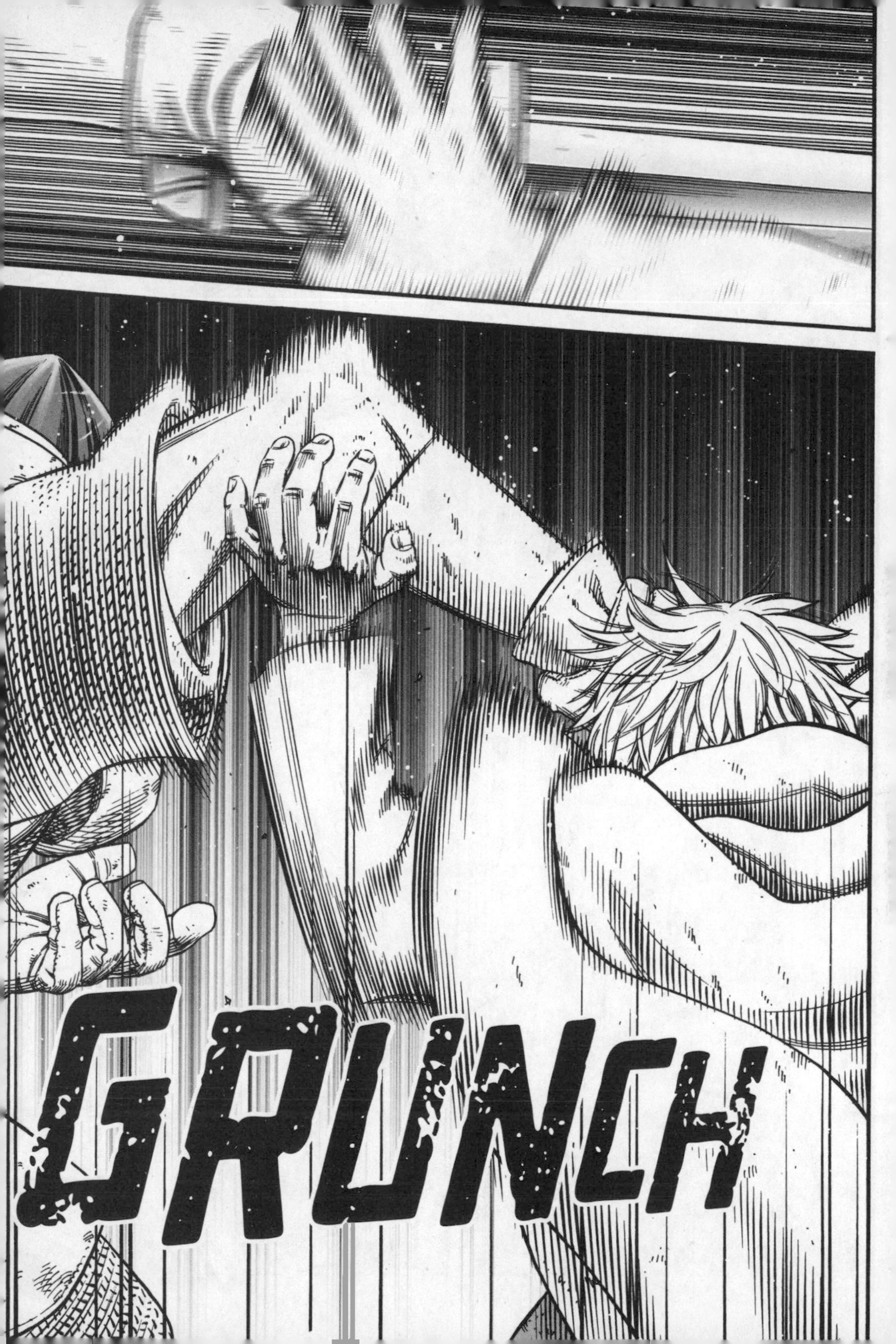
GRUNCH

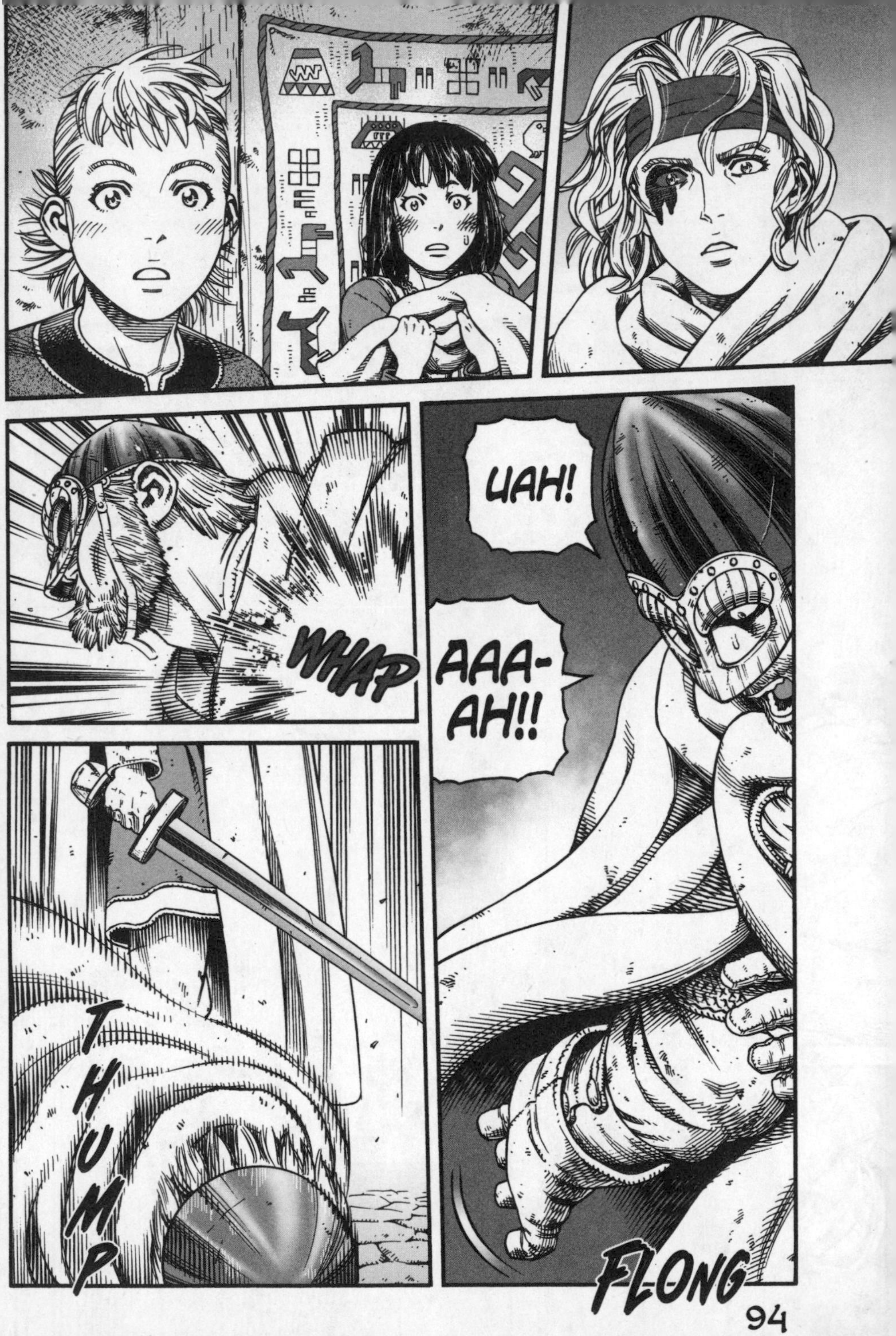
UAH!
AAA-AH!!
FLONG
WHAP
THUMP

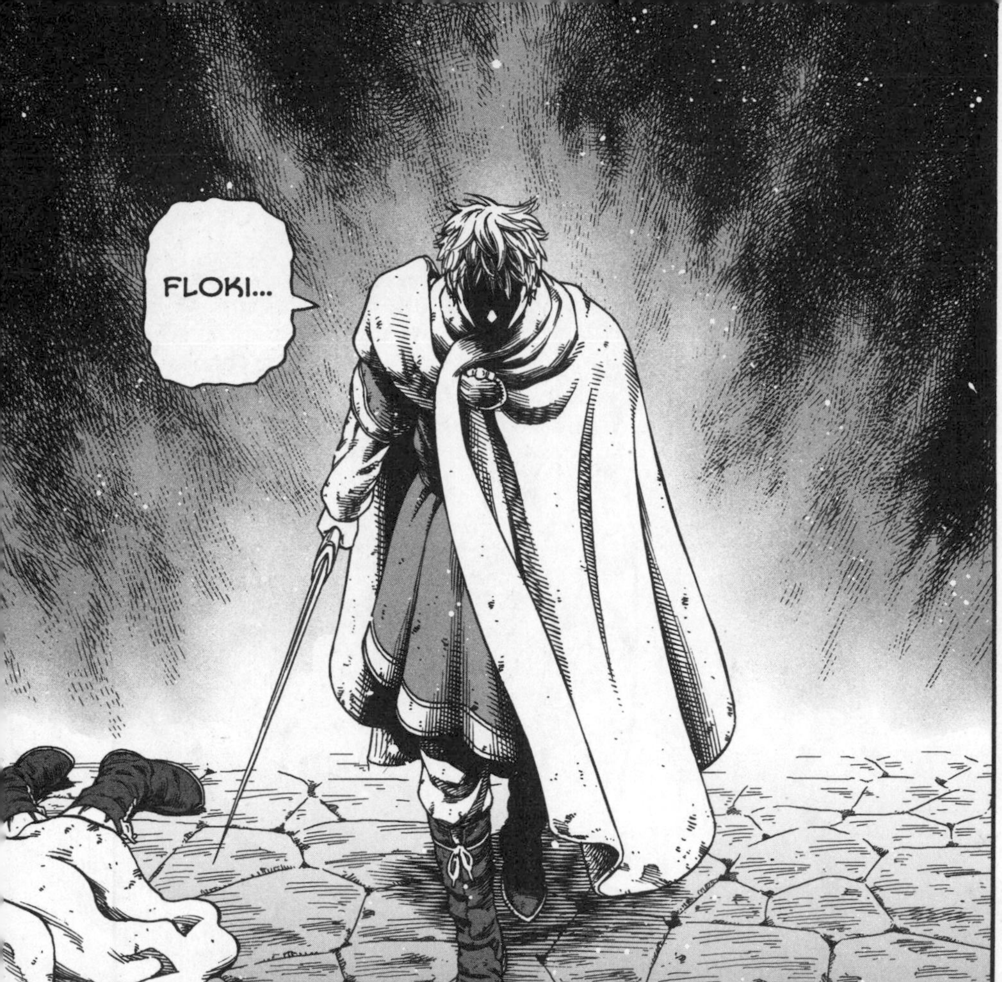
FLOKI...

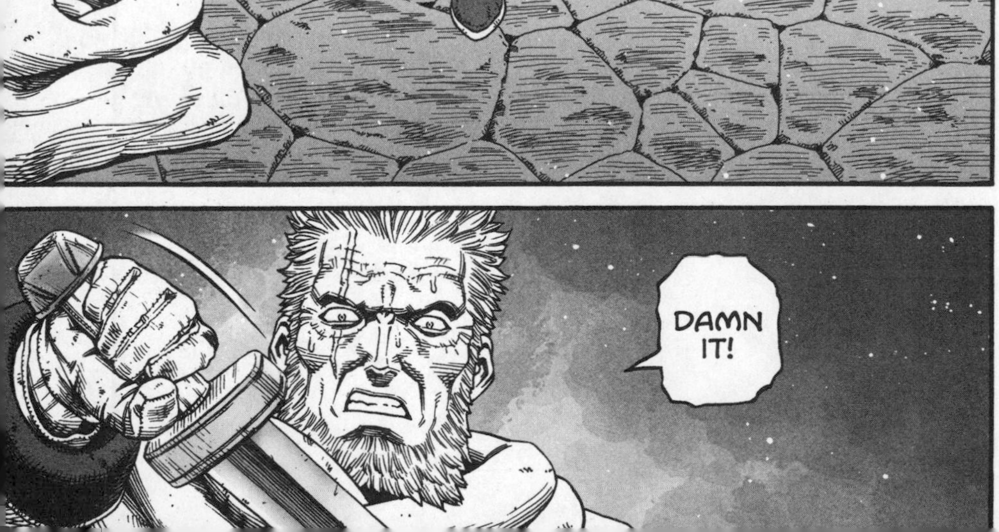
DAMN IT!

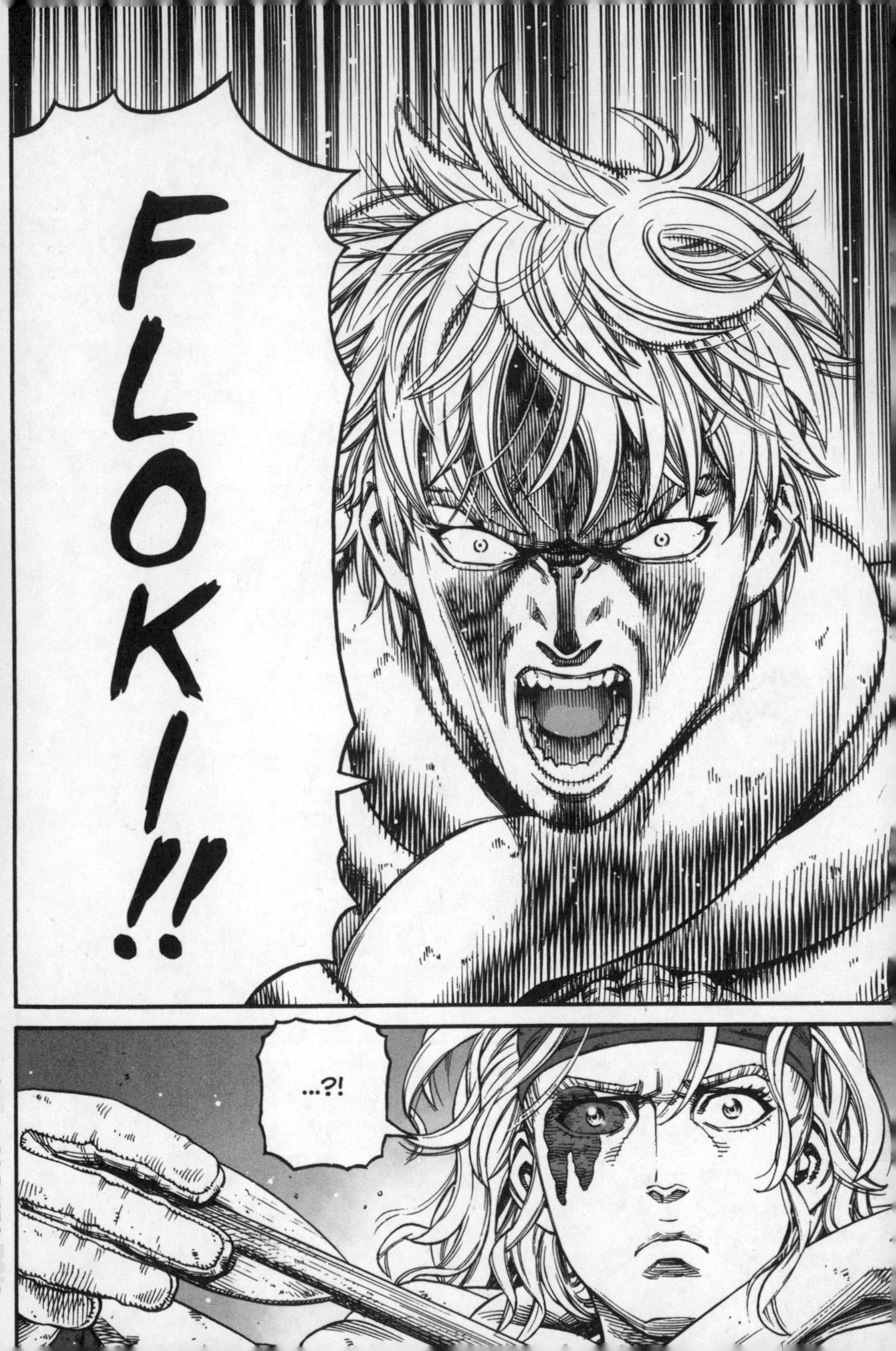
FLOKI!!
...?!

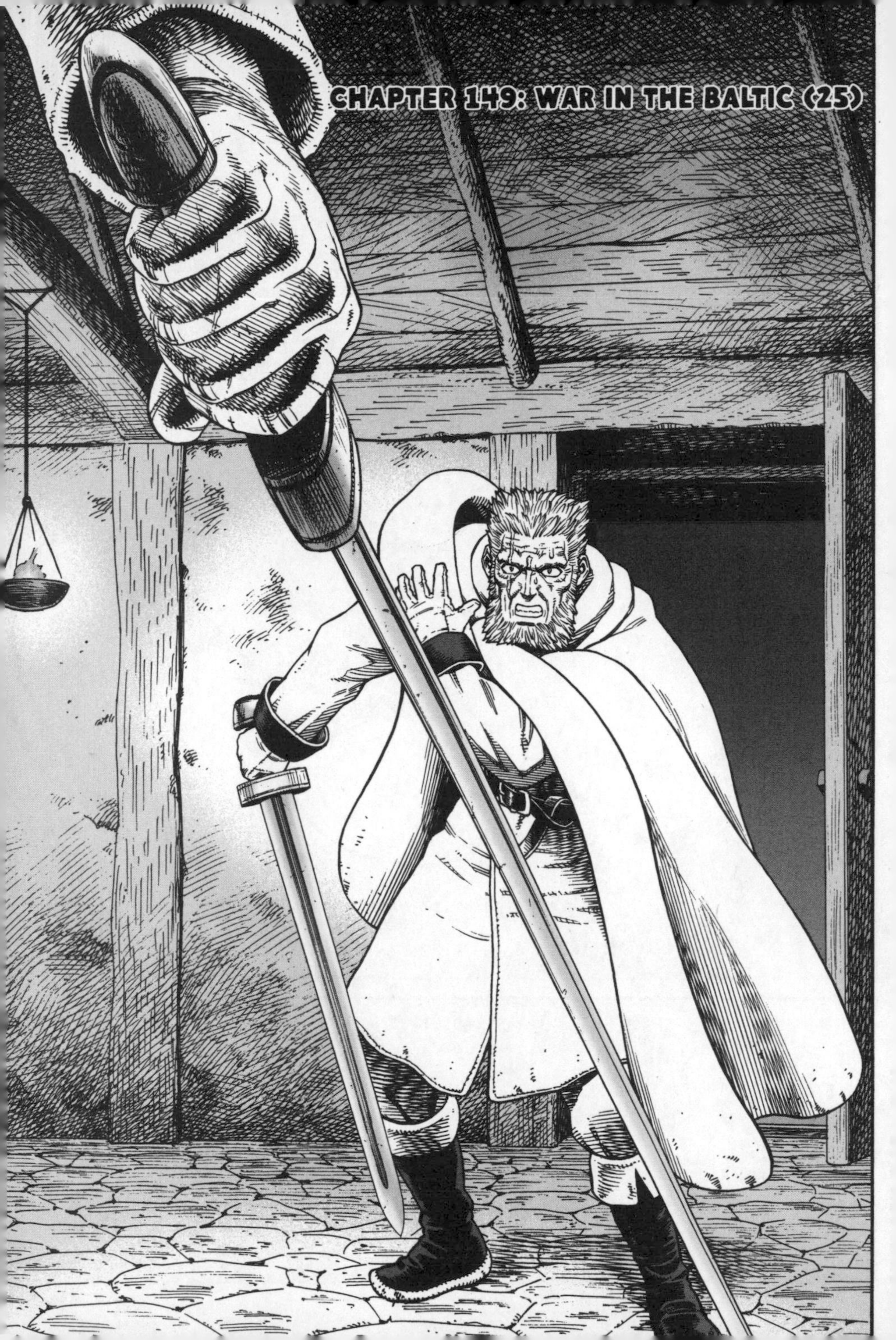
CHAPTER 149: WAR IN THE BALTIC (25)

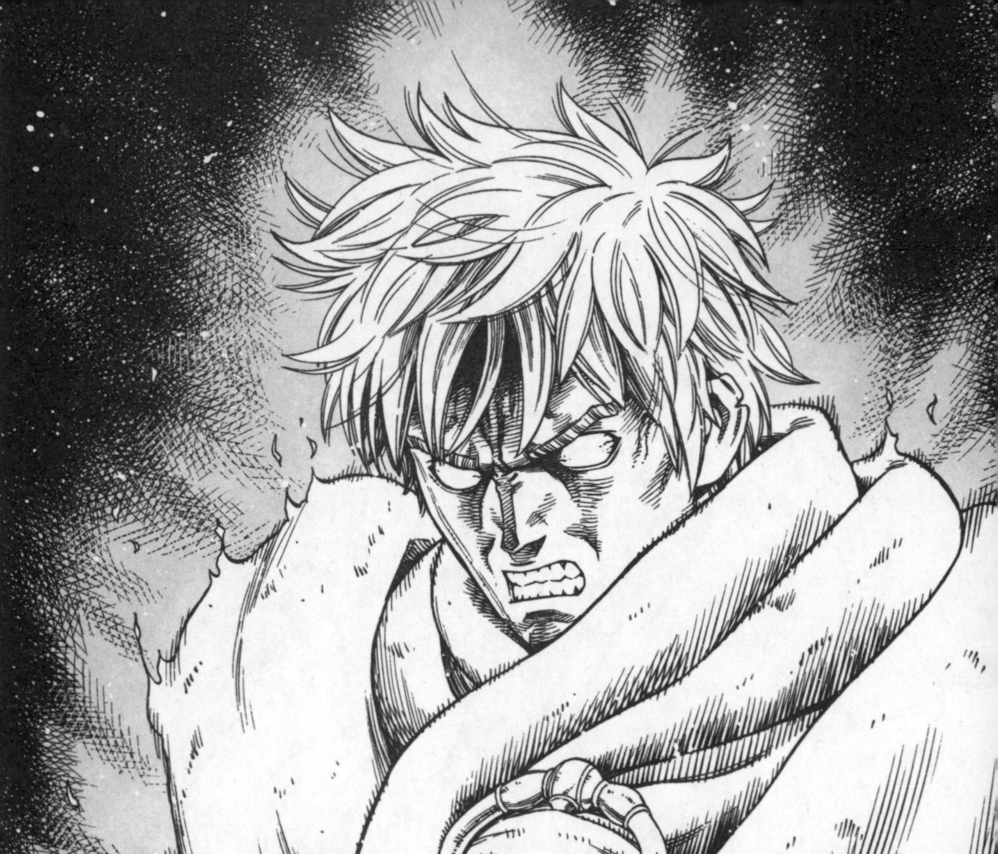

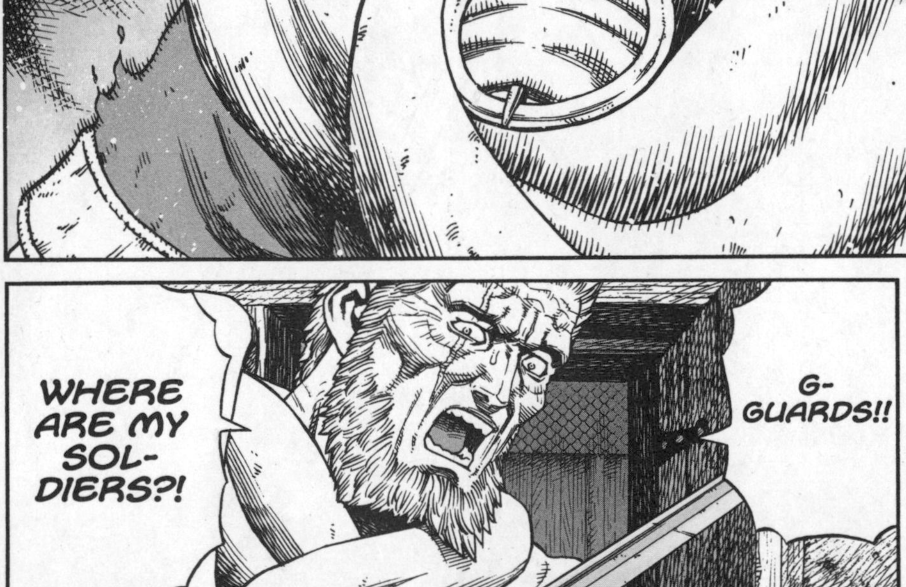
G- GUARDS!!
WHERE ARE MY SOL- DIERS?!

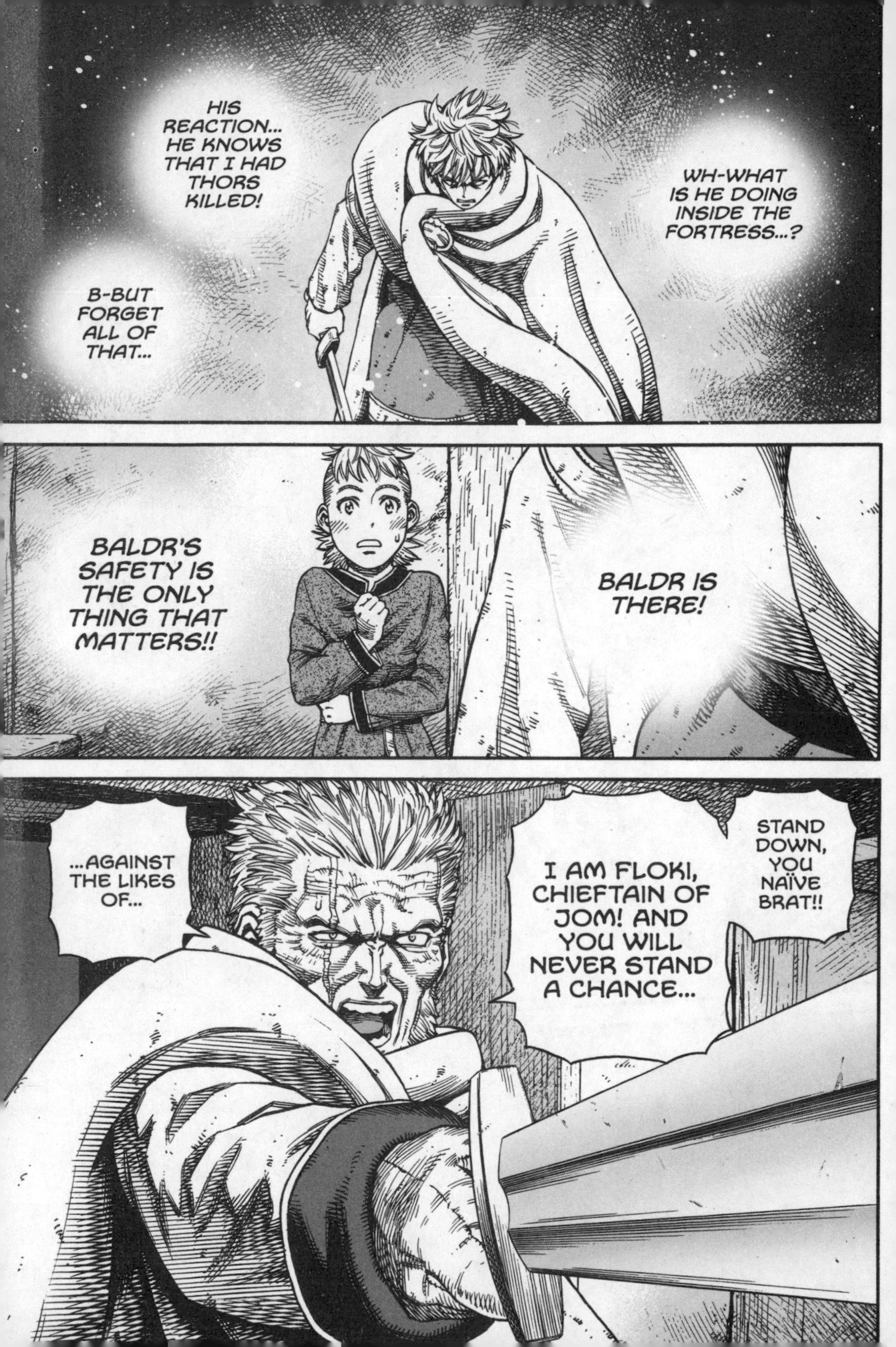
WH-WHAT IS HE DOING INSIDE THE FORTRESS...?
HIS REACTION... HE KNOWS THAT I HAD THORS KILLED!
B-BUT FORGET ALL OF THAT...
BALDR IS THERE!
BALDR'S SAFETY IS THE ONLY THING THAT MATTERS!!
STAND DOWN, YOU NAÏVE BRAT!!
I AM FLOKI, CHIEFTAIN OF JOM! AND YOU WILL NEVER STAND A CHANCE...
...AGAINST THE LIKES OF...

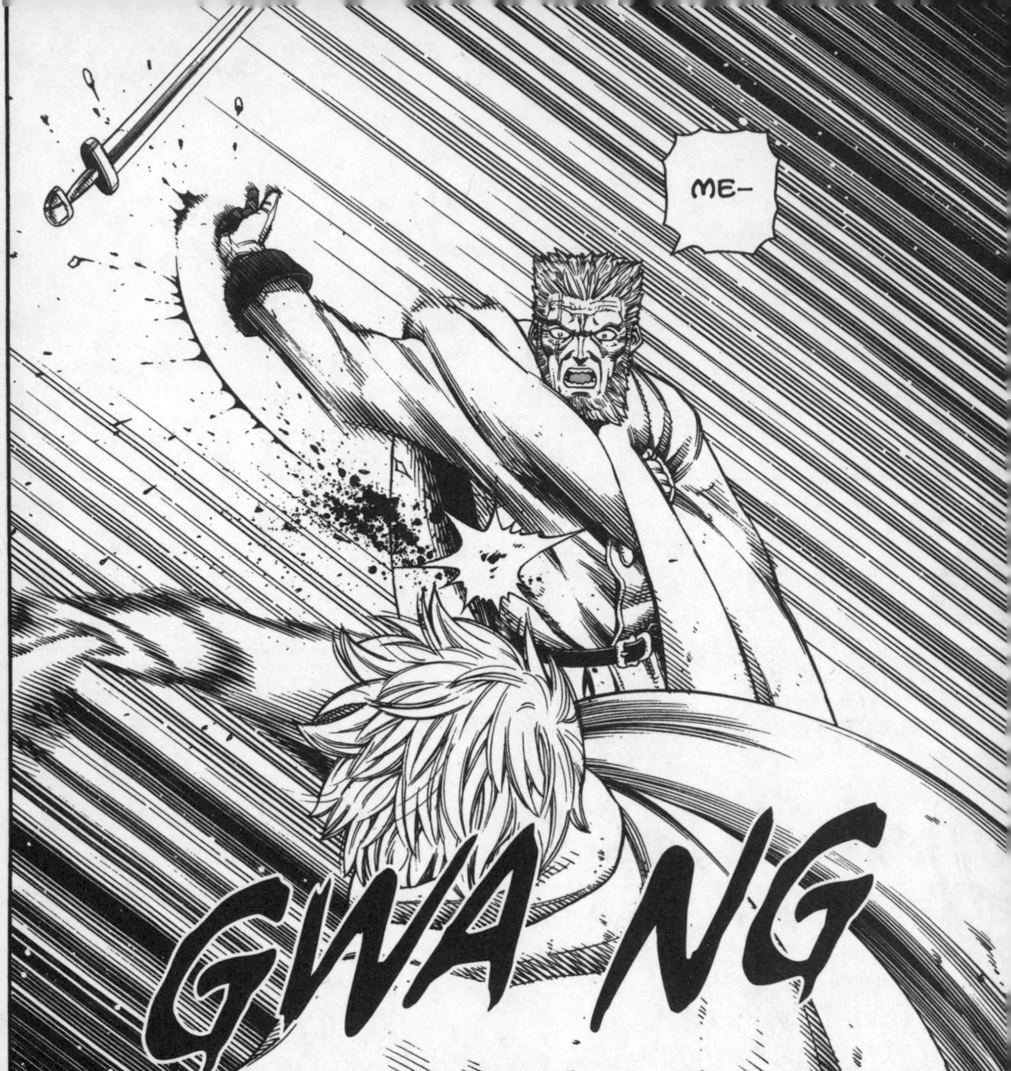
ME-
GWANG
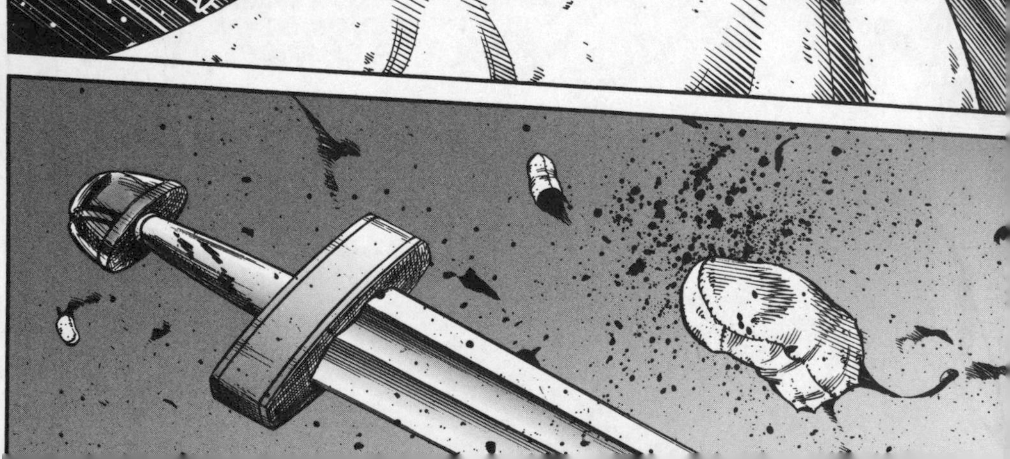

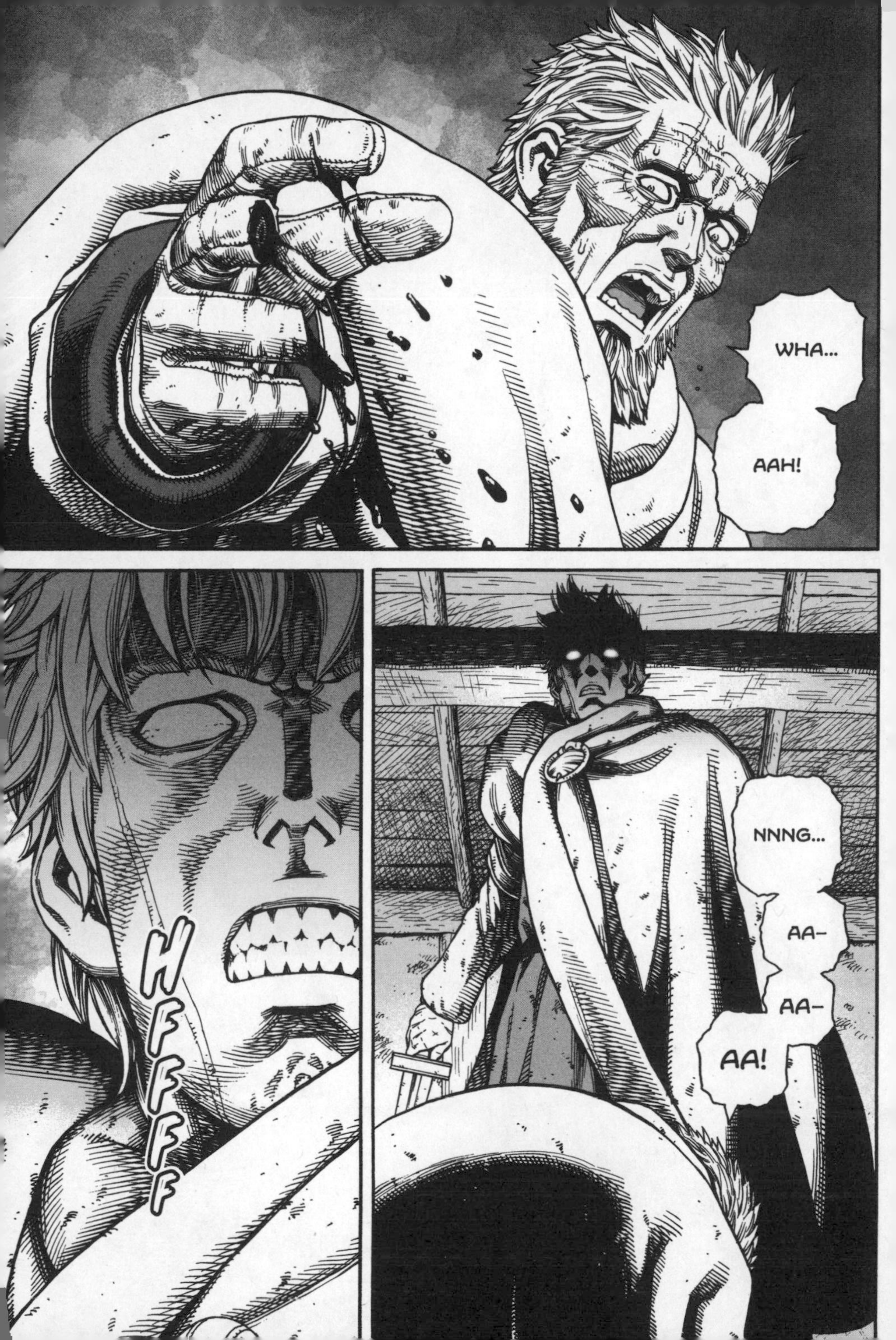
WHA...
AAH!
NNNG...
AA-
AA-
AA!
HFFFF

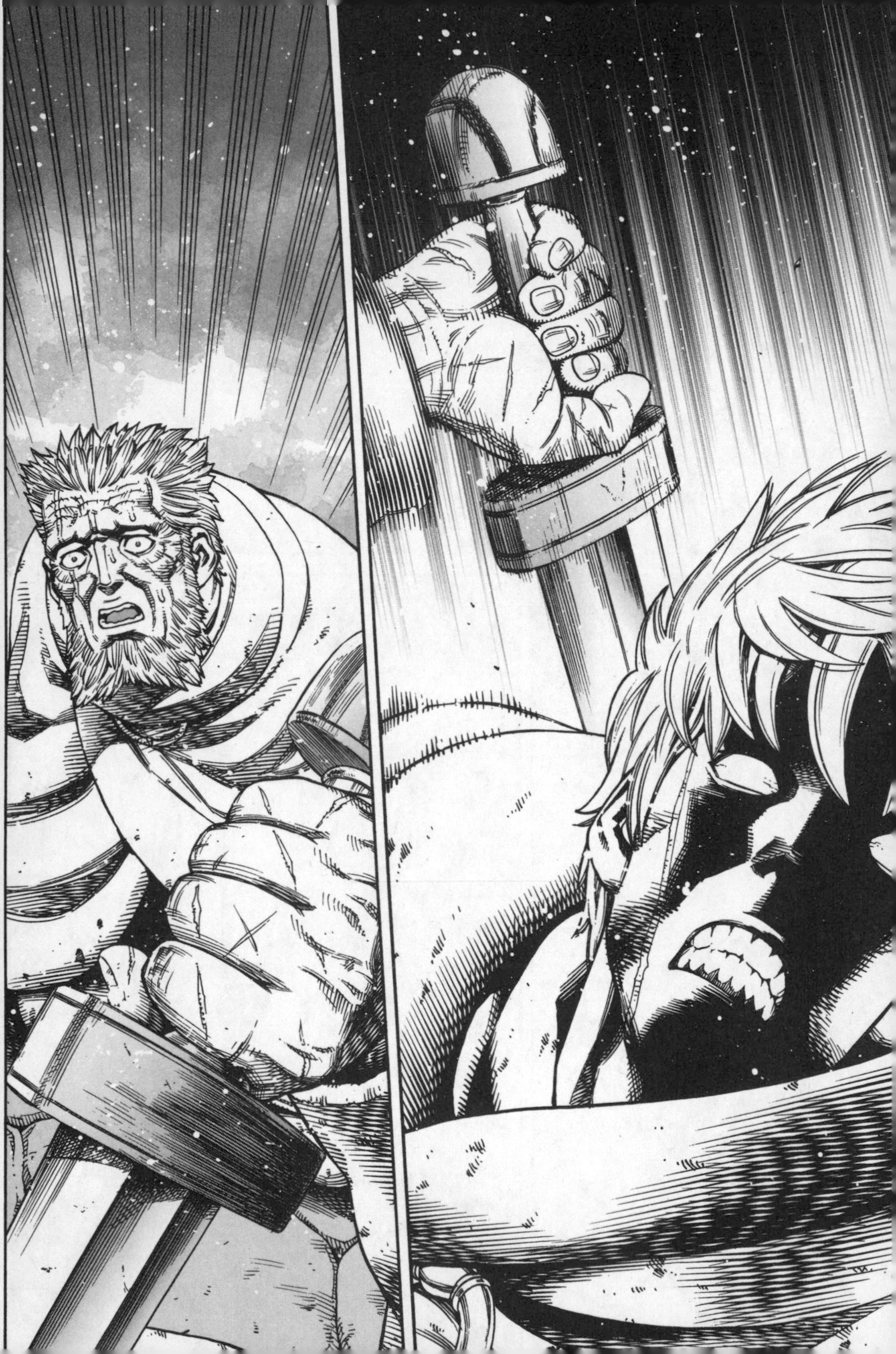

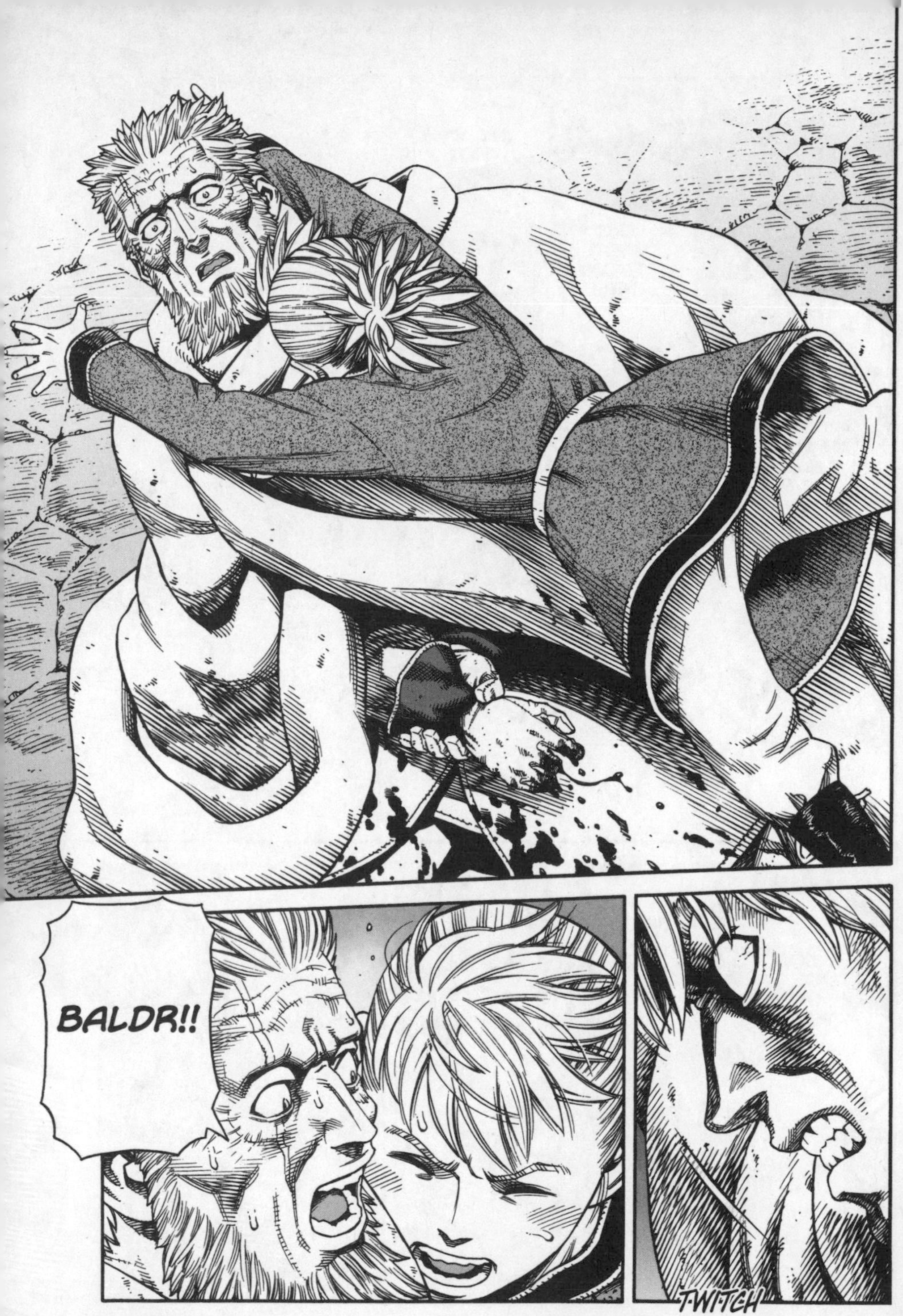
BALDR!!
T-WI-TCH

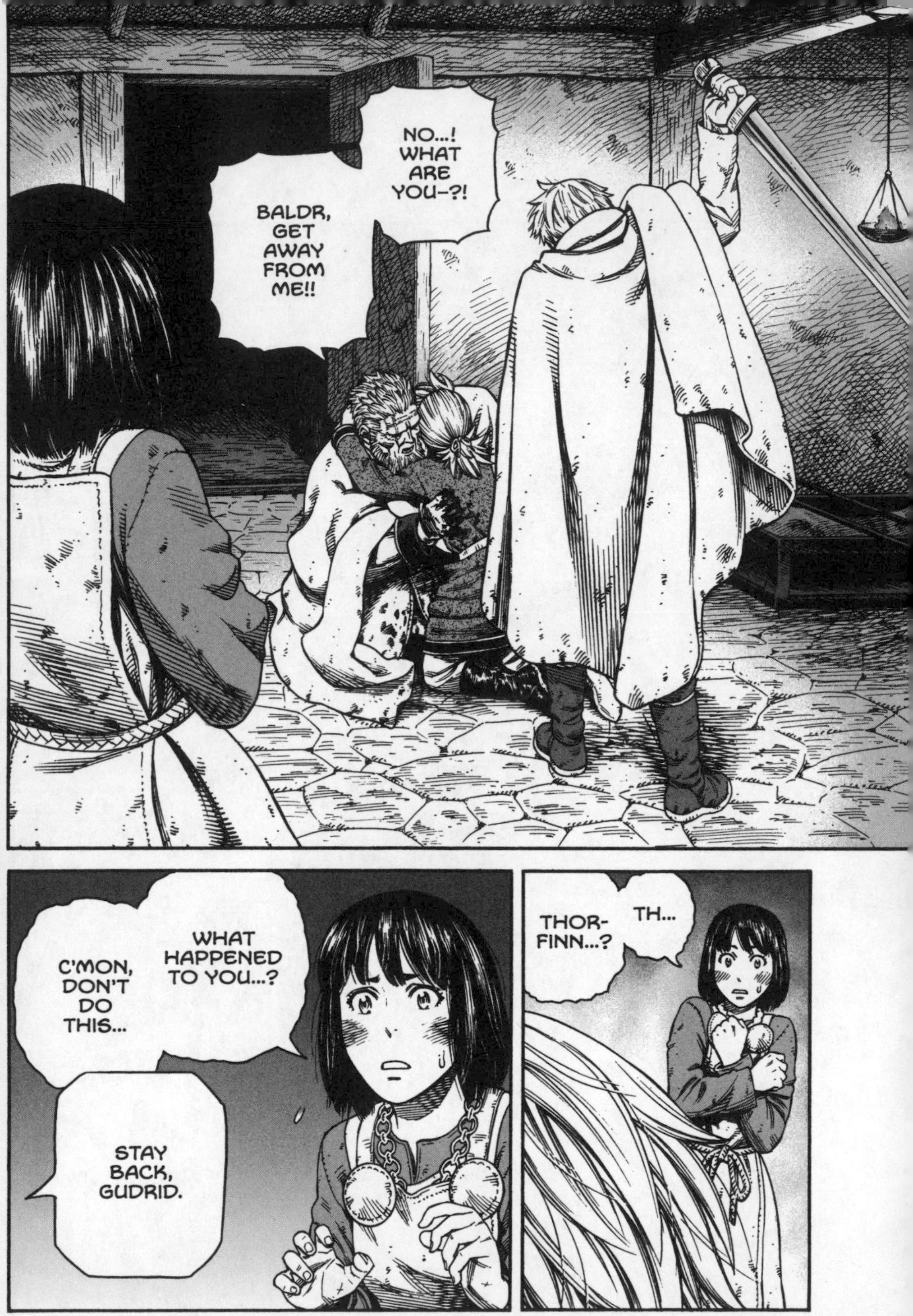
NO...! WHAT ARE YOU-?!
BALDR, GET AWAY FROM ME!!
TH...
THOR-FINN...?
WHAT HAPPENED TO YOU...?
C'MON, DON'T DO THIS...
STAY BACK, GUDRID.

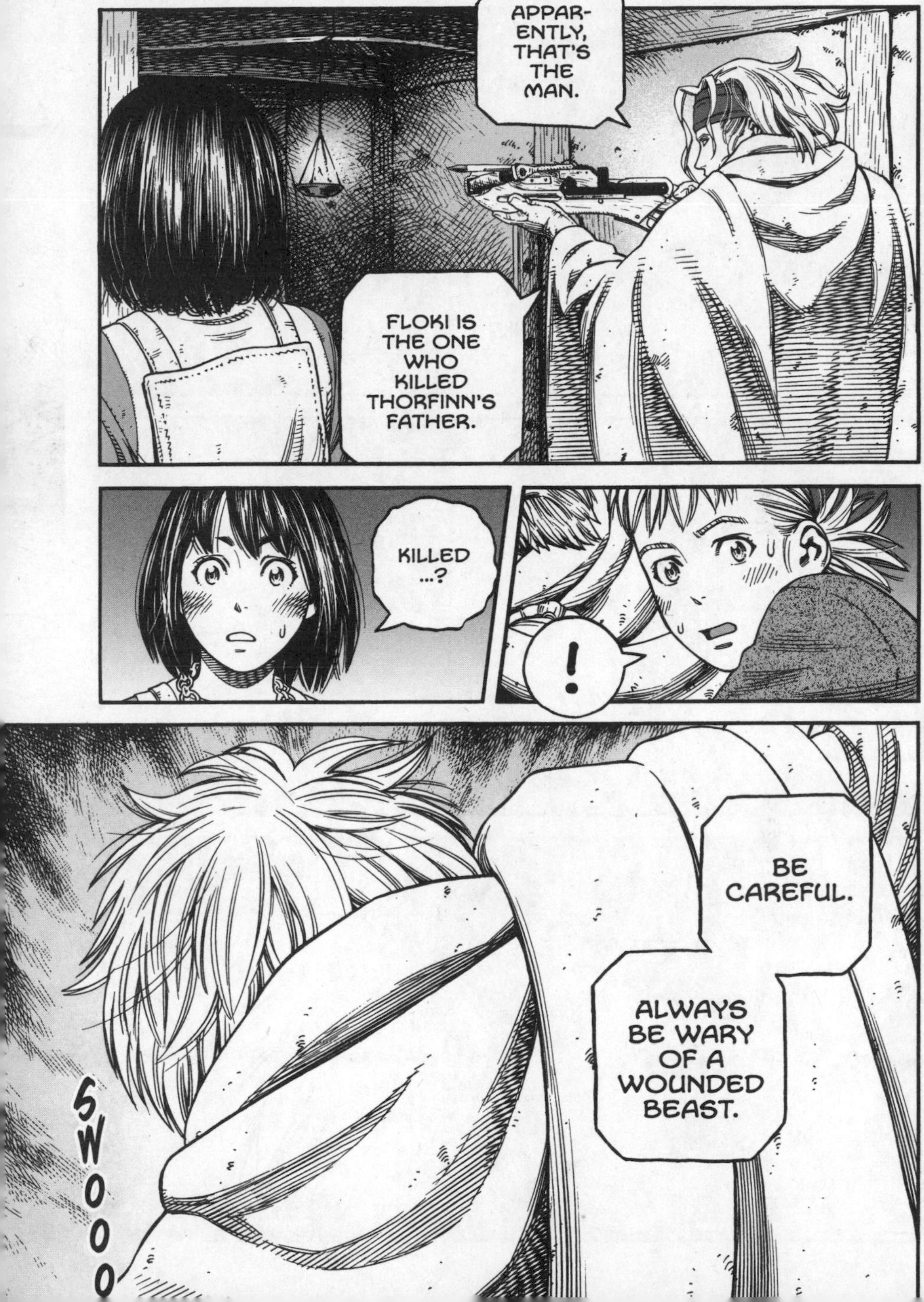
APPAR-ENTLY, THAT'S THE MAN.
FLOKI IS THE ONE WHO KILLED THORFINN'S FATHER.
!
KILLED ...?
BE CAREFUL.
ALWAYS BE WARY OF A WOUNDED BEAST.
SWOOO

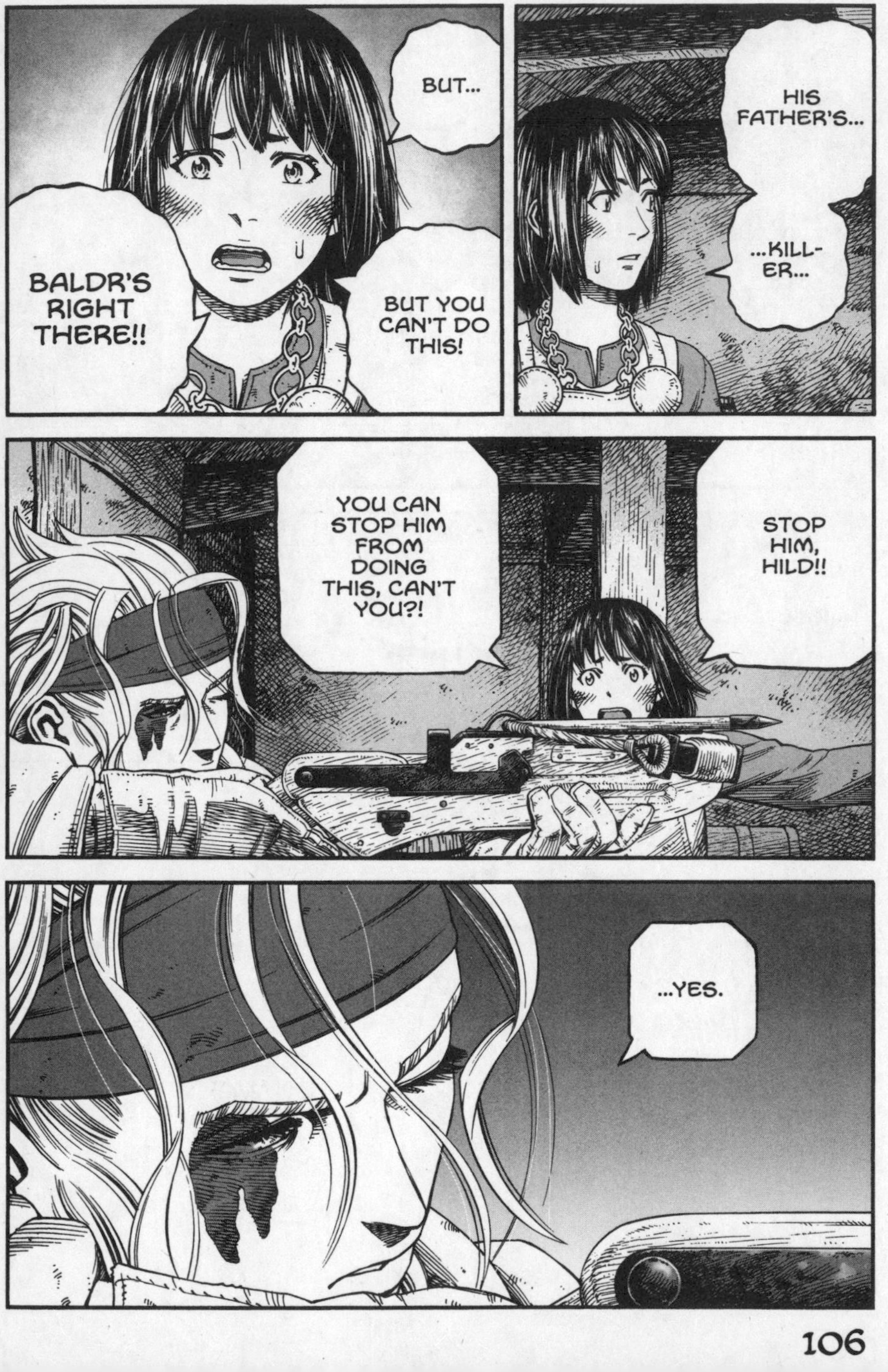
HIS FATHER'S...
...KILL-ER...
BUT...
BUT YOU CAN'T DO THIS!
BALDR'S RIGHT THERE!!
STOP HIM, HILD!!
YOU CAN STOP HIM FROM DOING THIS, CAN'T YOU?!
...YES.

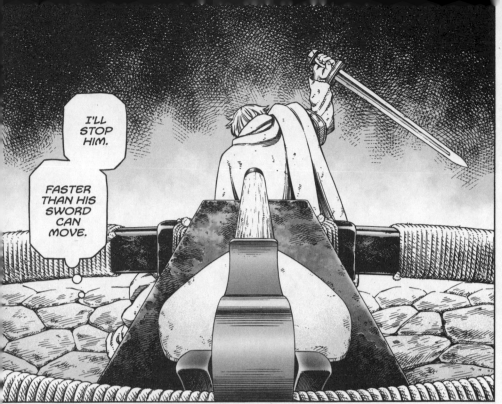

I'LL STOP HIM.

FASTER THAN HIS SWORD CAN MOVE.

THOR-FINN...

...

I'M SURE THAT WHAT GRAND-FATHER DID TO YOU IS UNFORGIV-ABLE...

BUT, IF THAT'S TRUE...

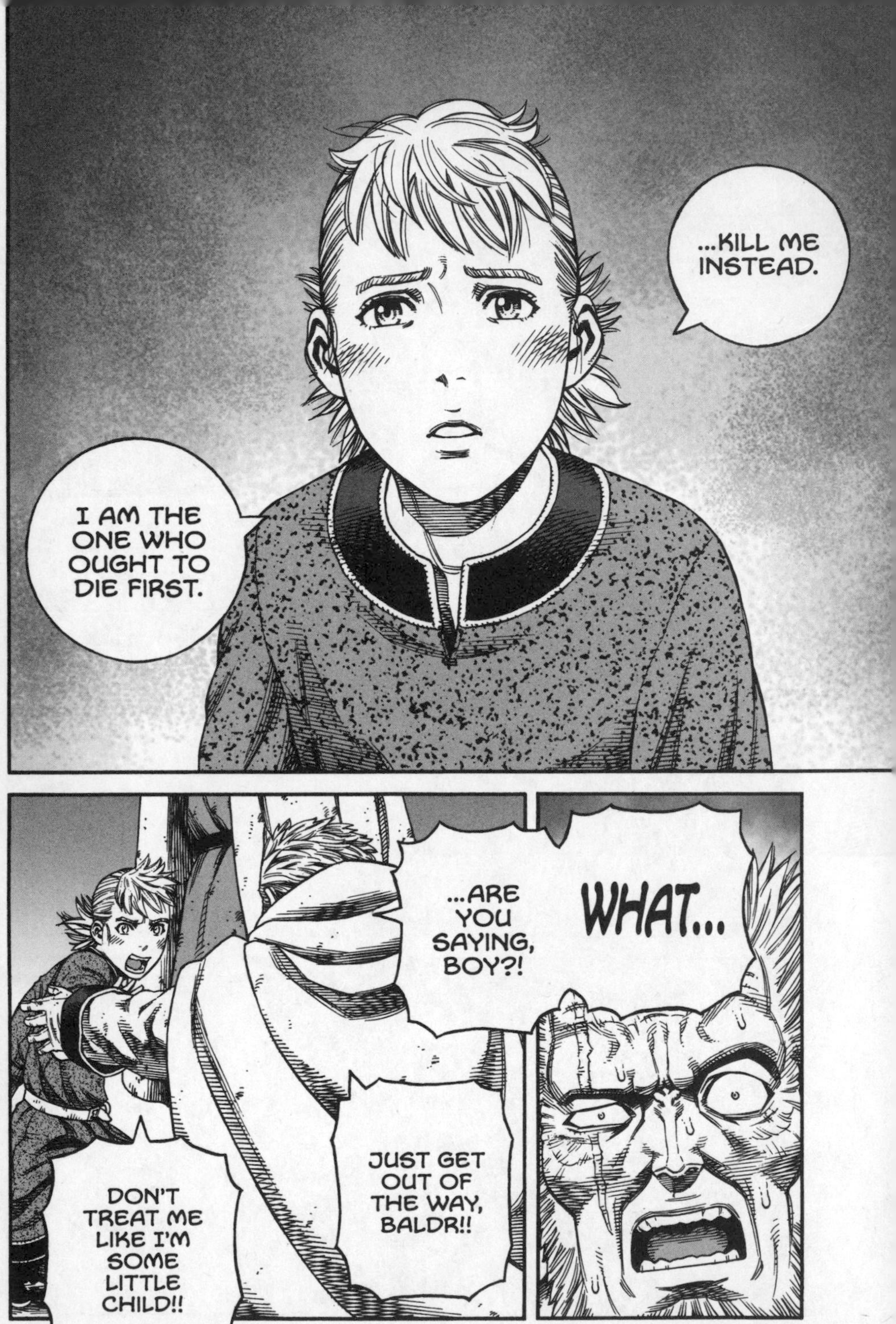
...KILL ME INSTEAD.
I AM THE ONE WHO OUGHT TO DIE FIRST.
WHAT...
...ARE YOU SAYING, BOY?!
JUST GET OUT OF THE WAY, BALDR!!
DON'T TREAT ME LIKE I'M SOME LITTLE CHILD!!

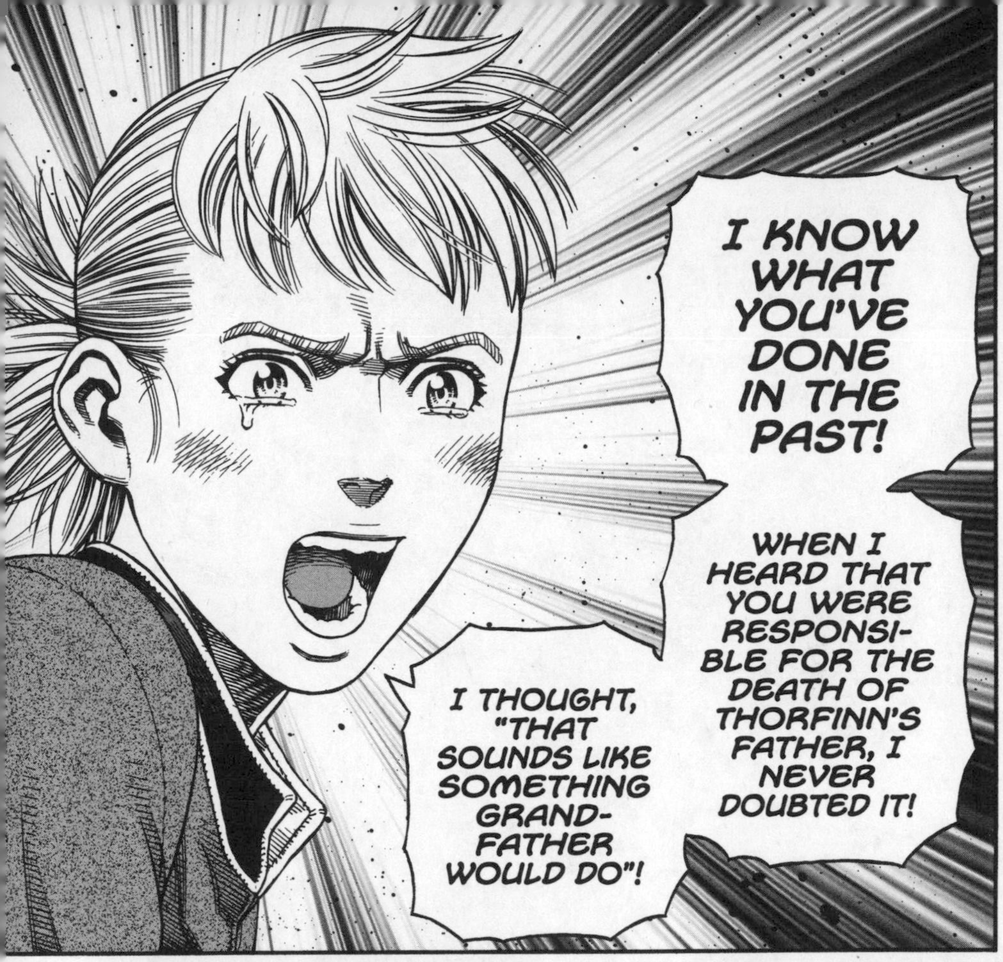
I KNOW WHAT YOU'VE DONE IN THE PAST!
WHEN I HEARD THAT YOU WERE RESPONSIBLE FOR THE DEATH OF THORFINN'S FATHER, I NEVER DOUBTED IT!
I THOUGHT, "THAT SOUNDS LIKE SOMETHING GRANDFATHER WOULD DO"!

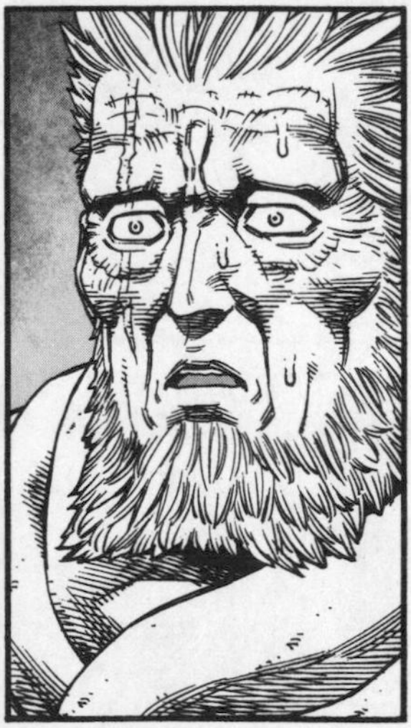

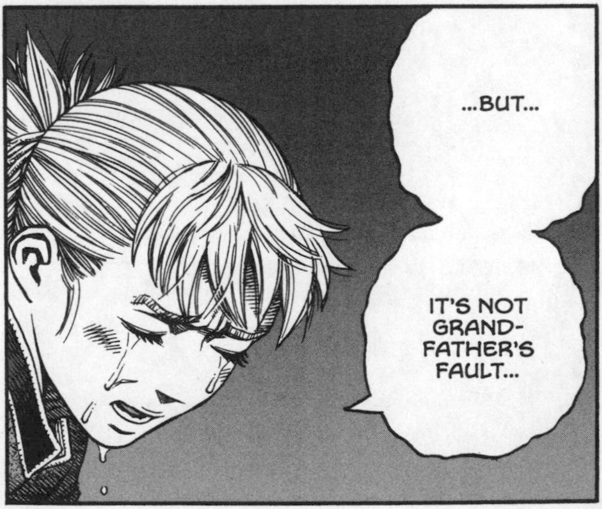
...BUT...
IT'S NOT GRANDFATHER'S FAULT...

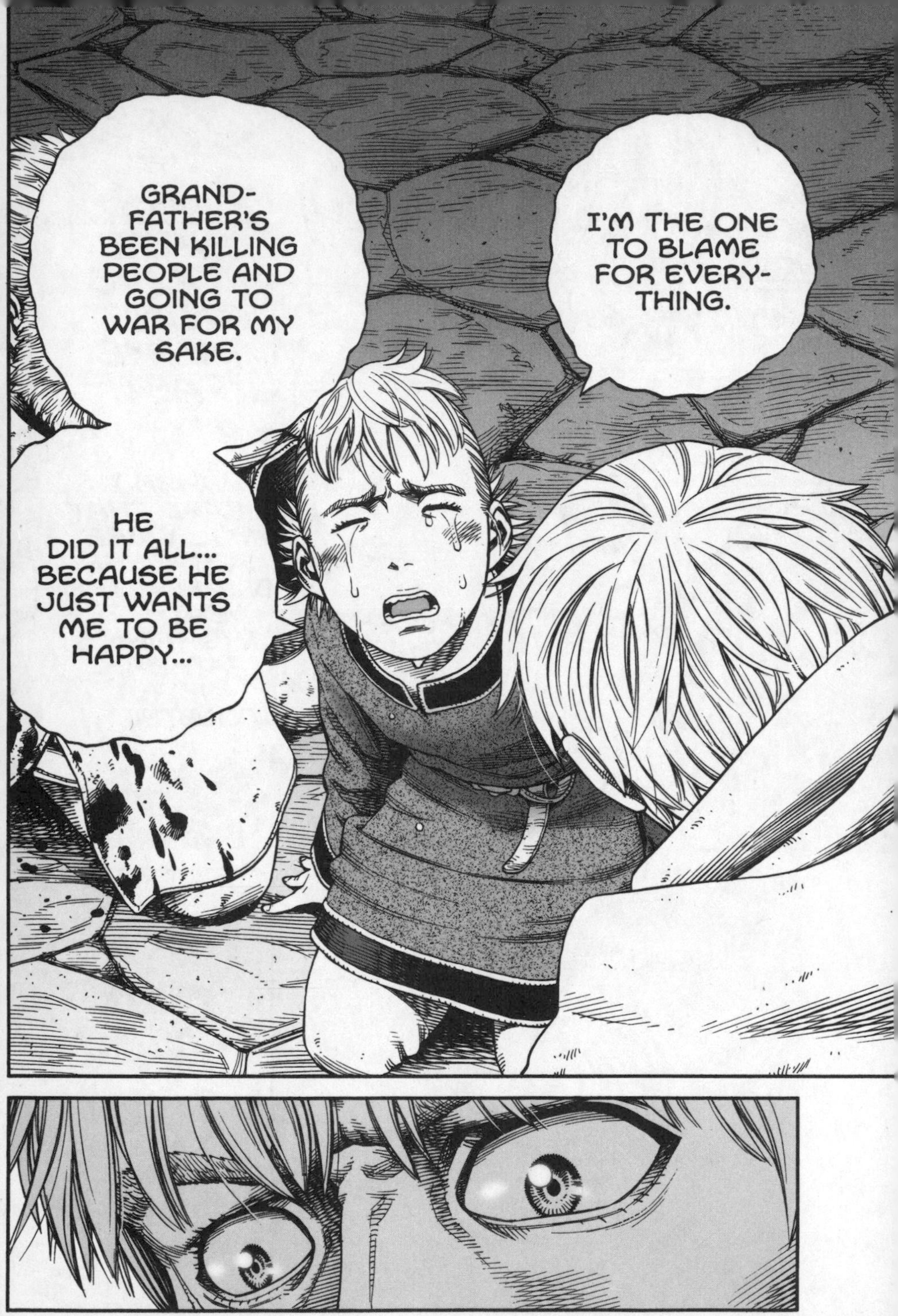
I'M THE ONE TO BLAME FOR EVERY-THING.
GRAND-FATHER'S BEEN KILLING PEOPLE AND GOING TO WAR FOR MY SAKE.
HE DID IT ALL... BECAUSE HE JUST WANTS ME TO BE HAPPY...

I'M SORRY...

I'M SORRY...

I'M SORRY I COULD NEVER STOP HIM...

...BALDR...

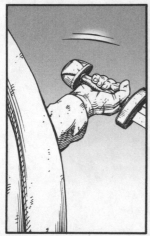

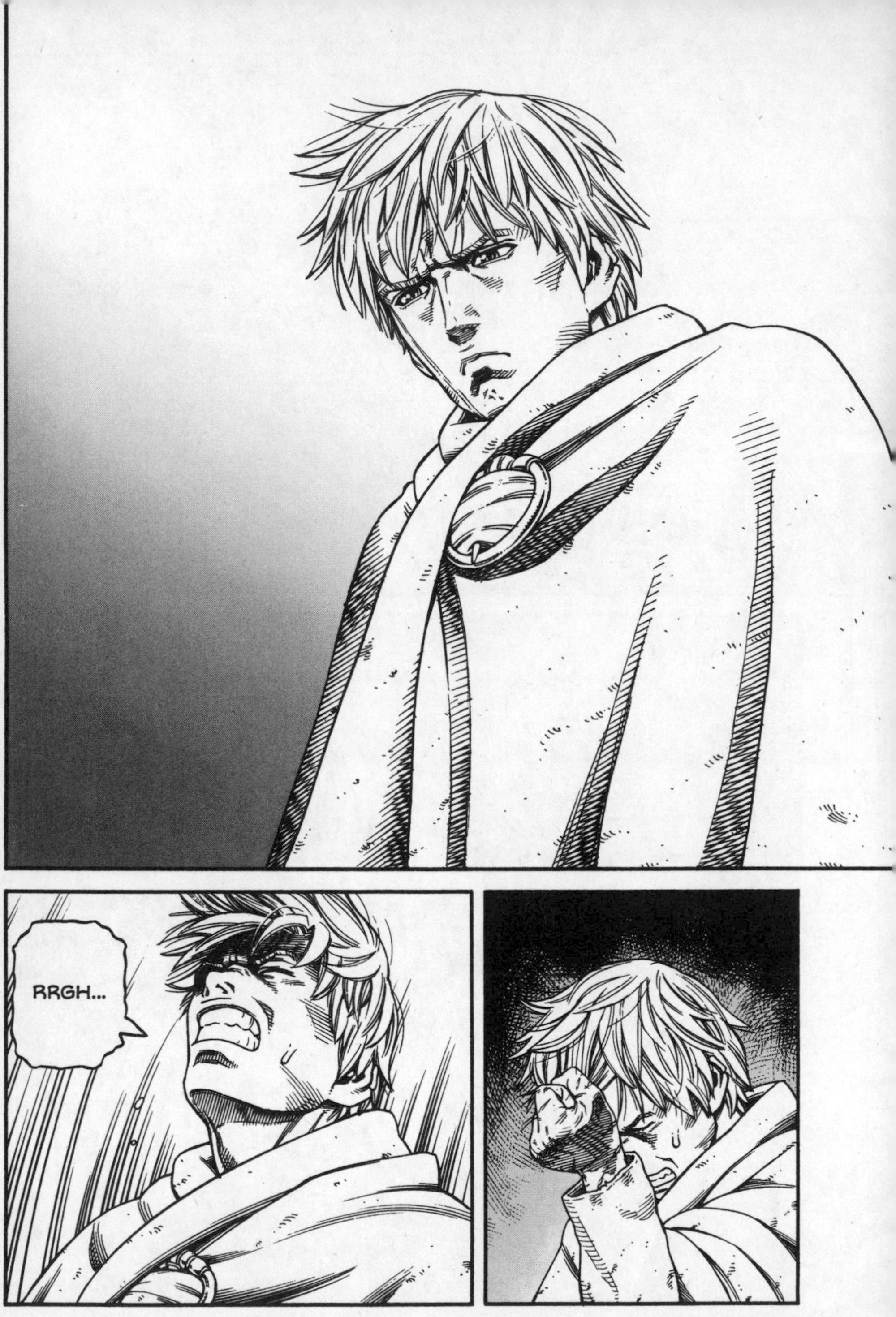
RRGH...

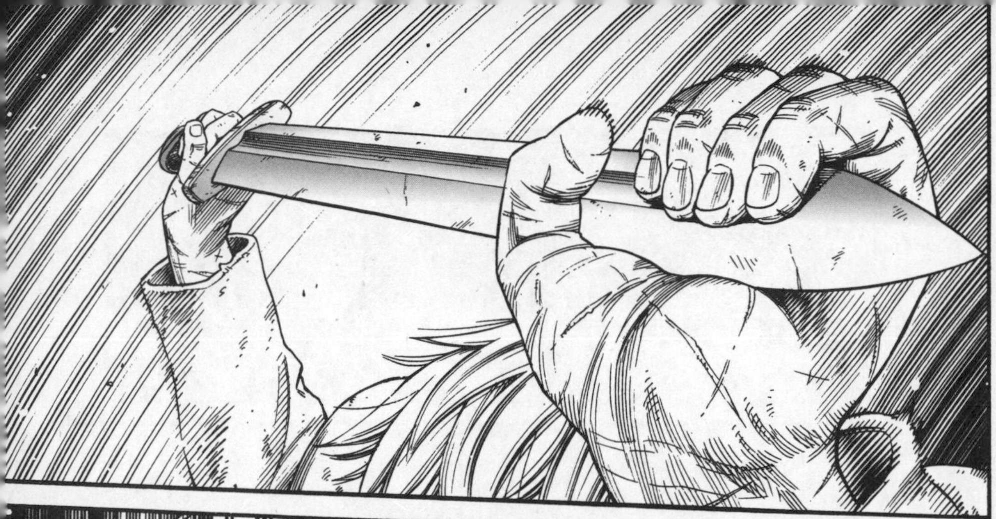
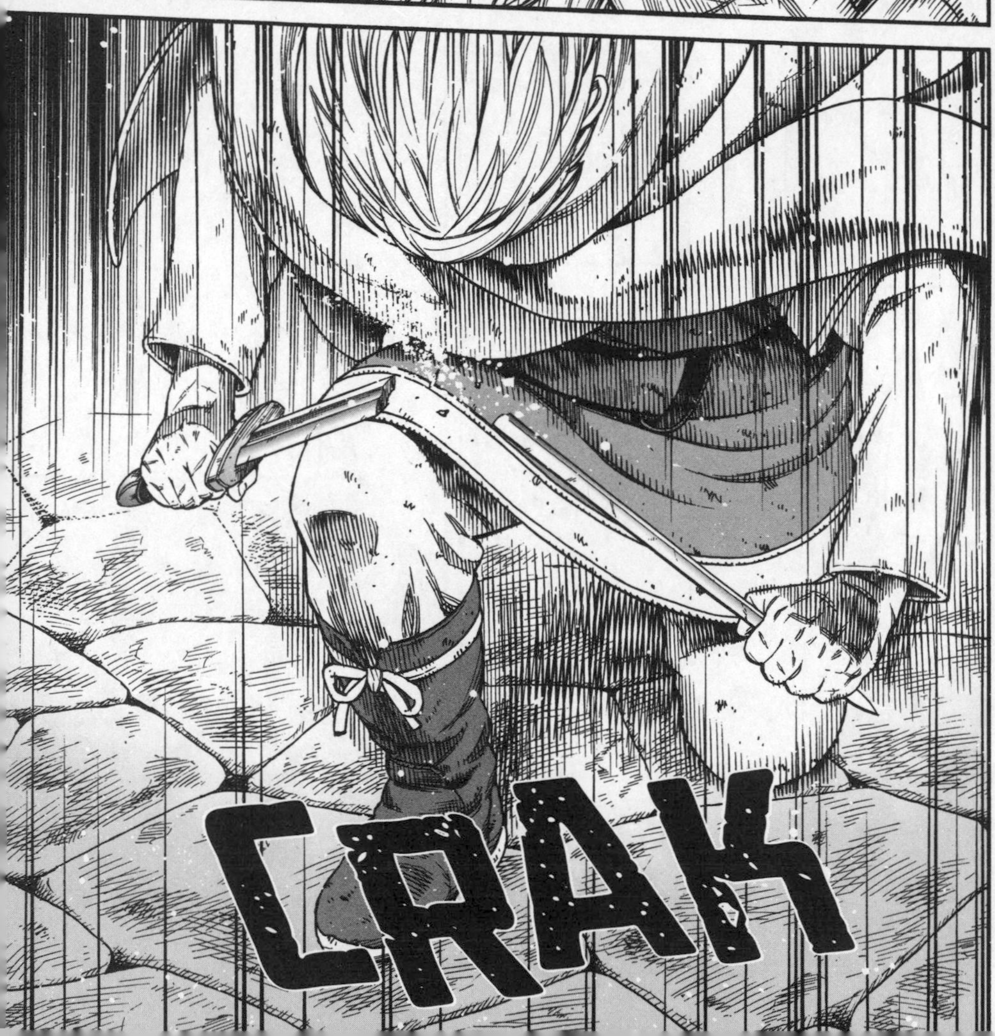
CRAK

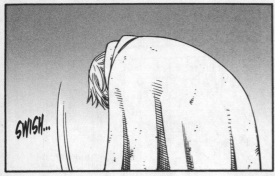

SWISH...

CLANG

KACLANG

PHEW...

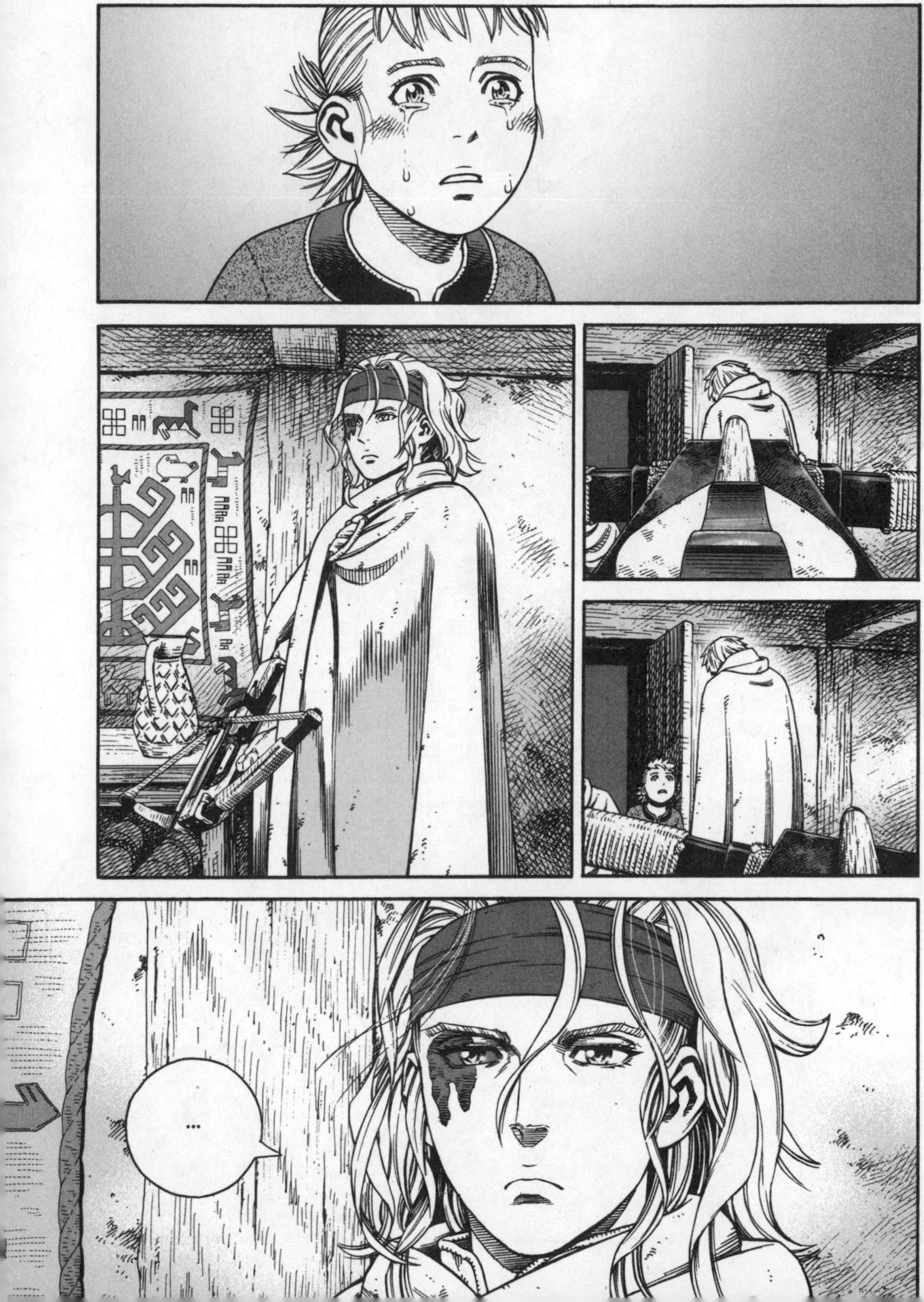
...

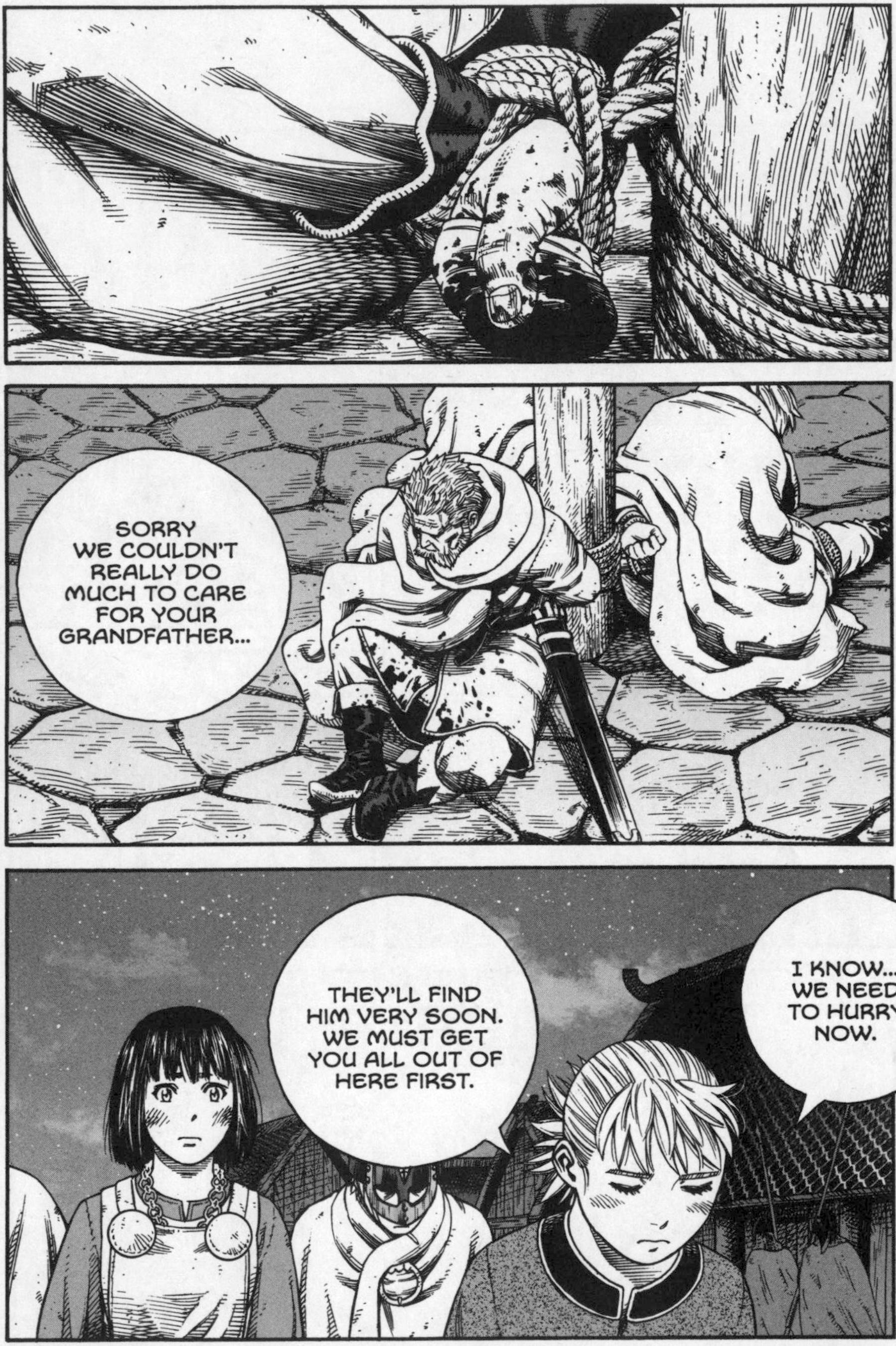
SORRY WE COULDN'T REALLY DO MUCH TO CARE FOR YOUR GRANDFATHER...
THEY'LL FIND HIM VERY SOON. WE MUST GET YOU ALL OUT OF HERE FIRST.
I KNOW... WE NEED TO HURRY NOW.

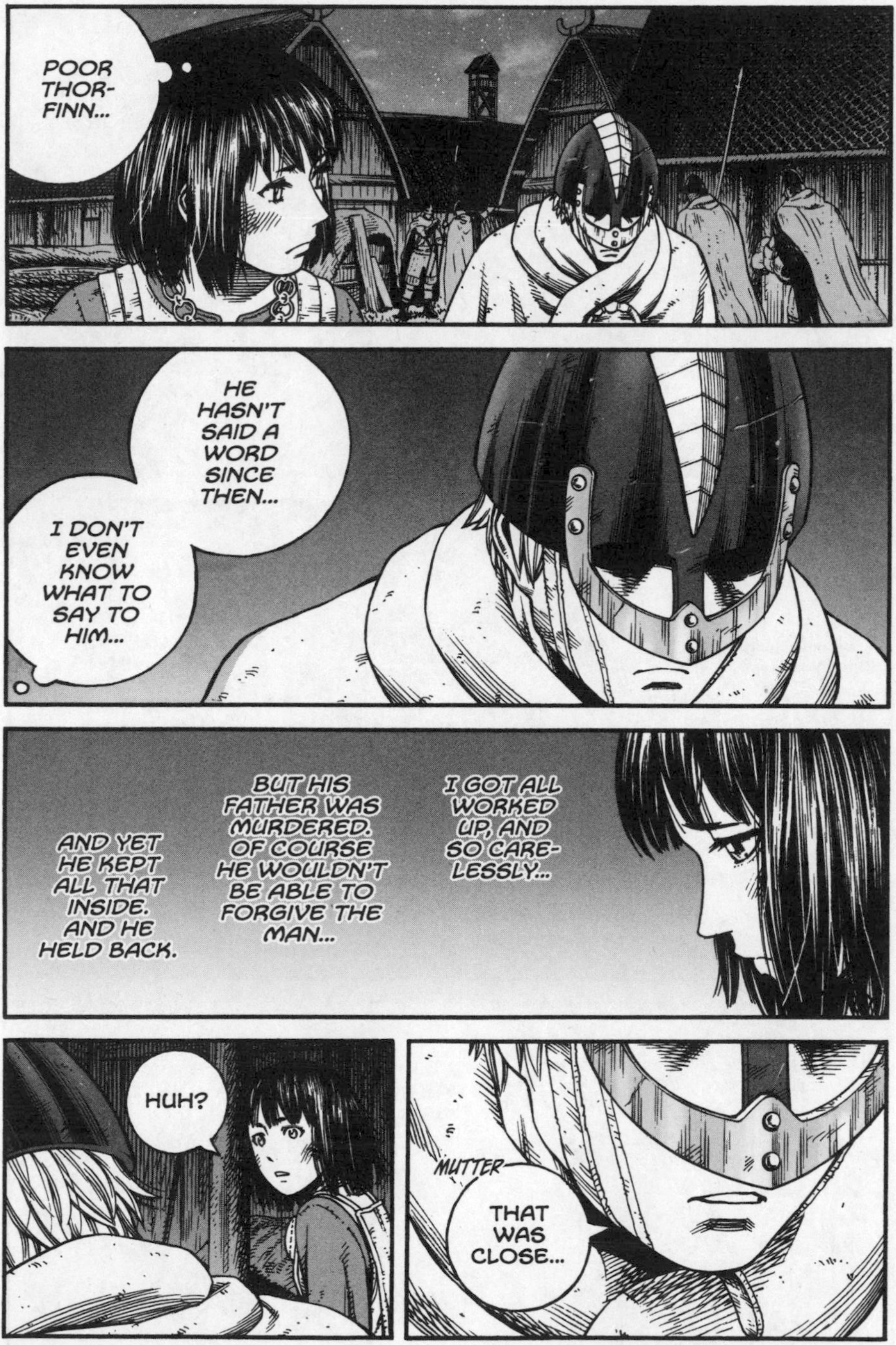
POOR THORFINN...
HE HASN'T SAID A WORD SINCE THEN...
I DON'T EVEN KNOW WHAT TO SAY TO HIM...
I GOT ALL WORKED UP, AND SO CARELESSLY...
BUT HIS FATHER WAS MURDERED. OF COURSE HE WOULDN'T BE ABLE TO FORGIVE THE MAN...
AND YET HE KEPT ALL THAT INSIDE. AND HE HELD BACK.
MUTTER
THAT WAS CLOSE...
HUH?

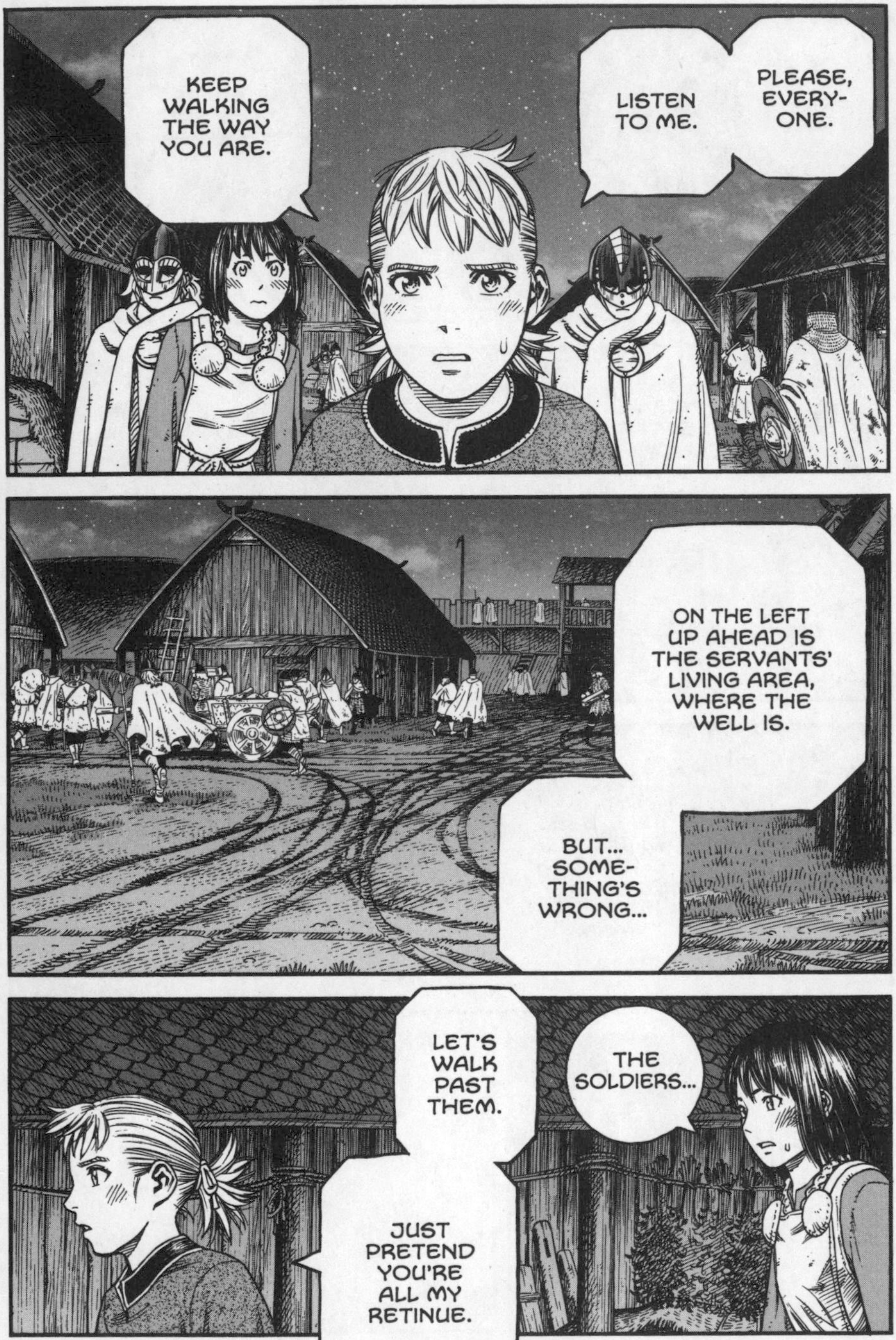
PLEASE, EVERY-ONE.
LISTEN TO ME.
KEEP WALKING THE WAY YOU ARE.
ON THE LEFT UP AHEAD IS THE SERVANTS' LIVING AREA, WHERE THE WELL IS.
BUT... SOME-THING'S WRONG...
THE SOLDIERS...
LET'S WALK PAST THEM.
JUST PRETEND YOU'RE ALL MY RETINUE.

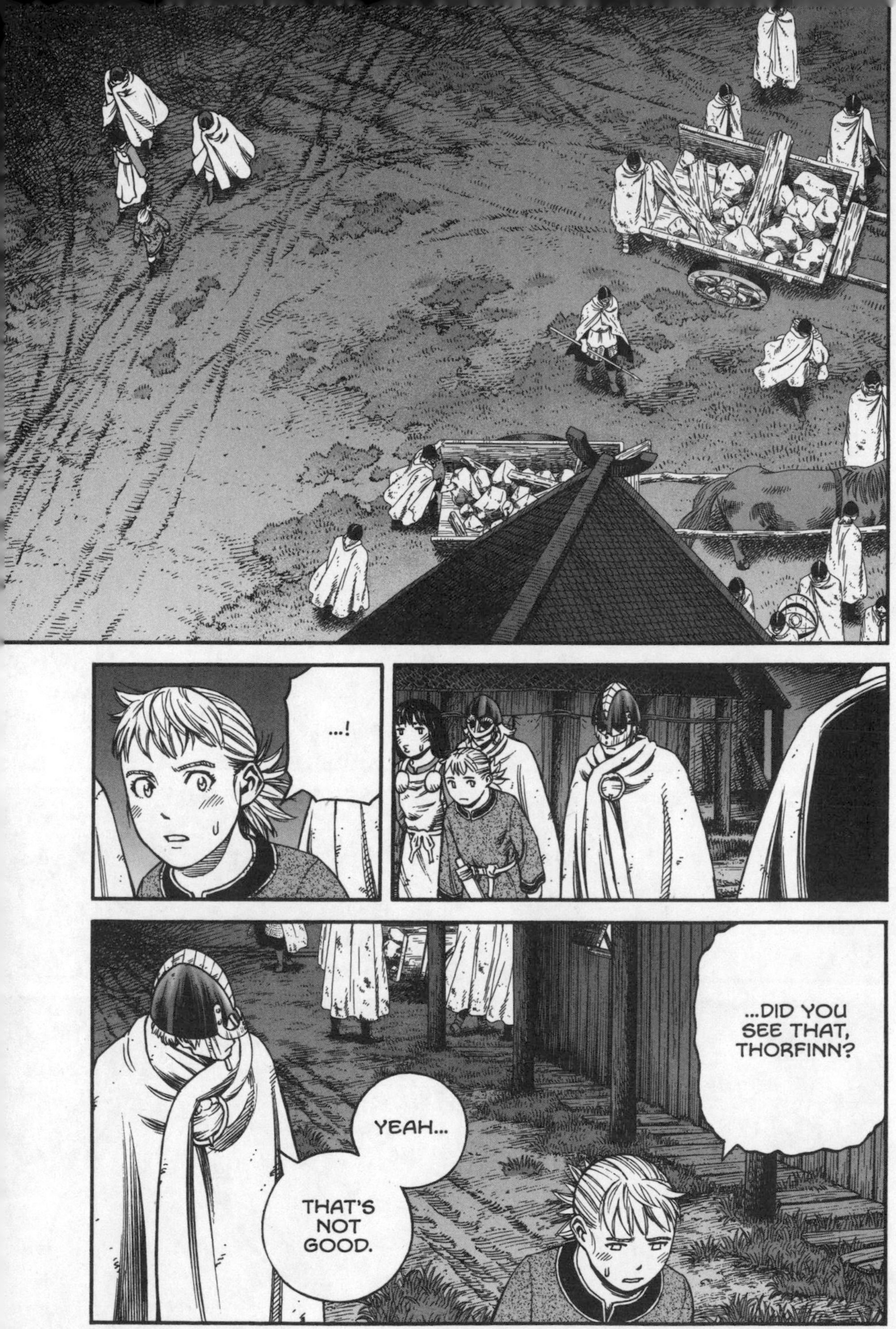
...!
...DID YOU SEE THAT, THORFINN?
YEAH...
THAT'S NOT GOOD.

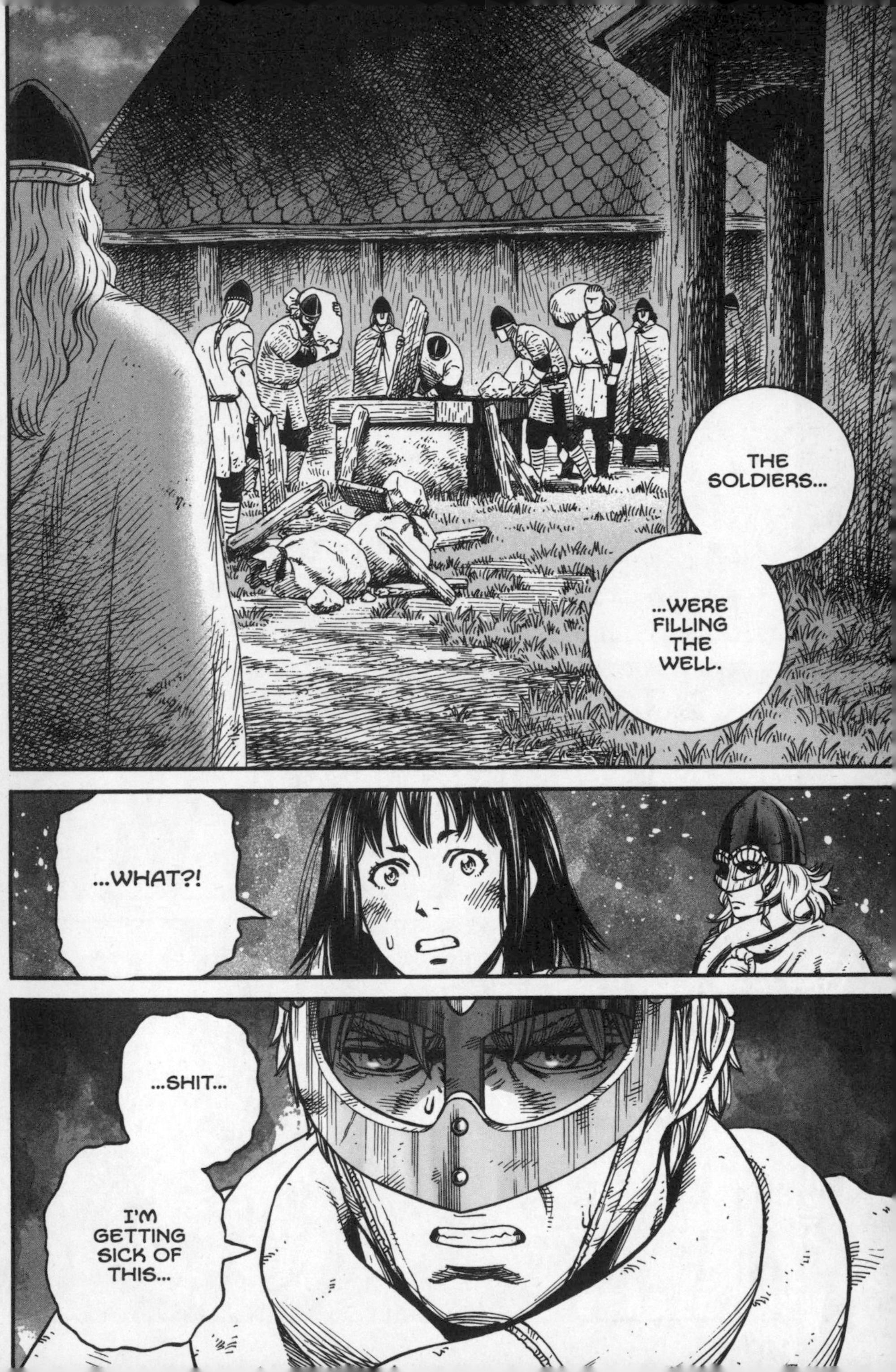
THE SOLDIERS...
...WERE FILLING THE WELL.
...WHAT?!
...SHIT...
I'M GETTING SICK OF THIS...

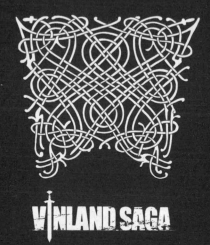

VINLAND SAGA

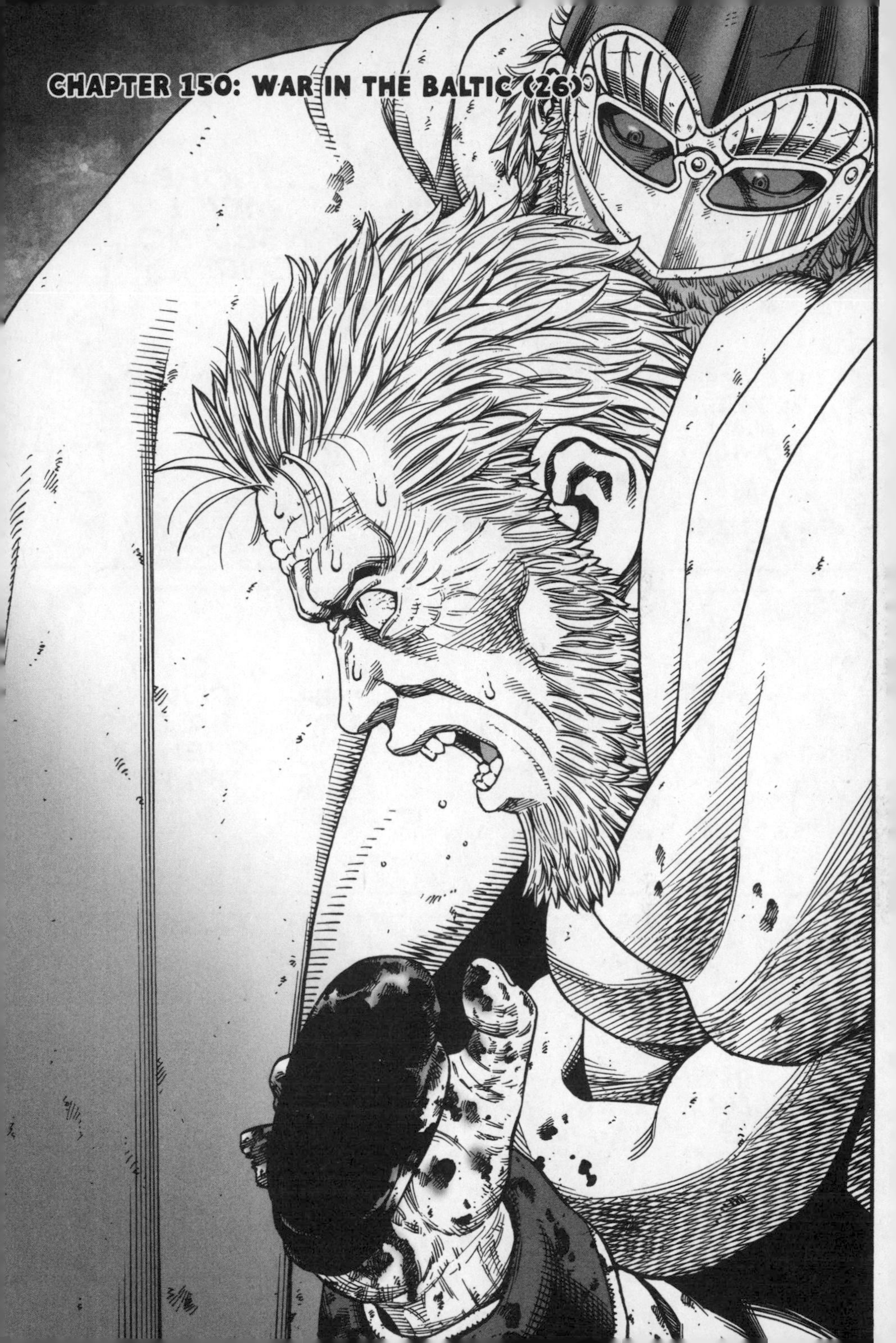
CHAPTER 150: WAR IN THE BALTIC (26)

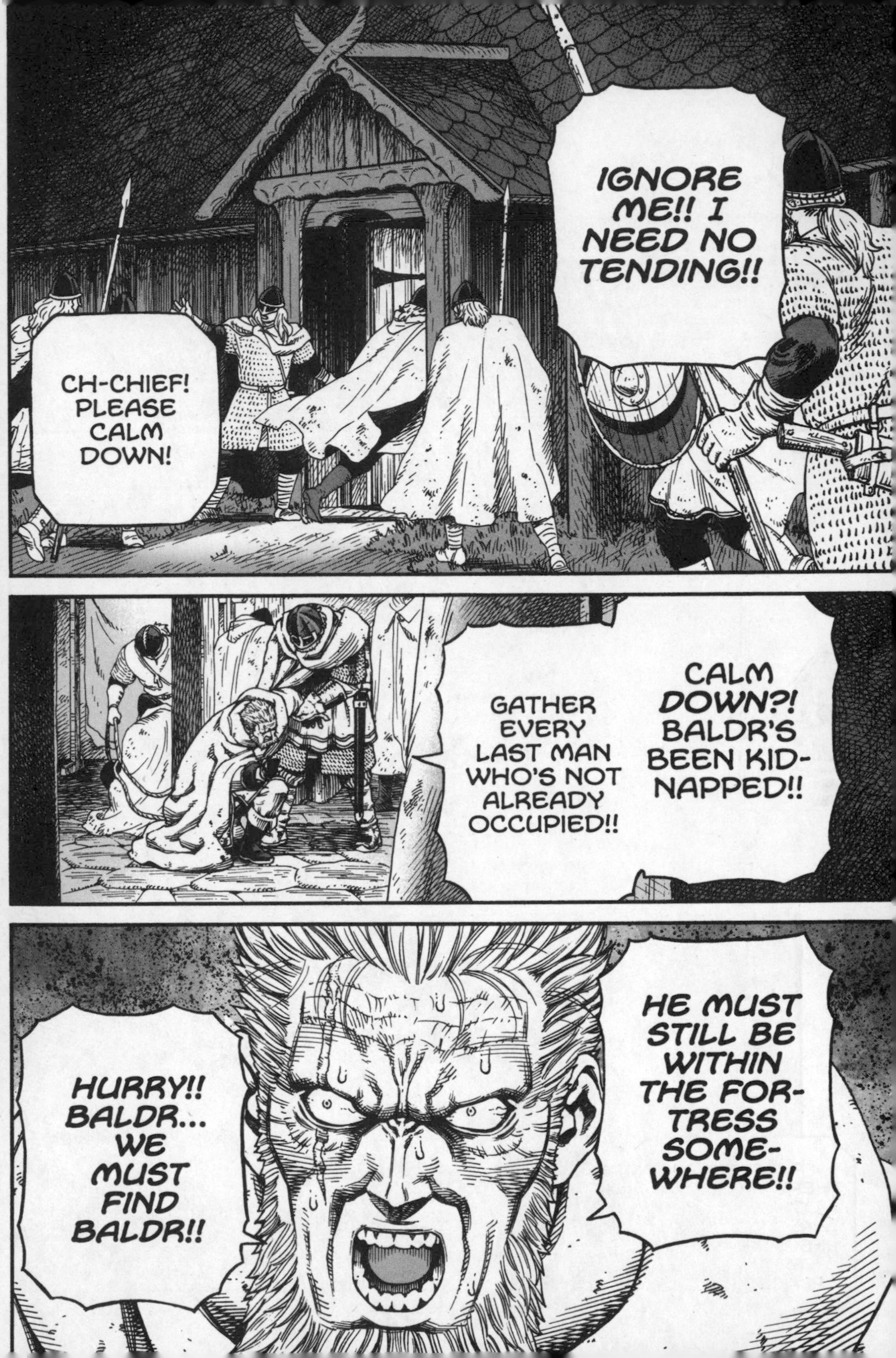
IGNORE ME!! I NEED NO TENDING!!
CH-CHIEF! PLEASE CALM DOWN!
CALM DOWN?! BALDR'S BEEN KID-NAPPED!!
GATHER EVERY LAST MAN WHO'S NOT ALREADY OCCUPIED!!
HE MUST STILL BE WITHIN THE FOR-TRESS SOME-WHERE!!
HURRY!! BALDR... WE MUST FIND BALDR!!

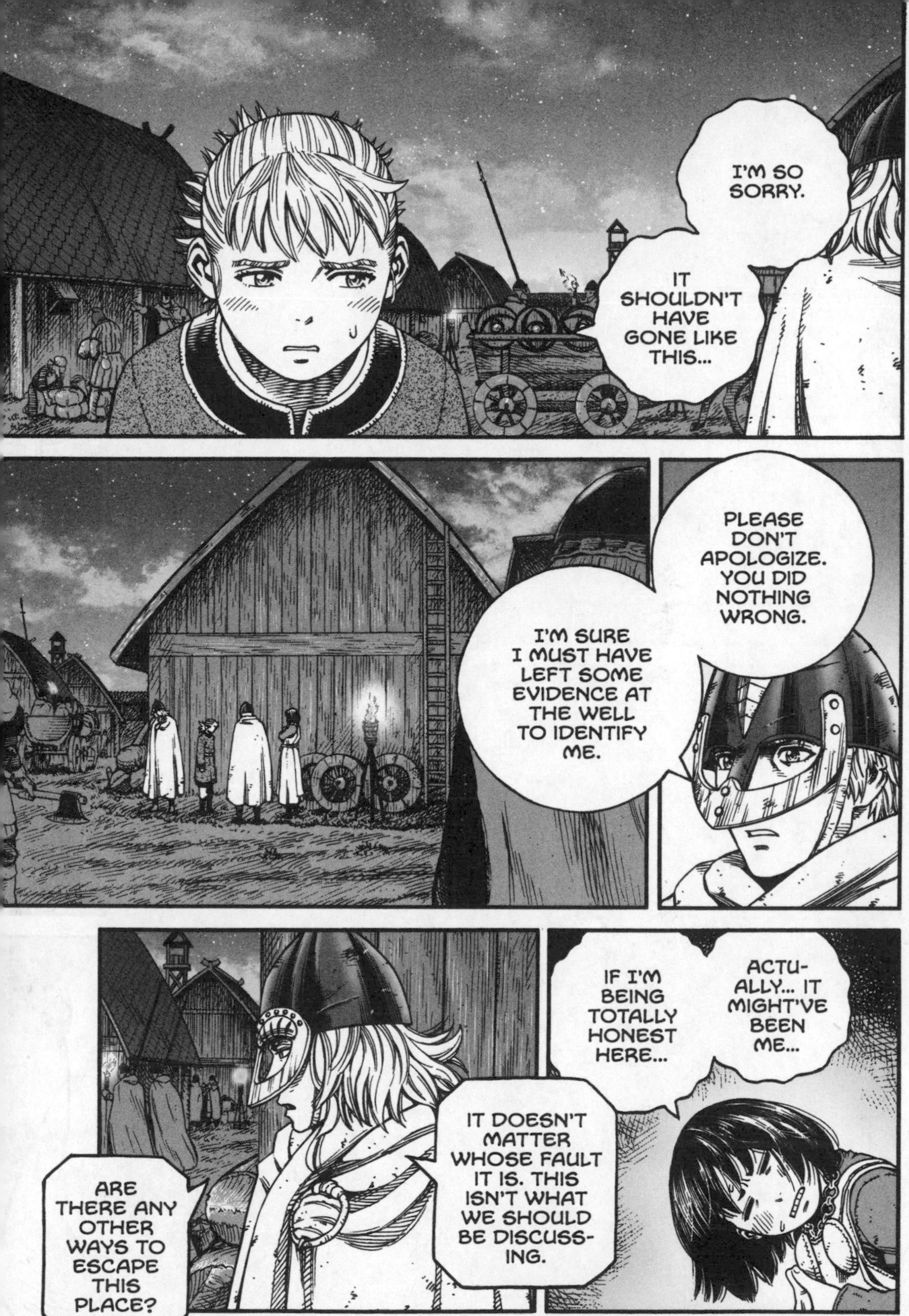
I'M SO SORRY.
IT SHOULDN'T HAVE GONE LIKE THIS...
PLEASE DON'T APOLOGIZE. YOU DID NOTHING WRONG.
I'M SURE I MUST HAVE LEFT SOME EVIDENCE AT THE WELL TO IDENTIFY ME.
ACTU-ALLY... IT MIGHT'VE BEEN ME...
IF I'M BEING TOTALLY HONEST HERE...
IT DOESN'T MATTER WHOSE FAULT IT IS. THIS ISN'T WHAT WE SHOULD BE DISCUSS-ING.
ARE THERE ANY OTHER WAYS TO ESCAPE THIS PLACE?

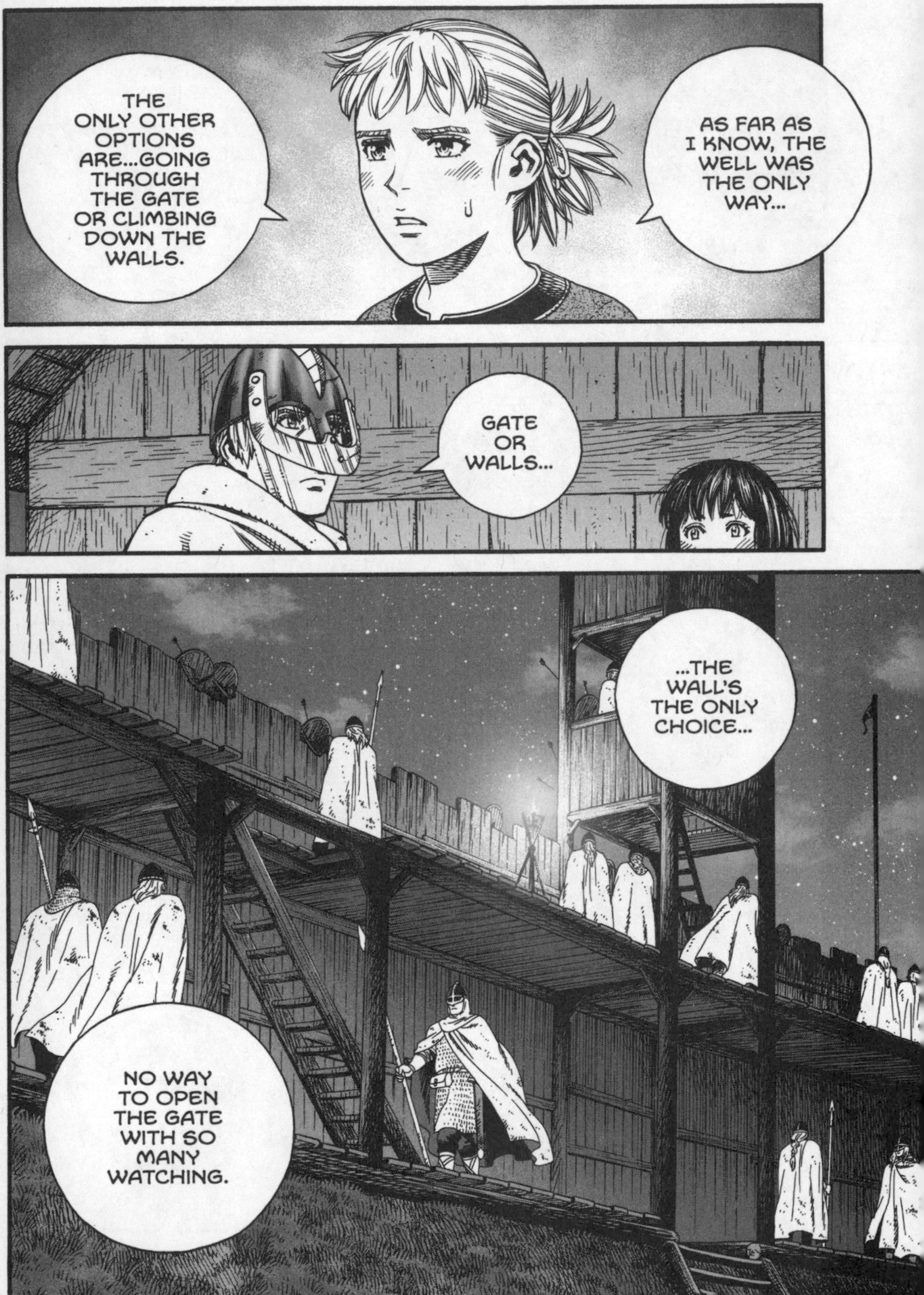
AS FAR AS I KNOW, THE WELL WAS THE ONLY WAY...
THE ONLY OTHER OPTIONS ARE...GOING THROUGH THE GATE OR CLIMBING DOWN THE WALLS.
GATE OR WALLS...
...THE WALL'S THE ONLY CHOICE...
NO WAY TO OPEN THE GATE WITH SO MANY WATCHING.

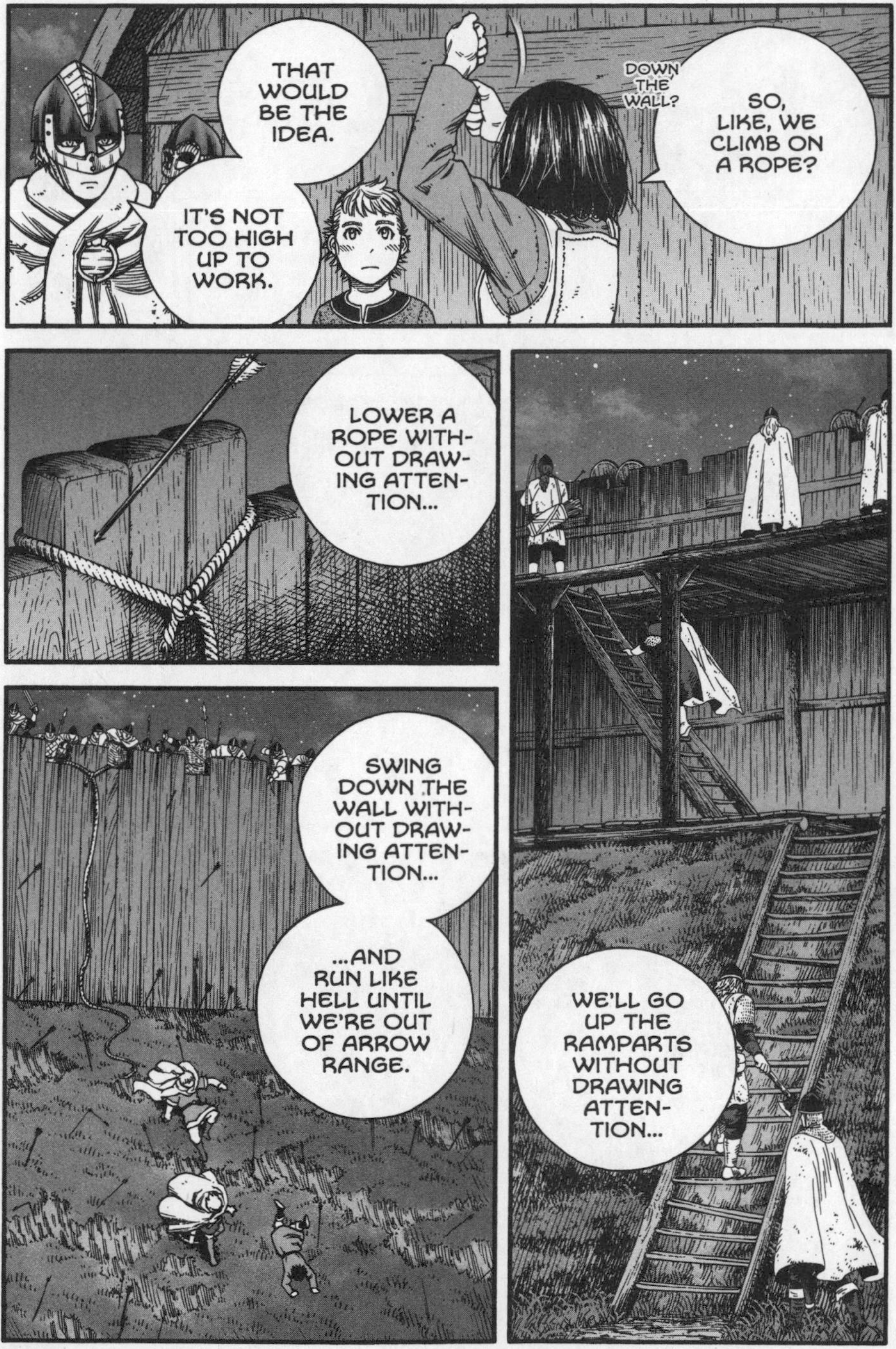
SO, LIKE, WE CLIMB ON A ROPE?
DOWN THE WALL?
THAT WOULD BE THE IDEA.
IT'S NOT TOO HIGH UP TO WORK.
WE'LL GO UP THE RAMPARTS WITHOUT DRAWING ATTEN- TION...
LOWER A ROPE WITH- OUT DRAW- ING ATTEN- TION...
SWING DOWN THE WALL WITH- OUT DRAW- ING ATTEN- TION...
...AND RUN LIKE HELL UNTIL WE'RE OUT OF ARROW RANGE.

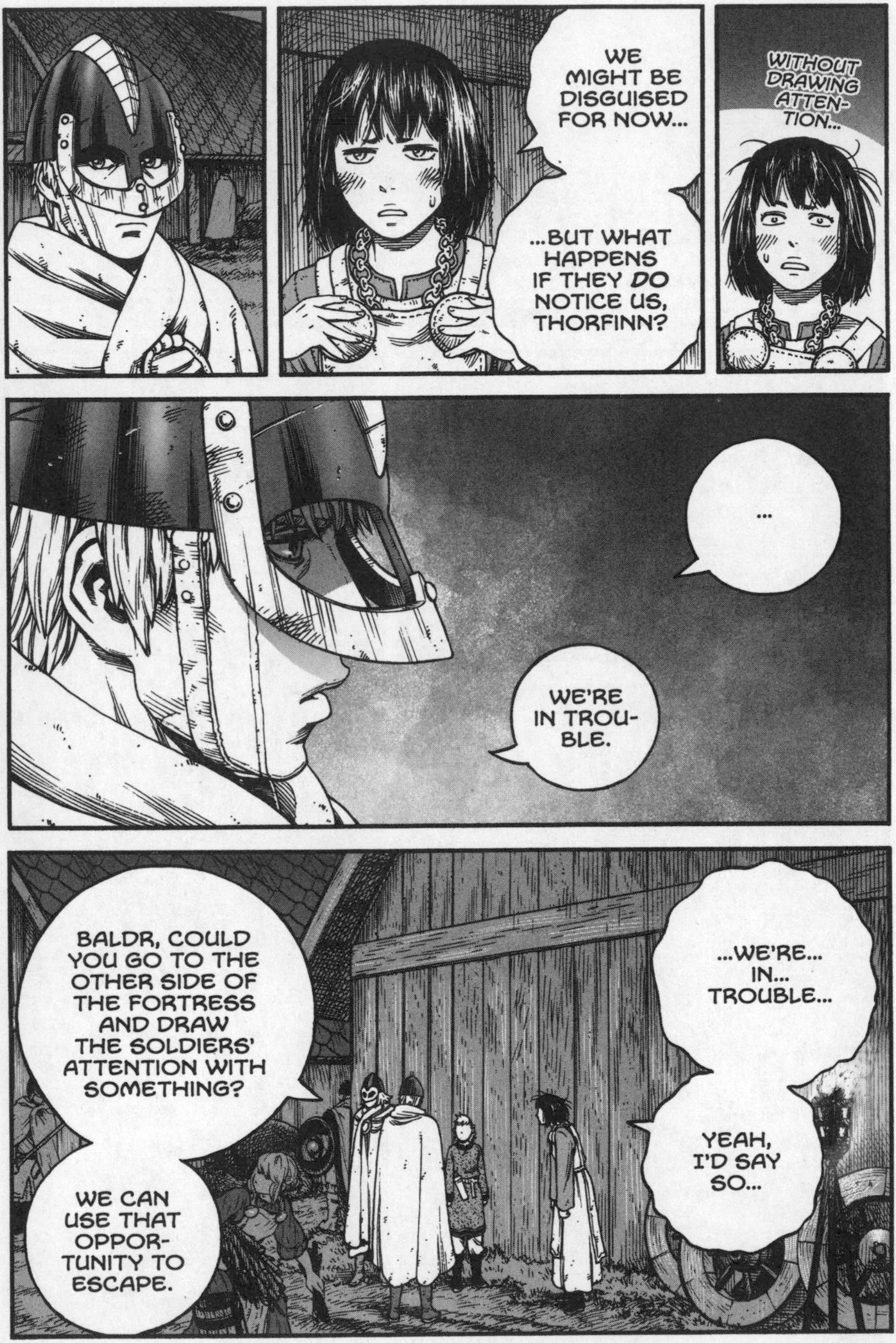
WITHOUT DRAWING ATTEN-TION...
WE MIGHT BE DISGUISED FOR NOW...
...BUT WHAT HAPPENS IF THEY *DO* NOTICE US, THORFINN?
...
WE'RE IN TROU-BLE.
...WE'RE... IN... TROUBLE...
YEAH, I'D SAY SO...
BALDR, COULD YOU GO TO THE OTHER SIDE OF THE FORTRESS AND DRAW THE SOLDIERS' ATTENTION WITH SOMETHING?
WE CAN USE THAT OPPOR-TUNITY TO ESCAPE.

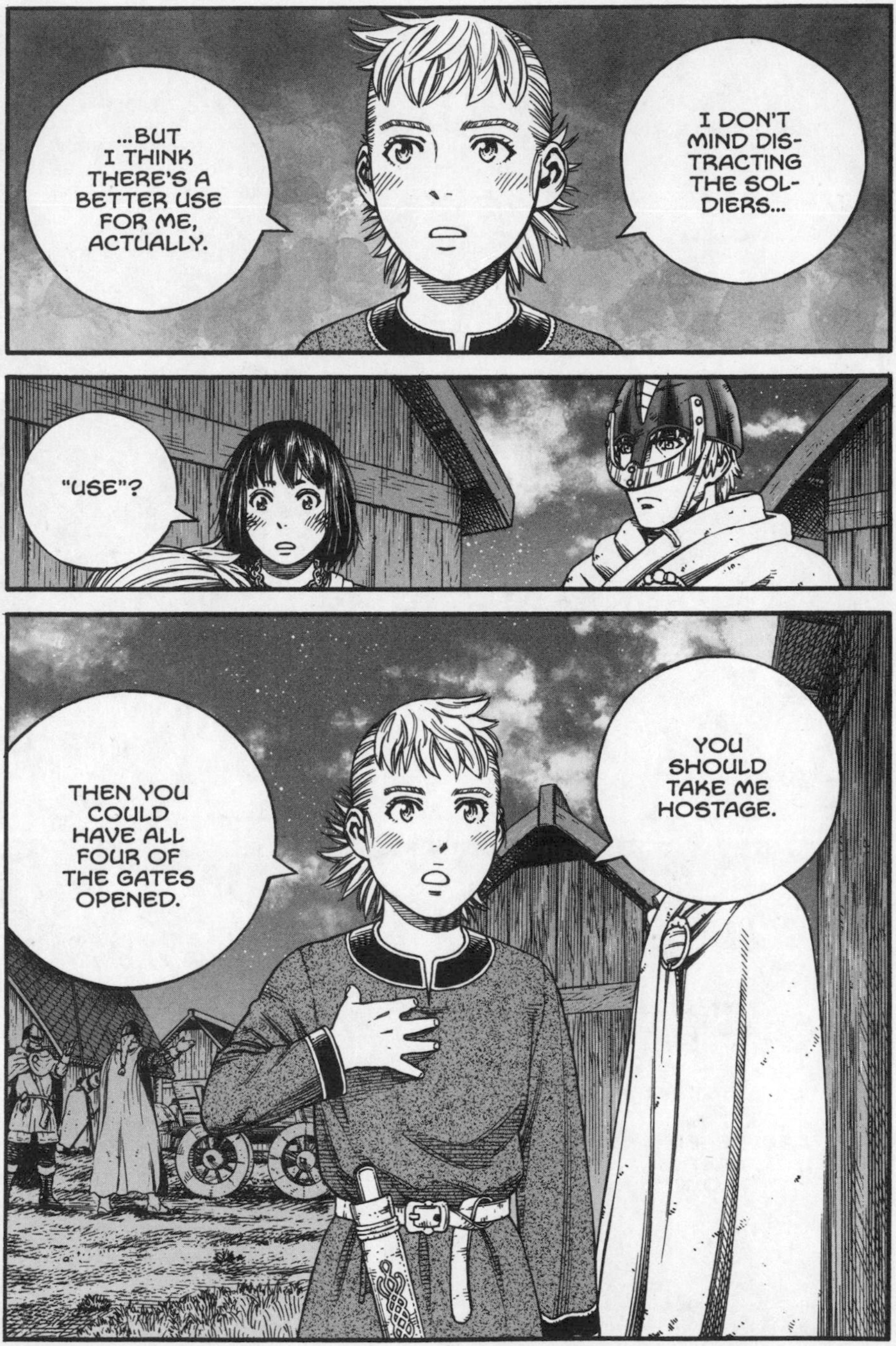
I DON'T MIND DIS-TRACTING THE SOL-DIERS...
...BUT I THINK THERE'S A BETTER USE FOR ME, ACTUALLY.
"USE"?
YOU SHOULD TAKE ME HOSTAGE.
THEN YOU COULD HAVE ALL FOUR OF THE GATES OPENED.

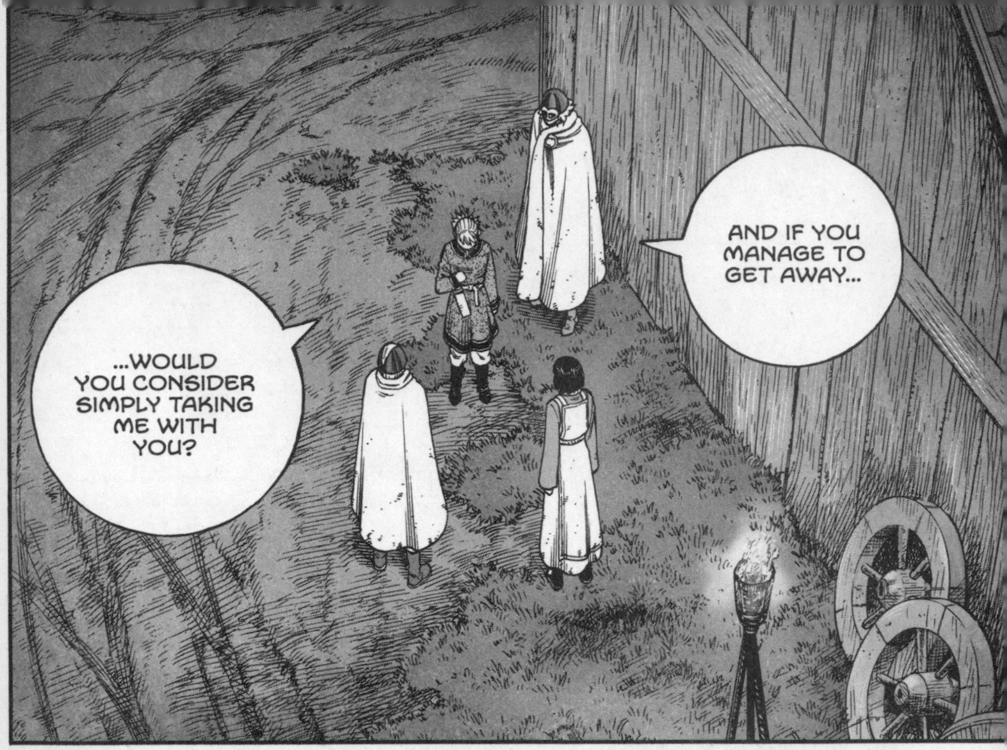
AND IF YOU MANAGE TO GET AWAY...
...WOULD YOU CONSIDER SIMPLY TAKING ME WITH YOU?
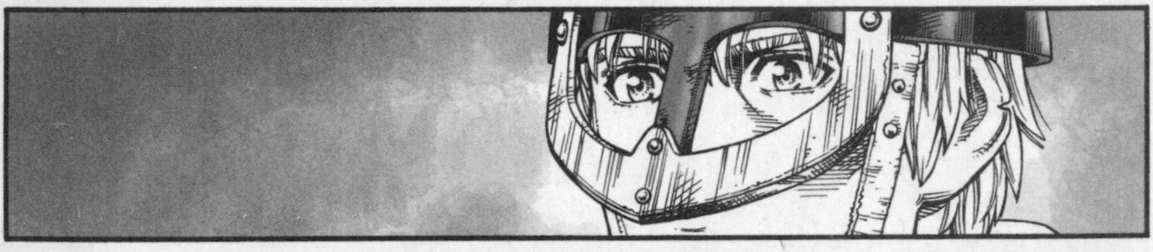
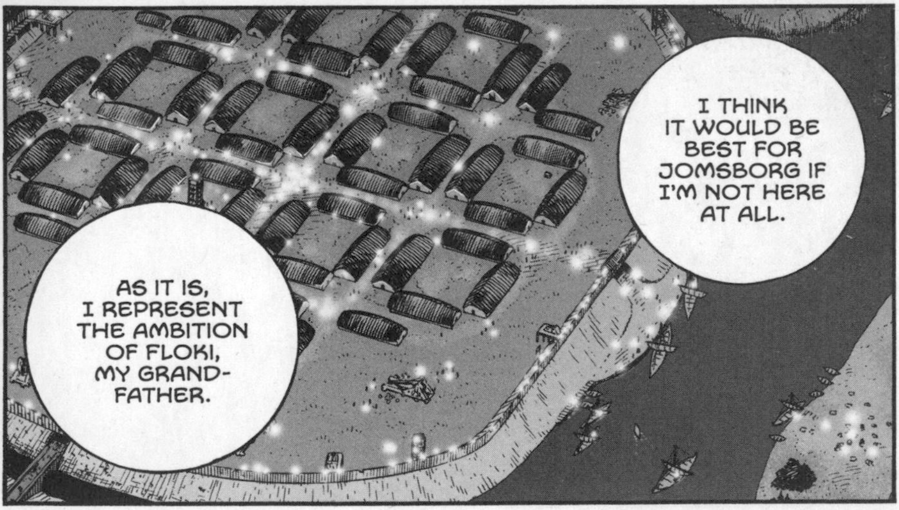
I THINK IT WOULD BE BEST FOR JOMSBORG IF I'M NOT HERE AT ALL.
AS IT IS, I REPRESENT THE AMBITION OF FLOKI, MY GRAND-FATHER.

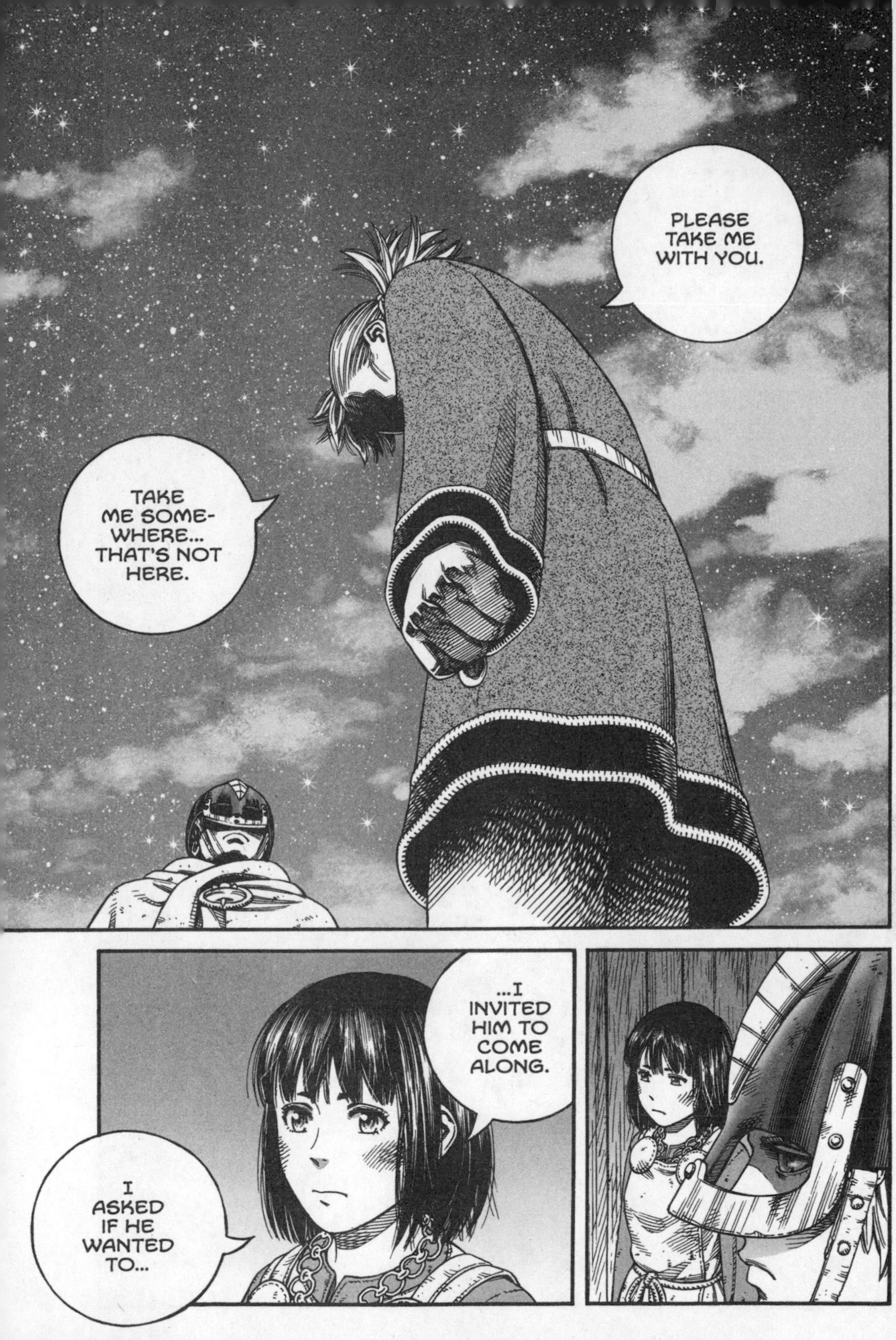
PLEASE TAKE ME WITH YOU.
TAKE ME SOME-WHERE... THAT'S NOT HERE.
...I INVITED HIM TO COME ALONG.
I ASKED IF HE WANTED TO...

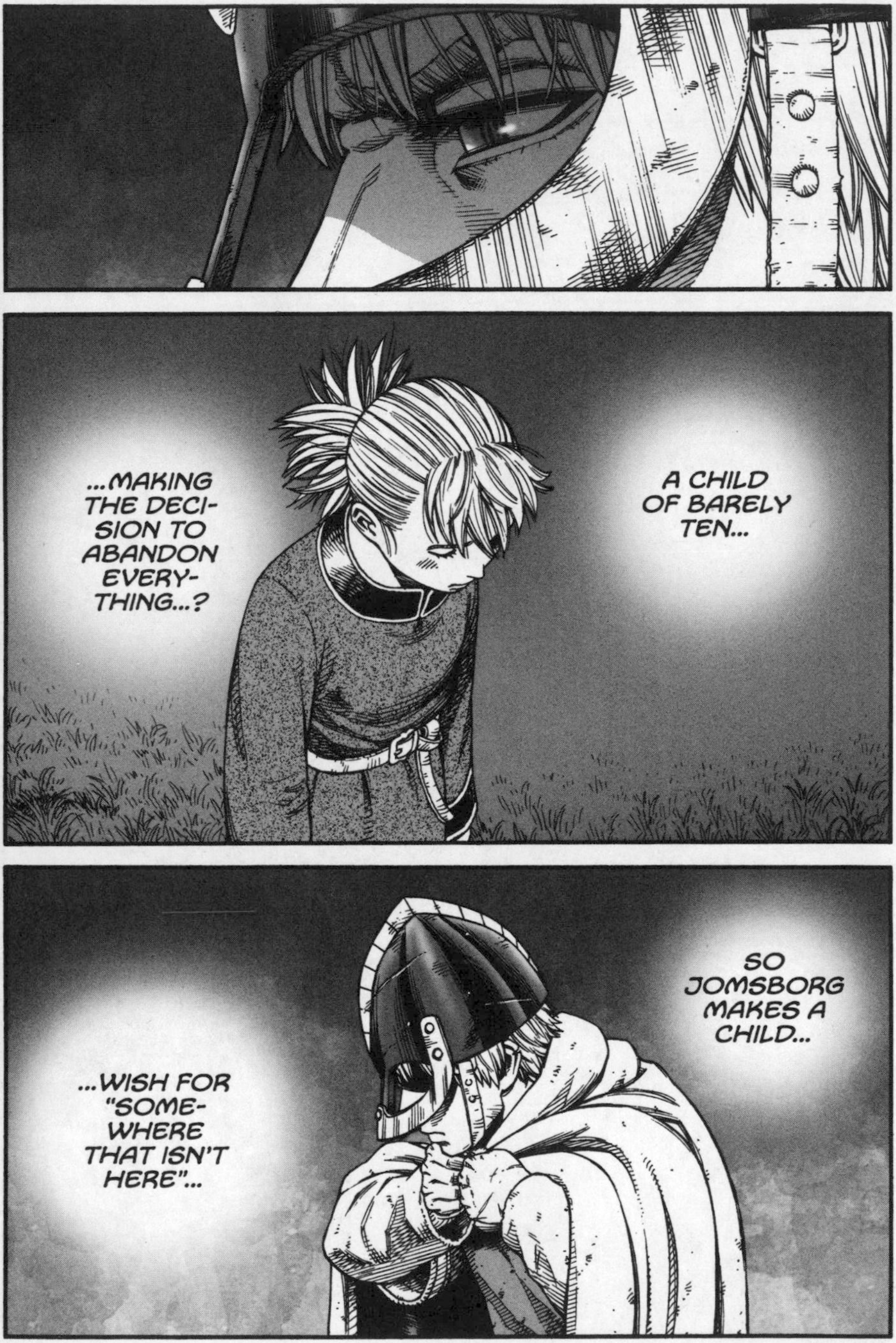
A CHILD OF BARELY TEN...
...MAKING THE DECI-SION TO ABANDON EVERY-THING...?
SO JOMSBORG MAKES A CHILD...
...WISH FOR "SOME-WHERE THAT ISN'T HERE"...

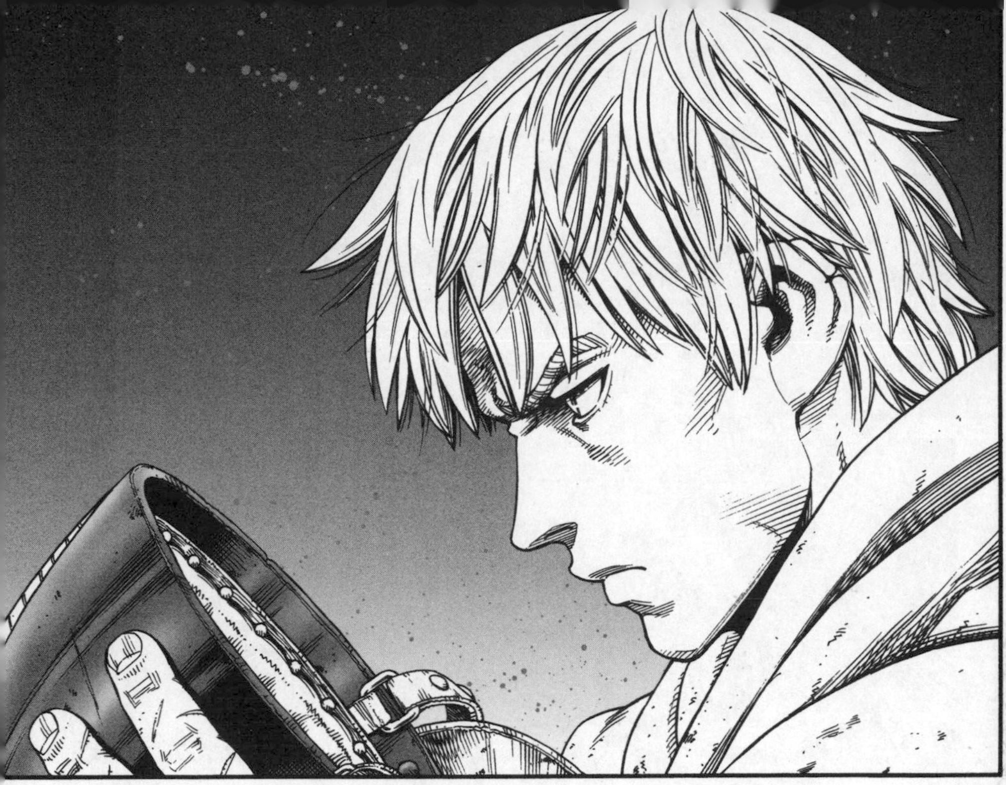

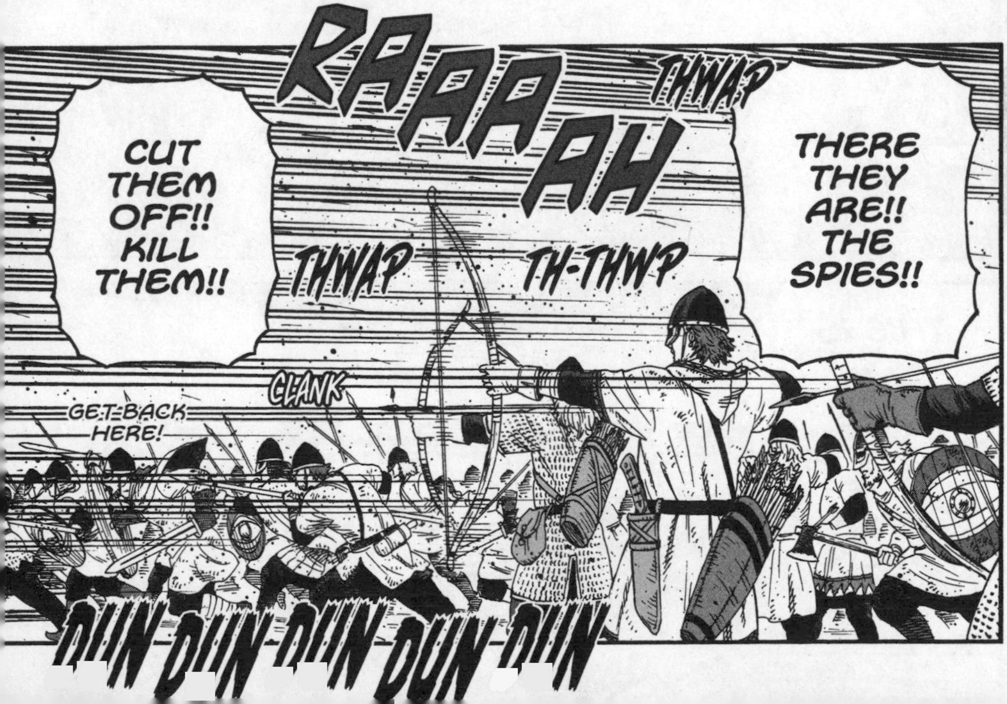
THERE THEY ARE!! THE SPIES!!
THWAP
RAAAAAH
TH-THWP
THWAP
CUT THEM OFF!! KILL THEM!!
CLANK
GET BACK HERE!
DUN DUN DUN DUN DUN

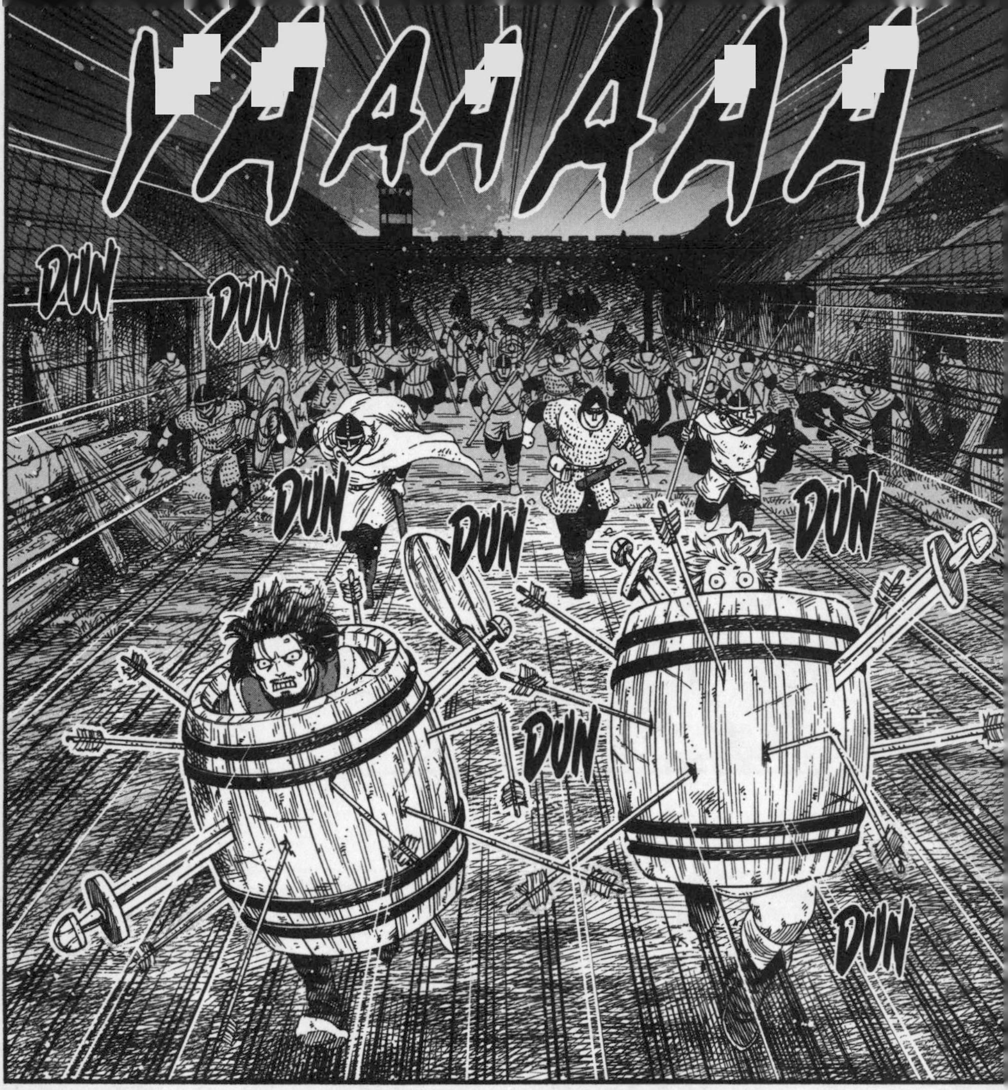
YAAAAAA
DUN
DUN
DUN
DUN
DUN
DUN
DUN
DUN

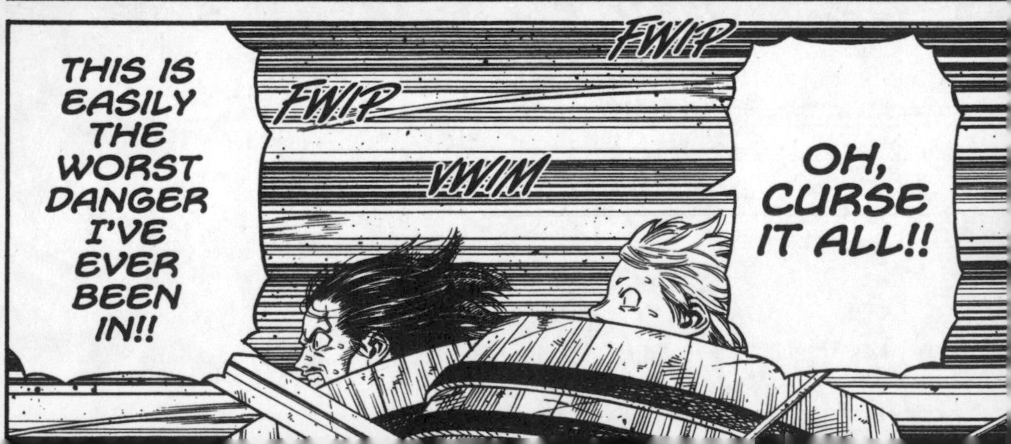
FWIP
OH, CURSE IT ALL!!
FWIP
VWM
THIS IS EASILY THE WORST DANGER I'VE EVER BEEN IN!!

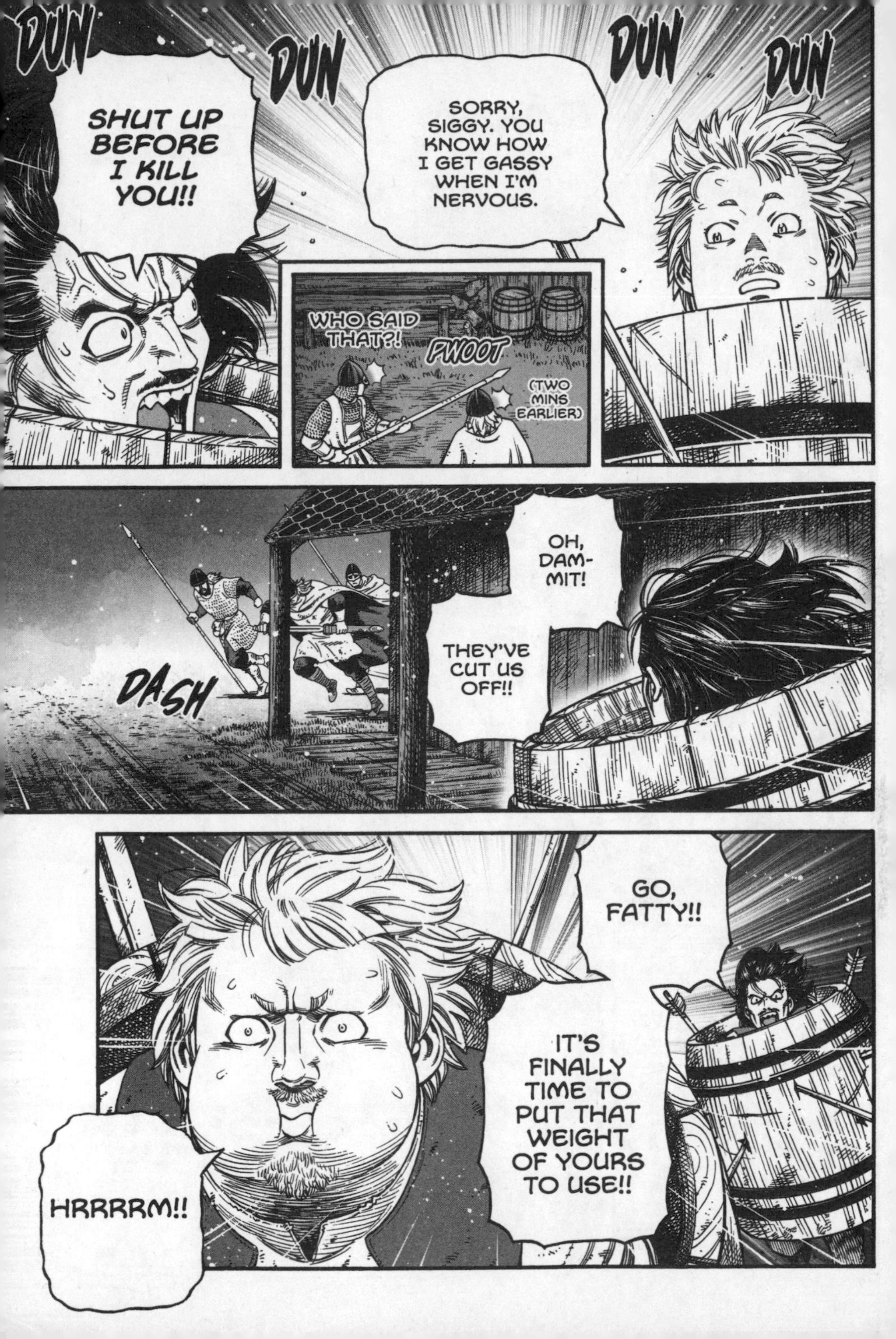
DUN
DUN
SORRY, SIGGY. YOU KNOW HOW I GET GASSY WHEN I'M NERVOUS.
(TWO MINS EARLIER)
PWOOT
WHO SAID THAT?!
DUN
DUN
SHUT UP BEFORE I KILL YOU!!
OH, DAM-MIT!
THEY'VE CUT US OFF!!
DASH
GO, FATTY!!
IT'S FINALLY TIME TO PUT THAT WEIGHT OF YOURS TO USE!!
HRRRRM!!

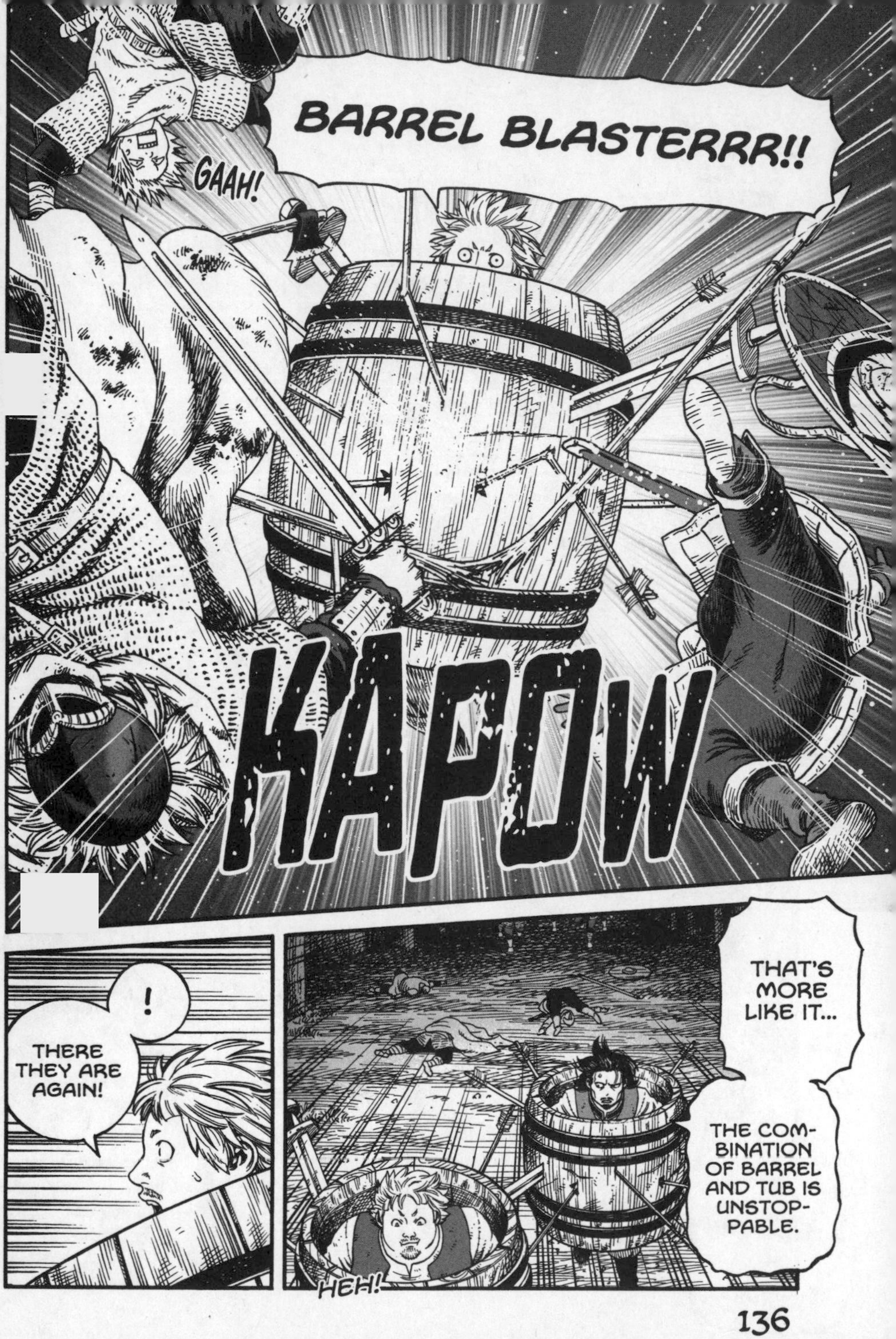
BARREL BLASTERRR!!
GAAH!
KAPOW
THAT'S MORE LIKE IT...
THE COM-BINATION OF BARREL AND TUB IS UNSTOP-PABLE.
HEH!
!
THERE THEY ARE AGAIN!

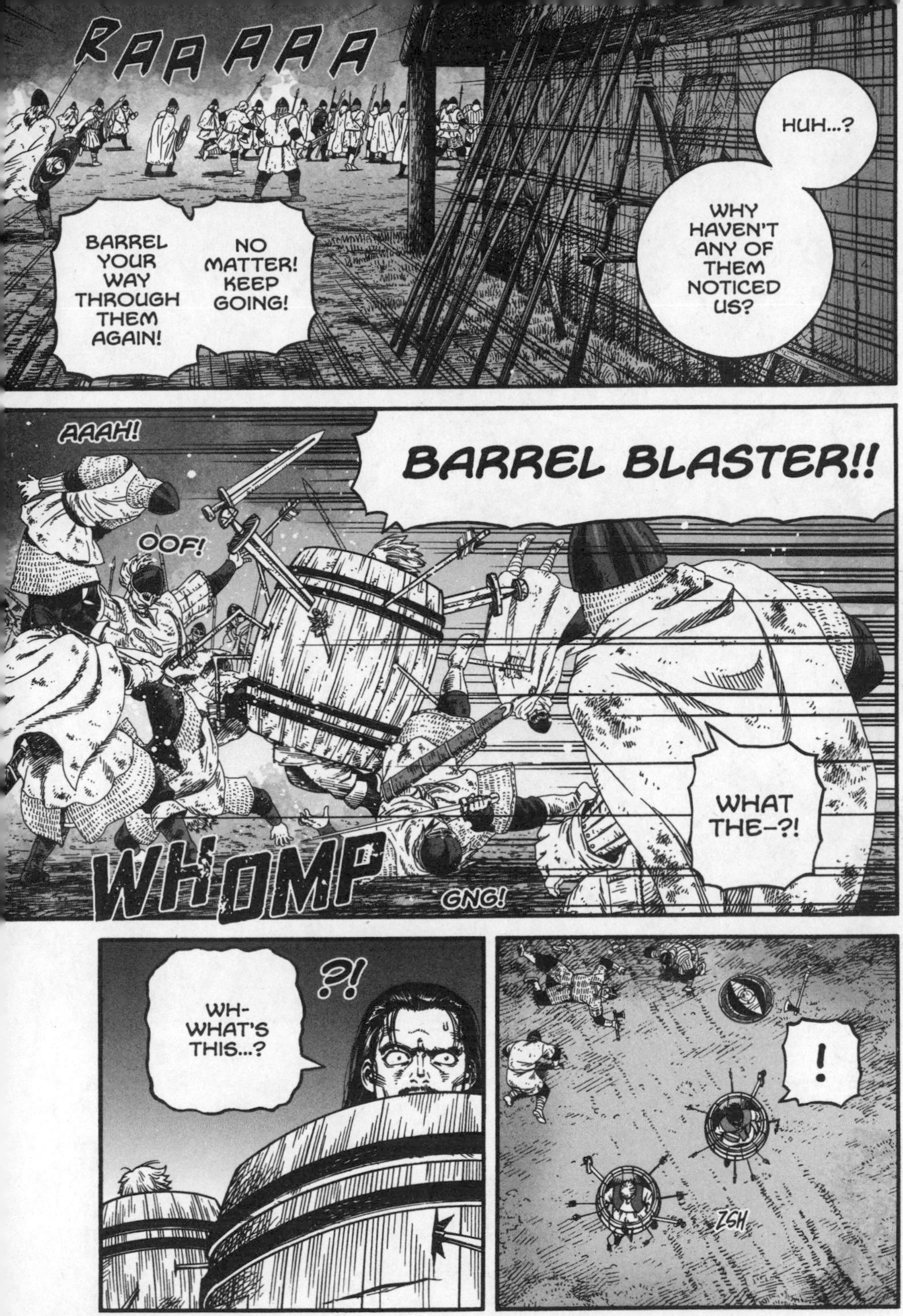
HUH...?
WHY HAVEN'T ANY OF THEM NOTICED US?
RAAAAA
NO MATTER! KEEP GOING!
BARREL YOUR WAY THROUGH THEM AGAIN!
BARREL BLASTER!!
AAAH!
OOF!
WHAT THE-?!
WHOMP
GNG!
!
ZSH
?!
WH-WHAT'S THIS...?

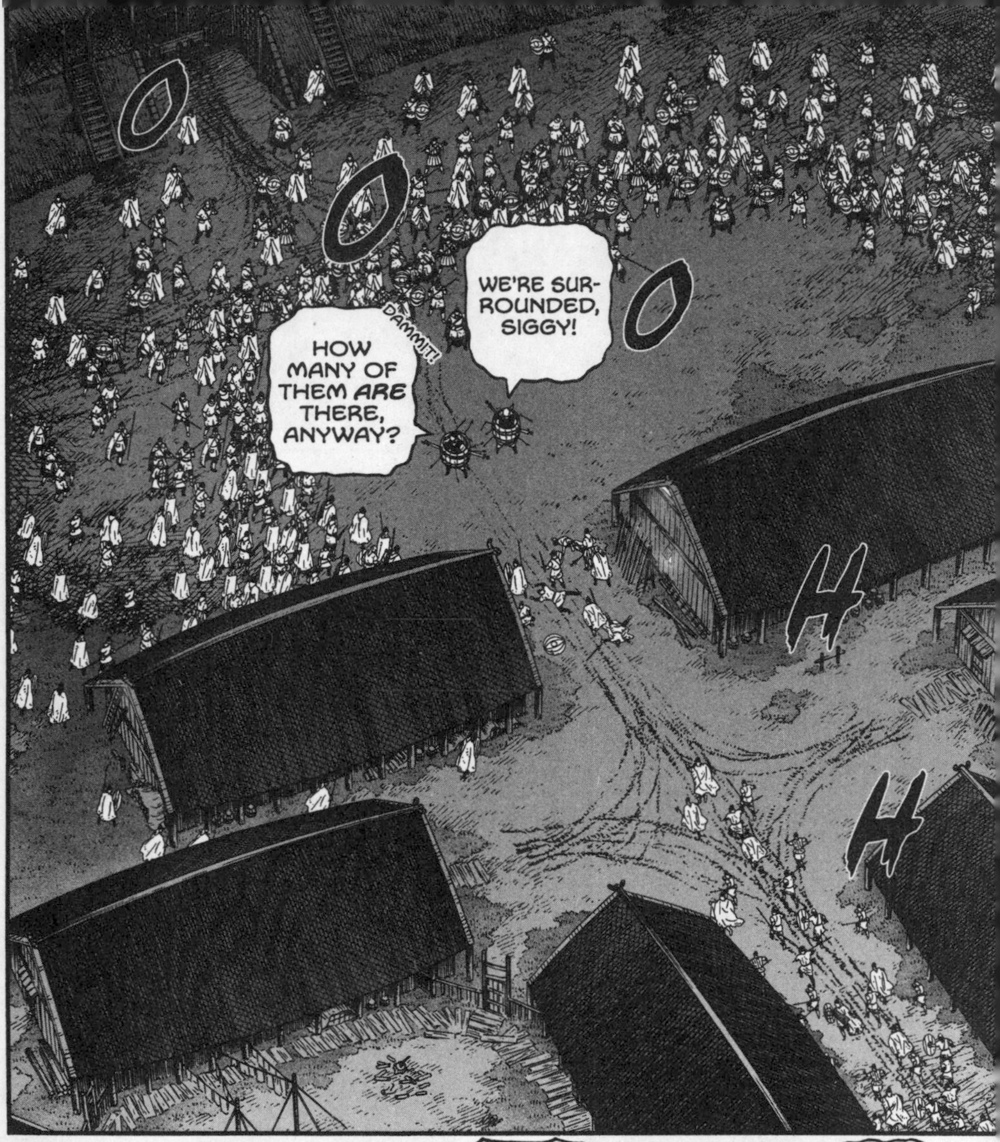
WE'RE SUR-
ROUNDED,
SIGGY!
DAMMIT!
HOW
MANY OF
THEM ARE
THERE,
ANYWAY?

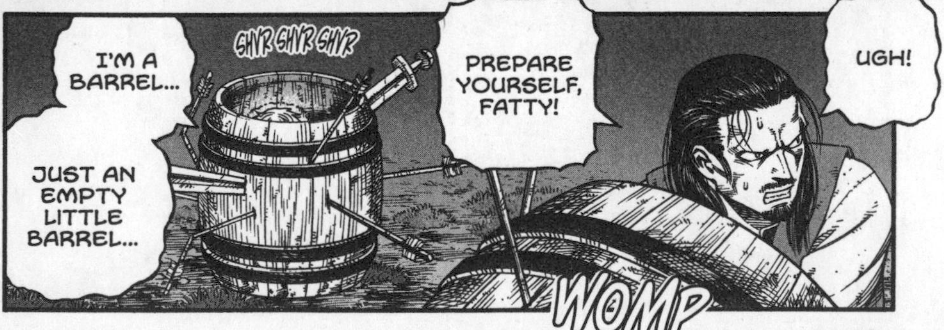
UGH!
PREPARE
YOURSELF,
FATTY!
SHYR SHYR SHYR
I'M A
BARREL...
JUST AN
EMPTY
LITTLE
BARREL...
WOMP

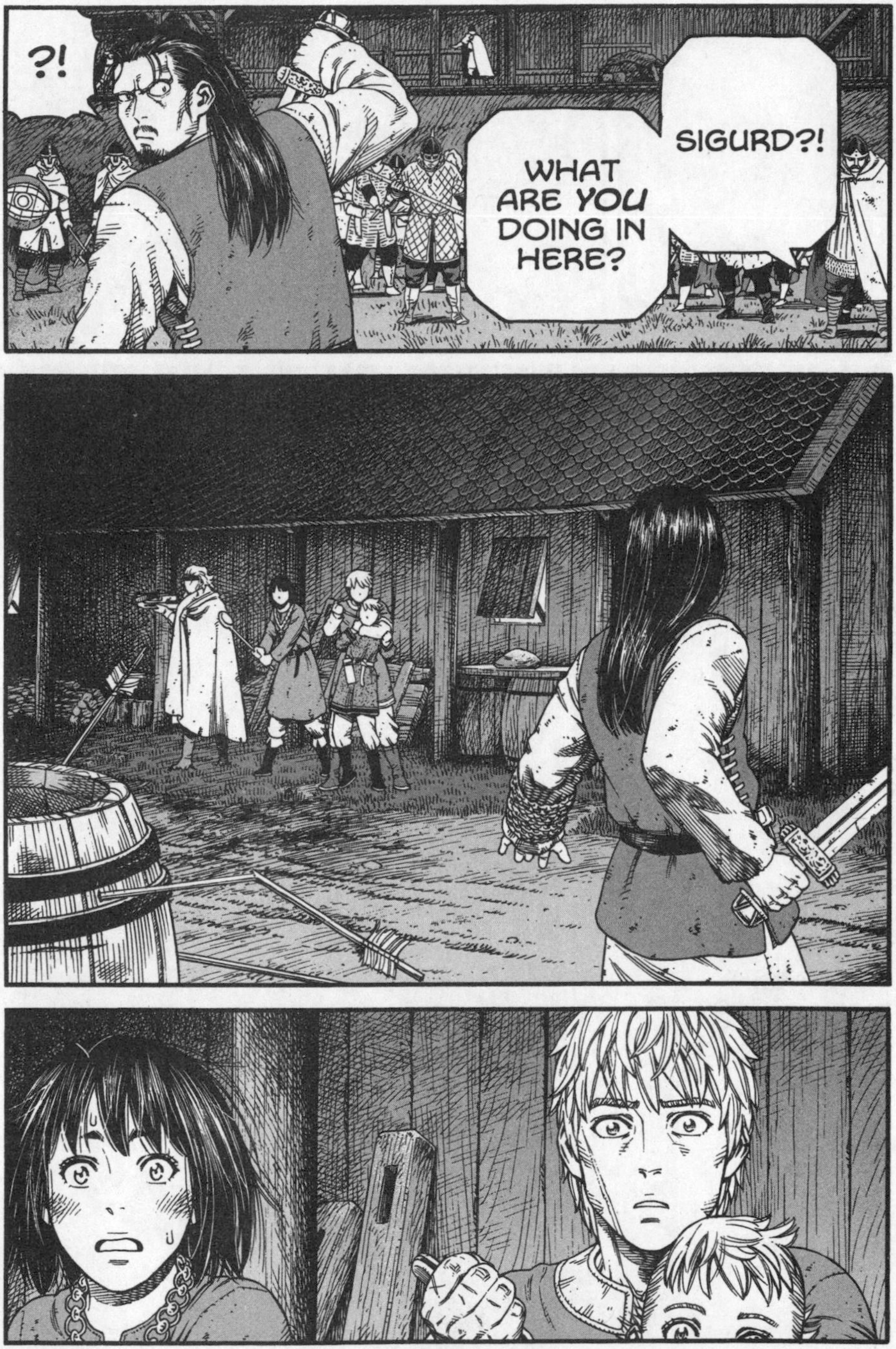
SIGURD?!
WHAT ARE YOU DOING IN HERE?
?!

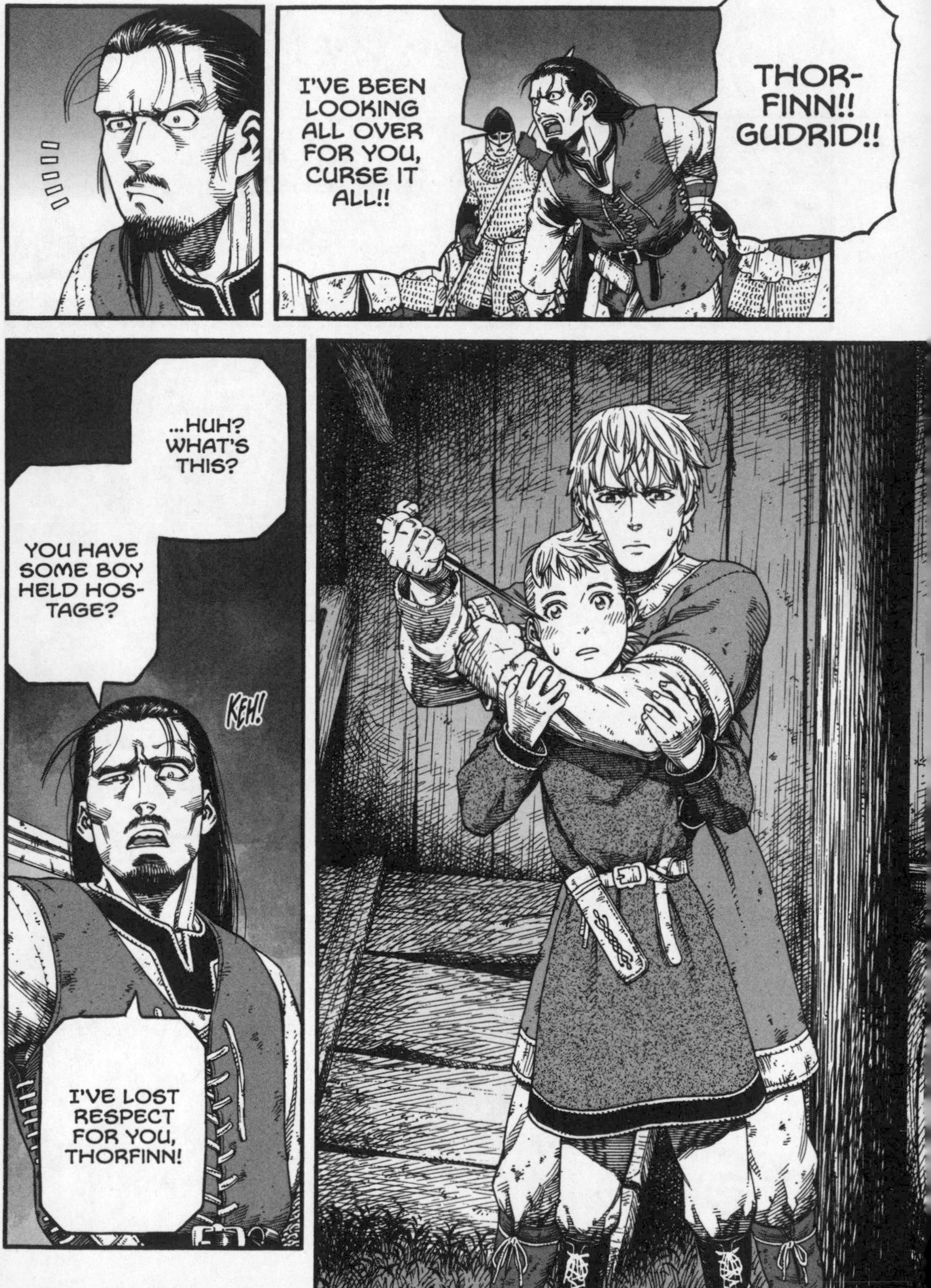
THOR-FINN!! GUDRID!!
I'VE BEEN LOOKING ALL OVER FOR YOU, CURSE IT ALL!!
...HUH? WHAT'S THIS?
YOU HAVE SOME BOY HELD HOS-TAGE?
KEH!
I'VE LOST RESPECT FOR YOU, THORFINN!

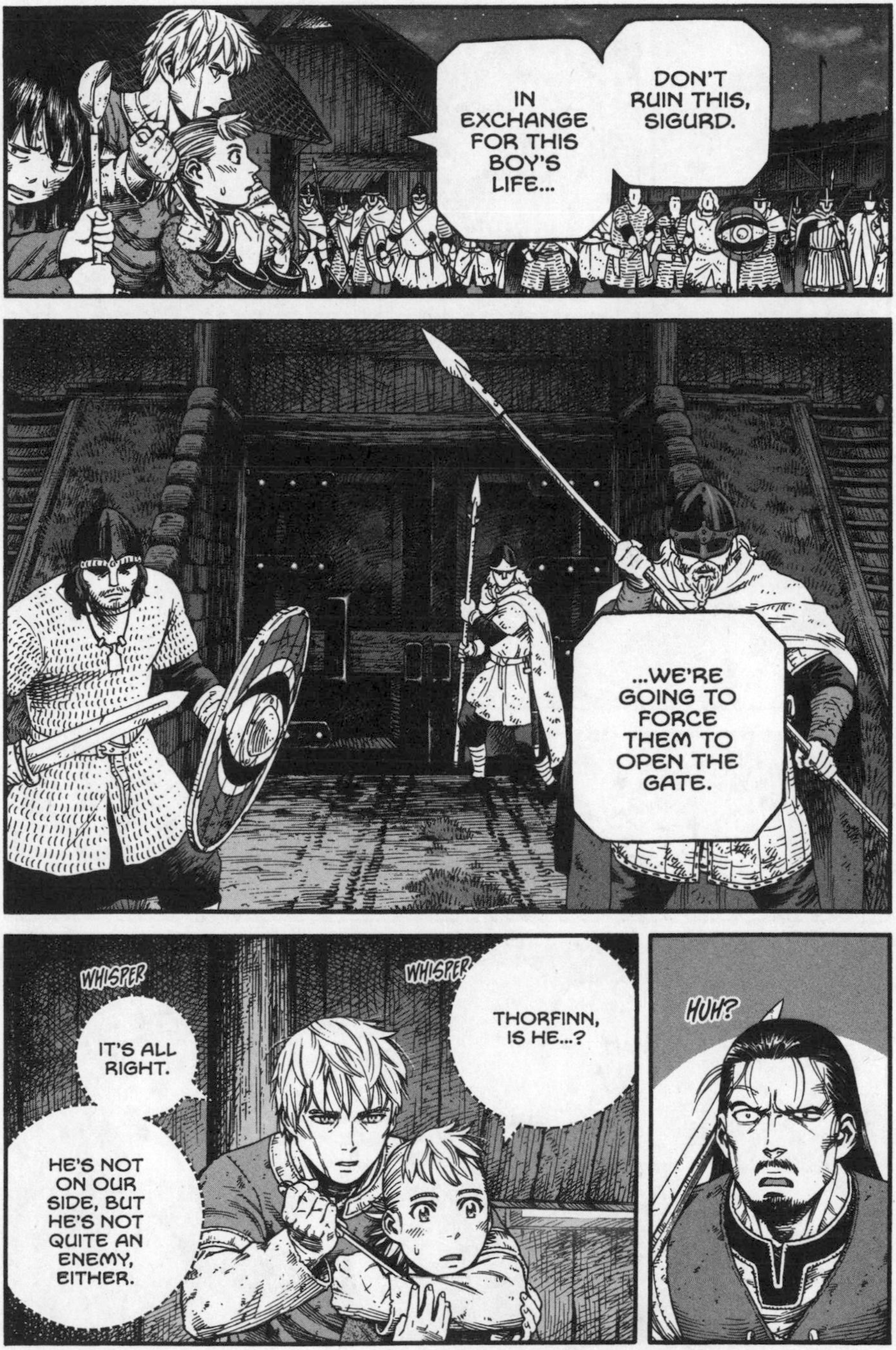
DON'T RUIN THIS, SIGURD.
IN EXCHANGE FOR THIS BOY'S LIFE...
...WE'RE GOING TO FORCE THEM TO OPEN THE GATE.
HUH?
WHISPER
THORFINN, IS HE...?
WHISPER
IT'S ALL RIGHT.
HE'S NOT ON OUR SIDE, BUT HE'S NOT QUITE AN ENEMY, EITHER.

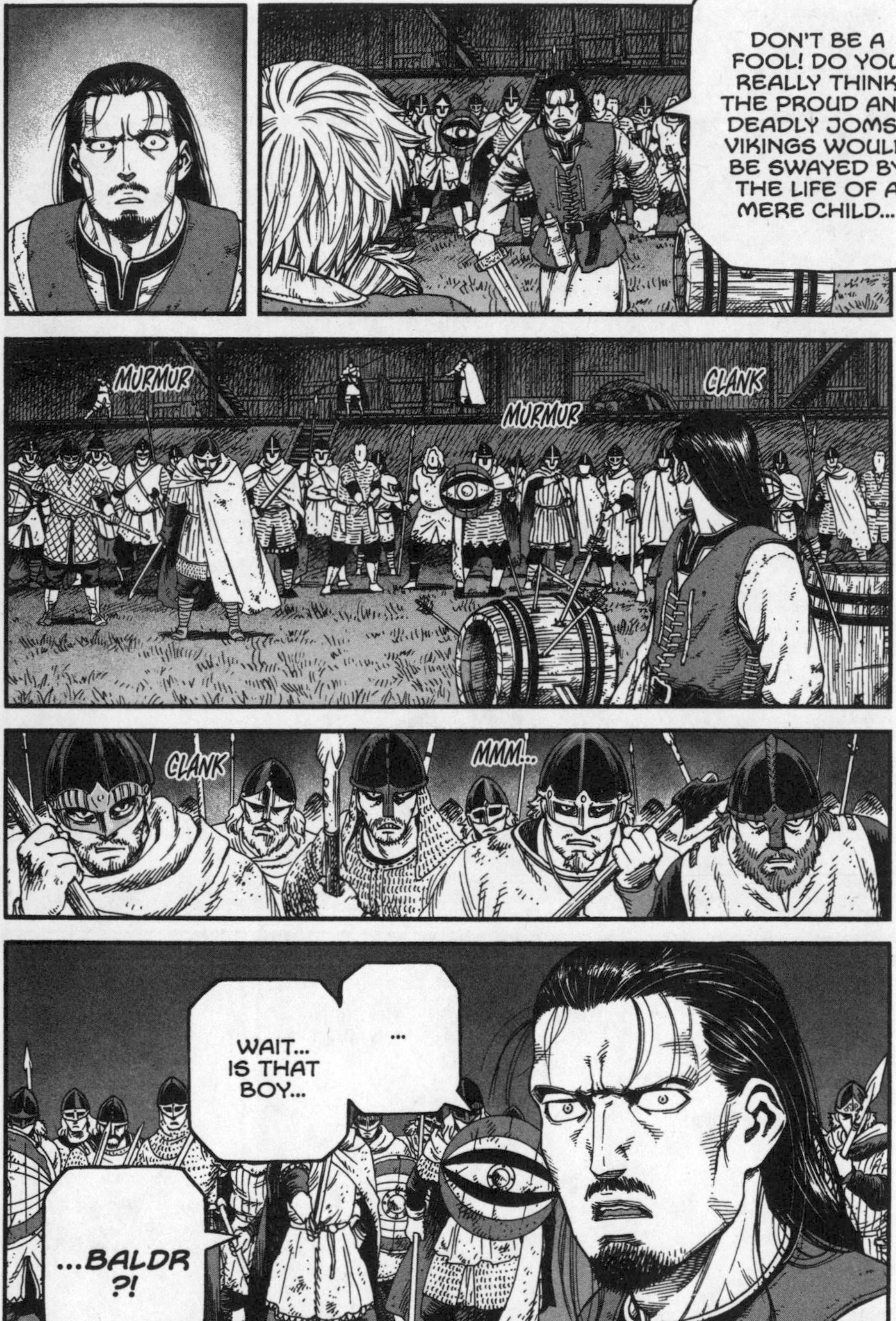
DON'T BE A FOOL! DO YOU REALLY THINK THE PROUD AND DEADLY JOMS-VIKINGS WOULD BE SWAYED BY THE LIFE OF A MERE CHILD...
CLANK
MURMUR
MURMUR
MMM...
CLANK
...
WAIT... IS THAT BOY...
...BALDR ?!

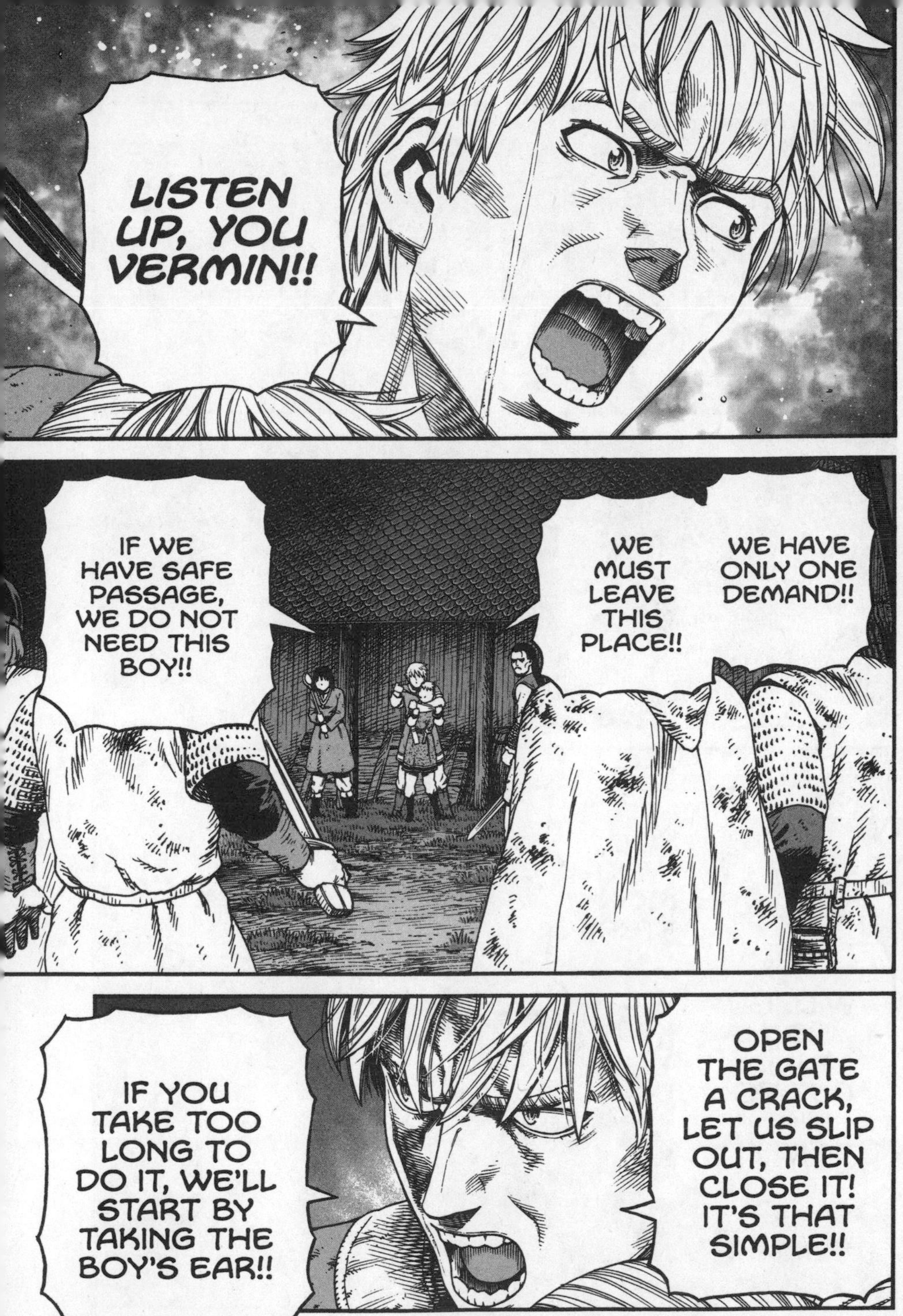
LISTEN UP, YOU VERMIN!!
WE HAVE ONLY ONE DEMAND!!
WE MUST LEAVE THIS PLACE!!
IF WE HAVE SAFE PASSAGE, WE DO NOT NEED THIS BOY!!
OPEN THE GATE A CRACK, LET US SLIP OUT, THEN CLOSE IT! IT'S THAT SIMPLE!!
IF YOU TAKE TOO LONG TO DO IT, WE'LL START BY TAKING THE BOY'S EAR!!

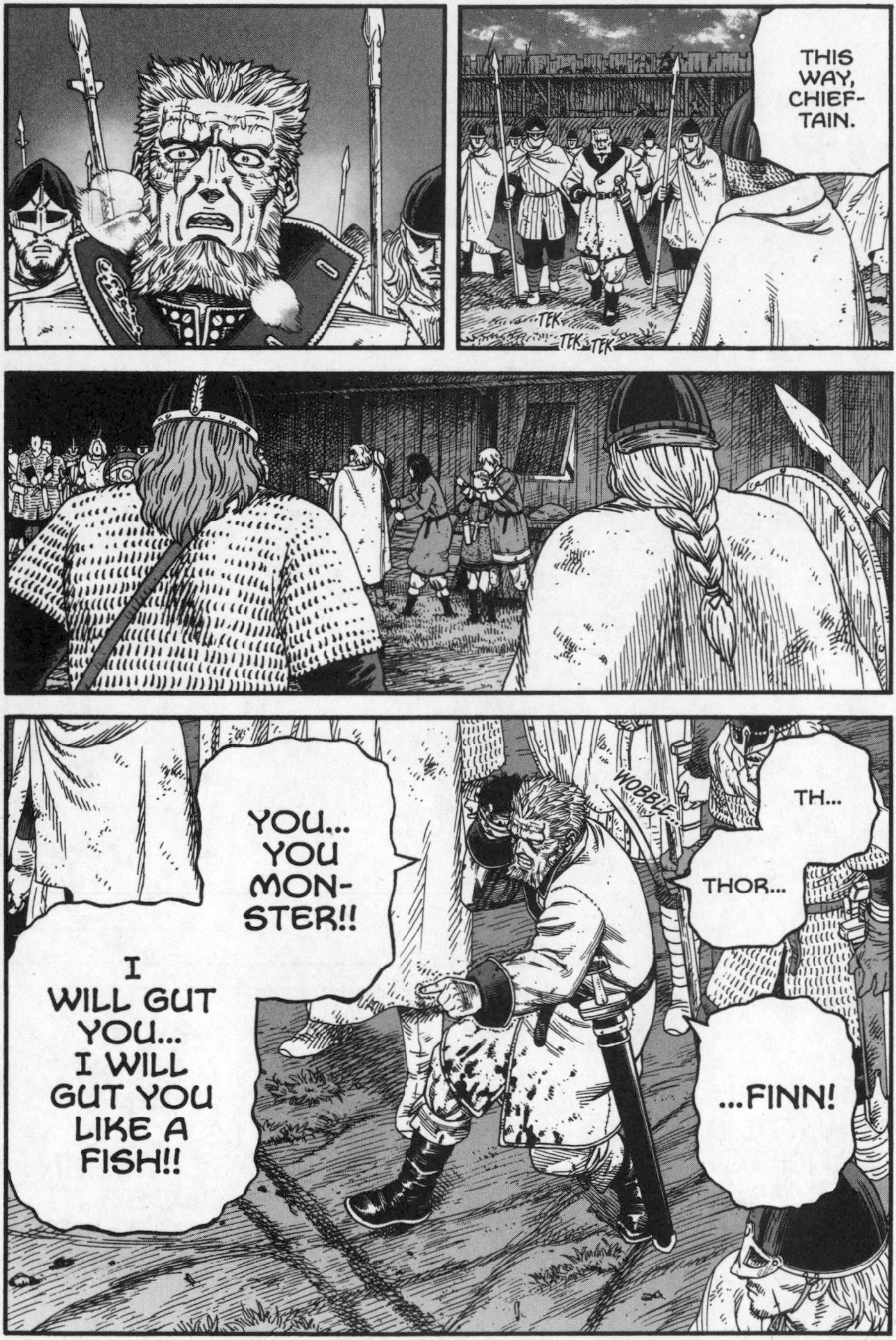
THIS WAY, CHIEF-TAIN.
TEK
TEK TEK
TH...
THOR...
WOBBLE...
...FINN!
YOU... YOU MON-STER!!
I WILL GUT YOU... I WILL GUT YOU LIKE A FISH!!

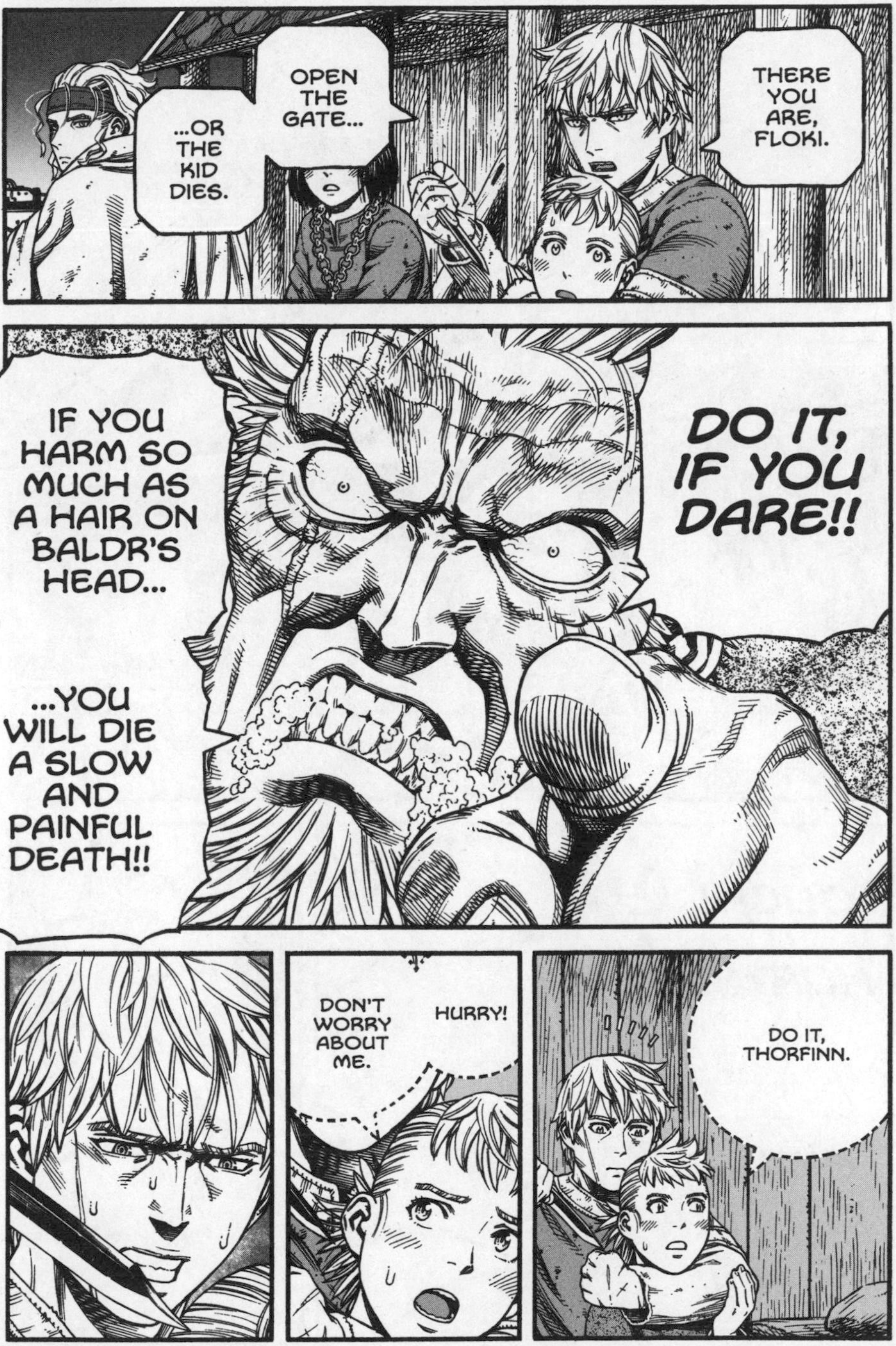
THERE YOU ARE, FLOKI.
OPEN THE GATE...
...OR THE KID DIES.
DO IT, IF YOU DARE!!
IF YOU HARM SO MUCH AS A HAIR ON BALDR'S HEAD...
...YOU WILL DIE A SLOW AND PAINFUL DEATH!!
DO IT, THORFINN.
HURRY!
DON'T WORRY ABOUT ME.

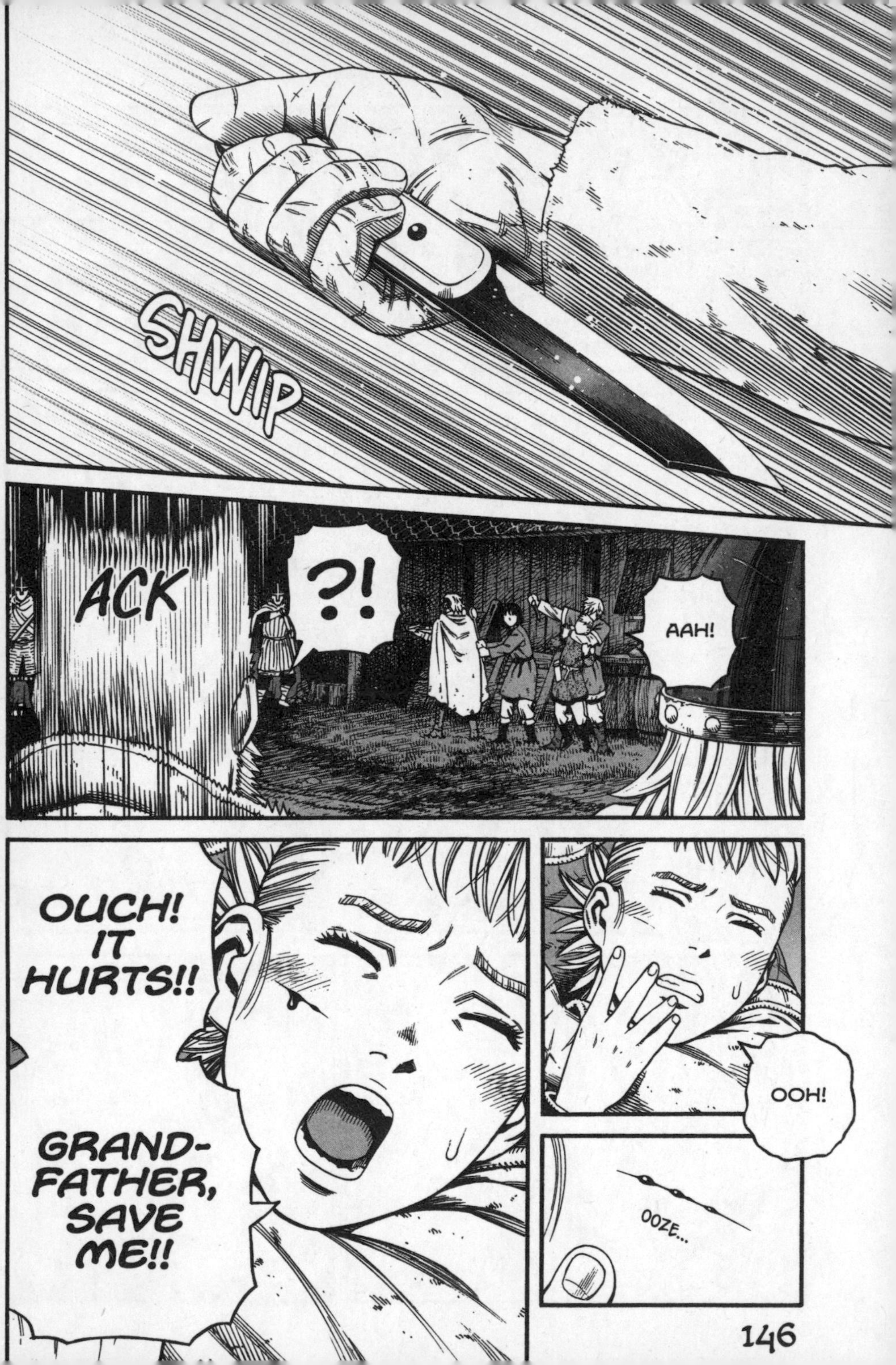
SHWIP
AAH!
?!
ACK
OOH!
OOZE...
OUCH! IT HURTS!!
GRAND-FATHER, SAVE ME!!

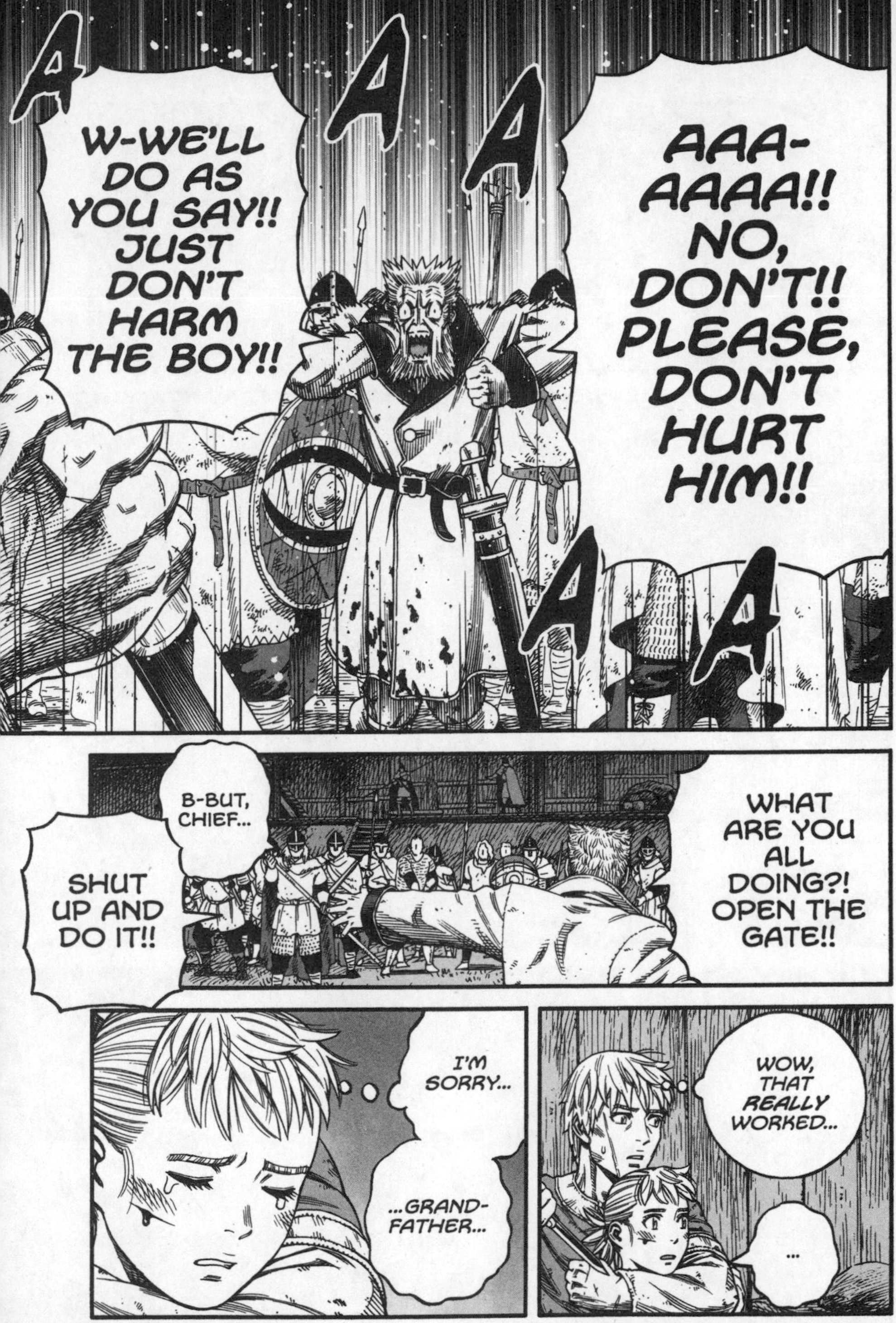
AAA-AAAA!! NO, DON'T!! PLEASE, DON'T HURT HIM!!
W-WE'LL DO AS YOU SAY!! JUST DON'T HARM THE BOY!!
A A A A A A
WHAT ARE YOU ALL DOING?! OPEN THE GATE!!
B-BUT, CHIEF...
SHUT UP AND DO IT!!
WOW, THAT REALLY WORKED...
...
I'M SORRY...
...GRAND-FATHER...

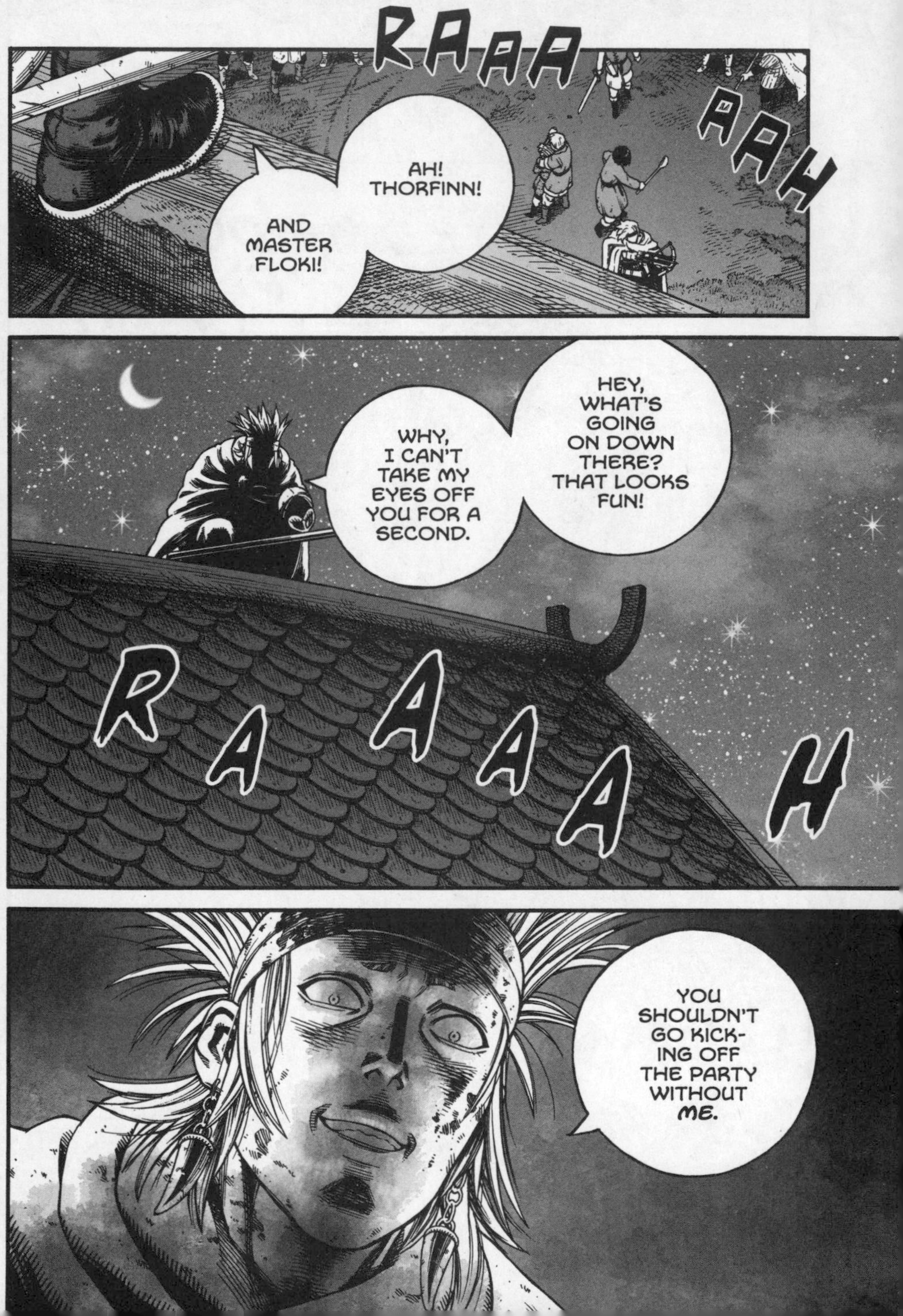
RAAAAAH
AH! THORFINN!
AND MASTER FLOKI!
HEY, WHAT'S GOING ON DOWN THERE? THAT LOOKS FUN!
WHY, I CAN'T TAKE MY EYES OFF YOU FOR A SECOND.
RAAAAAH
YOU SHOULDN'T GO KICKING OFF THE PARTY WITHOUT *ME.*

VINLAND SAGA

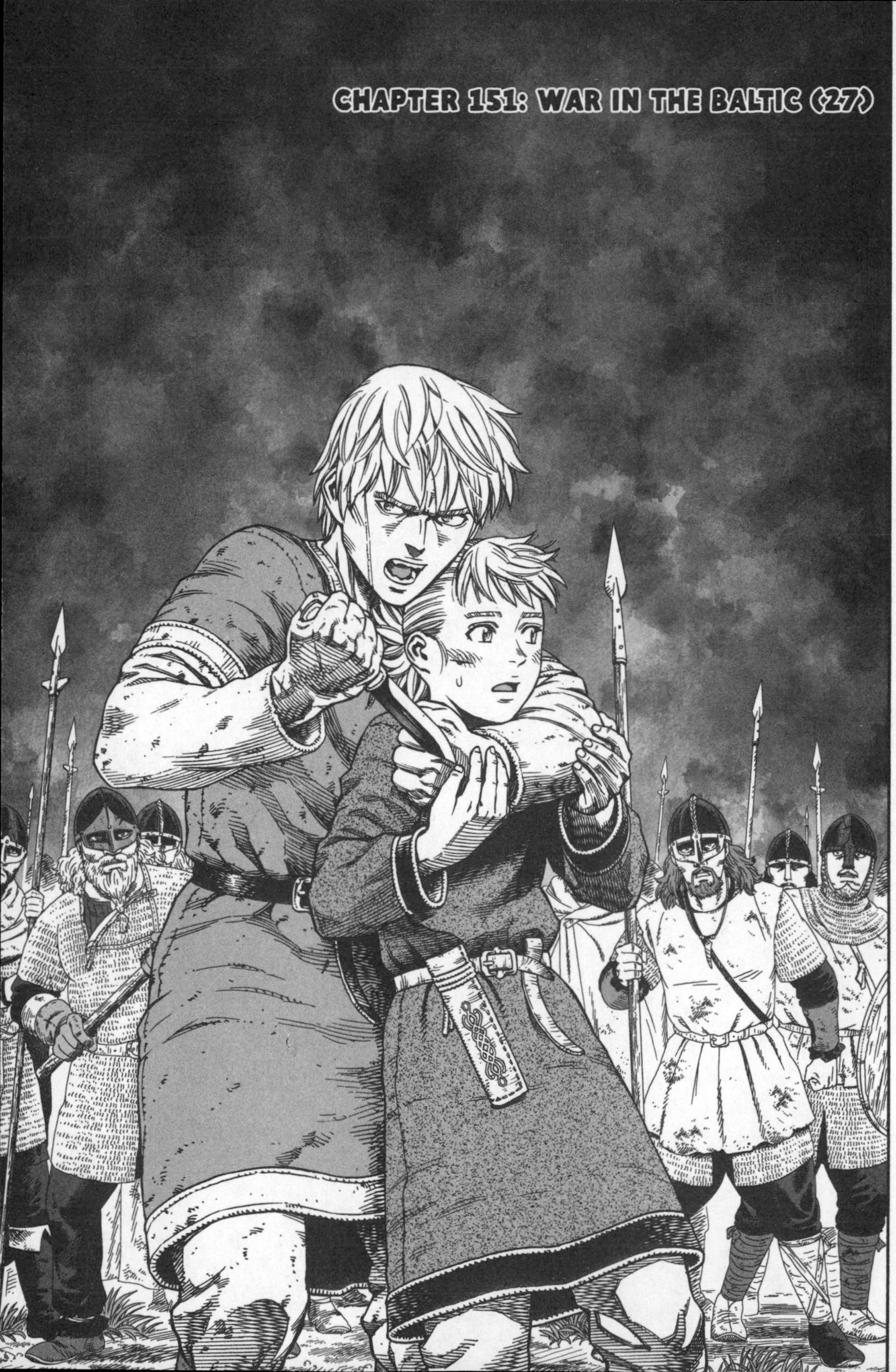
CHAPTER 151: WAR IN THE BALTIC (27)

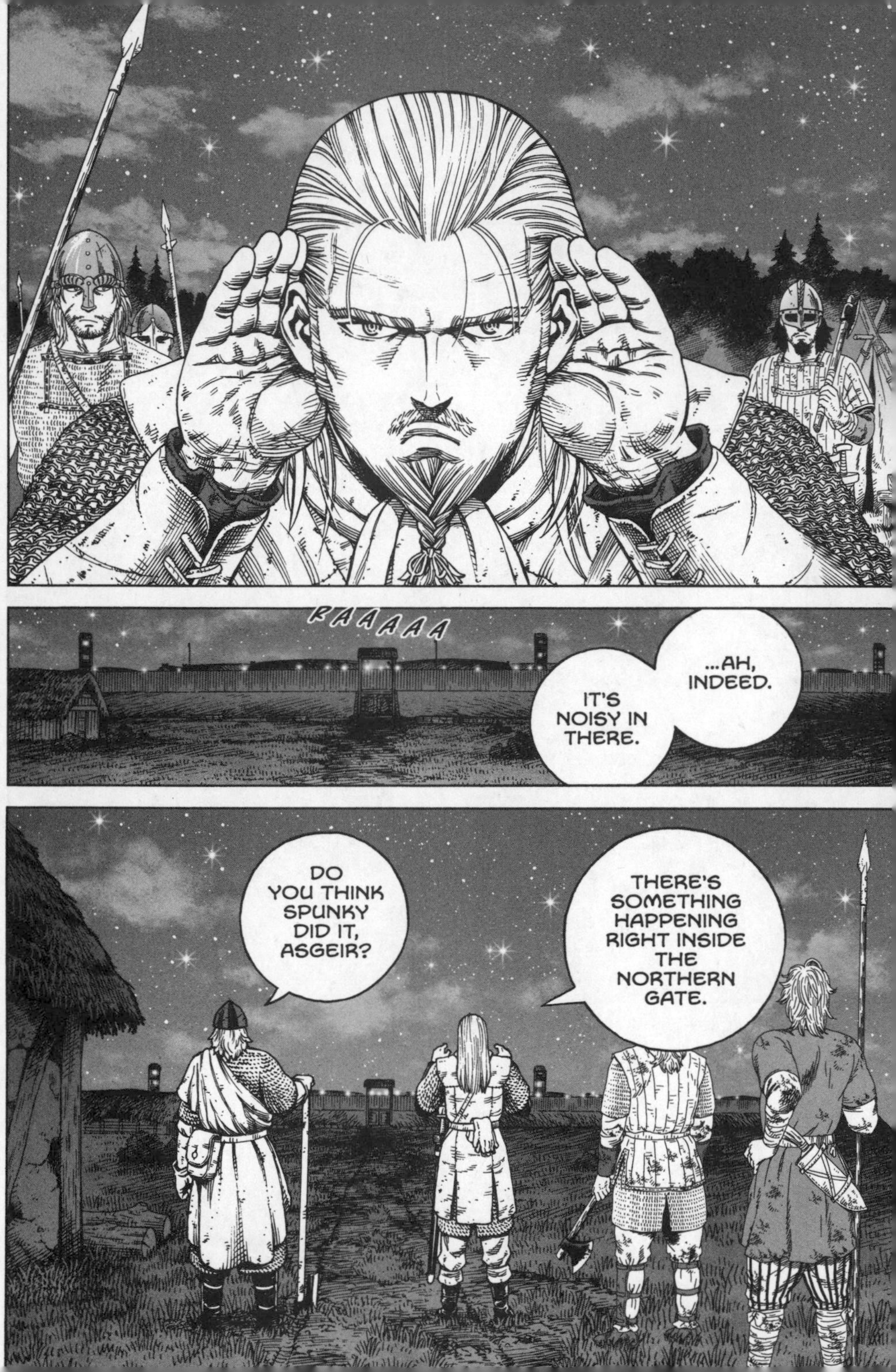
RAAAAAA
...AH, INDEED.
IT'S NOISY IN THERE.
THERE'S SOMETHING HAPPENING RIGHT INSIDE THE NORTHERN GATE.
DO YOU THINK SPUNKY DID IT, ASGEIR?

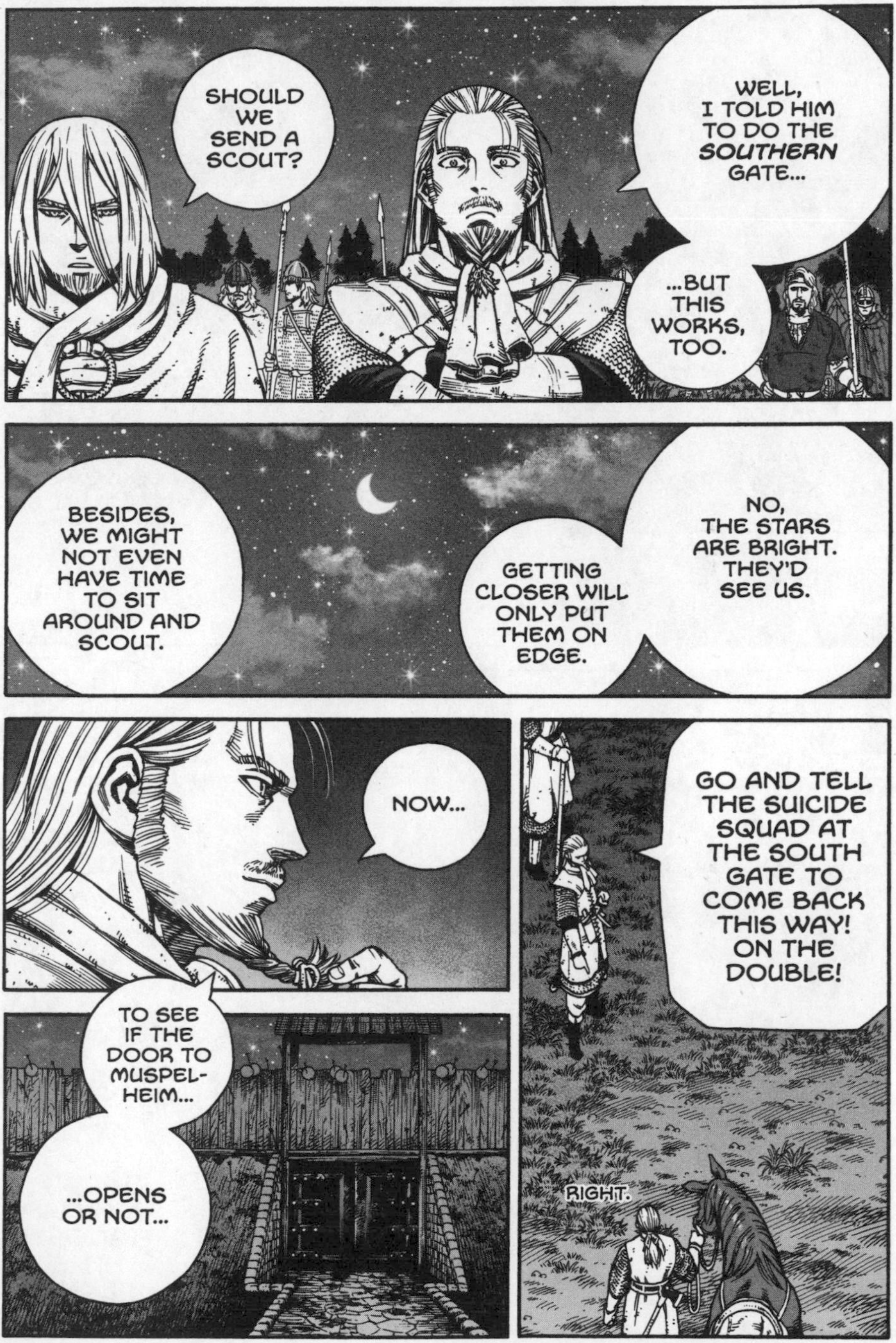
WELL, I TOLD HIM TO DO THE *SOUTHERN* GATE...
...BUT THIS WORKS, TOO.
SHOULD WE SEND A SCOUT?
NO, THE STARS ARE BRIGHT. THEY'D SEE US.
GETTING CLOSER WILL ONLY PUT THEM ON EDGE.
BESIDES, WE MIGHT NOT EVEN HAVE TIME TO SIT AROUND AND SCOUT.
GO AND TELL THE SUICIDE SQUAD AT THE SOUTH GATE TO COME BACK THIS WAY! ON THE DOUBLE!
RIGHT.
NOW...
TO SEE IF THE DOOR TO MUSPEL-HEIM...
...OPENS OR NOT...

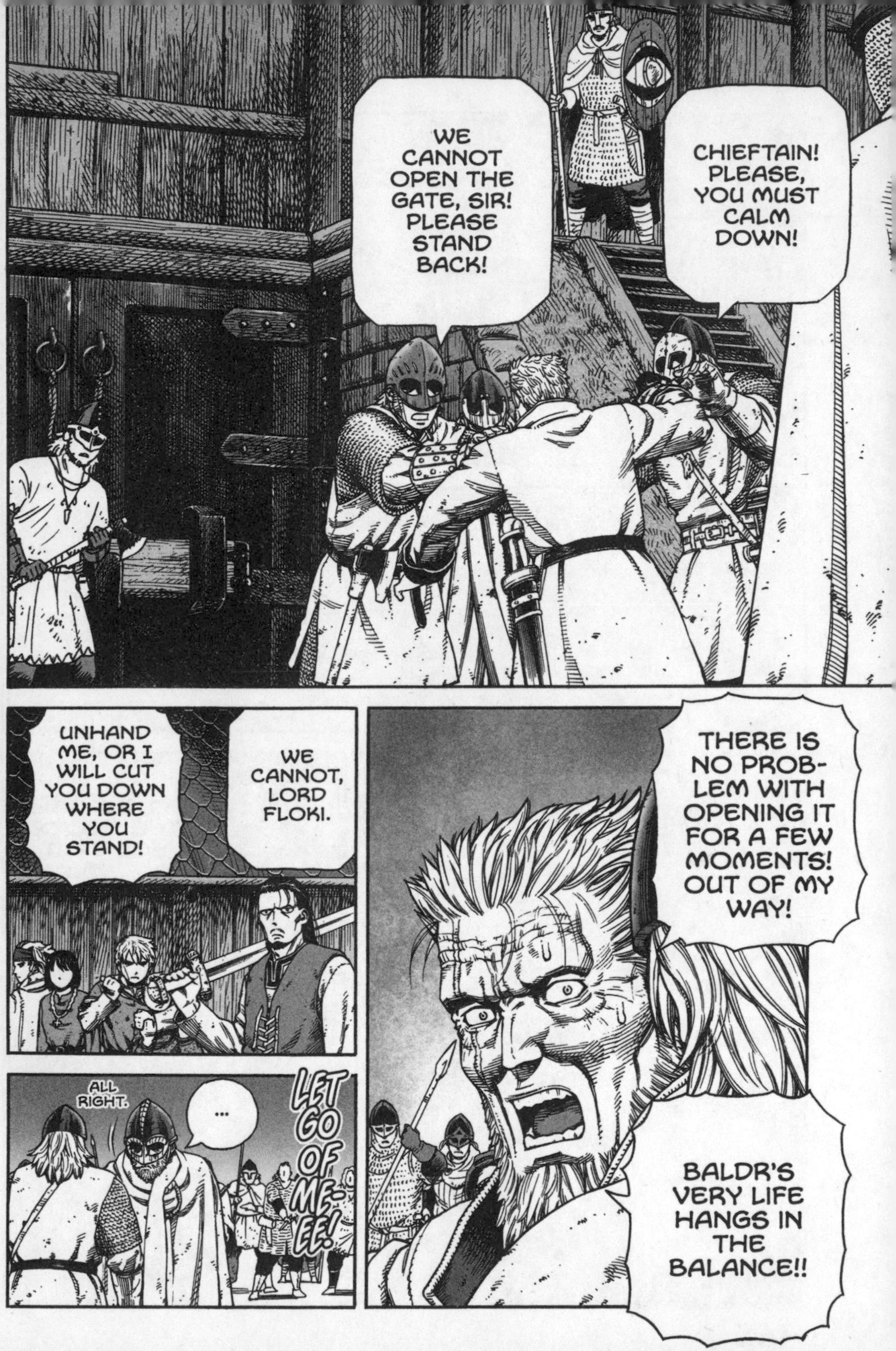
CHIEFTAIN! PLEASE, YOU MUST CALM DOWN!
WE CANNOT OPEN THE GATE, SIR! PLEASE STAND BACK!
THERE IS NO PROB-LEM WITH OPENING IT FOR A FEW MOMENTS! OUT OF MY WAY!
BALDR'S VERY LIFE HANGS IN THE BALANCE!!
WE CANNOT, LORD FLOKI.
UNHAND ME, OR I WILL CUT YOU DOWN WHERE YOU STAND!
LET GO OF ME-EE!
...
ALL RIGHT.

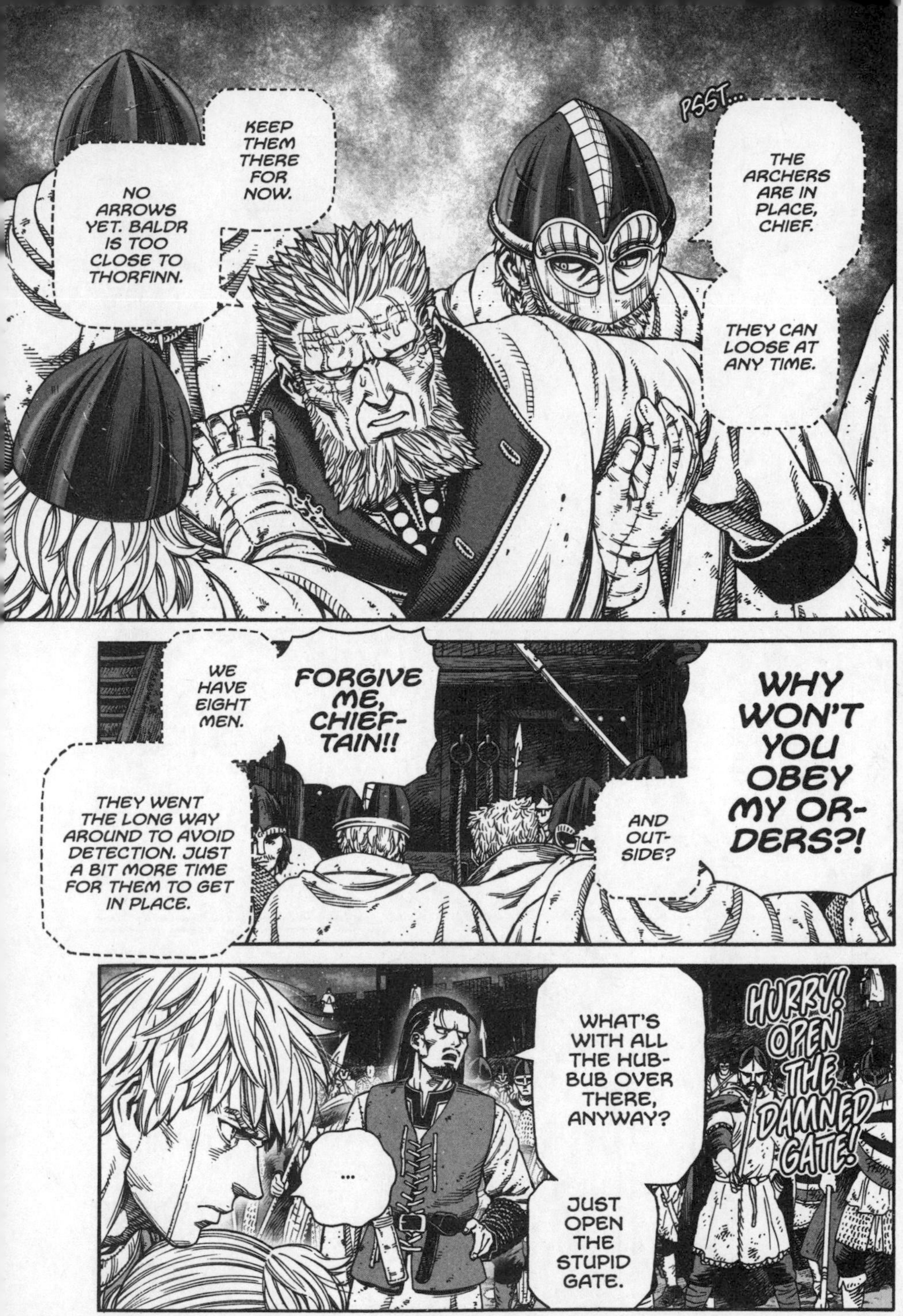
PSST...
THE ARCHERS ARE IN PLACE, CHIEF.
THEY CAN LOOSE AT ANY TIME.
KEEP THEM THERE FOR NOW.
NO ARROWS YET. BALDR IS TOO CLOSE TO THORFINN.
WHY WON'T YOU OBEY MY ORDERS?!
FORGIVE ME, CHIEFTAIN!!
AND OUTSIDE?
WE HAVE EIGHT MEN.
THEY WENT THE LONG WAY AROUND TO AVOID DETECTION. JUST A BIT MORE TIME FOR THEM TO GET IN PLACE.
HURRY! OPEN THE DAMNED GATE!
WHAT'S WITH ALL THE HUBBUB OVER THERE, ANYWAY?
JUST OPEN THE STUPID GATE.
...

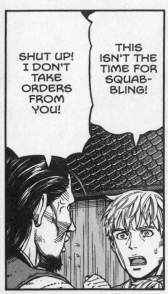

WE CAN'T WAIT. LET'S GO.
YOU OPEN THE GATE, SIGURD.
WHAT?
WHO DO YOU THINK YOU'RE ORDERING AROUND?!
ZSH
THIS ISN'T THE TIME FOR SQUAB-BLING!
SHUT UP! I DON'T TAKE ORDERS FROM YOU!
IF WE WASTE MORE TIME, WE JUST GIVE THEM THE CHANCE TO SET A TRAP FOR US.
YOU WANT TO GET OUT OF THE FOR-TRESS, TOO, DON'T YOU? SO HELP US.
"PLEASE, WON'T YOU KINDLY OPEN THE GATE FOR ME, MISTER SIGURD?"
LET'S HEAR IT!!
...

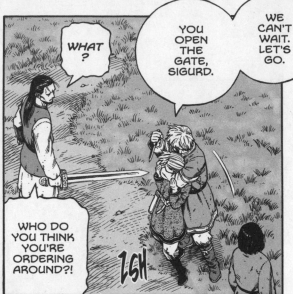

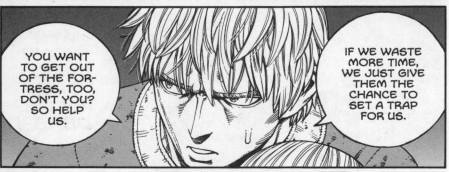

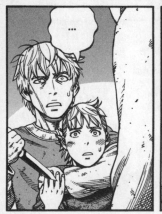

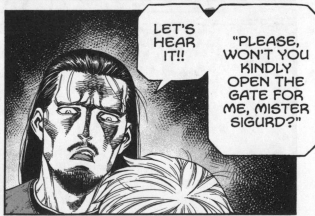

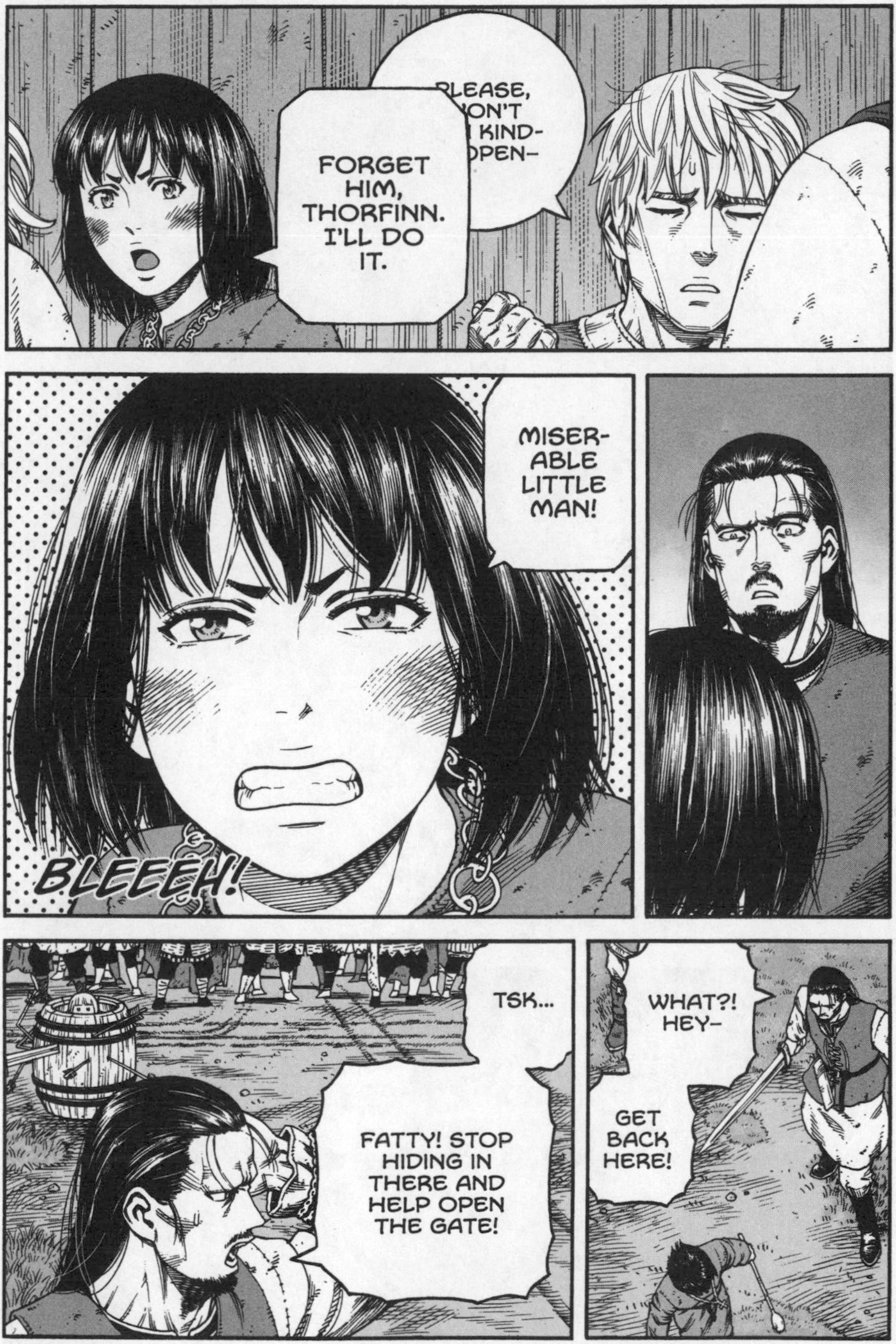
PLEASE, ON'T KIND- OPEN-
FORGET HIM, THORFINN. I'LL DO IT.
MISER-ABLE LITTLE MAN!
BLEEEH!
WHAT?! HEY-
GET BACK HERE!
TSK...
FATTY! STOP HIDING IN THERE AND HELP OPEN THE GATE!

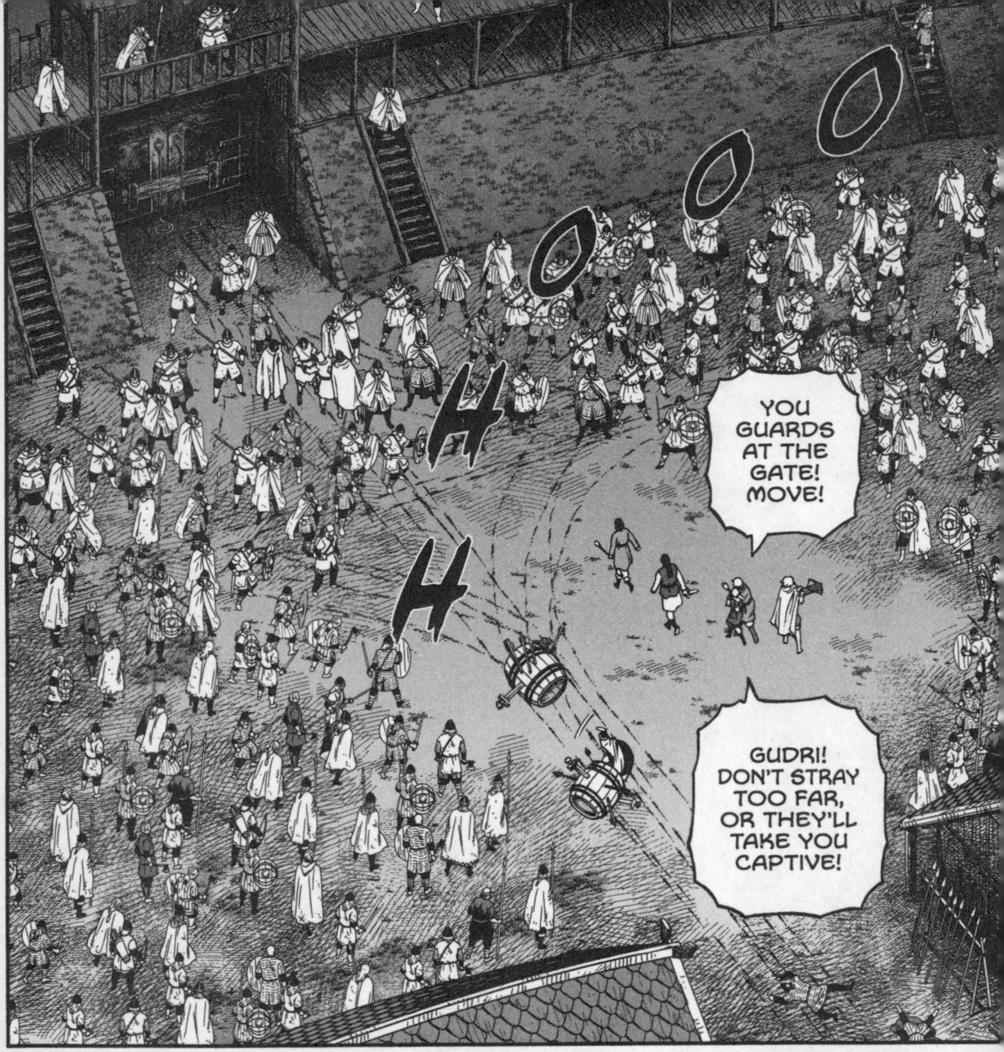
HHOOOO
YOU GUARDS AT THE GATE! MOVE!
GUDRI! DON'T STRAY TOO FAR, OR THEY'LL TAKE YOU CAPTIVE!

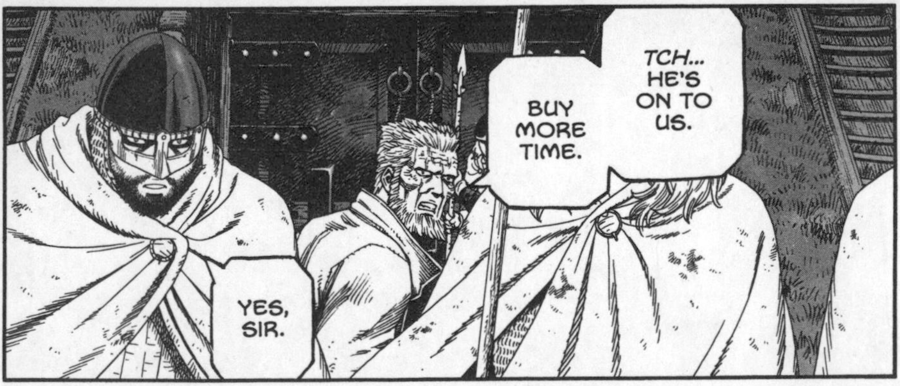
TCH... HE'S ON TO US.
BUY MORE TIME.
YES, SIR.

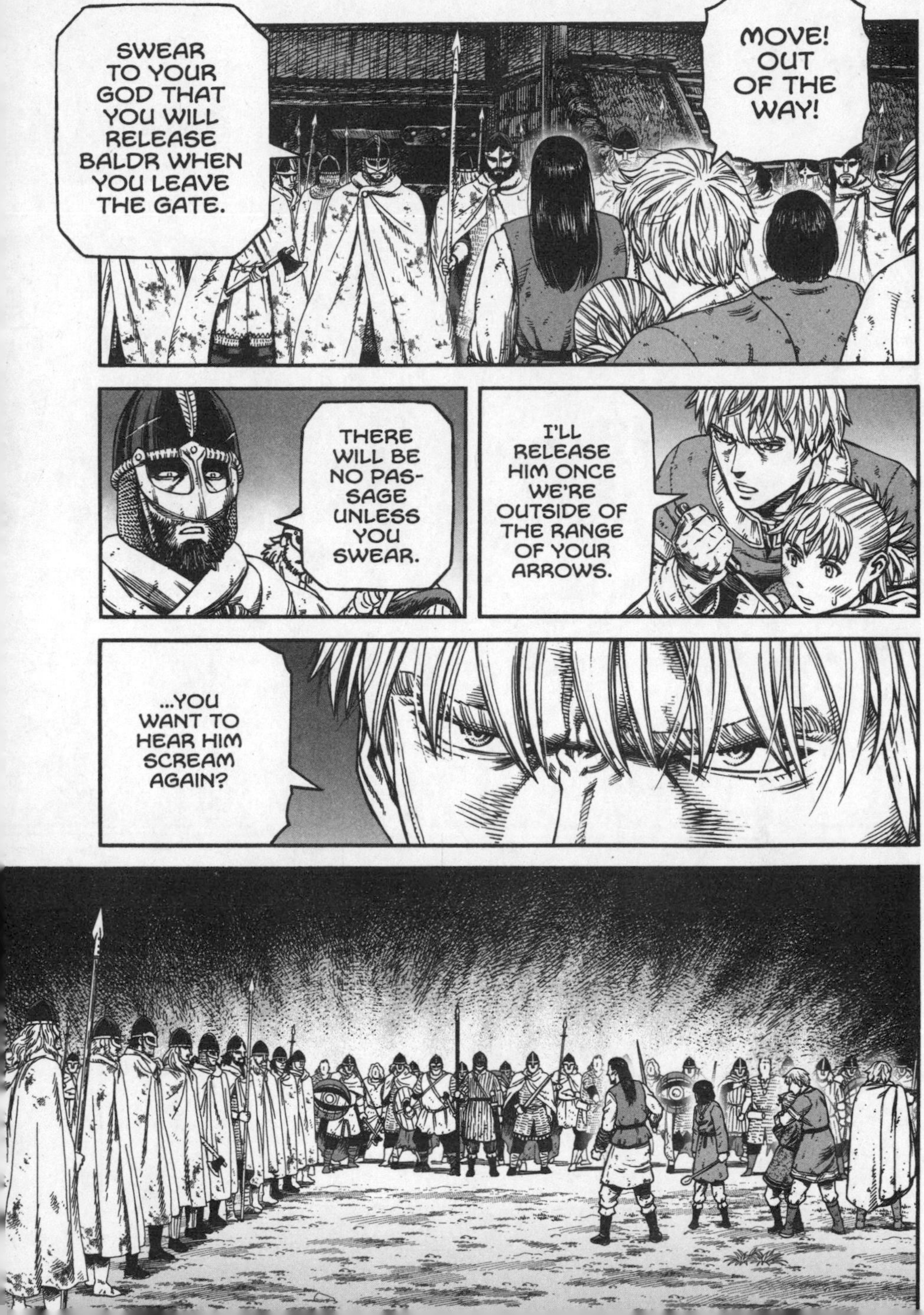
MOVE! OUT OF THE WAY!
SWEAR TO YOUR GOD THAT YOU WILL RELEASE BALDR WHEN YOU LEAVE THE GATE.
I'LL RELEASE HIM ONCE WE'RE OUTSIDE OF THE RANGE OF YOUR ARROWS.
THERE WILL BE NO PAS-SAGE UNLESS YOU SWEAR.
...YOU WANT TO HEAR HIM SCREAM AGAIN?

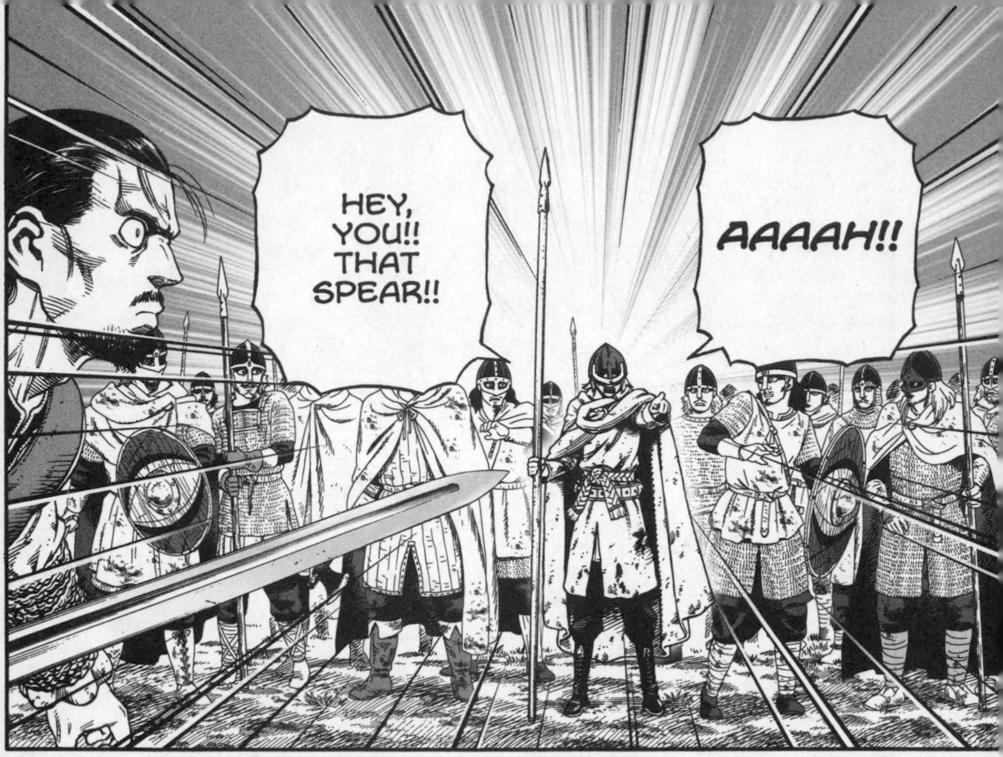
AAAAH!!
HEY, YOU!! THAT SPEAR!!

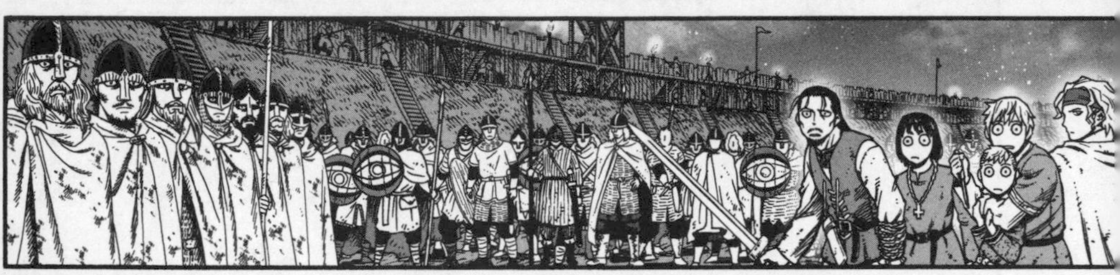

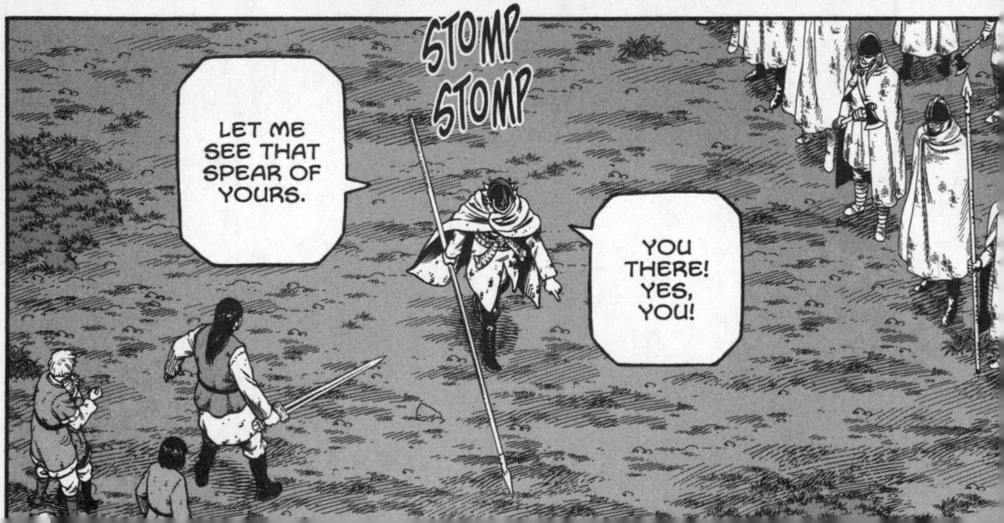
STOMP STOMP
YOU THERE! YES, YOU!
LET ME SEE THAT SPEAR OF YOURS.

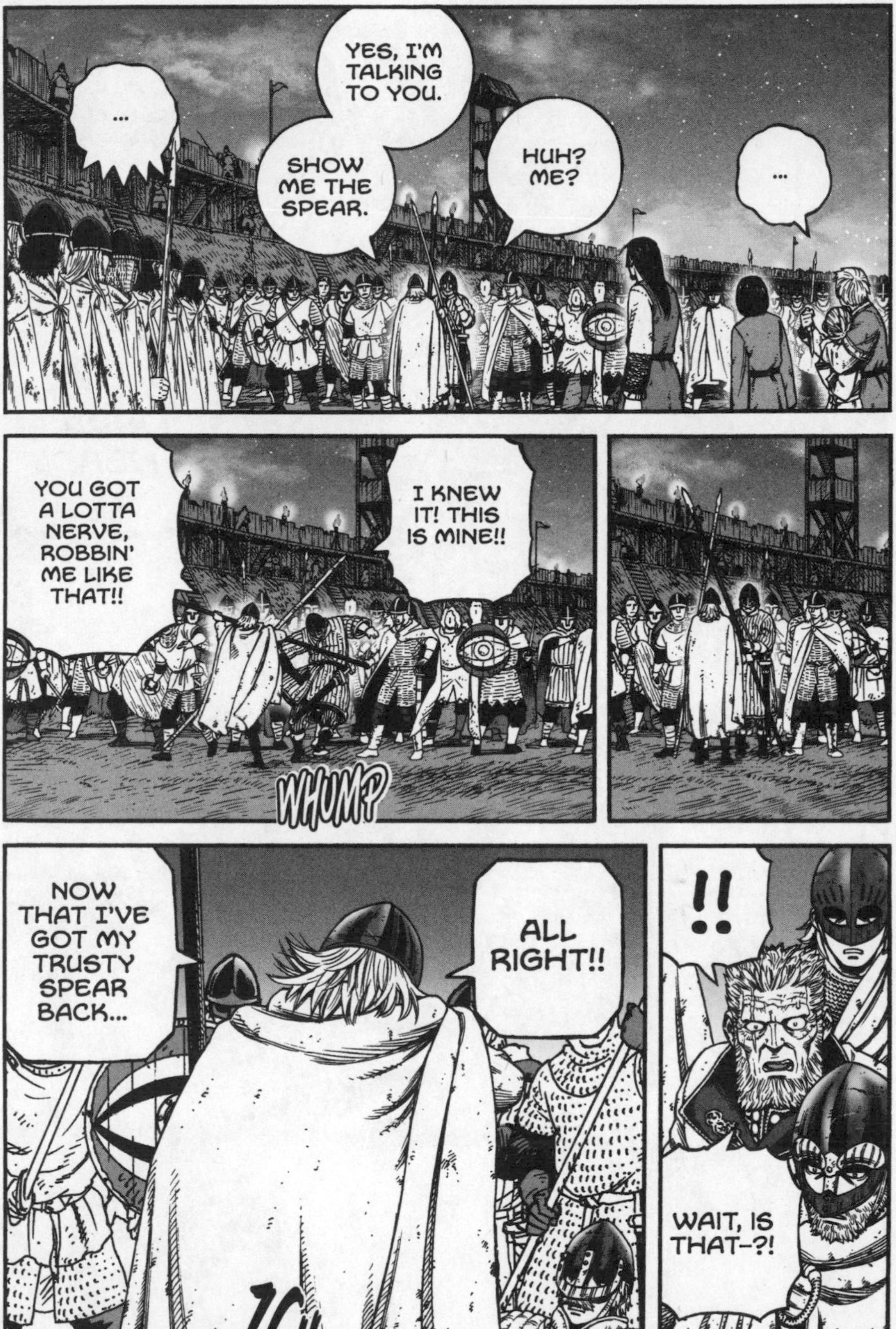
...
HUH? ME?
YES, I'M TALKING TO YOU.
SHOW ME THE SPEAR.
...
I KNEW IT! THIS IS MINE!!
YOU GOT A LOTTA NERVE, ROBBIN' ME LIKE THAT!!
WHUMP
!!
WAIT, IS THAT-?!
ALL RIGHT!!
NOW THAT I'VE GOT MY TRUSTY SPEAR BACK...
Z-SH

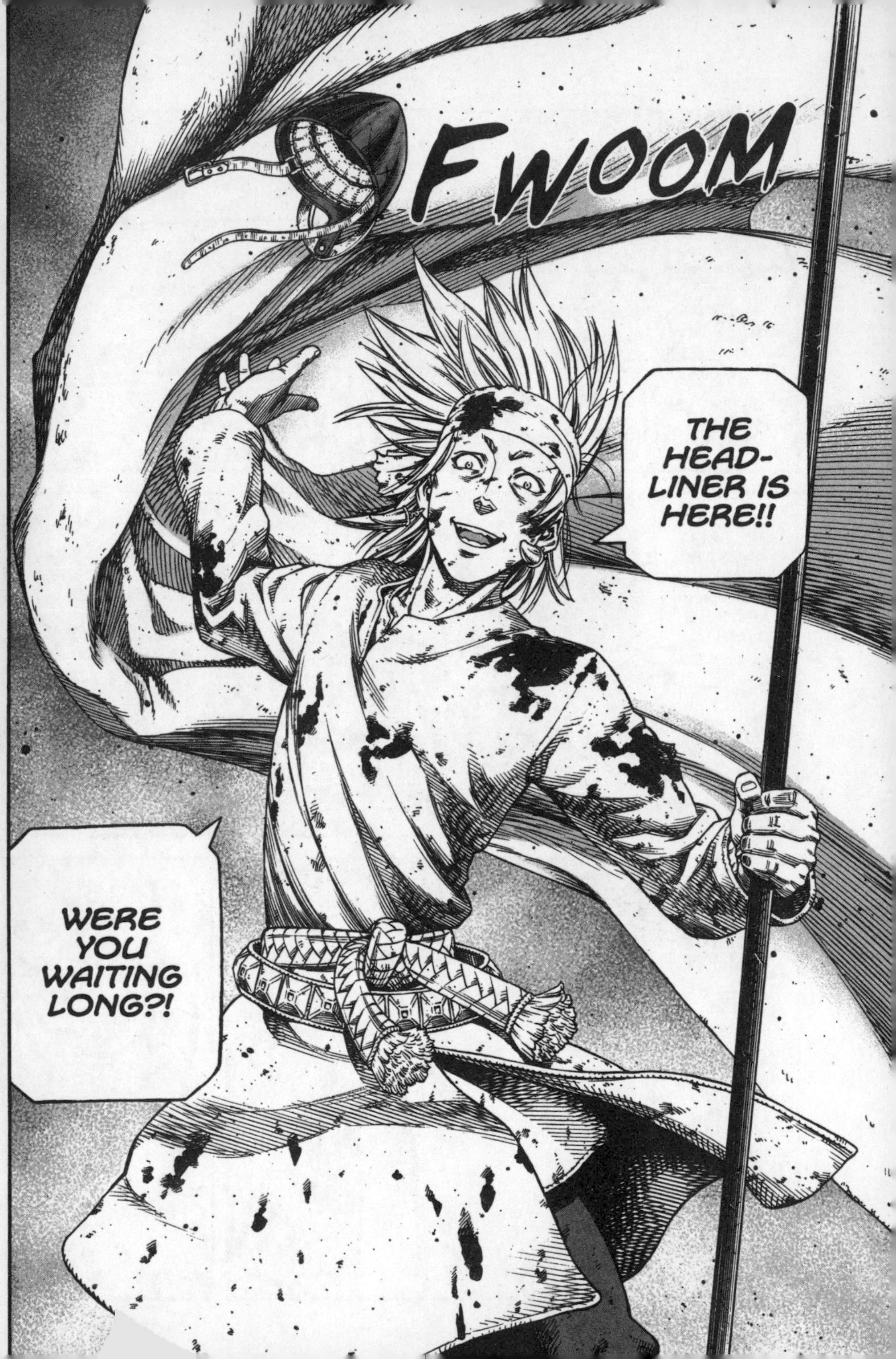
FWOOM
THE HEAD-LINER IS HERE!!
WERE YOU WAITING LONG?!

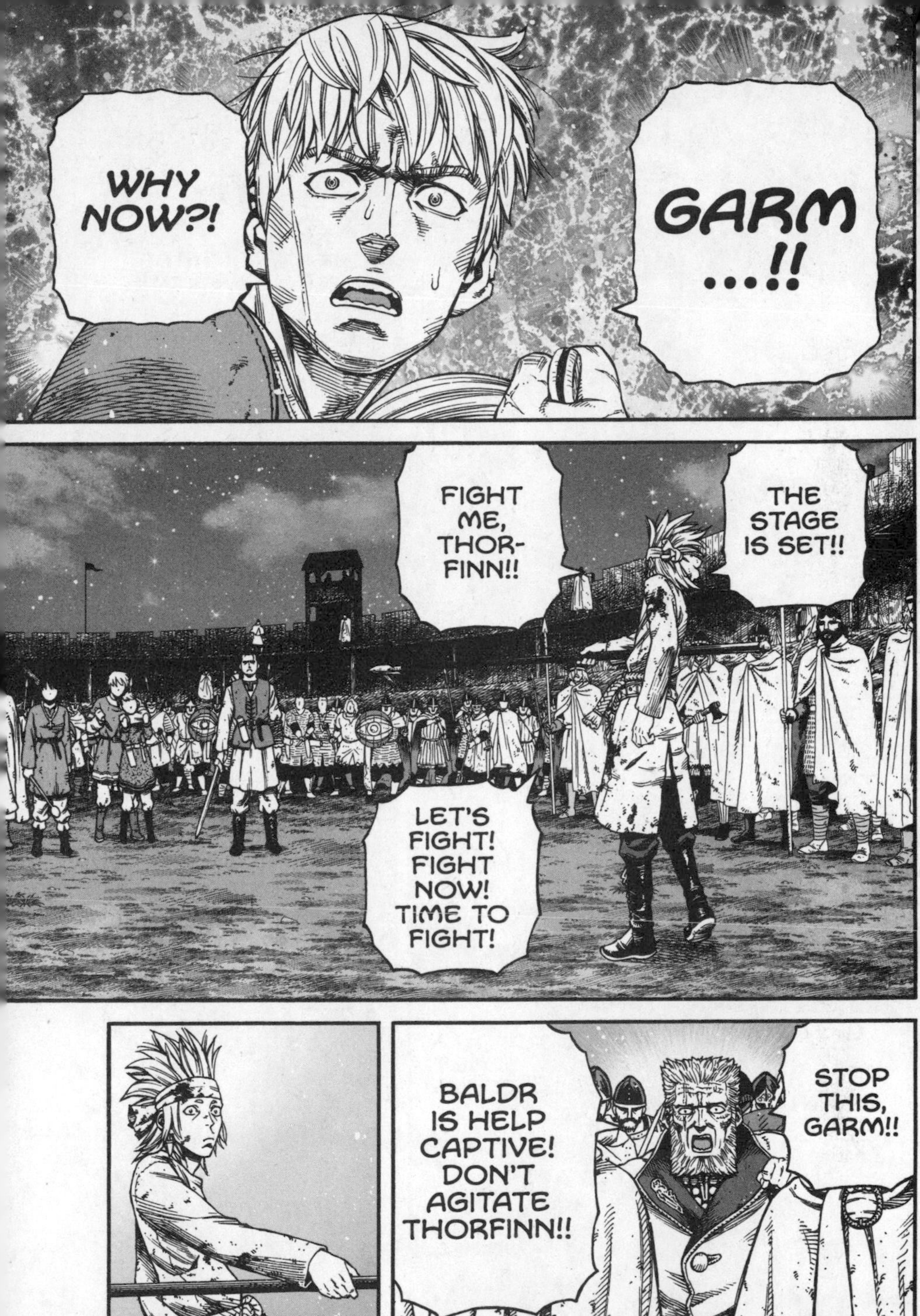
GARM ...!!
WHY NOW?!
THE STAGE IS SET!!
FIGHT ME, THORFINN!!
LET'S FIGHT! FIGHT NOW! TIME TO FIGHT!
STOP THIS, GARM!!
BALDR IS HELP CAPTIVE! DON'T AGITATE THORFINN!!

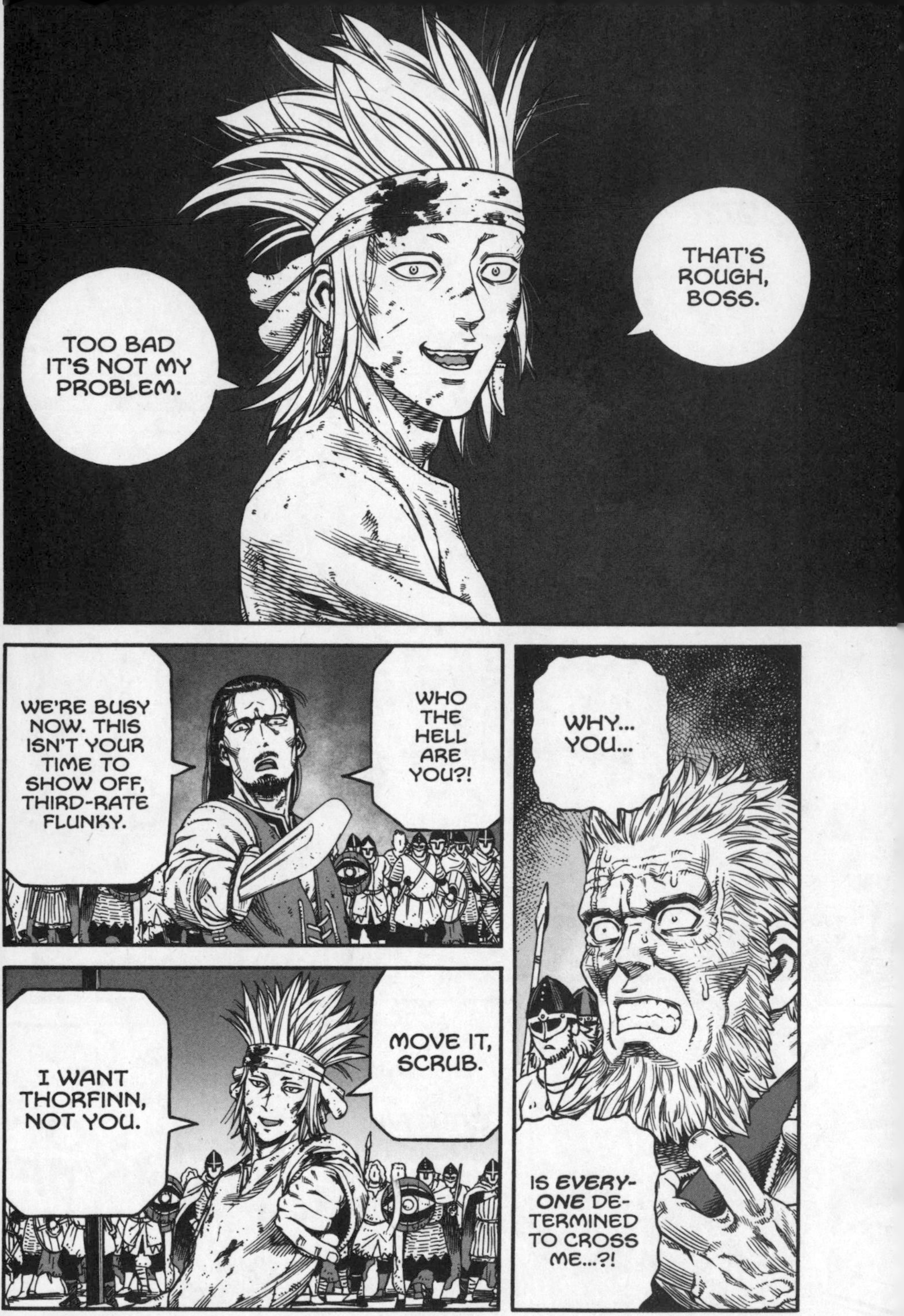
THAT'S ROUGH, BOSS.
TOO BAD IT'S NOT MY PROBLEM.
WHY... YOU...
IS *EVERY-ONE* DE-TERMINED TO CROSS ME...?!
WHO THE HELL ARE YOU?!
WE'RE BUSY NOW. THIS ISN'T YOUR TIME TO SHOW OFF, THIRD-RATE FLUNKY.
MOVE IT, SCRUB.
I WANT THORFINN, NOT YOU.

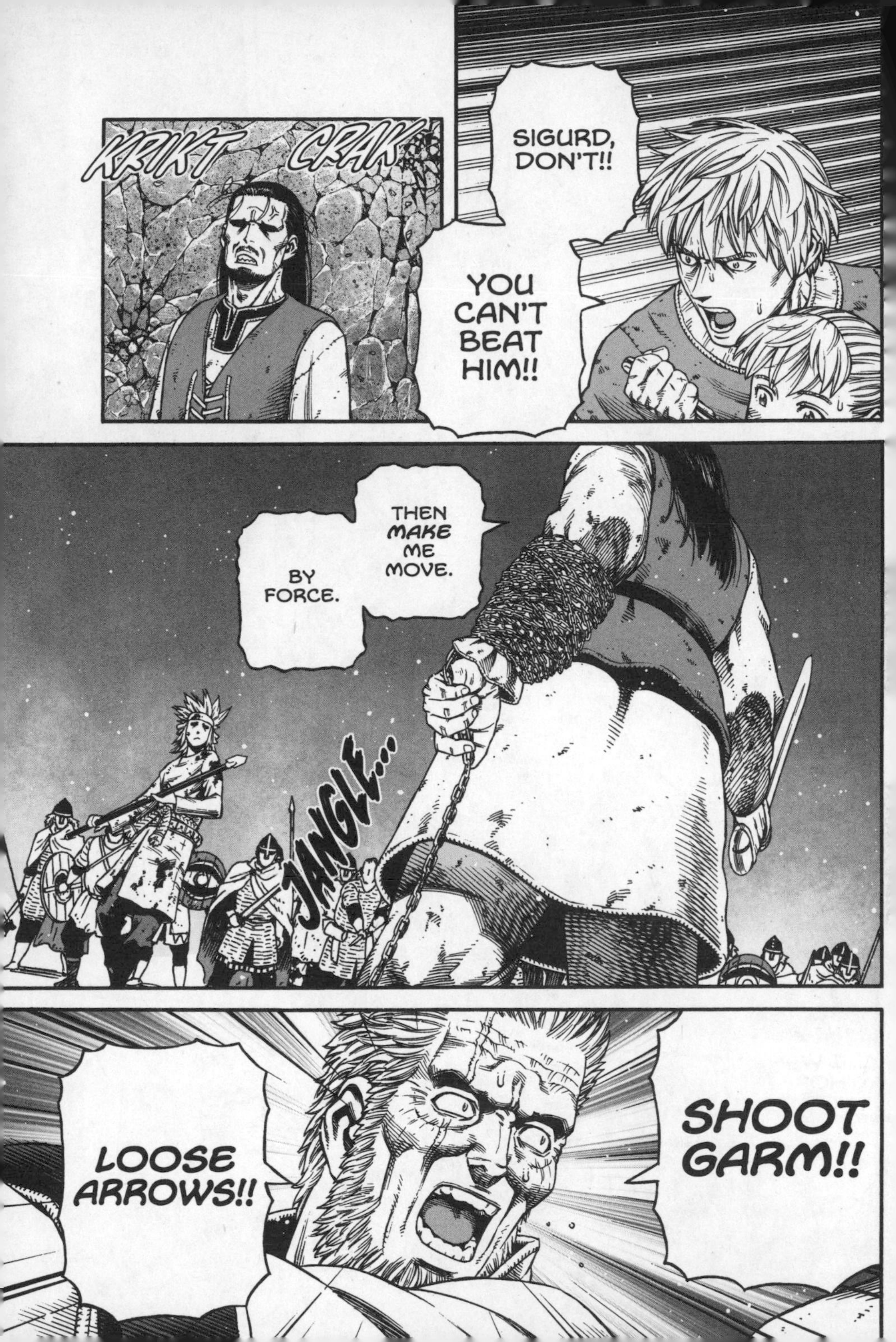
SIGURD, DON'T!!
YOU CAN'T BEAT HIM!!
KRIKT
CRAK
THEN MAKE ME MOVE.
BY FORCE.
JANGLE...
SHOOT GARM!!
LOOSE ARROWS!!

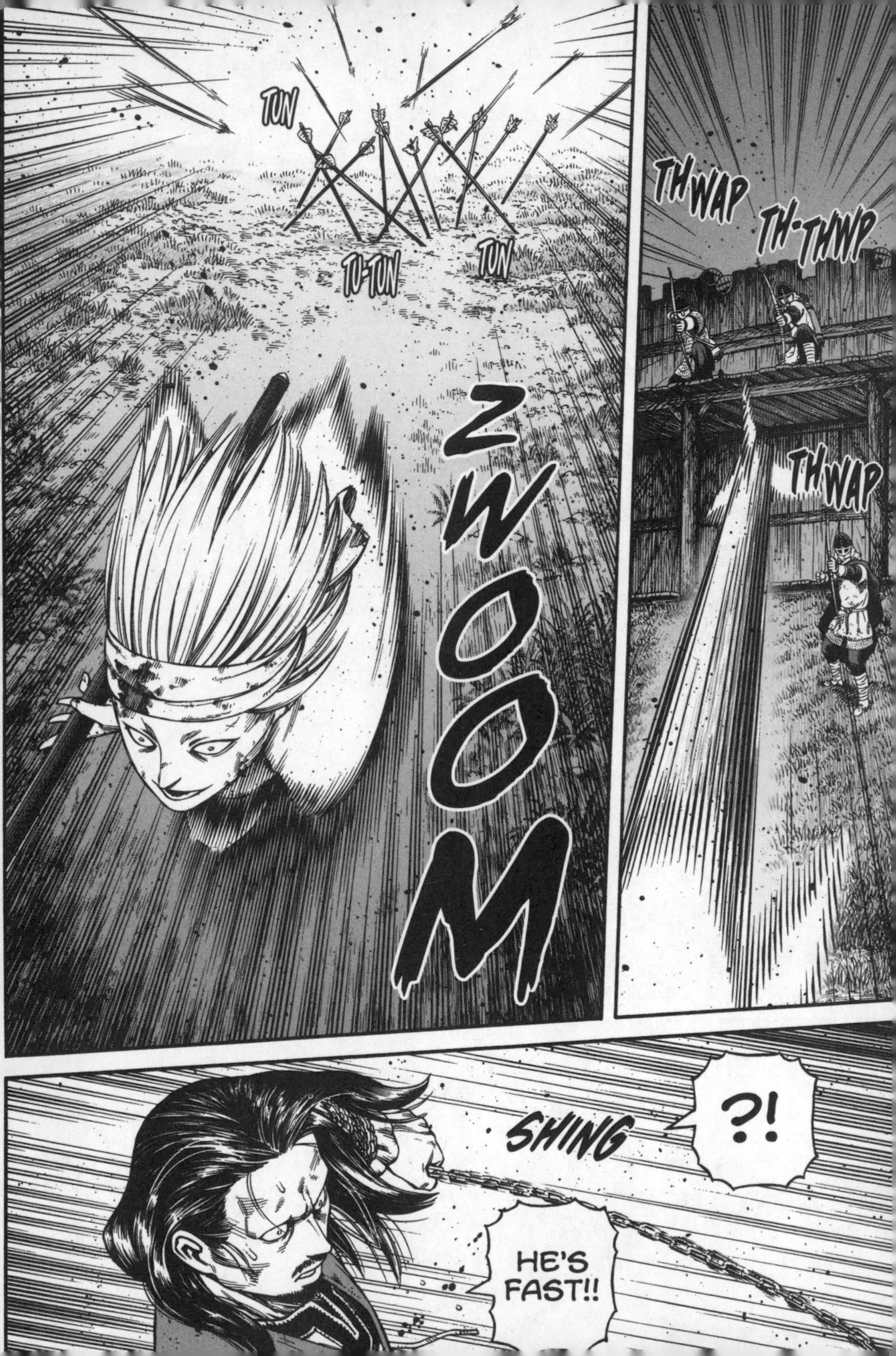
THWAP
TH-THWP
THWAP
TUN
TO-TUN
TUN
ZWOOM
SHING
?!
HE'S FAST!!

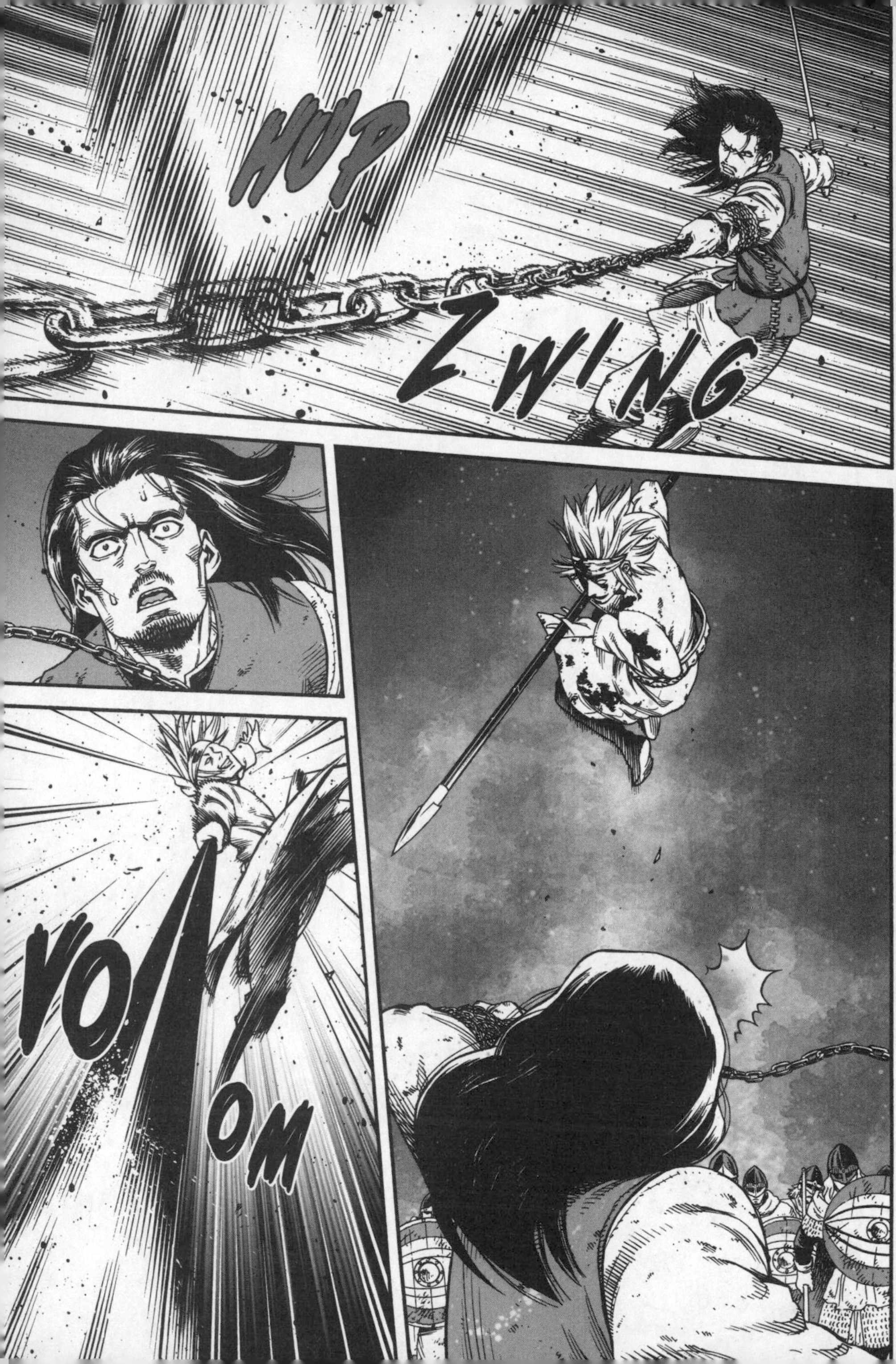
HUP
ZWING
VOOM

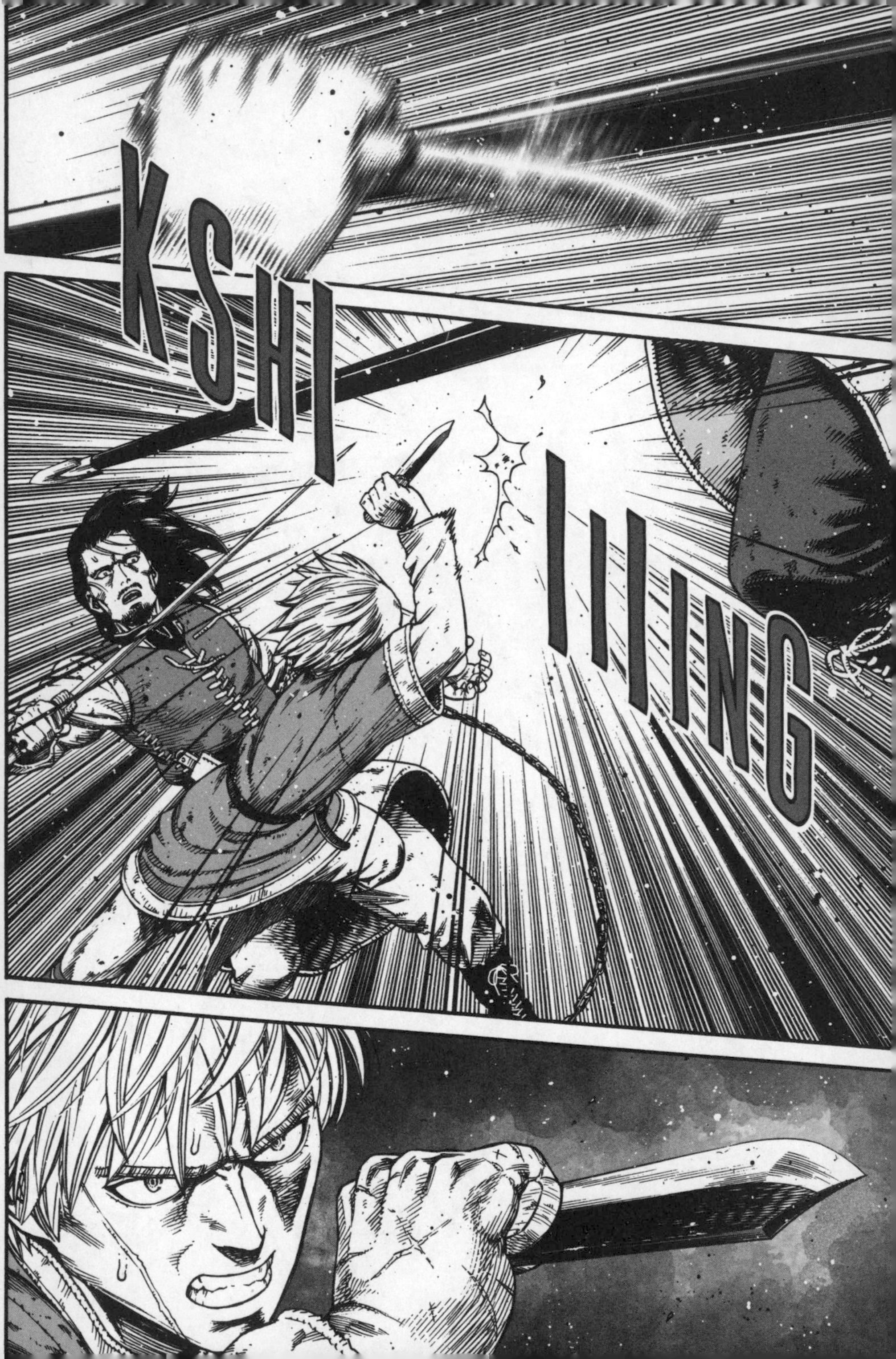
KSHI
IIING

VINLAND SAGA

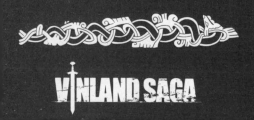

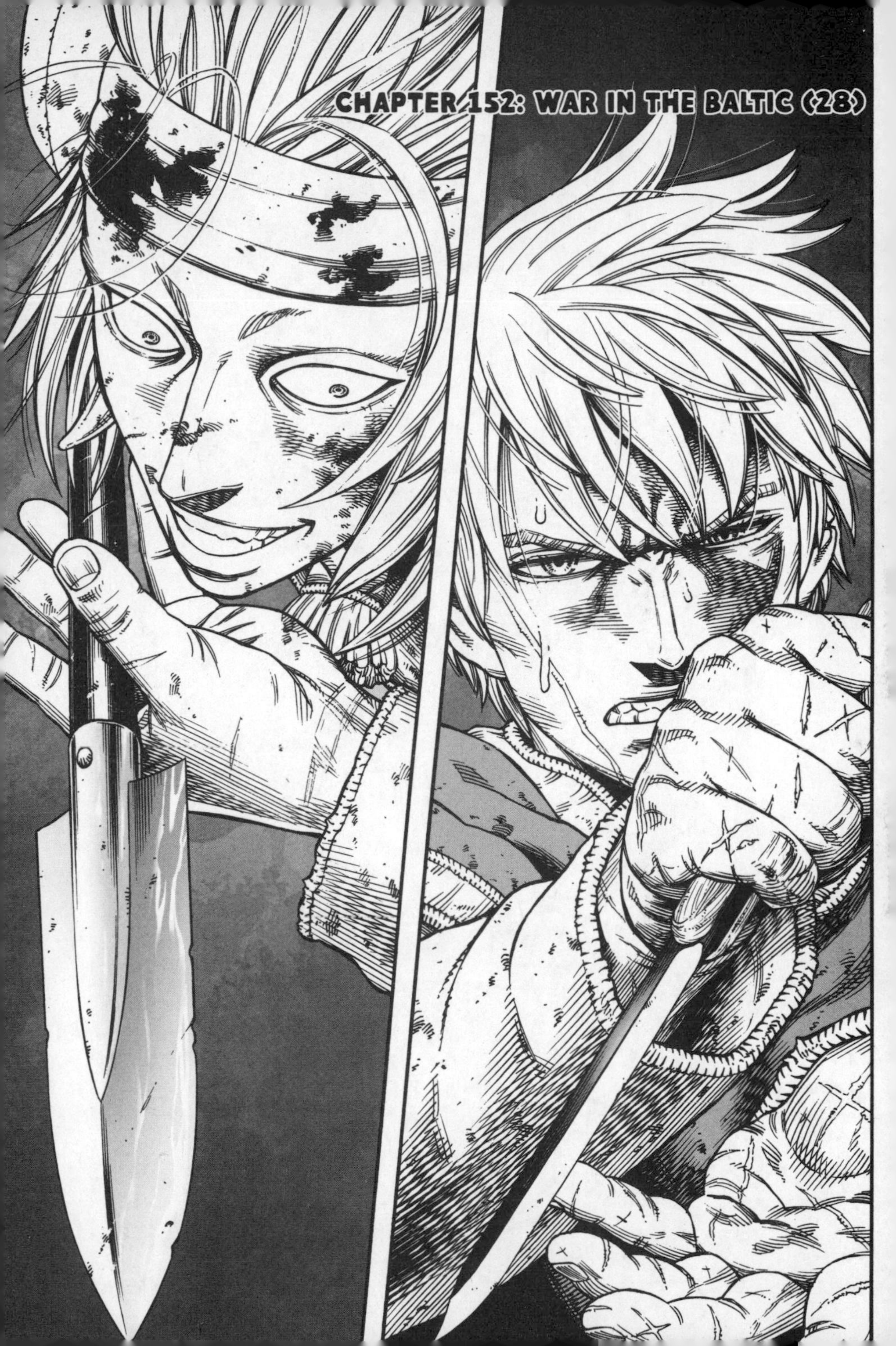
CHAPTER 152: WAR IN THE BALTIC (28)

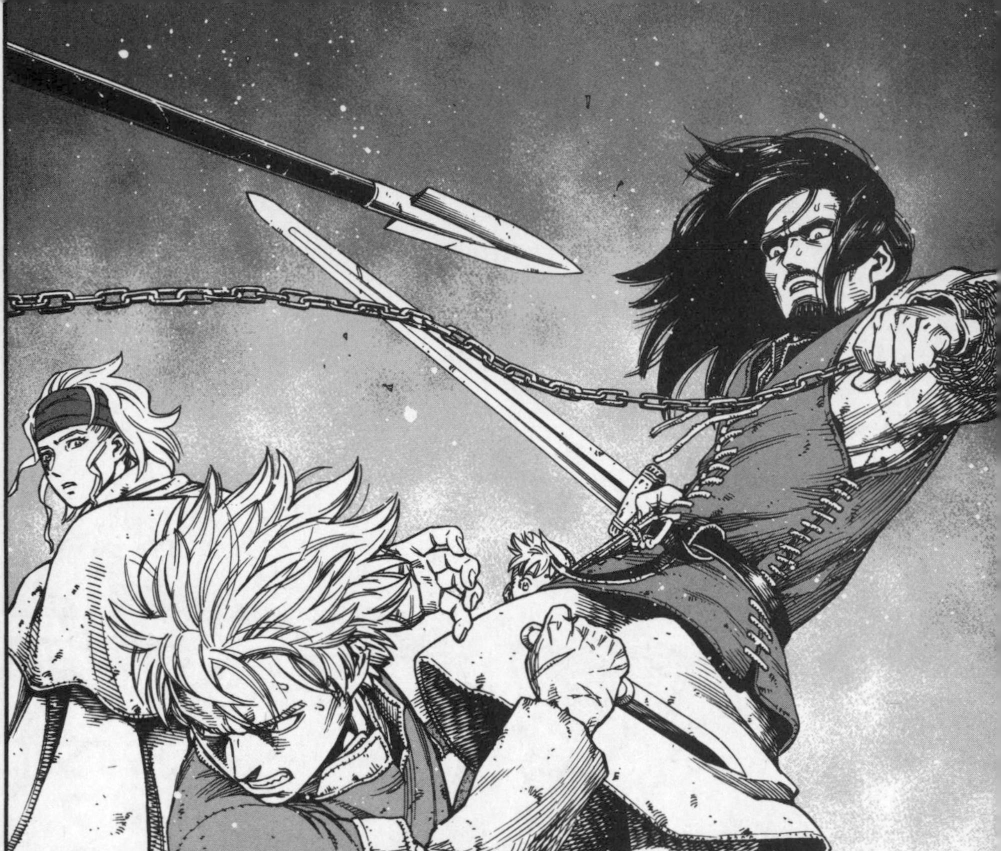

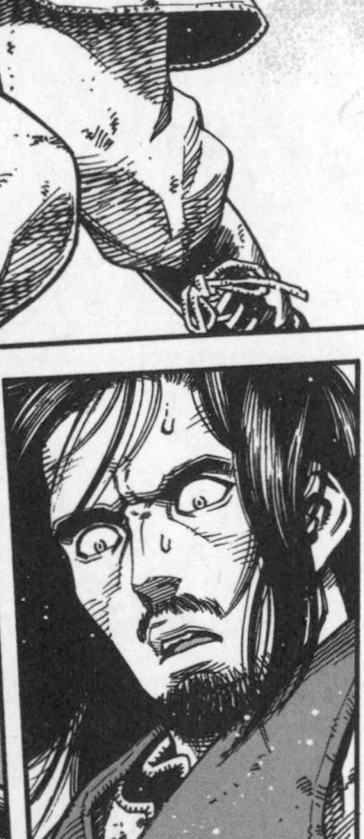

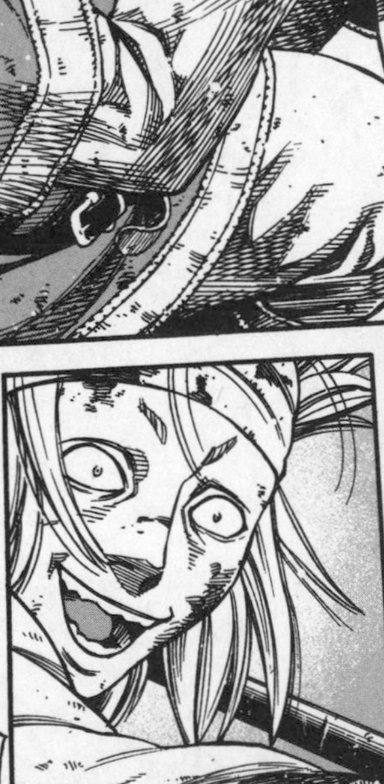

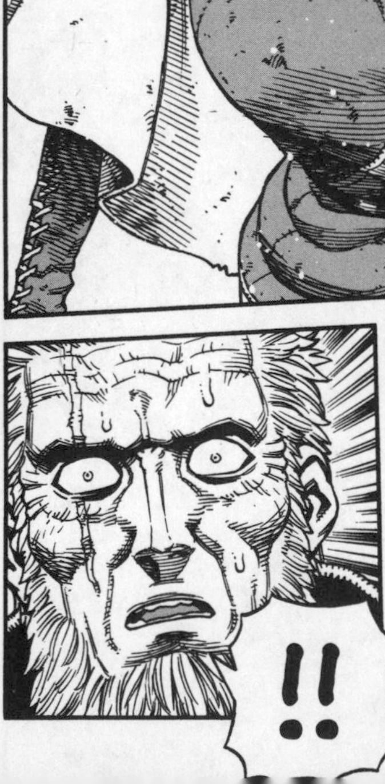
!!

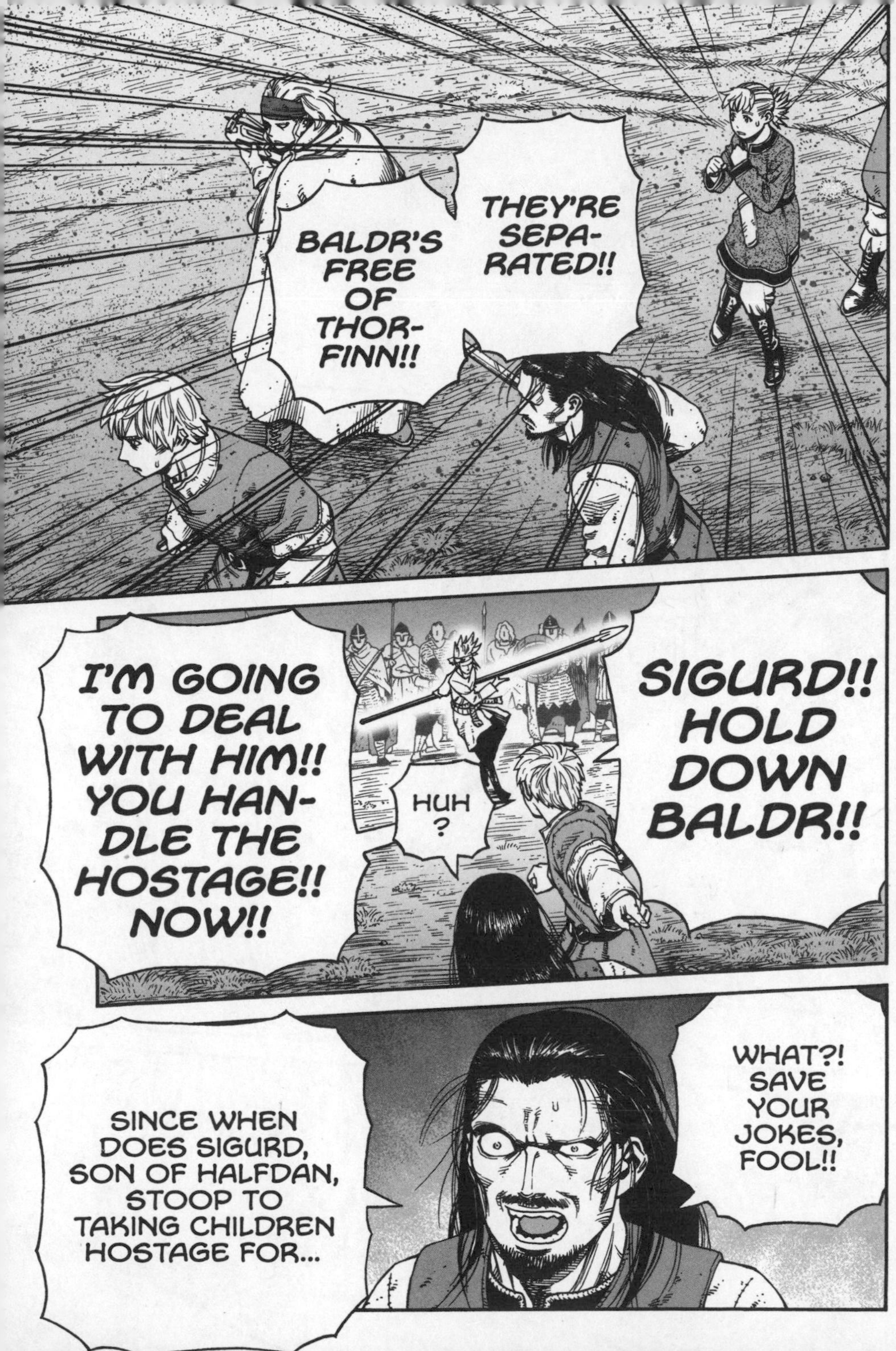
THEY'RE SEPA-RATED!!
BALDR'S FREE OF THOR-FINN!!
SIGURD!! HOLD DOWN BALDR!!
HUH?
I'M GOING TO DEAL WITH HIM!! YOU HAN-DLE THE HOSTAGE!! NOW!!
WHAT?! SAVE YOUR JOKES, FOOL!!
SINCE WHEN DOES SIGURD, SON OF HALFDAN, STOOP TO TAKING CHILDREN HOSTAGE FOR...

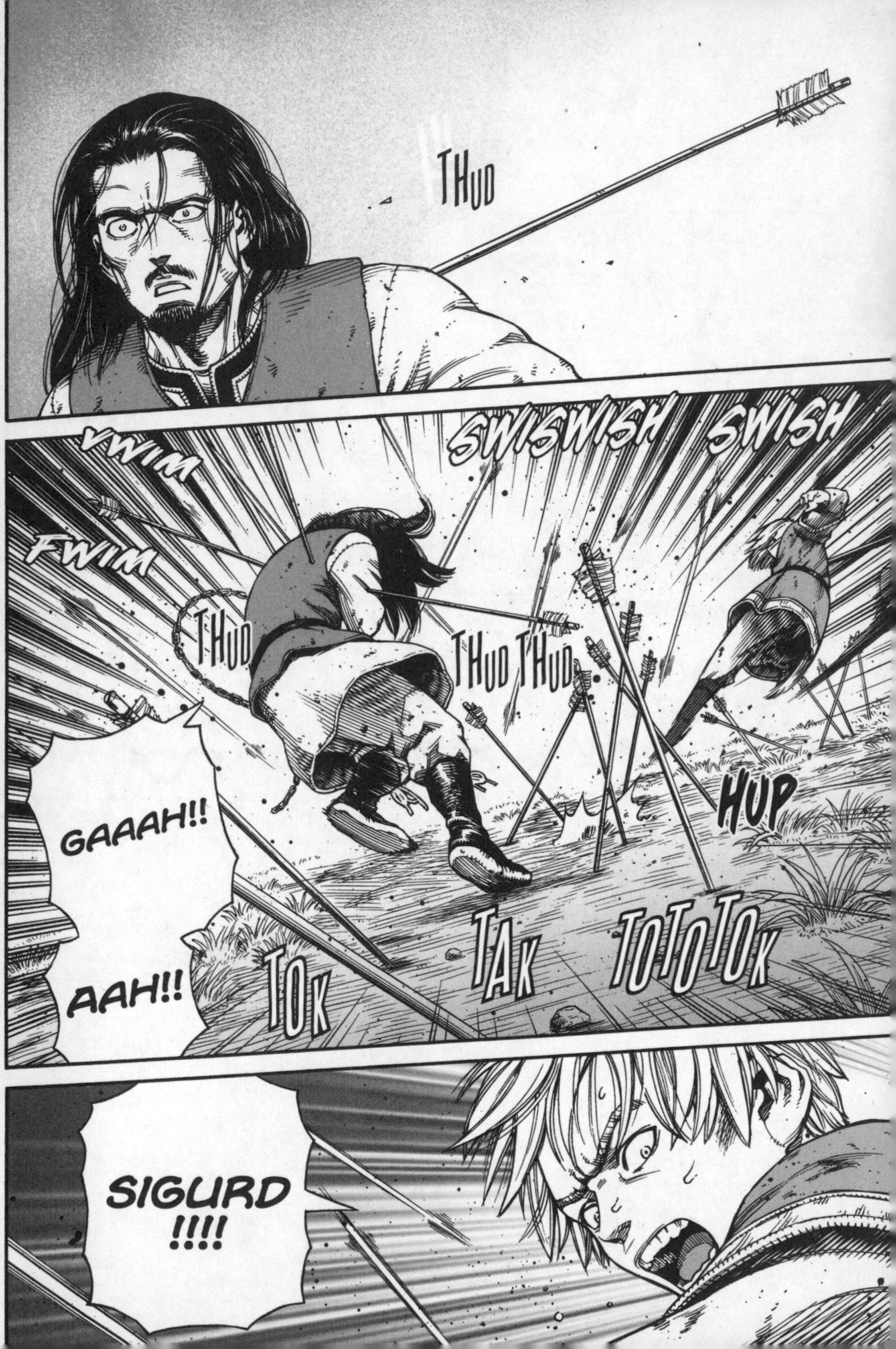
THUD
SWISH
SWISWISH
VWIM
FWIM
THUD THUD
THUD
HUP
TOTOTOTOK
TAK
GAAAH!!
AAH!!
TOK
SIGURD !!!!

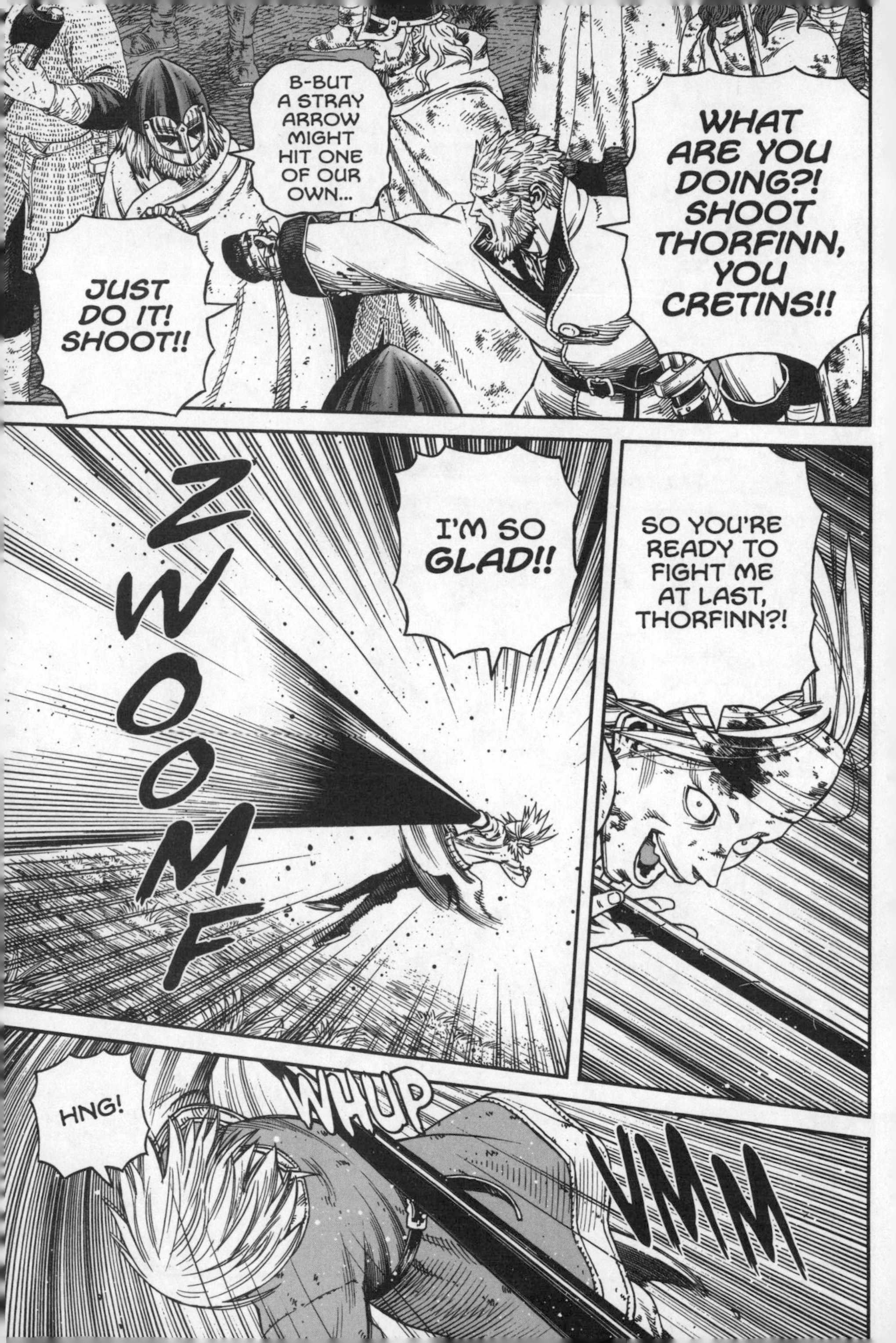
WHAT ARE YOU DOING?! SHOOT THORFINN, YOU CRETINS!!
B-BUT A STRAY ARROW MIGHT HIT ONE OF OUR OWN...
JUST DO IT! SHOOT!!
SO YOU'RE READY TO FIGHT ME AT LAST, THORFINN?!
I'M SO GLAD!!
ZWOOMF
VMM
WHUP
HNG!

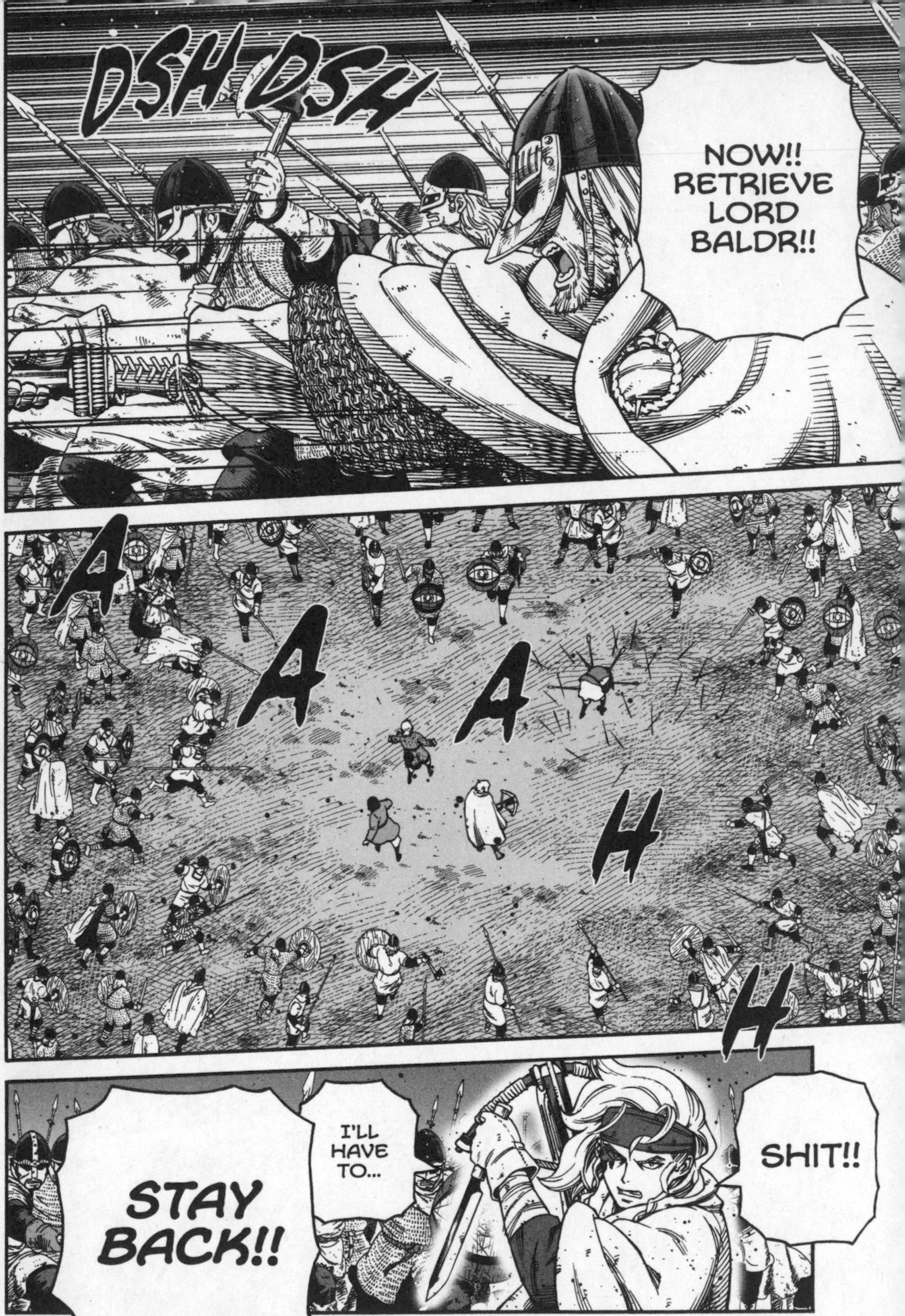
NOW!! RETRIEVE LORD BALDR!!
DSH DSH
AAAHH
SHIT!!
I'LL HAVE TO...
STAY BACK!!

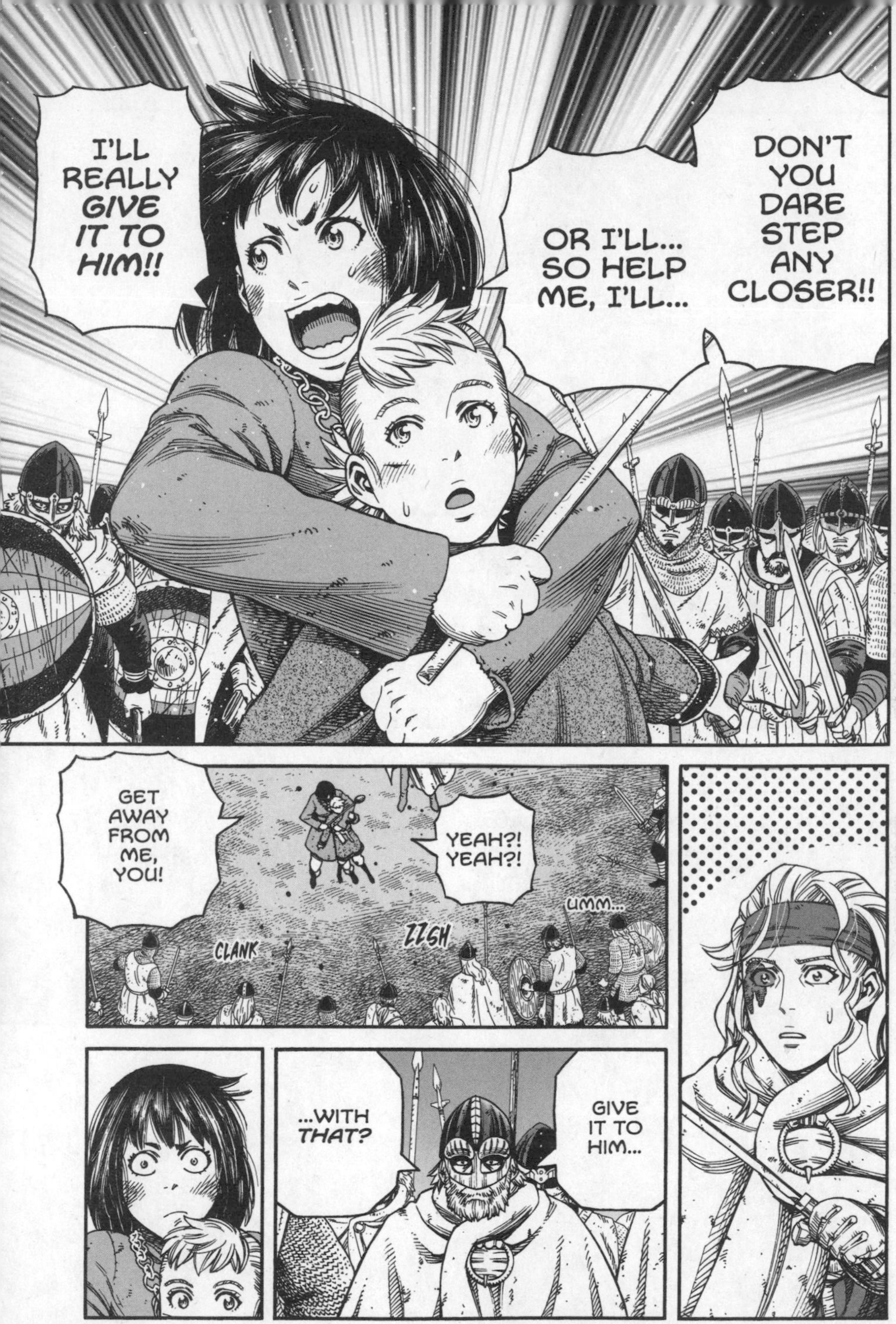
DON'T YOU DARE STEP ANY CLOSER!!
OR I'LL... SO HELP ME, I'LL...
I'LL REALLY GIVE IT TO HIM!!
YEAH?! YEAH?!
GET AWAY FROM ME, YOU!
UMM...
ZZSH
CLANK
GIVE IT TO HIM...
...WITH THAT?

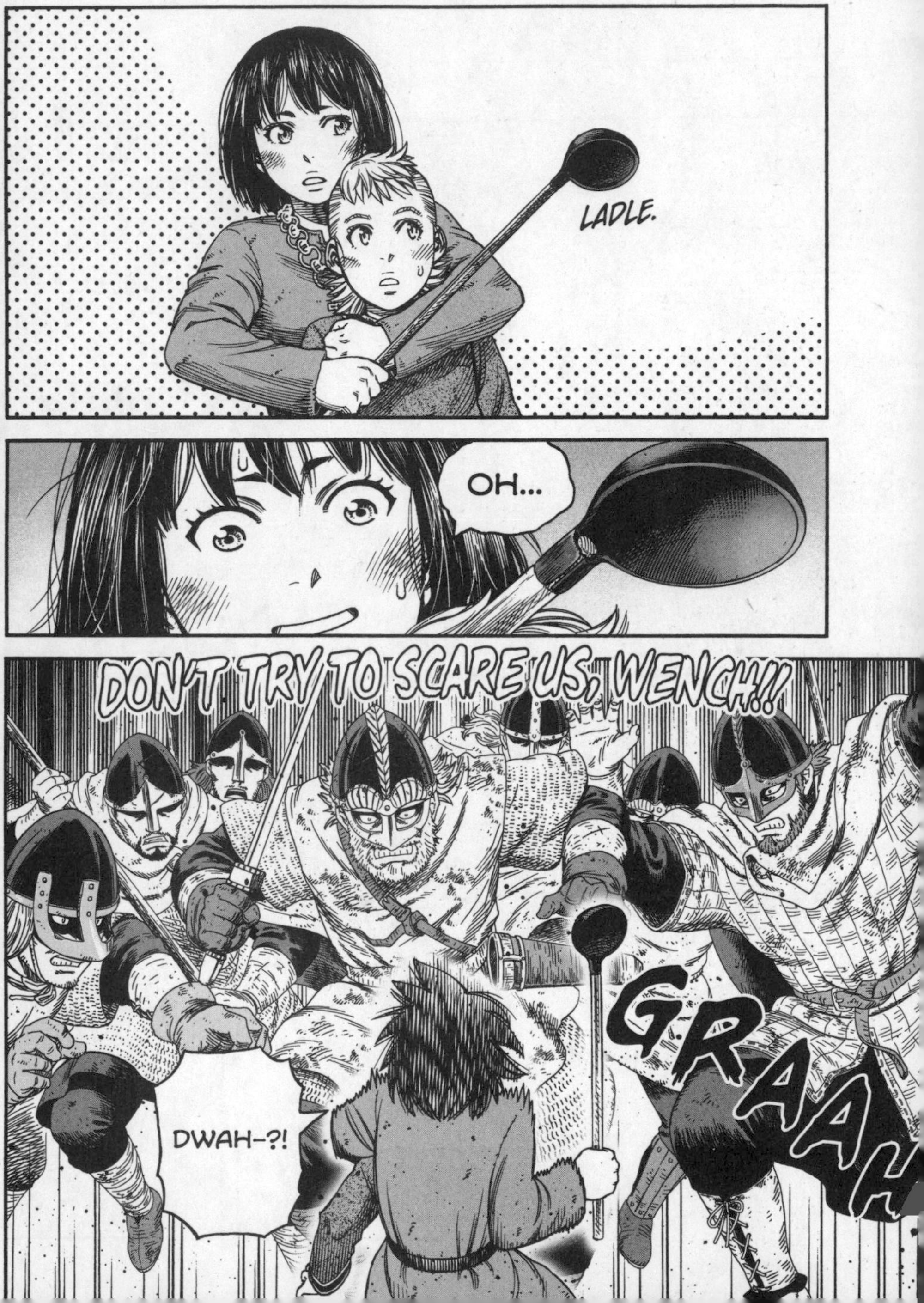
LADLE.
OH...
DON'T TRY TO SCARE US, WENCH!!
GRAAAH
DWAH-?!

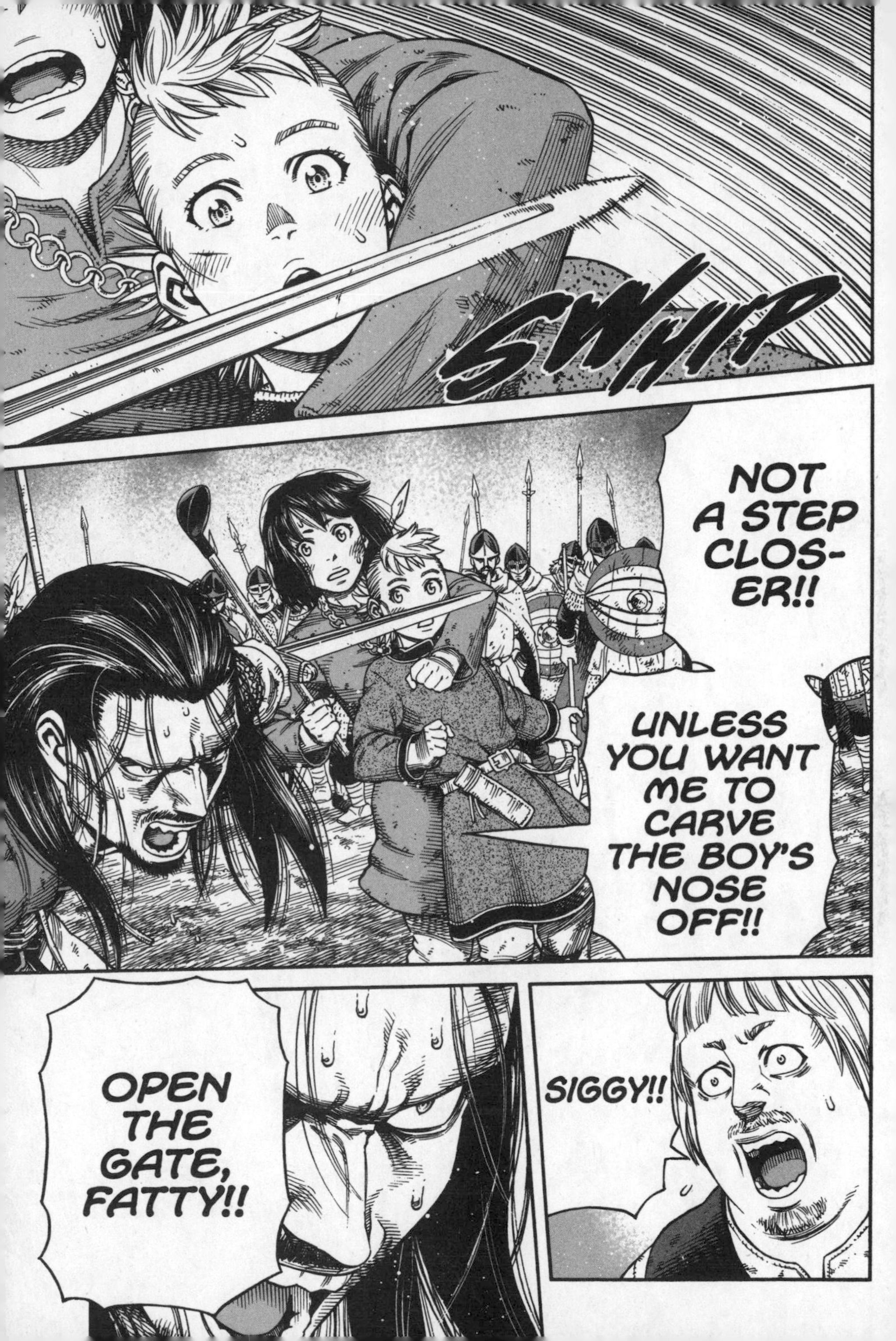
SWHIP
NOT A STEP CLOSER!!
UNLESS YOU WANT ME TO CARVE THE BOY'S NOSE OFF!!
SIGGY!!
OPEN THE GATE, FATTY!!

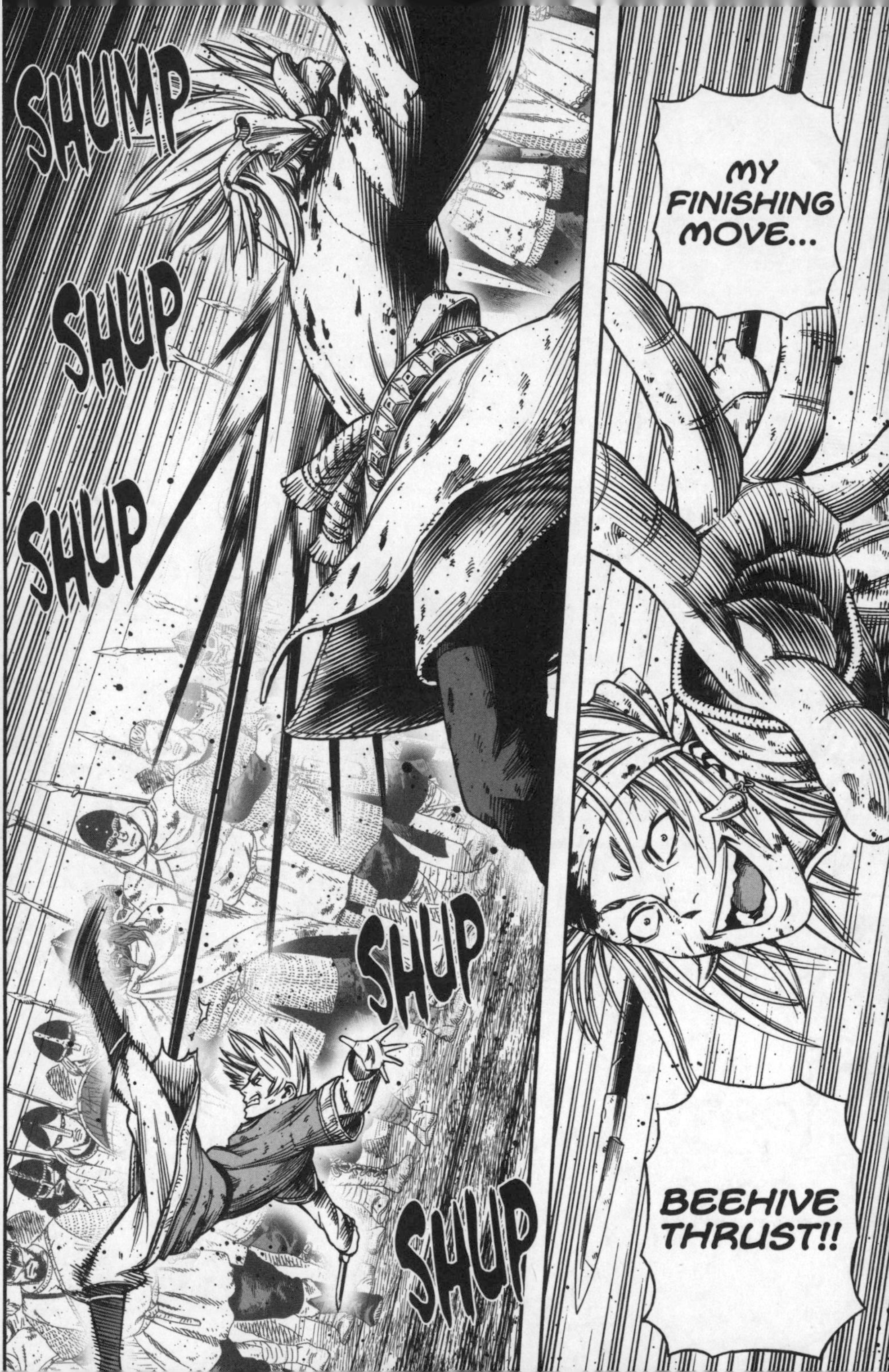
MY FINISHING MOVE...
BEEHIVE THRUST!!
SHUMP
SHUP
SHUP
SHUP
SHUP

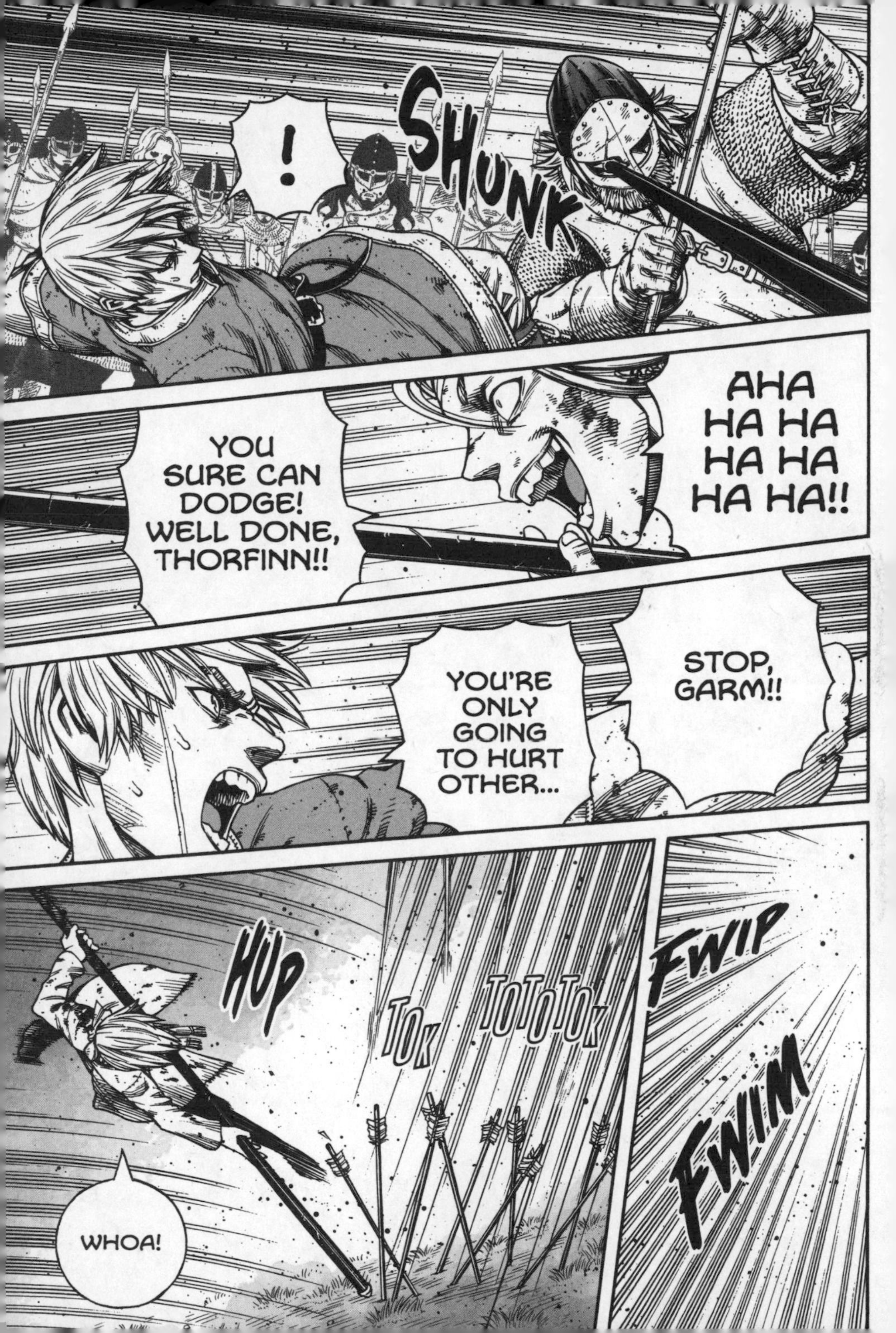
SHUNK
!
AHA HA HA HA HA HA HA!!
YOU SURE CAN DODGE! WELL DONE, THORFINN!!
STOP, GARM!!
YOU'RE ONLY GOING TO HURT OTHER...
FWIP
FWIM
TOTOTOTOK
TOK
HUP
WHOA!

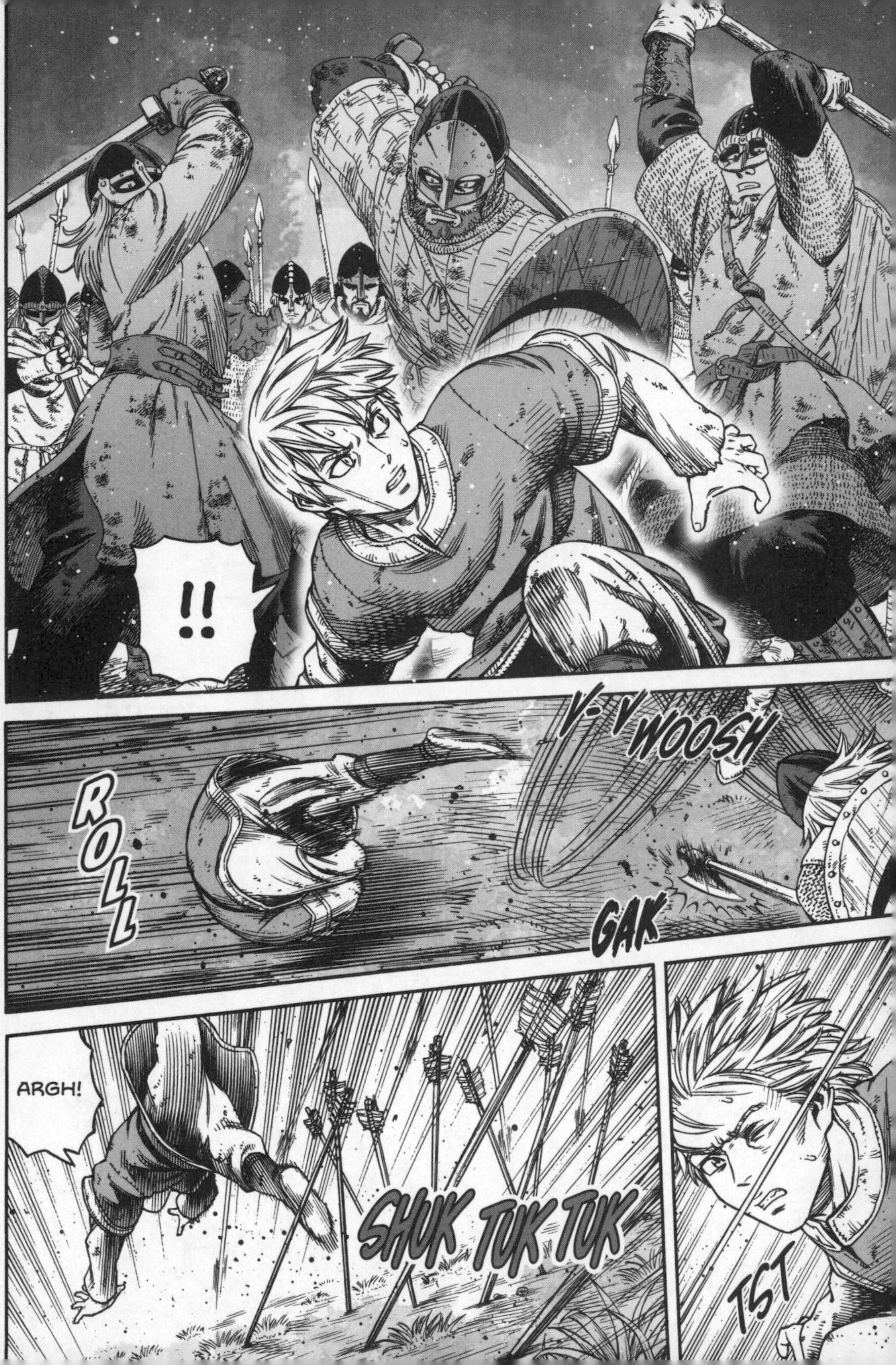
!!
V-V WOOSH
GAK
ROLL
TST
ARGH!
SHUK TUK TUK

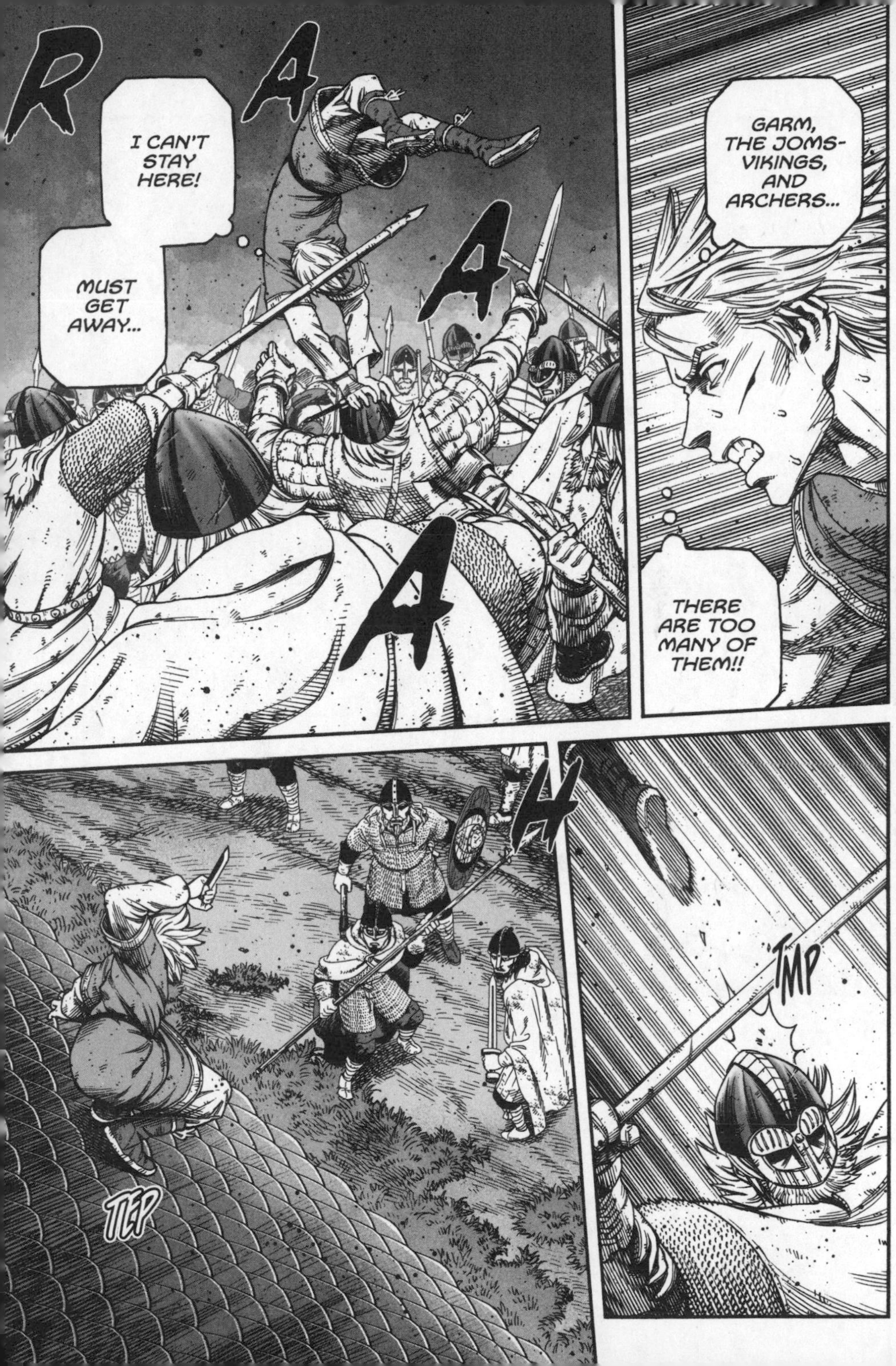
GARM, THE JOMS-VIKINGS, AND ARCHERS...
THERE ARE TOO MANY OF THEM!!
RAAAA
I CAN'T STAY HERE!
MUST GET AWAY...
TMP
H
TLEP

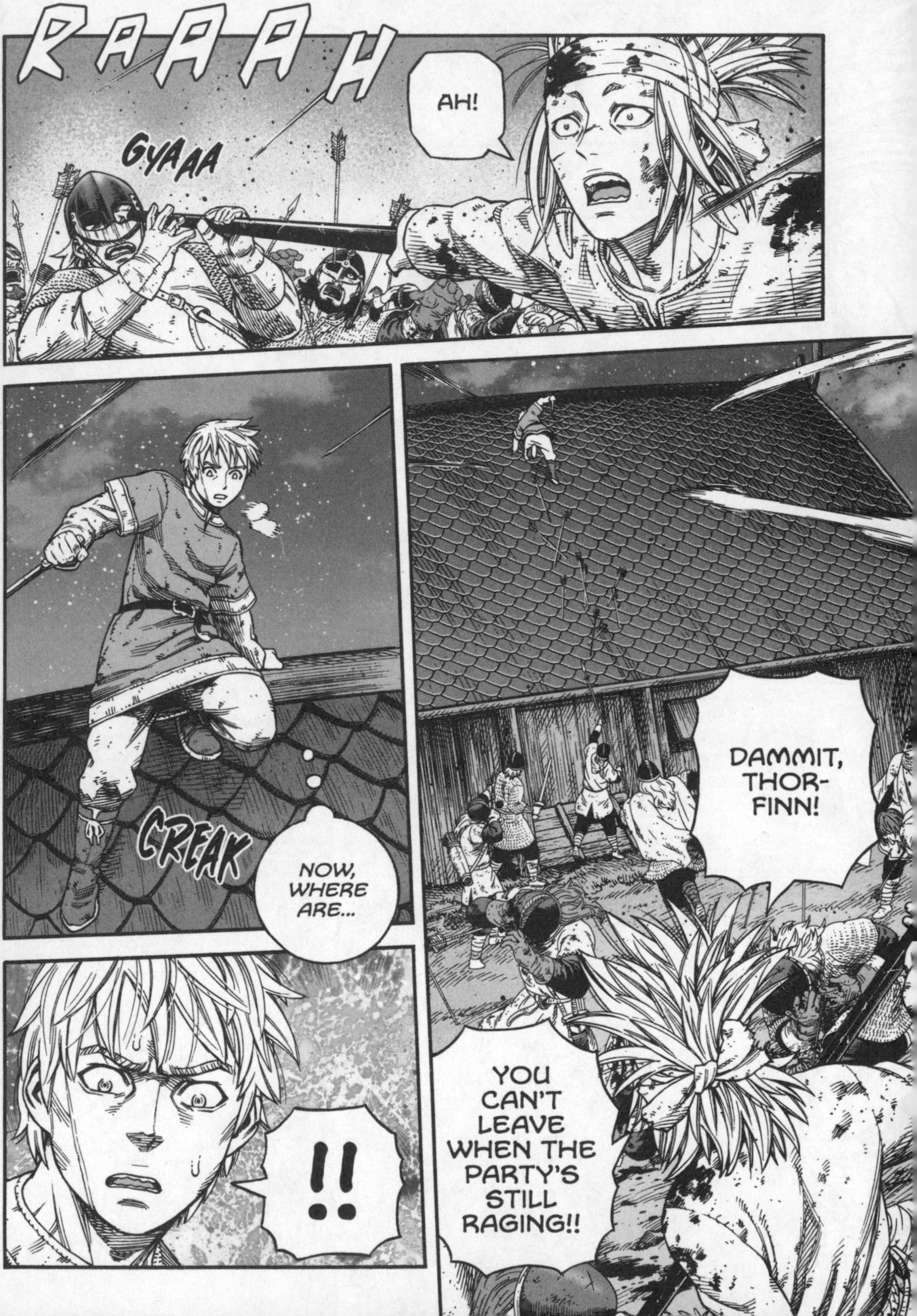
AH!
RAAAAH
GYAAA
DAMMIT, THORFINN!
YOU CAN'T LEAVE WHEN THE PARTY'S STILL RAGING!!
CREAK
NOW, WHERE ARE...
!!

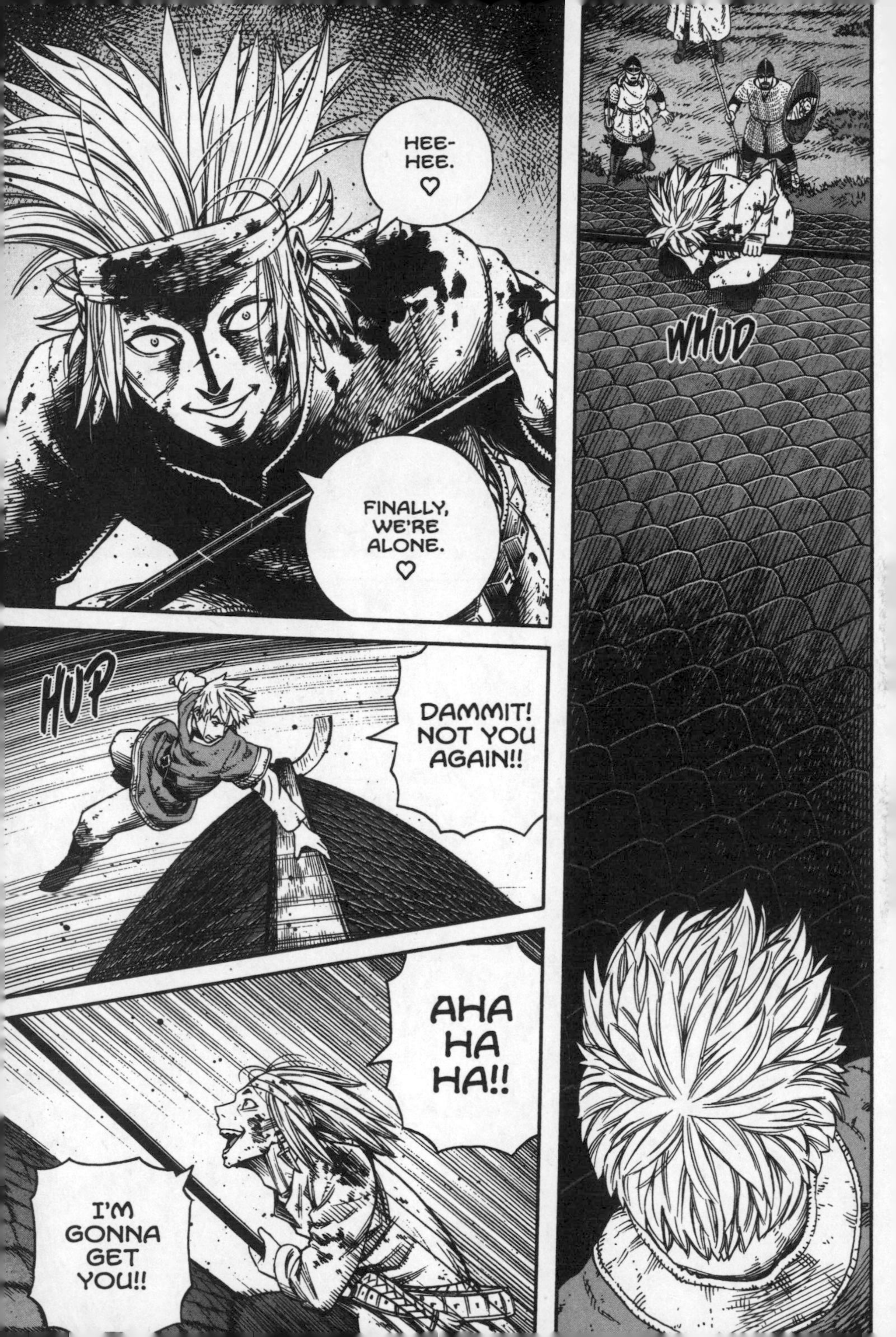
WHUD
HEE-HEE. ♡
FINALLY, WE'RE ALONE. ♡
DAMMIT! NOT YOU AGAIN!!
HUP
AHA HA HA!!
I'M GONNA GET YOU!!

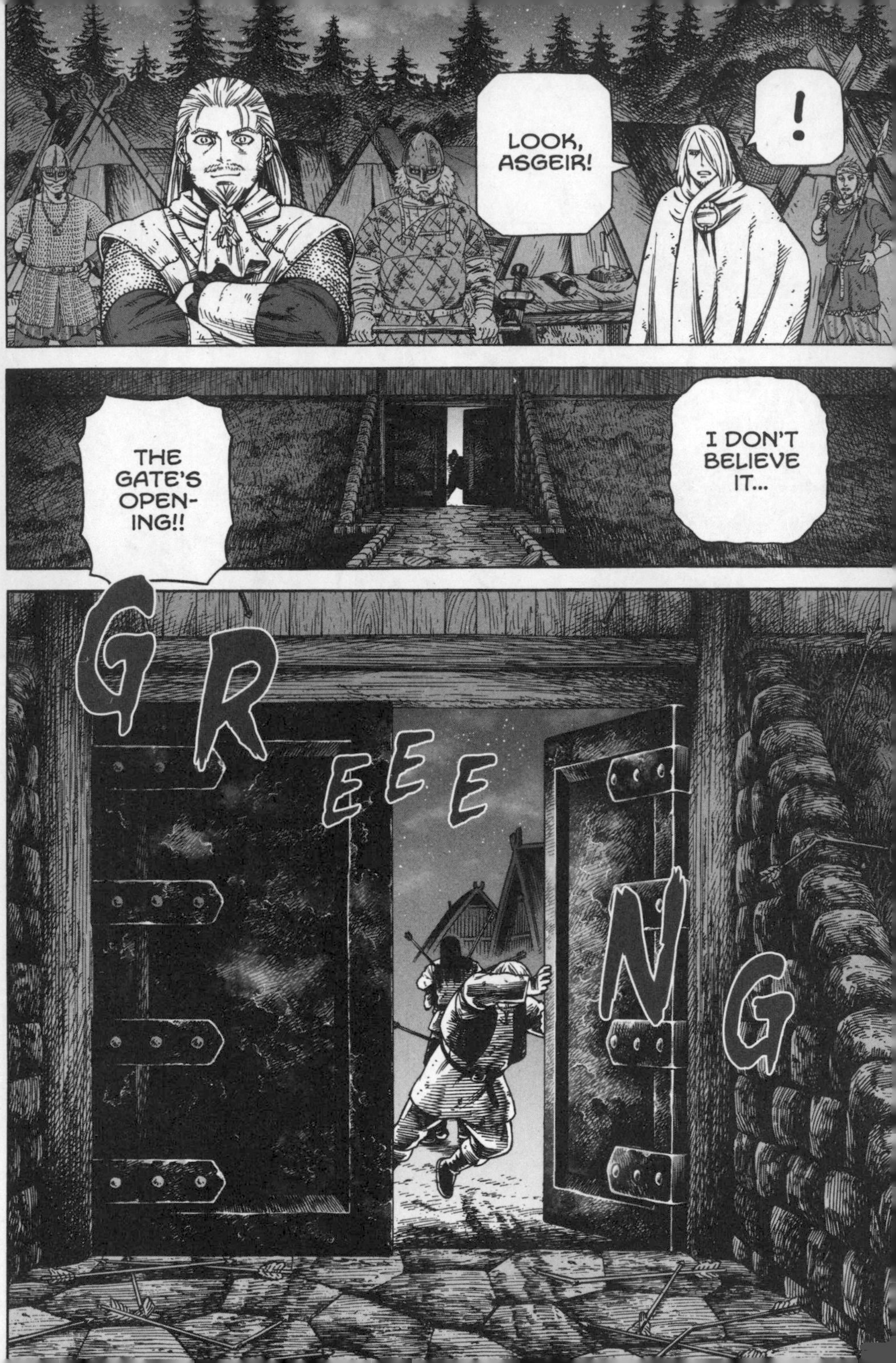
LOOK, ASGEIR!
!
THE GATE'S OPENING!!
I DON'T BELIEVE IT...
GREEENG

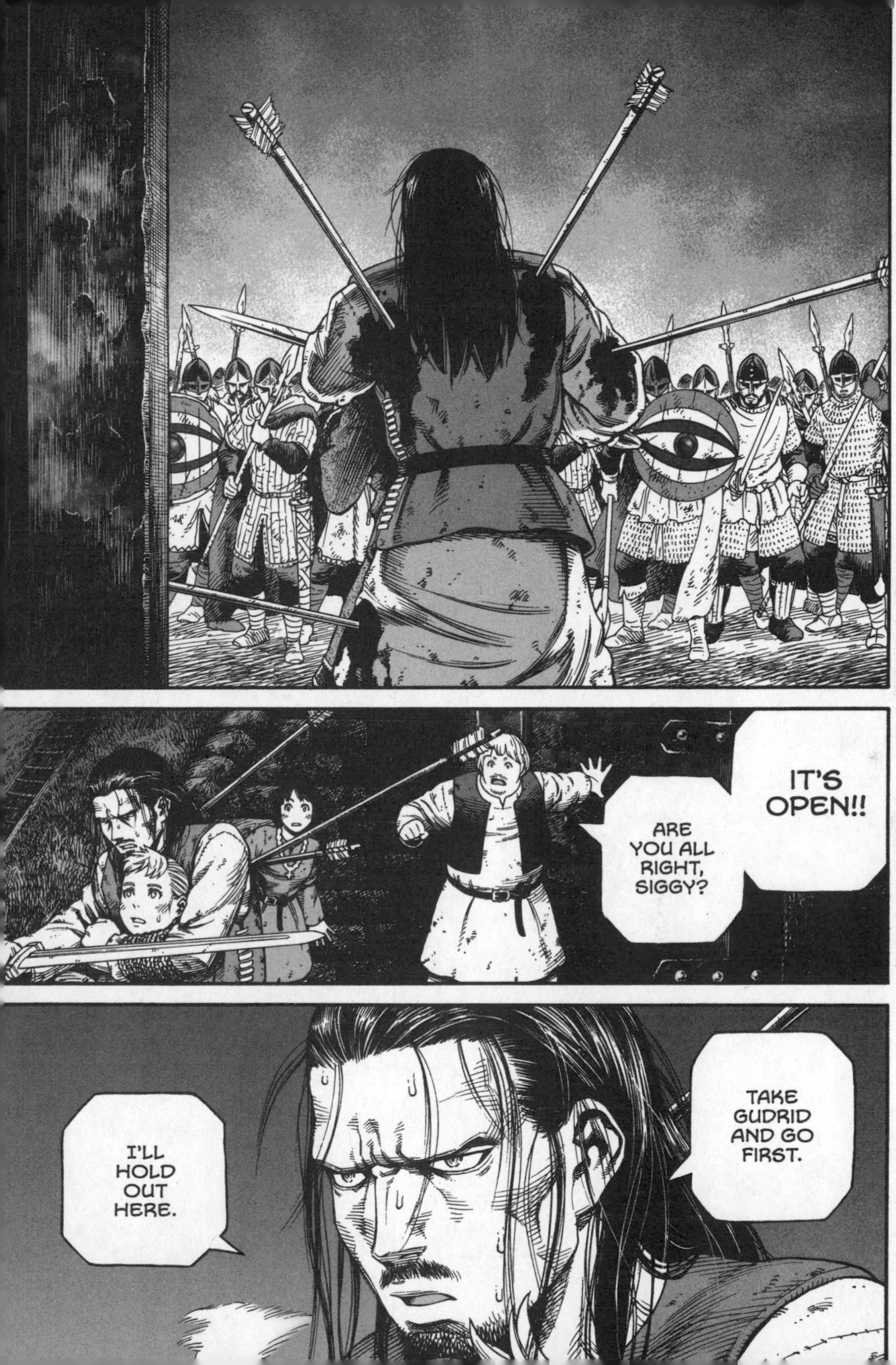
IT'S OPEN!!
ARE YOU ALL RIGHT, SIGGY?
TAKE GUDRID AND GO FIRST.
I'LL HOLD OUT HERE.

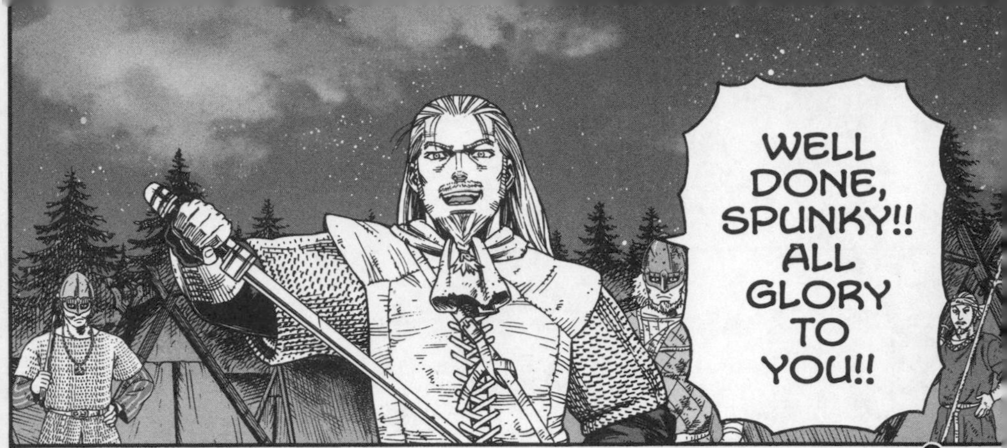
WELL DONE, SPUNKY!! ALL GLORY TO YOU!!
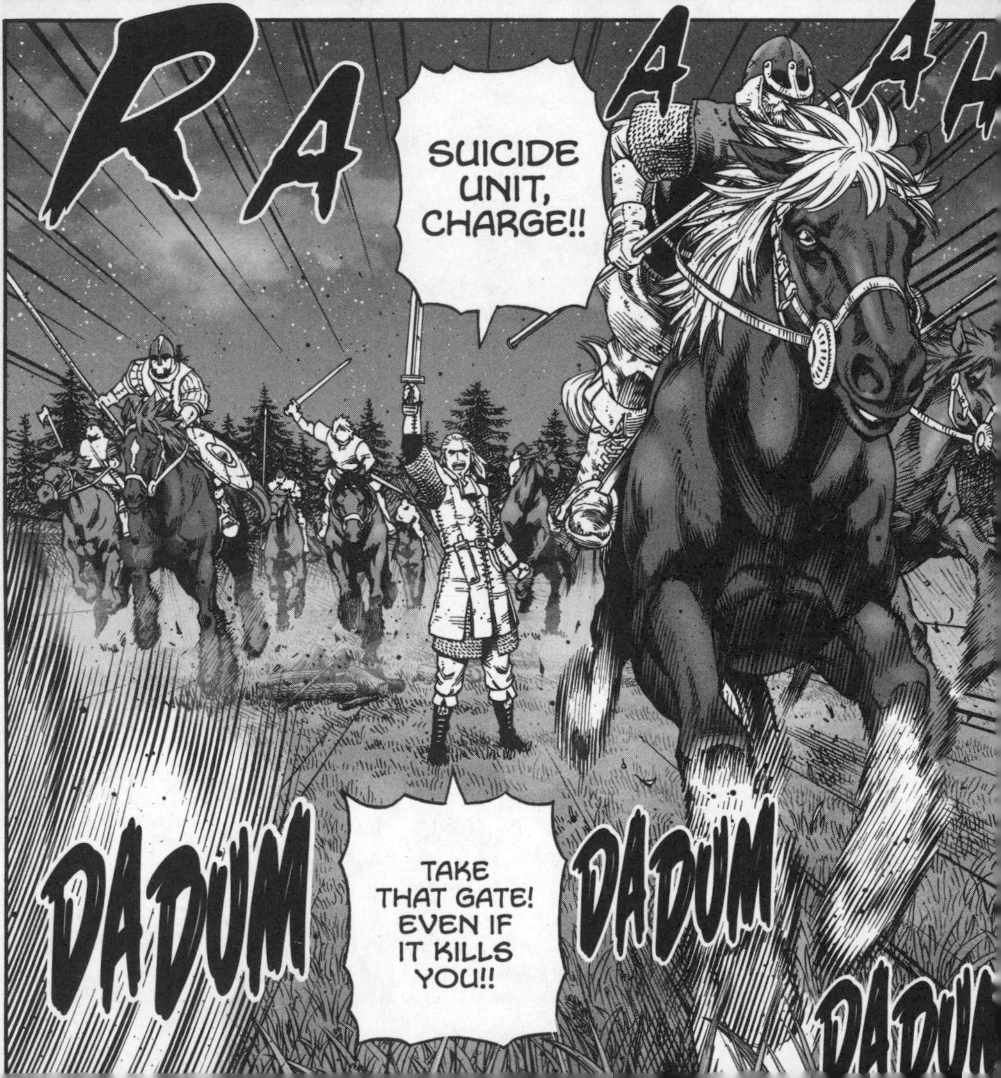
RAAAAH
SUICIDE UNIT, CHARGE!!
DADUM
TAKE THAT GATE! EVEN IF IT KILLS YOU!!
DADUM
DADUM

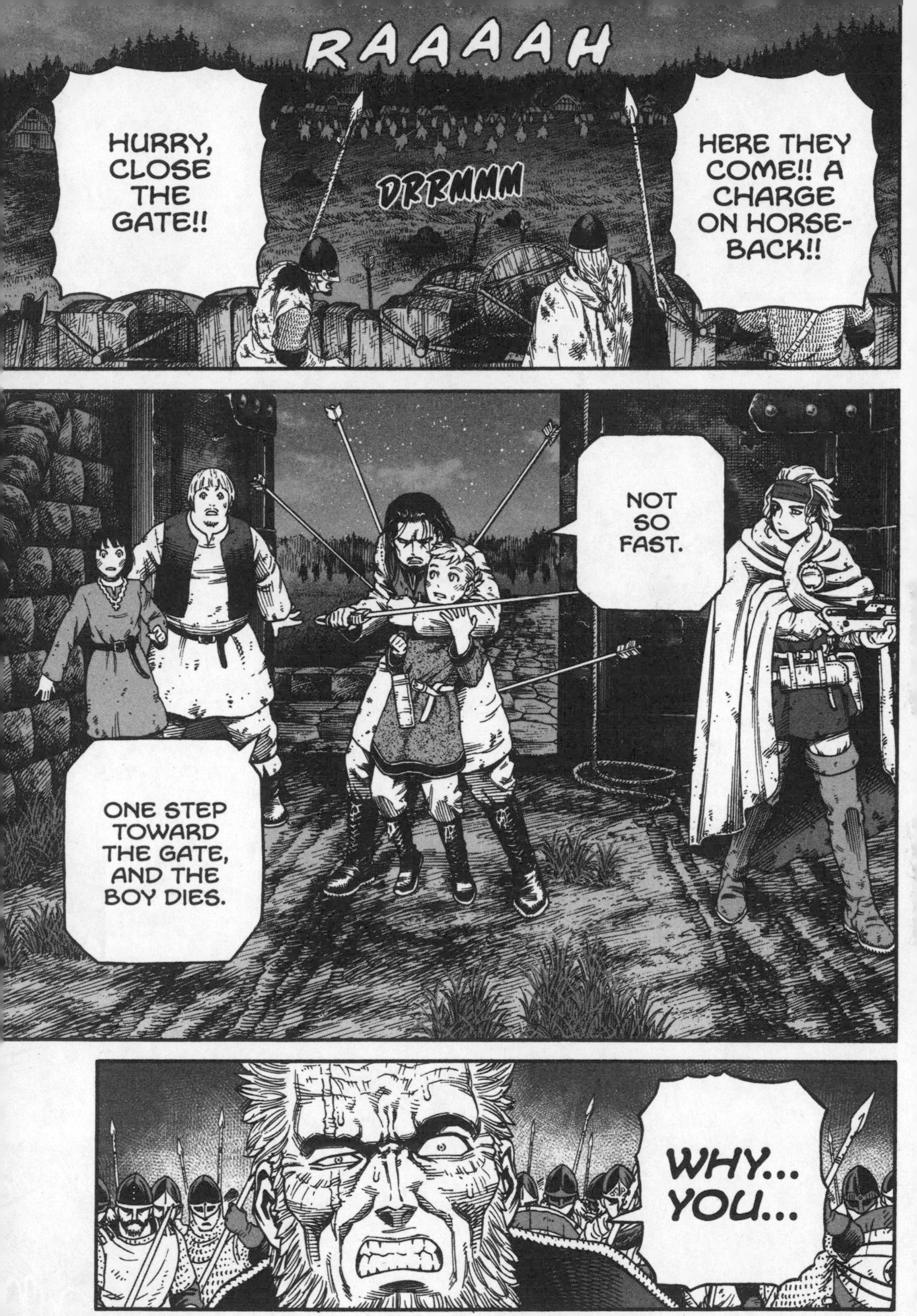
RAAAAH
HERE THEY COME!! A CHARGE ON HORSE-BACK!!
DRRMMM
HURRY, CLOSE THE GATE!!
NOT SO FAST.
ONE STEP TOWARD THE GATE, AND THE BOY DIES.
WHY... YOU...

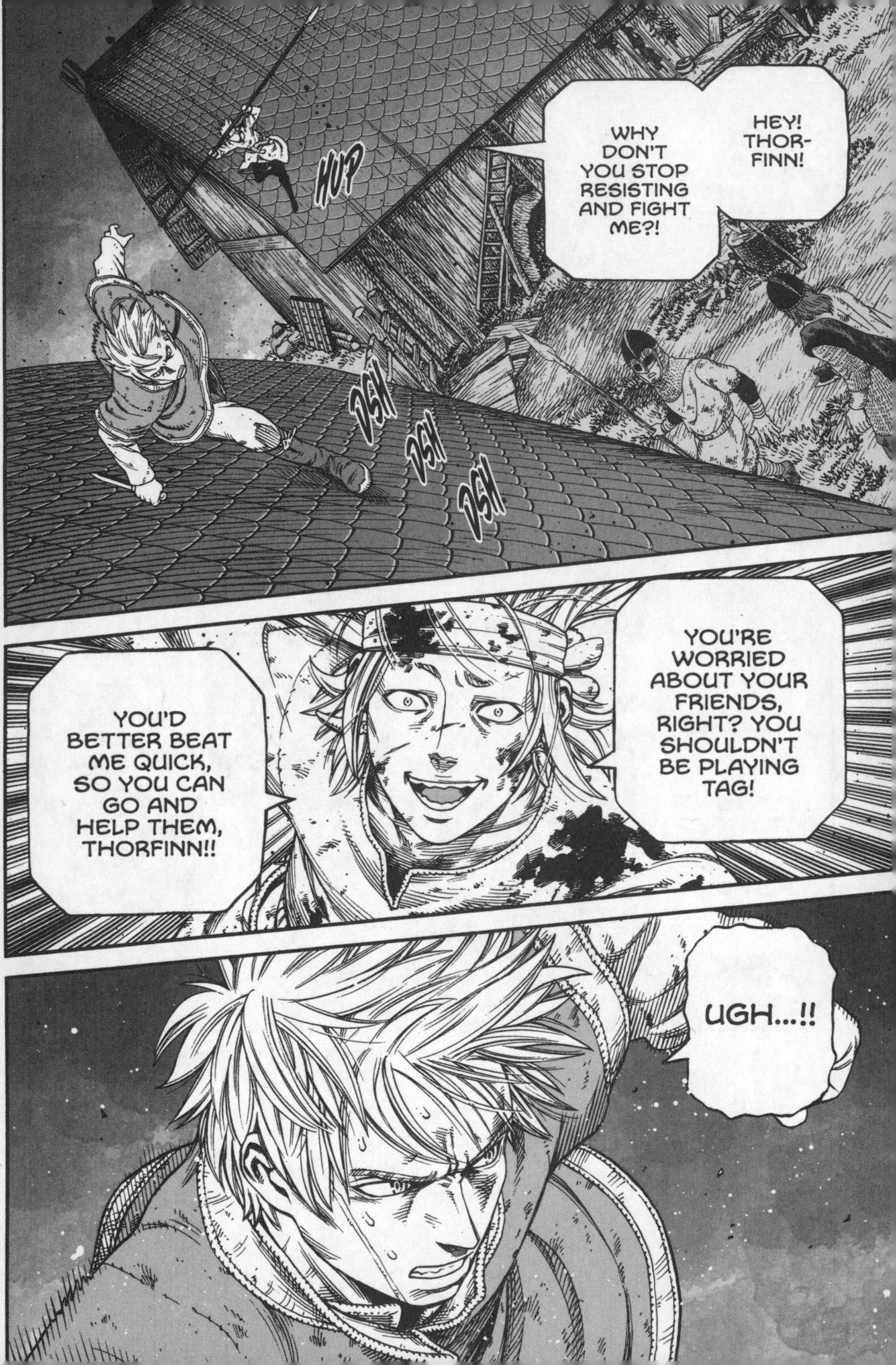
HEY! THORFINN!
WHY DON'T YOU STOP RESISTING AND FIGHT ME?!
HUP
DSH
DSH
DSH
YOU'RE WORRIED ABOUT YOUR FRIENDS, RIGHT? YOU SHOULDN'T BE PLAYING TAG!
YOU'D BETTER BEAT ME QUICK, SO YOU CAN GO AND HELP THEM, THORFINN!!
UGH...!!

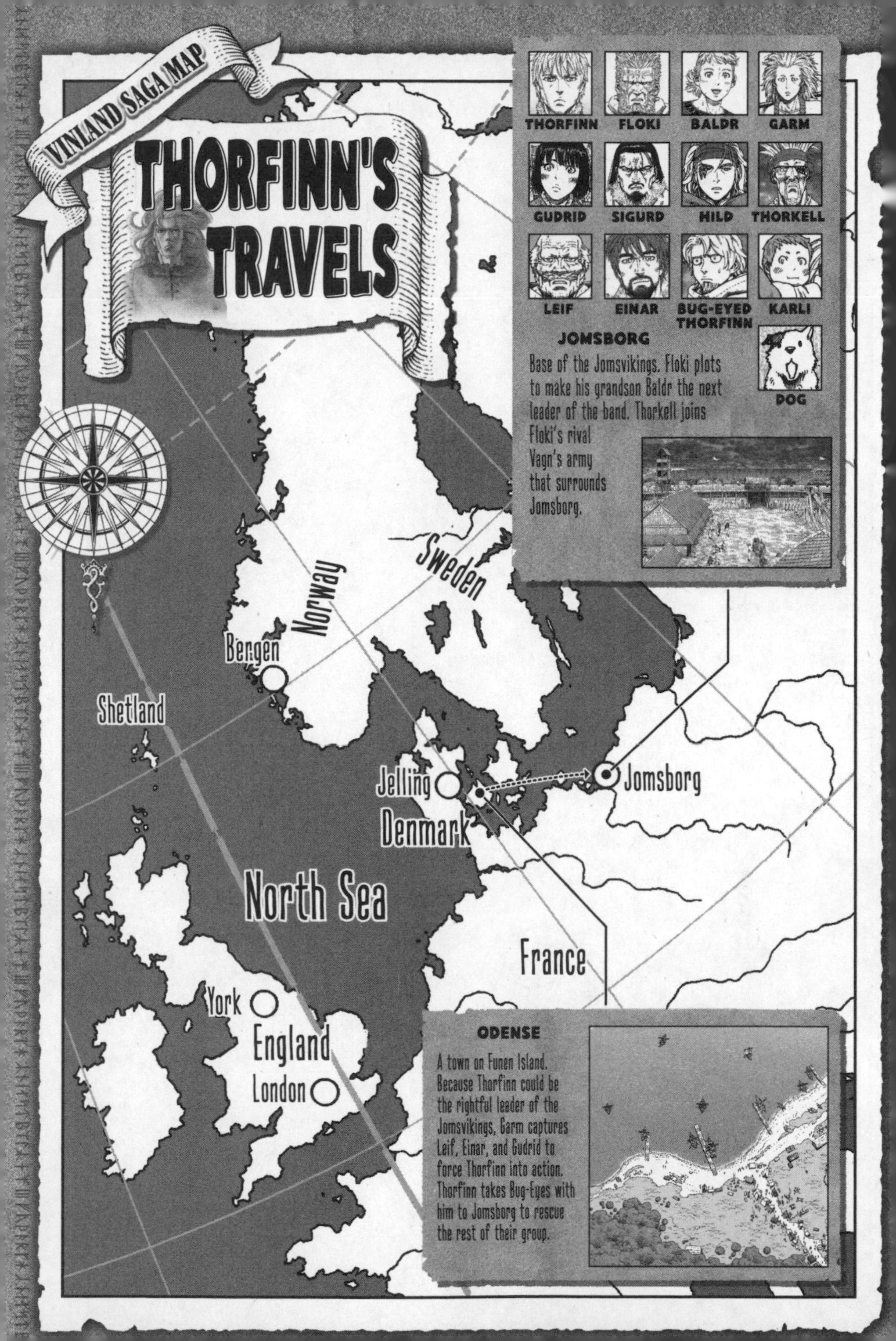
VINLAND SAGA MAP
THORFINN'S TRAVELS
THORFINN
FLOKI
BALDR
GARM
GUDRID
SIGURD
HILD
THORKELL
LEIF
EINAR
BUG-EYED THORFINN
KARLI
DOG
JOMSBORG
Base of the Jomsvikings. Floki plots to make his grandson Baldr the next leader of the band. Thorkell joins Floki's rival Vagn's army that surrounds Jomsborg.
Sweden
Norway
Bergen
Shetland
Jelling
Jomsborg
Denmark
North Sea
France
York
England
London
ODENSE
A town on Funen Island. Because Thorfinn could be the rightful leader of the Jomsvikings, Garm captures Leif, Einar, and Gudrid to force Thorfinn into action. Thorfinn takes Bug-Eyes with him to Jomsborg to rescue the rest of their group.

It's actually not clear exactly where Jomsborg existed. Some people say that the modern-day town of Wolin in Poland marks the location. According to Icelandic records, Jomsborg had a port "big enough to moor 360 ships." Apparently, the Vikings who made this mighty port their base were very stoic and disciplined, and did not allow women into the town. They pursued no agriculture; warfare was their export. It was a professional mercenary group that took part in war for payment. They threw themselves into combat with little thought for death, and never retreated. Hmm! I'm...not so sure about this! Is that not a bit too perfect?! You see, these perfect warriors were the ideal image of the Norsemen at the time—so ideal, in fact, that their existence is doubted by some. It makes you think, ahh, boys will be boys. A mere thousand years isn't going to change the things boys look up to. Everyone wants to be the hero in battle. Anyway!...I'm sorry. I'll try to be an adult.

MAKOTO YUKIMURA

VINLAND SAGA

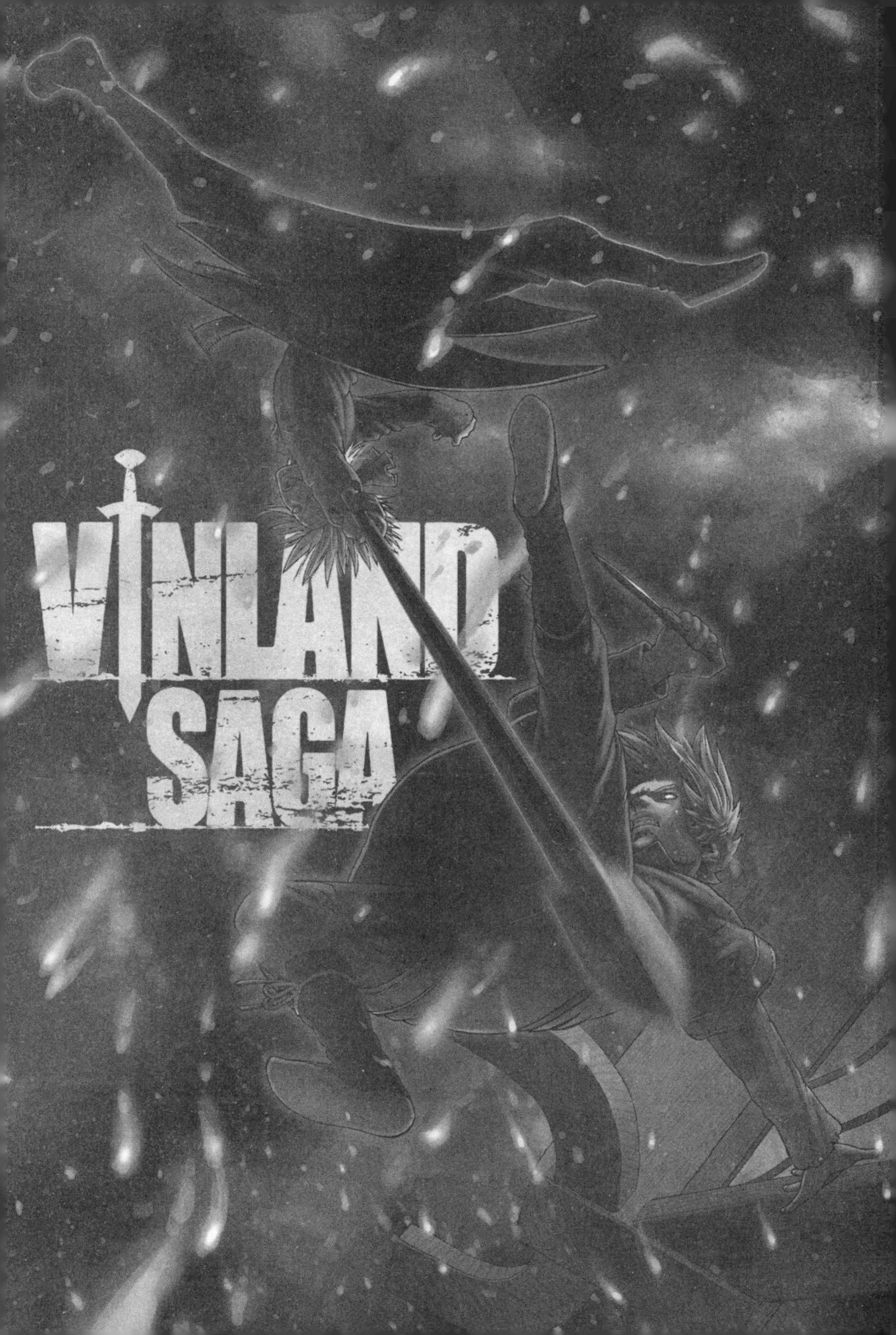
VINLAND
SAGA

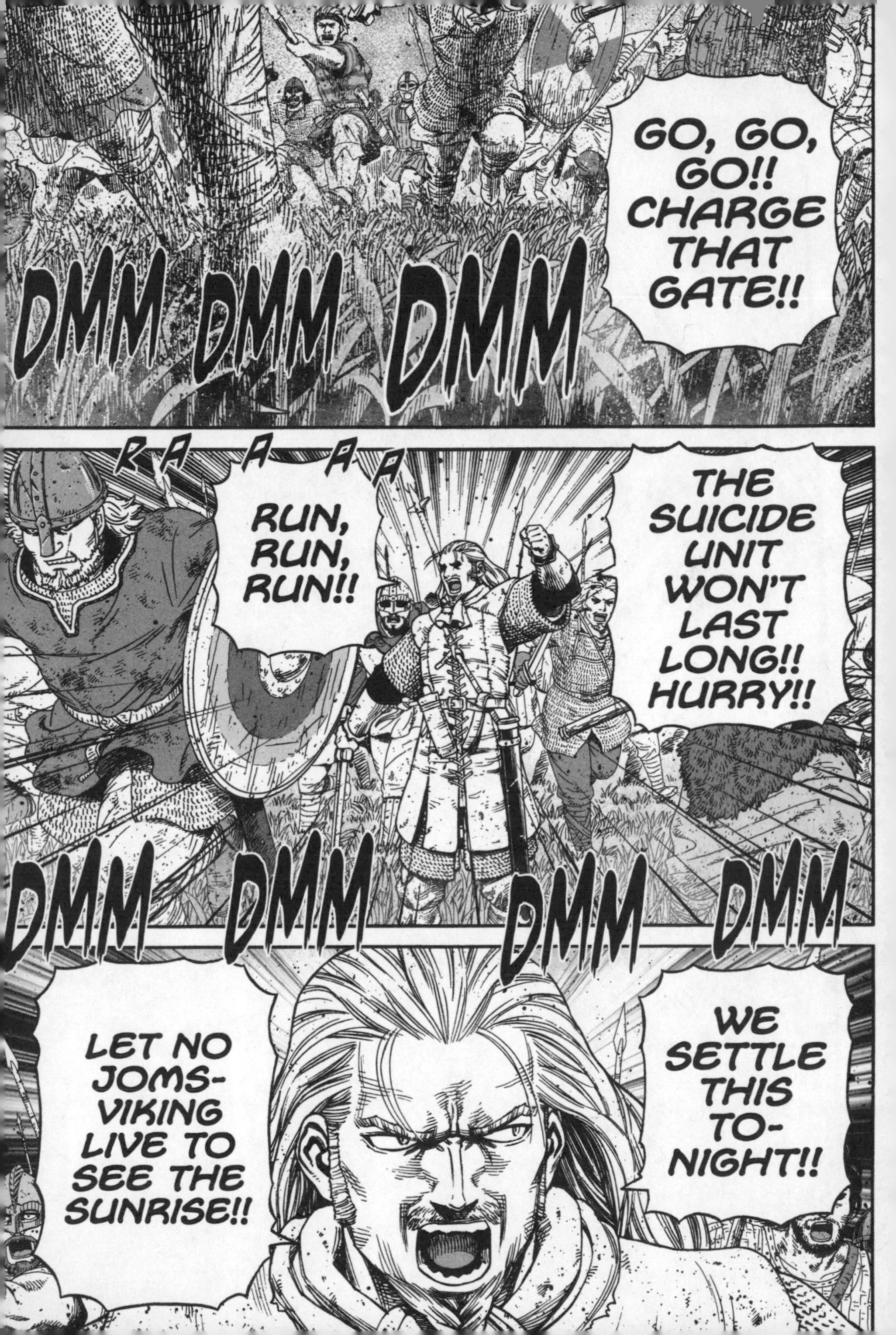
GO, GO, GO!! CHARGE THAT GATE!!
DMM DMM DMM
THE SUICIDE UNIT WON'T LAST LONG!! HURRY!!
RUN, RUN, RUN!!
RAAAA
DMM DMM DMM DMM
WE SETTLE THIS TO-NIGHT!!
LET NO JOMS-VIKING LIVE TO SEE THE SUNRISE!!

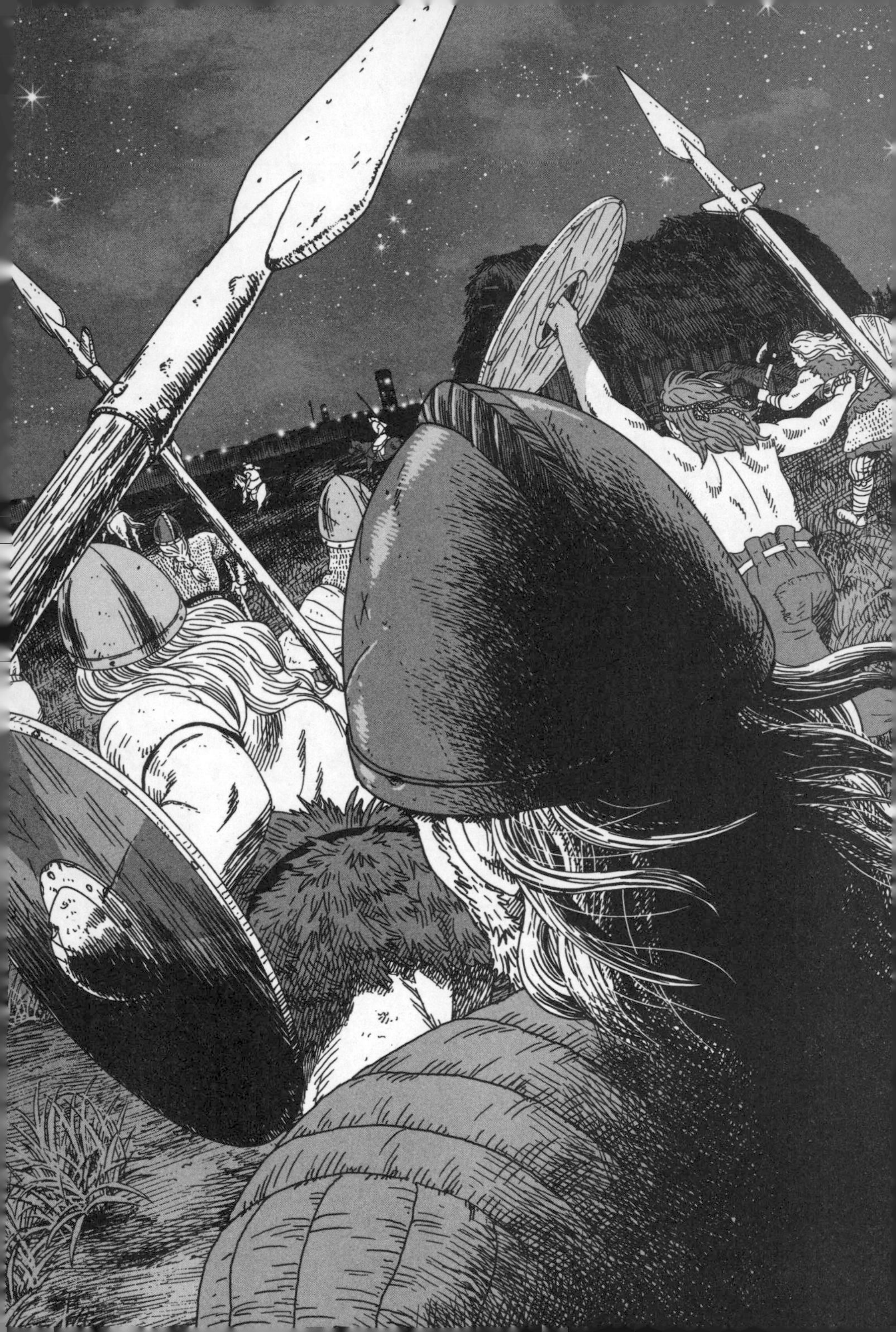

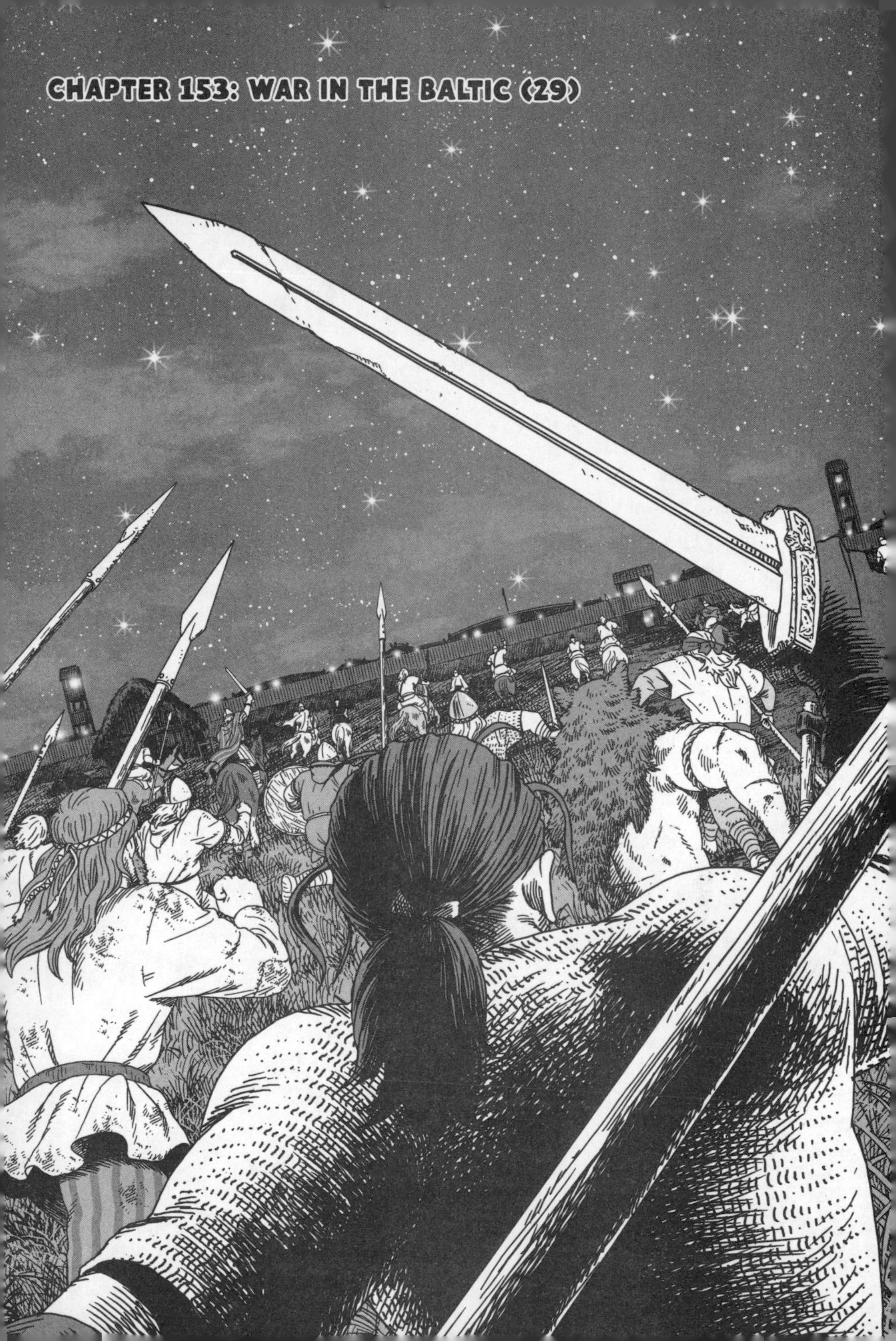
CHAPTER 153: WAR IN THE BALTIC (29)

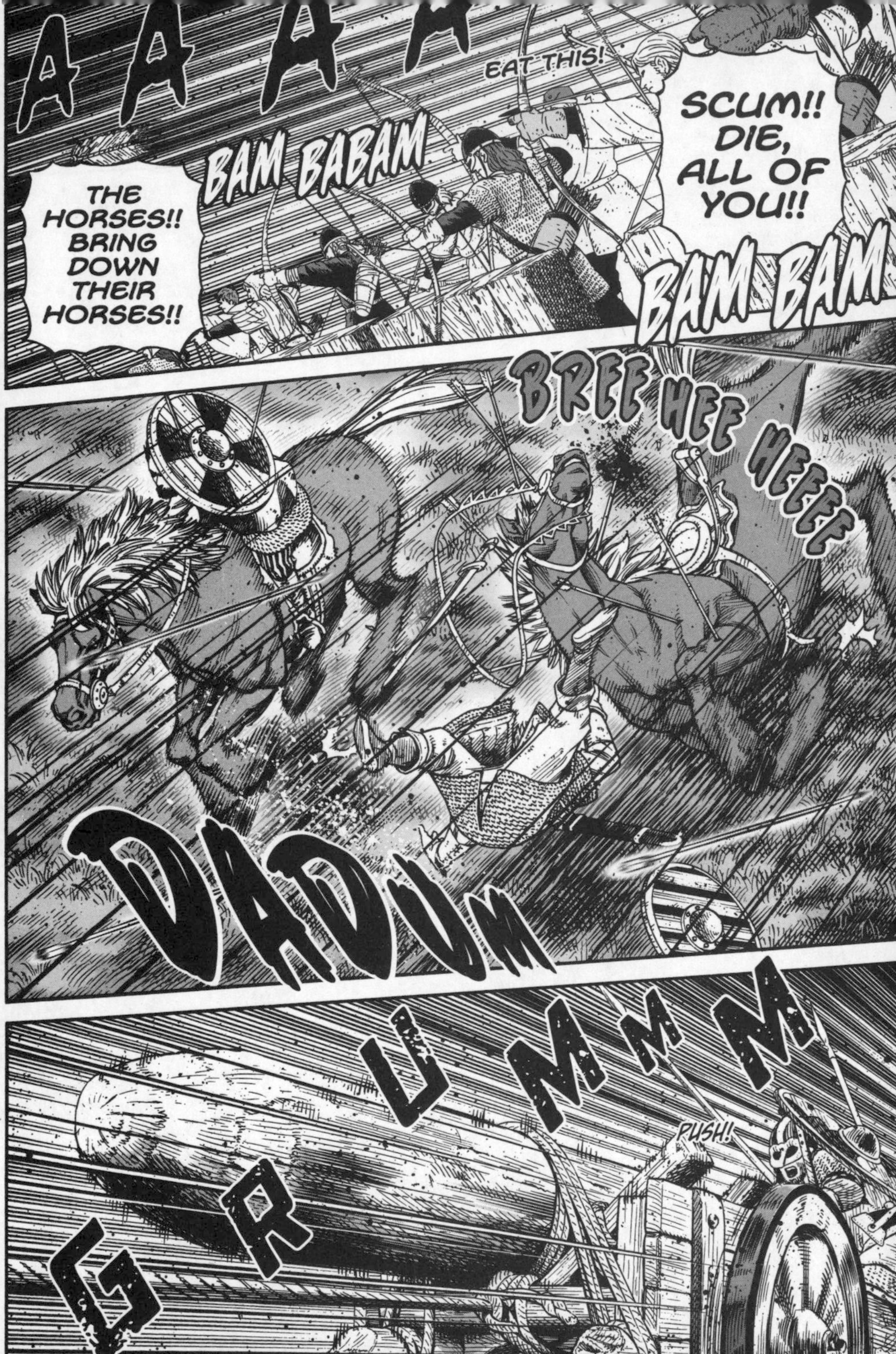
SCUM!! DIE, ALL OF YOU!!
EAT THIS!
A A A
BAM BAM
BAM BABAM
THE HORSES!! BRING DOWN THEIR HORSES!!
BREE HEE HEEEE
DADUM
PUSH!
G R U M M M

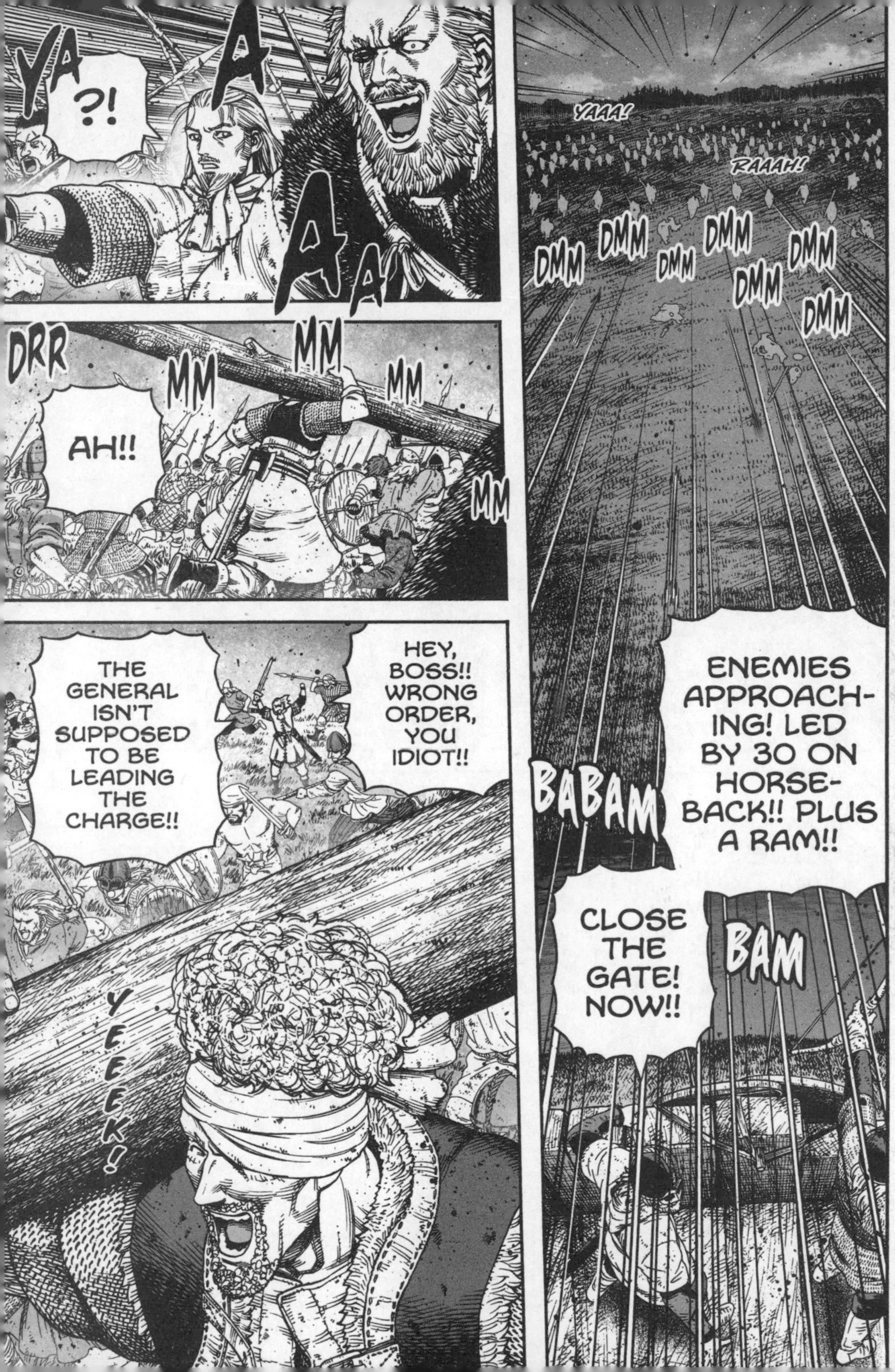
YAAA!
RAAAH!
DMM DMM DMM DMM DMM DMM DMM
ENEMIES APPROACH-ING! LED BY 30 ON HORSE-BACK!! PLUS A RAM!!
BABAM
CLOSE THE GATE! NOW!!
BAM
YAAAA
?!
DRR MM MM MM MM
AH!!
HEY, BOSS!! WRONG ORDER, YOU IDIOT!!
THE GENERAL ISN'T SUPPOSED TO BE LEADING THE CHARGE!!
YEEEK!

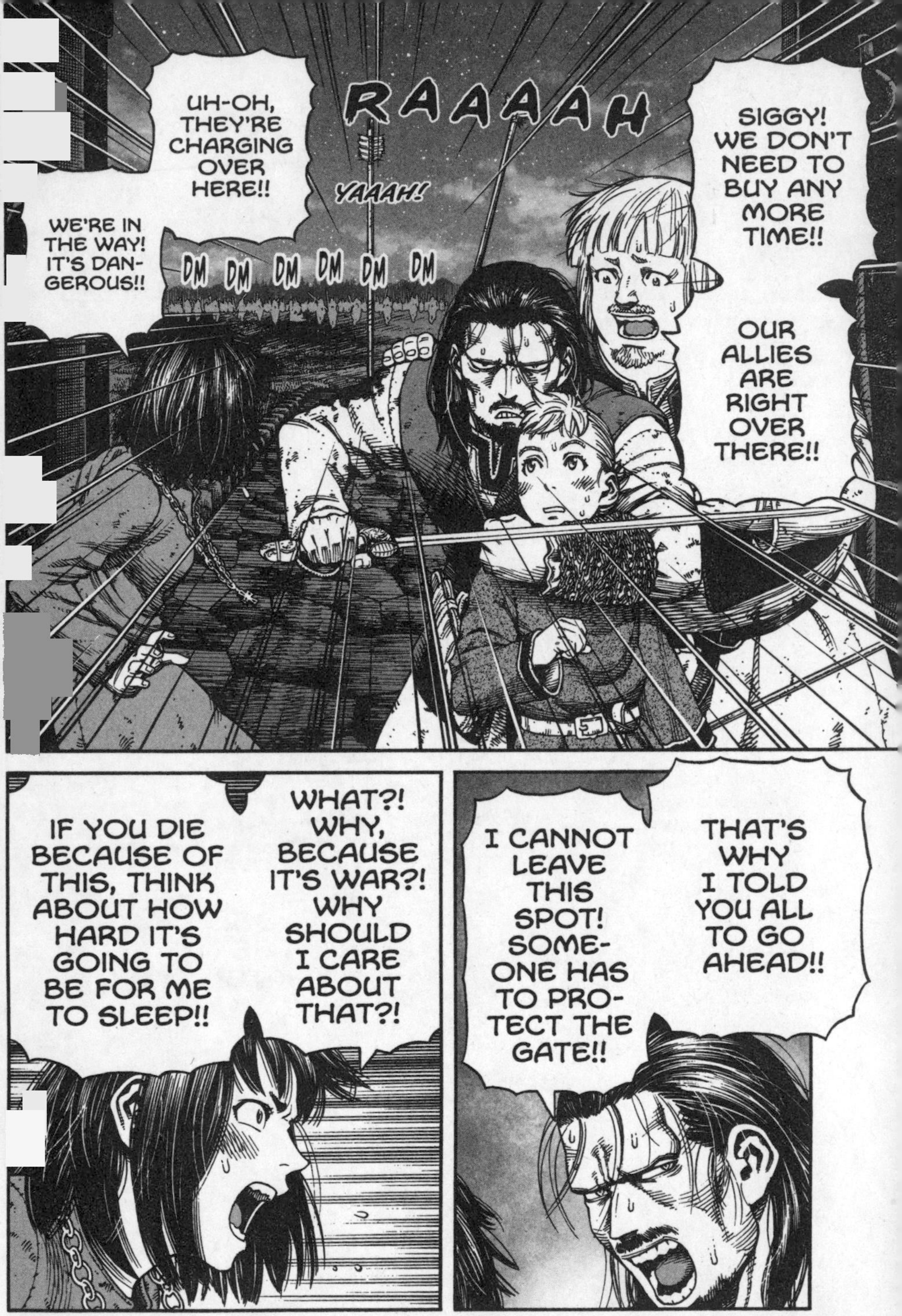
SIGGY! WE DON'T NEED TO BUY ANY MORE TIME!!
OUR ALLIES ARE RIGHT OVER THERE!!
RAAAAH
YAAAH!
UH-OH, THEY'RE CHARGING OVER HERE!!
WE'RE IN THE WAY! IT'S DAN-GEROUS!!
DM DM DM DM DM DM
THAT'S WHY I TOLD YOU ALL TO GO AHEAD!!
I CANNOT LEAVE THIS SPOT! SOME-ONE HAS TO PRO-TECT THE GATE!!
WHAT?! WHY, BECAUSE IT'S WAR?! WHY SHOULD I CARE ABOUT THAT?!
IF YOU DIE BECAUSE OF THIS, THINK ABOUT HOW HARD IT'S GOING TO BE FOR ME TO SLEEP!!

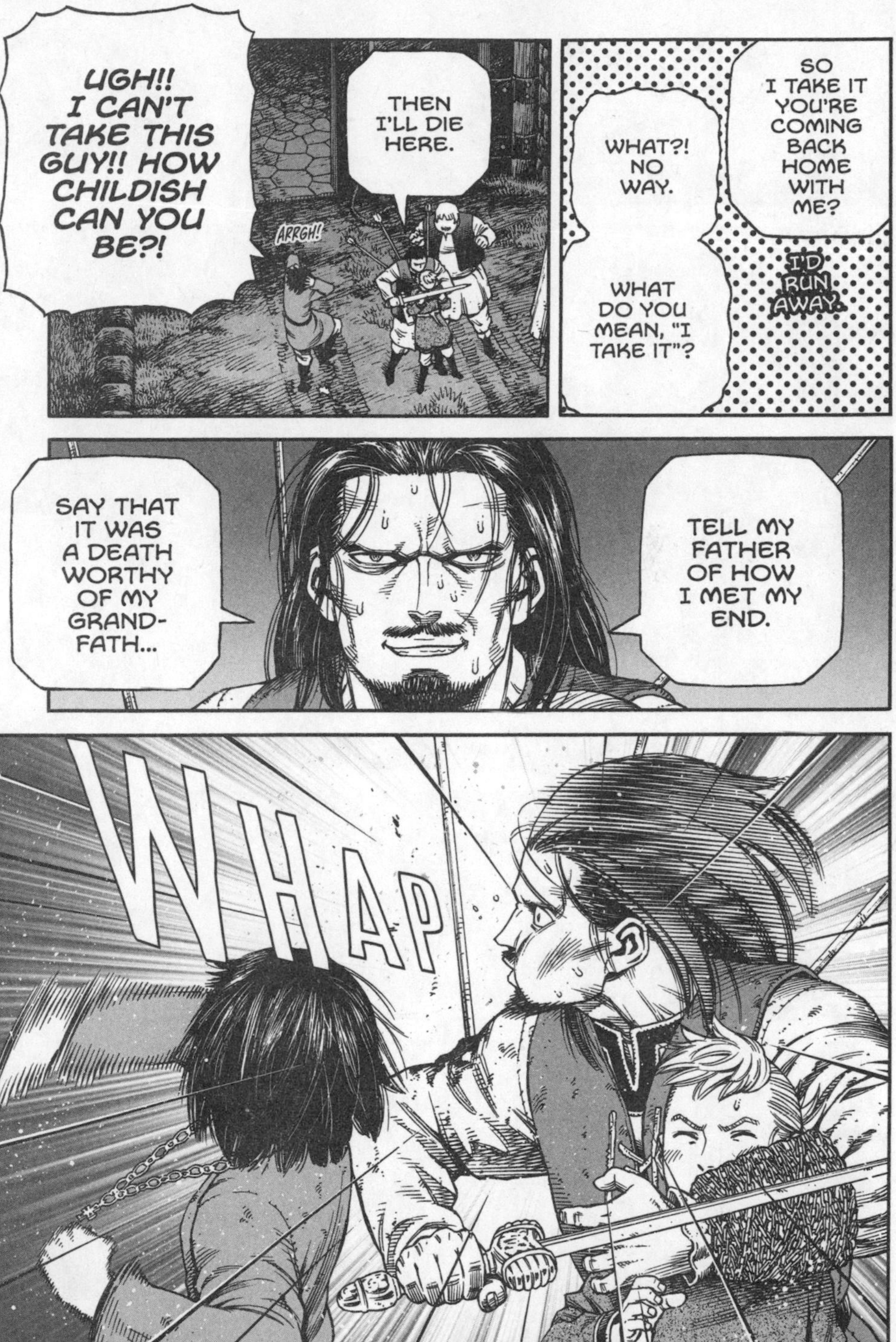
SO I TAKE IT YOU'RE COMING BACK HOME WITH ME?
I'D RUN AWAY.
WHAT?! NO WAY.
WHAT DO YOU MEAN, "I TAKE IT"?
THEN I'LL DIE HERE.
ARRGH!
UGH!! I CAN'T TAKE THIS GUY!! HOW CHILDISH CAN YOU BE?!
TELL MY FATHER OF HOW I MET MY END.
SAY THAT IT WAS A DEATH WORTHY OF MY GRAND-FATH...
WHAP

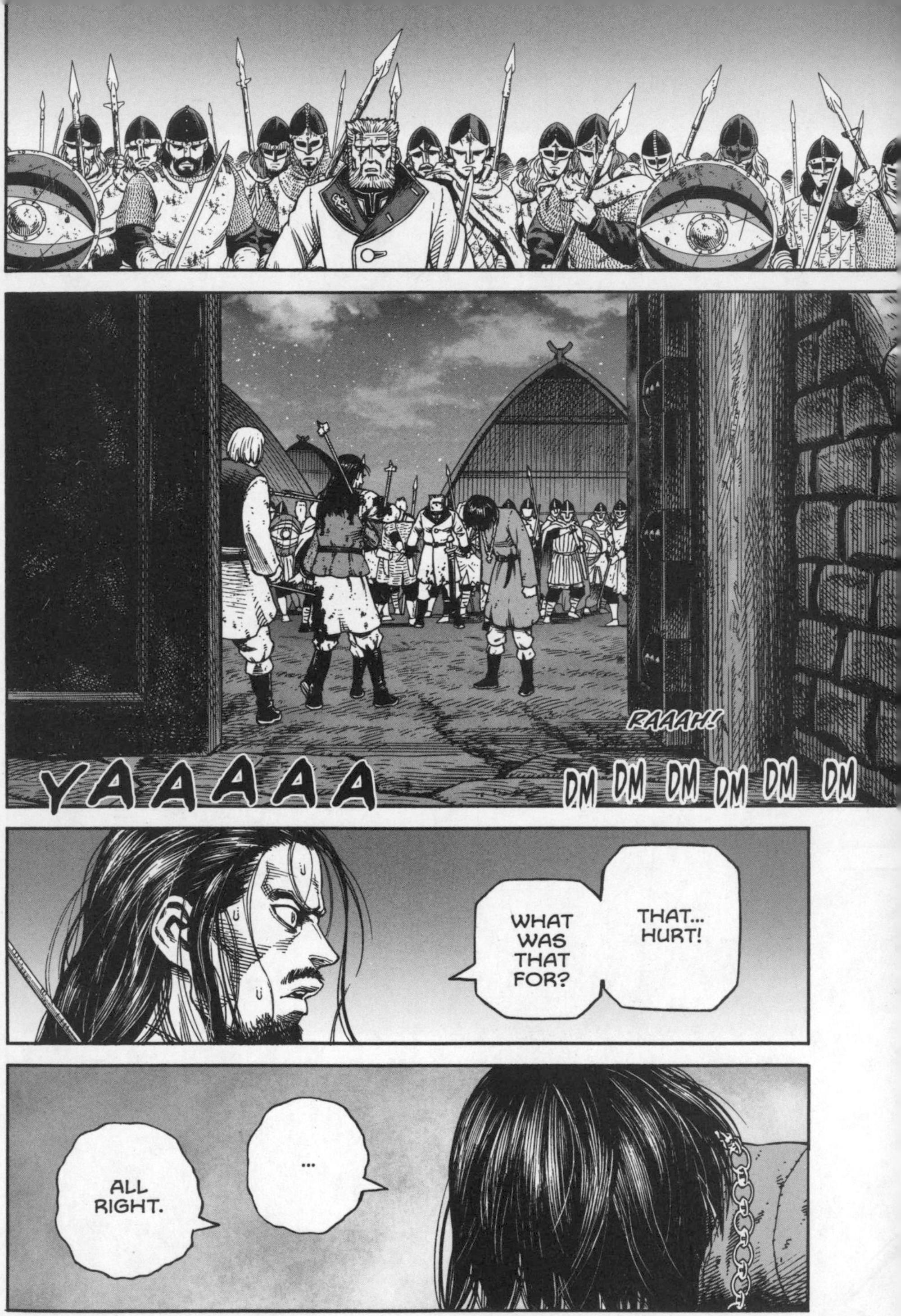
RAAAH!
DM DM DM DM DM DM
YAAAAA
THAT... HURT!
WHAT WAS THAT FOR?
...
ALL RIGHT.

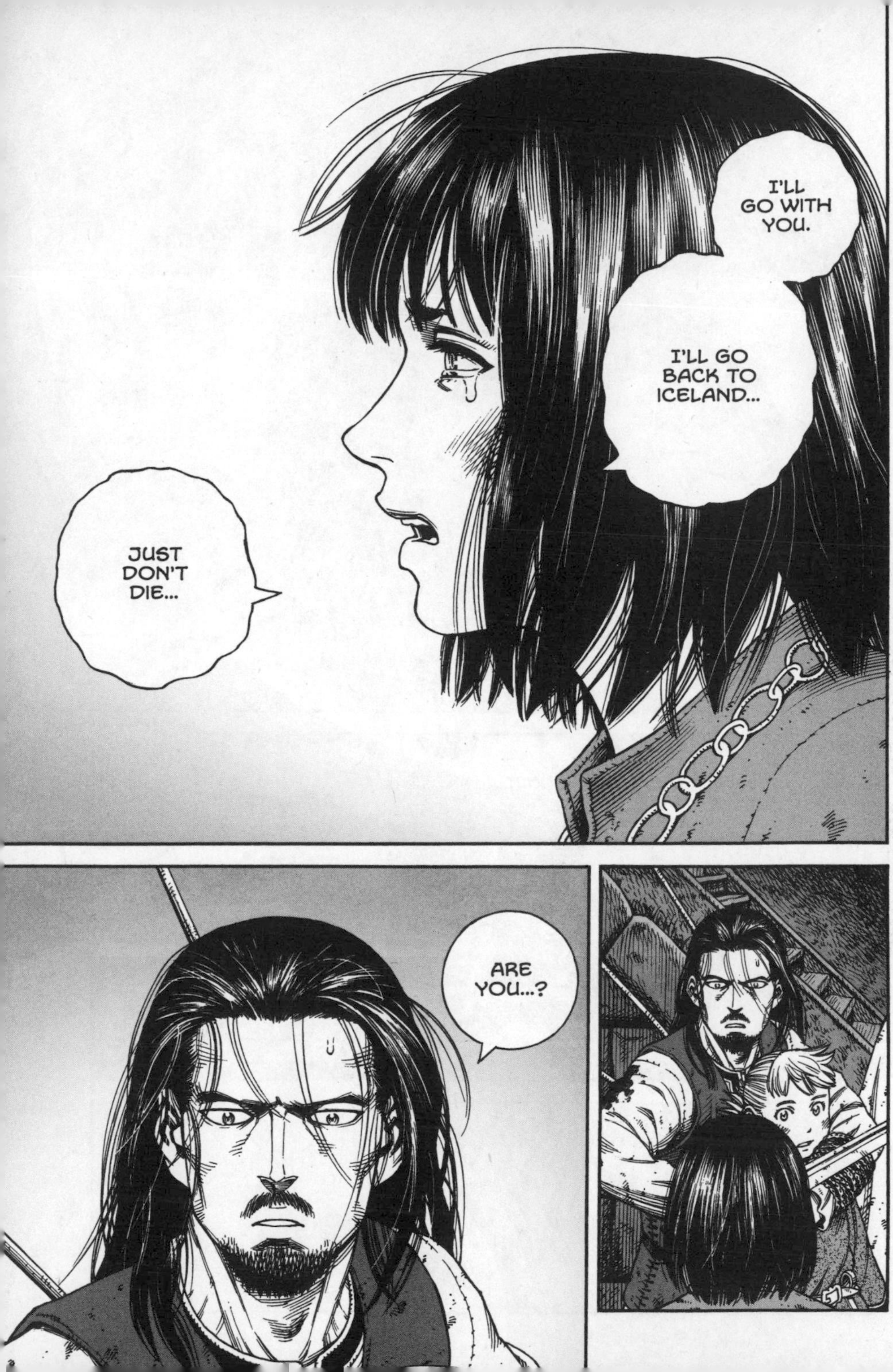
I'LL GO WITH YOU.
I'LL GO BACK TO ICELAND...
JUST DON'T DIE...
ARE YOU...?

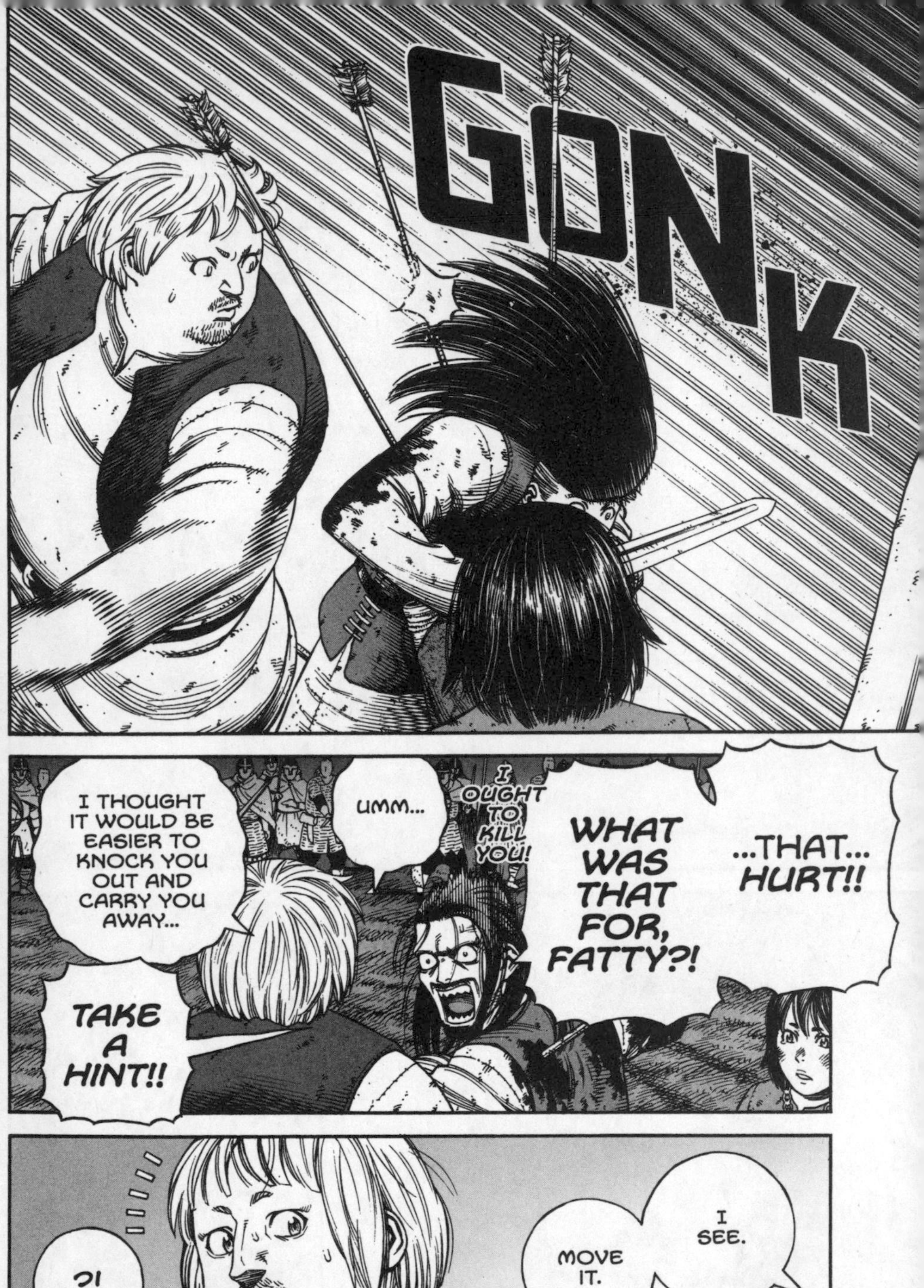
GONK
...THAT... HURT!!
WHAT WAS THAT FOR, FATTY?!
I OUGHT TO KILL YOU!
UMM...
I THOUGHT IT WOULD BE EASIER TO KNOCK YOU OUT AND CARRY YOU AWAY...
TAKE A HINT!!
I SEE.
MOVE IT.
?!

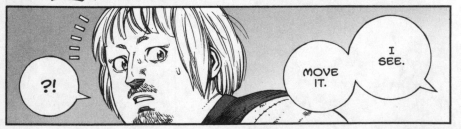

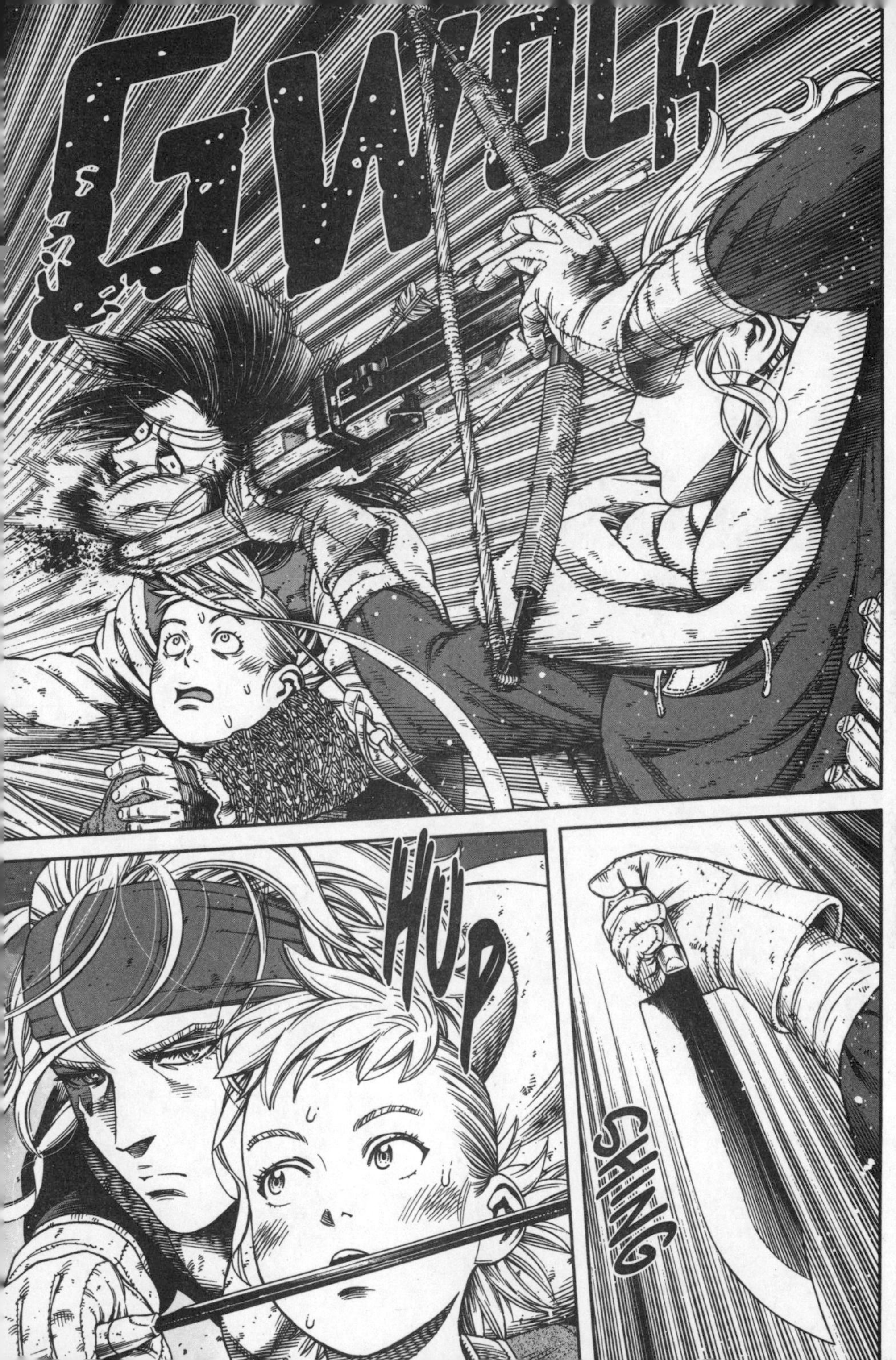
GWOLK
SHING
HUP

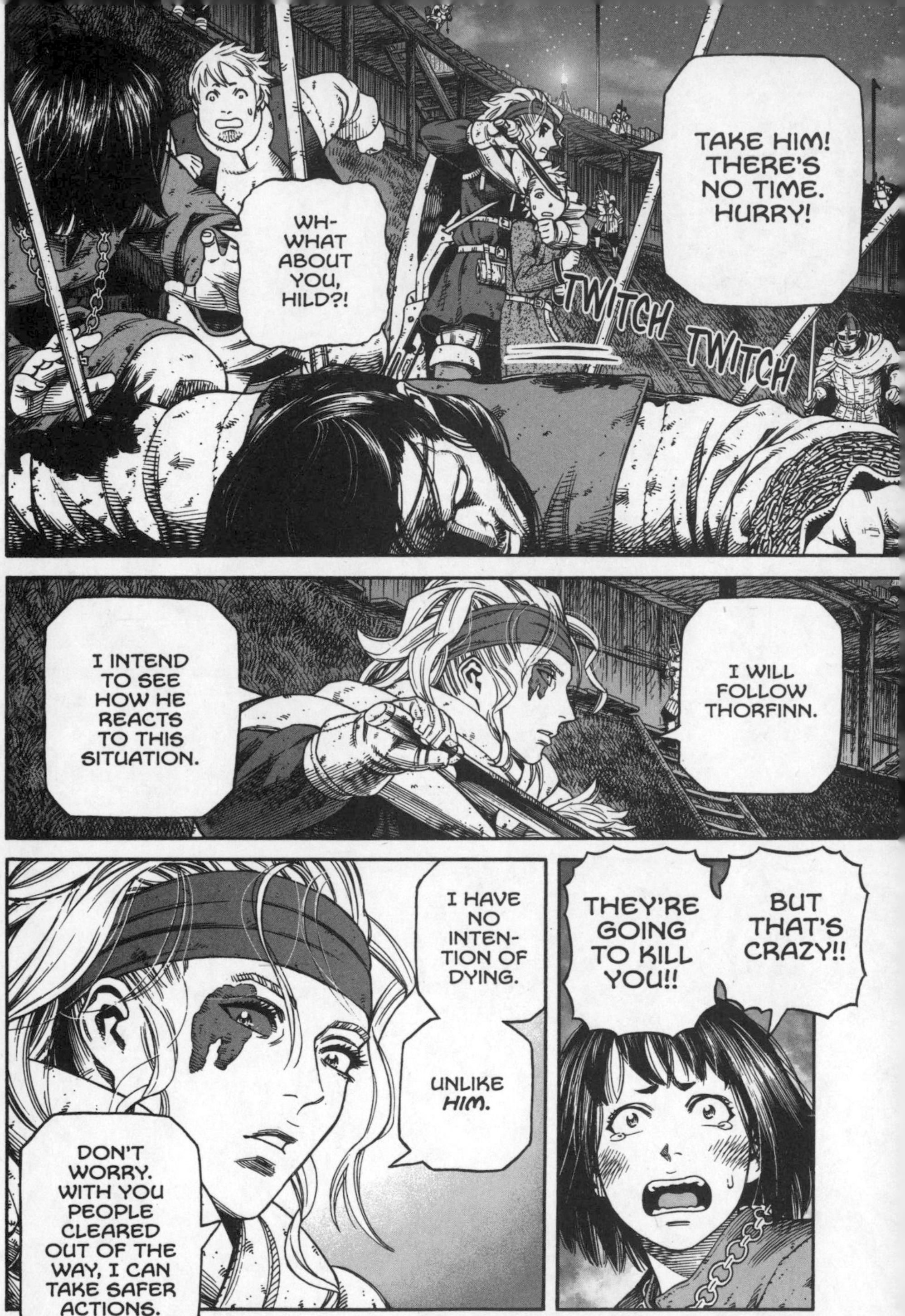
TAKE HIM! THERE'S NO TIME. HURRY!
WH- WHAT ABOUT YOU, HILD?!
TWITCH TWITCH
I WILL FOLLOW THORFINN.
I INTEND TO SEE HOW HE REACTS TO THIS SITUATION.
BUT THAT'S CRAZY!!
THEY'RE GOING TO KILL YOU!!
I HAVE NO INTEN- TION OF DYING.
UNLIKE *HIM.*
DON'T WORRY. WITH YOU PEOPLE CLEARED OUT OF THE WAY, I CAN TAKE SAFER ACTIONS.

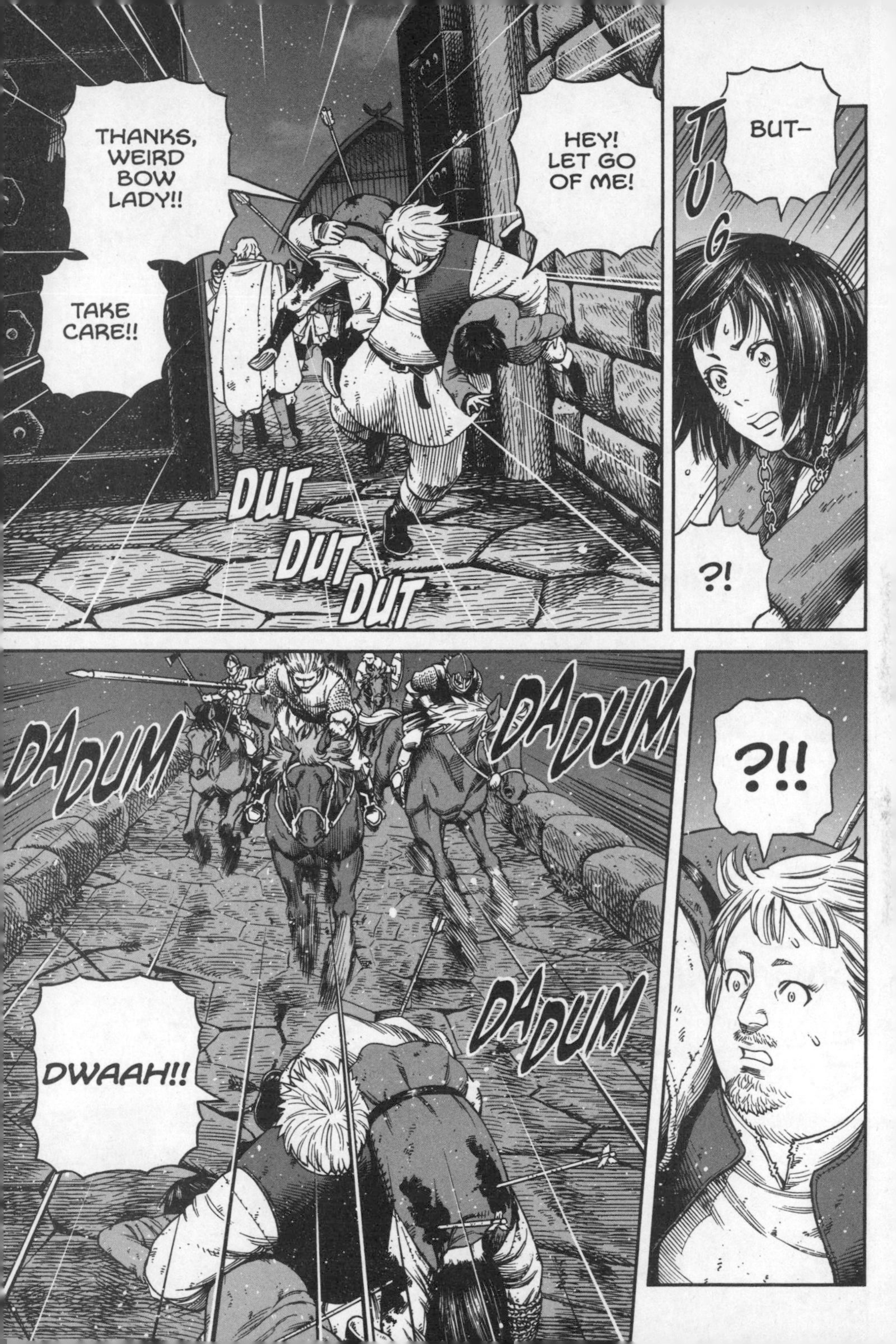
BUT–
TUG
?!
HEY! LET GO OF ME!
THANKS, WEIRD BOW LADY!!
TAKE CARE!!
DUT DUT DUT
?!!
DADUM
DADUM
DADUM
DWAAH!!

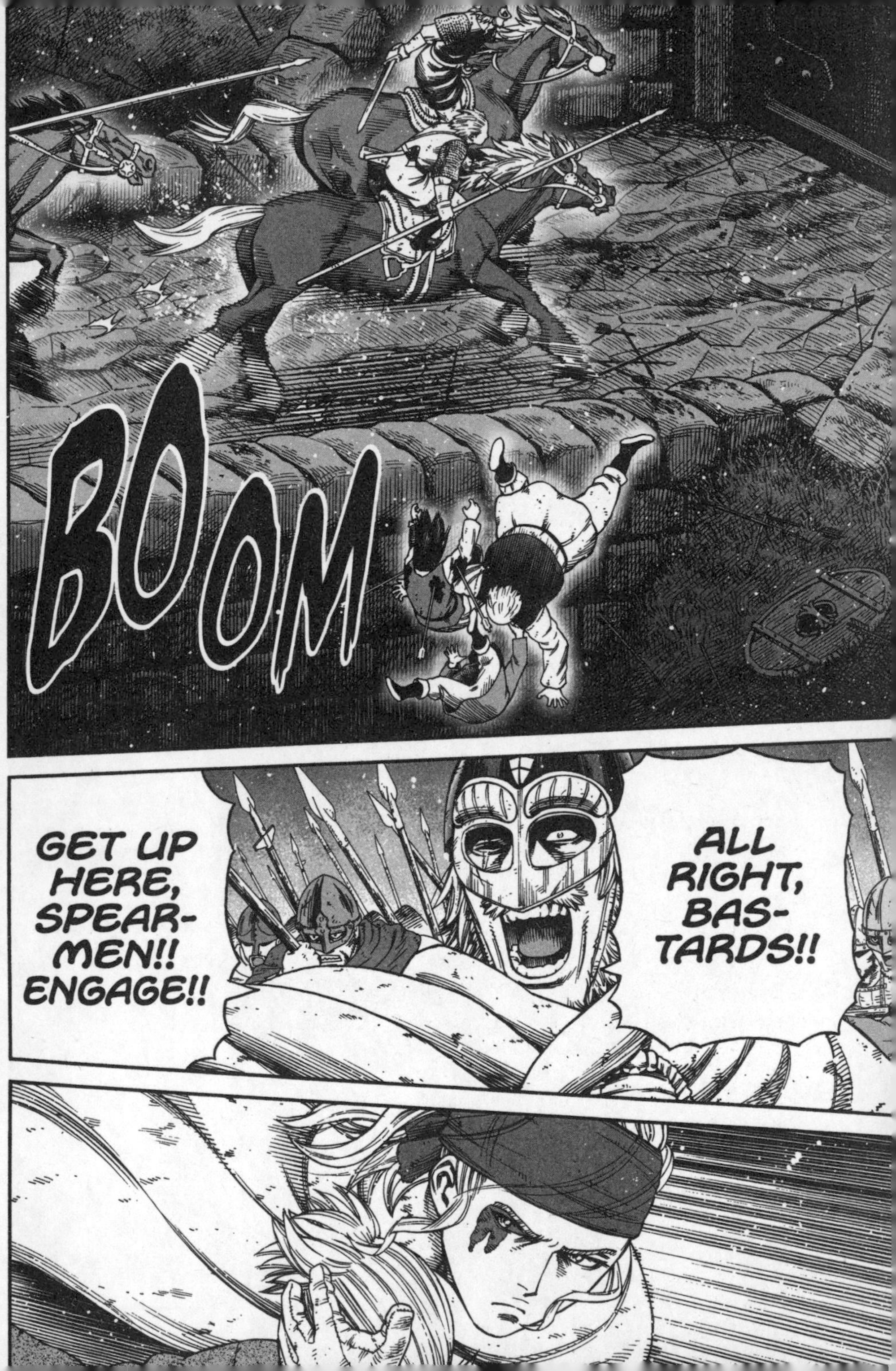
BOOM
ALL RIGHT, BAS-TARDS!!
GET UP HERE, SPEAR-MEN!! ENGAGE!!

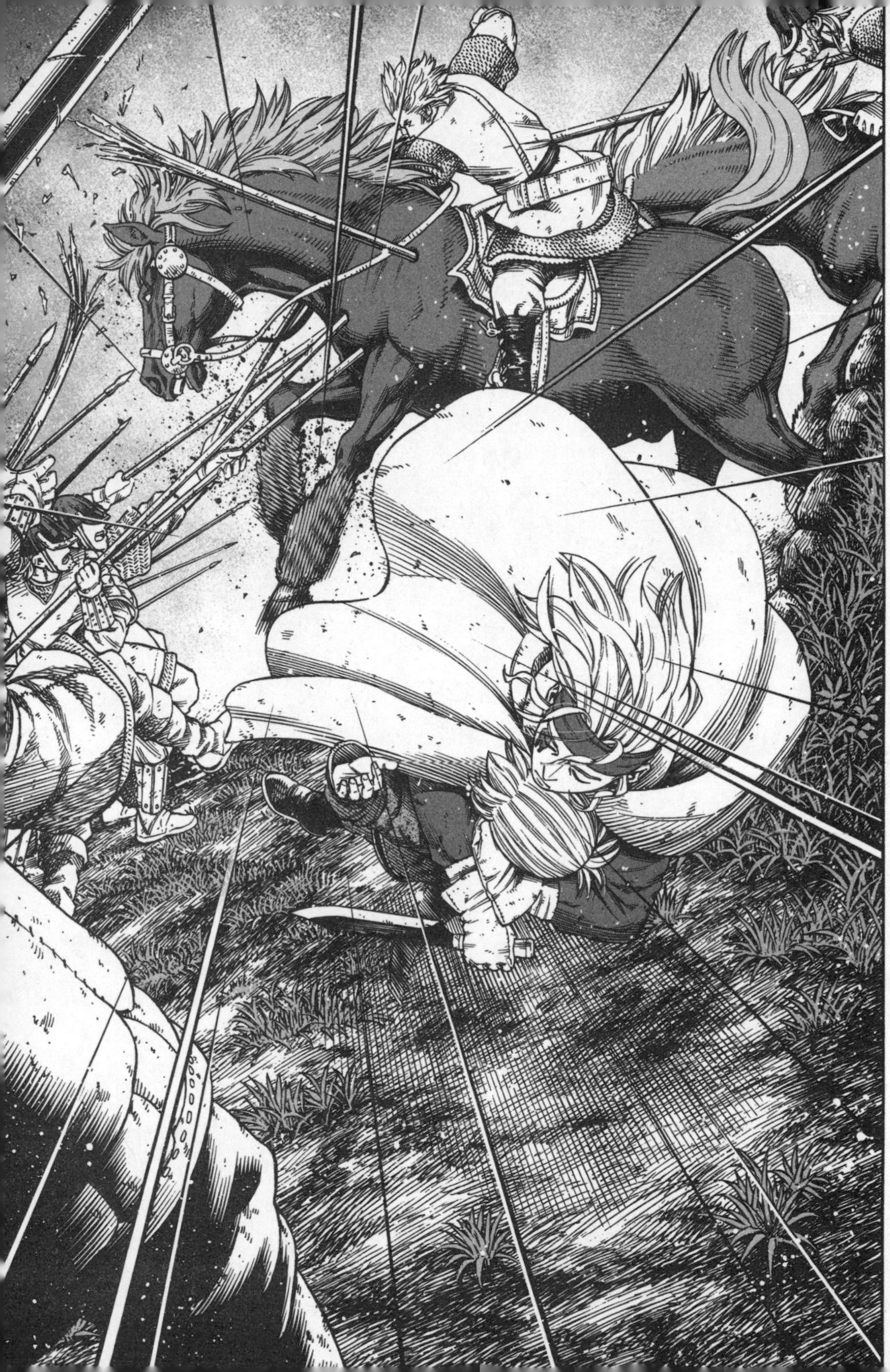

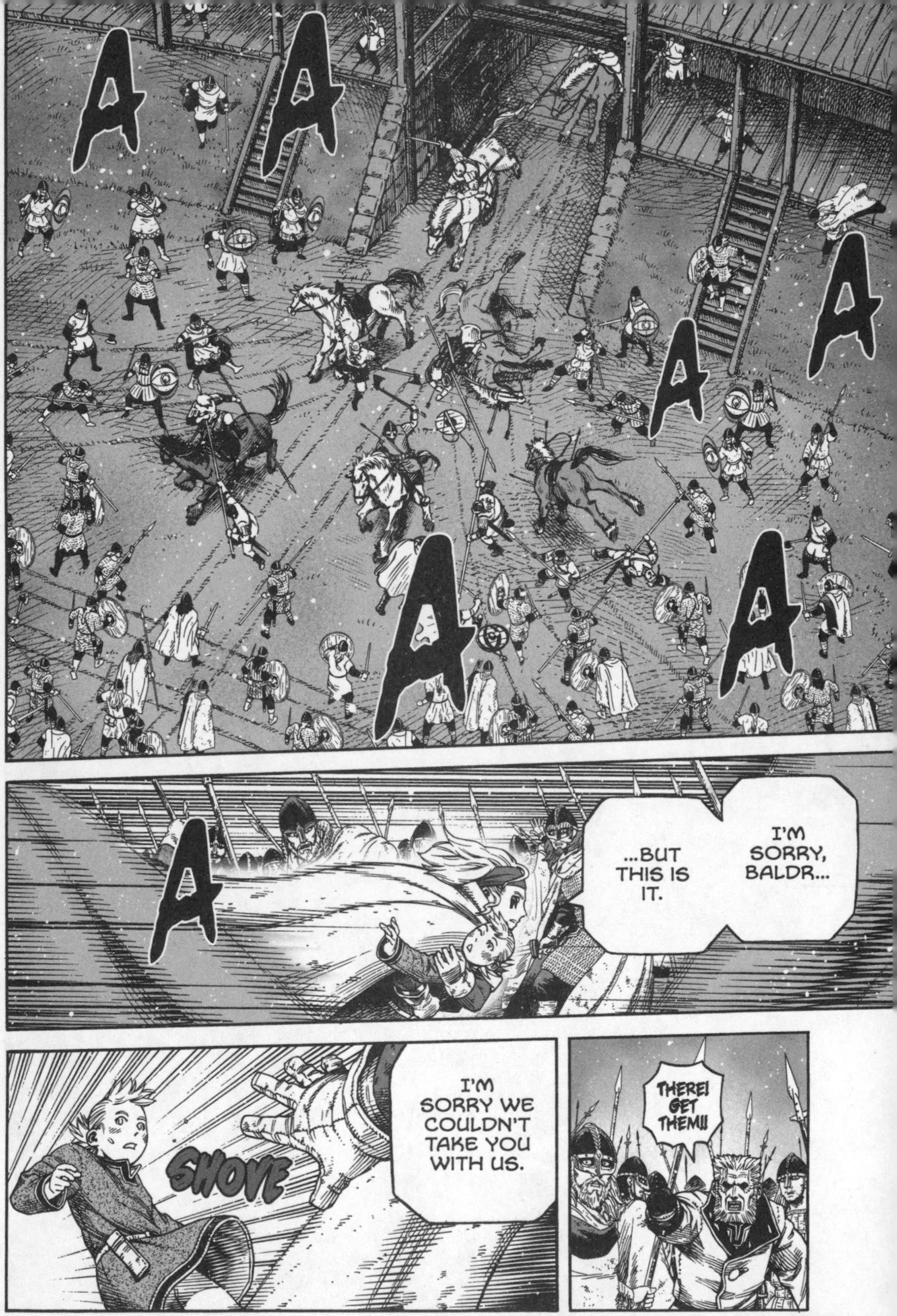
AAAAAA
I'M SORRY, BALDR...
...BUT THIS IS IT.
A
THERE! GET THEM!!
I'M SORRY WE COULDN'T TAKE YOU WITH US.
SHOVE

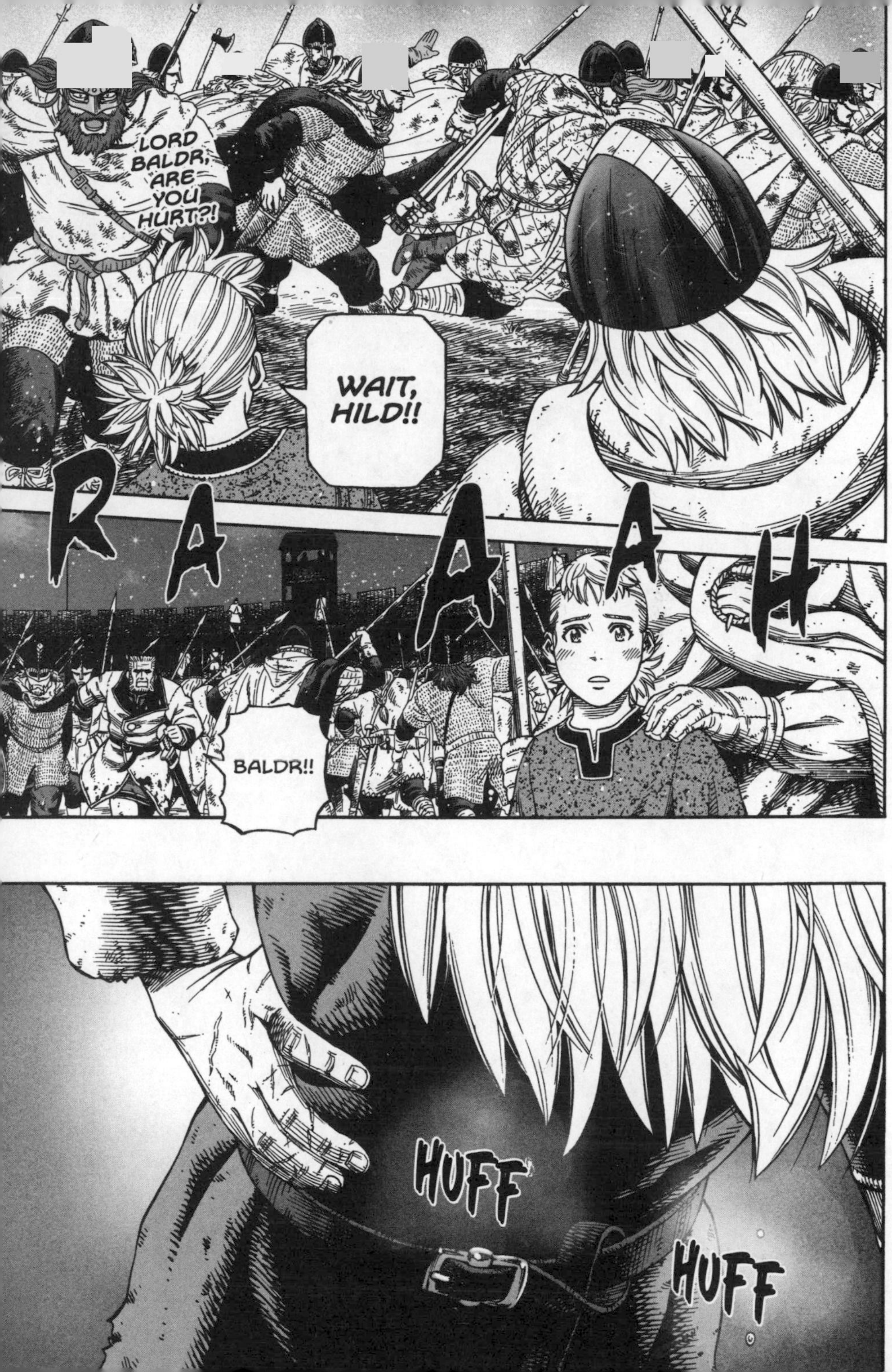
LORD BALDR, ARE YOU HURT?!
WAIT, HILD!!
RAAAAH
BALDR!!
HUFF
HUFF

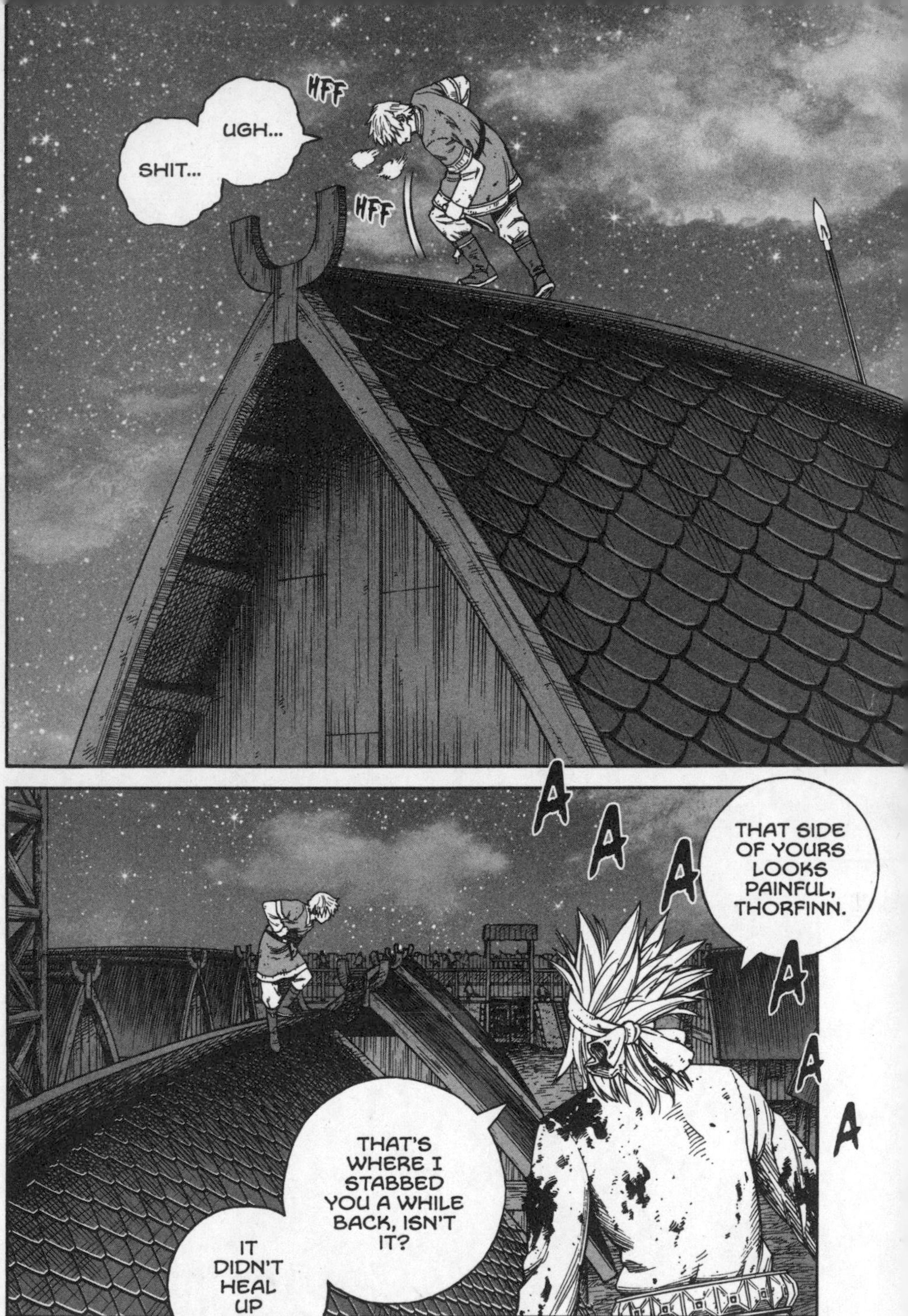
HFF
UGH... SHIT...
HFF
AAAAAA
THAT SIDE OF YOURS LOOKS PAINFUL, THORFINN.
THAT'S WHERE I STABBED YOU A WHILE BACK, ISN'T IT?
IT DIDN'T HEAL UP YET?

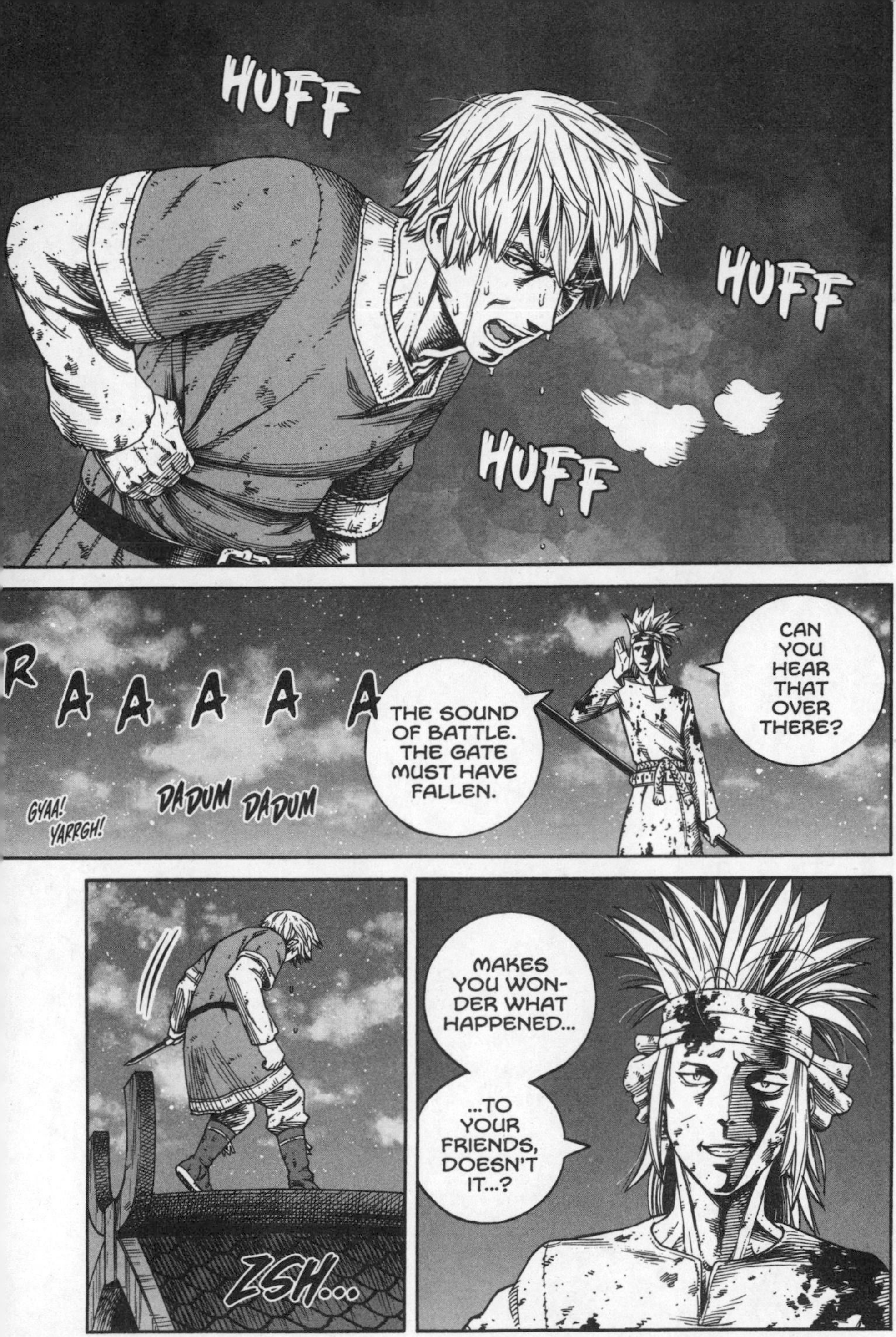
HUFF
HUFF
HUFF
CAN YOU HEAR THAT OVER THERE?
THE SOUND OF BATTLE. THE GATE MUST HAVE FALLEN.
RAAAAA
DADUM DADUM
GYAA! YARRGH!
MAKES YOU WONDER WHAT HAPPENED...
...TO YOUR FRIENDS, DOESN'T IT...?
ZSH...

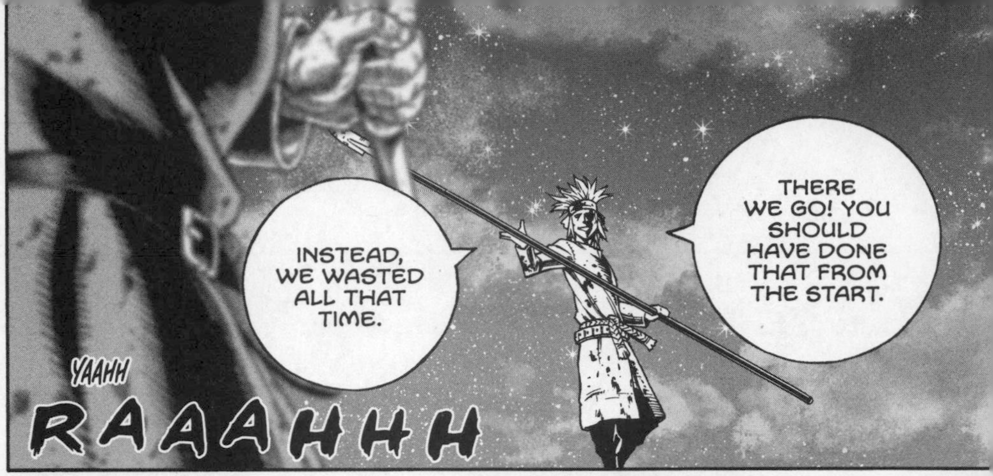
THERE WE GO! YOU SHOULD HAVE DONE THAT FROM THE START.
INSTEAD, WE WASTED ALL THAT TIME.
YAAHH
RAAAHHH

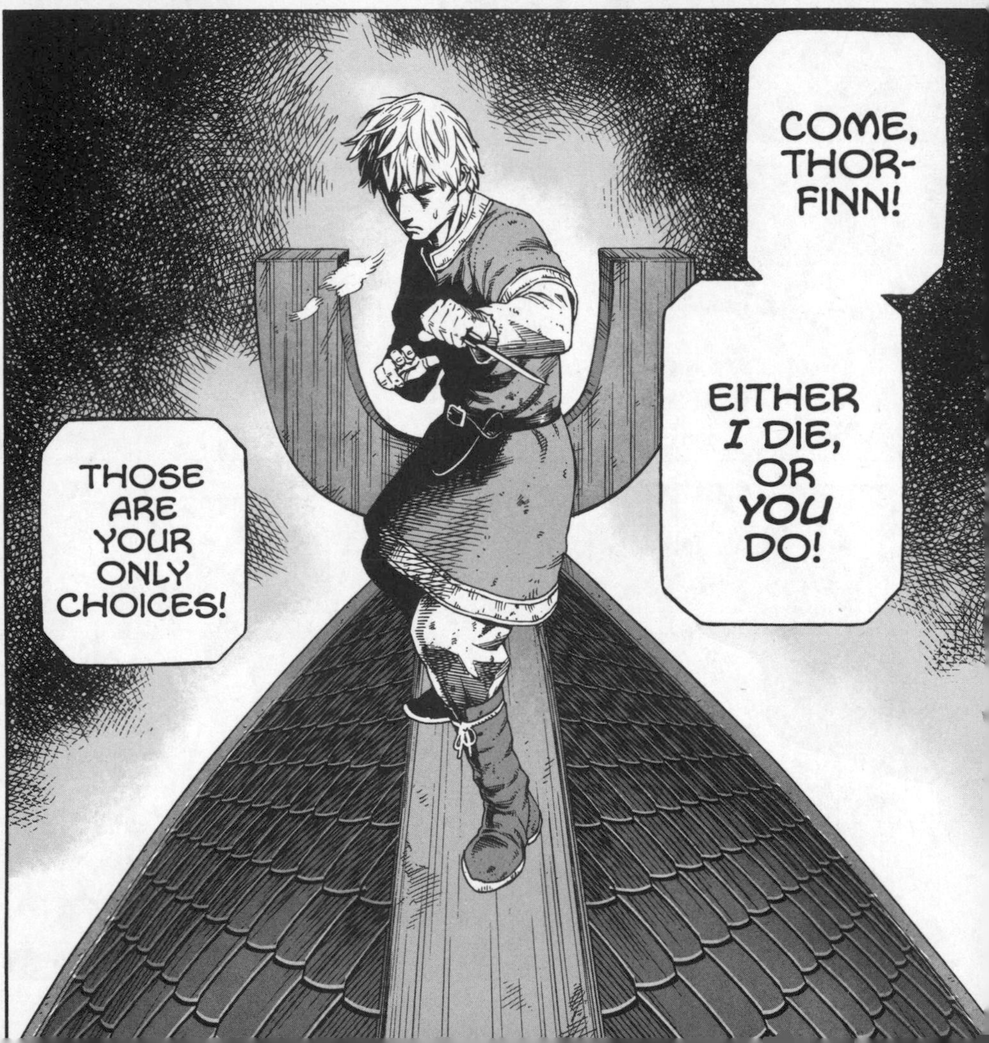
COME, THOR-FINN!
EITHER *I* DIE, OR *YOU* DO!
THOSE ARE YOUR ONLY CHOICES!

CHAPTER 155 • END

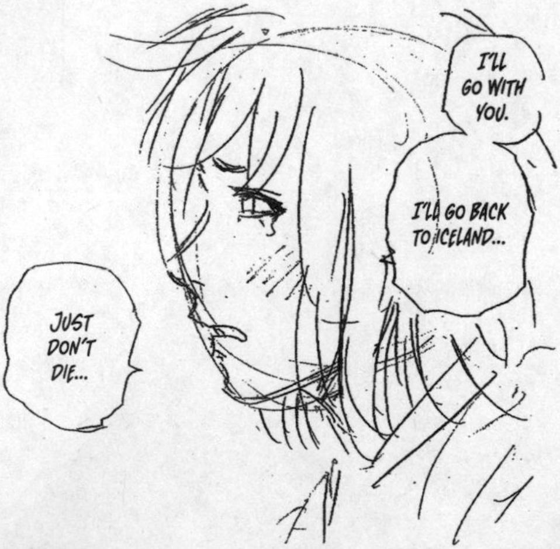
I'LL GO WITH YOU.
I'LL GO BACK TO ICELAND...
JUST DON'T DIE...

CHAPTER 154: WAR IN THE BALTIC (30)

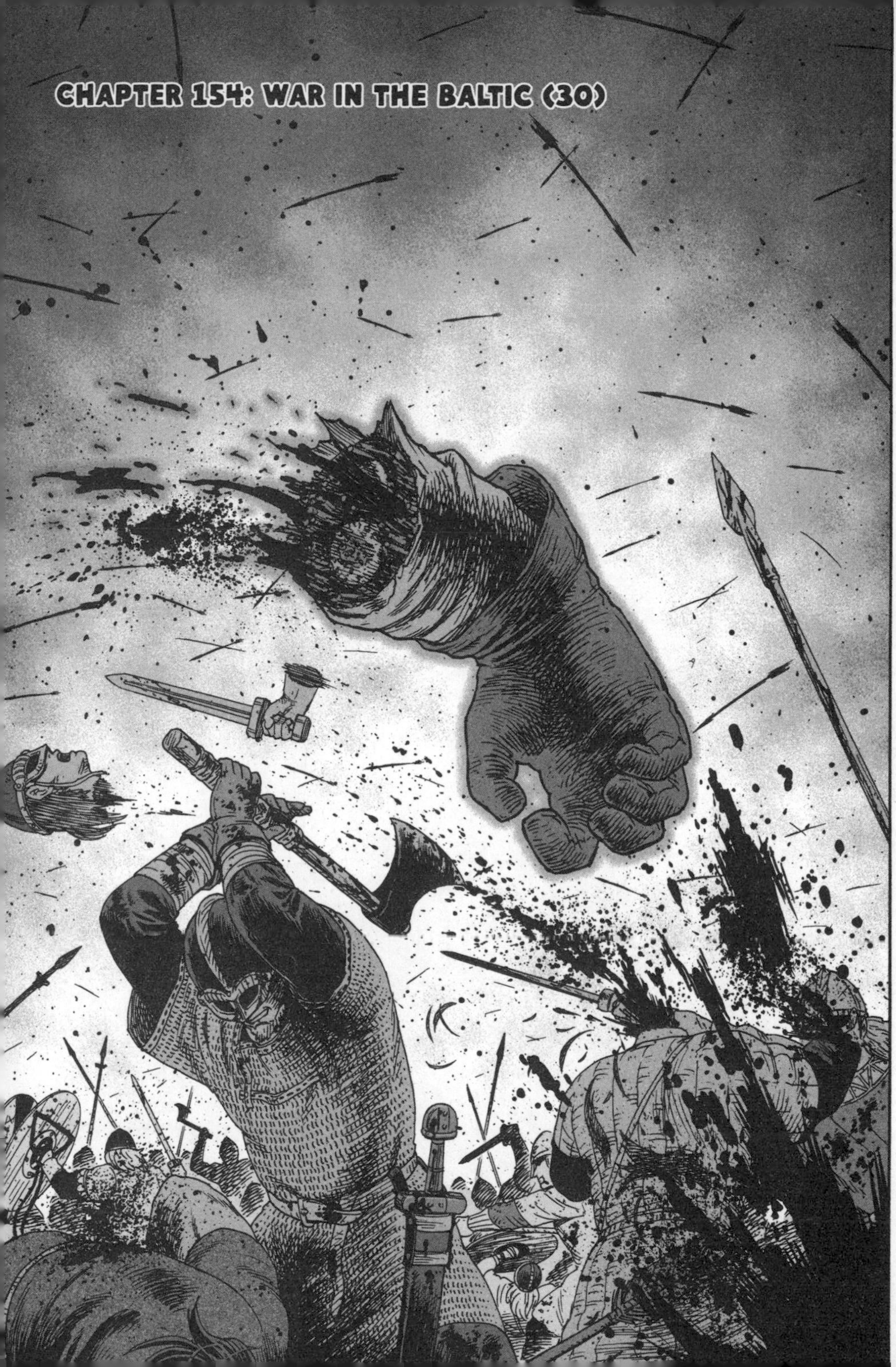

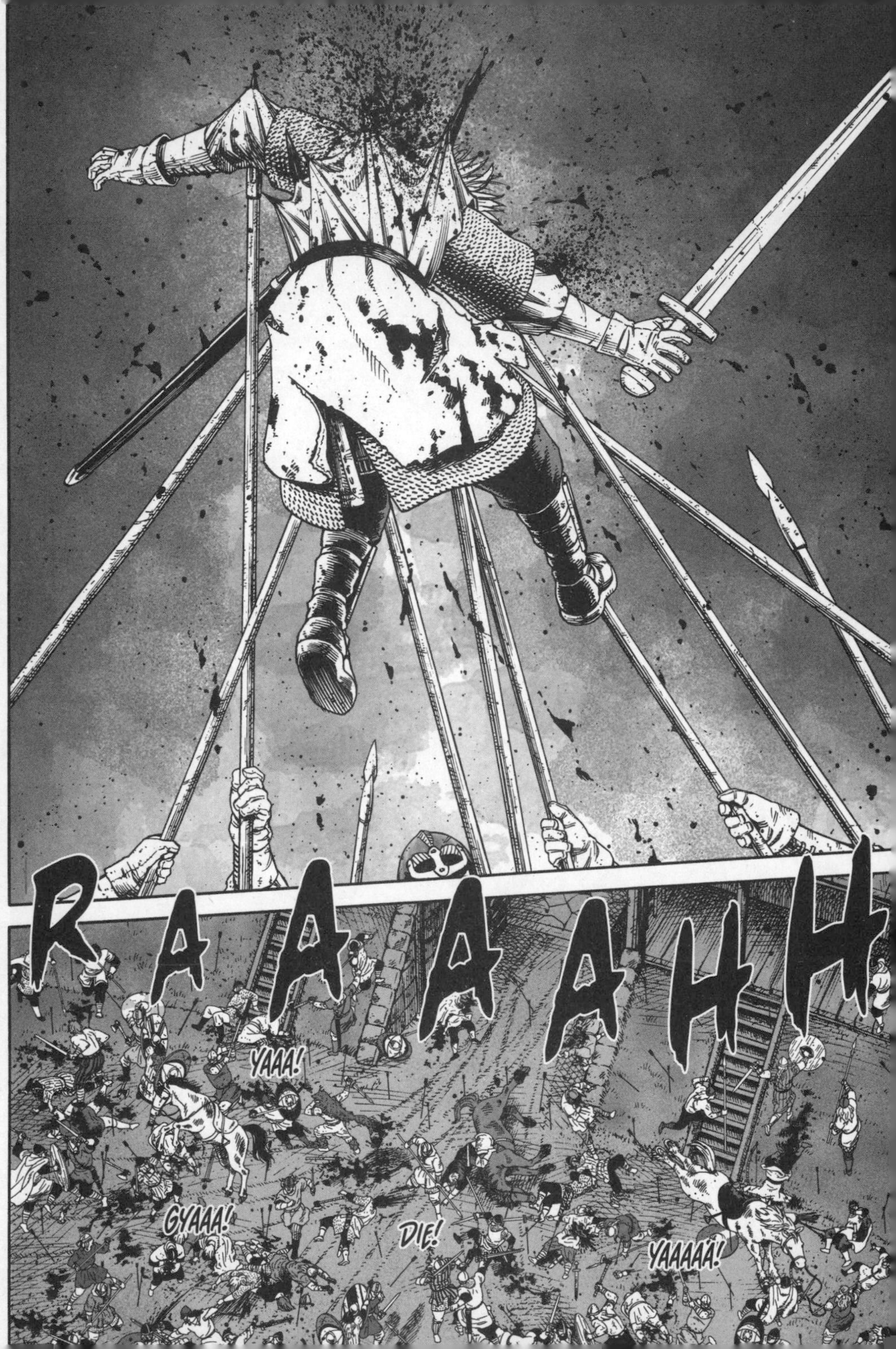
RAAAAHH
YAAA!
YAAAAA!
DIE!
GYAAA!

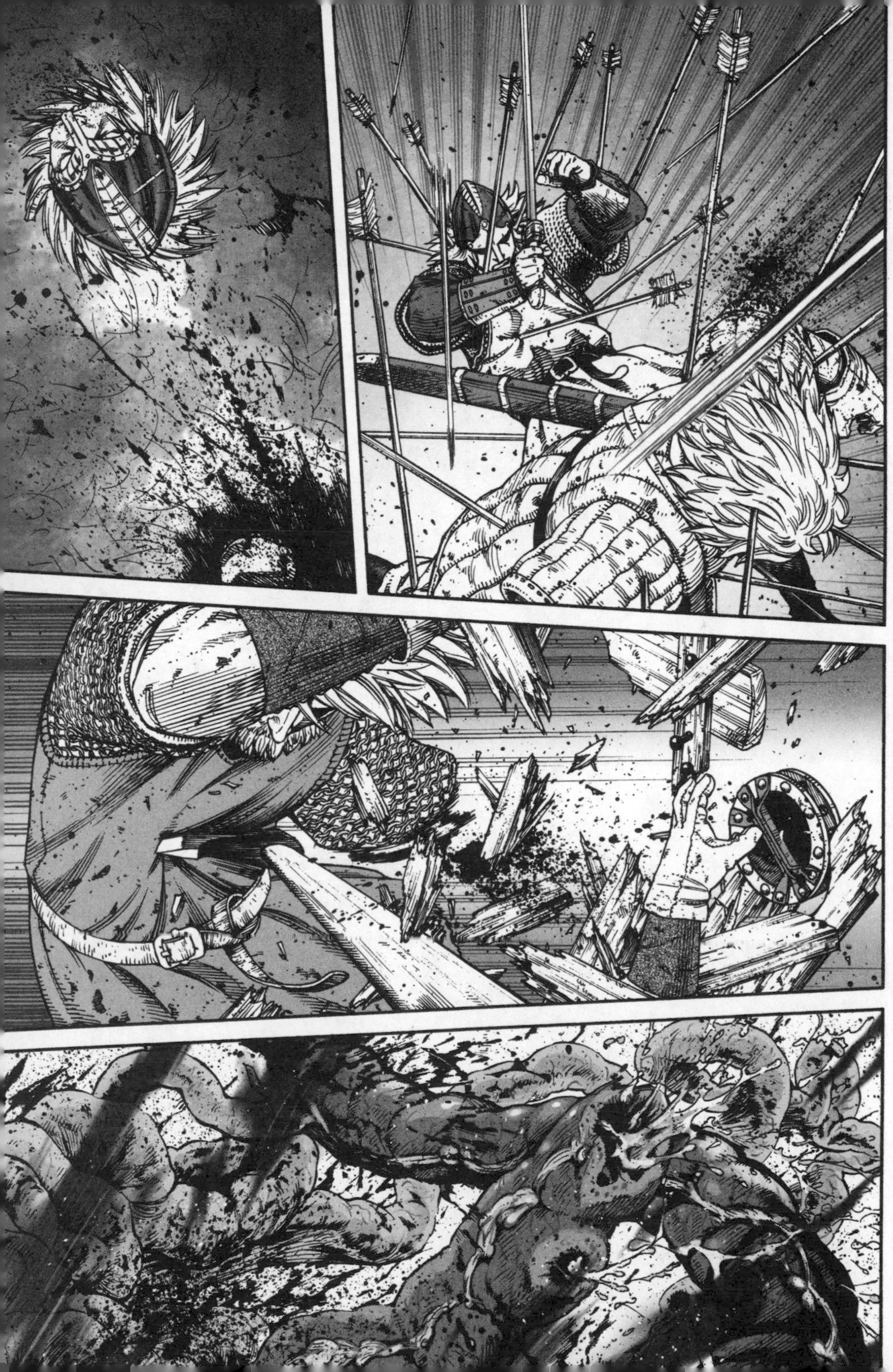

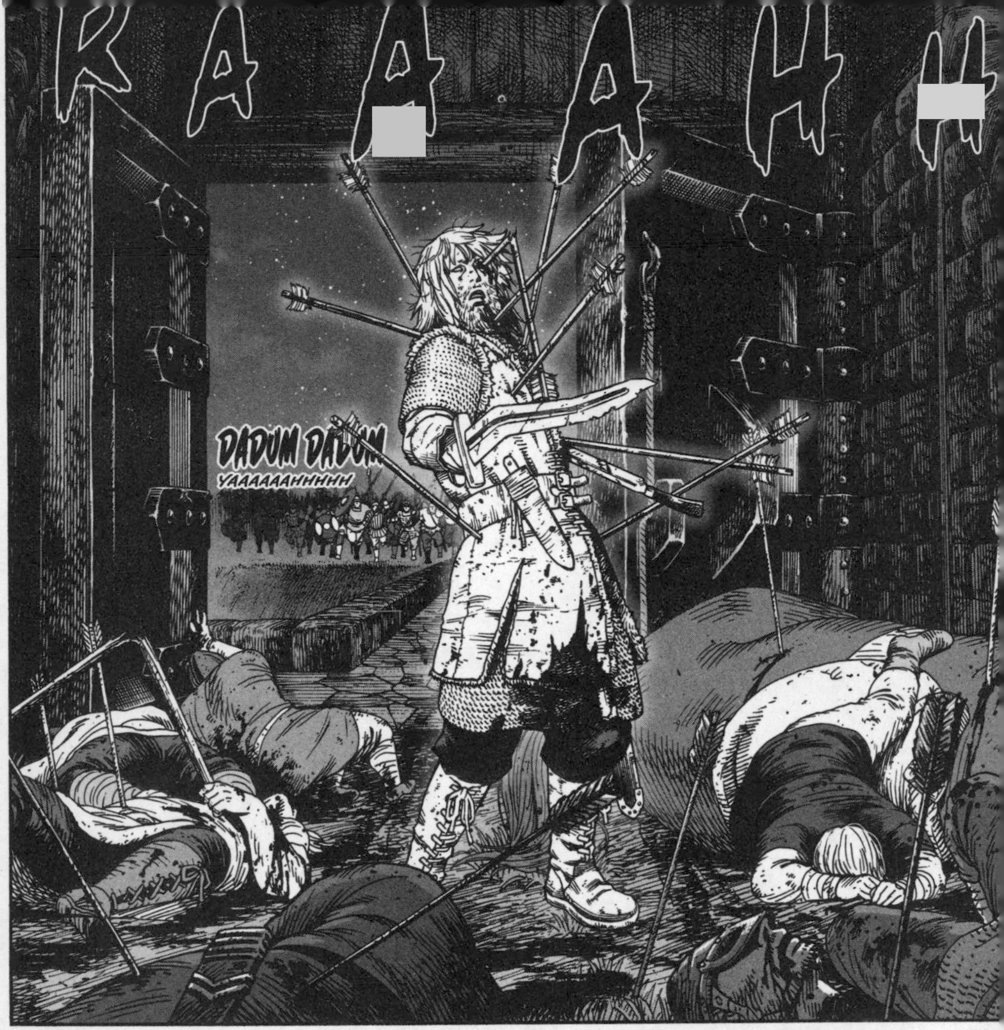
KAAAH
DADUM DADUM
YAAAAAAHHHHHH

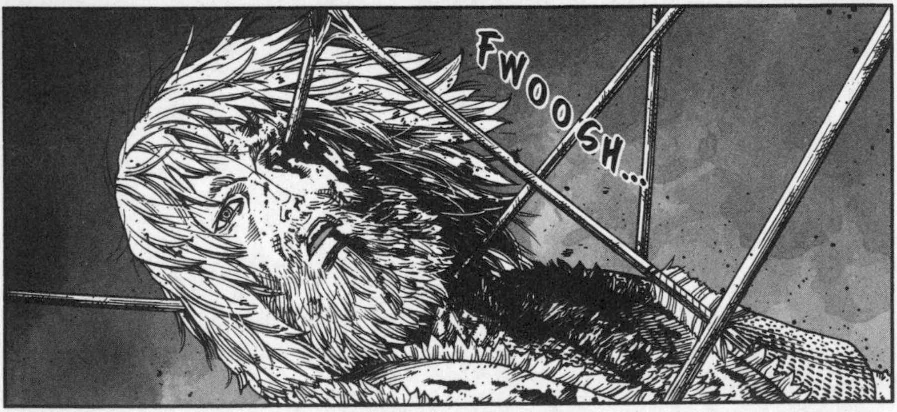
FWOOSH...

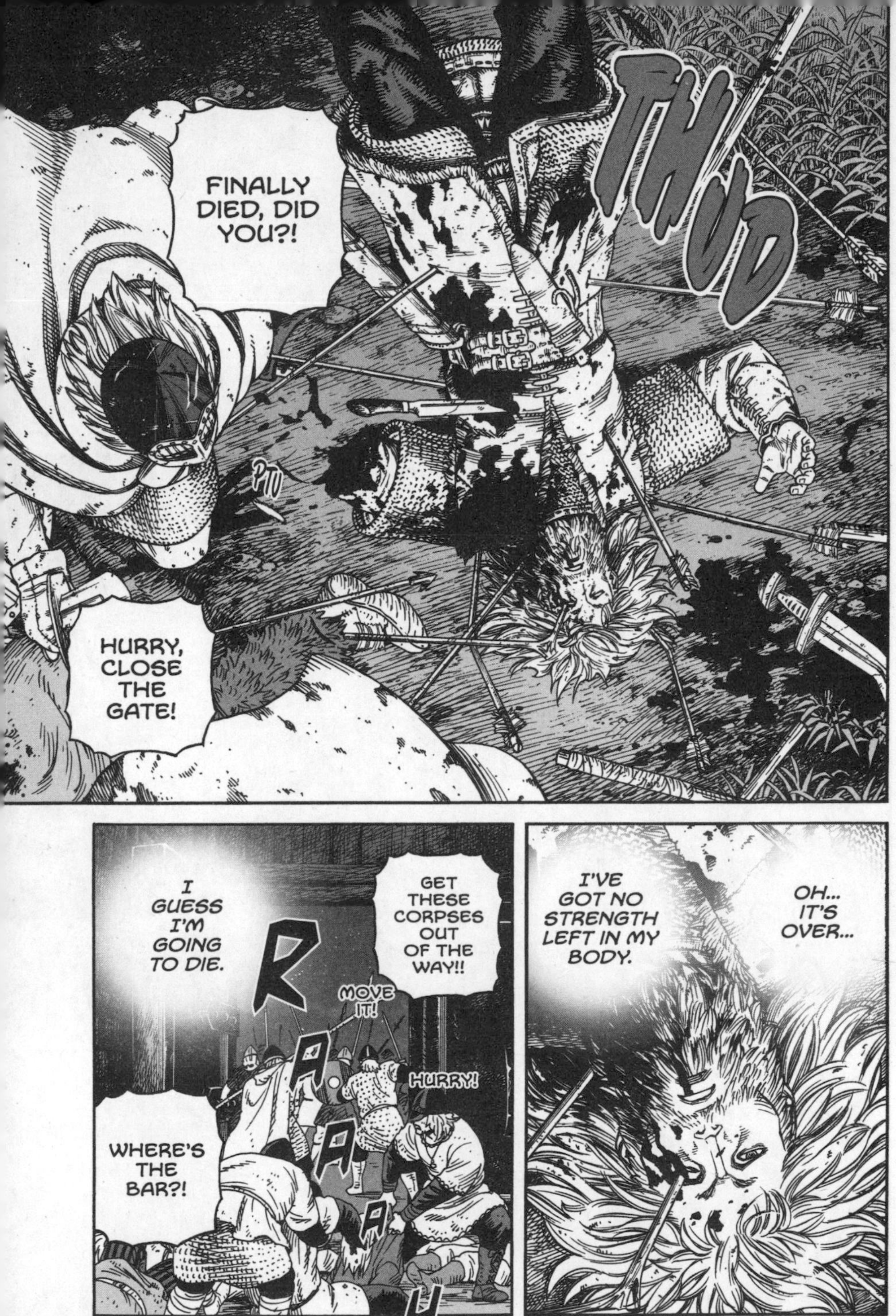
THUD
FINALLY DIED, DID YOU?!
PTU
HURRY, CLOSE THE GATE!
OH... IT'S OVER...
I'VE GOT NO STRENGTH LEFT IN MY BODY.
GET THESE CORPSES OUT OF THE WAY!!
I GUESS I'M GOING TO DIE.
RAAAAH
MOVE IT!
HURRY!
WHERE'S THE BAR?!

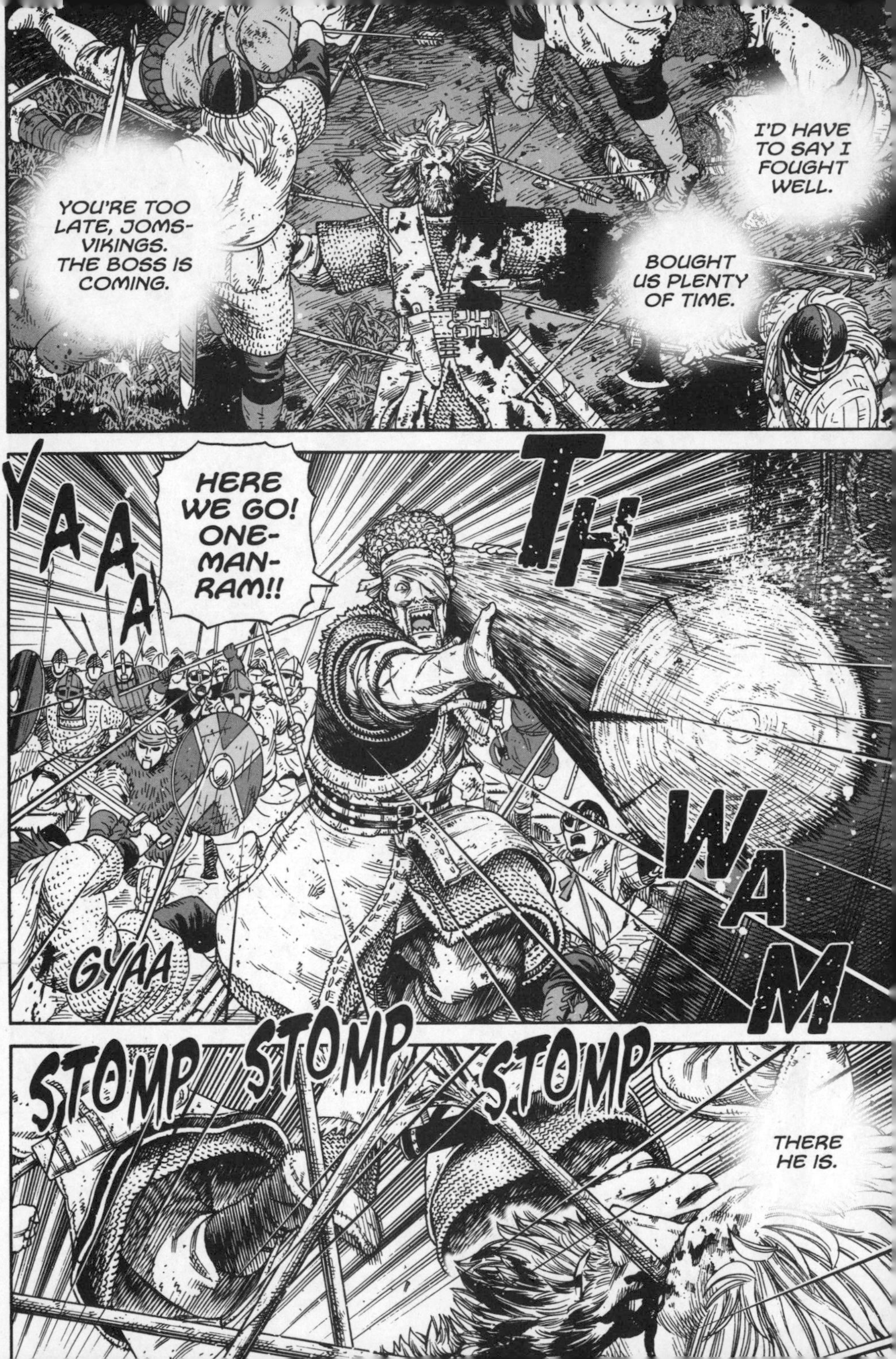
I'D HAVE TO SAY I FOUGHT WELL.
BOUGHT US PLENTY OF TIME.
YOU'RE TOO LATE, JOMS-VIKINGS. THE BOSS IS COMING.
THWAM
HERE WE GO! ONE-MAN-RAM!!
YAAAA
GYAA
THERE HE IS.
STOMP
STOMP
STOMP

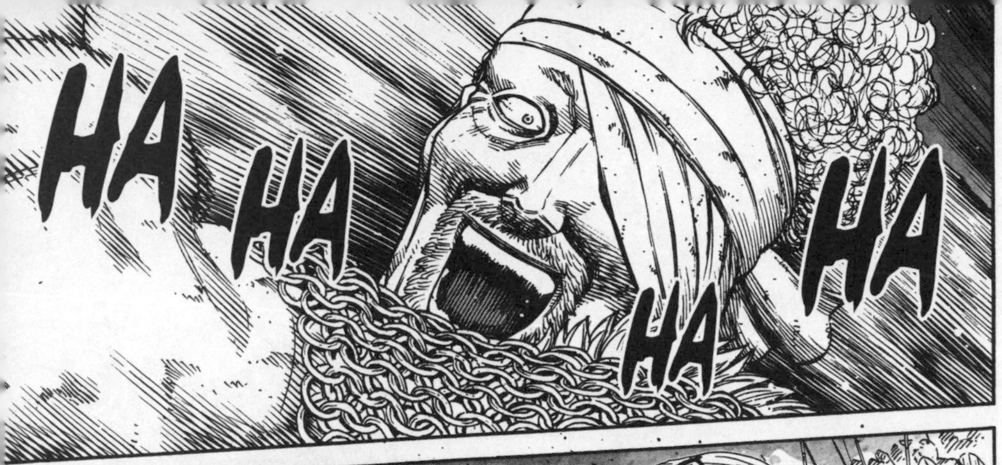
HA HA HA HA
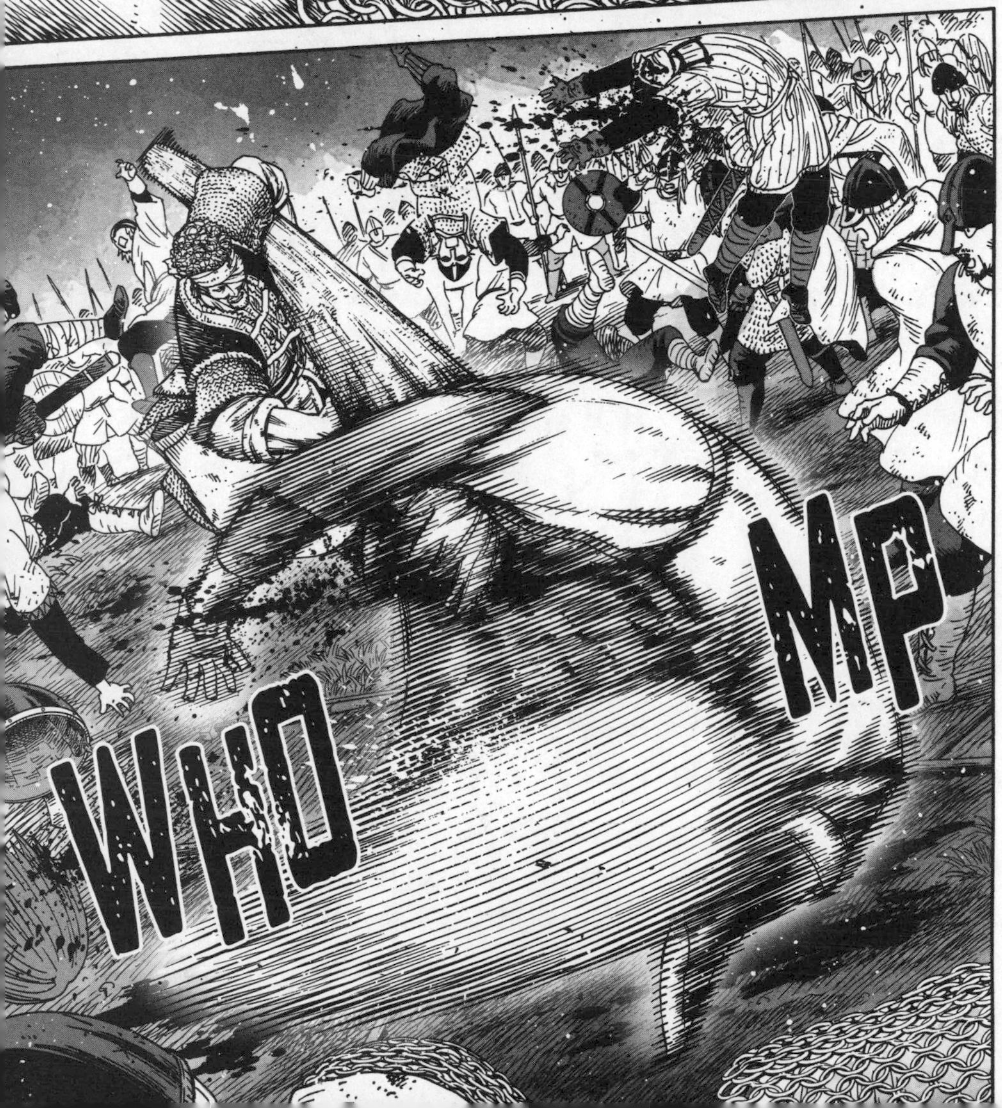
WHOMP

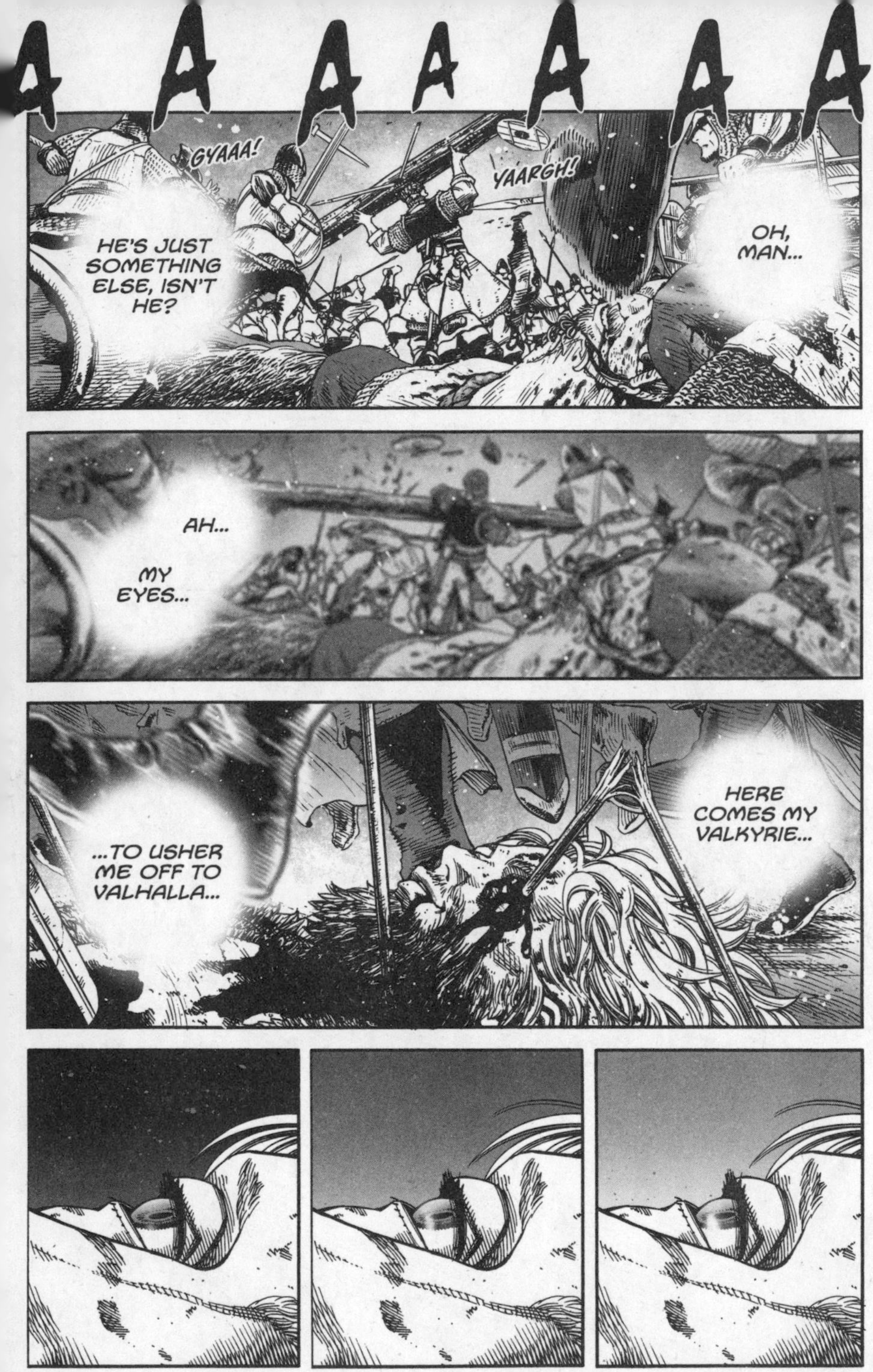
AAAAAAA
YAARGH!
GYAAA!
OH, MAN...
HE'S JUST SOMETHING ELSE, ISN'T HE?
AH...
MY EYES...
HERE COMES MY VALKYRIE...
...TO USHER ME OFF TO VALHALLA...

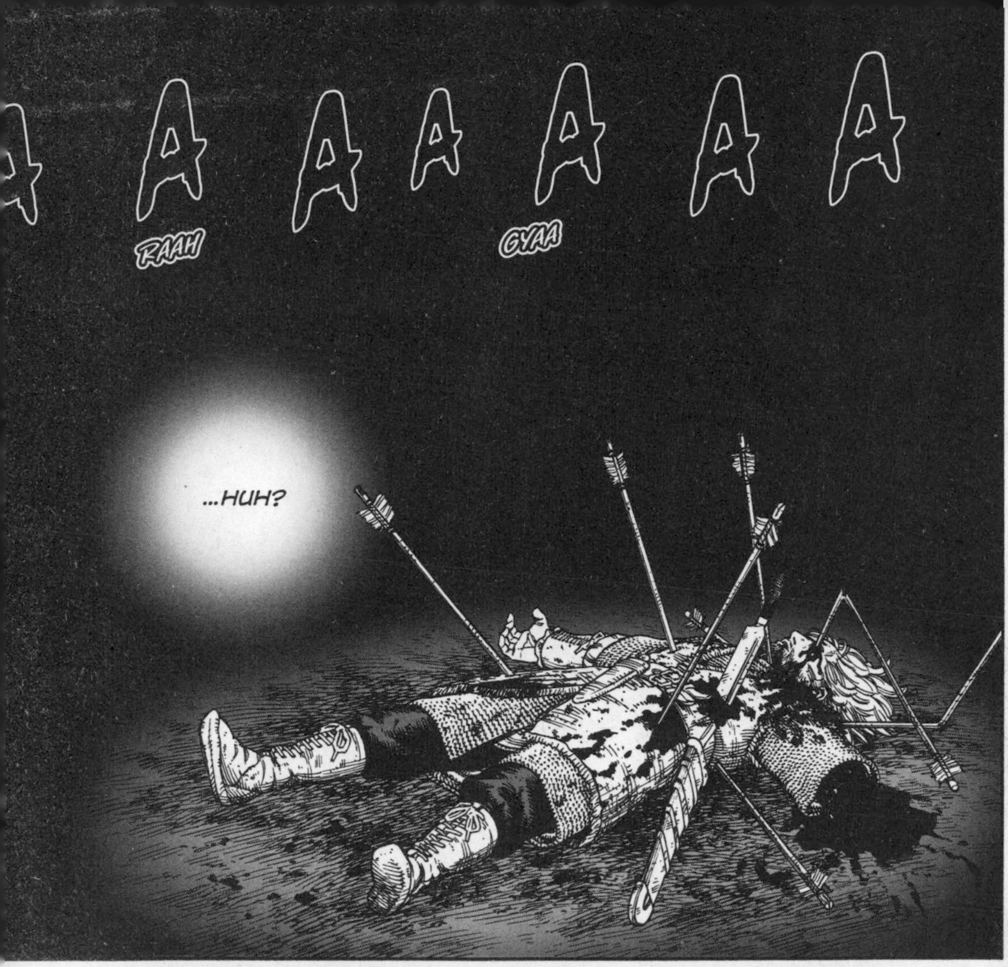
AAAAAAA
RAAH
GYAA
...HUH?

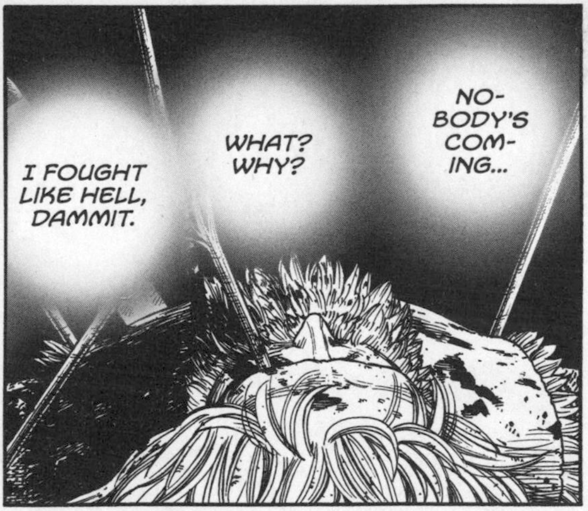
NO-BODY'S COM-ING...
WHAT? WHY?
I FOUGHT LIKE HELL, DAMMIT.

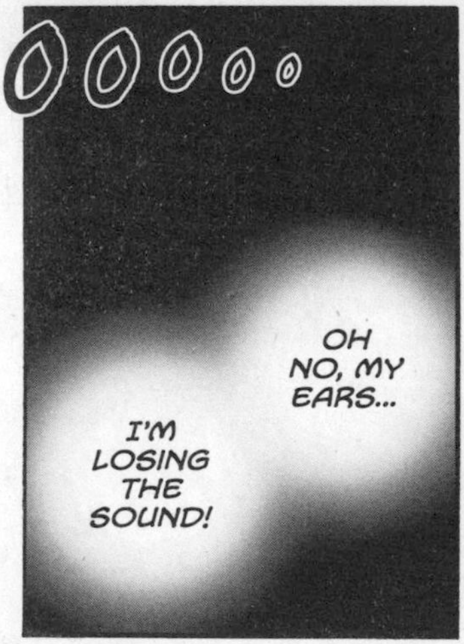
OOOOO
OH NO, MY EARS...
I'M LOSING THE SOUND!

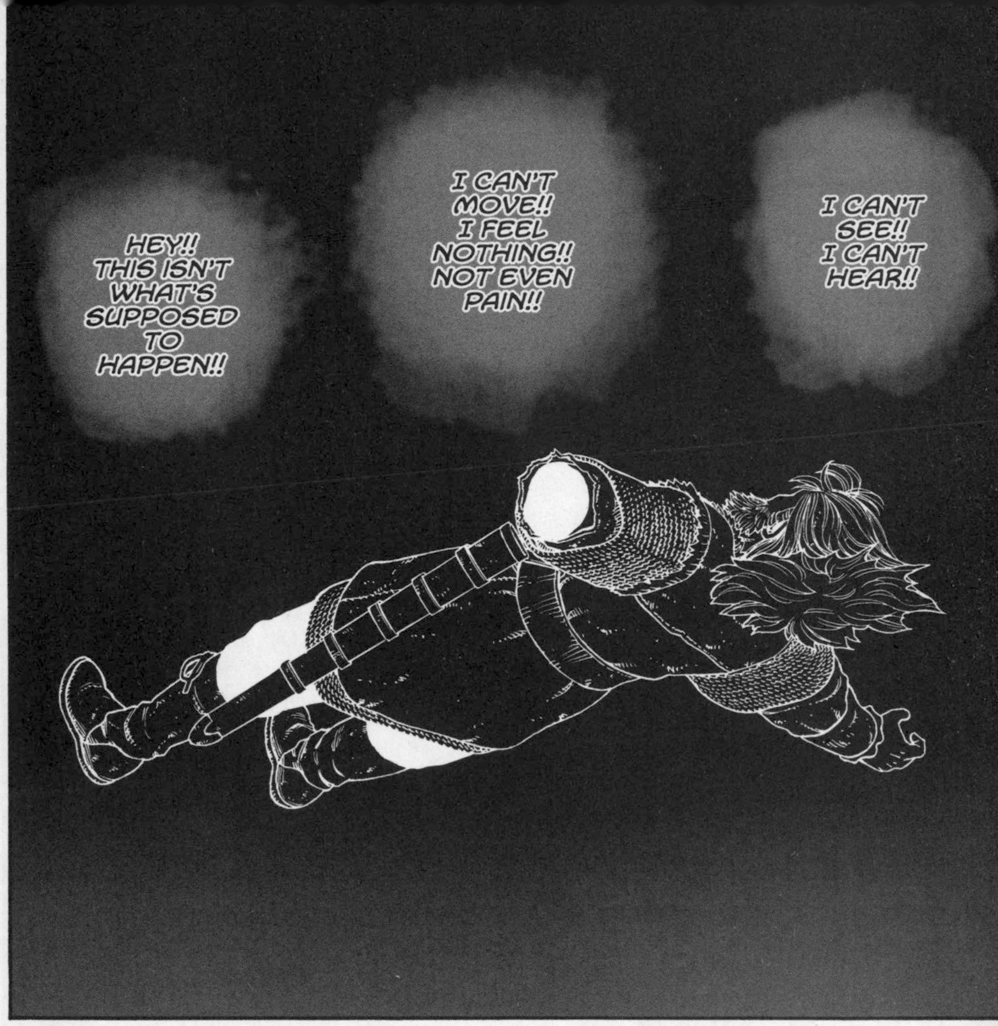
I CAN'T SEE!! I CAN'T HEAR!!
I CAN'T MOVE!! I FEEL NOTHING!! NOT EVEN PAIN!!
HEY!! THIS ISN'T WHAT'S SUPPOSED TO HAPPEN!!

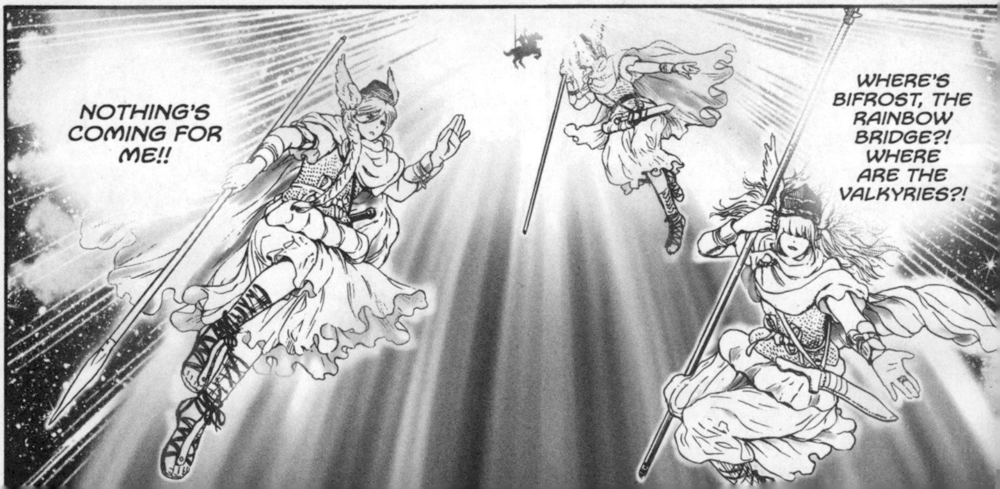
WHERE'S BIFROST, THE RAINBOW BRIDGE?! WHERE ARE THE VALKYRIES?!
NOTHING'S COMING FOR ME!!

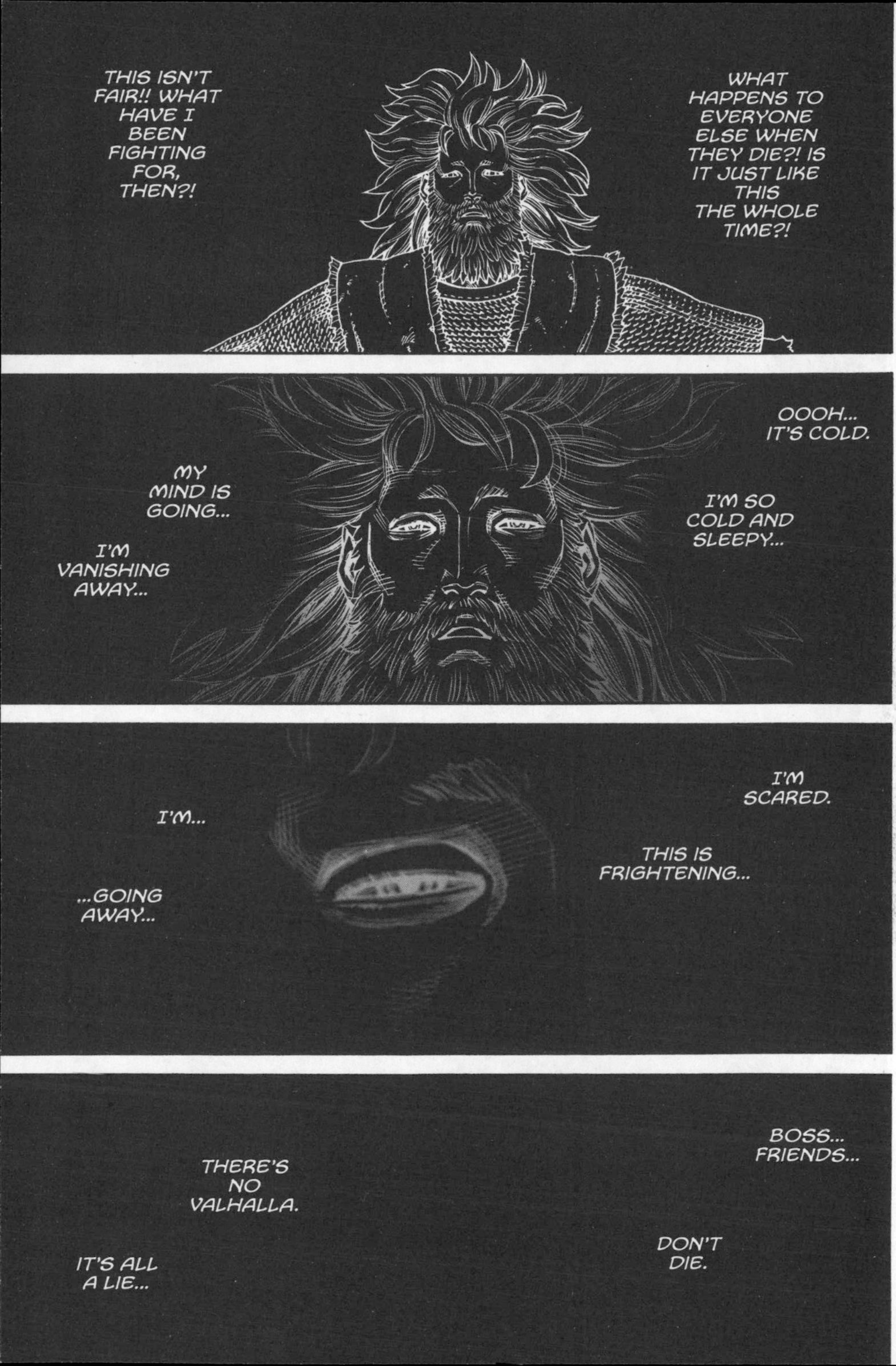
THIS ISN'T FAIR!! WHAT HAVE I BEEN FIGHTING FOR, THEN?!
WHAT HAPPENS TO EVERYONE ELSE WHEN THEY DIE?! IS IT JUST LIKE THIS THE WHOLE TIME?!
MY MIND IS GOING...
I'M VANISHING AWAY...
OOOH... IT'S COLD.
I'M SO COLD AND SLEEPY...
I'M...
...GOING AWAY...
I'M SCARED.
THIS IS FRIGHTENING...
THERE'S NO VALHALLA.
IT'S ALL A LIE...
BOSS... FRIENDS...
DON'T DIE.

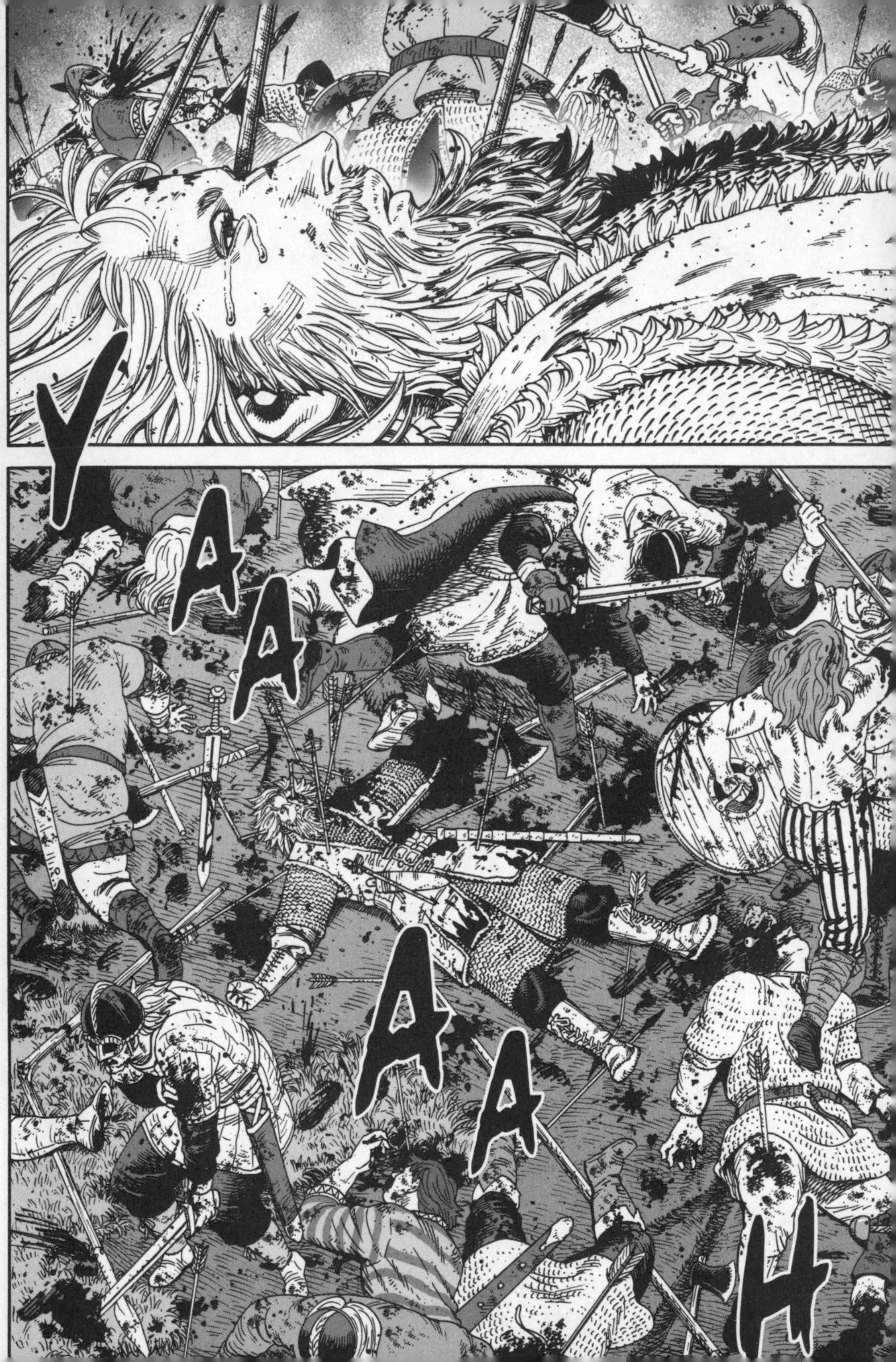
YAAAAH

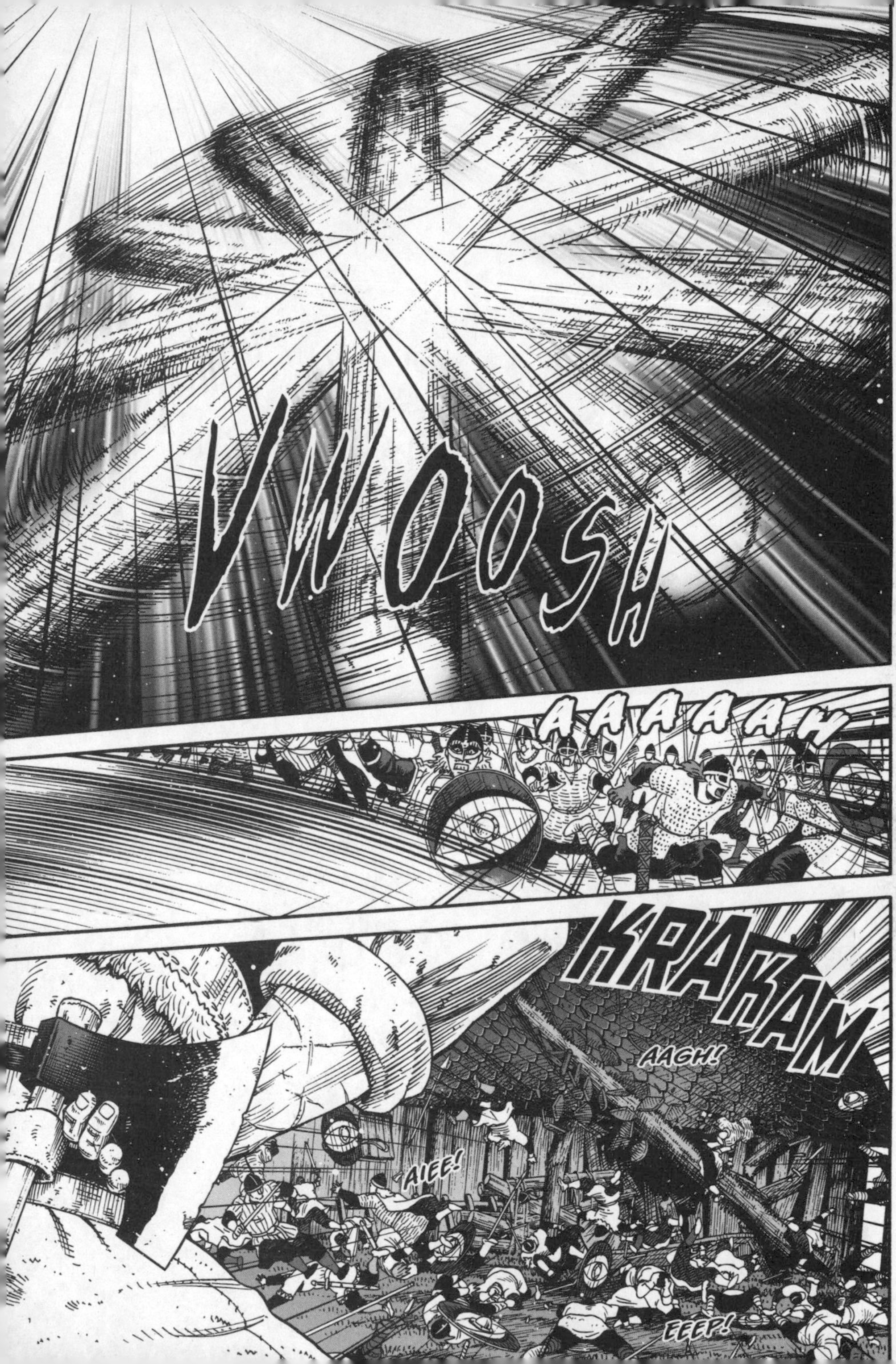
VWOOSH
AAAAAH
KRAKAM
AAGH!
AIEE!
EEEP!

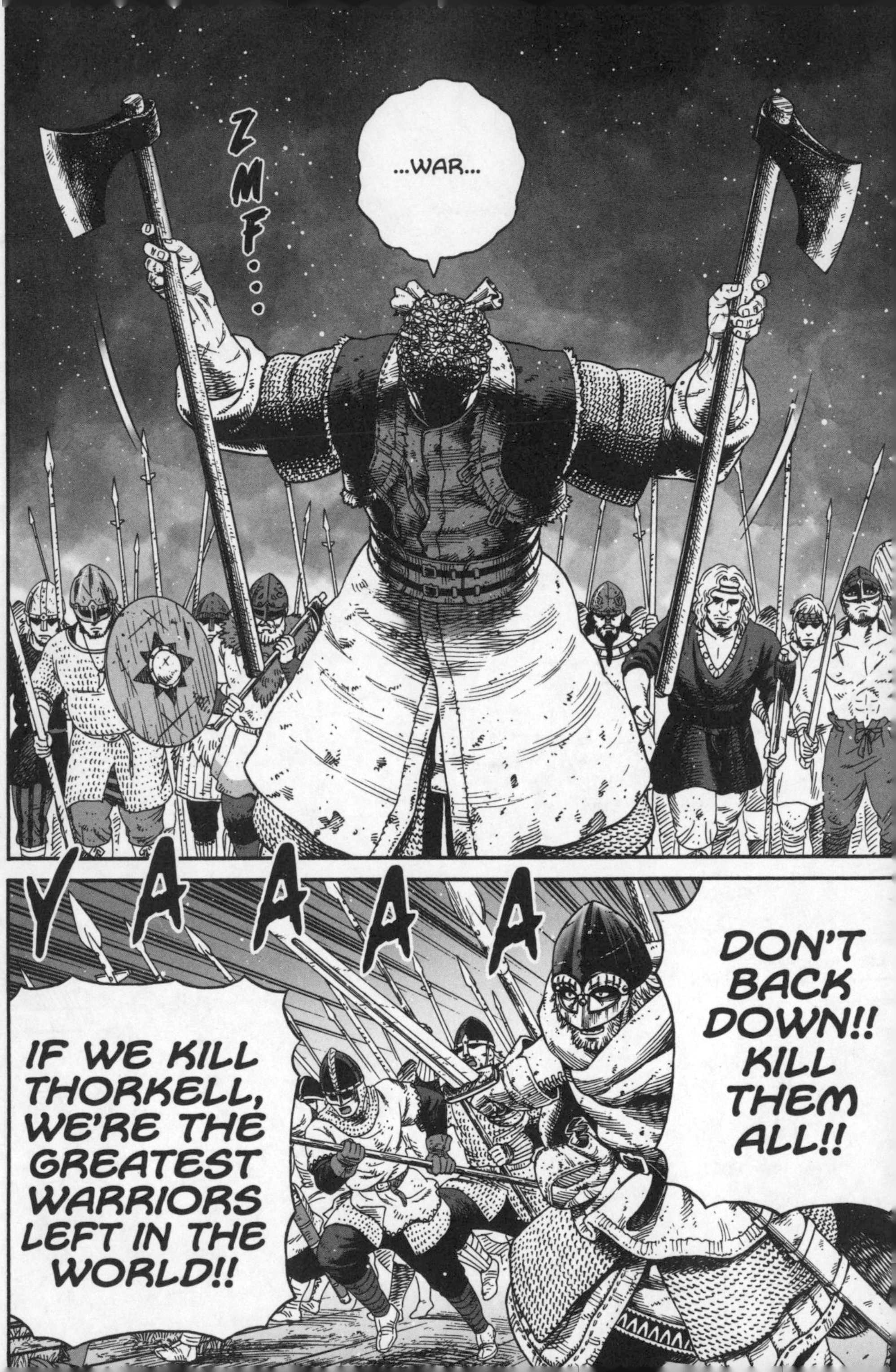
...WAR...
ZMF...
YAAAAA
DON'T BACK DOWN!! KILL THEM ALL!!
IF WE KILL THORKELL, WE'RE THE GREATEST WARRIORS LEFT IN THE WORLD!!

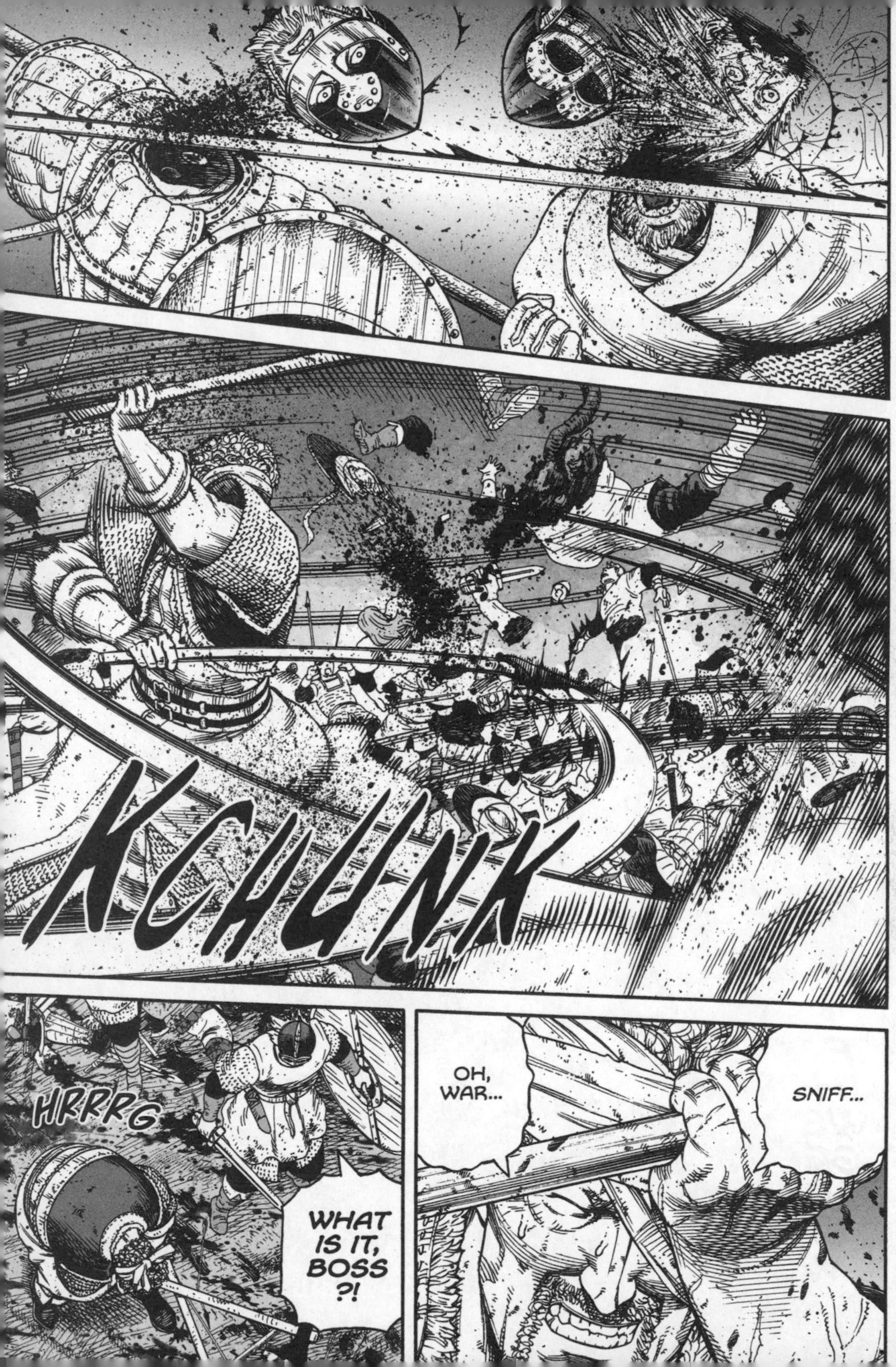
KCHUNK
SNIFF...
OH, WAR...
HRRRG
WHAT IS IT, BOSS?!

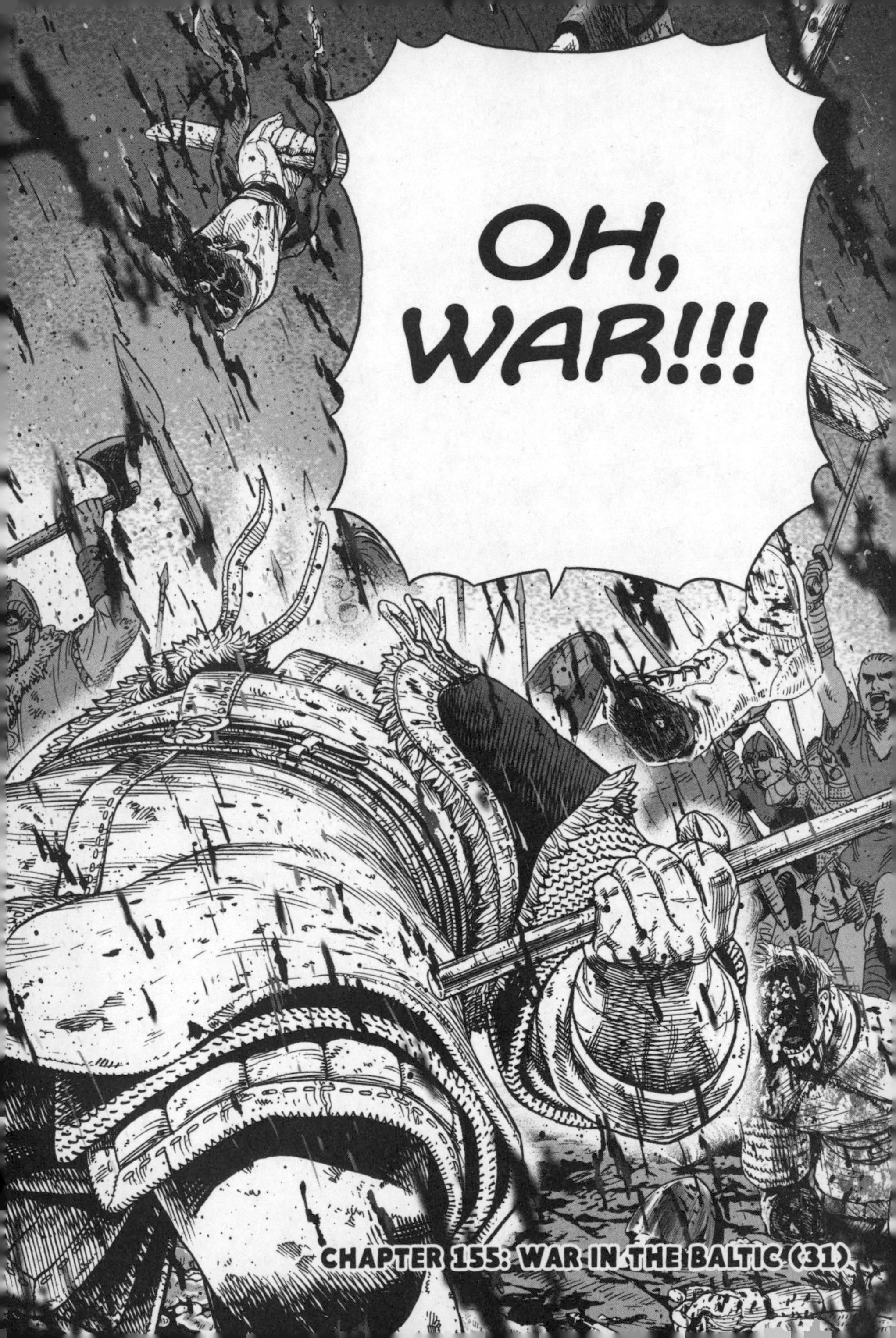
OH, WAR!!!
CHAPTER 155: WAR IN THE BALTIC (31)

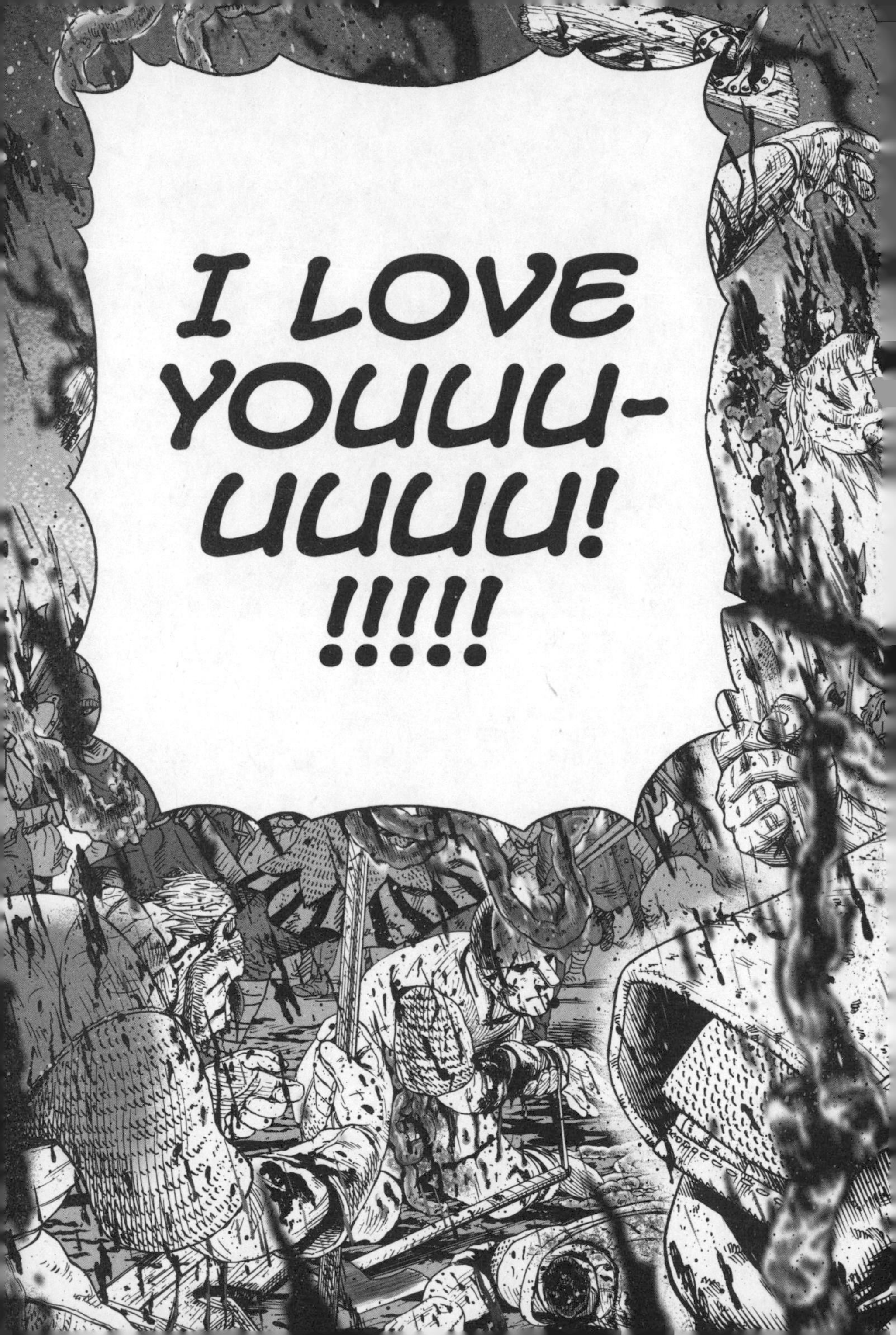
I LOVE YOUUU-UUUUU!!!!!!

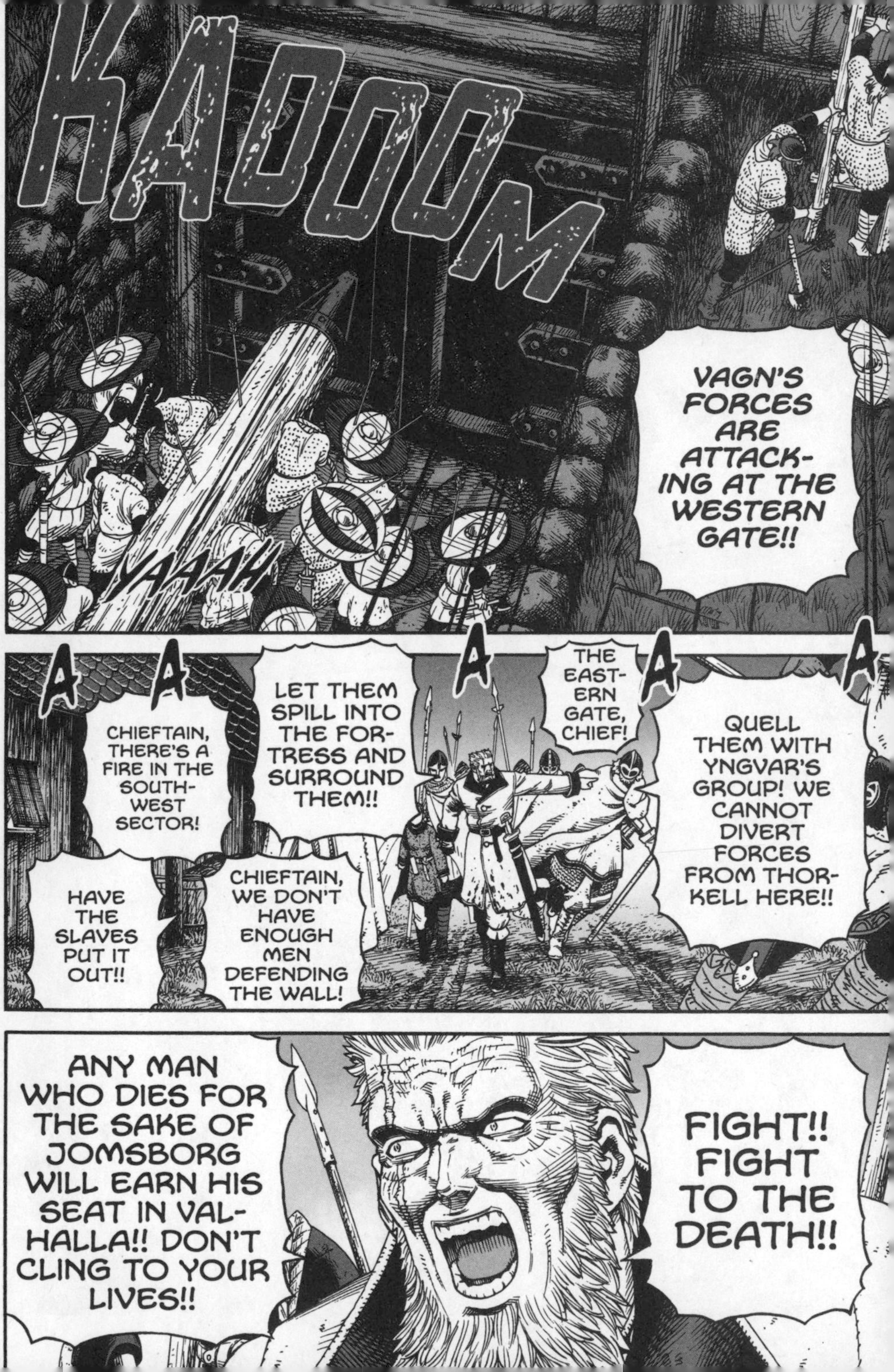
KADOOOM
VAGN'S FORCES ARE ATTACKING AT THE WESTERN GATE!!
YAAAH
A
A
A
A
A
THE EASTERN GATE, CHIEF!
QUELL THEM WITH YNGVAR'S GROUP! WE CANNOT DIVERT FORCES FROM THORKELL HERE!!
CHIEFTAIN, WE DON'T HAVE ENOUGH MEN DEFENDING THE WALL!
LET THEM SPILL INTO THE FORTRESS AND SURROUND THEM!!
CHIEFTAIN, THERE'S A FIRE IN THE SOUTHWEST SECTOR!
HAVE THE SLAVES PUT IT OUT!!
FIGHT!! FIGHT TO THE DEATH!!
ANY MAN WHO DIES FOR THE SAKE OF JOMSBORG WILL EARN HIS SEAT IN VALHALLA!! DON'T CLING TO YOUR LIVES!!

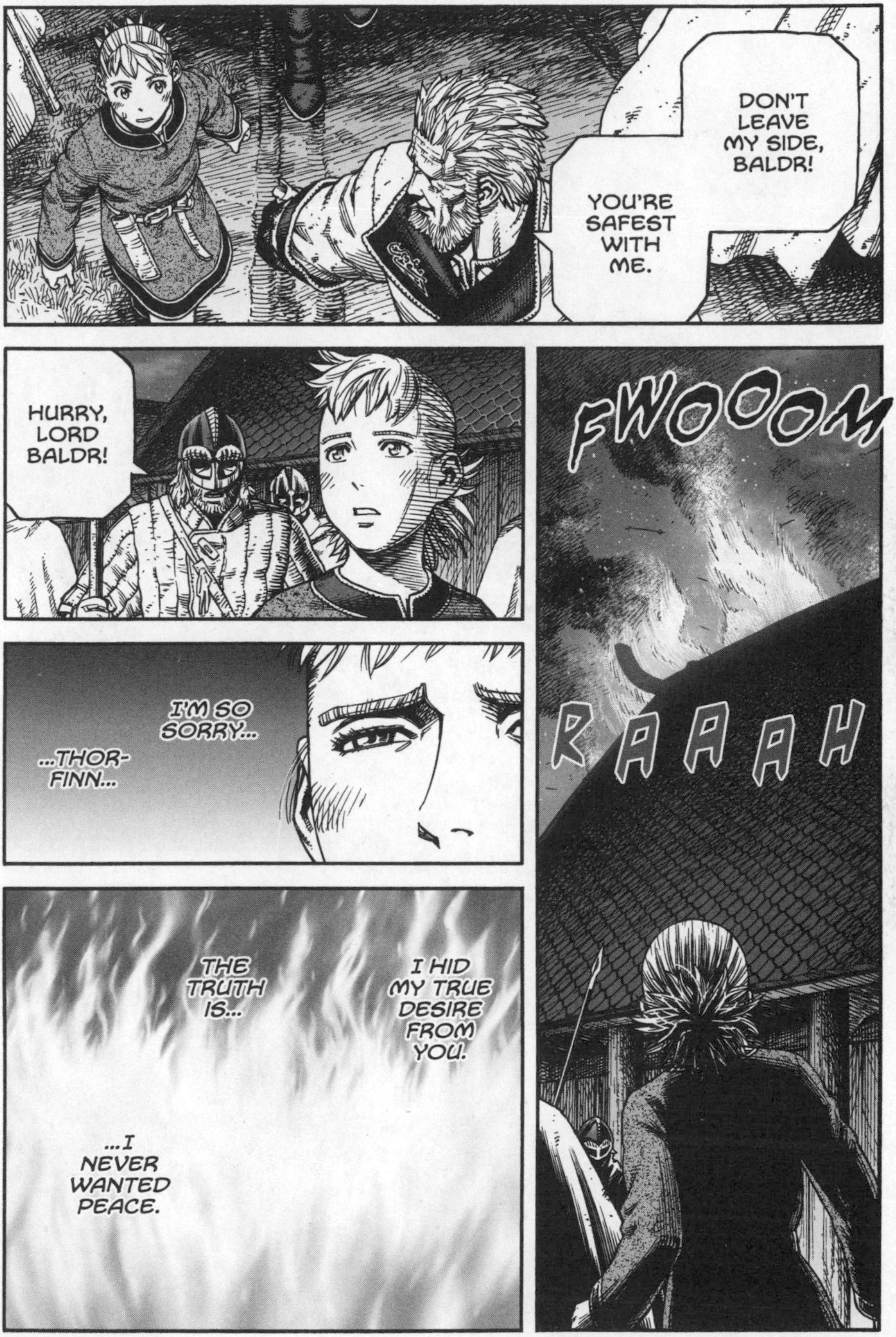
DON'T LEAVE MY SIDE, BALDR!
YOU'RE SAFEST WITH ME.
FWOOOM
RAAAH
HURRY, LORD BALDR!
I'M SO SORRY...
...THOR-FINN...
THE TRUTH IS...
I HID MY TRUE DESIRE FROM YOU.
...I NEVER WANTED PEACE.

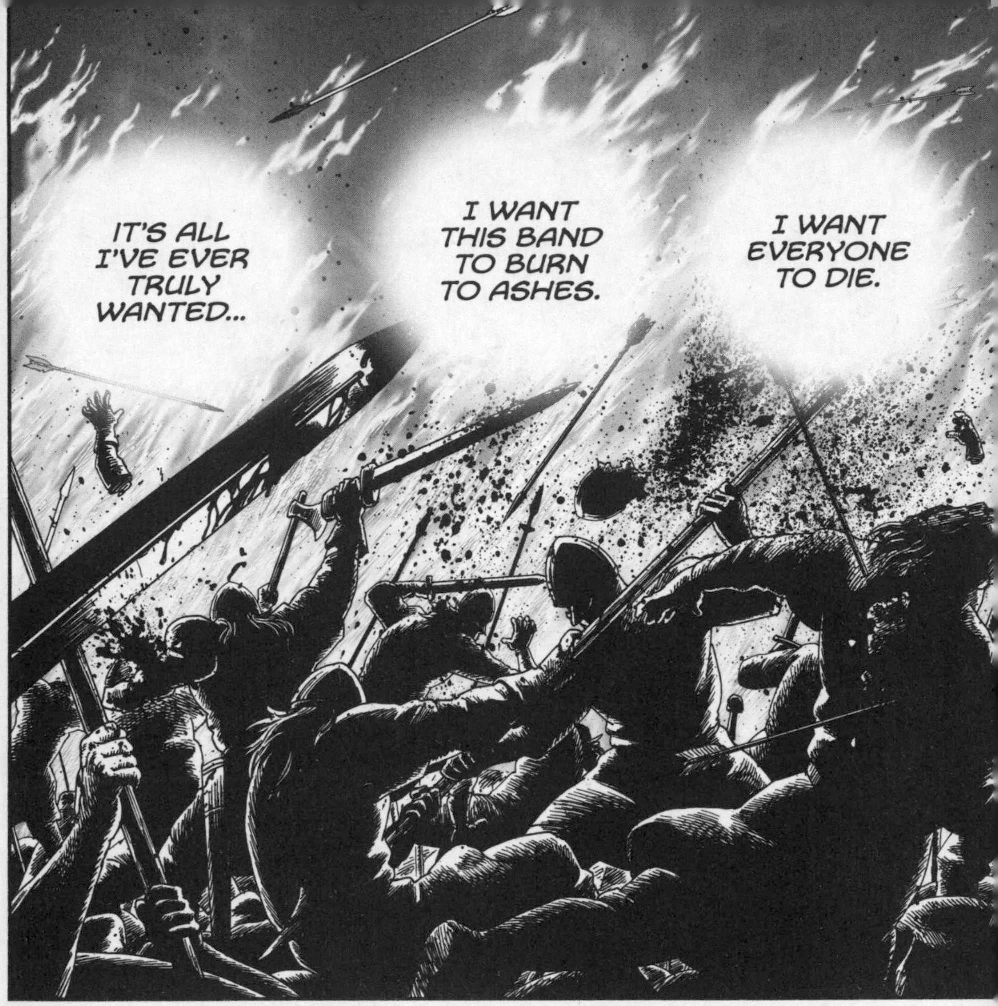
I WANT EVERYONE TO DIE.
I WANT THIS BAND TO BURN TO ASHES.
IT'S ALL I'VE EVER TRULY WANTED...

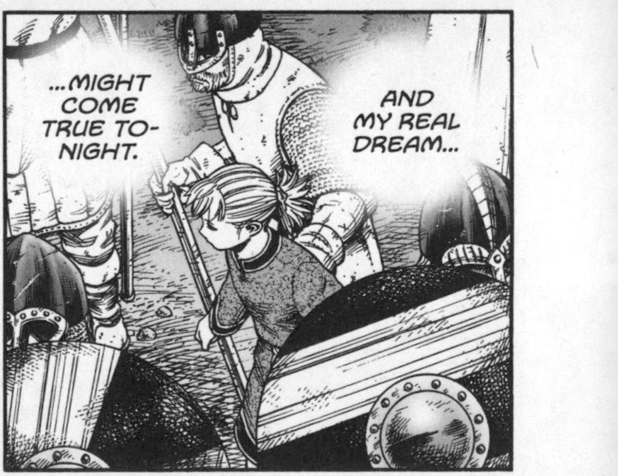
AND MY REAL DREAM...
...MIGHT COME TRUE TO-NIGHT.

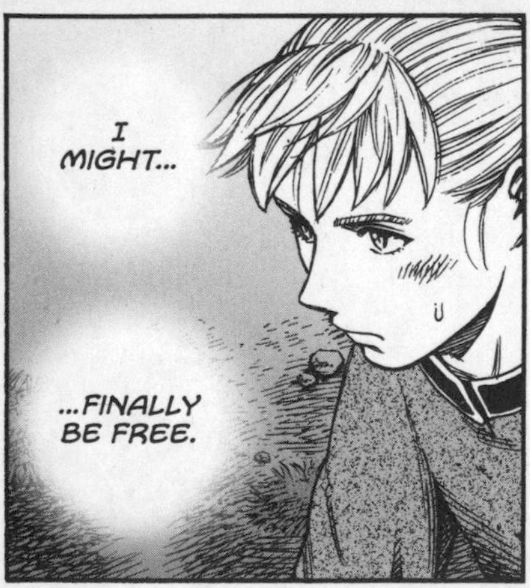
I MIGHT...
...FINALLY BE FREE.

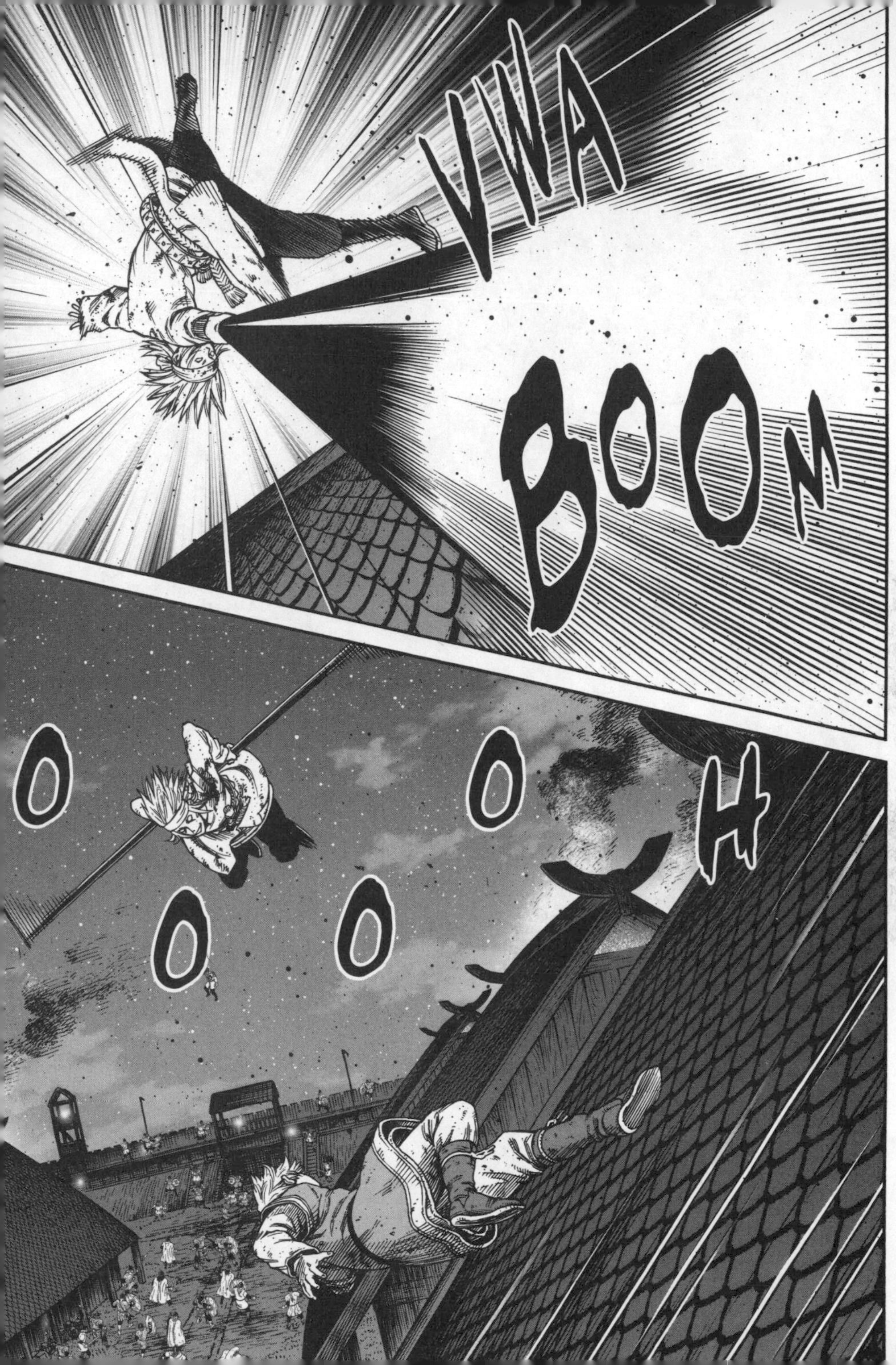
VWA
BOOM
OOOOOH

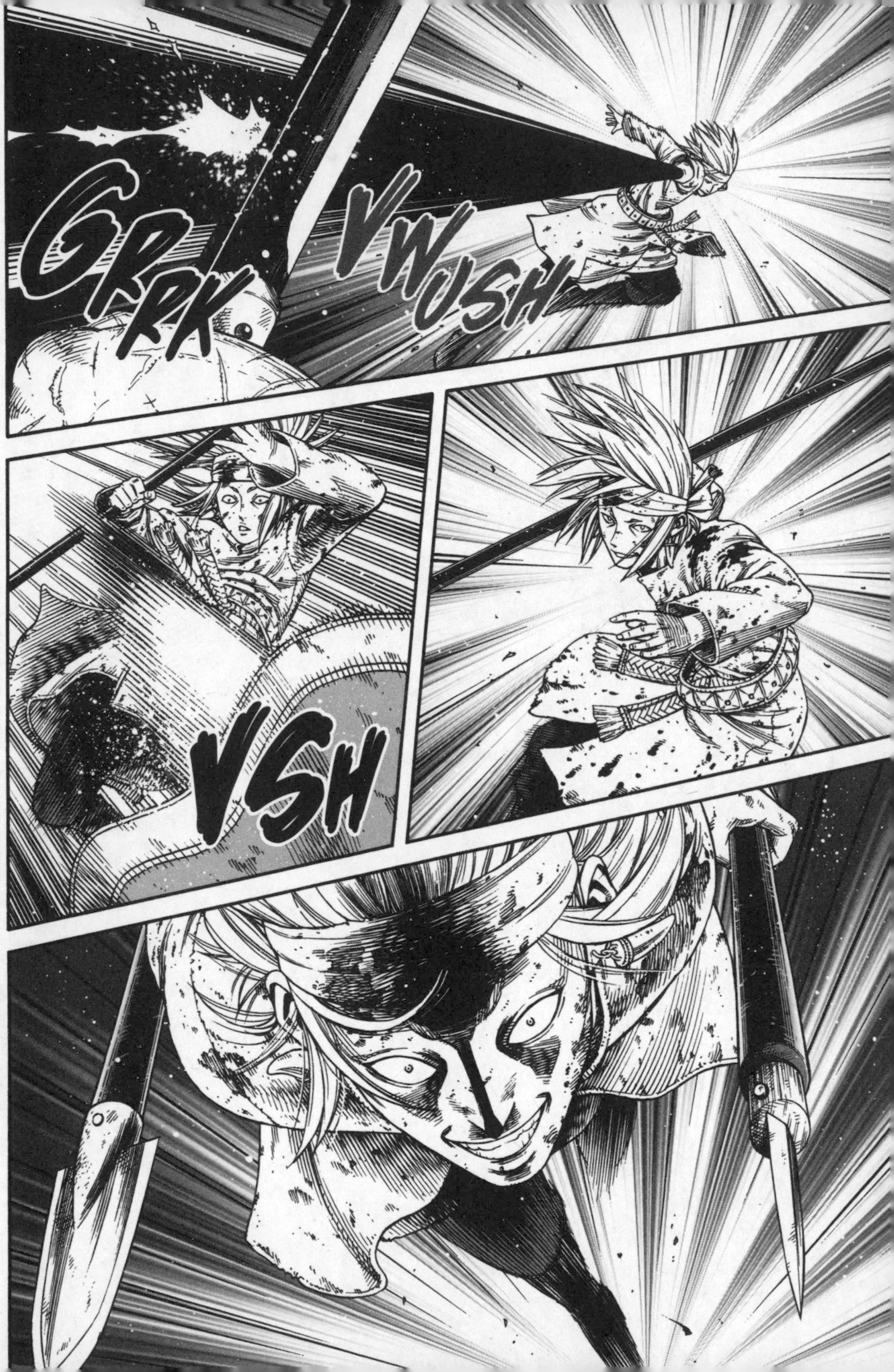
VWUSH
GRRK
VSH

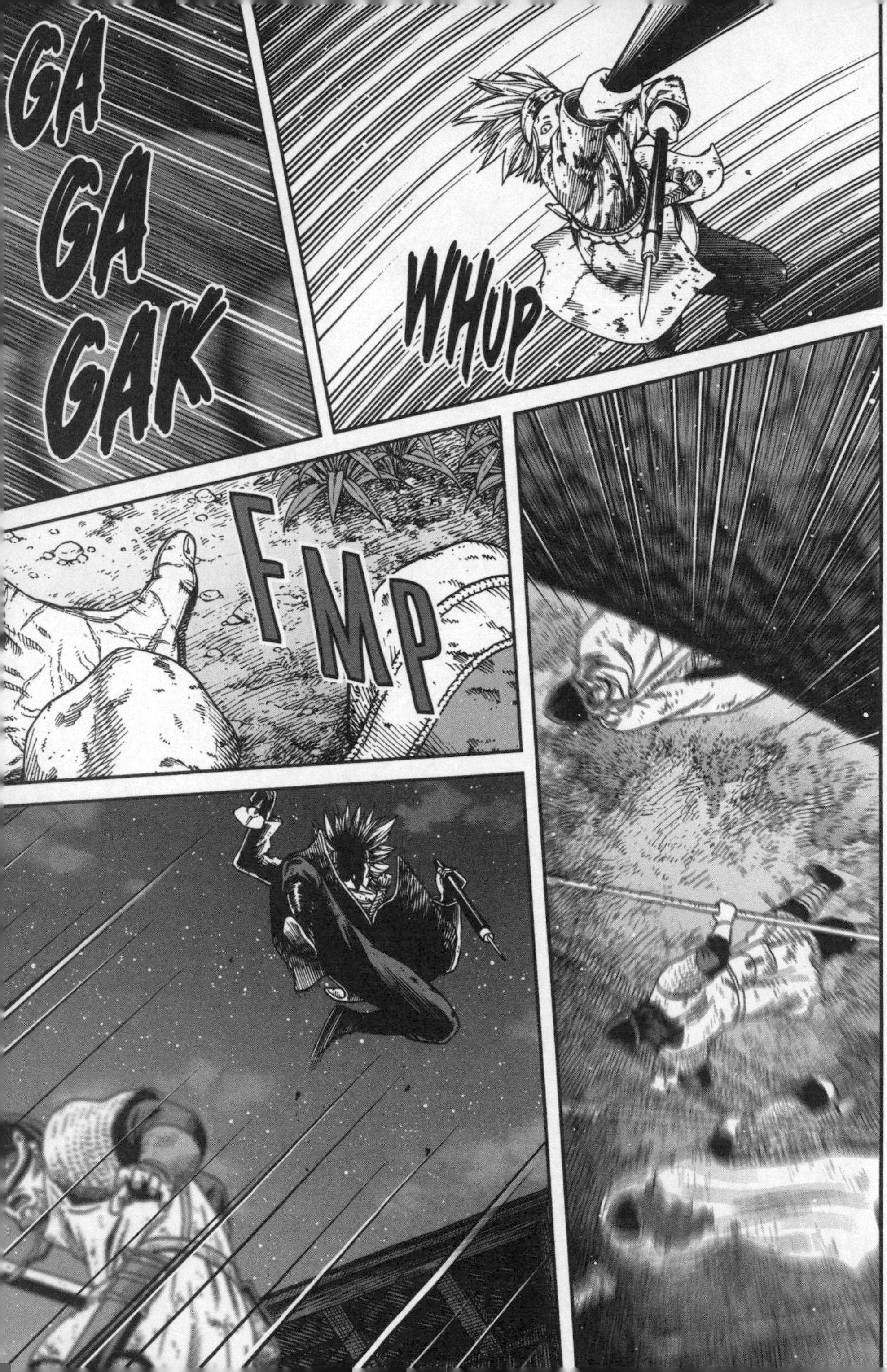
WHUP
GA
GA
GAK
FMP

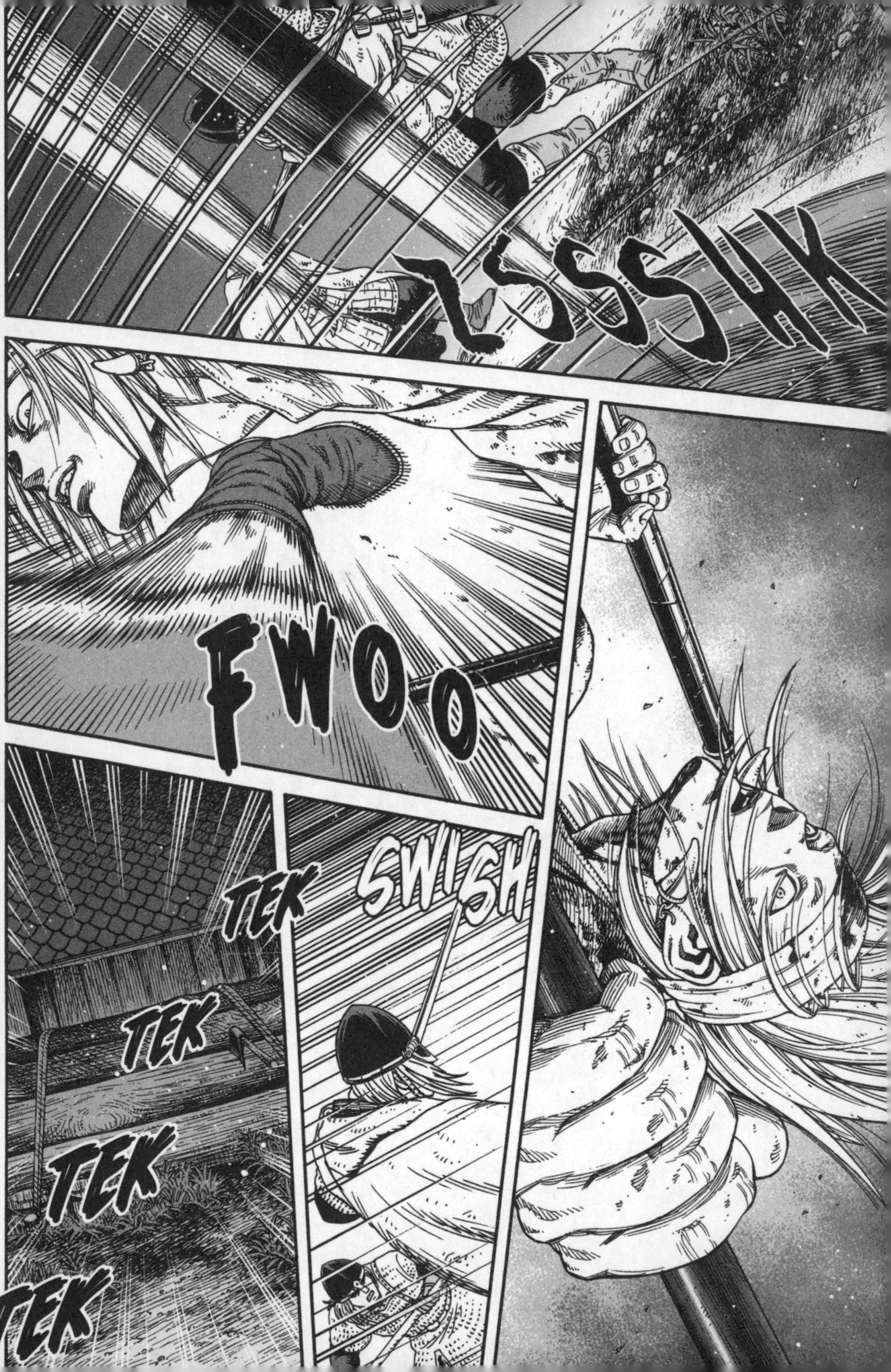
ZSSSHK
FWOO
SWISH
TEK
TEK
TEK
TEK

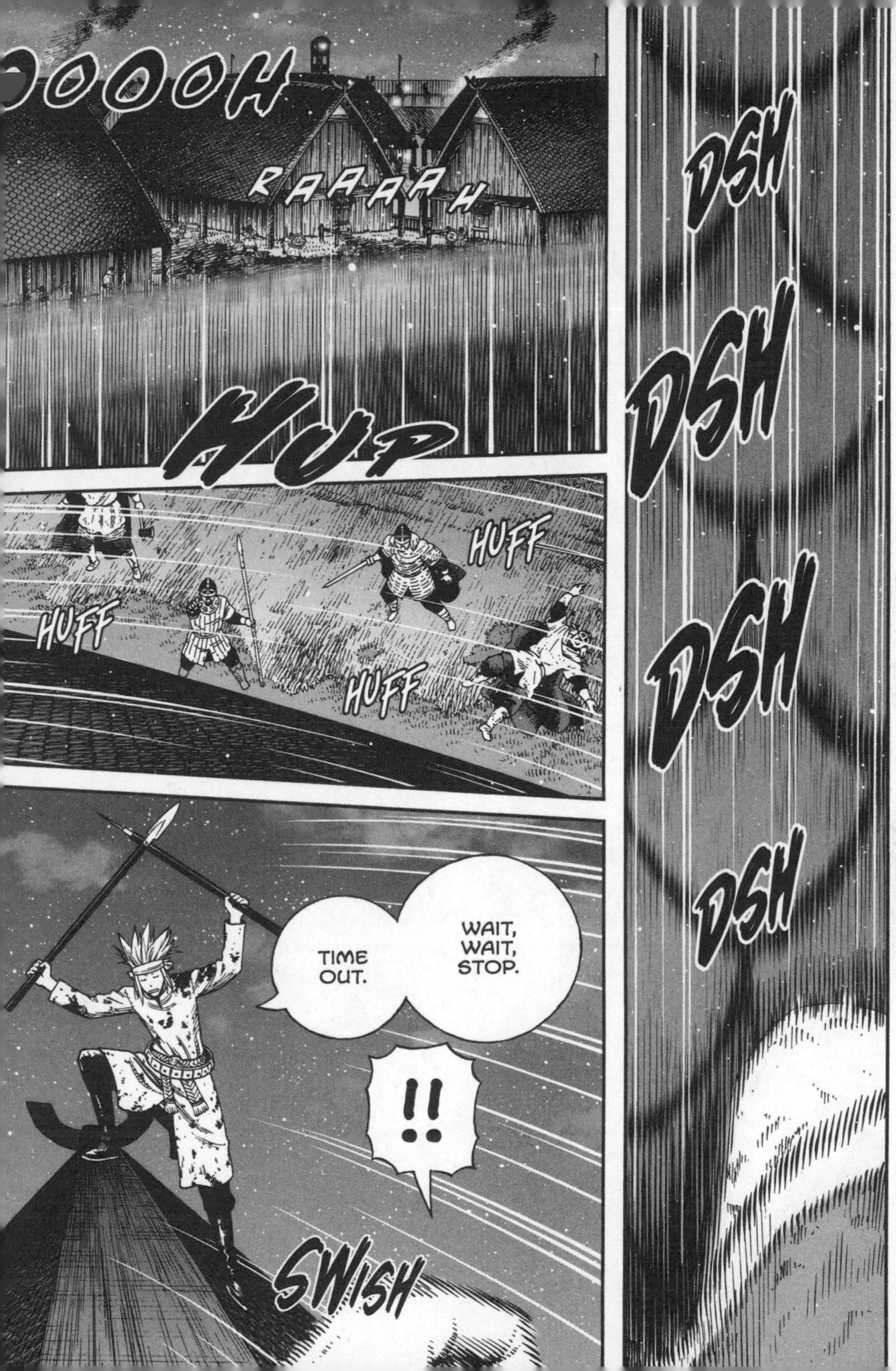
DSH
DSH
DSH
DSH
OOOOH
RAAAAAH
HUP
HUFF
HUFF
HUFF
WAIT, WAIT, STOP.
TIME OUT.
!!
SWISH

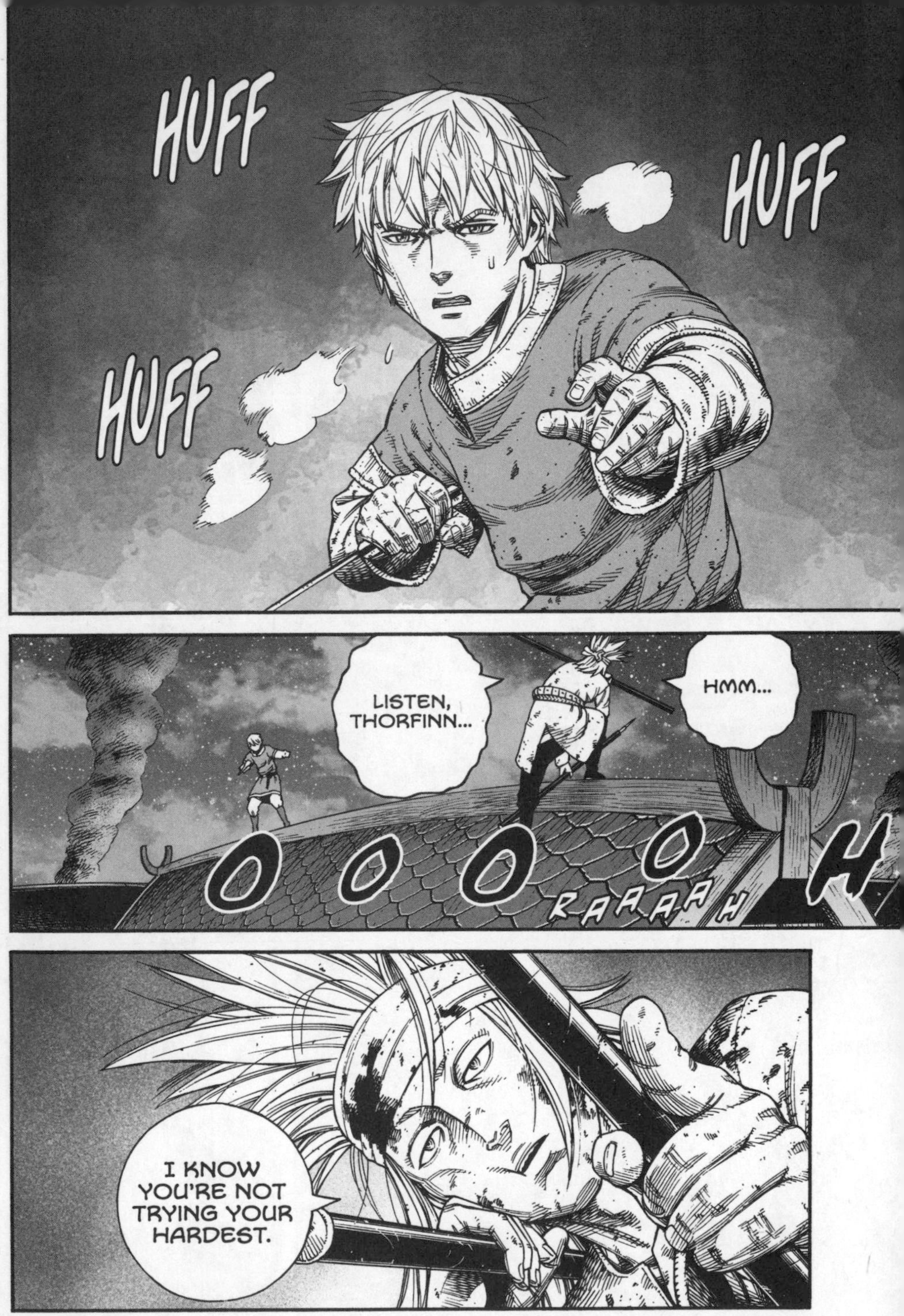
HUFF
HUFF
HUFF
HMM...
LISTEN, THORFINN...
OOOOOH
RAAAAH
I KNOW YOU'RE NOT TRYING YOUR HARDEST.

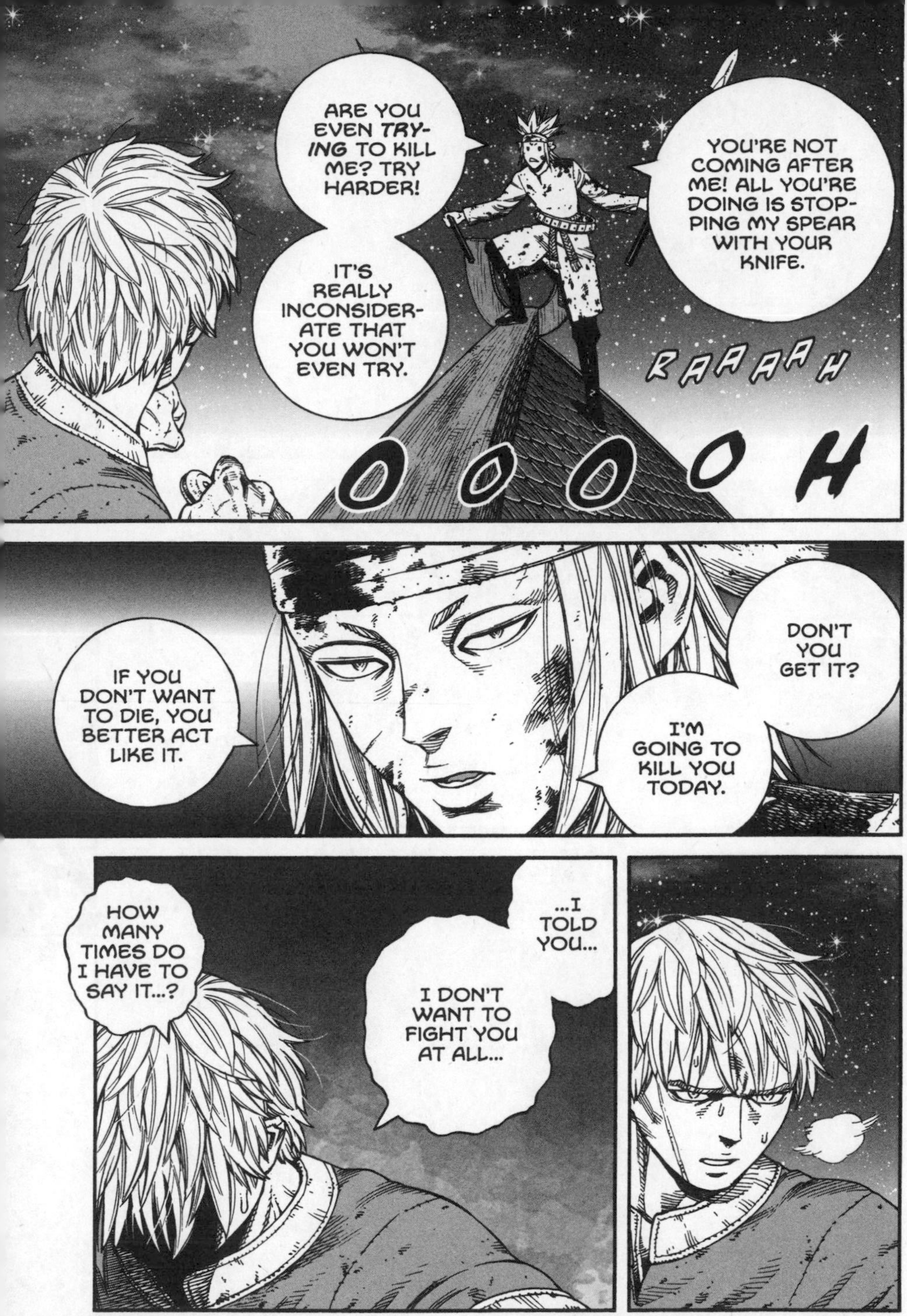
YOU'RE NOT COMING AFTER ME! ALL YOU'RE DOING IS STOP-PING MY SPEAR WITH YOUR KNIFE.
ARE YOU EVEN *TRY-ING* TO KILL ME? TRY HARDER!
IT'S REALLY INCONSIDER-ATE THAT YOU WON'T EVEN TRY.
RAAAAH
OOOOOH
DON'T YOU GET IT?
I'M GOING TO KILL YOU TODAY.
IF YOU DON'T WANT TO DIE, YOU BETTER ACT LIKE IT.
...I TOLD YOU...
I DON'T WANT TO FIGHT YOU AT ALL...
HOW MANY TIMES DO I HAVE TO SAY IT...?

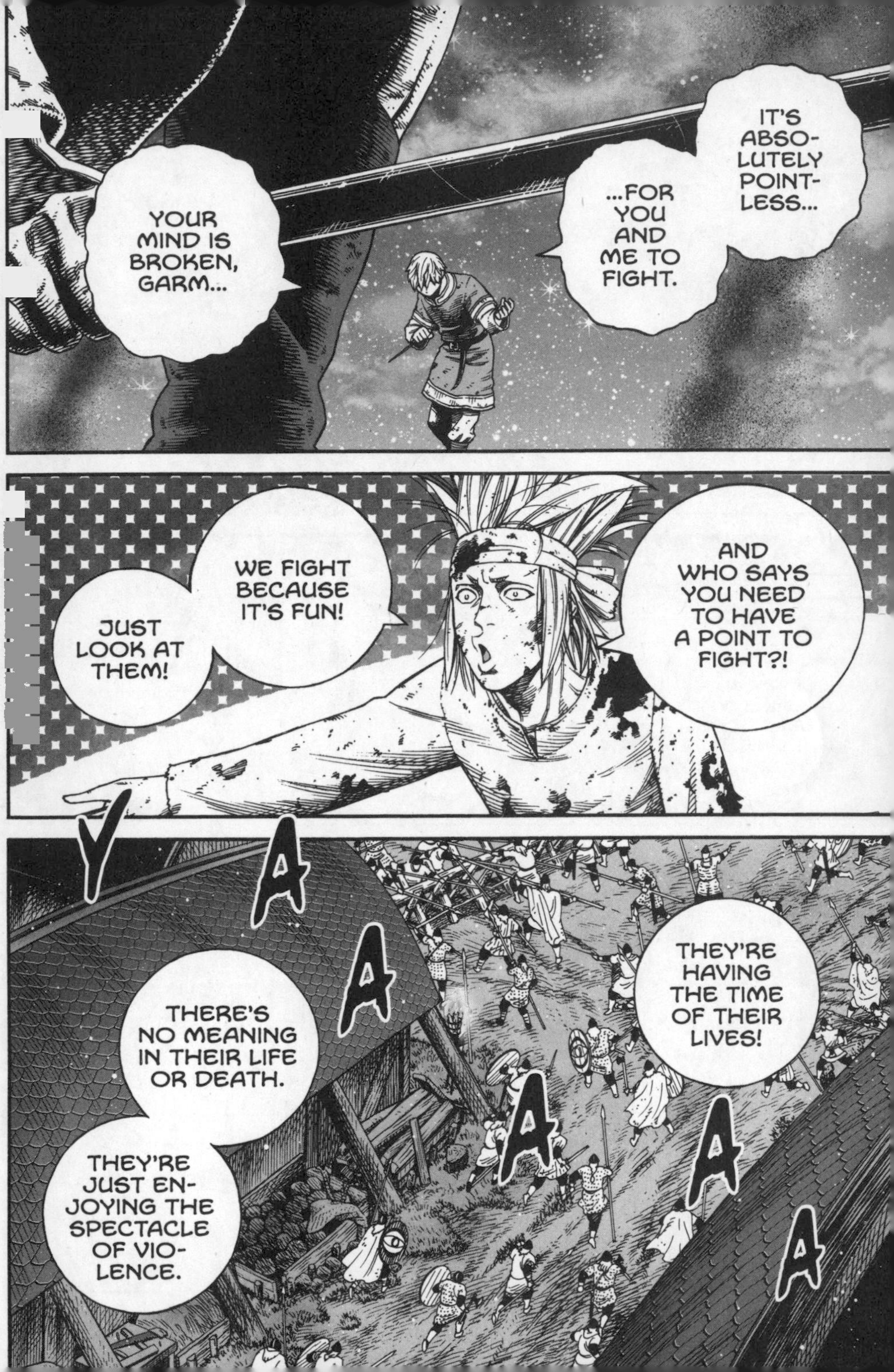
IT'S ABSOLUTELY POINTLESS...
...FOR YOU AND ME TO FIGHT.
YOUR MIND IS BROKEN, GARM...
AND WHO SAYS YOU NEED TO HAVE A POINT TO FIGHT?!
WE FIGHT BECAUSE IT'S FUN!
JUST LOOK AT THEM!
YAAAAAA
THEY'RE HAVING THE TIME OF THEIR LIVES!
THERE'S NO MEANING IN THEIR LIFE OR DEATH.
THEY'RE JUST ENJOYING THE SPECTACLE OF VIOLENCE.

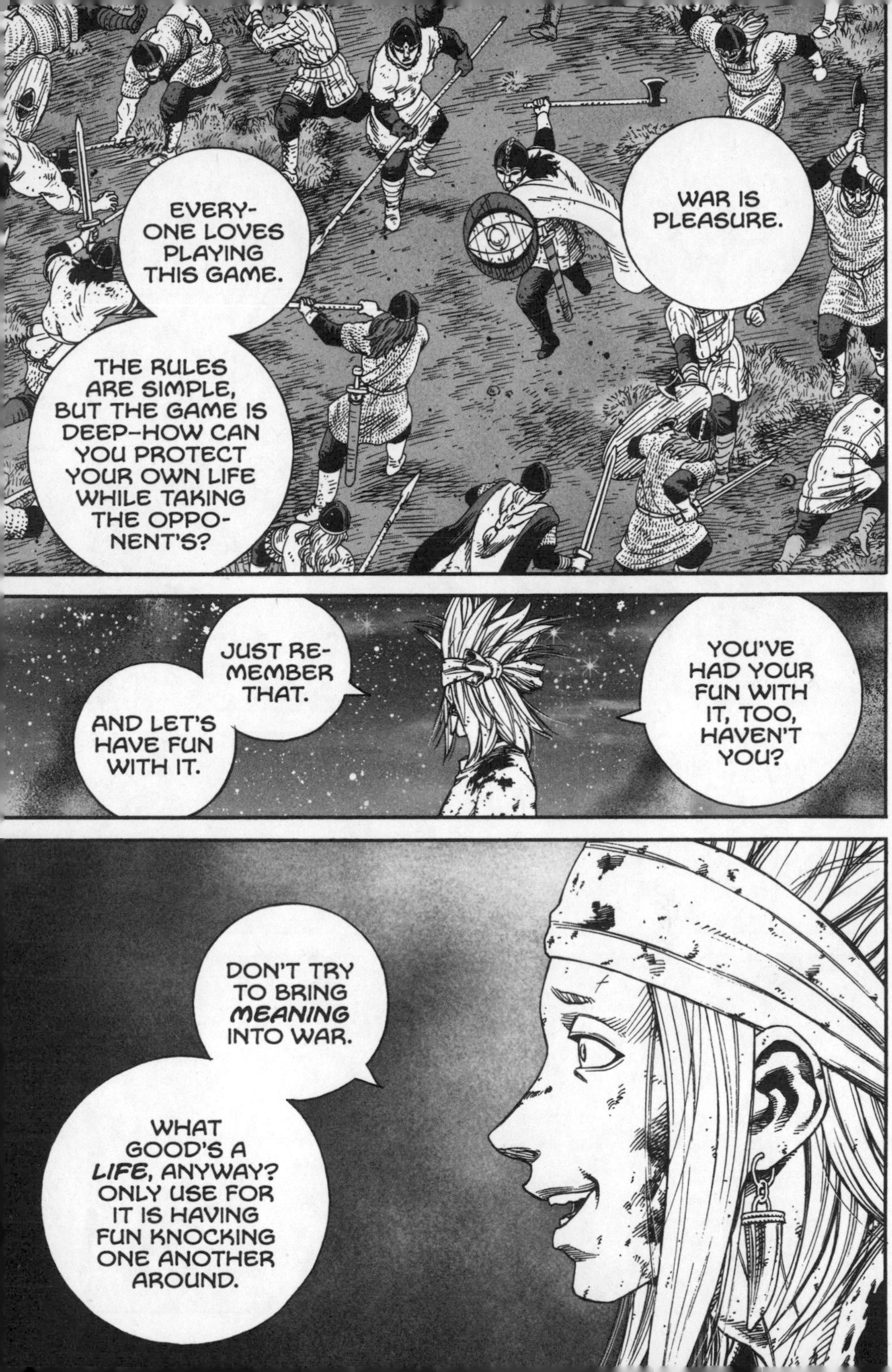
WAR IS PLEASURE.
EVERY-ONE LOVES PLAYING THIS GAME.
THE RULES ARE SIMPLE, BUT THE GAME IS DEEP—HOW CAN YOU PROTECT YOUR OWN LIFE WHILE TAKING THE OPPO-NENT'S?
YOU'VE HAD YOUR FUN WITH IT, TOO, HAVEN'T YOU?
JUST RE-MEMBER THAT.
AND LET'S HAVE FUN WITH IT.
DON'T TRY TO BRING *MEANING* INTO WAR.
WHAT GOOD'S A *LIFE*, ANYWAY? ONLY USE FOR IT IS HAVING FUN KNOCKING ONE ANOTHER AROUND.

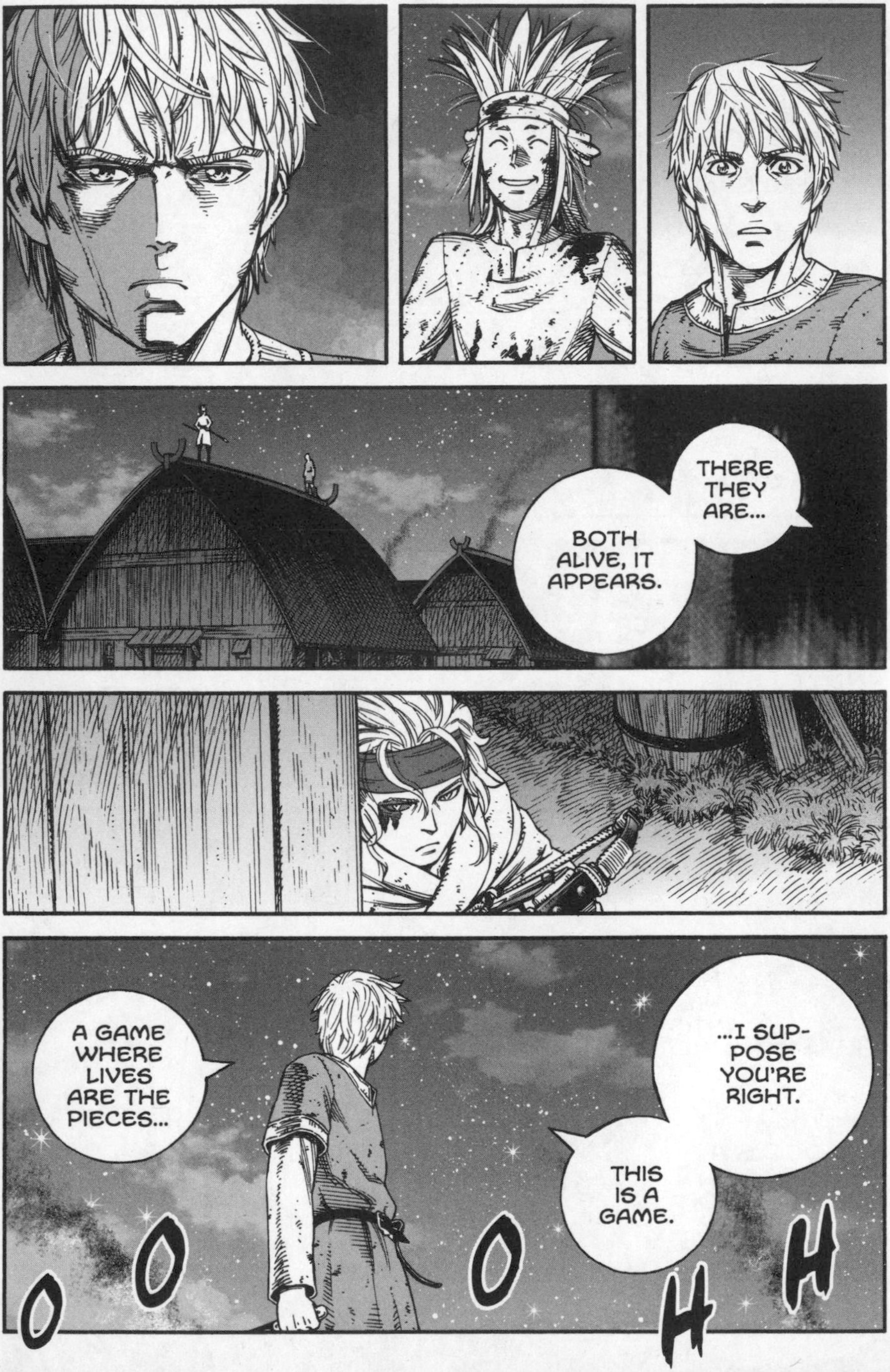
THERE THEY ARE...
BOTH ALIVE, IT APPEARS.
...I SUP-POSE YOU'RE RIGHT.
THIS IS A GAME.
A GAME WHERE LIVES ARE THE PIECES...
OOOHH

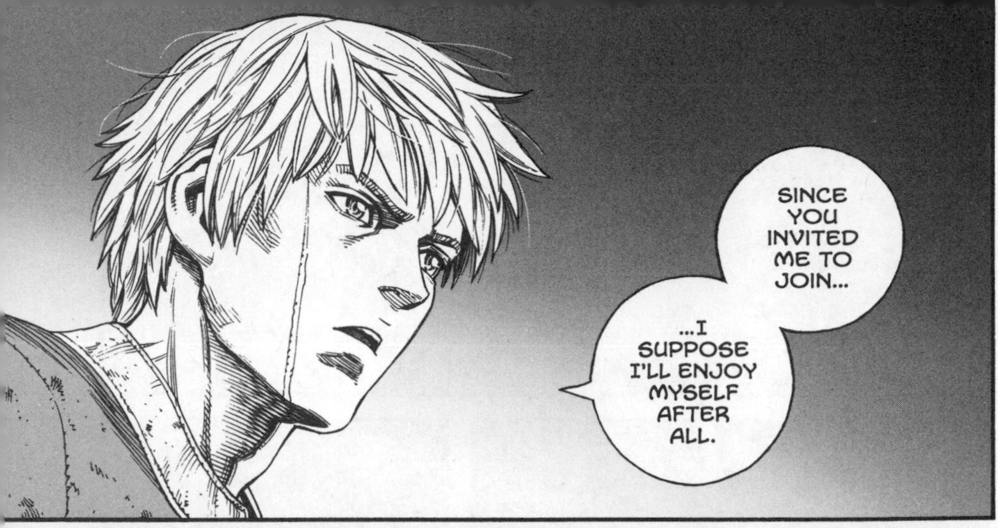
SINCE YOU INVITED ME TO JOIN...
...I SUPPOSE I'LL ENJOY MYSELF AFTER ALL.
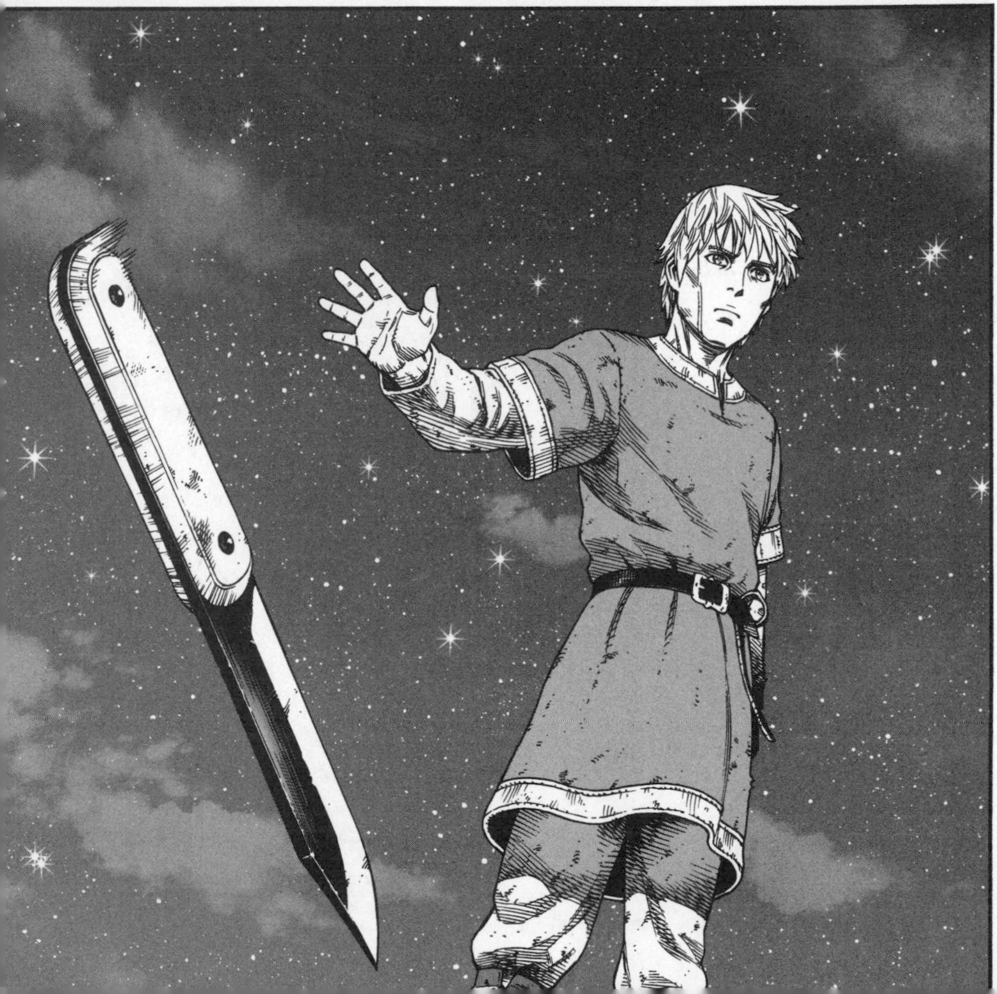

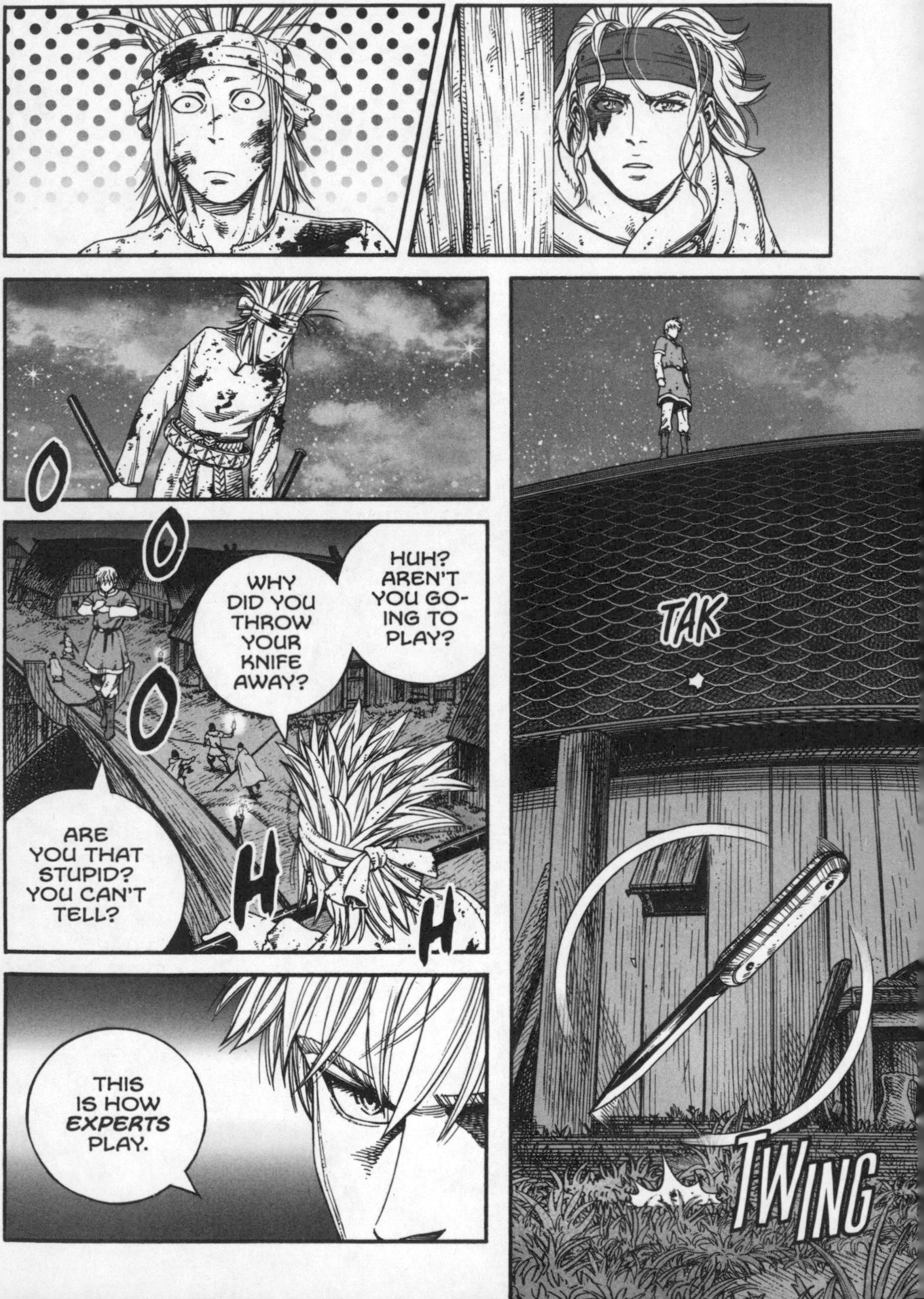
TAK
TWING
HUH? AREN'T YOU GO-ING TO PLAY?
WHY DID YOU THROW YOUR KNIFE AWAY?
ARE YOU THAT STUPID? YOU CAN'T TELL?
H
H
THIS IS HOW EXPERTS PLAY.

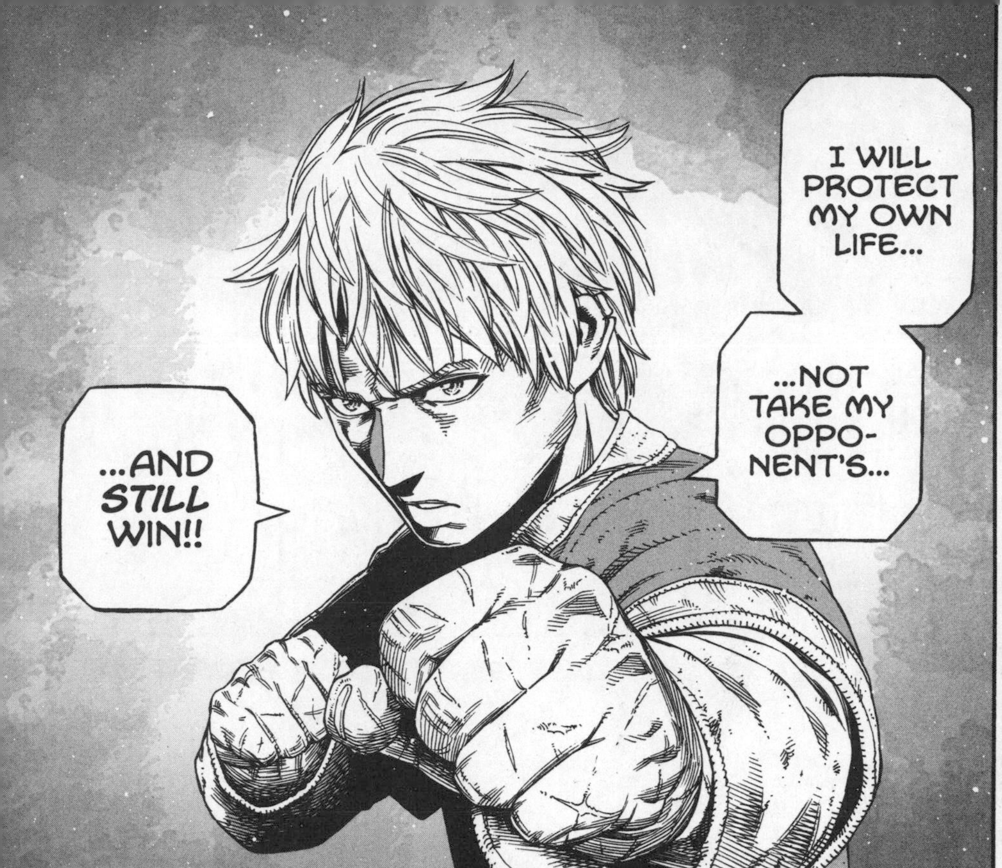
I WILL PROTECT MY OWN LIFE...
...NOT TAKE MY OPPO-NENT'S...
...AND STILL WIN!!

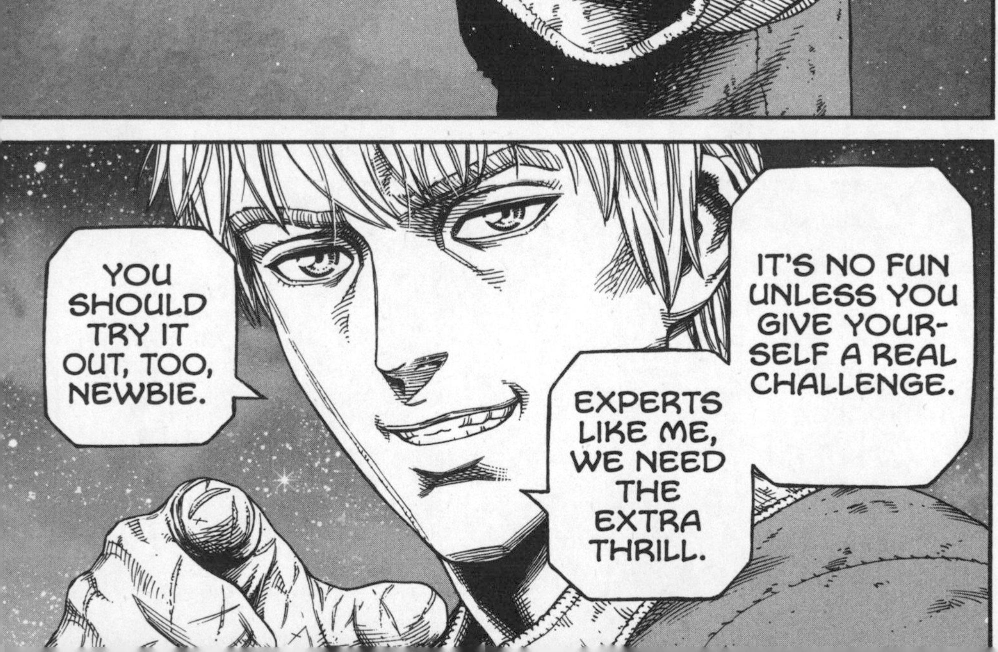
IT'S NO FUN UNLESS YOU GIVE YOUR-SELF A REAL CHALLENGE.
EXPERTS LIKE ME, WE NEED THE EXTRA THRILL.
YOU SHOULD TRY IT OUT, TOO, NEWBIE.

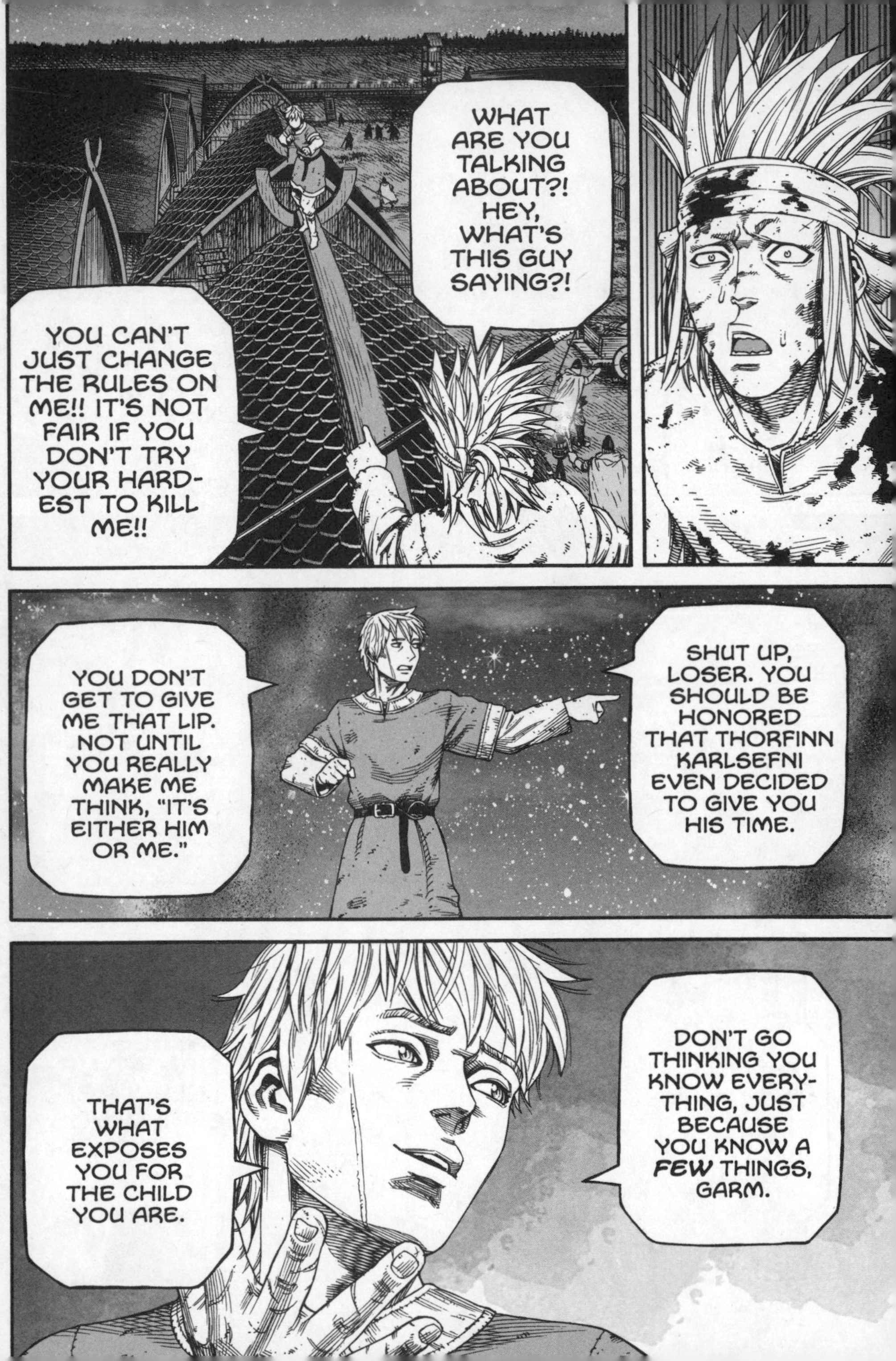
WHAT ARE YOU TALKING ABOUT?! HEY, WHAT'S THIS GUY SAYING?!
YOU CAN'T JUST CHANGE THE RULES ON ME!! IT'S NOT FAIR IF YOU DON'T TRY YOUR HARD-EST TO KILL ME!!
SHUT UP, LOSER. YOU SHOULD BE HONORED THAT THORFINN KARLSEFNI EVEN DECIDED TO GIVE YOU HIS TIME.
YOU DON'T GET TO GIVE ME THAT LIP. NOT UNTIL YOU REALLY MAKE ME THINK, "IT'S EITHER HIM OR ME."
DON'T GO THINKING YOU KNOW EVERY-THING, JUST BECAUSE YOU KNOW A *FEW* THINGS, GARM.
THAT'S WHAT EXPOSES YOU FOR THE CHILD YOU ARE.

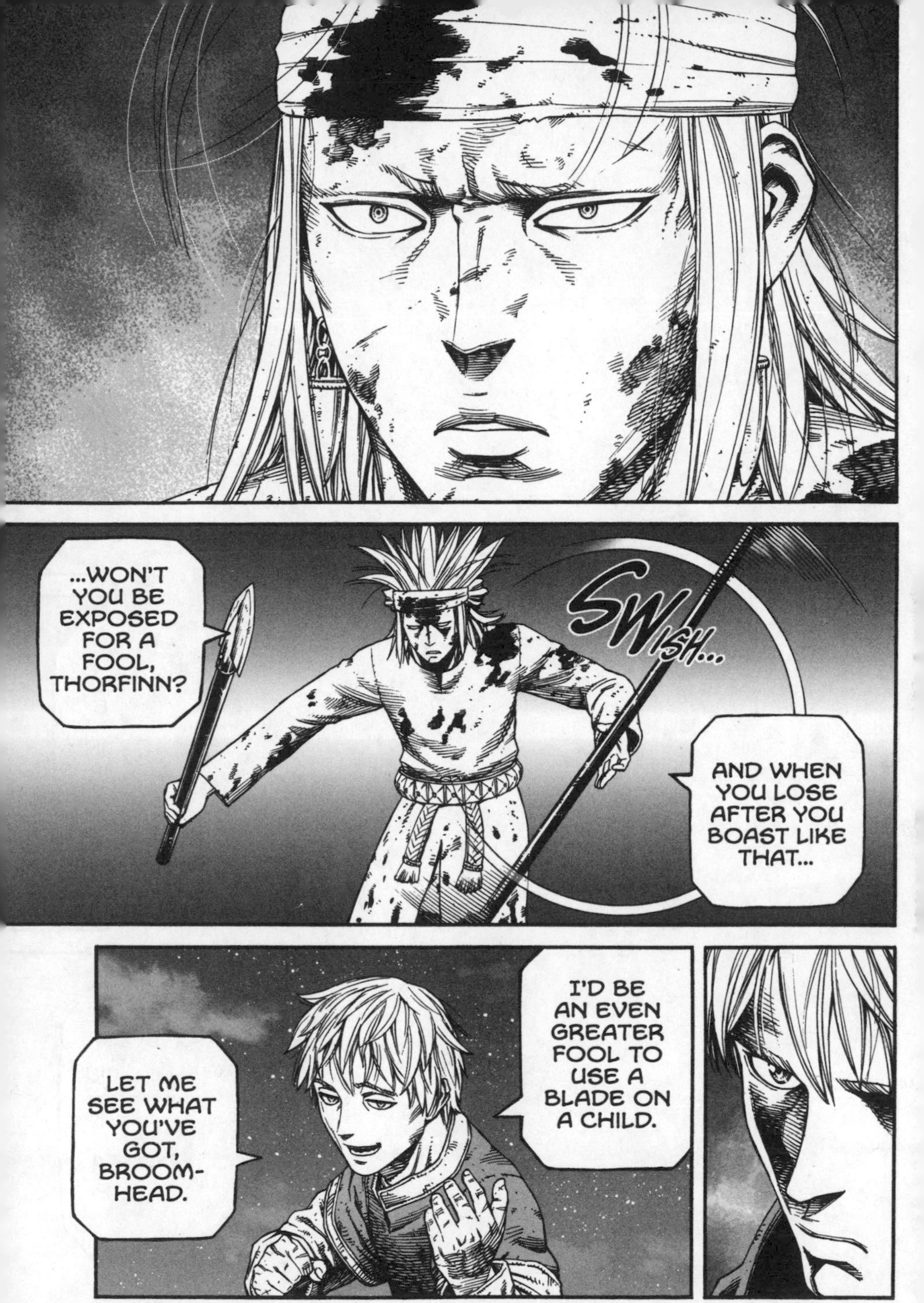
SWISH...
AND WHEN YOU LOSE AFTER YOU BOAST LIKE THAT...
...WON'T YOU BE EXPOSED FOR A FOOL, THORFINN?
I'D BE AN EVEN GREATER FOOL TO USE A BLADE ON A CHILD.
LET ME SEE WHAT YOU'VE GOT, BROOM-HEAD.

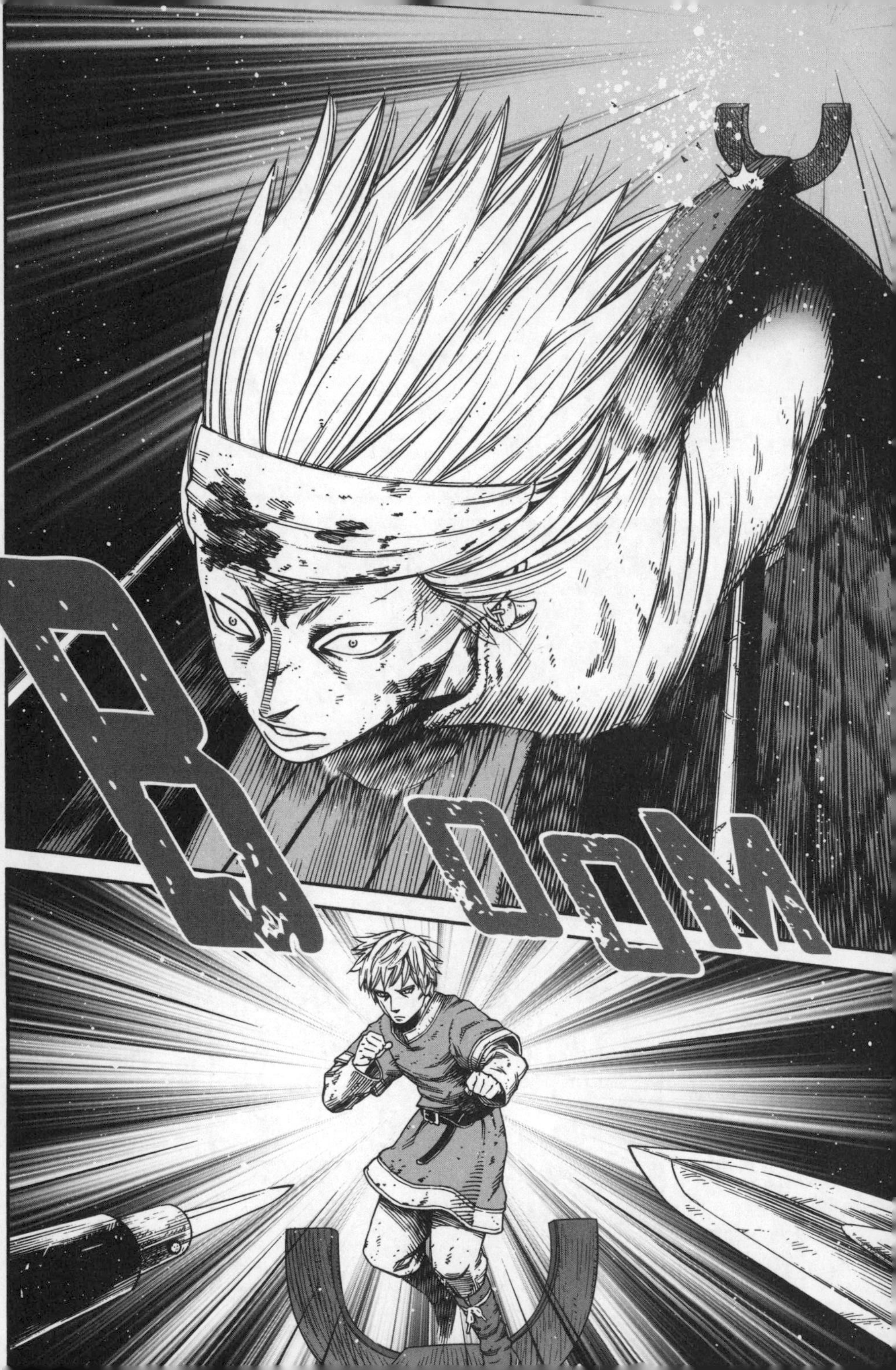
BOOM

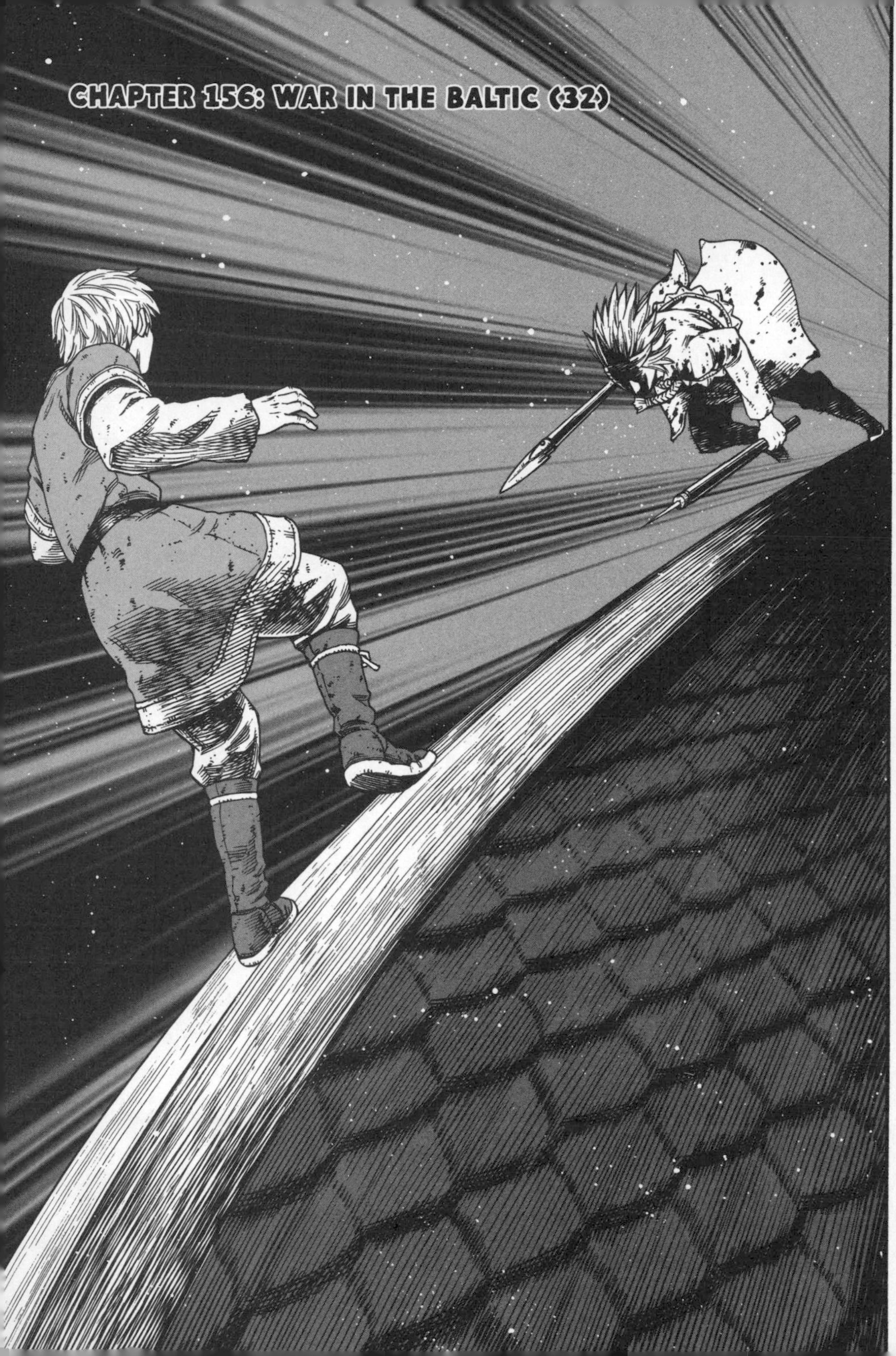
CHAPTER 156: WAR IN THE BALTIC (32)

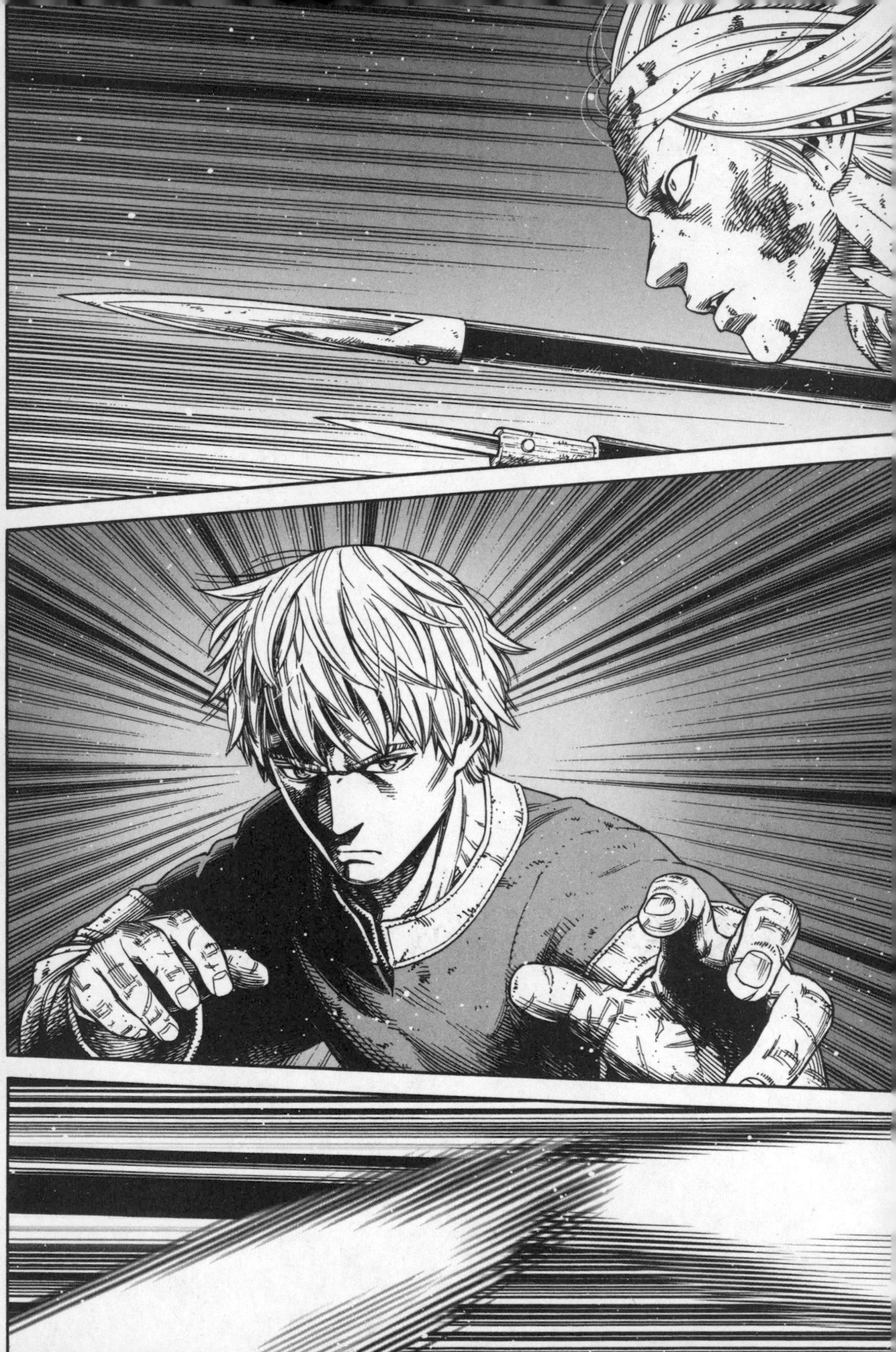

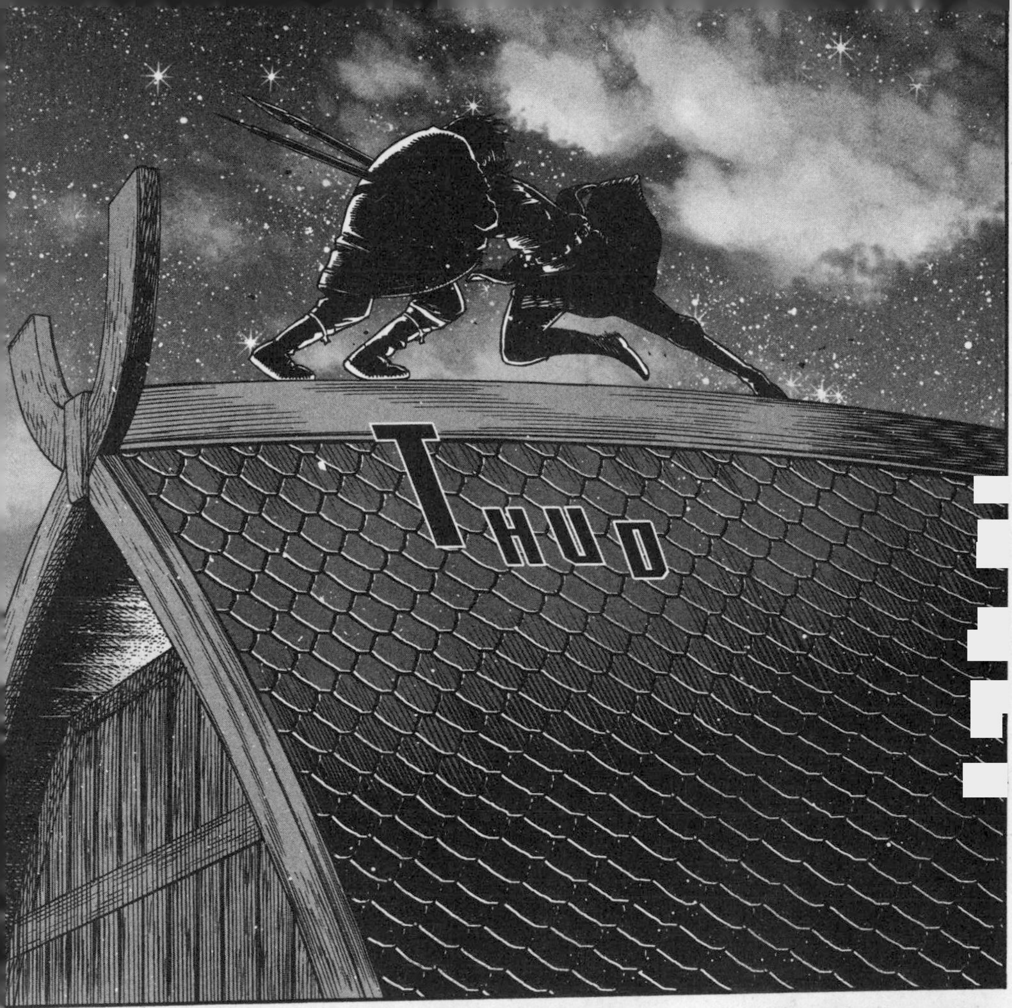
THUD
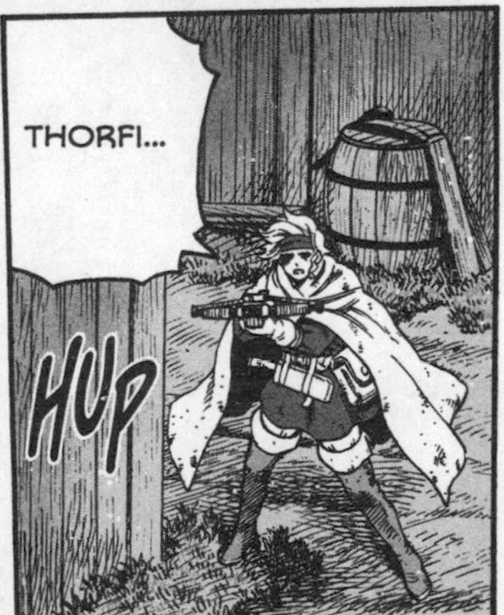
THORFI...
HUP
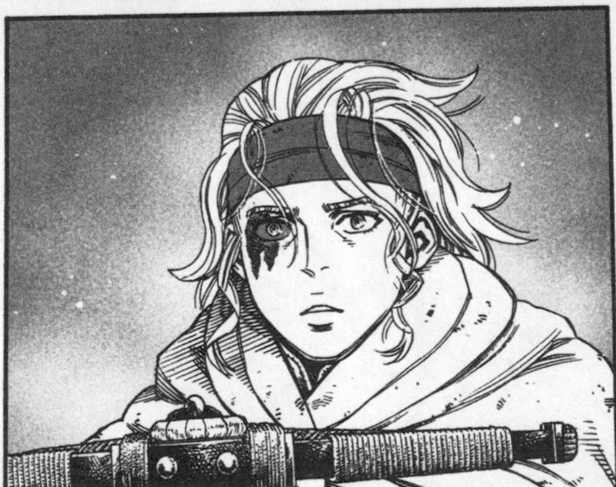

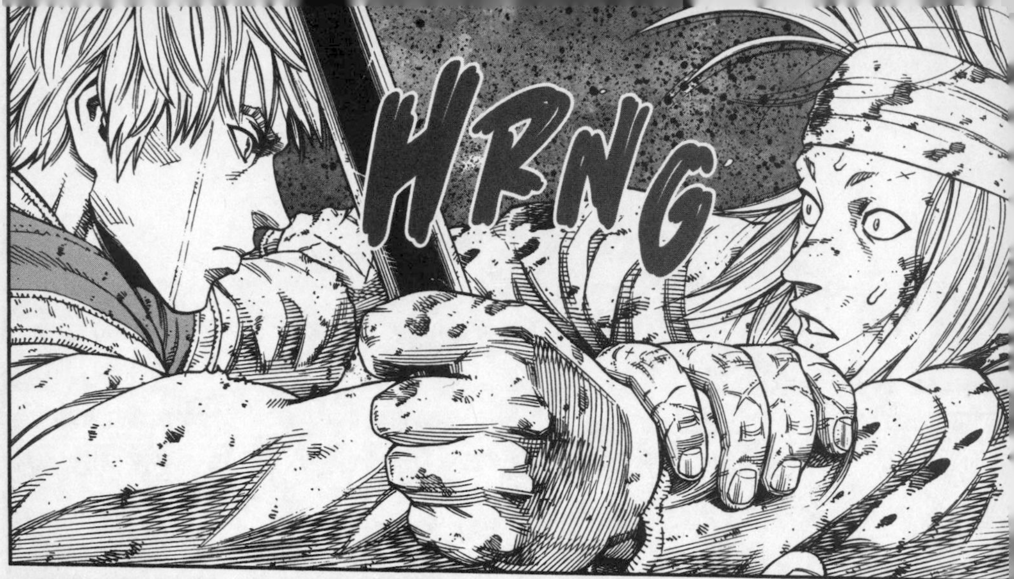
HRNG
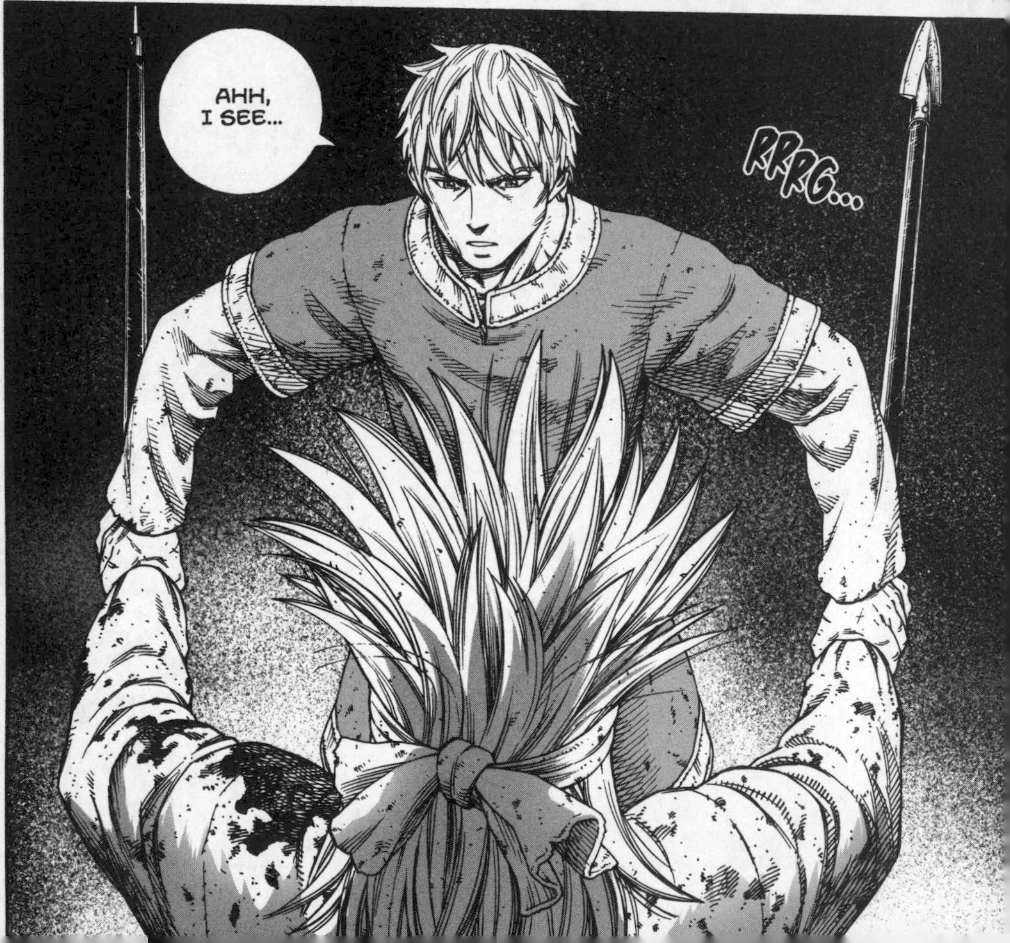
AHH, I SEE...
RRRG...

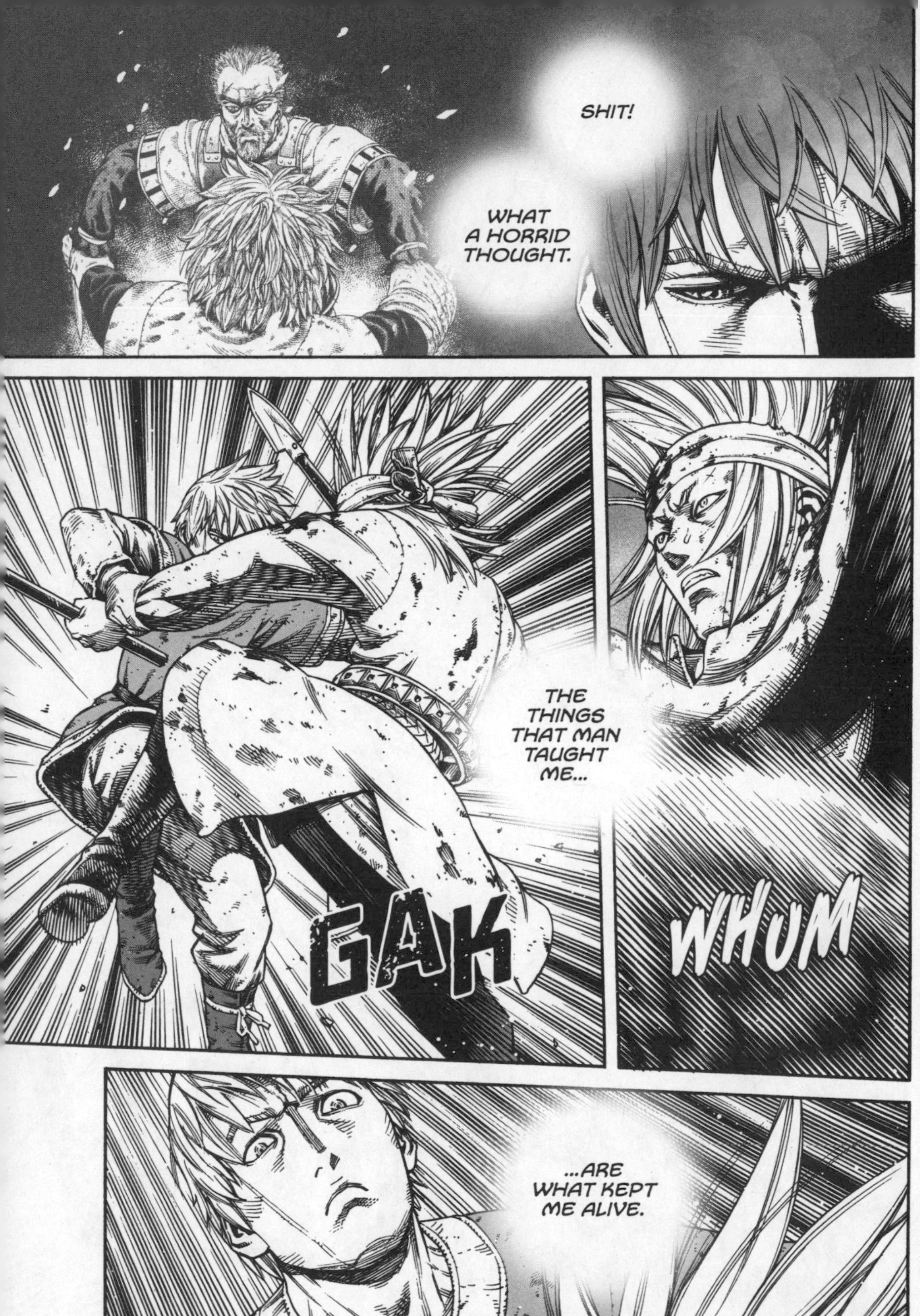
SHIT!
WHAT A HORRID THOUGHT.
THE THINGS THAT MAN TAUGHT ME...
WHUM
GAK
...ARE WHAT KEPT ME ALIVE.

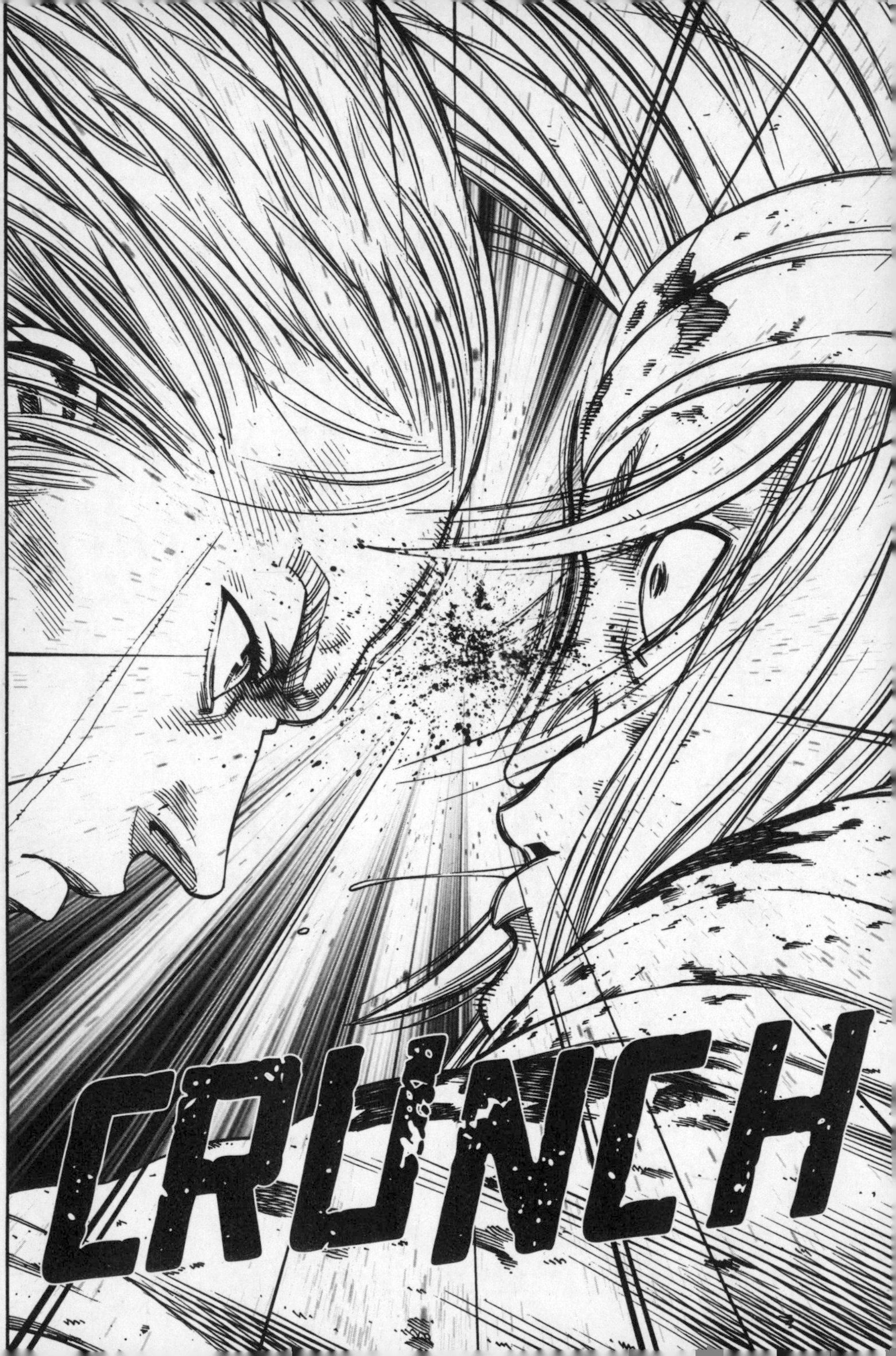
CRUNCH

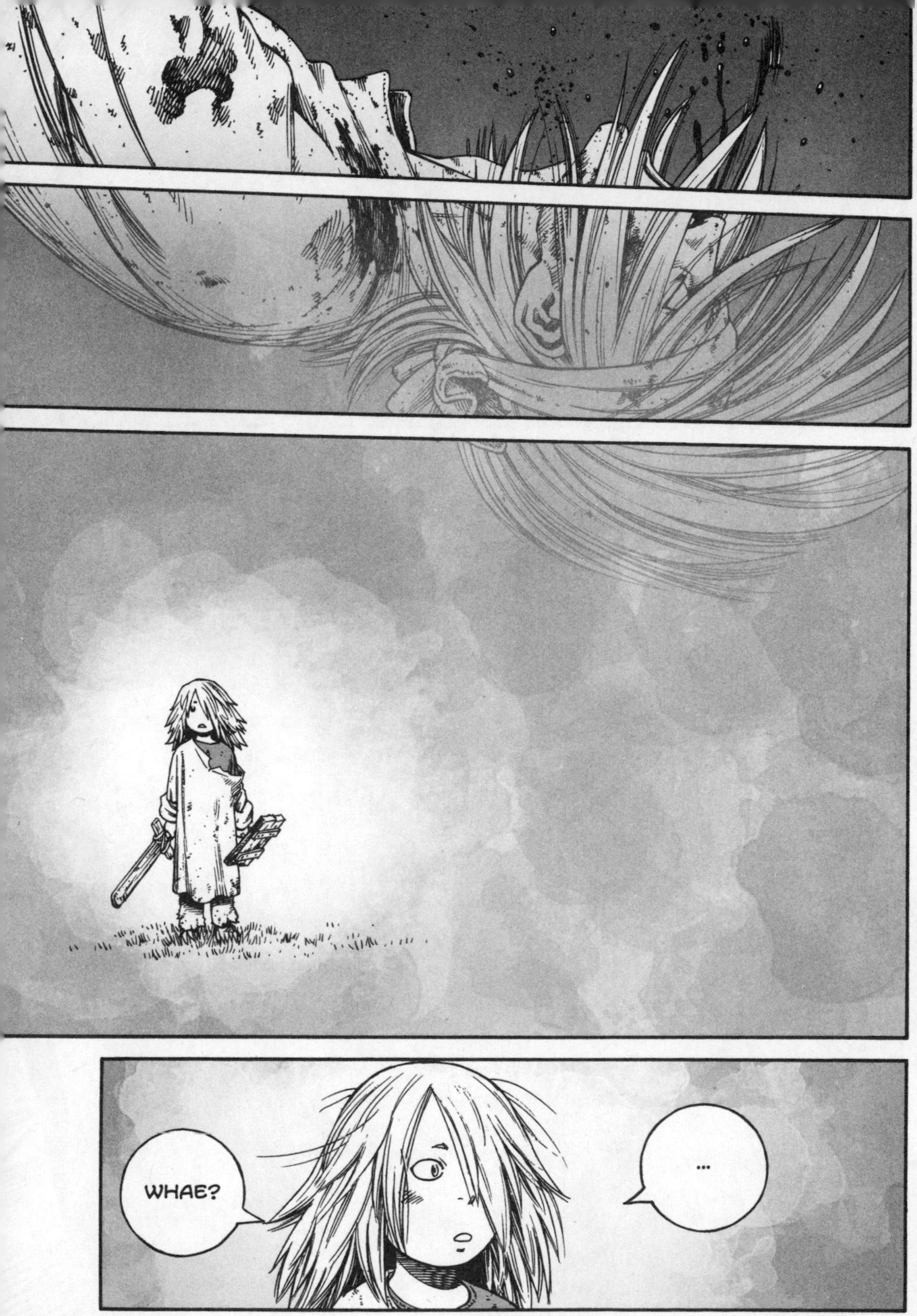
…
WHAE?

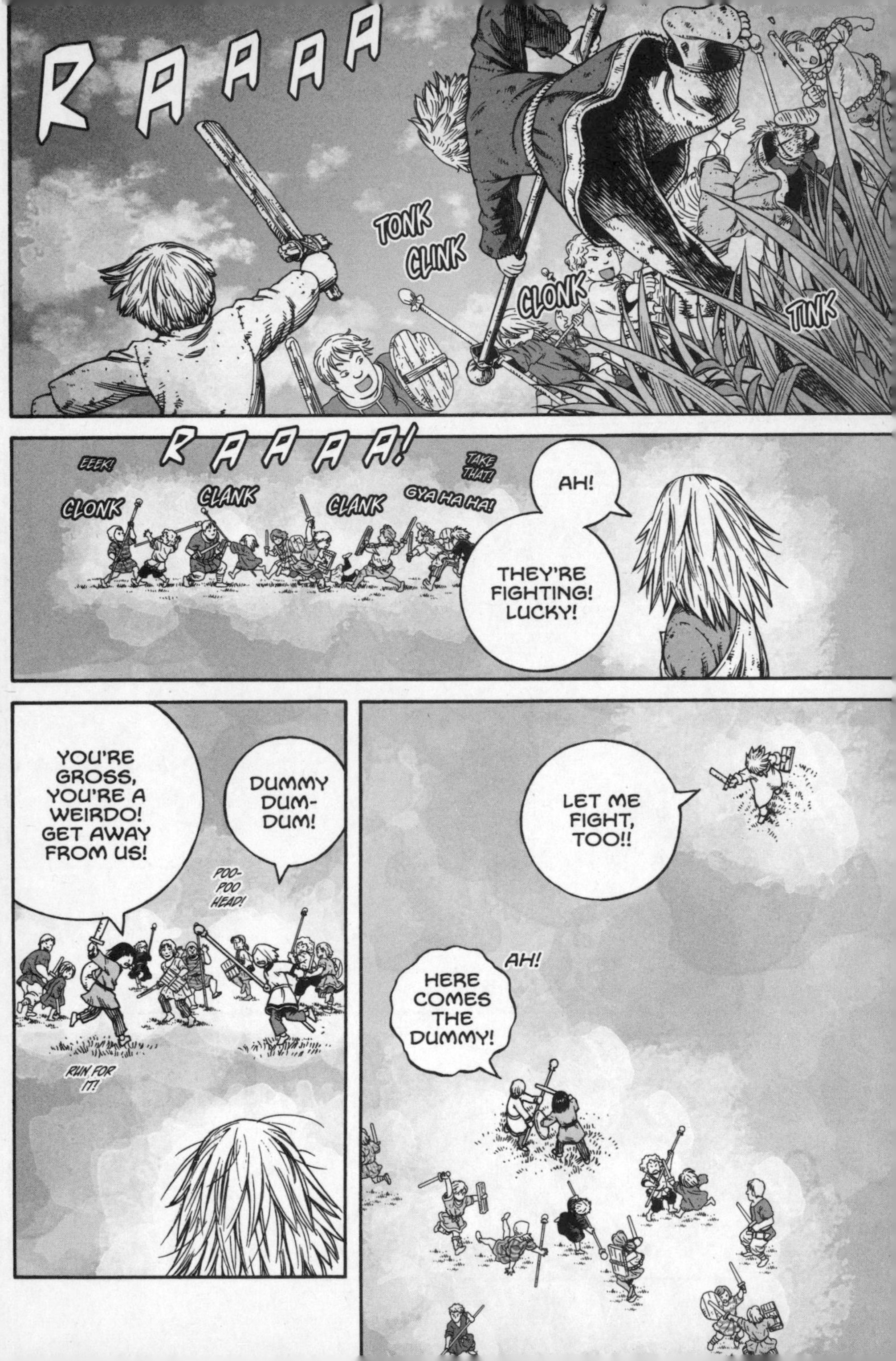
RAAAA
TONK
CLINK
CLONK
TINK
AH!
THEY'RE FIGHTING! LUCKY!
RAAAA!
TAKE THAT!
GYA HA HA!
CLANK
CLANK
EEEK!
CLONK
LET ME FIGHT, TOO!!
AH!
HERE COMES THE DUMMY!
DUMMY DUM-DUM!
YOU'RE GROSS, YOU'RE A WEIRDO! GET AWAY FROM US!
POO-POO HEAD!
RUN FOR IT!

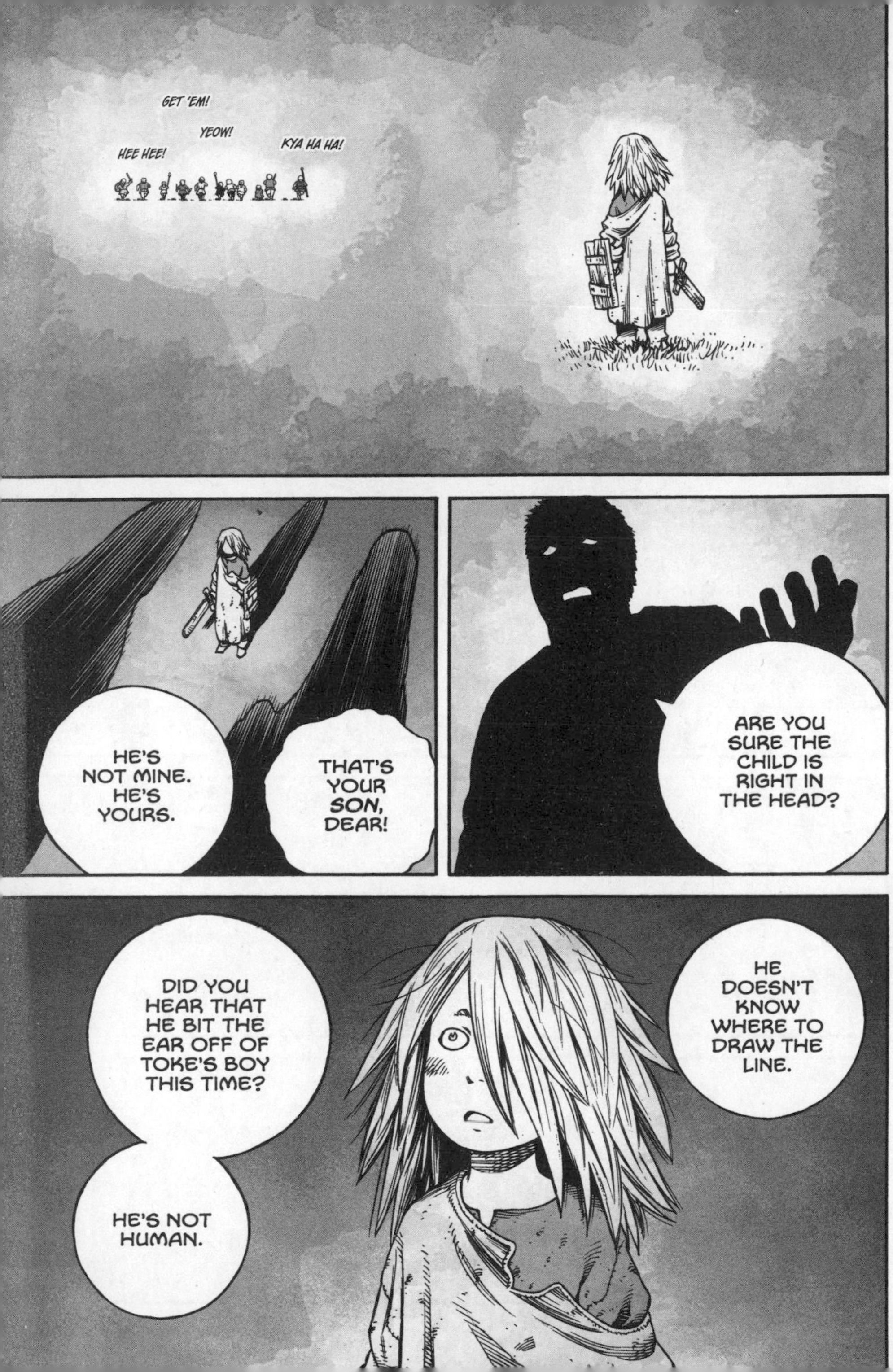
KYA HA HA!
YEOW!
GET 'EM!
HEE HEE!
ARE YOU SURE THE CHILD IS RIGHT IN THE HEAD?
THAT'S YOUR SON, DEAR!
HE'S NOT MINE. HE'S YOURS.
HE DOESN'T KNOW WHERE TO DRAW THE LINE.
DID YOU HEAR THAT HE BIT THE EAR OFF OF TOKE'S BOY THIS TIME?
HE'S NOT HUMAN.

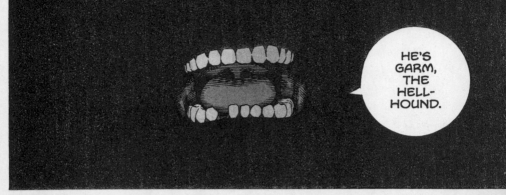

HE'S GARM, THE HELL-HOUND.

CLANK

GARM THE DOG BOY!

SWISH

CLONK

GET LOST, GARM!

TAKE THIS!

HI-YA!

HA HA HA!

KYA HA HA HA!

LOSER!

C'MON, LET'S GO.

LITTLE CREEP!

HEY, GARM.

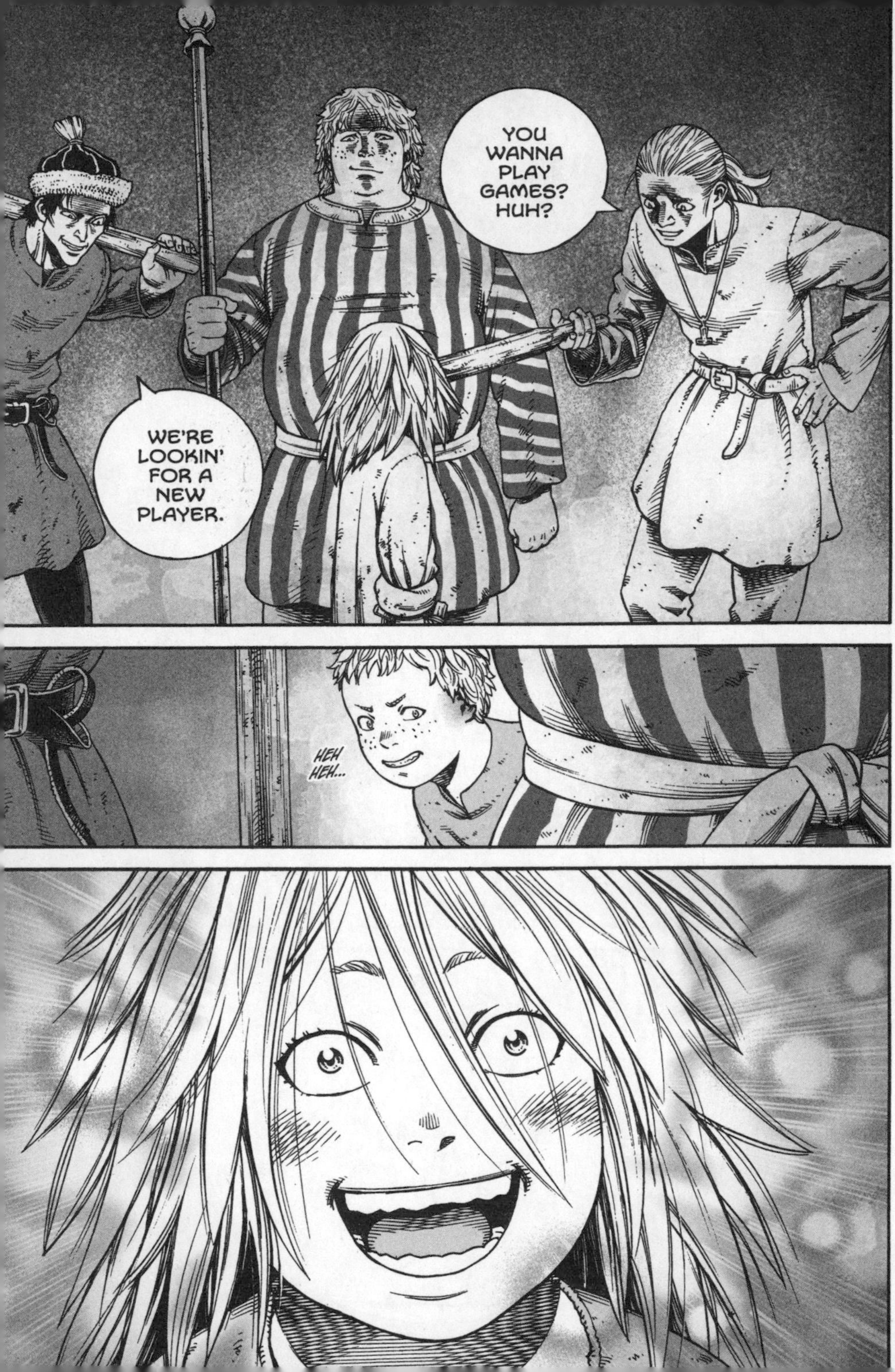
YOU WANNA PLAY GAMES? HUH?
WE'RE LOOKIN' FOR A NEW PLAYER.
HEH HEH...

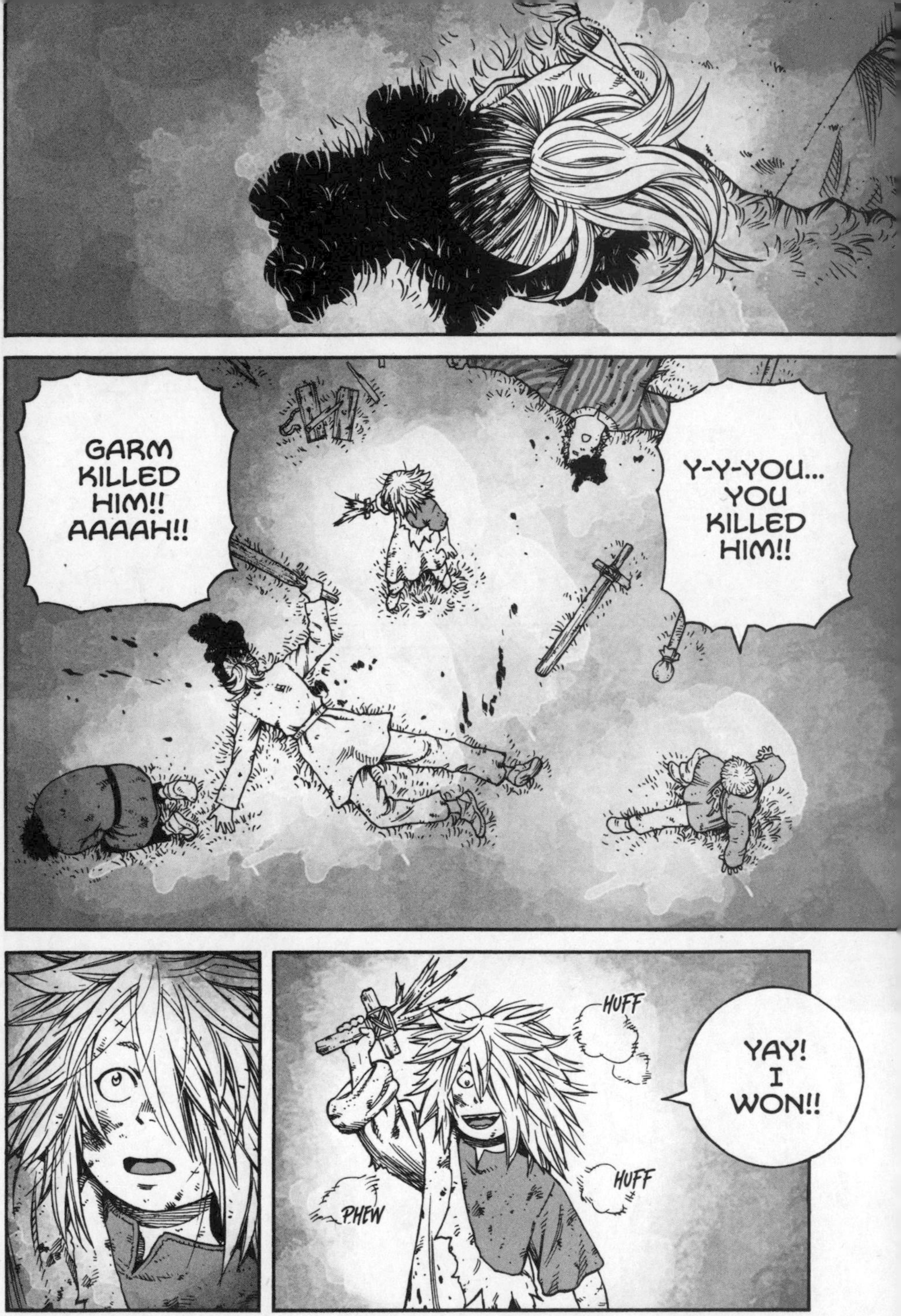
Y-Y-YOU... YOU KILLED HIM!!
GARM KILLED HIM!! AAAAH!!
HUFF
YAY! I WON!!
HUFF
PHEW

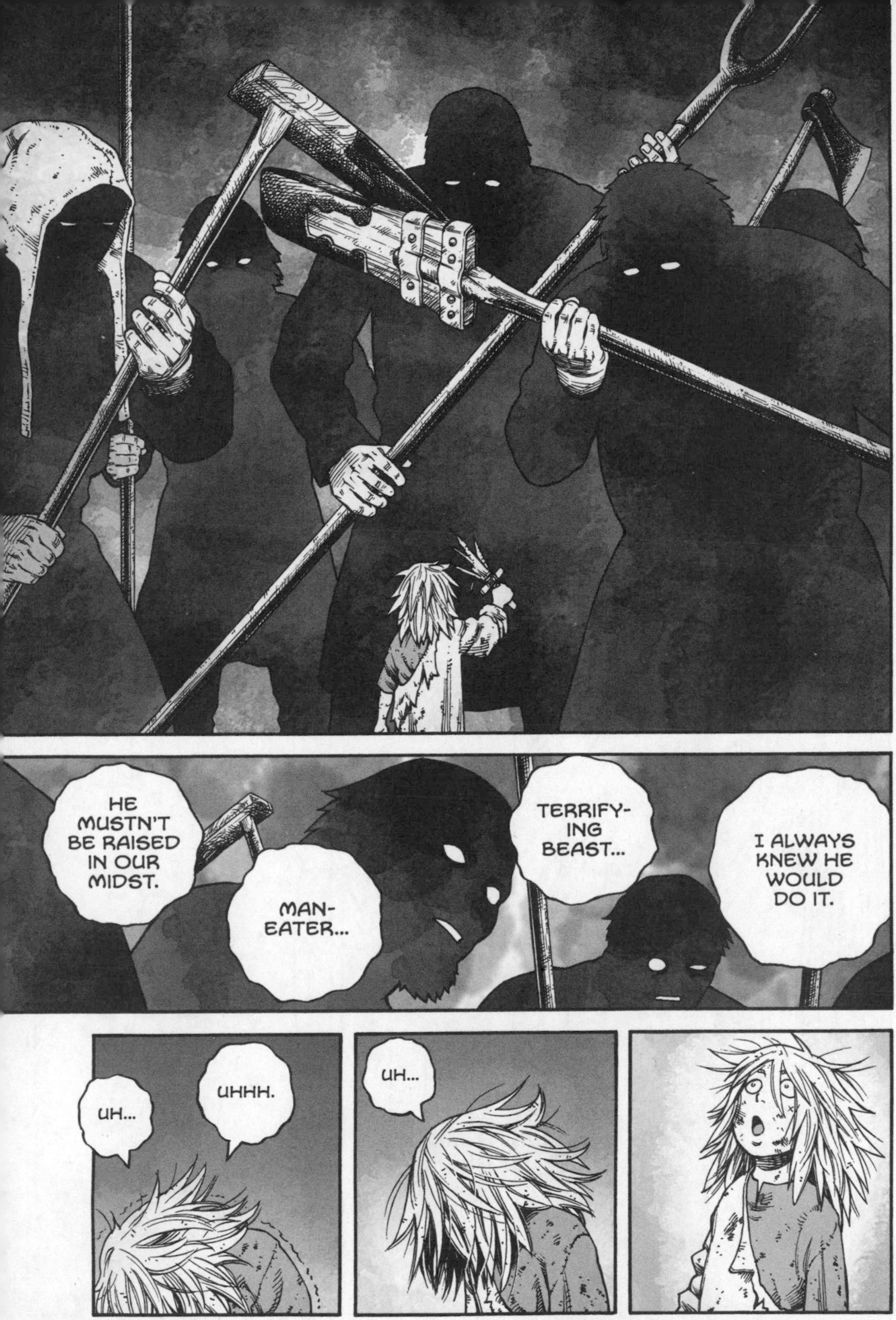
I ALWAYS KNEW HE WOULD DO IT.
TERRIFY-ING BEAST...
MAN-EATER...
HE MUSTN'T BE RAISED IN OUR MIDST.
UH...
UHHH.
UH...

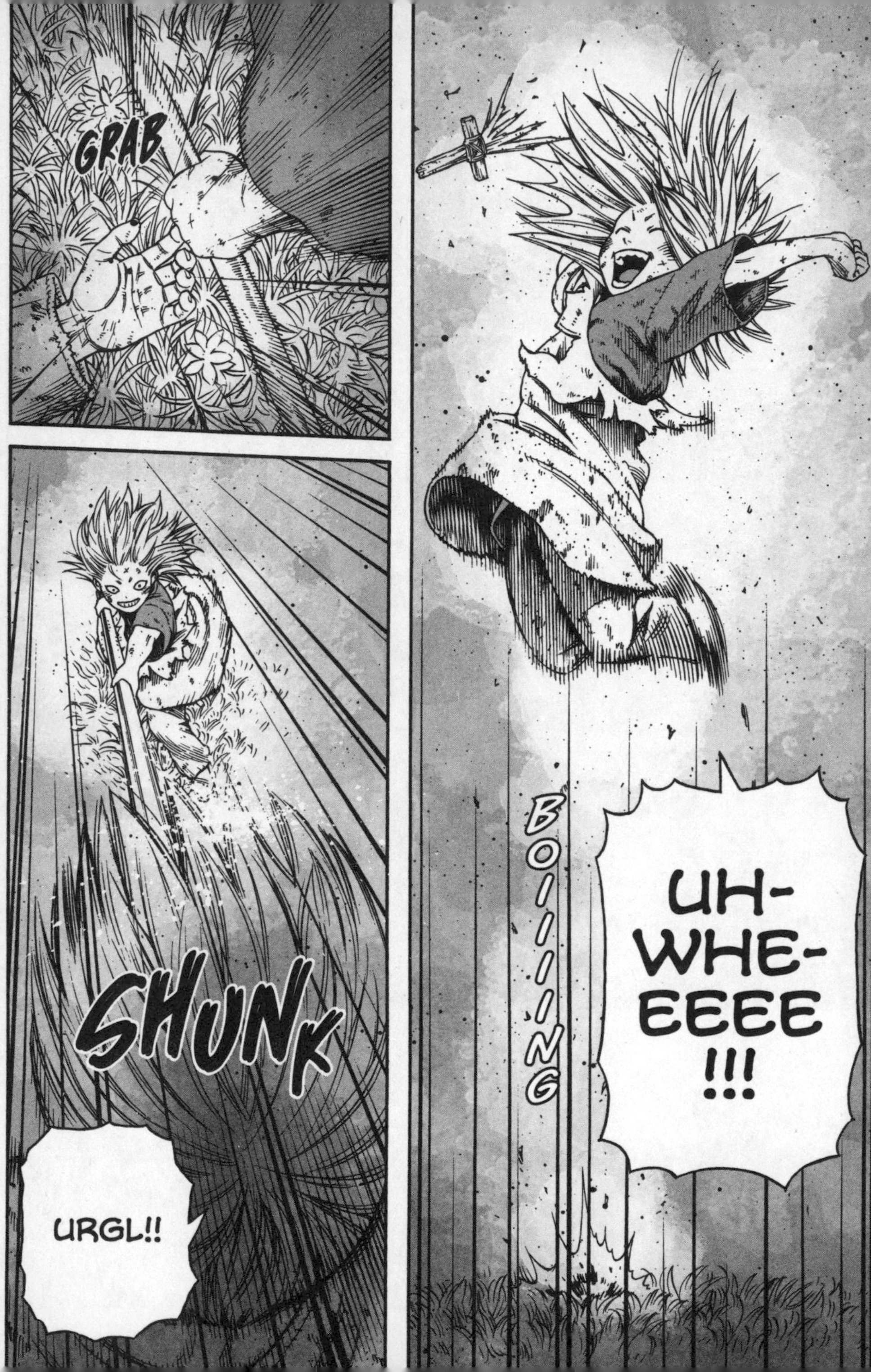
GRAB
SHUNK
URGL!!
BOIIIING
UH-WHE-EEEE!!!

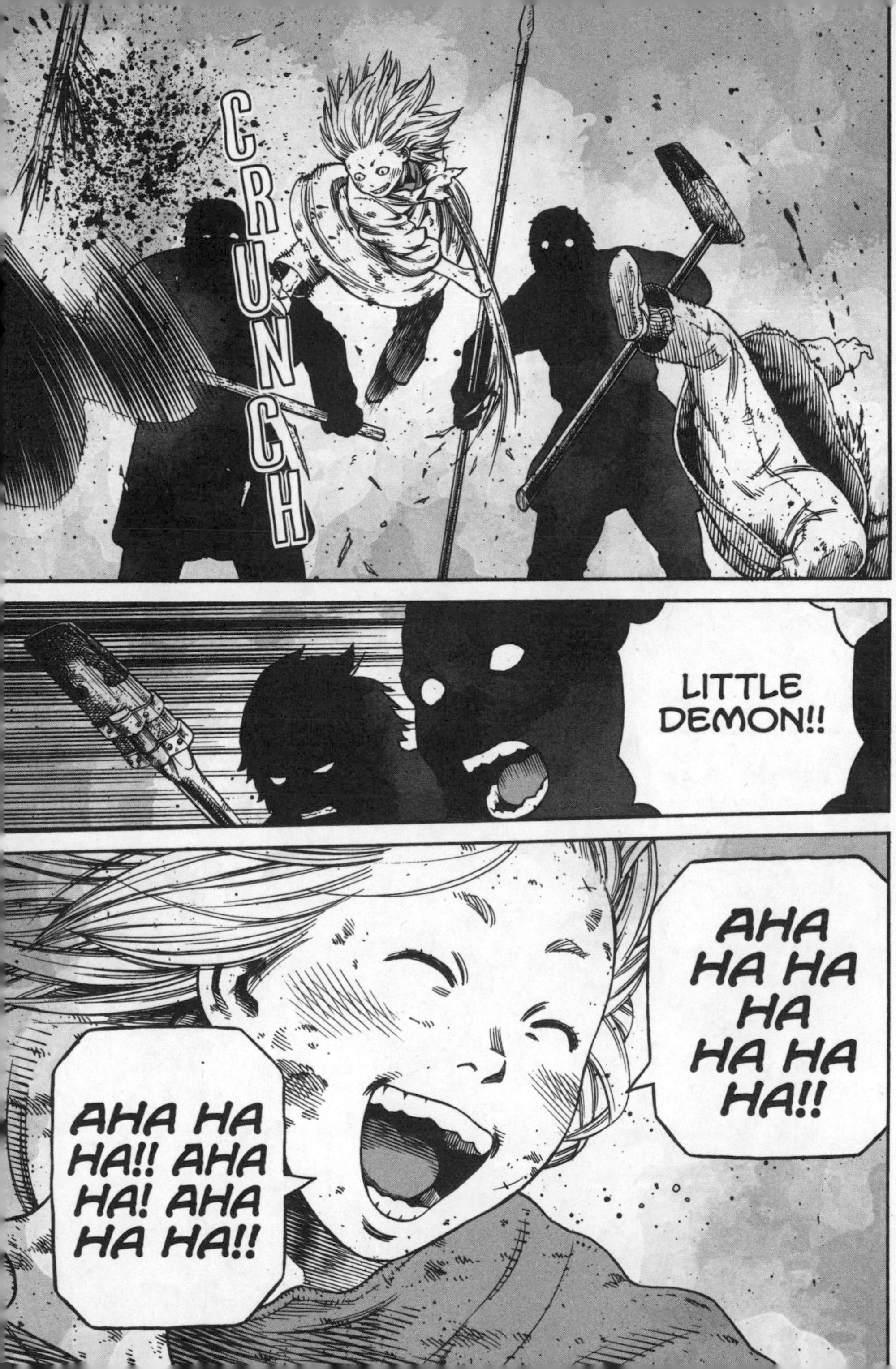
CRUNCH
LITTLE DEMON!!
AHA HA HA HA HA HA HA HA!!
AHA HA HA!! AHA HA! AHA HA HA!!

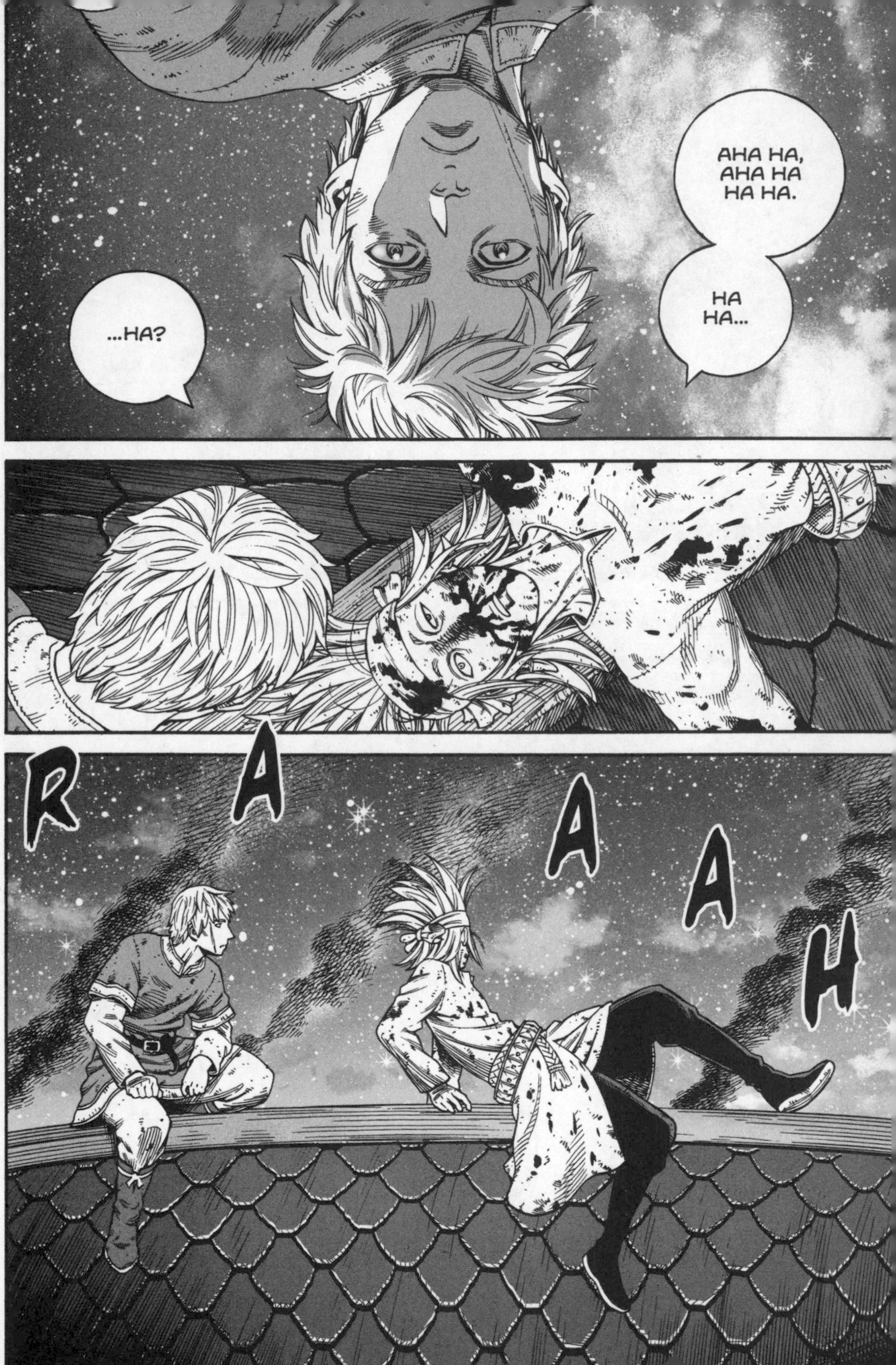
AHA HA, AHA HA HA HA.
HA HA...
...HA?
RAAAAH

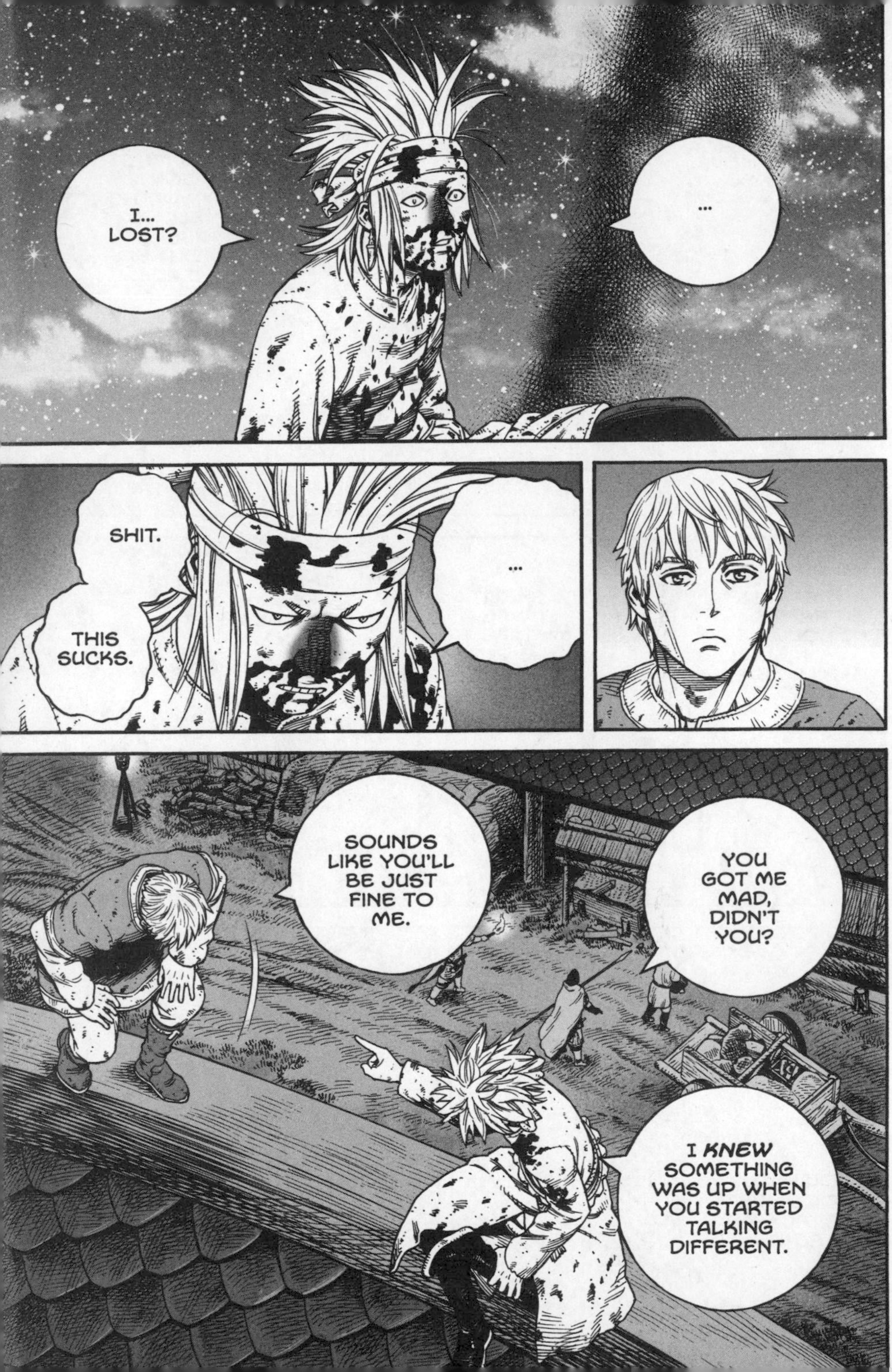
...
I... LOST?
...
SHIT.
THIS SUCKS.
YOU GOT ME MAD, DIDN'T YOU?
SOUNDS LIKE YOU'LL BE JUST FINE TO ME.
I *KNEW* SOMETHING WAS UP WHEN YOU STARTED TALKING DIFFERENT.

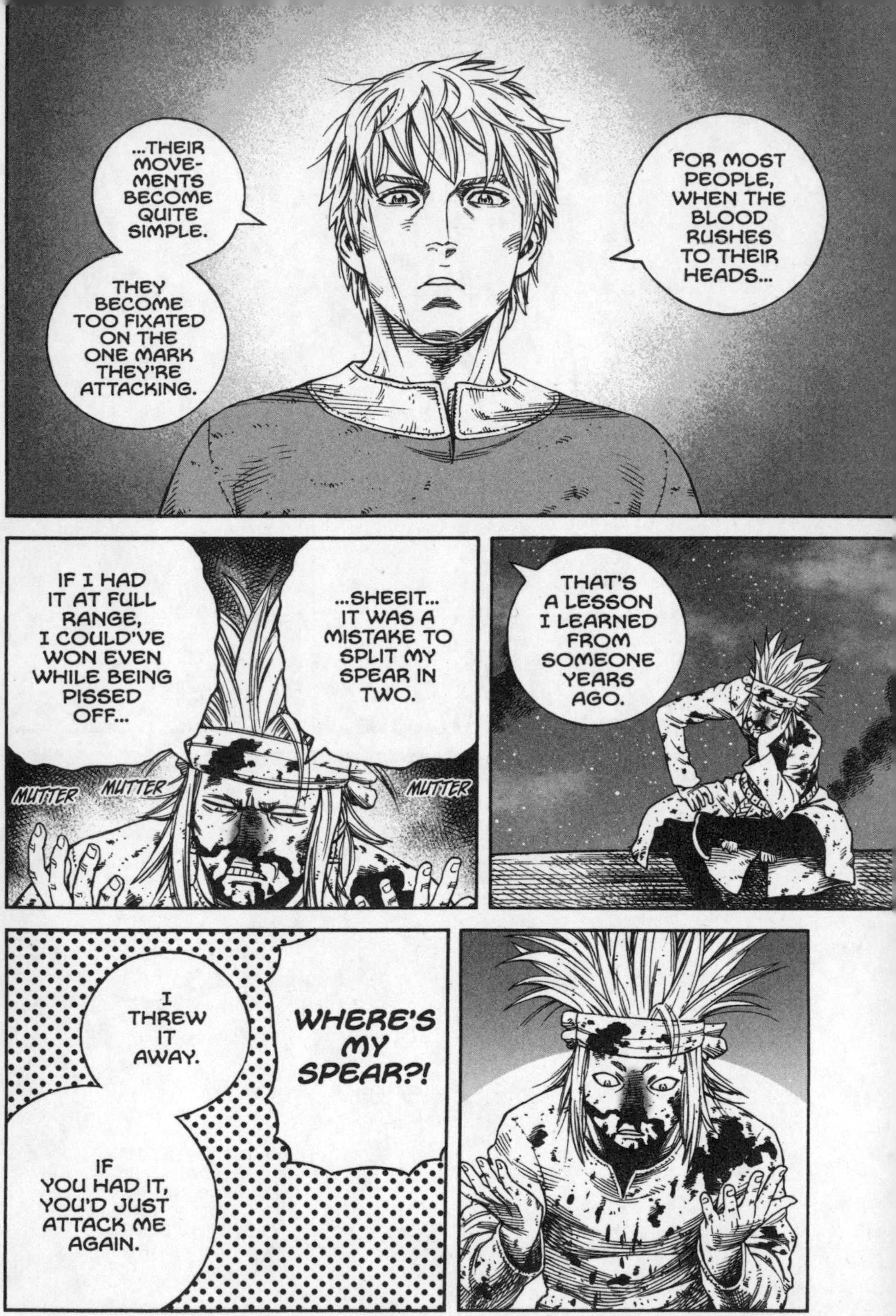
FOR MOST PEOPLE, WHEN THE BLOOD RUSHES TO THEIR HEADS...
...THEIR MOVEMENTS BECOME QUITE SIMPLE.
THEY BECOME TOO FIXATED ON THE ONE MARK THEY'RE ATTACKING.
THAT'S A LESSON I LEARNED FROM SOMEONE YEARS AGO.
...SHEEIT... IT WAS A MISTAKE TO SPLIT MY SPEAR IN TWO.
IF I HAD IT AT FULL RANGE, I COULD'VE WON EVEN WHILE BEING PISSED OFF...
MUTTER
MUTTER
MUTTER
WHERE'S MY SPEAR?!
I THREW IT AWAY.
IF YOU HAD IT, YOU'D JUST ATTACK ME AGAIN.

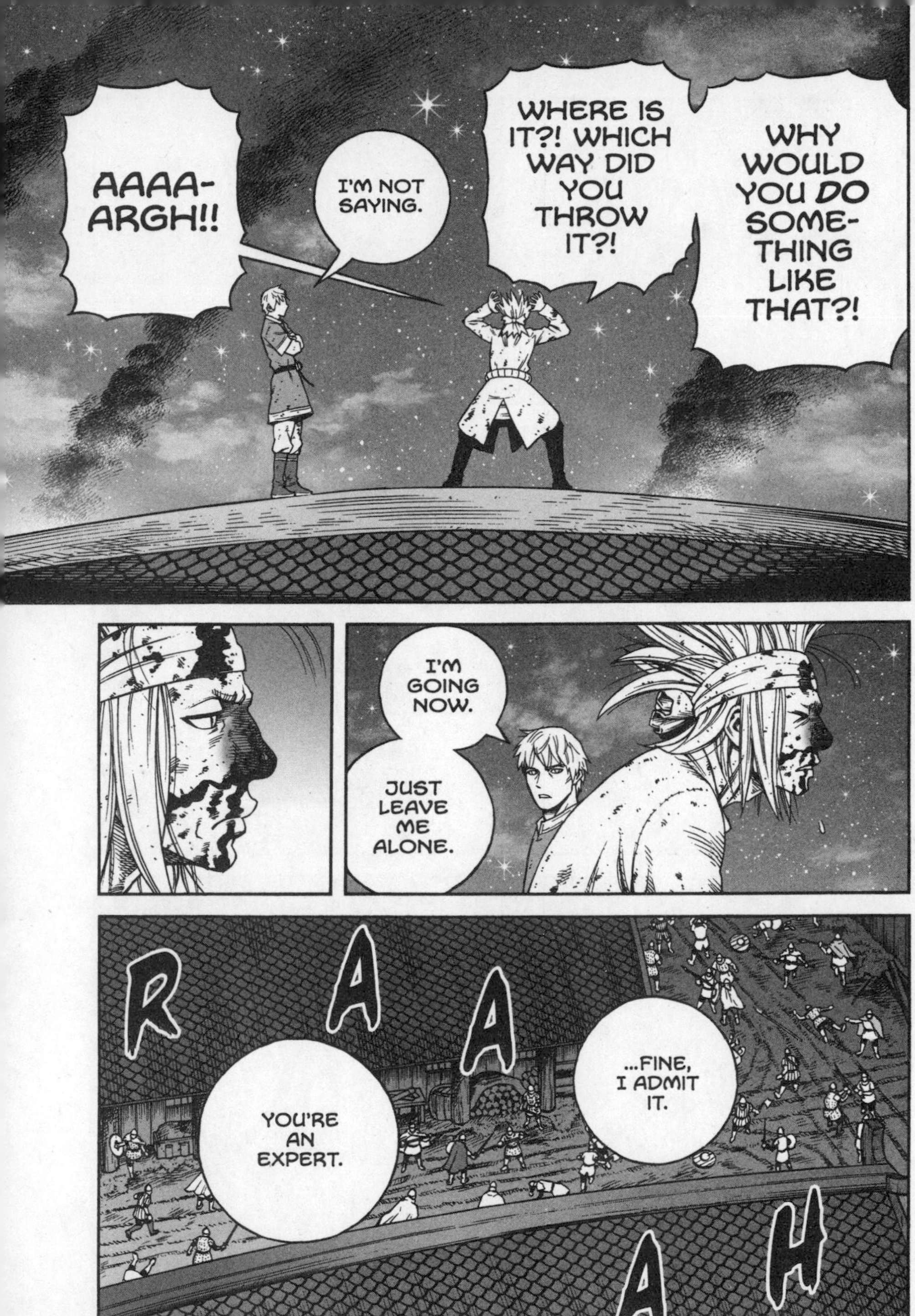
WHY WOULD YOU DO SOME-THING LIKE THAT?!
WHERE IS IT?! WHICH WAY DID YOU THROW IT?!
I'M NOT SAYING.
AAAA-ARGH!!
I'M GOING NOW.
JUST LEAVE ME ALONE.
RAAAAH
...FINE, I ADMIT IT.
YOU'RE AN EXPERT.

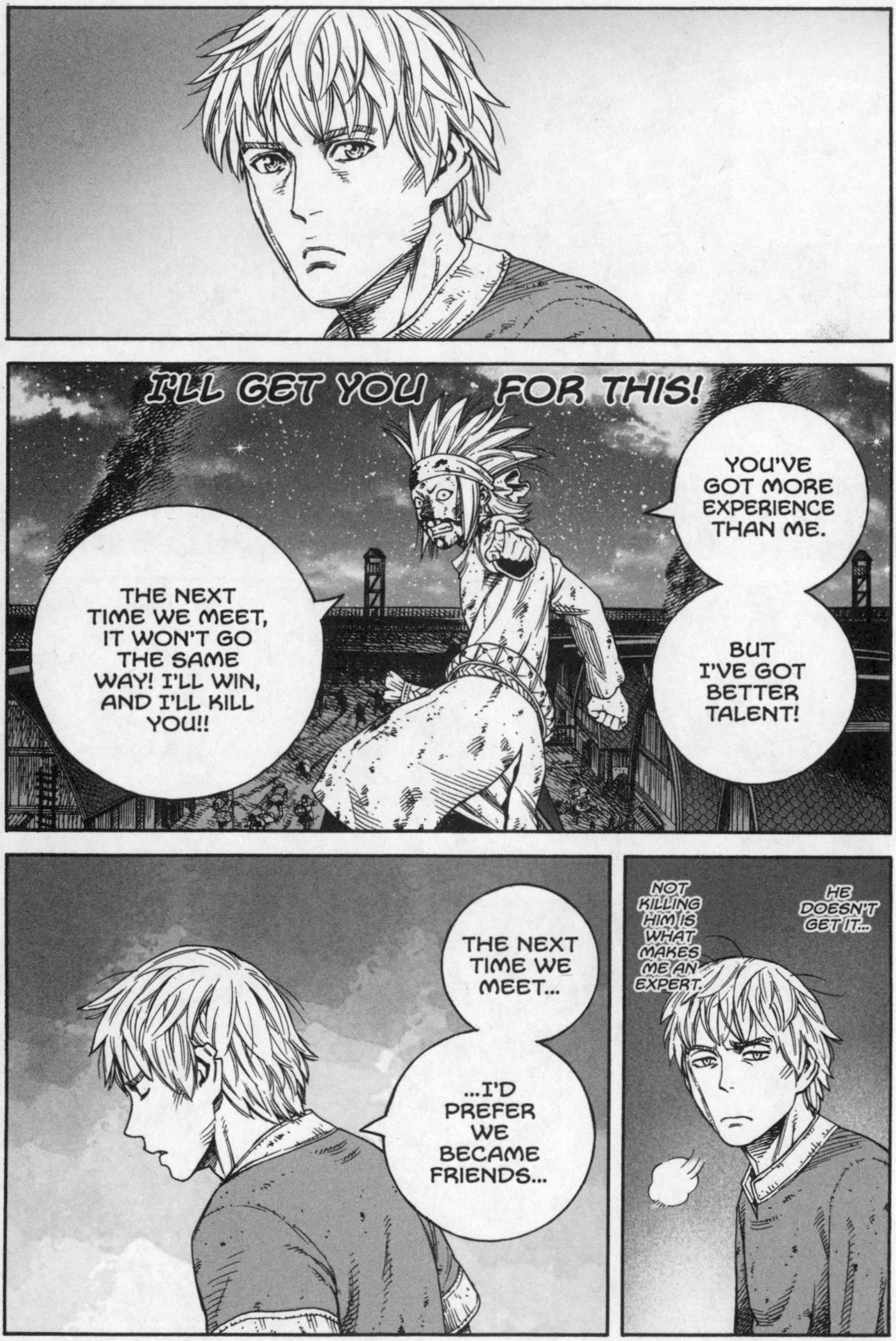
I'LL GET YOU FOR THIS!
YOU'VE GOT MORE EXPERIENCE THAN ME.
BUT I'VE GOT BETTER TALENT!
THE NEXT TIME WE MEET, IT WON'T GO THE SAME WAY! I'LL WIN, AND I'LL KILL YOU!!
HE DOESN'T GET IT...
NOT KILLING HIM IS WHAT MAKES ME AN EXPERT.
THE NEXT TIME WE MEET...
...I'D PREFER WE BECAME FRIENDS...

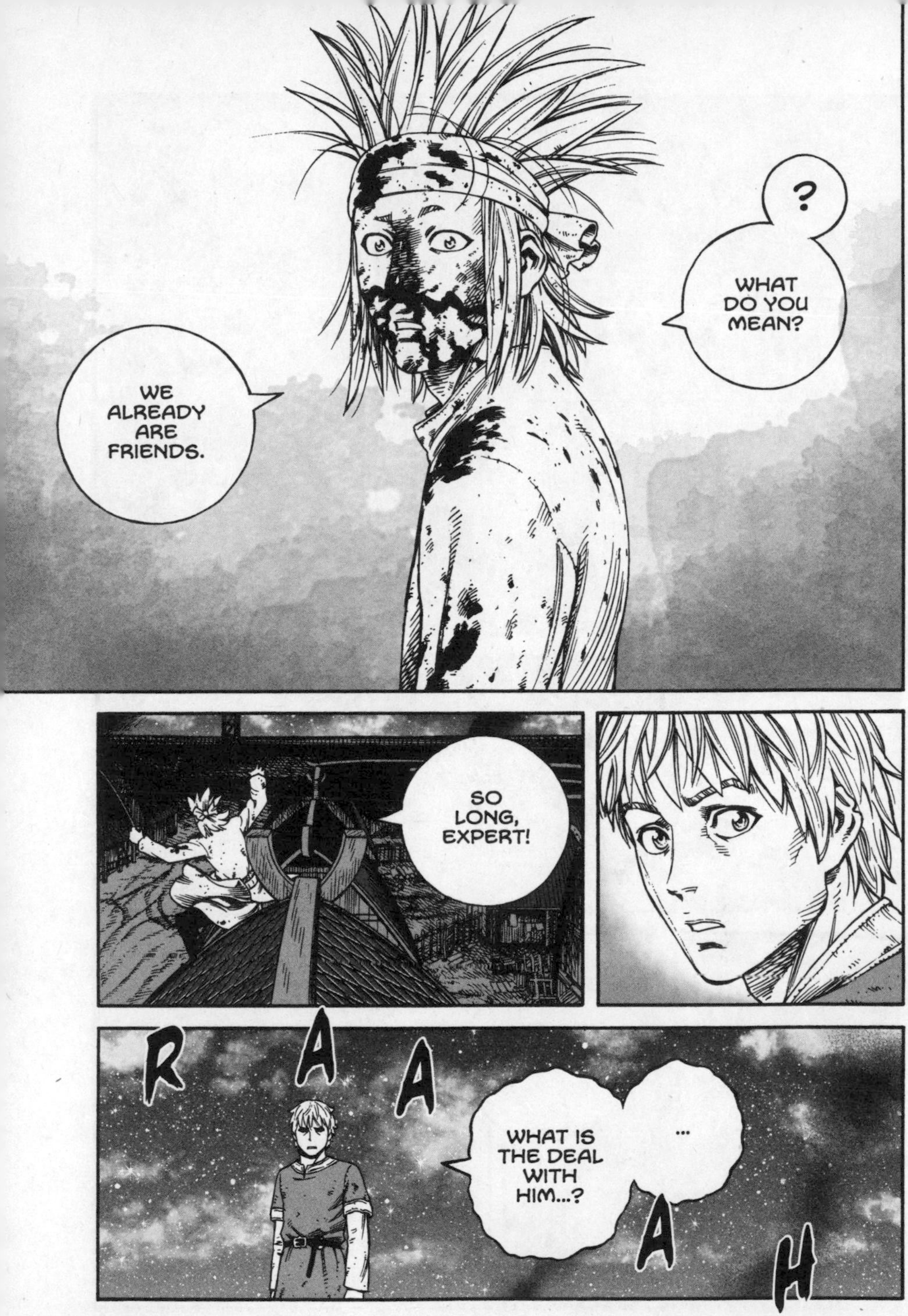
?
WHAT DO YOU MEAN?
WE ALREADY ARE FRIENDS.
SO LONG, EXPERT!
RAAAAH
...
WHAT IS THE DEAL WITH HIM...?

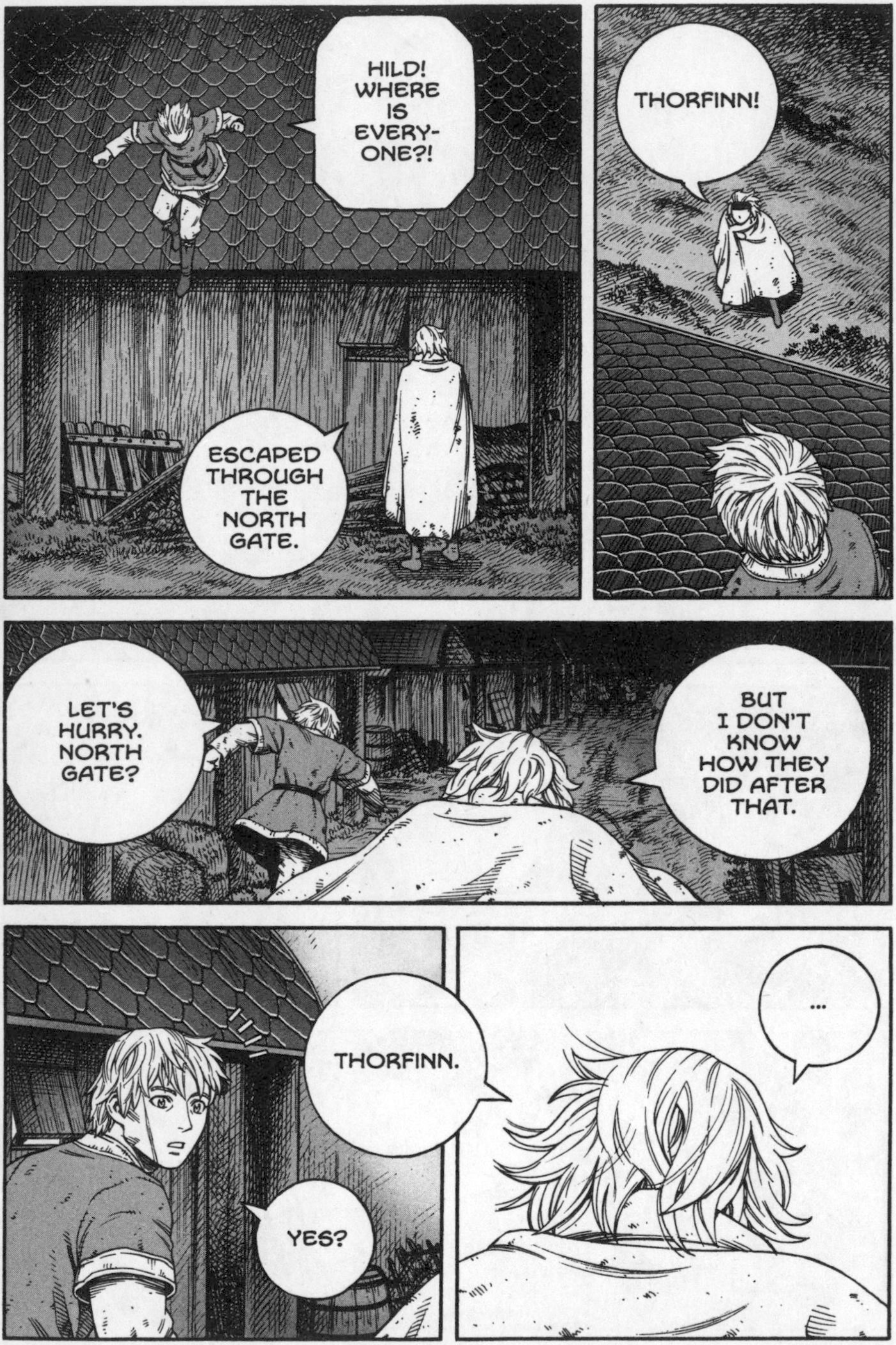
THORFINN!
HILD! WHERE IS EVERYONE?!
ESCAPED THROUGH THE NORTH GATE.
BUT I DON'T KNOW HOW THEY DID AFTER THAT.
LET'S HURRY. NORTH GATE?
...
THORFINN.
YES?

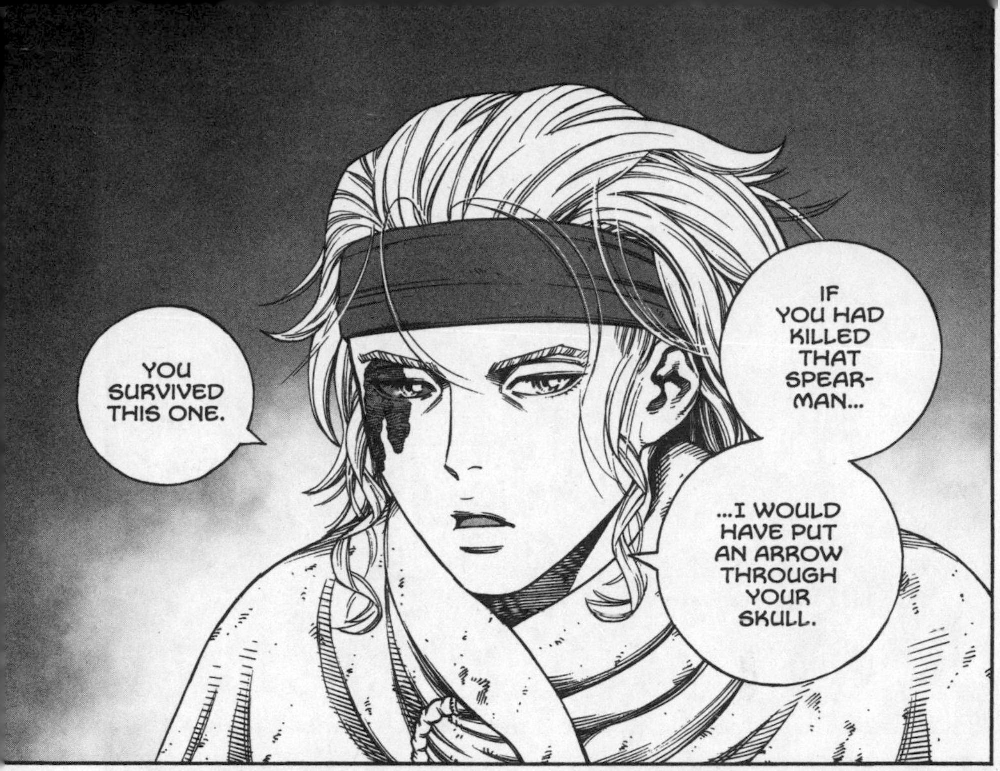
IF YOU HAD KILLED THAT SPEAR-MAN...
...I WOULD HAVE PUT AN ARROW THROUGH YOUR SKULL.
YOU SURVIVED THIS ONE.
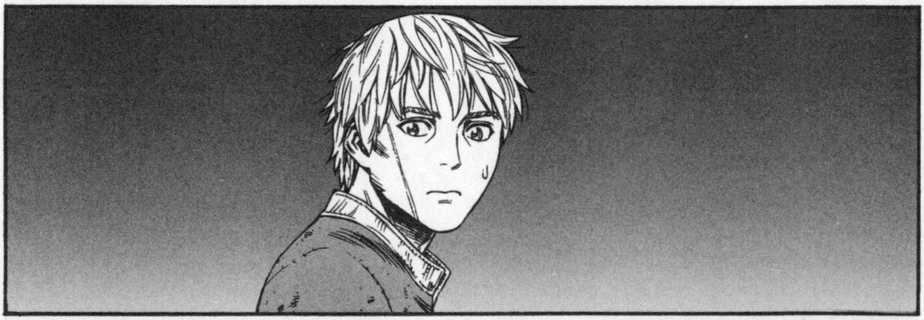
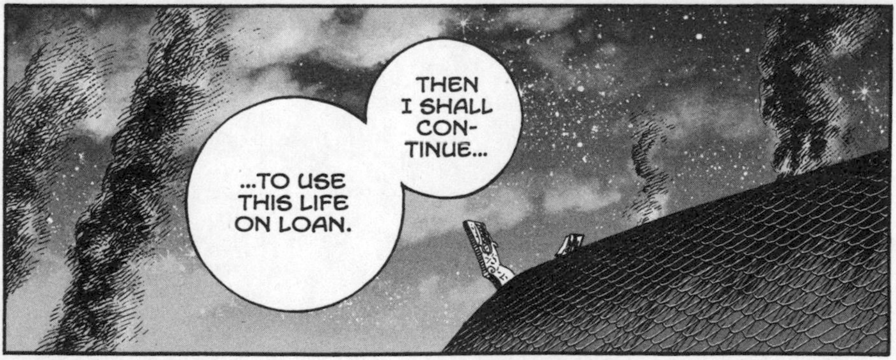
THEN I SHALL CON-TINUE...
...TO USE THIS LIFE ON LOAN.

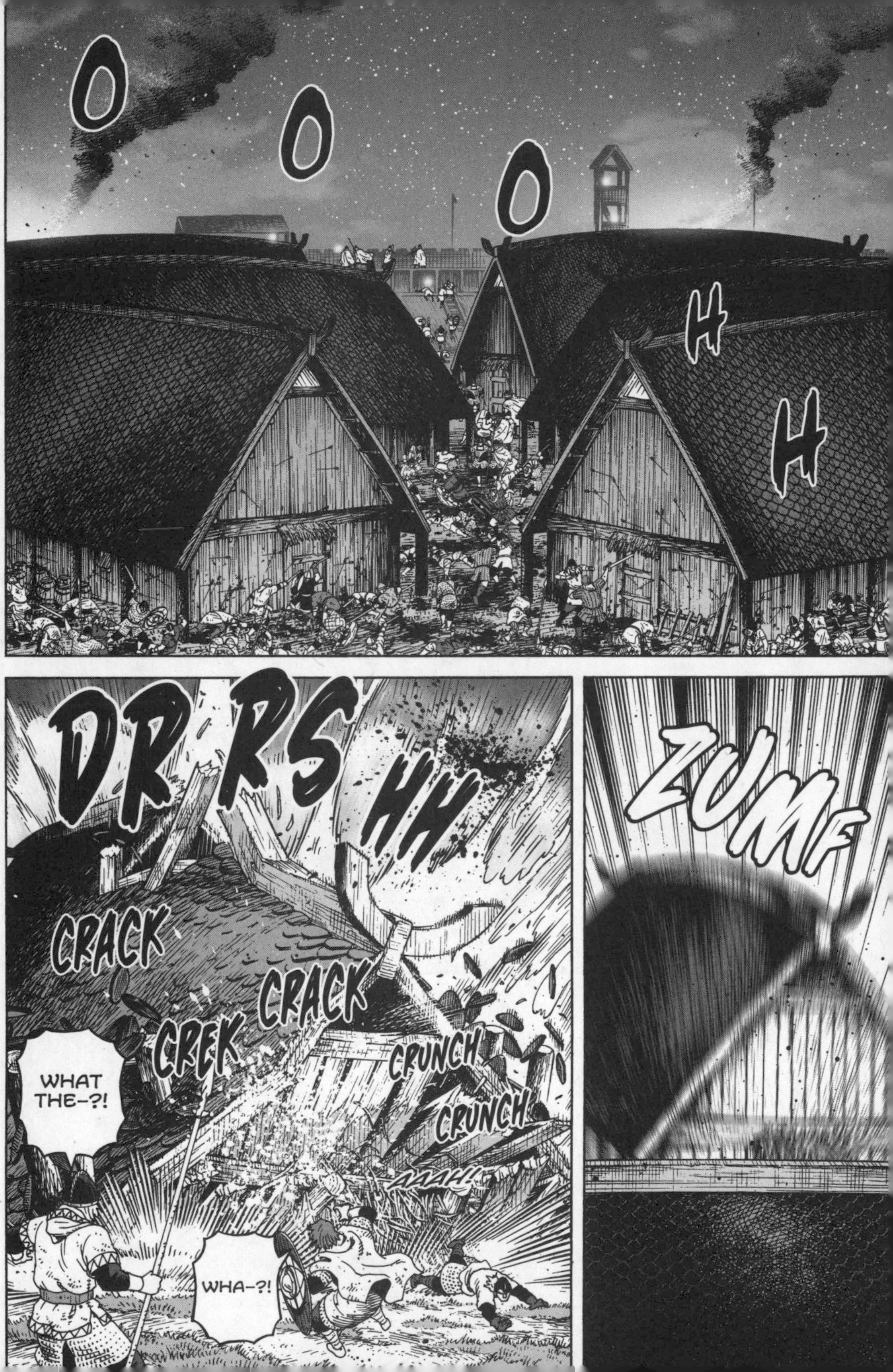
OOOHH
ZUMF
DRRSHH
CRACK
CREK
CRACK
CRUNCH
CRUNCH
AAAH!
WHAT THE-?!
WHA-?!

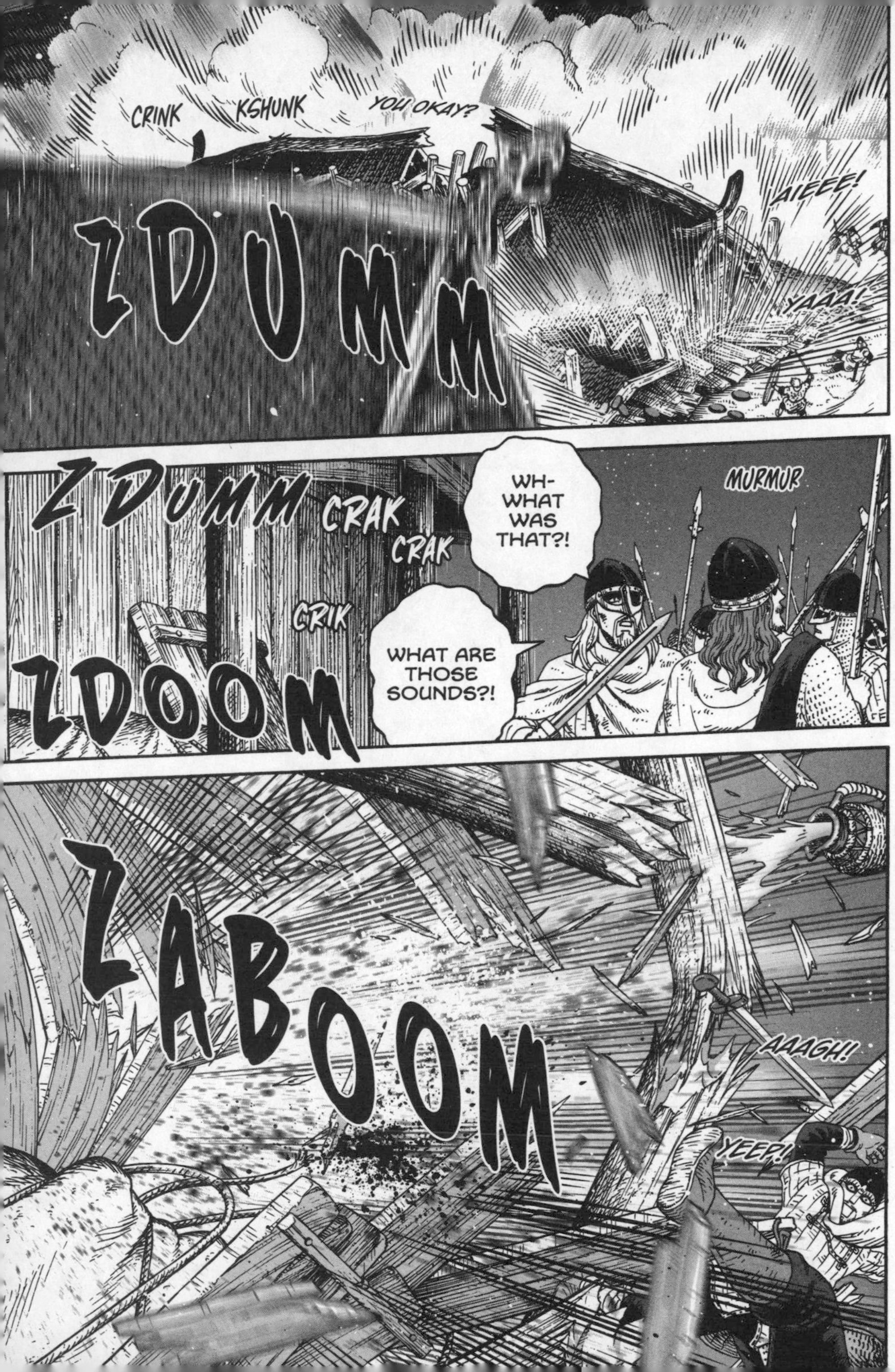
CRINK
KSHUNK
YOU OKAY?
AIEEE!
ZDUMM
YAAA!
MURMUR
WH- WHAT WAS THAT?!
CRAK
CRAK
ZDUMM
WHAT ARE THOSE SOUNDS?!
CRIK
ZDOOM
ZABOOM
AAAGH!
YEEP!

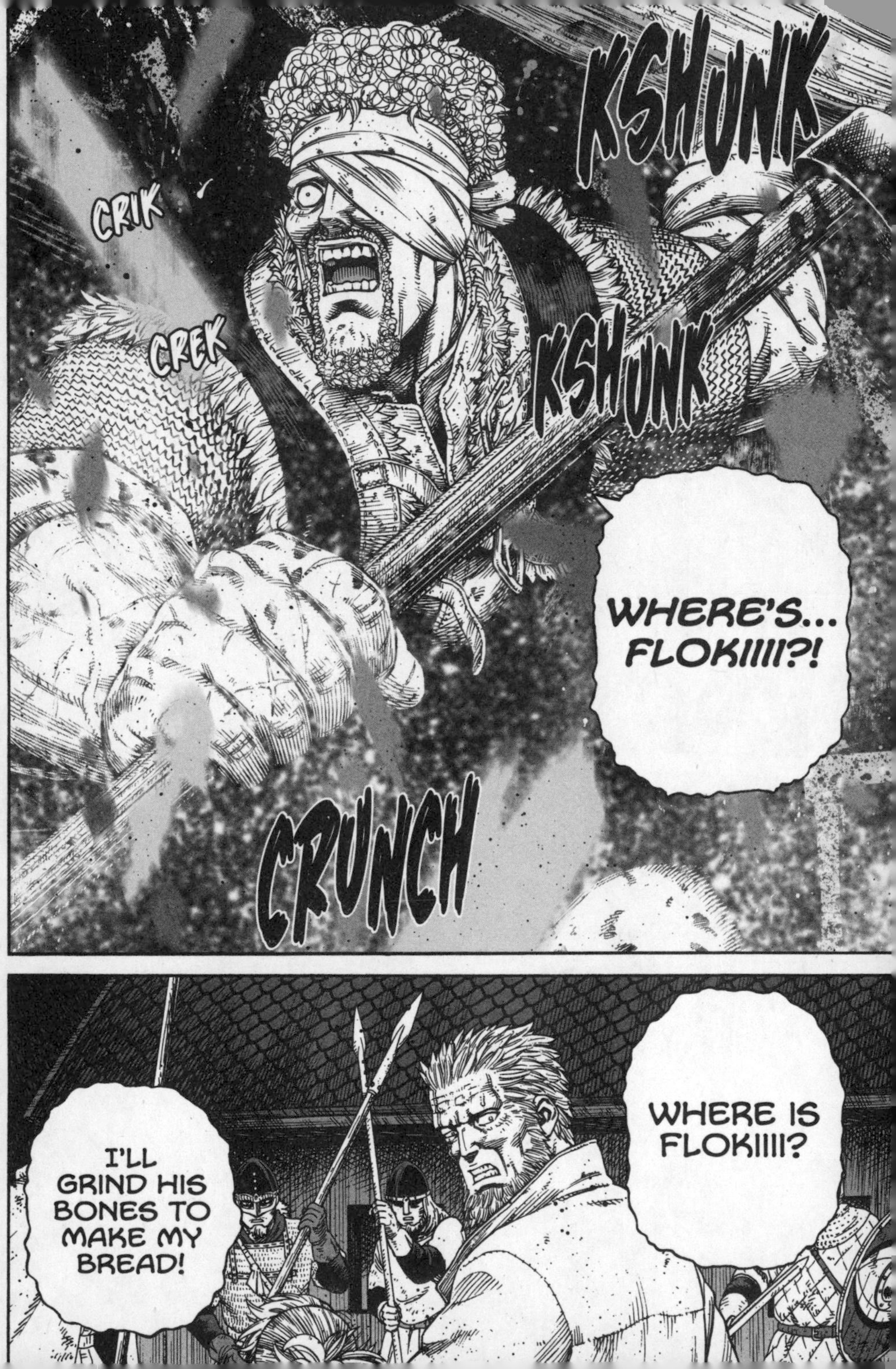
KSHUNK
KSHUNK
CRIK
CREK
WHERE'S... FLOKIIII?!
CRUNCH
WHERE IS FLOKIIII?
I'LL GRIND HIS BONES TO MAKE MY BREAD!

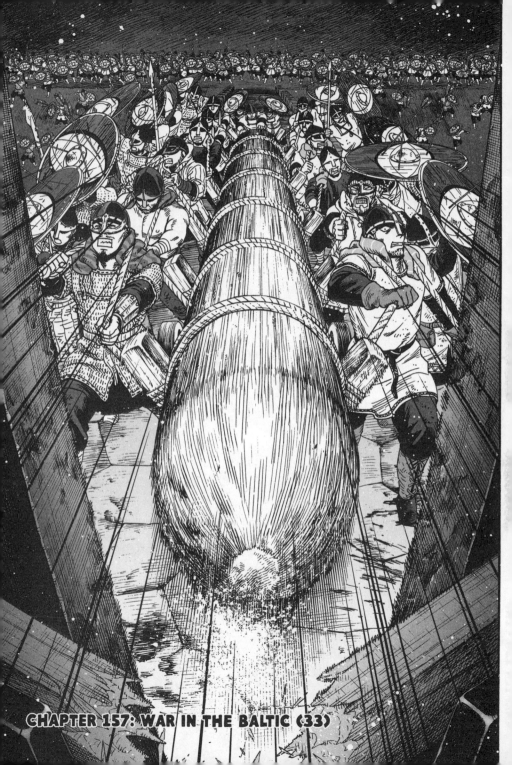

CHAPTER 157: WAR IN THE BALTIC (33)

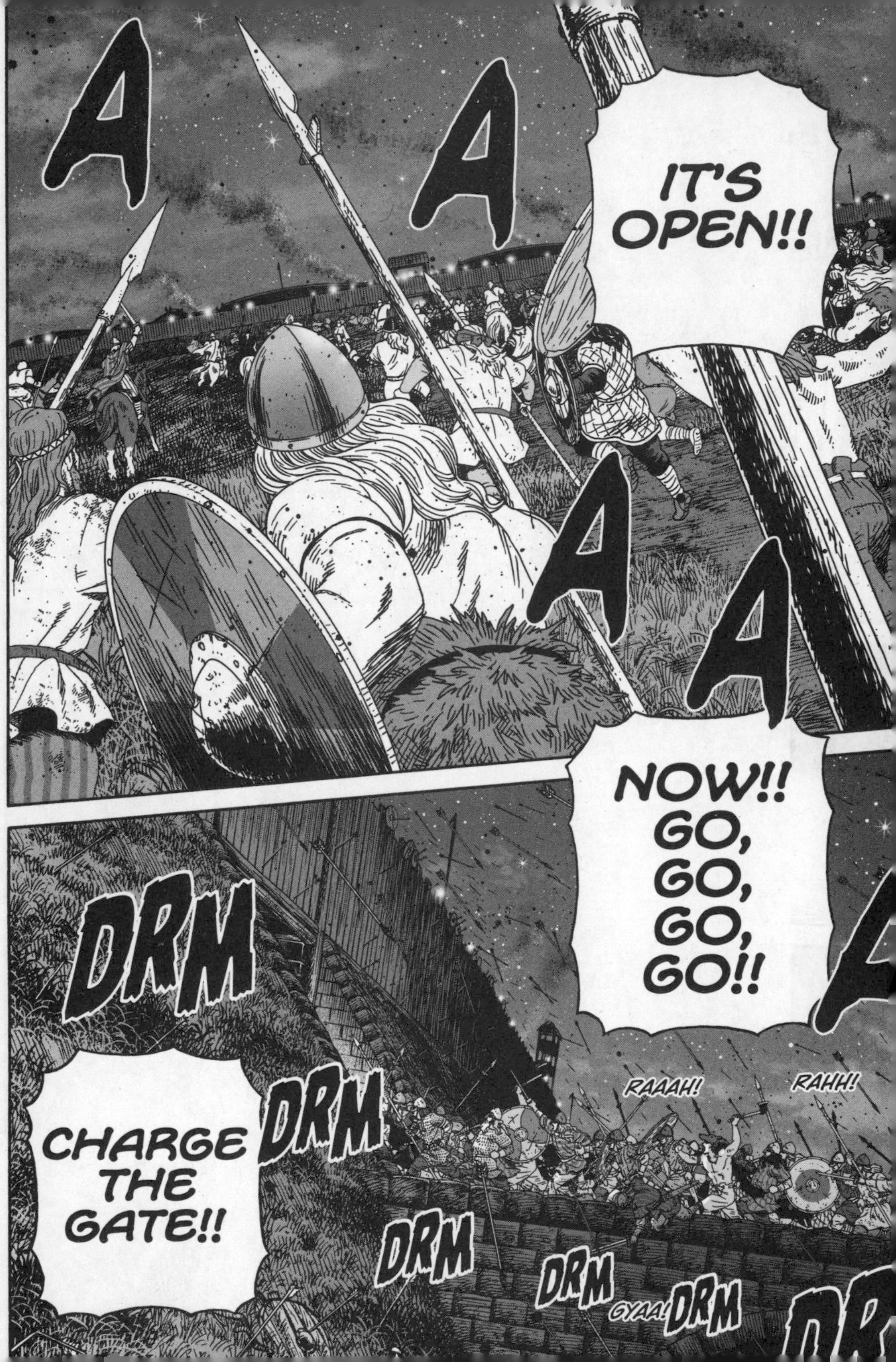

A
A
IT'S OPEN!!
A
A
A
NOW!! GO, GO, GO, GO!!
DRM
CHARGE THE GATE!!
DRM
RAAAH!
RAHH!
DRM
DRM
GYAA!
DRM

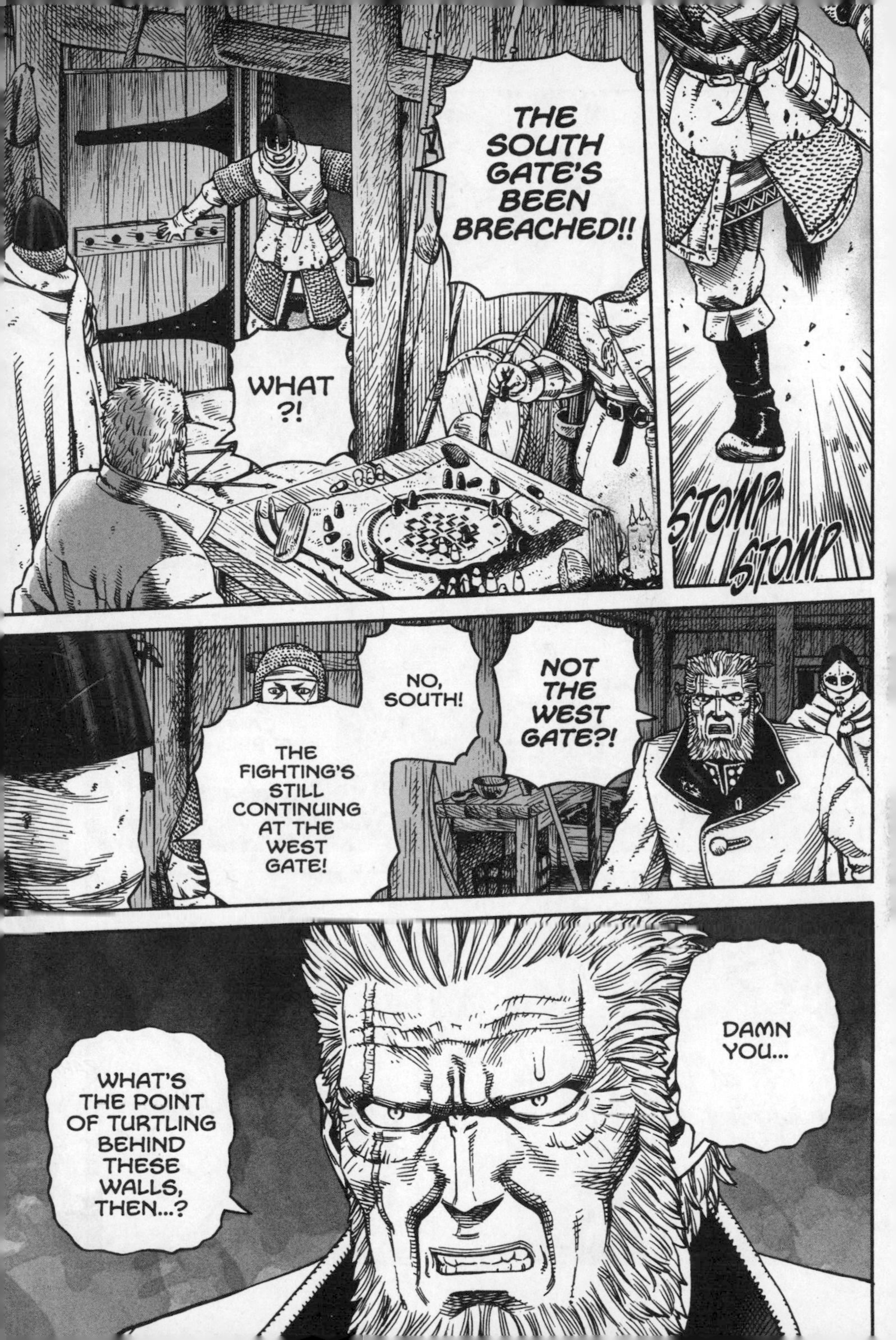
STOMP STOMP
THE SOUTH GATE'S BEEN BREACHED!!
WHAT?!
NOT THE WEST GATE?!
NO, SOUTH!
THE FIGHTING'S STILL CONTINUING AT THE WEST GATE!
DAMN YOU...
WHAT'S THE POINT OF TURTLING BEHIND THESE WALLS, THEN...?

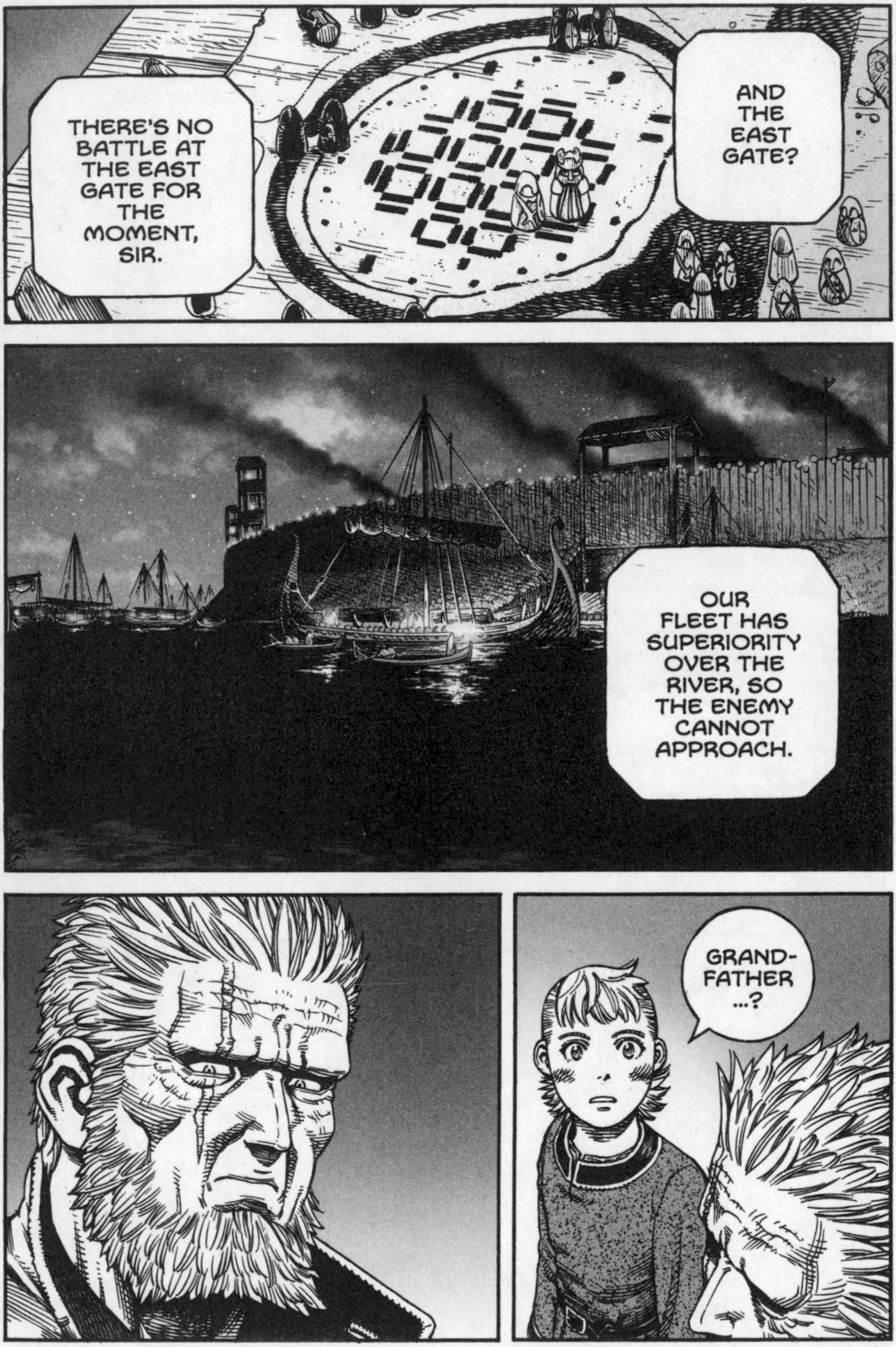
AND THE EAST GATE?
THERE'S NO BATTLE AT THE EAST GATE FOR THE MOMENT, SIR.
OUR FLEET HAS SUPERIORITY OVER THE RIVER, SO THE ENEMY CANNOT APPROACH.
GRAND-FATHER ...?

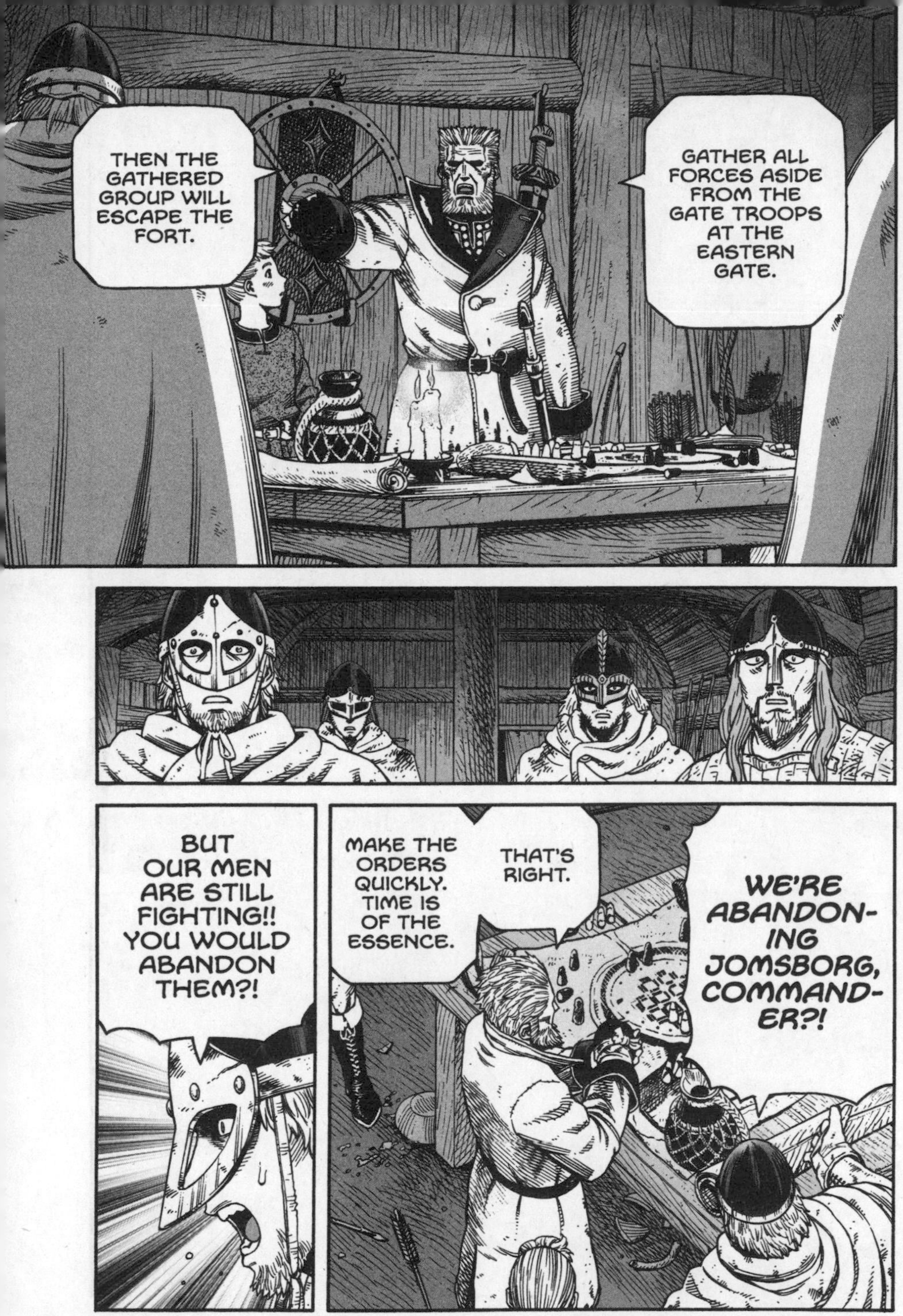
GATHER ALL FORCES ASIDE FROM THE GATE TROOPS AT THE EASTERN GATE.
THEN THE GATHERED GROUP WILL ESCAPE THE FORT.
WE'RE ABANDON-ING JOMSBORG, COMMAND-ER?!
THAT'S RIGHT.
MAKE THE ORDERS QUICKLY. TIME IS OF THE ESSENCE.
BUT OUR MEN ARE STILL FIGHTING!! YOU WOULD ABANDON THEM?!

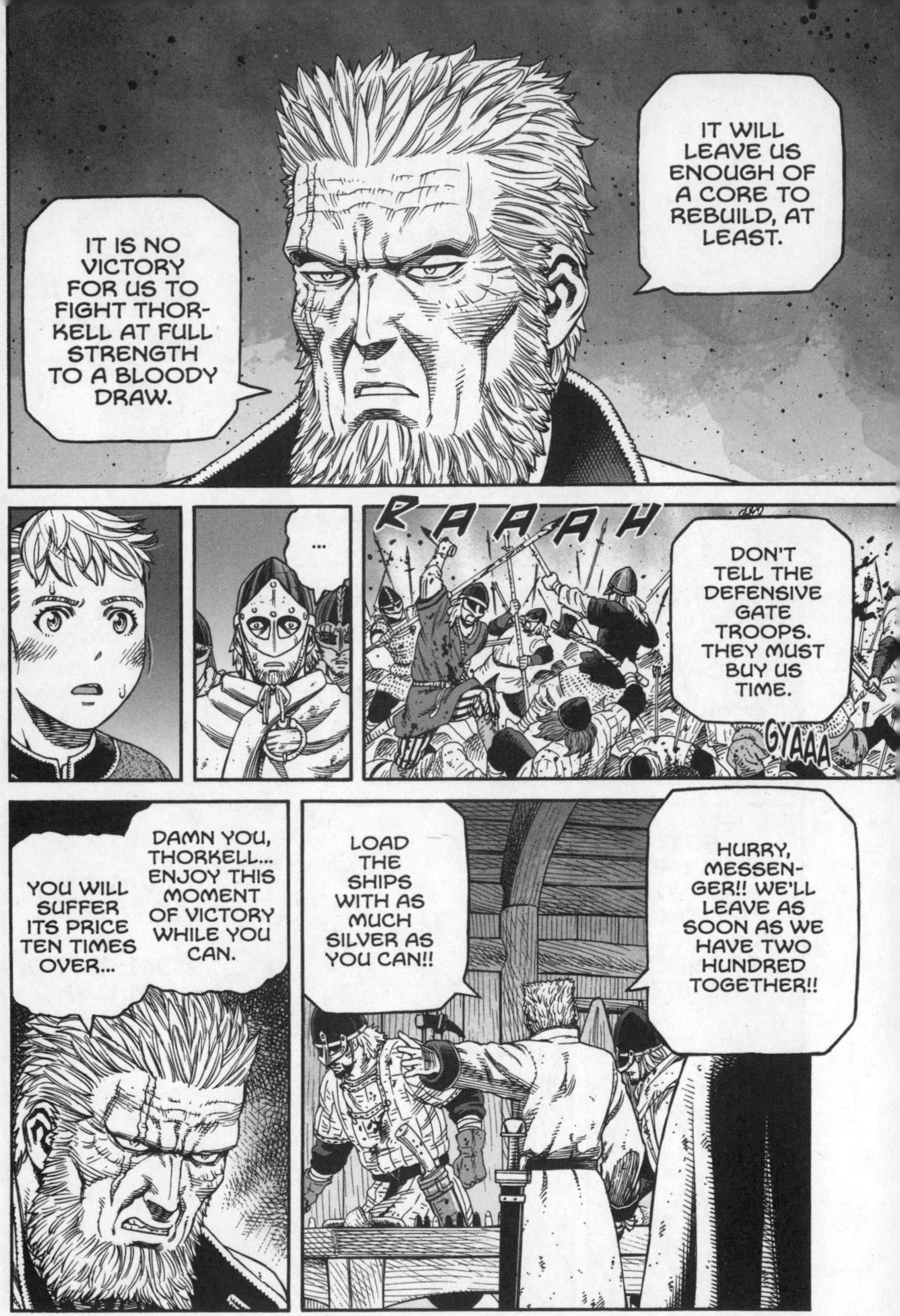
IT WILL LEAVE US ENOUGH OF A CORE TO REBUILD, AT LEAST.
IT IS NO VICTORY FOR US TO FIGHT THORKELL AT FULL STRENGTH TO A BLOODY DRAW.
RAAAAH
DON'T TELL THE DEFENSIVE GATE TROOPS. THEY MUST BUY US TIME.
GYAAA
...
HURRY, MESSENGER!! WE'LL LEAVE AS SOON AS WE HAVE TWO HUNDRED TOGETHER!!
LOAD THE SHIPS WITH AS MUCH SILVER AS YOU CAN!!
DAMN YOU, THORKELL... ENJOY THIS MOMENT OF VICTORY WHILE YOU CAN.
YOU WILL SUFFER ITS PRICE TEN TIMES OVER...

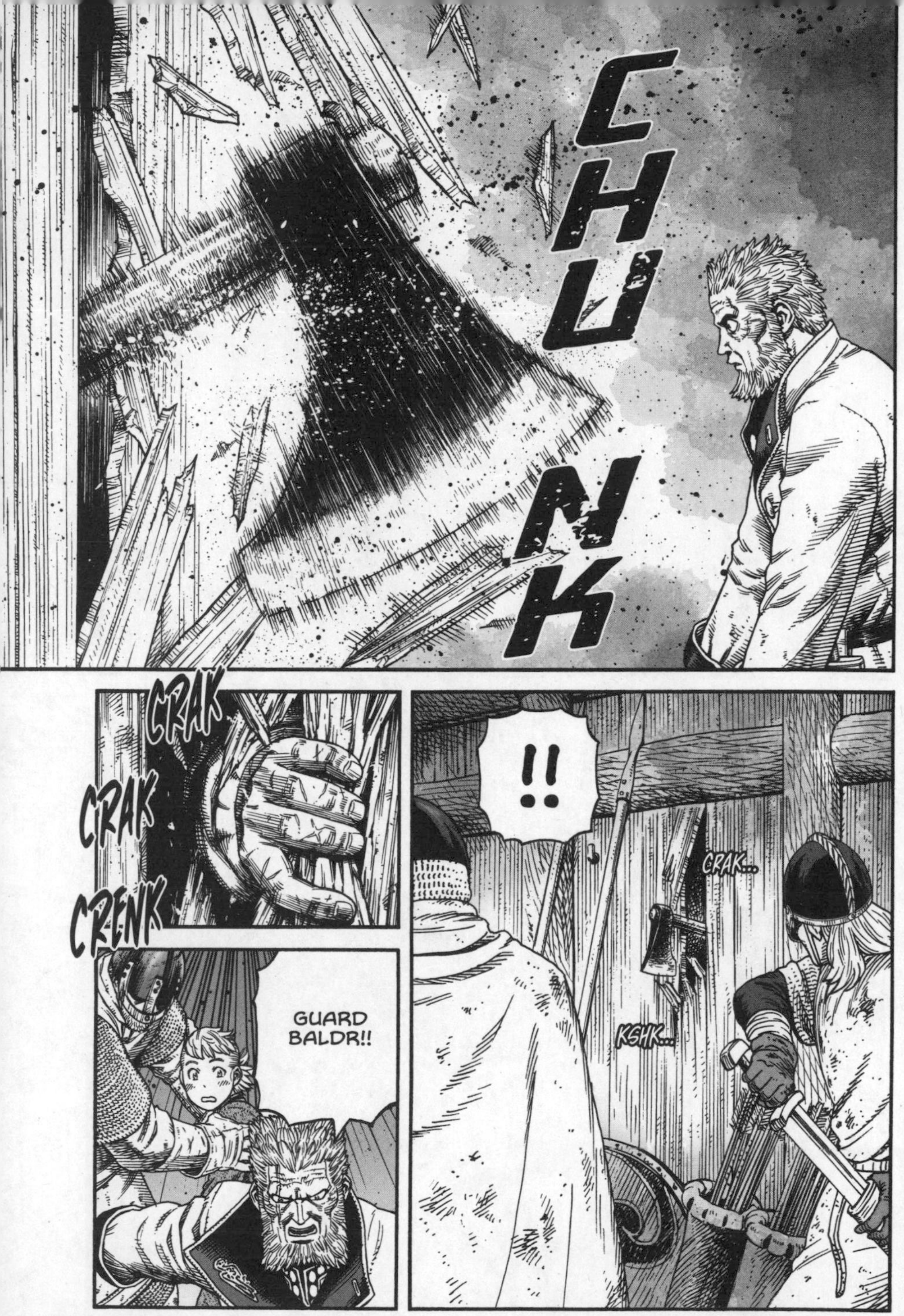
CHUNK
!!
CRAK...
KSHK...
CRAK
CRAK
CRENK
GUARD BALDR!!

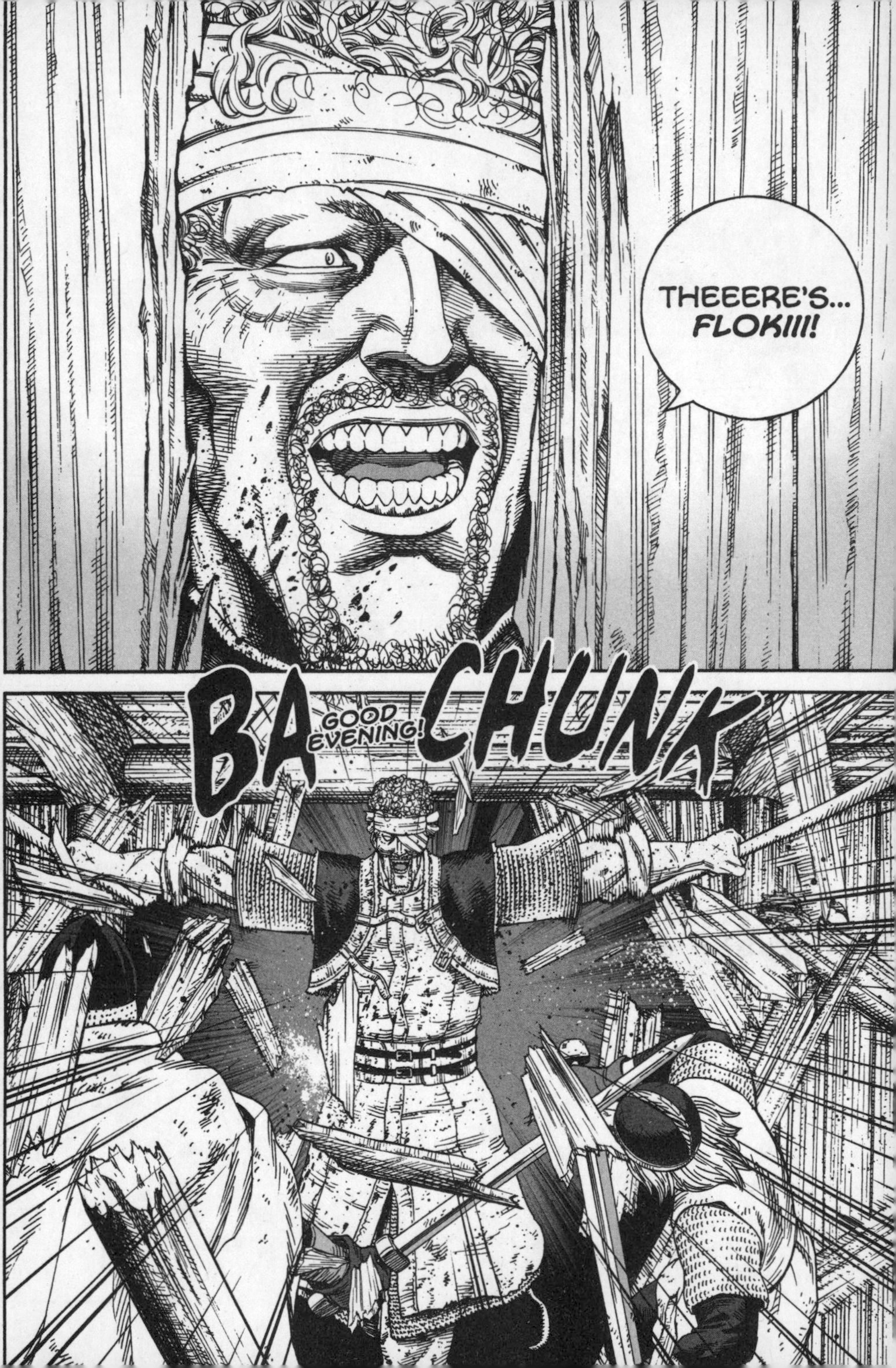
THEEERE'S... FLOKIII!
BA CHUNK
GOOD EVENING!

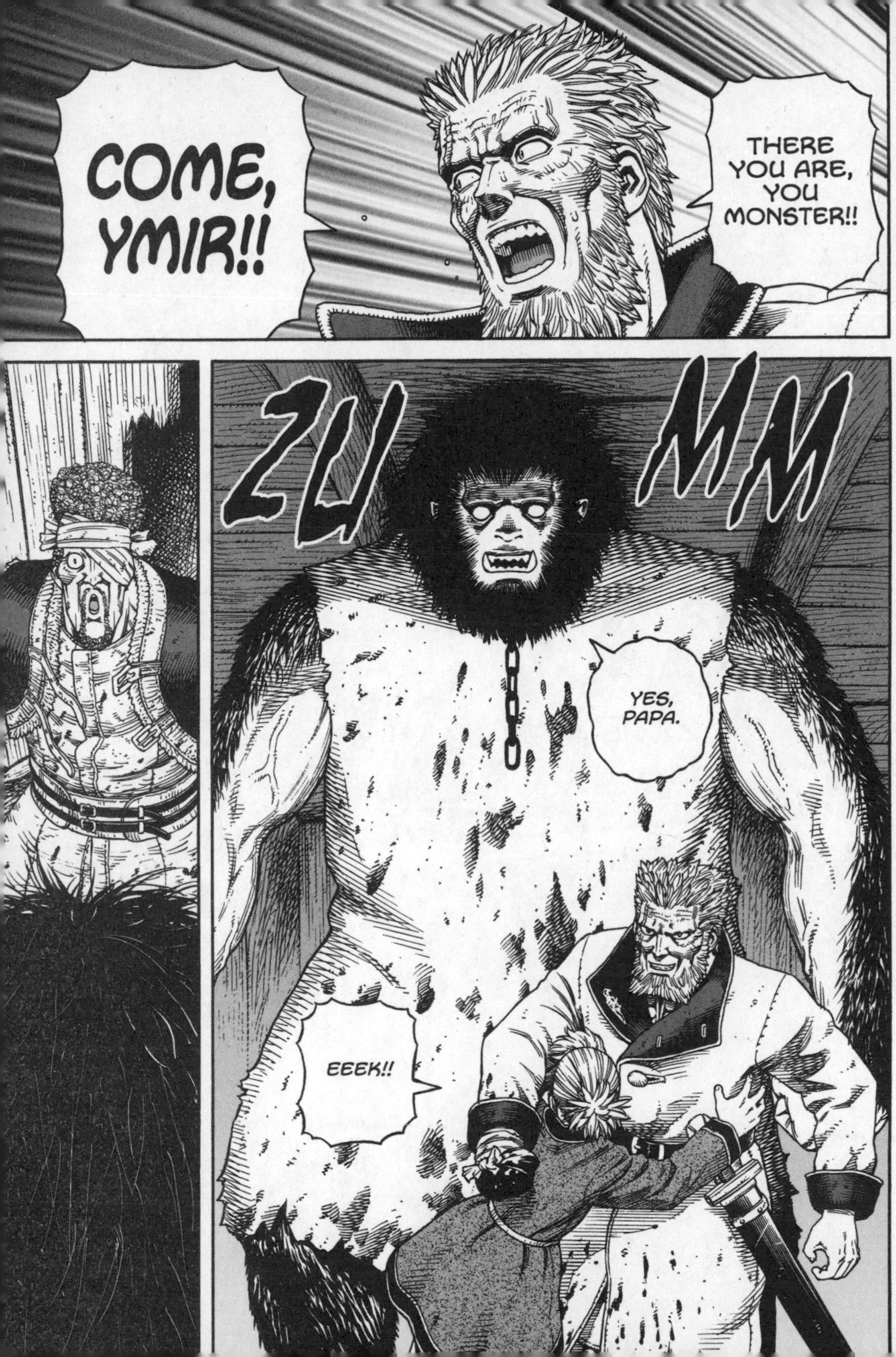
THERE YOU ARE, YOU MONSTER!!
COME, YMIR!!
ZUMM
YES, PAPA.
EEEK!!

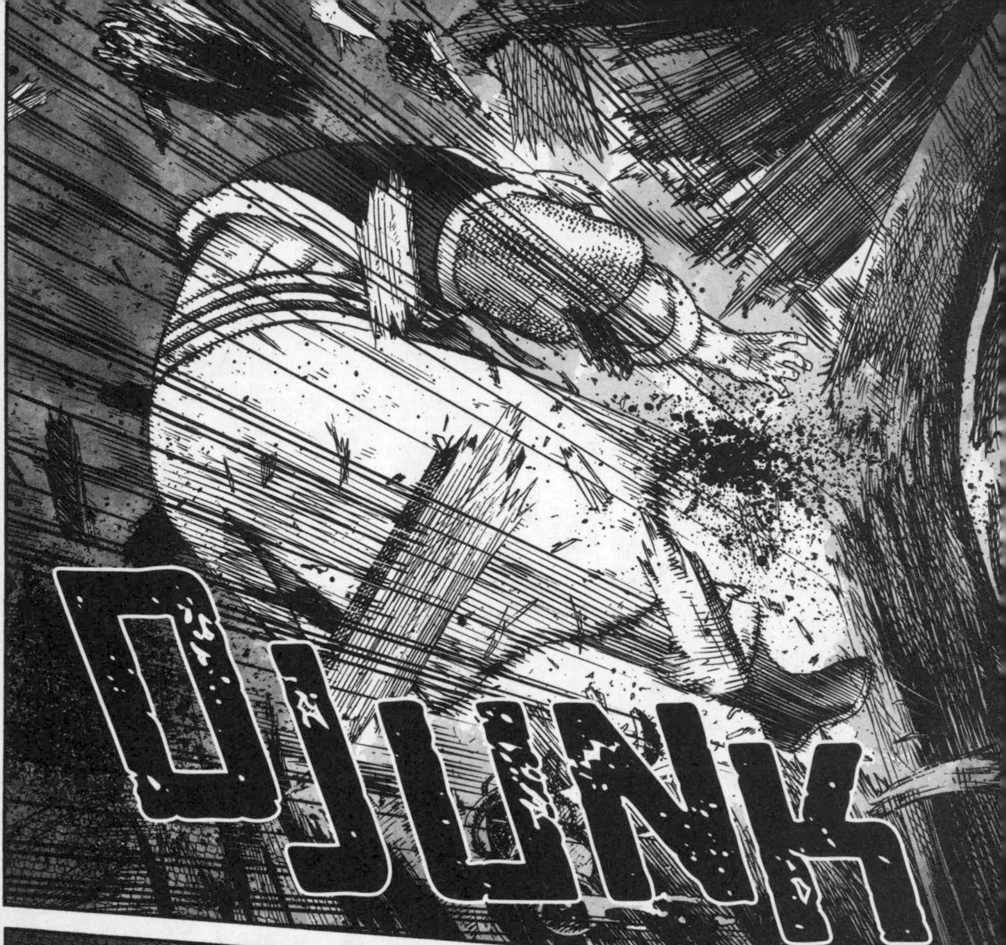
DJUNK
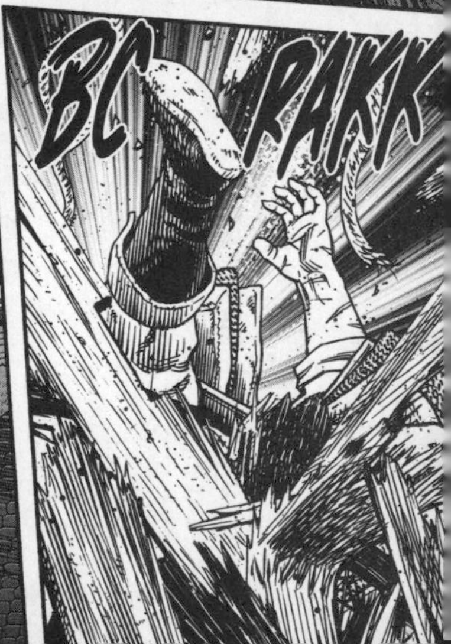
BC RAKK
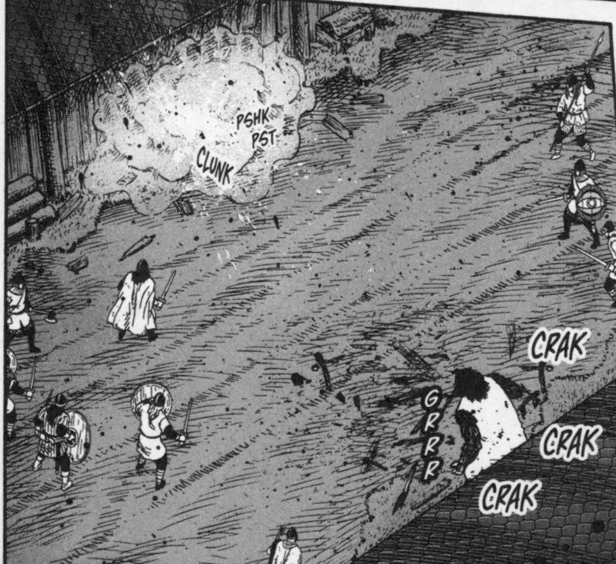
PSHK
PST
CLUNK
CRAK
GRRR
CRAK
CRAK

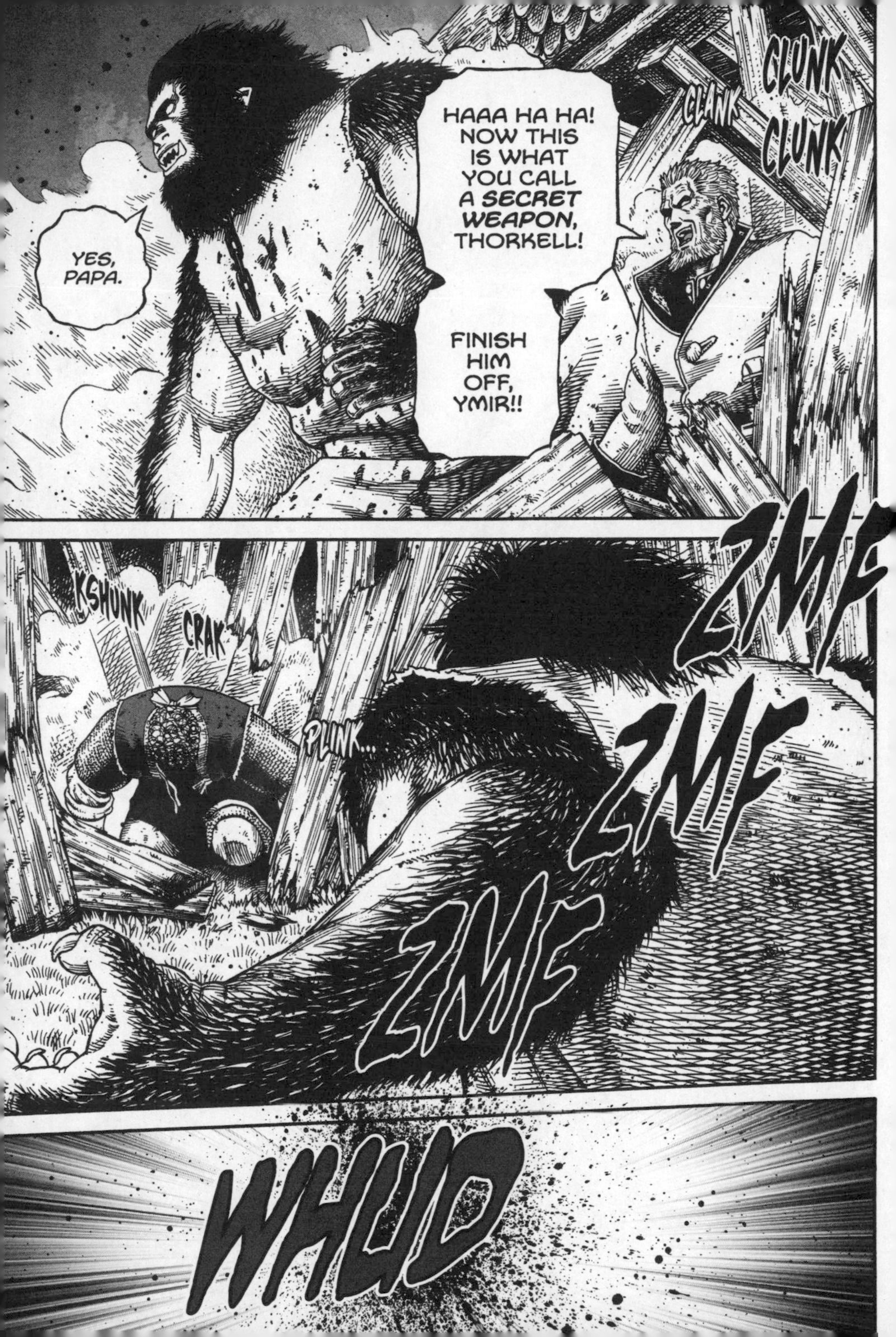
CLUNK
CLANK
CLUNK
HAAA HA HA! NOW THIS IS WHAT YOU CALL A *SECRET WEAPON*, THORKELL!
FINISH HIM OFF, YMIR!!
YES, PAPA.
ZMF
ZMF
ZMF
PLINK...
CRAK
KSHUNK
WHUD

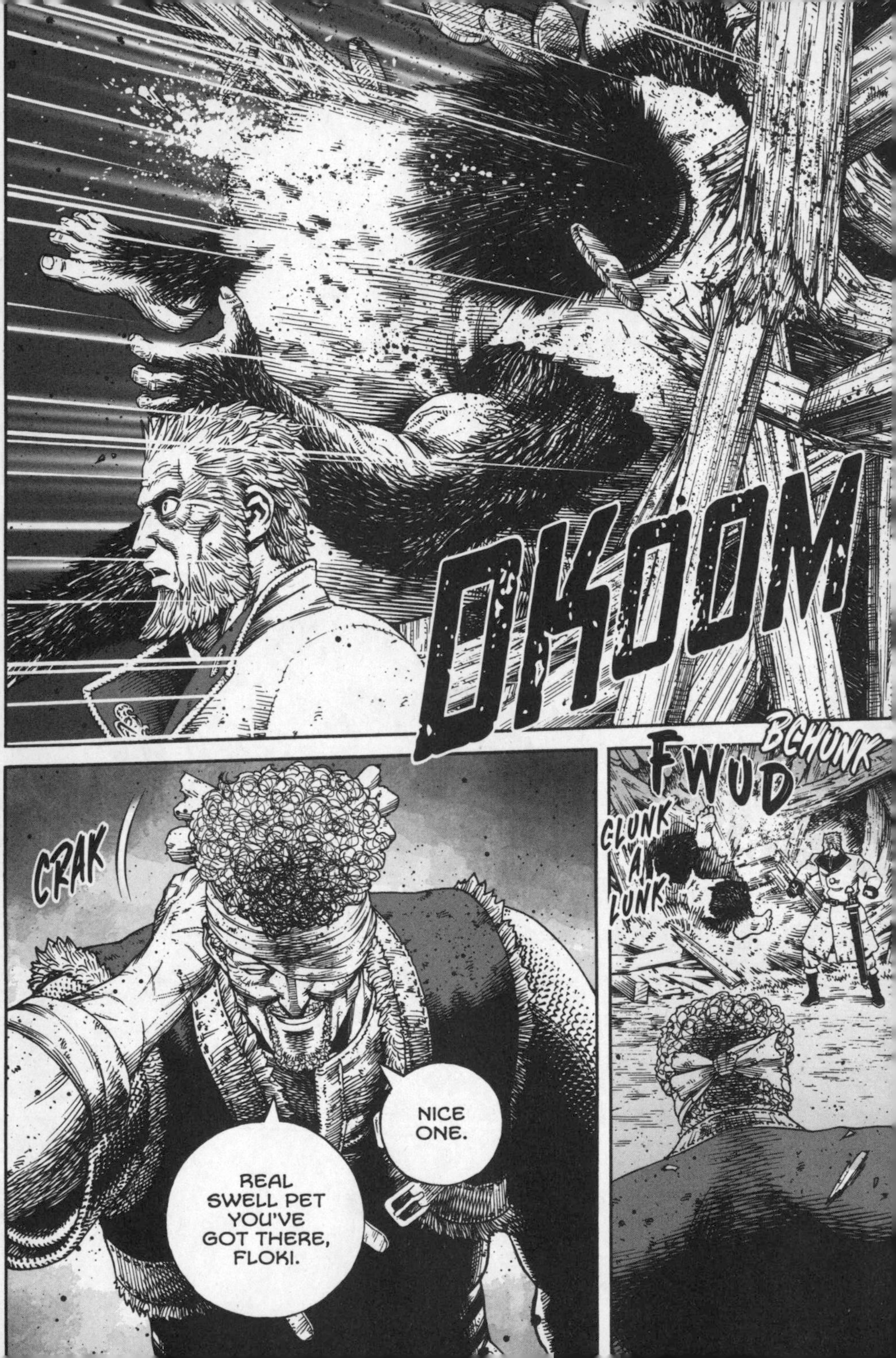
DKOOM
BCHUNK
FWUD
CLUNK A LUNK
CRAK
NICE ONE.
REAL SWELL PET YOU'VE GOT THERE, FLOKI.

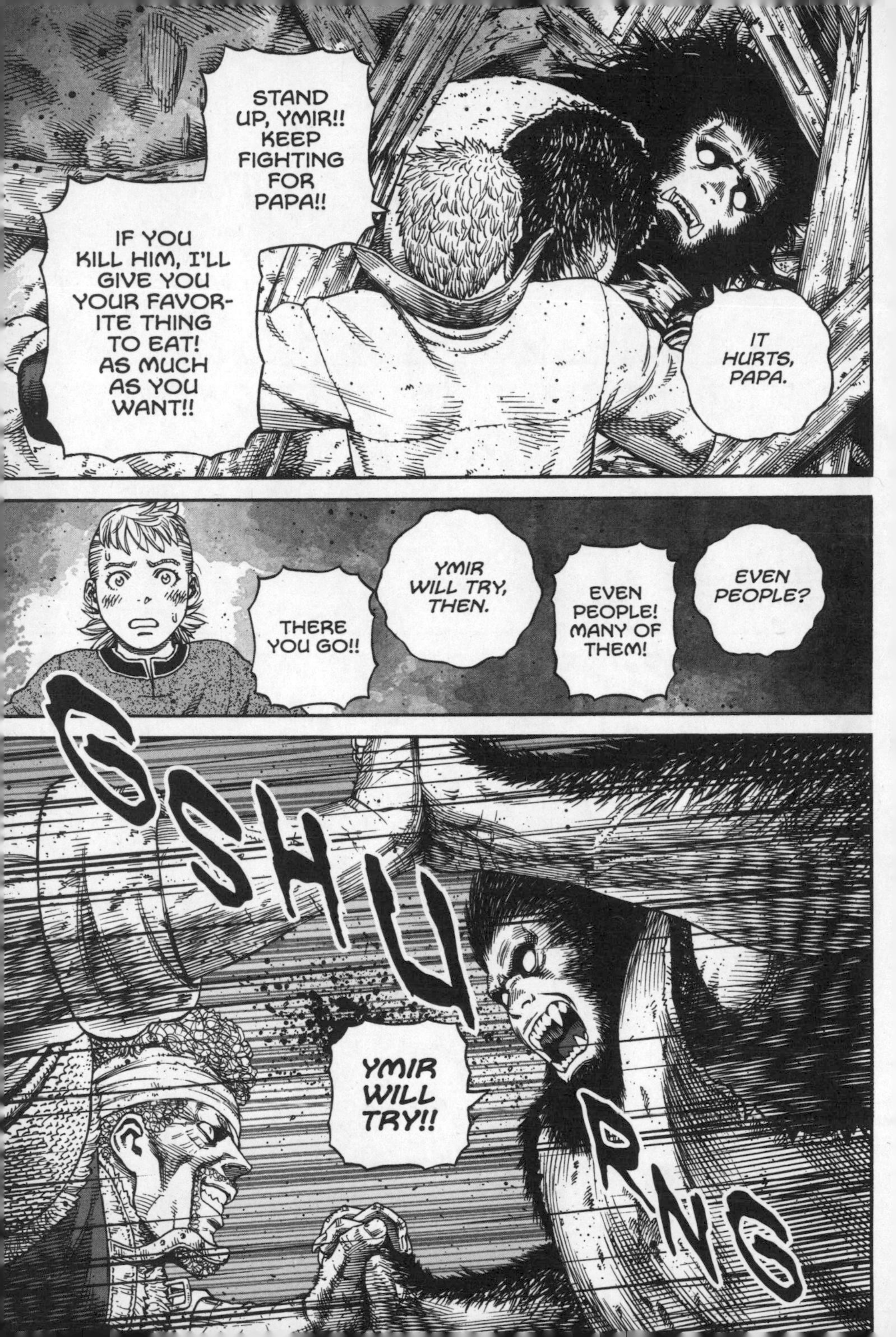
IT HURTS, PAPA.
STAND UP, YMIR!! KEEP FIGHTING FOR PAPA!!
IF YOU KILL HIM, I'LL GIVE YOU YOUR FAVORITE THING TO EAT! AS MUCH AS YOU WANT!!
EVEN PEOPLE?
EVEN PEOPLE! MANY OF THEM!
YMIR WILL TRY, THEN.
THERE YOU GO!!
YMIR WILL TRY!!
GSHURNG

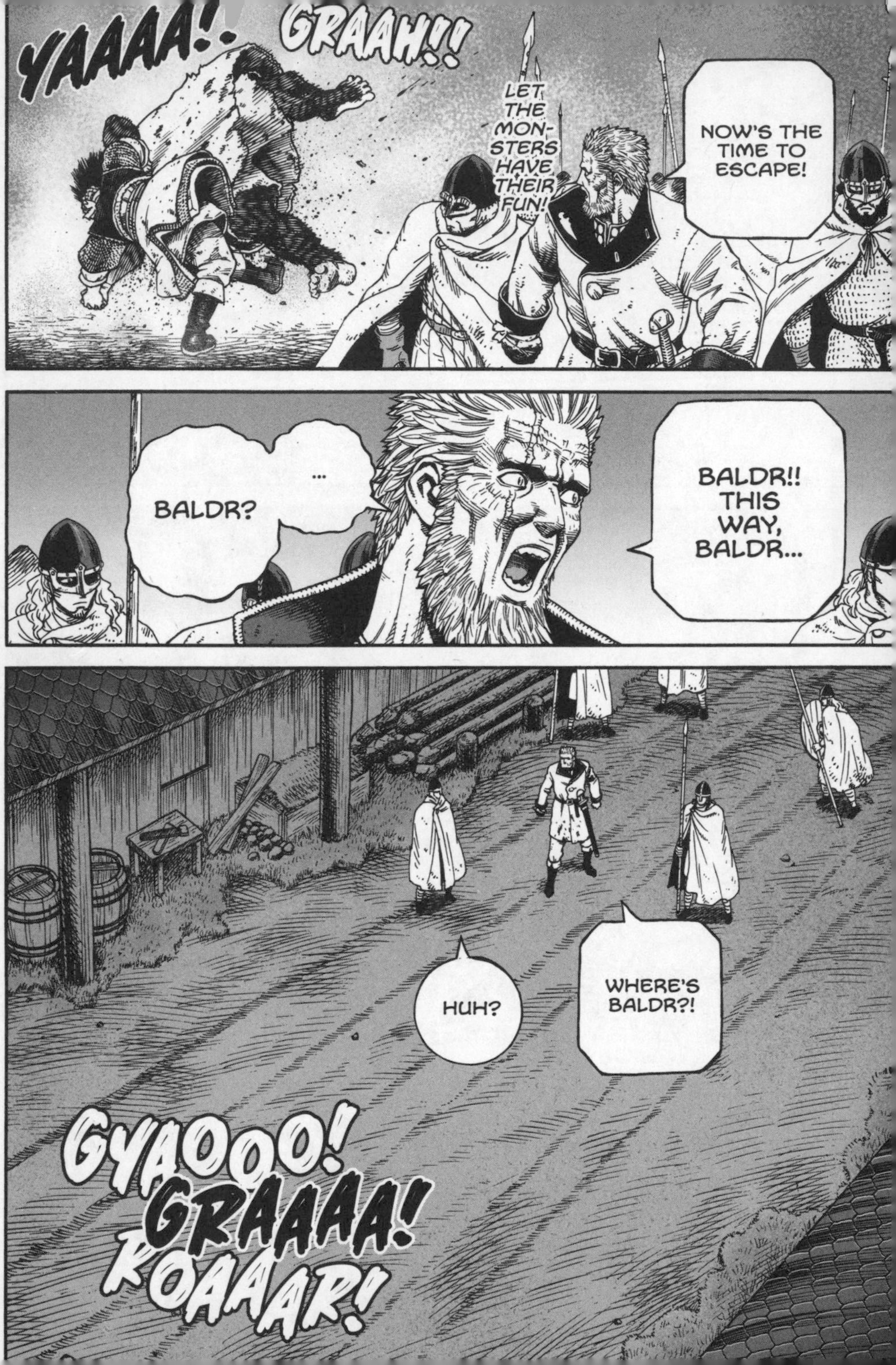
NOW'S THE TIME TO ESCAPE!
LET THE MON-STERS HAVE THEIR FUN!
GRAAH!!
YAAAA!
BALDR!! THIS WAY, BALDR...
... BALDR?
WHERE'S BALDR?!
HUH?
GYAOOO!
GRAAAA!
KOAAAR!

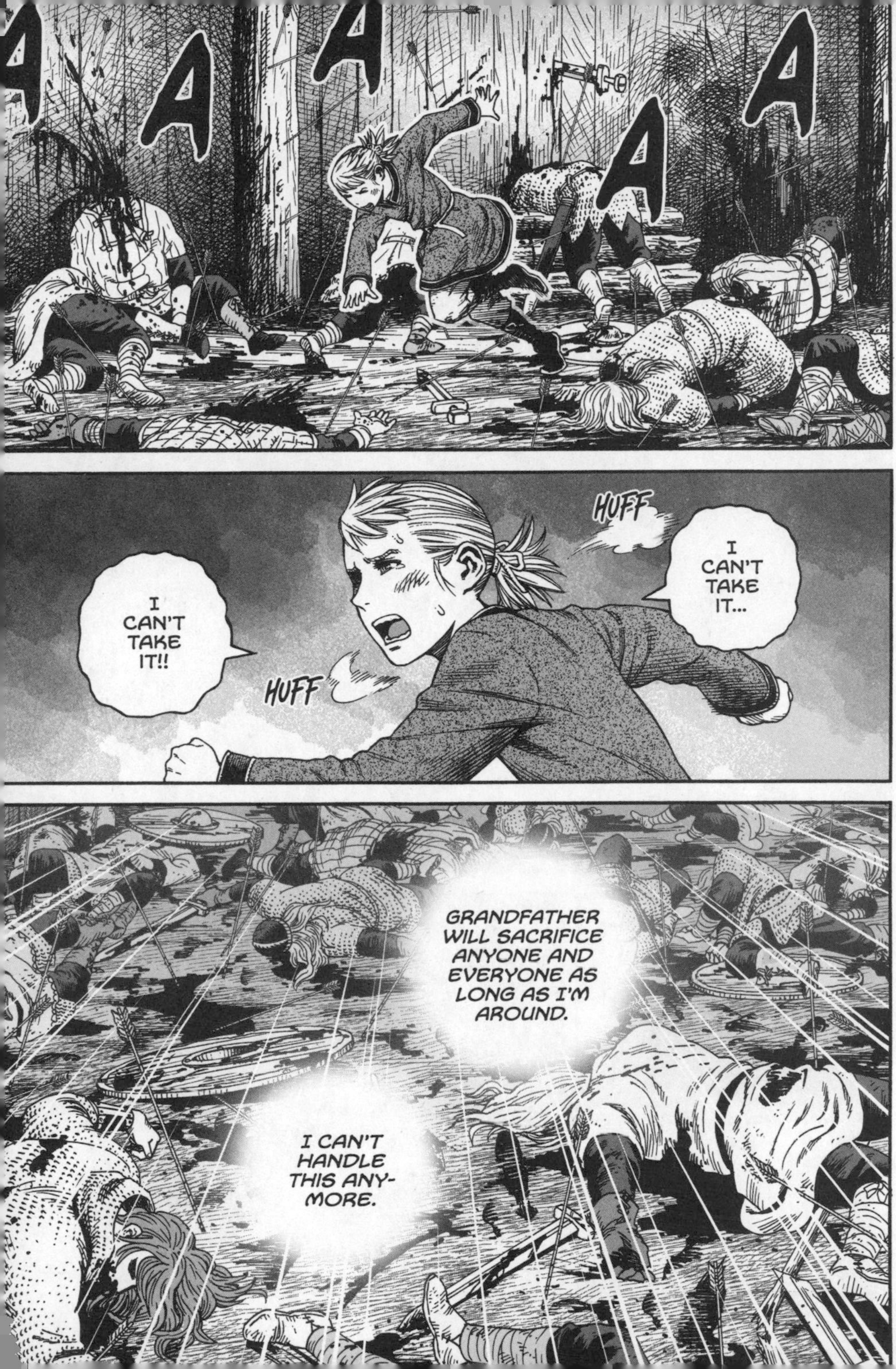
AAAAA
HUFF
I CAN'T TAKE IT...
I CAN'T TAKE IT!!
HUFF
GRANDFATHER WILL SACRIFICE ANYONE AND EVERYONE AS LONG AS I'M AROUND.
I CAN'T HANDLE THIS ANY-MORE.

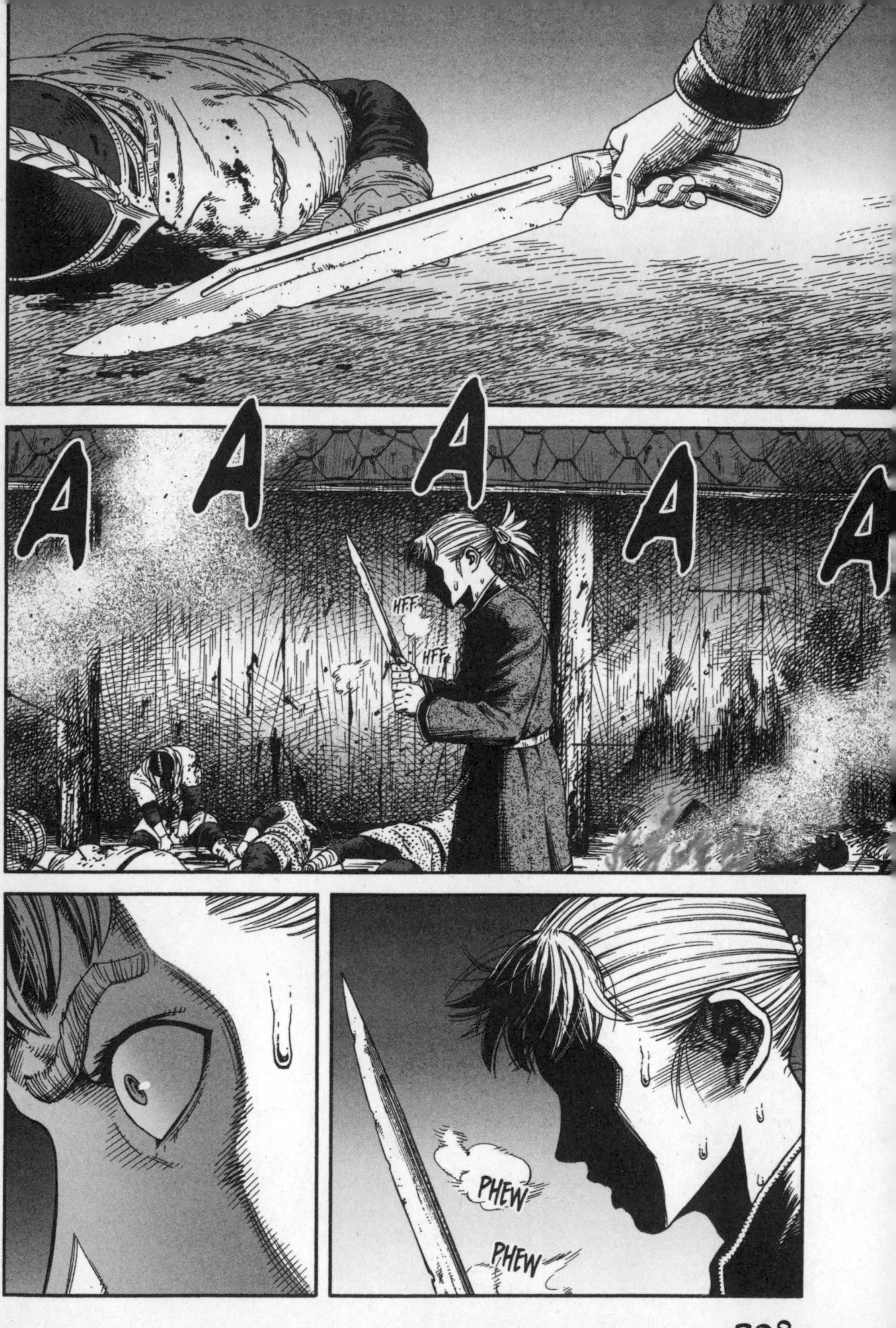
A A A A A
HFF
HFF
PHEW
PHEW

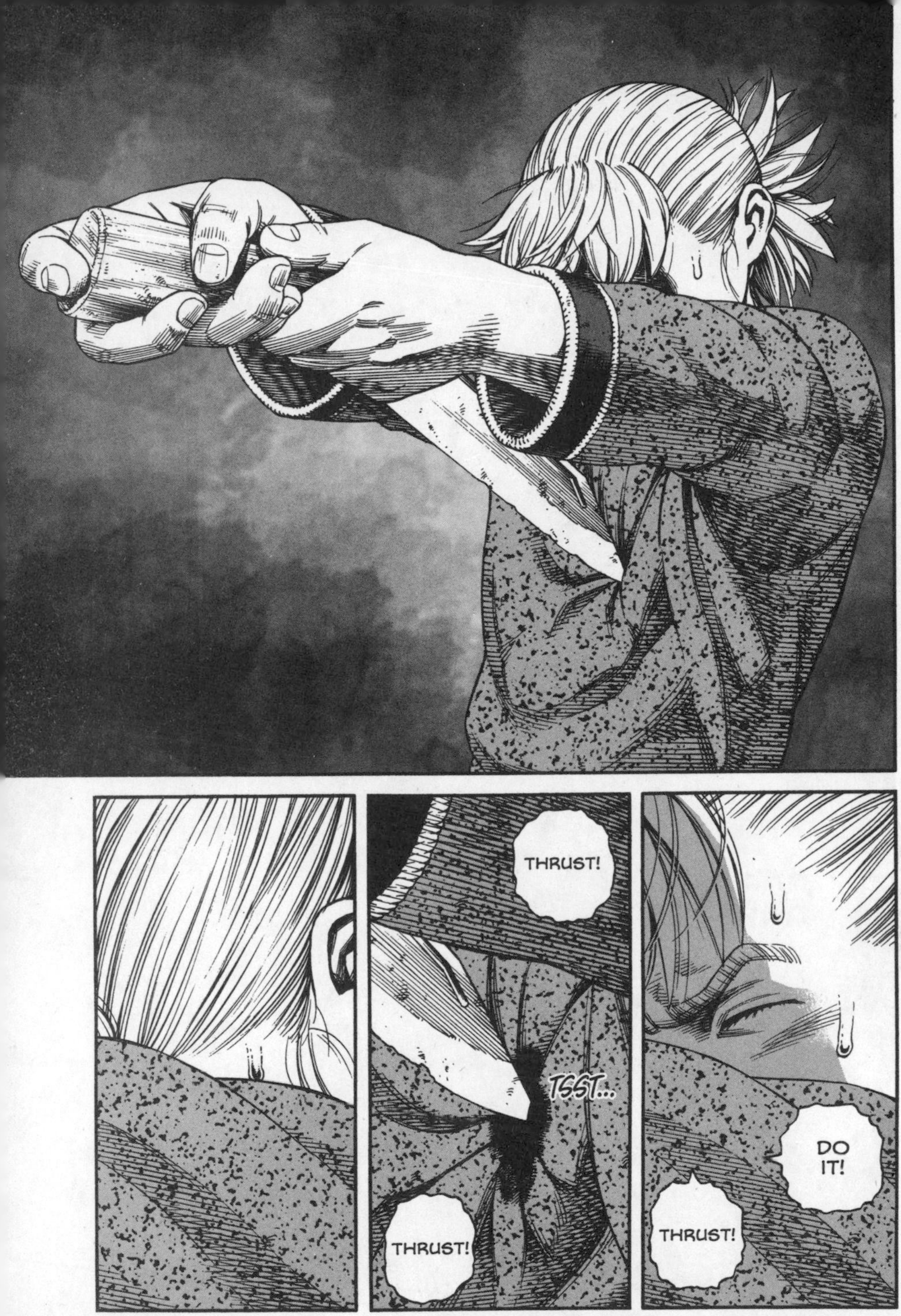
DO IT!
THRUST!
THRUST!
TSST...
THRUST!

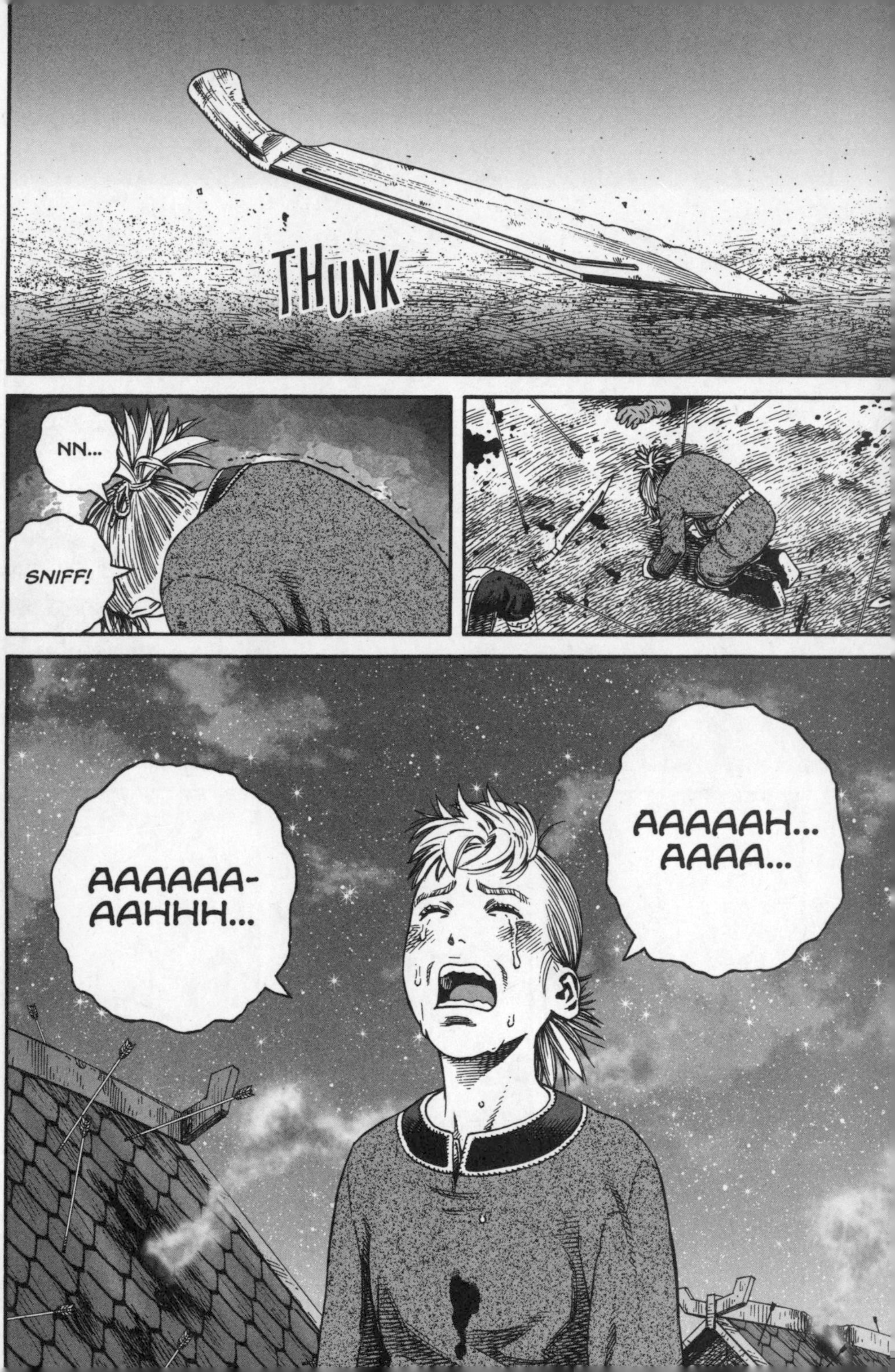
THUNK
NN...
SNIFF!
AAAAAH... AAAA...
AAAAAA-AAHHH...

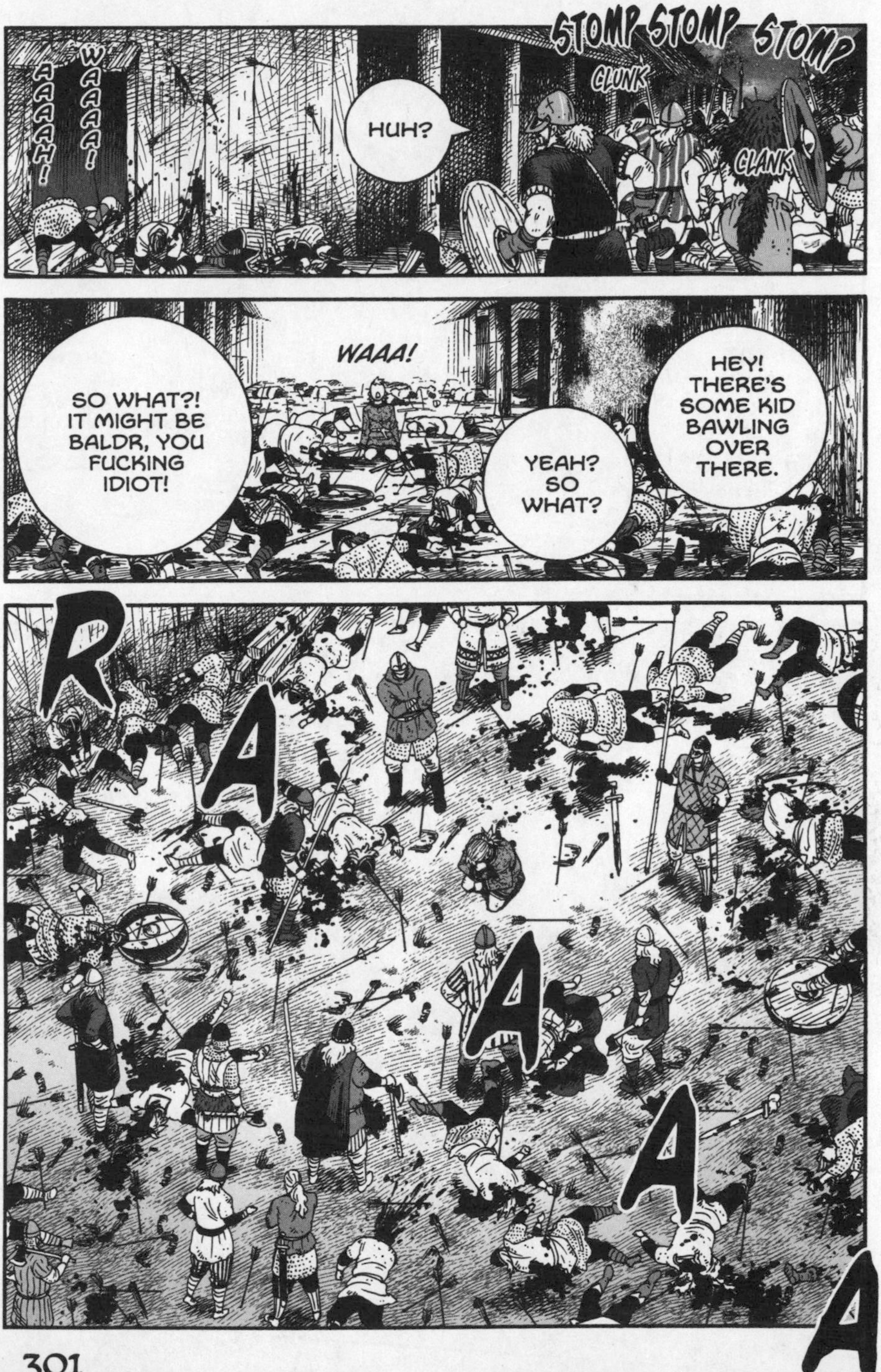
STOMP STOMP STOMP
CLUNK
CLANK
HUH?
WAAAAA!
AAAAAH!
HEY! THERE'S SOME KID BAWLING OVER THERE.
YEAH? SO WHAT?
WAAA!
SO WHAT?! IT MIGHT BE BALDR, YOU FUCKING IDIOT!
RAAAA

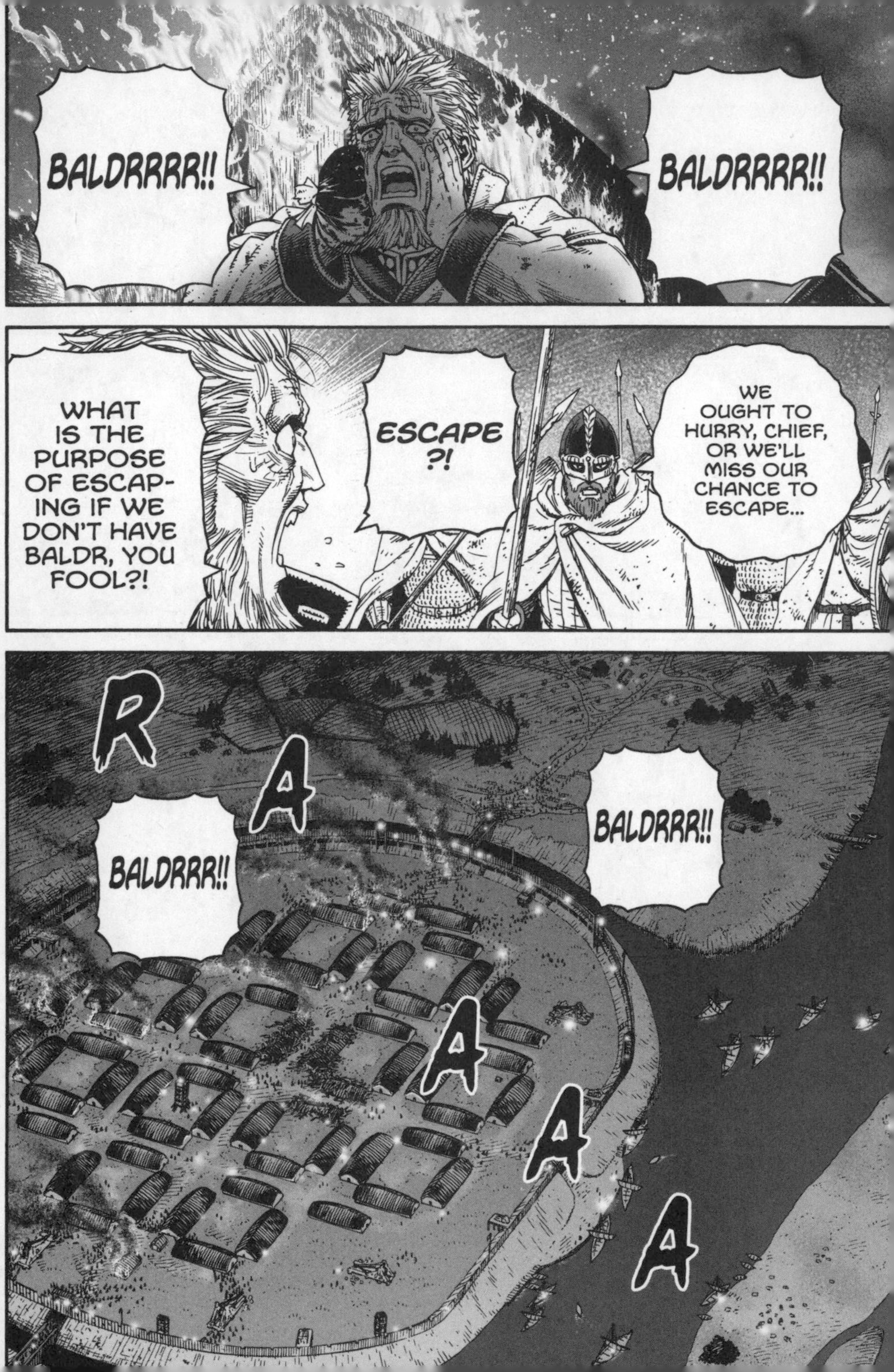
BALDRRRR!!
BALDRRRR!!
WE OUGHT TO HURRY, CHIEF, OR WE'LL MISS OUR CHANCE TO ESCAPE...
ESCAPE?!
WHAT IS THE PURPOSE OF ESCAP-ING IF WE DON'T HAVE BALDR, YOU FOOL?!
BALDRRR!!
BALDRRR!!
RAAAAA

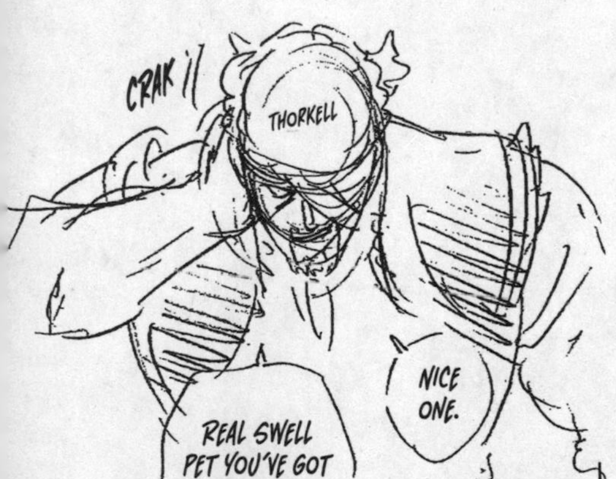
CRAK
THORKELL
NICE ONE.
REAL SWELL PET YOU'VE GOT THERE, FLOKI.

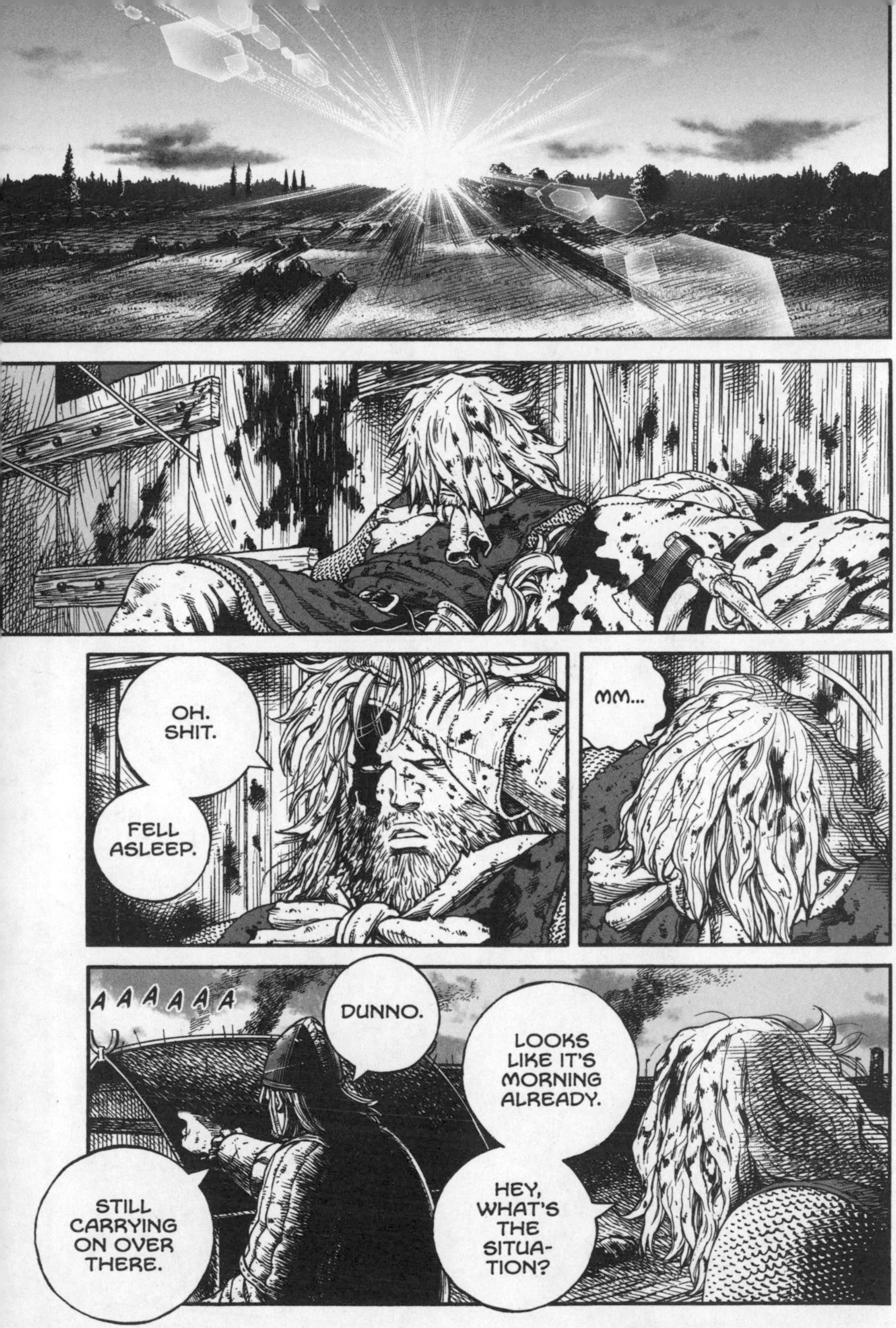
MM...
OH. SHIT.
FELL ASLEEP.
LOOKS LIKE IT'S MORNING ALREADY.
HEY, WHAT'S THE SITUATION?
DUNNO.
STILL CARRYING ON OVER THERE.
AAAAAA

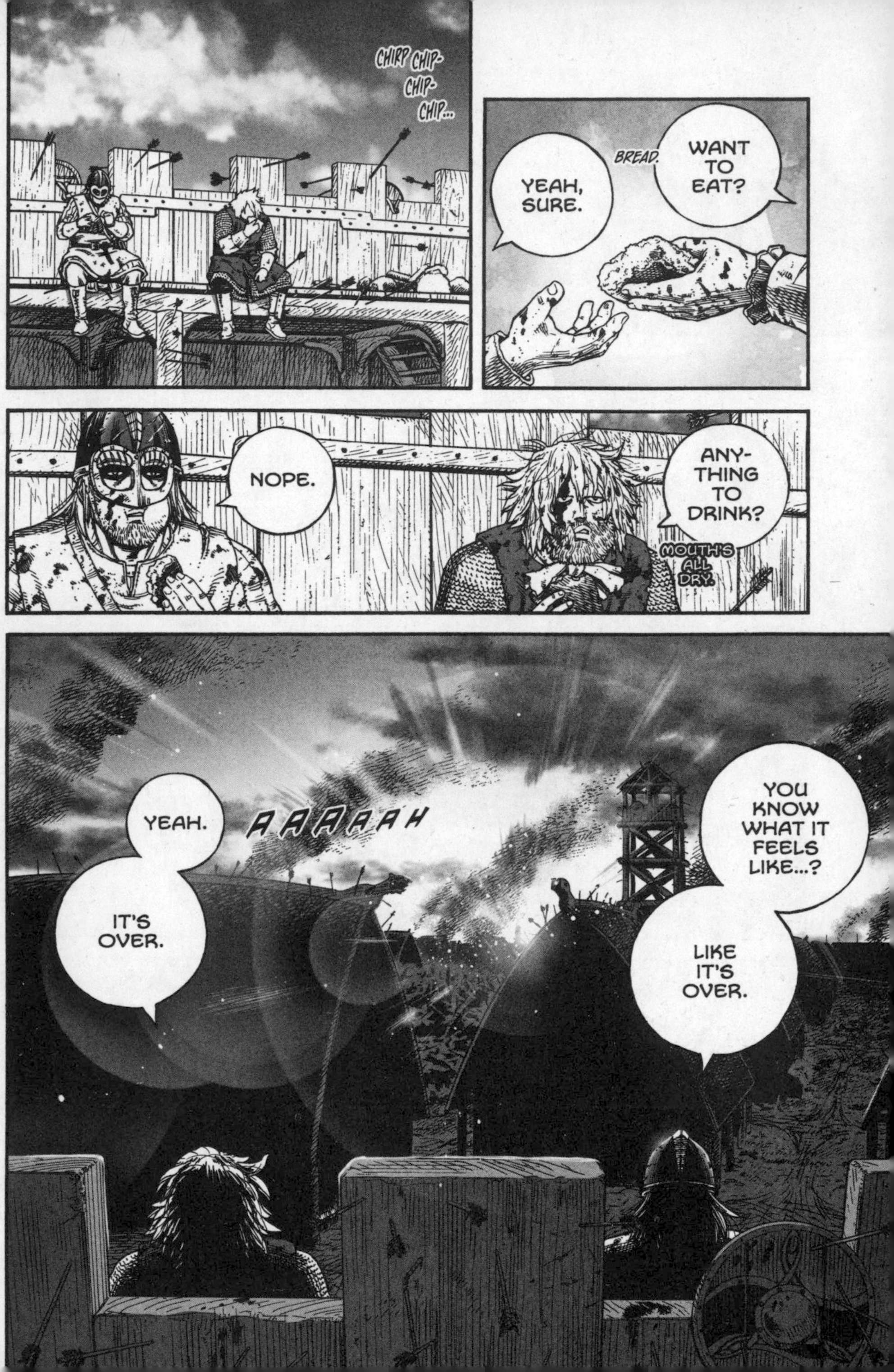
WANT TO EAT?
BREAD.
YEAH, SURE.
CHIRP CHIP-CHIP-CHIP...
ANY-THING TO DRINK?
MOUTH'S ALL DRY.
NOPE.
YOU KNOW WHAT IT FEELS LIKE...?
LIKE IT'S OVER.
AAAAAH
YEAH.
IT'S OVER.

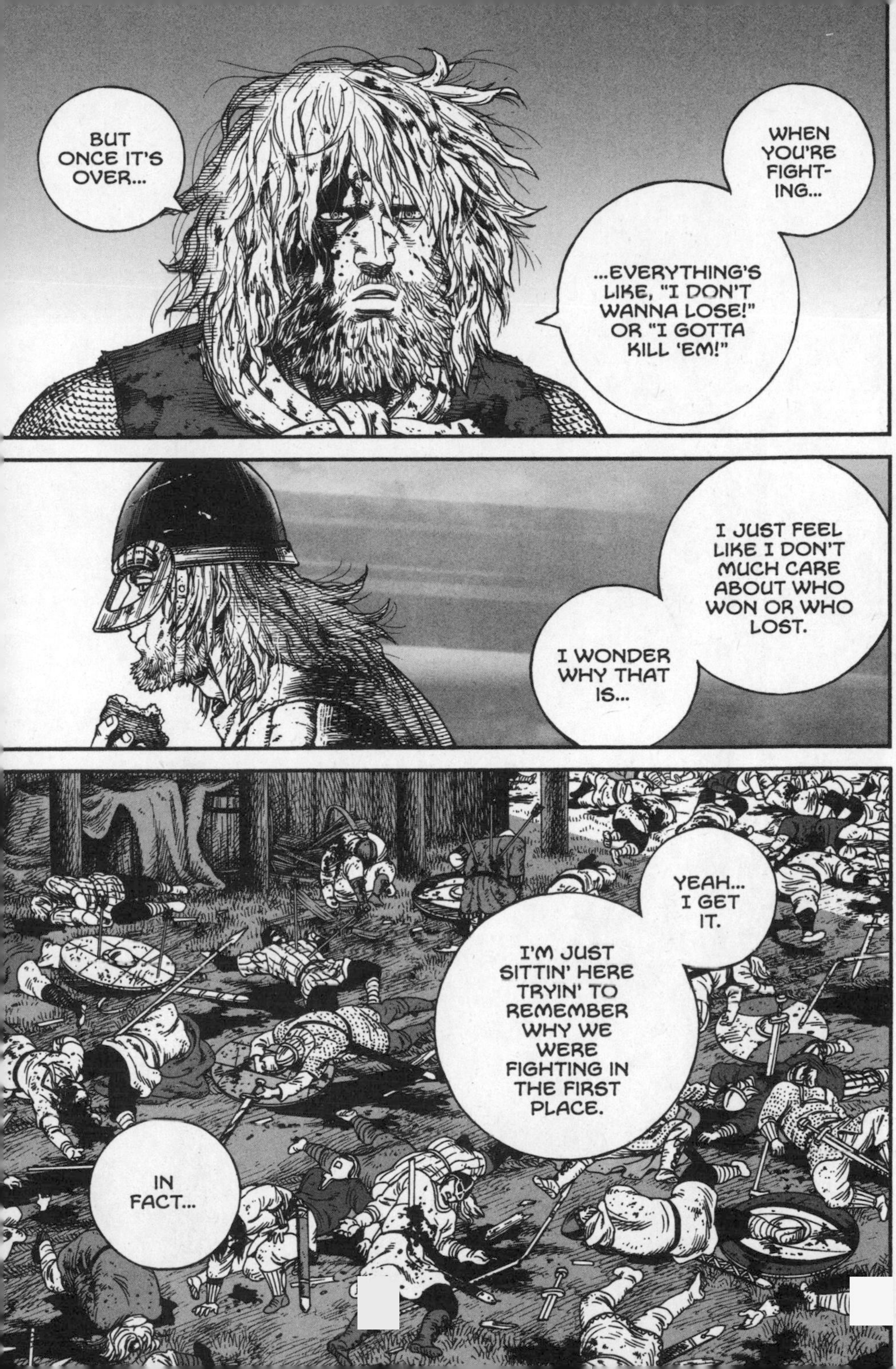
WHEN YOU'RE FIGHTING...
...EVERYTHING'S LIKE, "I DON'T WANNA LOSE!" OR "I GOTTA KILL 'EM!"
BUT ONCE IT'S OVER...
I JUST FEEL LIKE I DON'T MUCH CARE ABOUT WHO WON OR WHO LOST.
I WONDER WHY THAT IS...
YEAH... I GET IT.
I'M JUST SITTIN' HERE TRYIN' TO REMEMBER WHY WE WERE FIGHTING IN THE FIRST PLACE.
IN FACT...

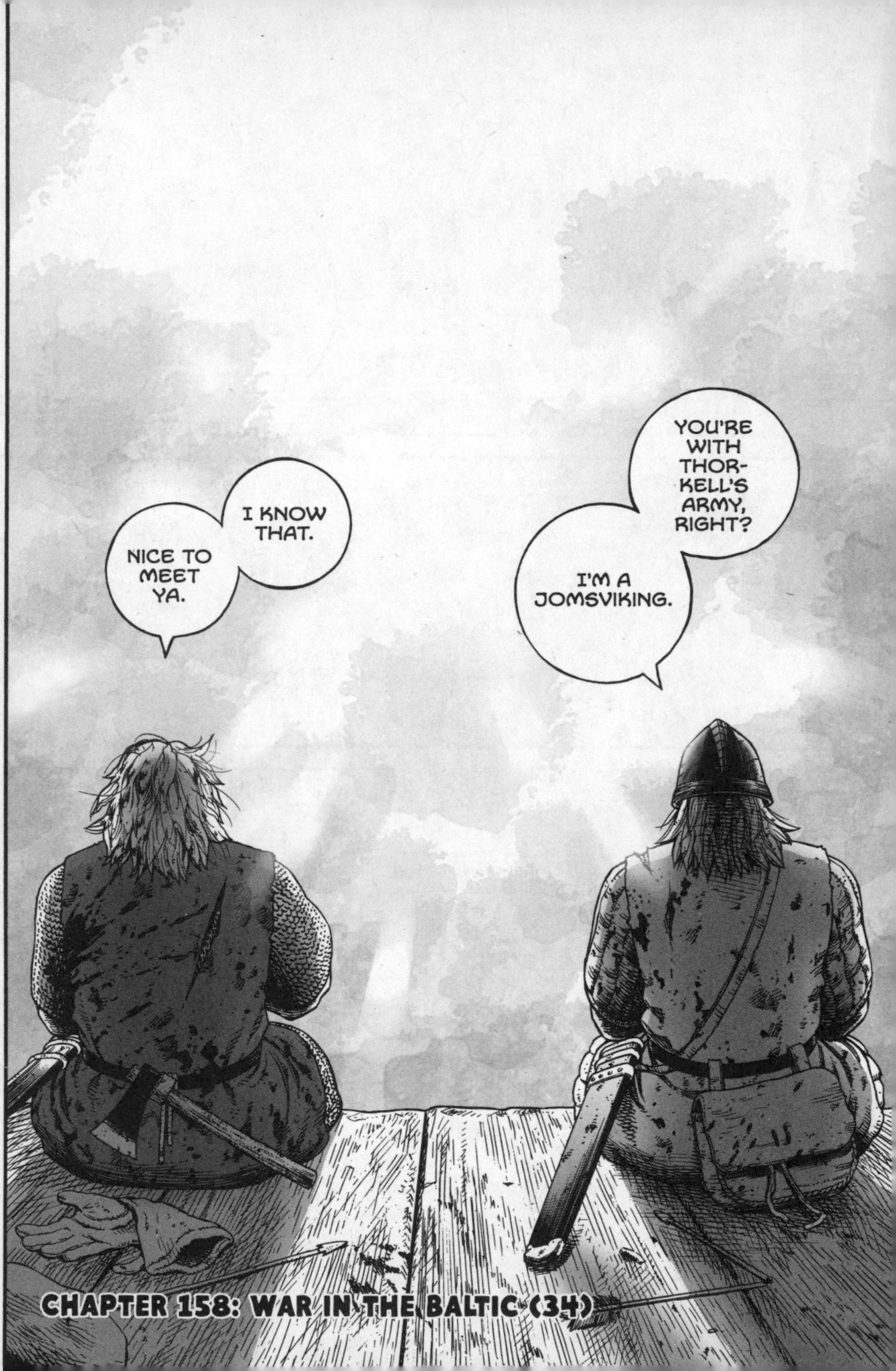
YOU'RE WITH THOR-KELL'S ARMY, RIGHT?
I'M A JOMSVIKING.
I KNOW THAT.
NICE TO MEET YA.
CHAPTER 158: WAR IN THE BALTIC (34)

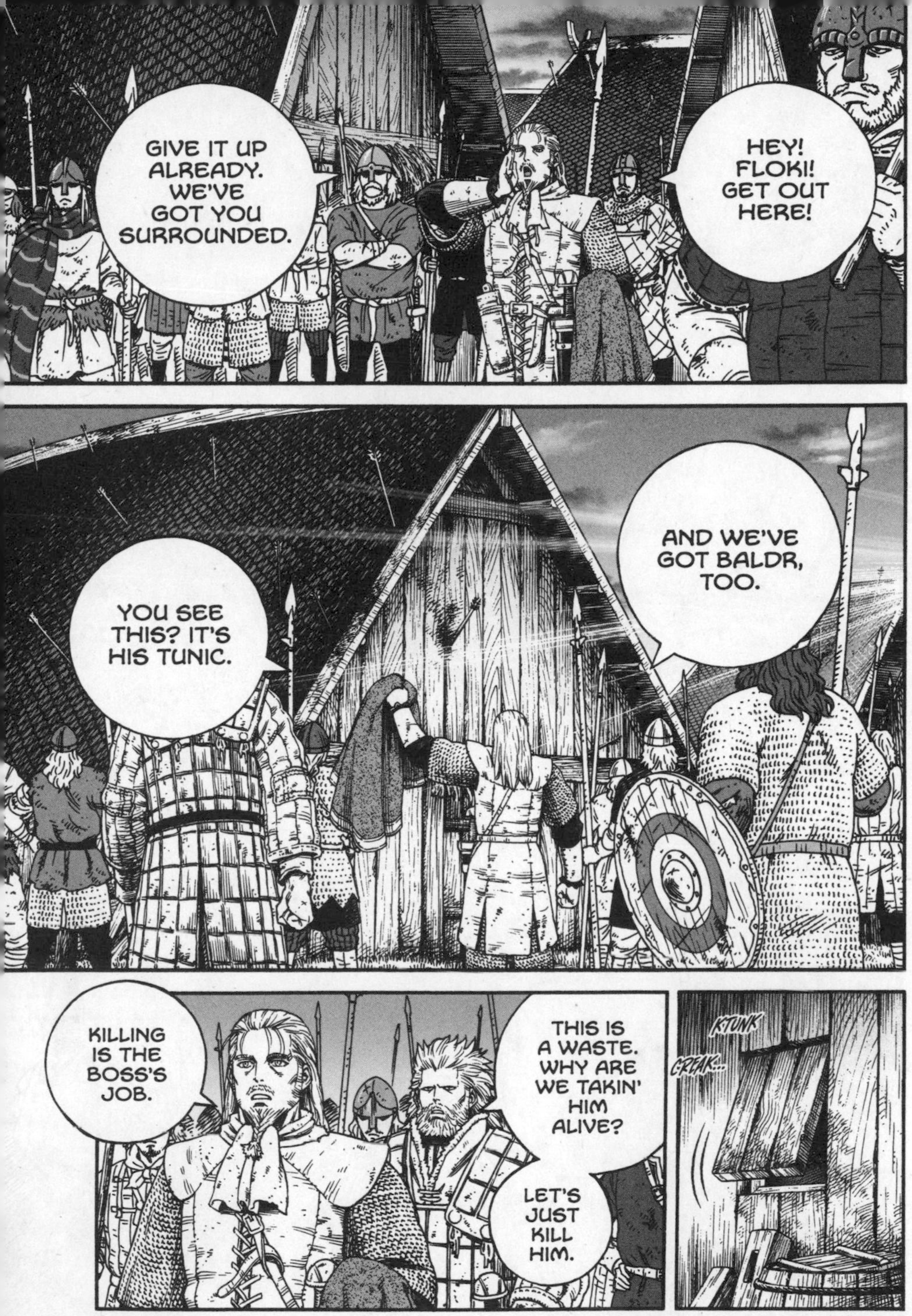
HEY! FLOKI! GET OUT HERE!
GIVE IT UP ALREADY. WE'VE GOT YOU SURROUNDED.
AND WE'VE GOT BALDR, TOO.
YOU SEE THIS? IT'S HIS TUNIC.
KTUNK
CREAK...
THIS IS A WASTE. WHY ARE WE TAKIN' HIM ALIVE?
LET'S JUST KILL HIM.
KILLING IS THE BOSS'S JOB.

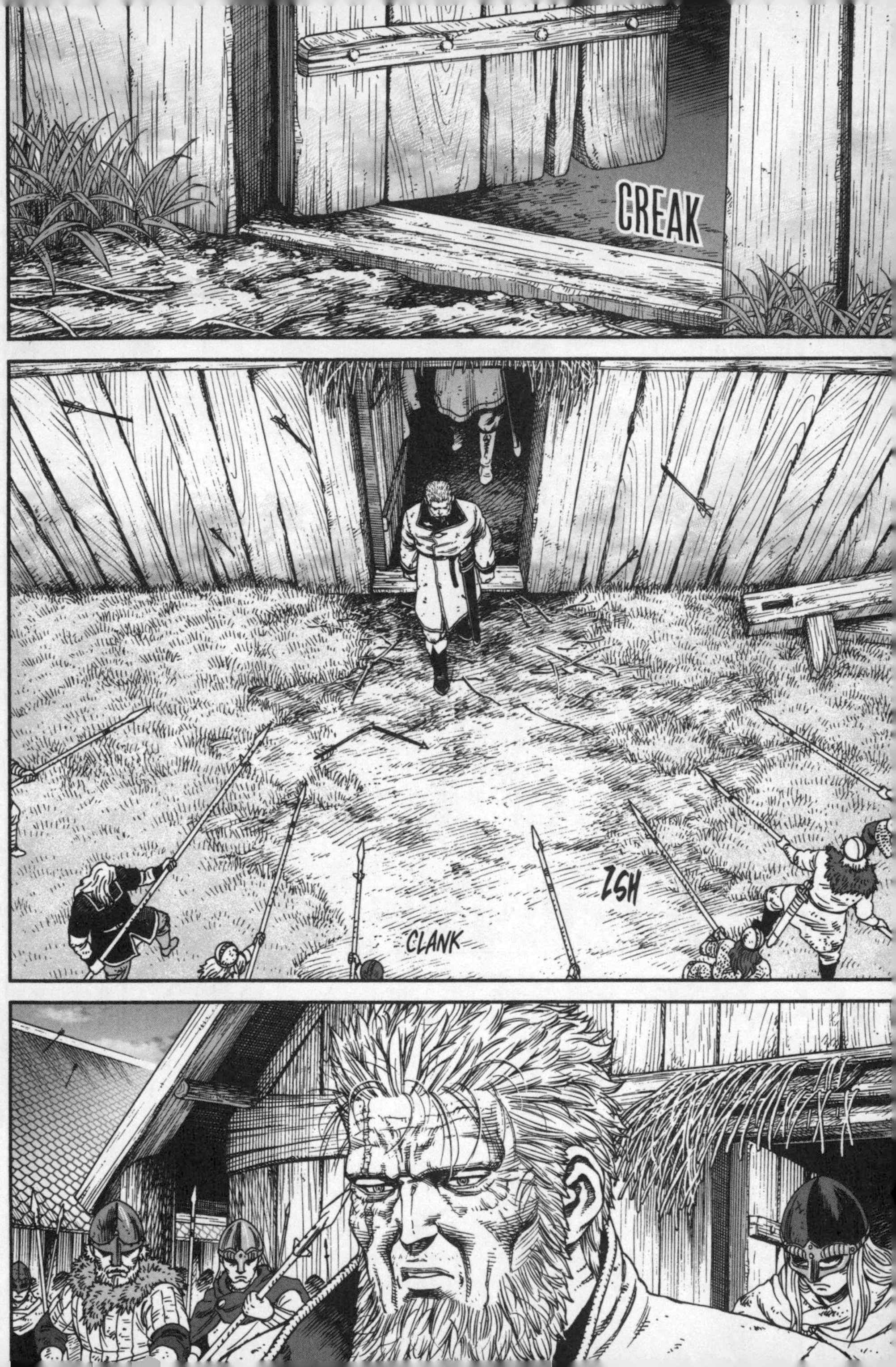
CREAK
ZSH
CLANK

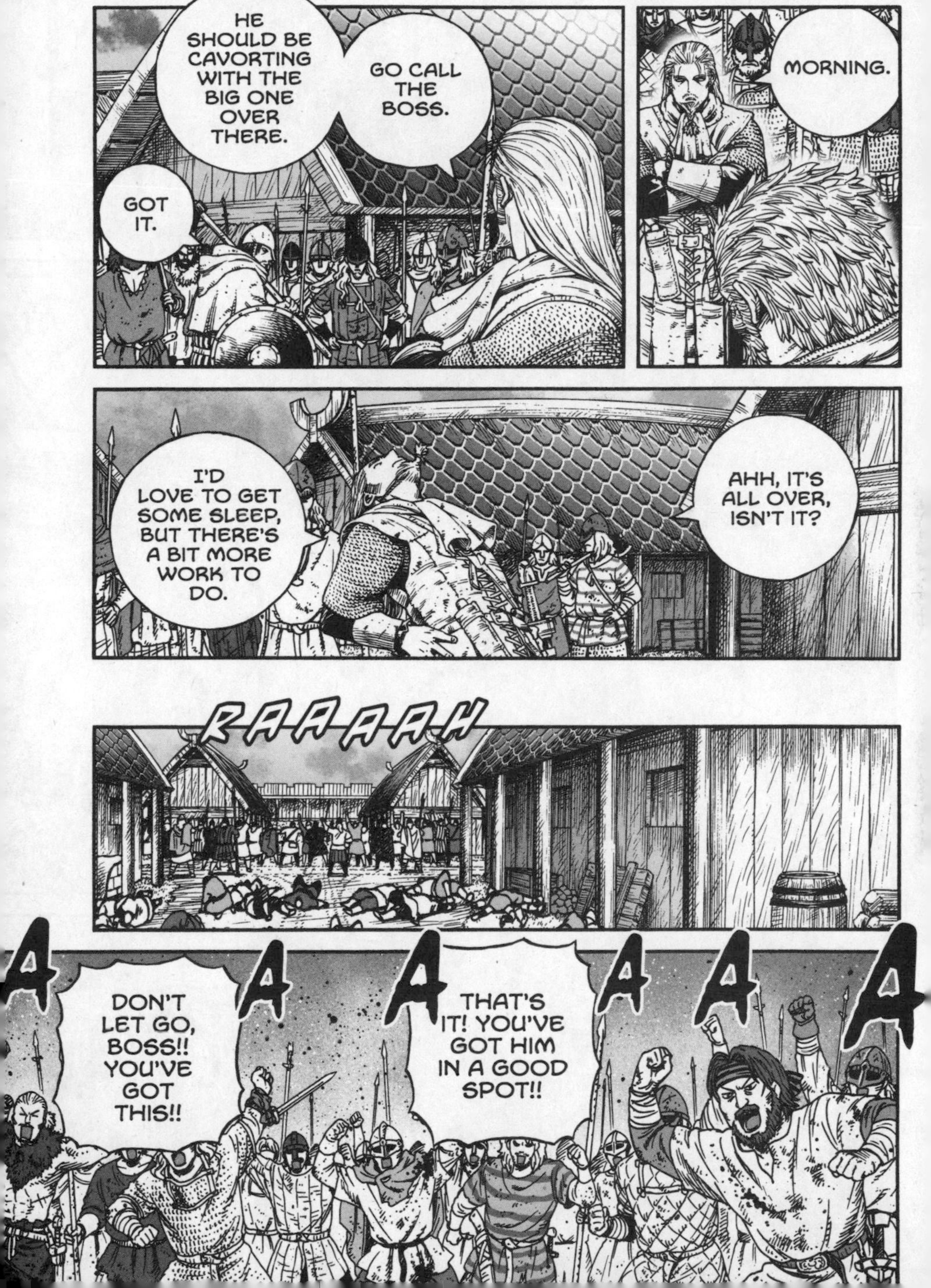
MORNING.
GO CALL THE BOSS.
HE SHOULD BE CAVORTING WITH THE BIG ONE OVER THERE.
GOT IT.
AHH, IT'S ALL OVER, ISN'T IT?
I'D LOVE TO GET SOME SLEEP, BUT THERE'S A BIT MORE WORK TO DO.
RAAAAAH
THAT'S IT! YOU'VE GOT HIM IN A GOOD SPOT!!
DON'T LET GO, BOSS!! YOU'VE GOT THIS!!
A A A A A A

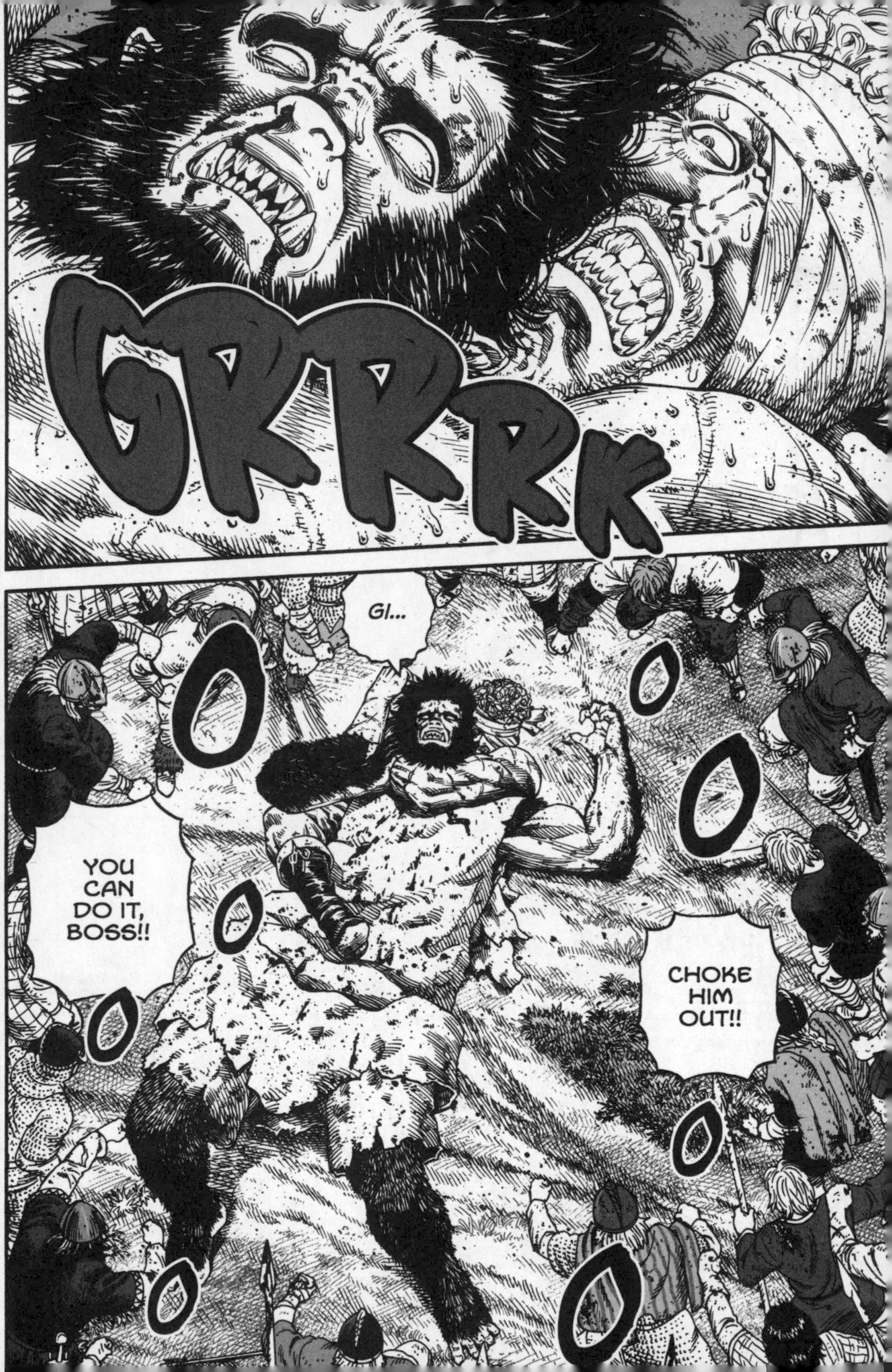
GRRRK
GI...
CHOKE HIM OUT!!
YOU CAN DO IT, BOSS!!

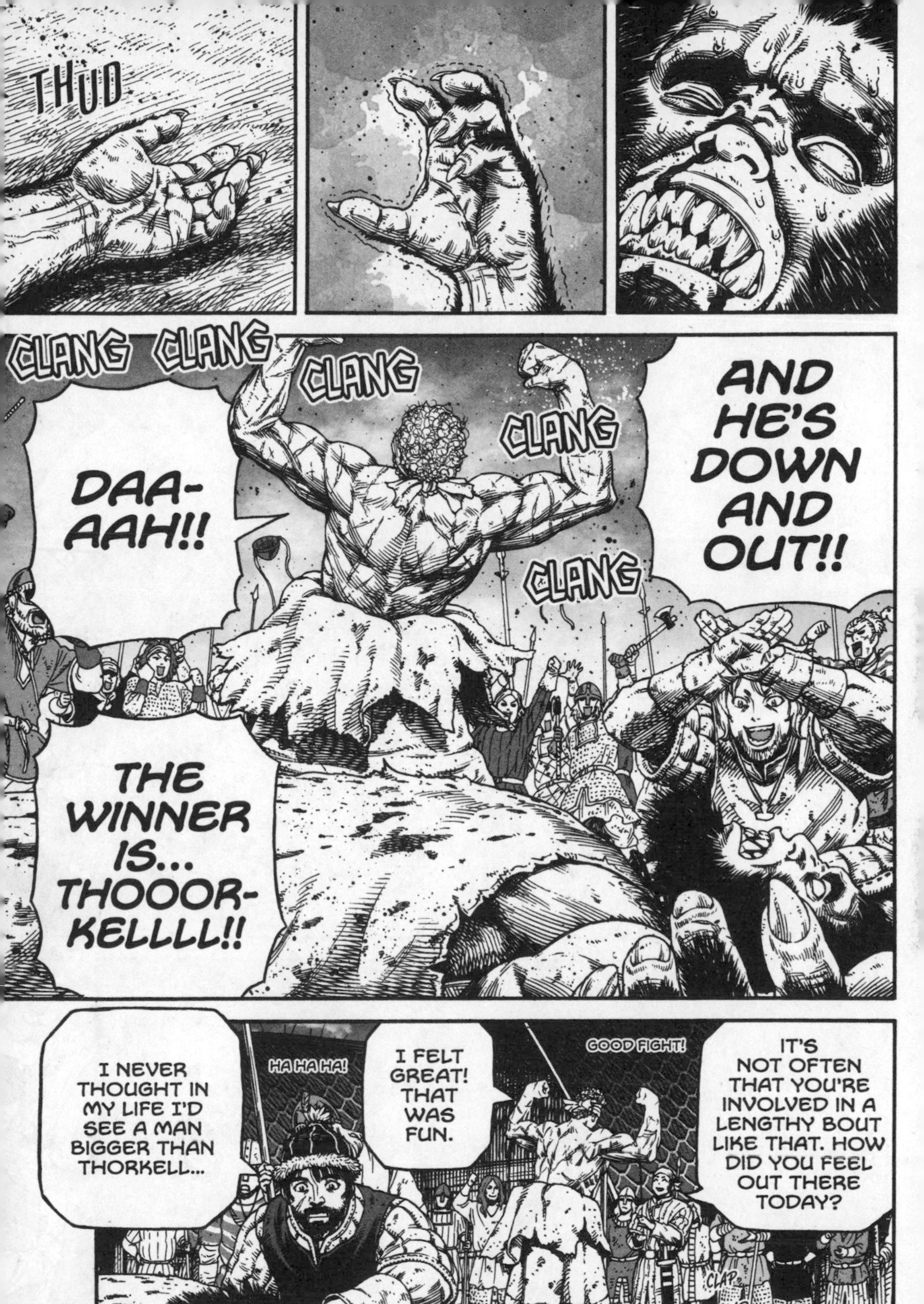
THUD
AND HE'S DOWN AND OUT!!
CLANG
CLANG
CLANG
CLANG
CLANG
DAA-AAH!!
THE WINNER IS... THOOOR-KELLLL!!
IT'S NOT OFTEN THAT YOU'RE INVOLVED IN A LENGTHY BOUT LIKE THAT. HOW DID YOU FEEL OUT THERE TODAY?
GOOD FIGHT!
I FELT GREAT! THAT WAS FUN.
HA HA HA!
I NEVER THOUGHT IN MY LIFE I'D SEE A MAN BIGGER THAN THORKELL...
CLAP
CLAP

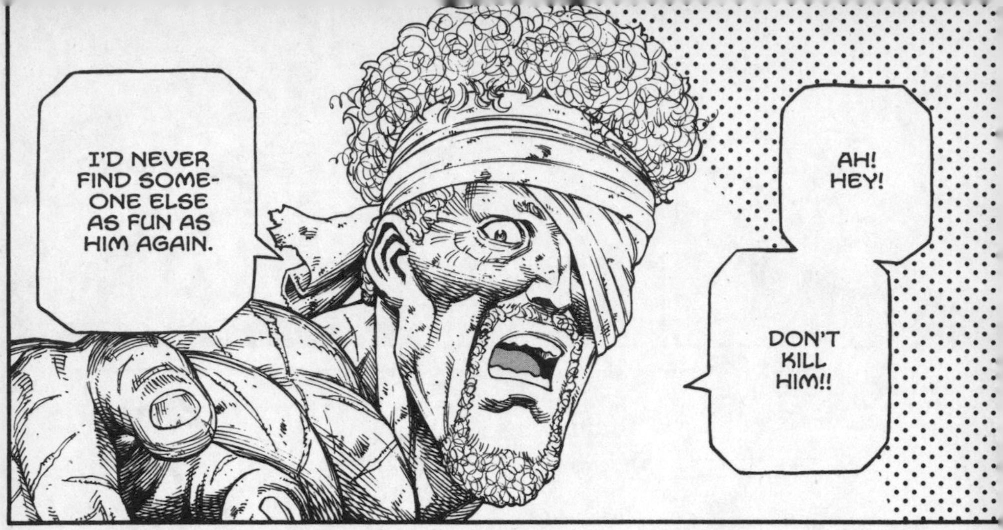
AH! HEY!
DON'T KILL HIM!!
I'D NEVER FIND SOME-ONE ELSE AS FUN AS HIM AGAIN.

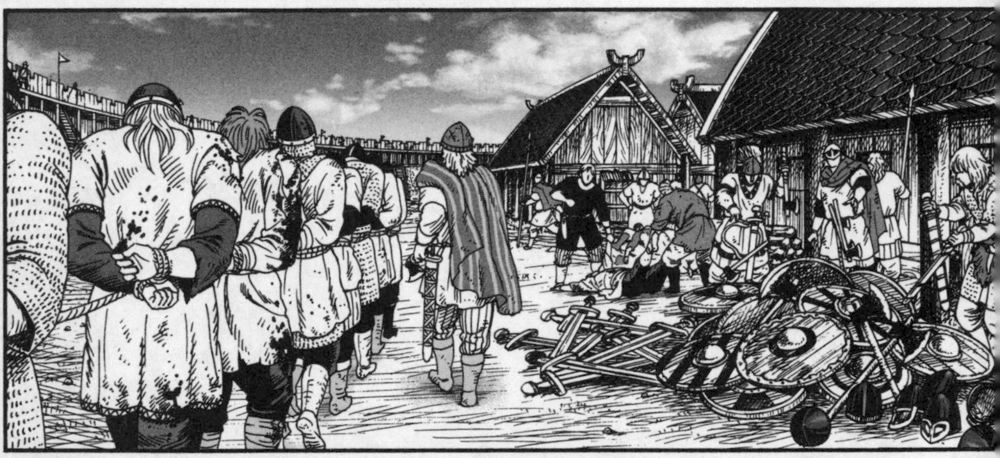

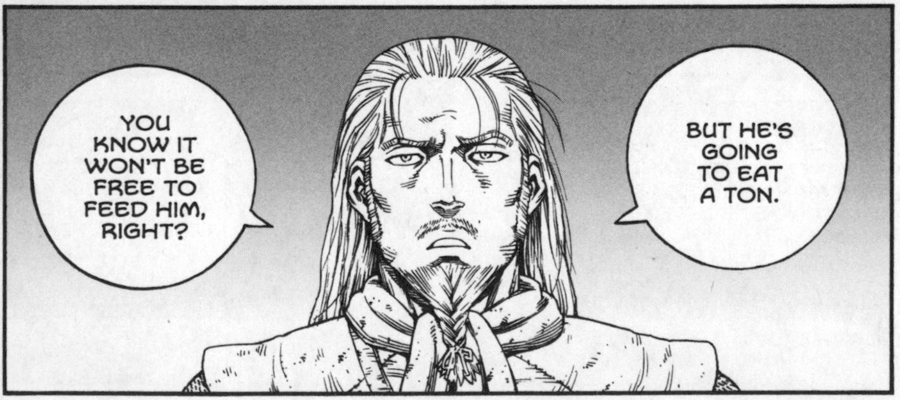
BUT HE'S GOING TO EAT A TON.
YOU KNOW IT WON'T BE FREE TO FEED HIM, RIGHT?

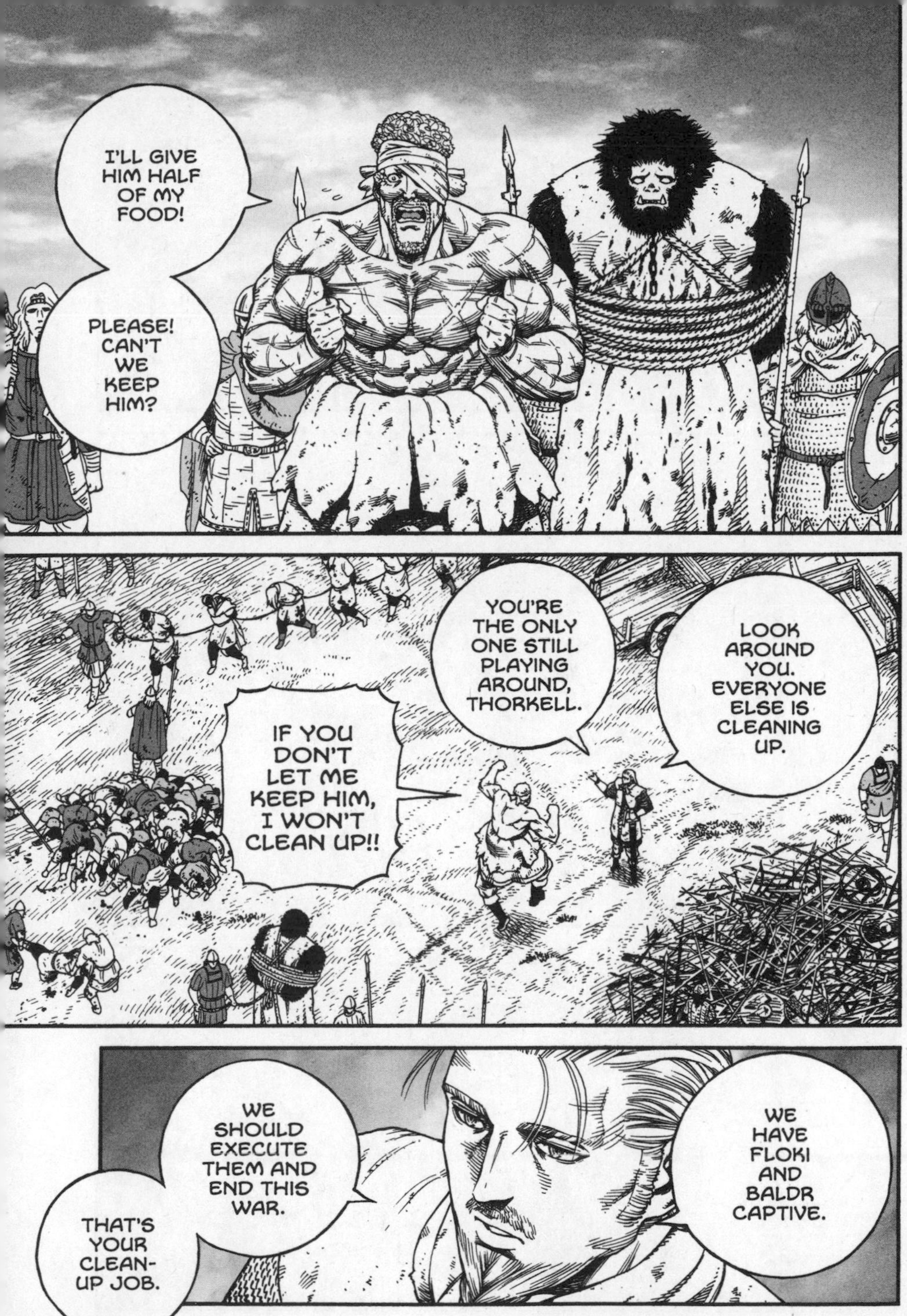
I'LL GIVE HIM HALF OF MY FOOD!
PLEASE! CAN'T WE KEEP HIM?
LOOK AROUND YOU. EVERYONE ELSE IS CLEANING UP.
YOU'RE THE ONLY ONE STILL PLAYING AROUND, THORKELL.
IF YOU DON'T LET ME KEEP HIM, I WON'T CLEAN UP!!
WE HAVE FLOKI AND BALDR CAPTIVE.
WE SHOULD EXECUTE THEM AND END THIS WAR.
THAT'S YOUR CLEAN-UP JOB.

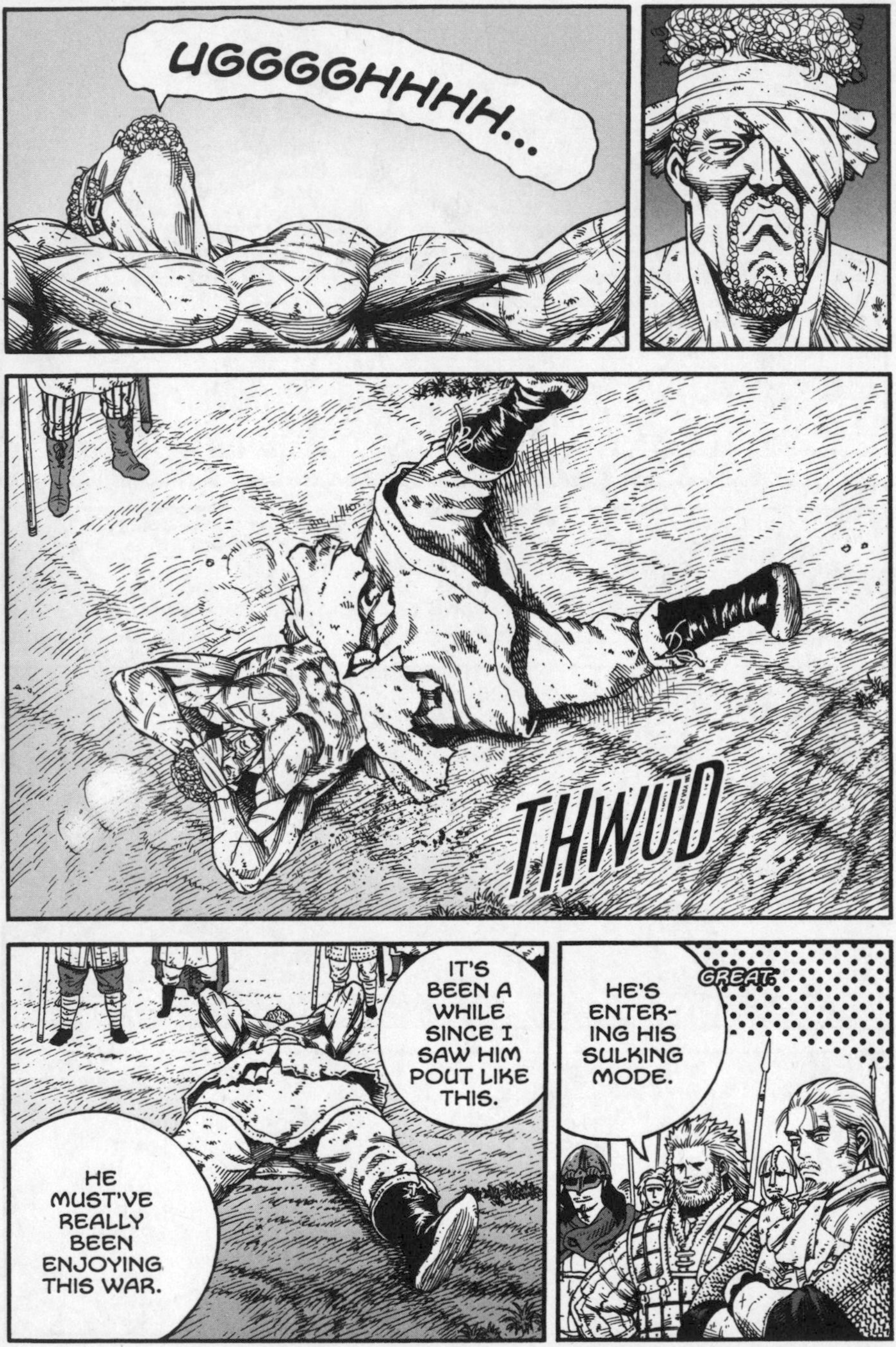
UGGGGHHHH...
THWUD
GREAT.
HE'S ENTERING HIS SULKING MODE.
IT'S BEEN A WHILE SINCE I SAW HIM POUT LIKE THIS.
HE MUST'VE REALLY BEEN ENJOYING THIS WAR.

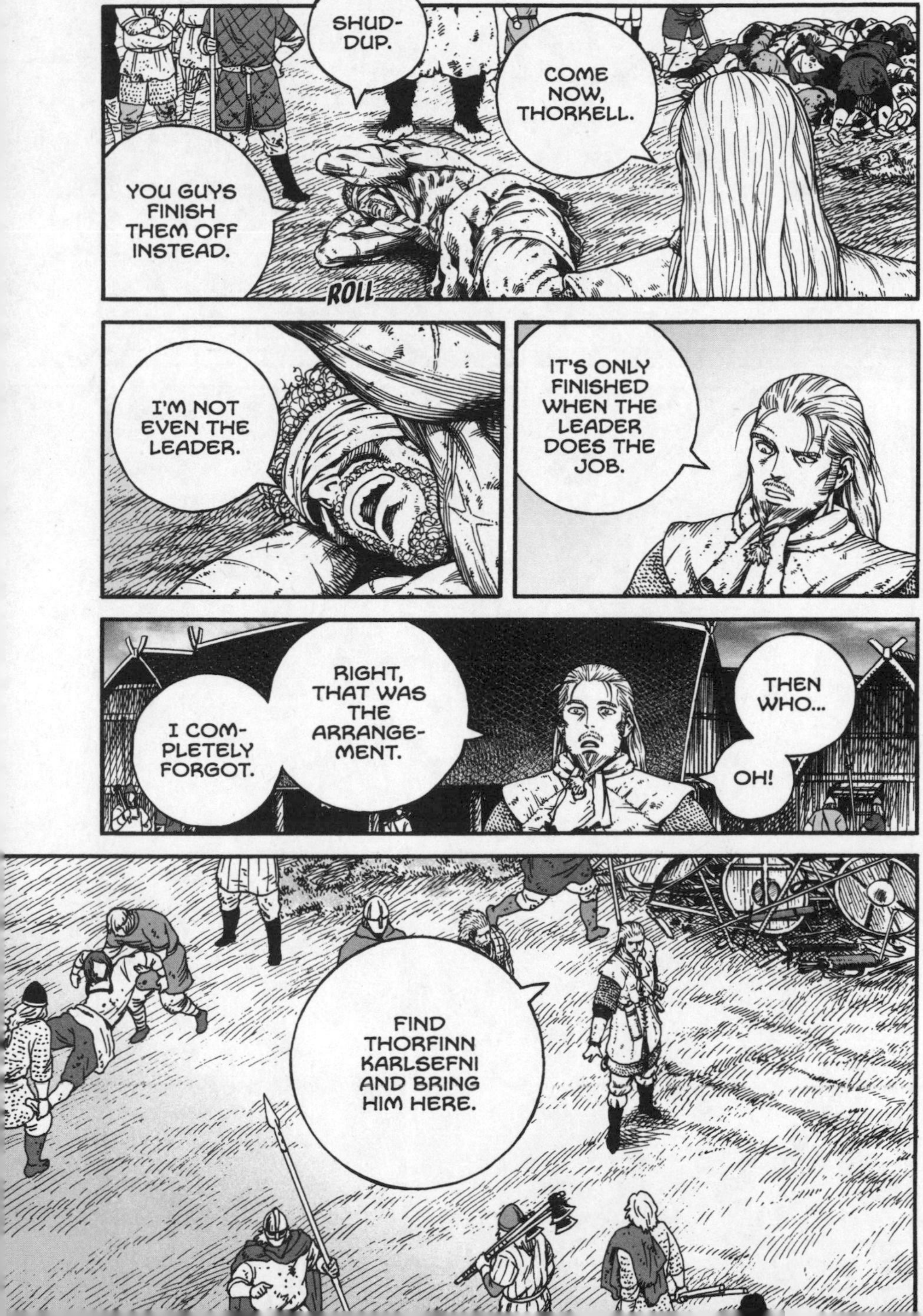
COME NOW, THORKELL.
SHUD-DUP.
YOU GUYS FINISH THEM OFF INSTEAD.
ROLL
IT'S ONLY FINISHED WHEN THE LEADER DOES THE JOB.
I'M NOT EVEN THE LEADER.
THEN WHO...
OH!
RIGHT, THAT WAS THE ARRANGE-MENT.
I COM-PLETELY FORGOT.
FIND THORFINN KARLSEFNI AND BRING HIM HERE.

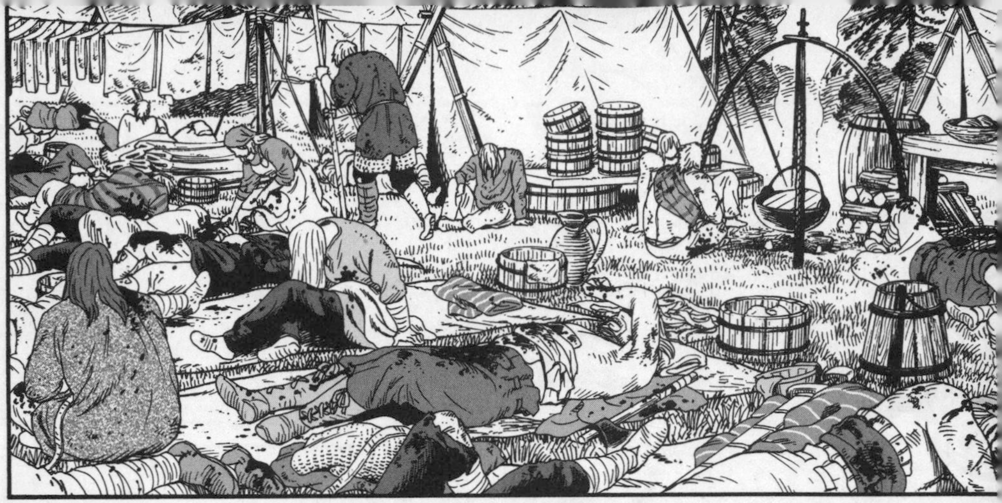

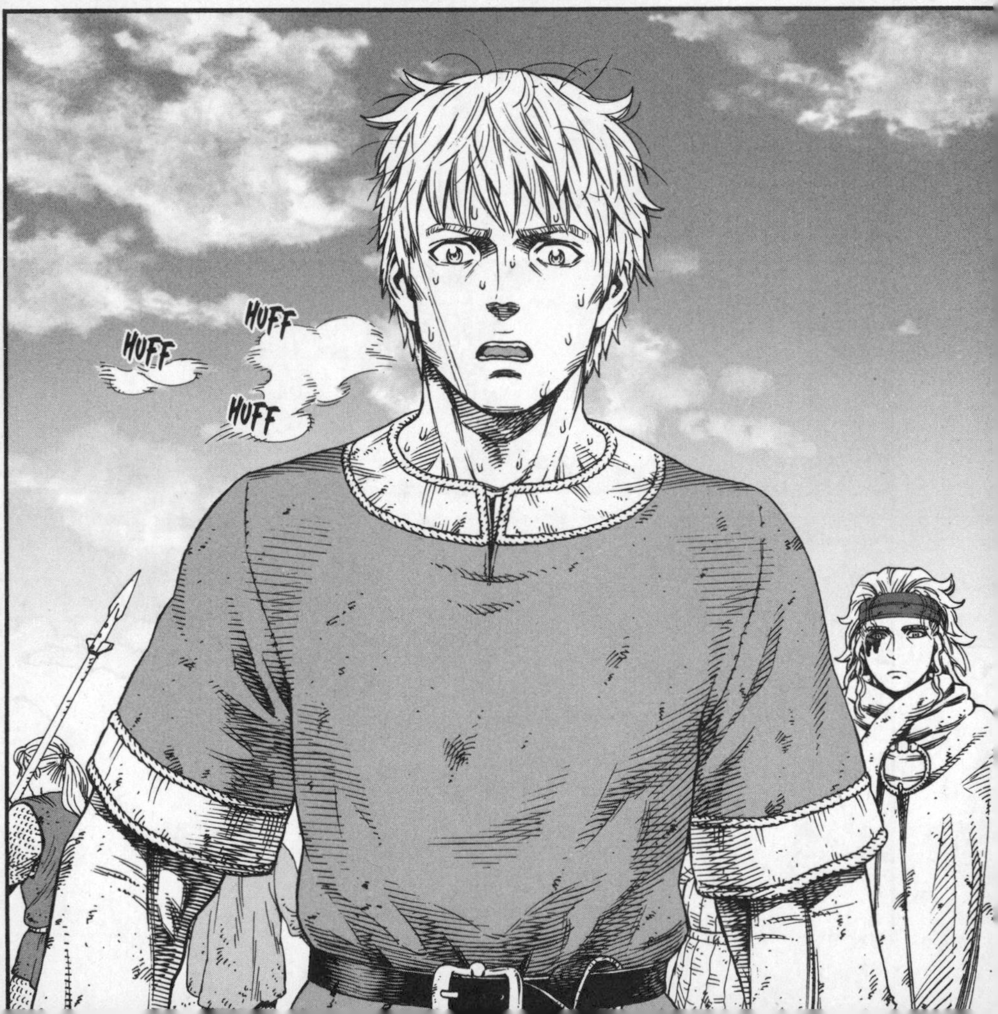
HUFF
HUFF
HUFF

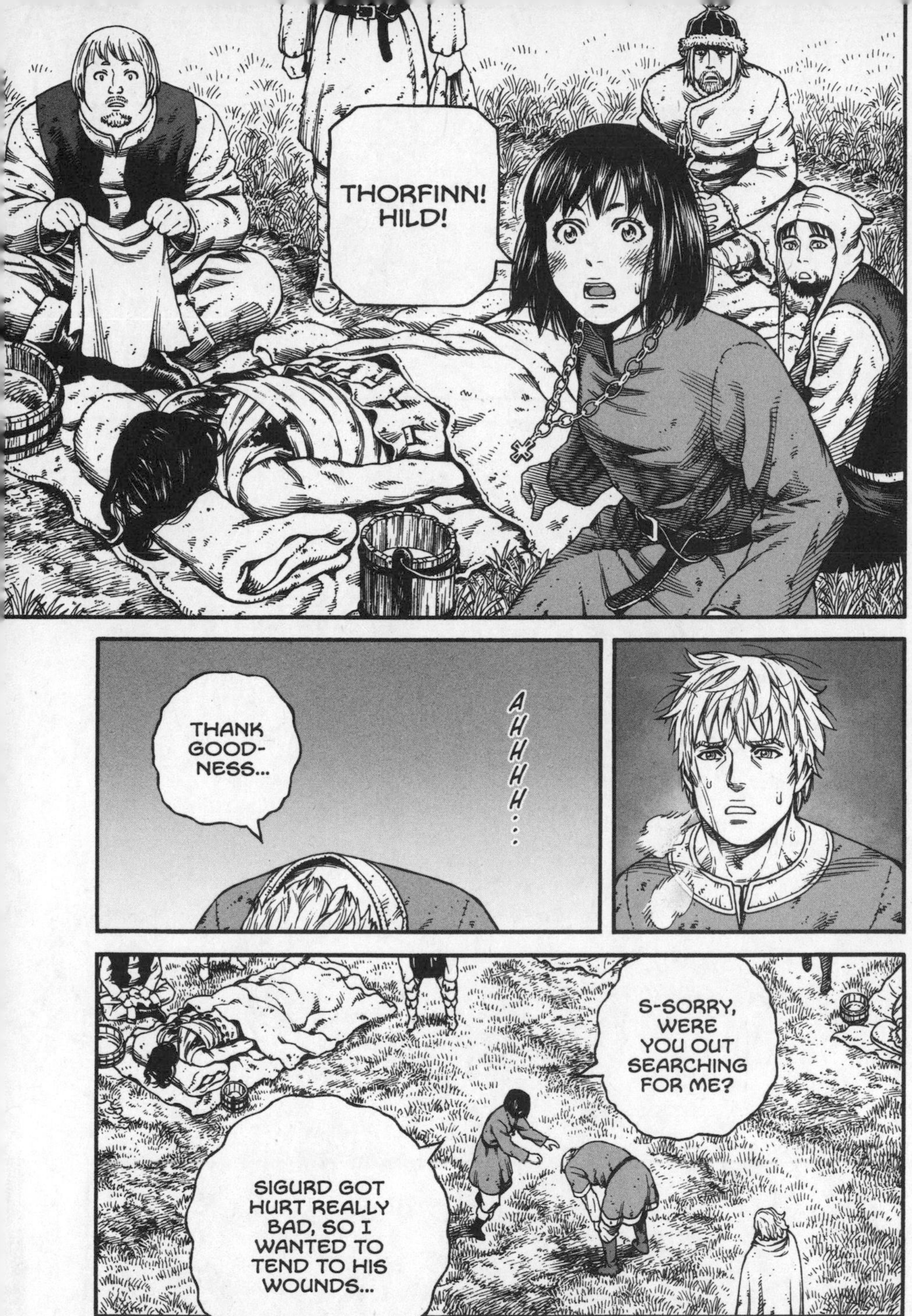
THORFINN! HILD!
AHHHH...
THANK GOOD-NESS...
S-SORRY, WERE YOU OUT SEARCHING FOR ME?
SIGURD GOT HURT REALLY BAD, SO I WANTED TO TEND TO HIS WOUNDS...

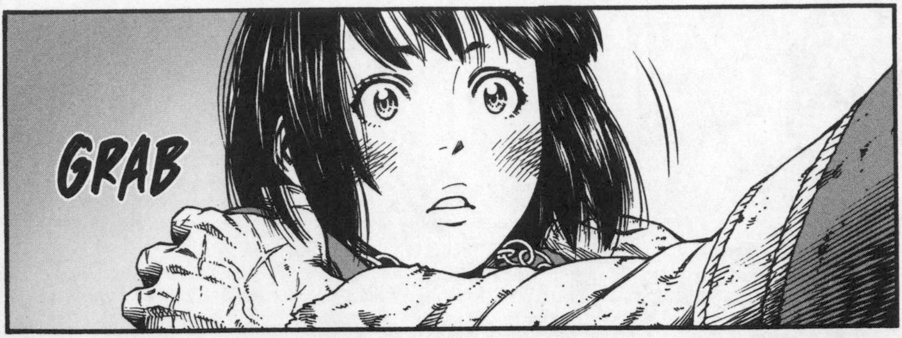
GRAB
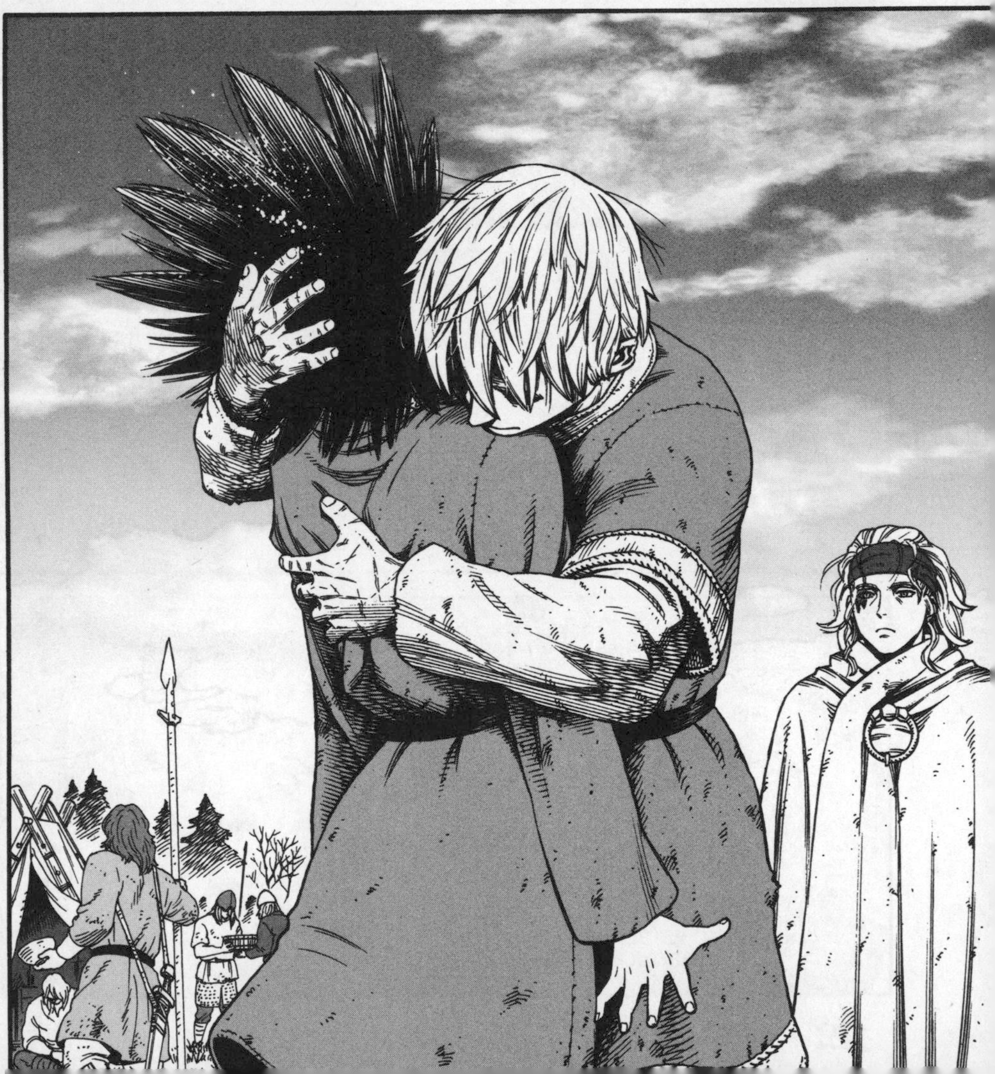

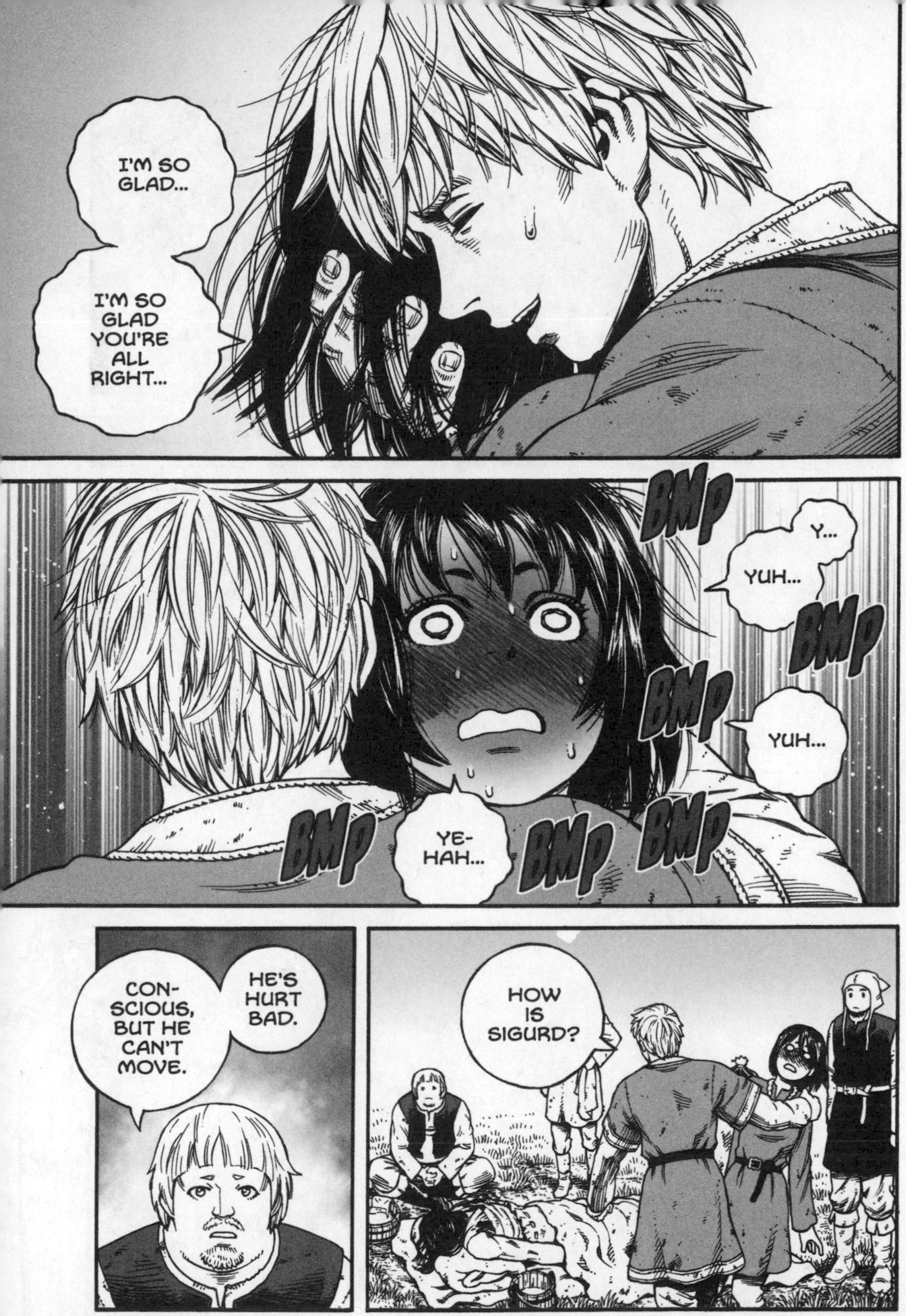
I'M SO GLAD...
I'M SO GLAD YOU'RE ALL RIGHT...
BMP
Y... YUH...
BMP
BMP
YUH...
BMP
BMP
YE-HAH...
BMP
HOW IS SIGURD?
HE'S HURT BAD.
CON-SCIOUS, BUT HE CAN'T MOVE.

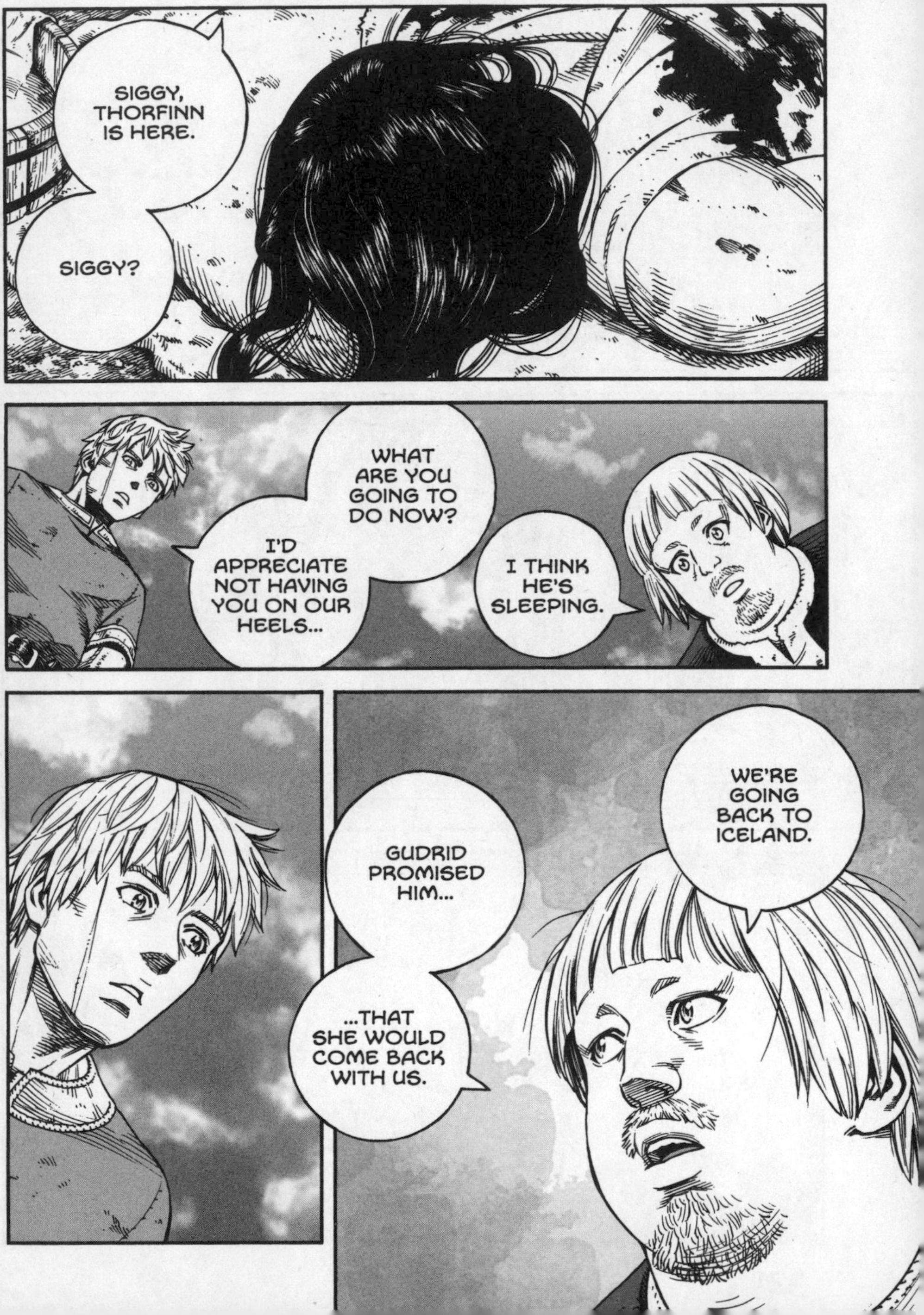
SIGGY, THORFINN IS HERE.
SIGGY?
I THINK HE'S SLEEPING.
WHAT ARE YOU GOING TO DO NOW?
I'D APPRECIATE NOT HAVING YOU ON OUR HEELS...
WE'RE GOING BACK TO ICELAND.
GUDRID PROMISED HIM...
...THAT SHE WOULD COME BACK WITH US.

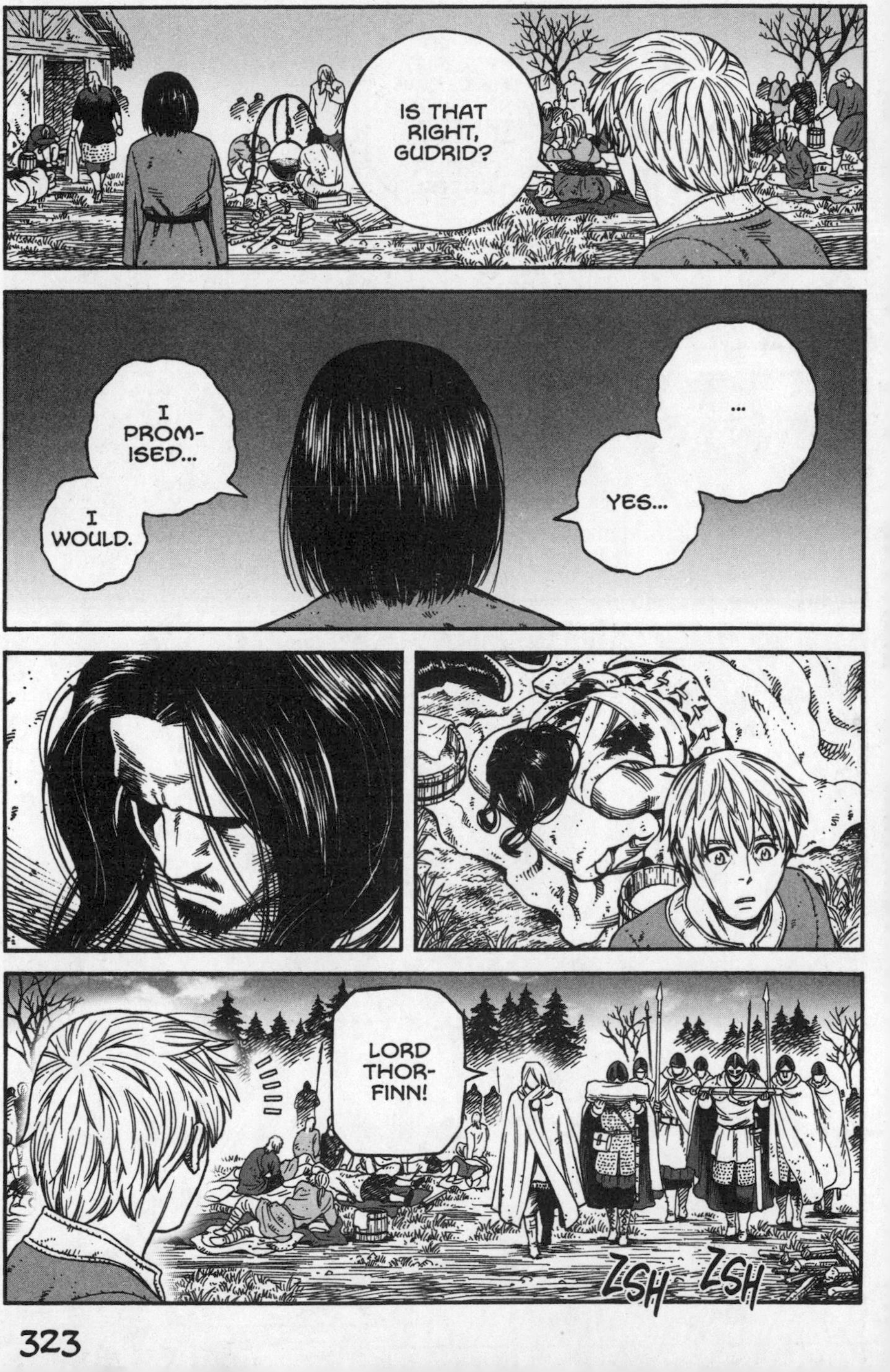
IS THAT RIGHT, GUDRID?
... YES...
I PROMISED... I WOULD.
LORD THORFINN!
ZSH ZSH

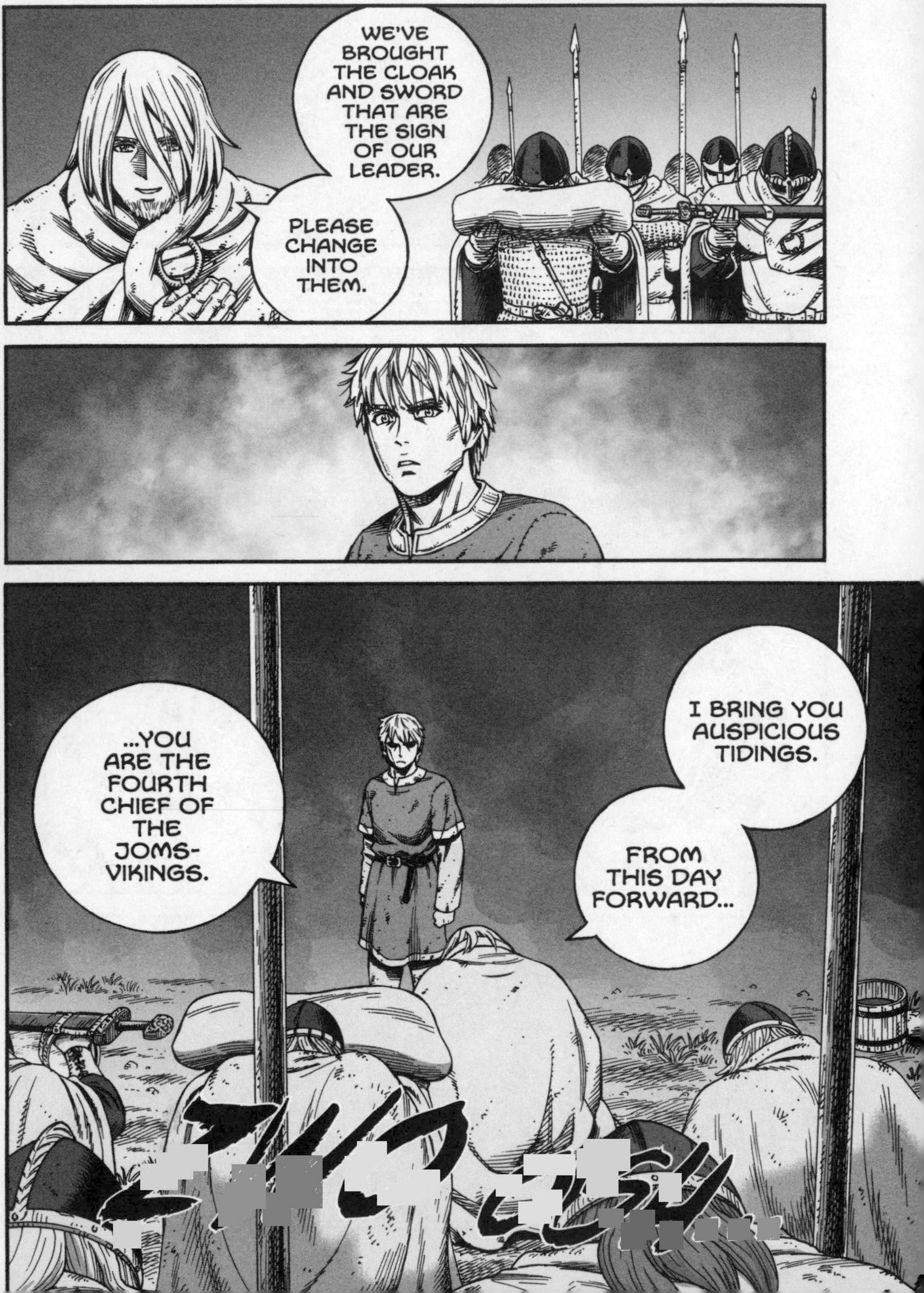
WE'VE BROUGHT THE CLOAK AND SWORD THAT ARE THE SIGN OF OUR LEADER.
PLEASE CHANGE INTO THEM.
I BRING YOU AUSPICIOUS TIDINGS.
FROM THIS DAY FORWARD...
...YOU ARE THE FOURTH CHIEF OF THE JOMS-VIKINGS.

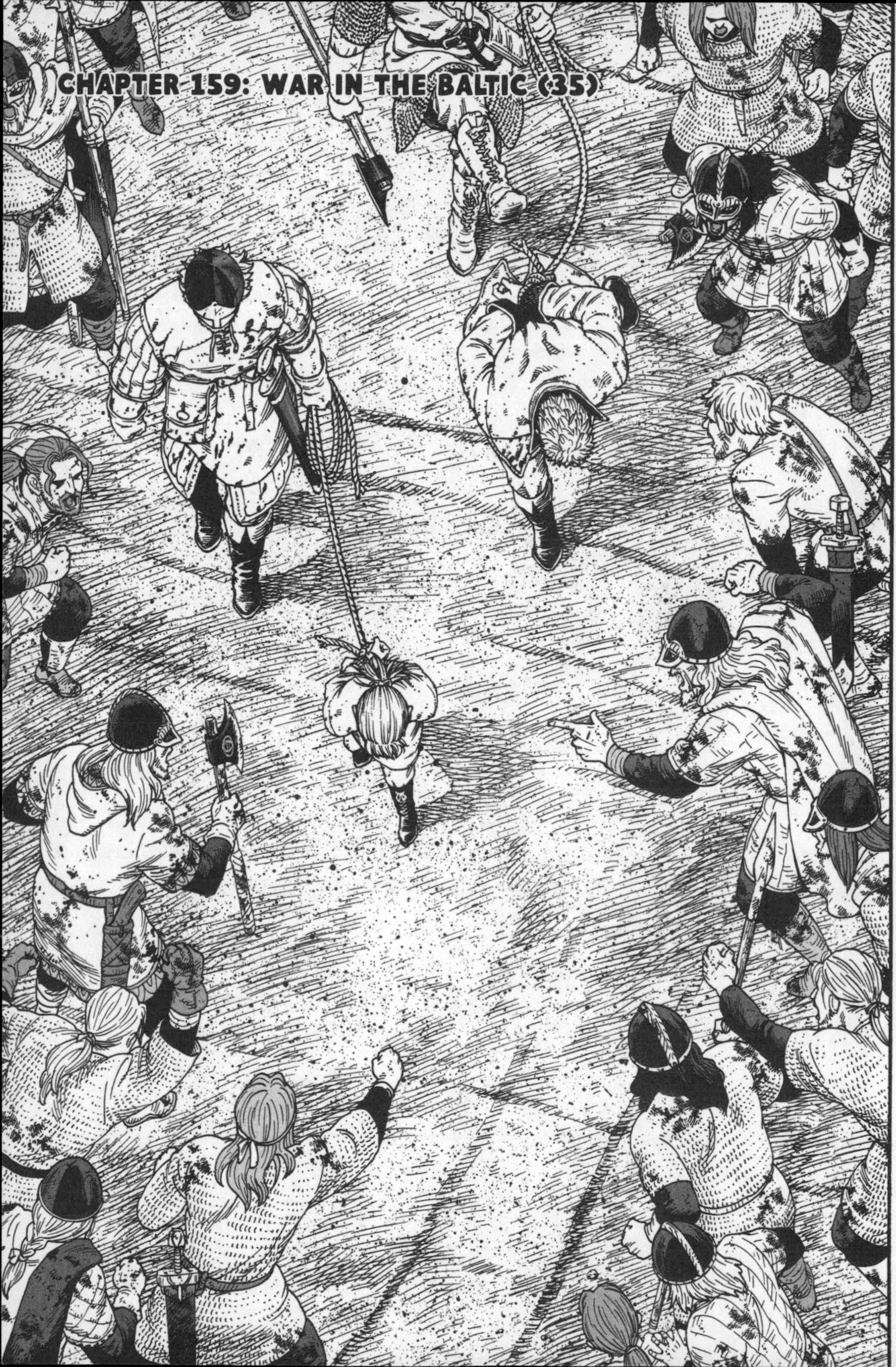
CHAPTER 159: WAR IN THE BALTIC (35)

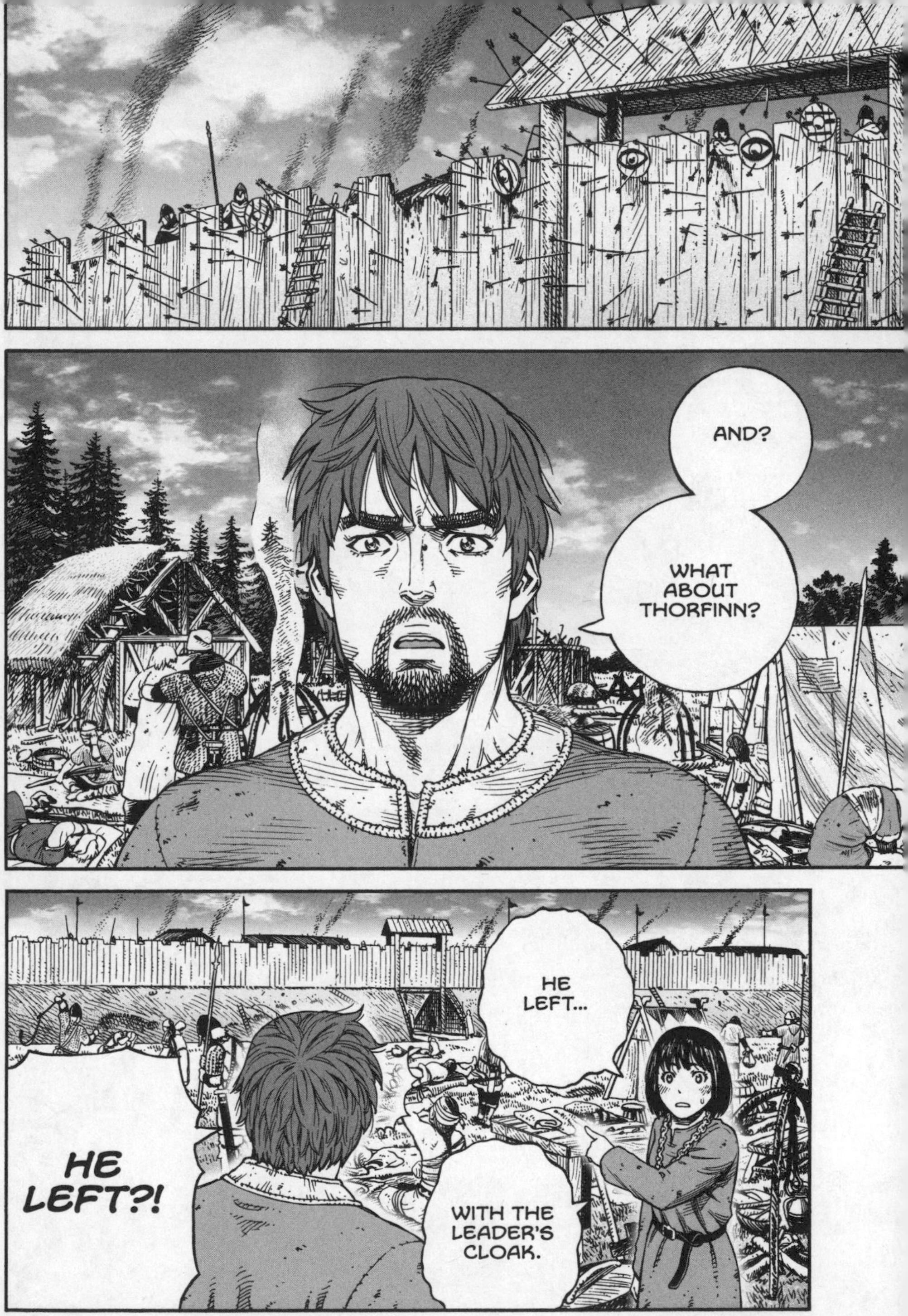
AND?
WHAT ABOUT THORFINN?
HE LEFT...
WITH THE LEADER'S CLOAK.
HE LEFT?!

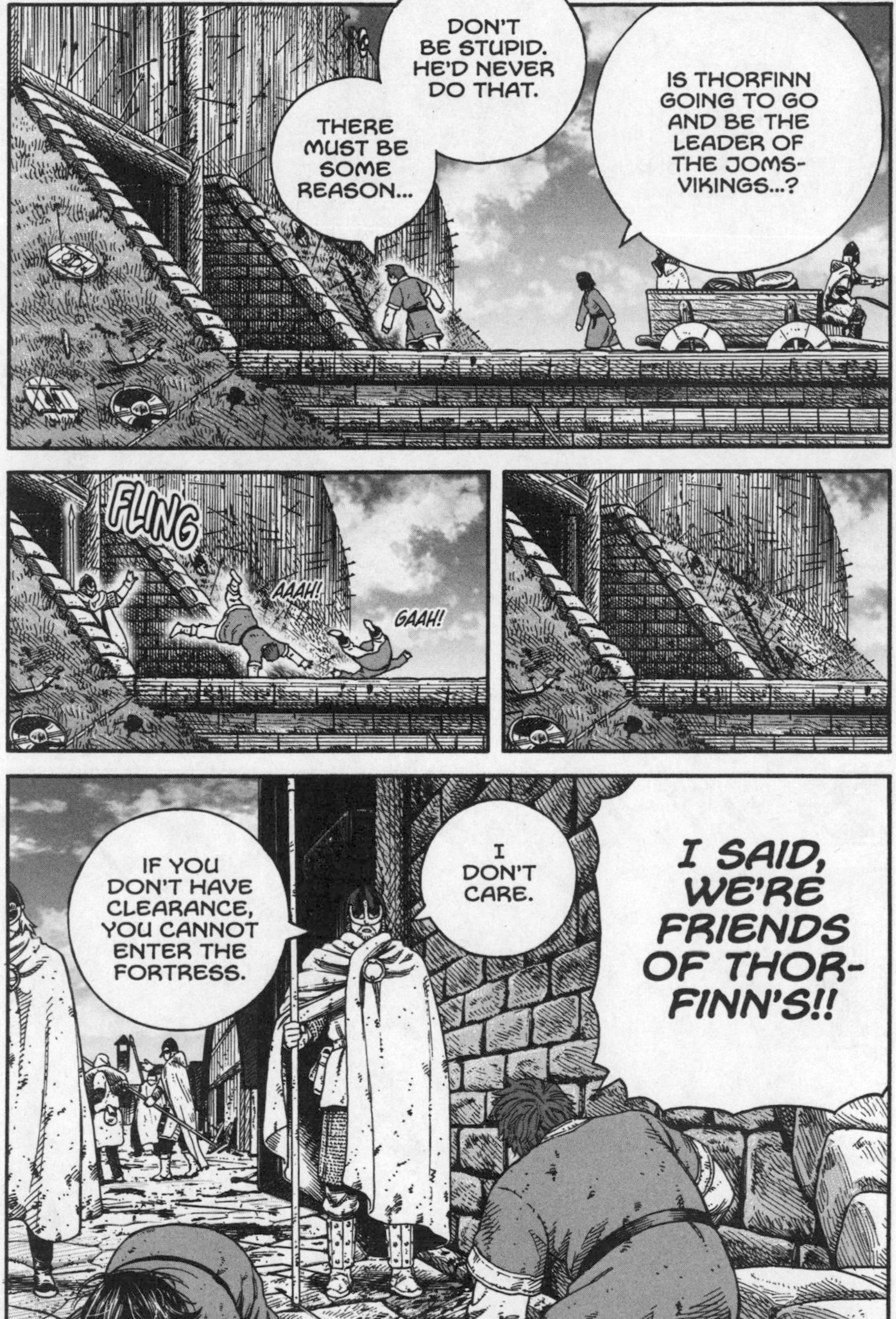
IS THORFINN GOING TO GO AND BE THE LEADER OF THE JOMS-VIKINGS...?
DON'T BE STUPID. HE'D NEVER DO THAT.
THERE MUST BE SOME REASON...
FLING
AAAH!
GAAH!
I SAID, WE'RE FRIENDS OF THOR-FINN'S!!
I DON'T CARE.
IF YOU DON'T HAVE CLEARANCE, YOU CANNOT ENTER THE FORTRESS.

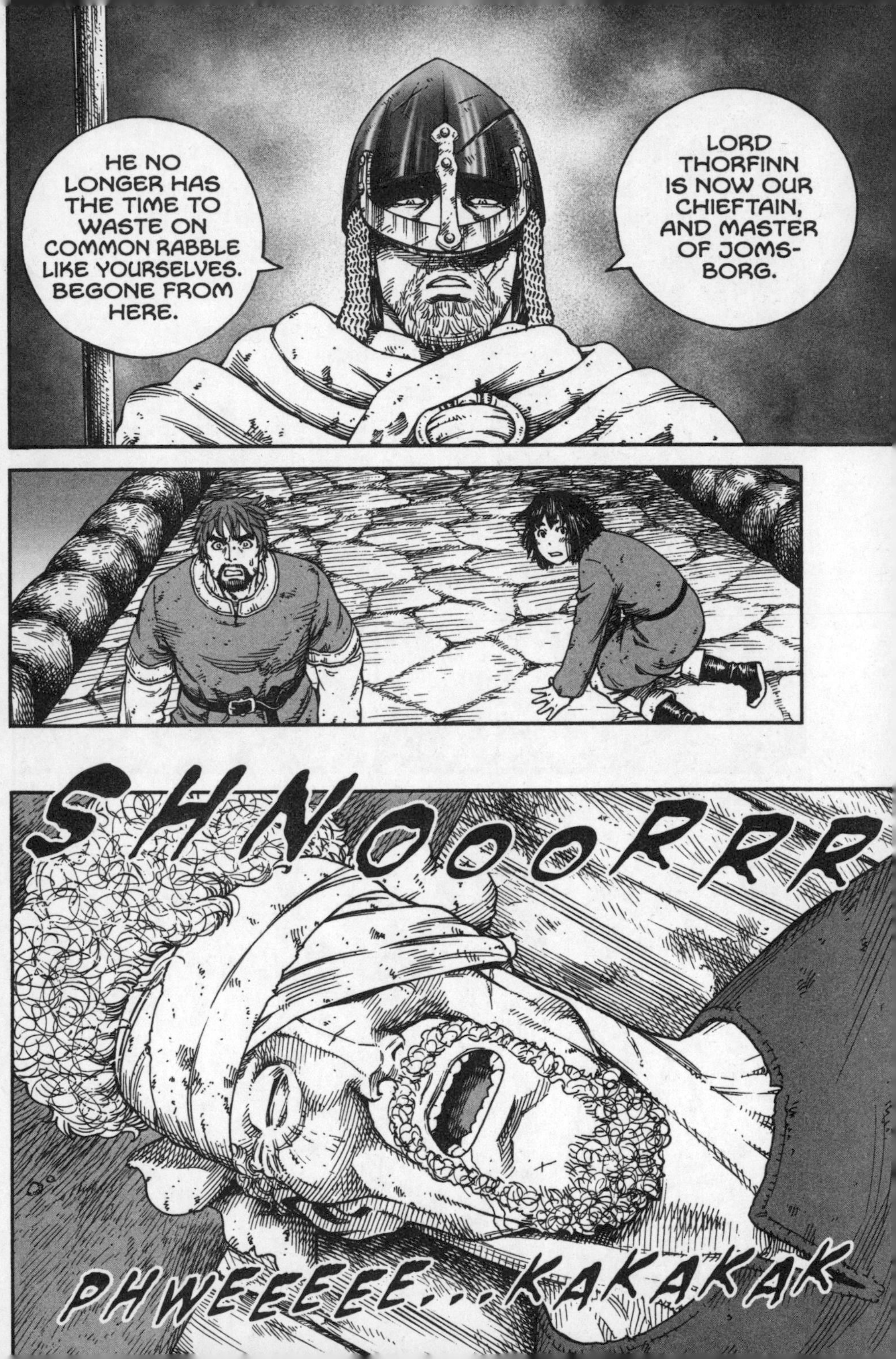
LORD THORFINN IS NOW OUR CHIEFTAIN, AND MASTER OF JOMS-BORG.
HE NO LONGER HAS THE TIME TO WASTE ON COMMON RABBLE LIKE YOURSELVES. BEGONE FROM HERE.
SHNOOORRR
PHWEEEEE...KAKAKAK

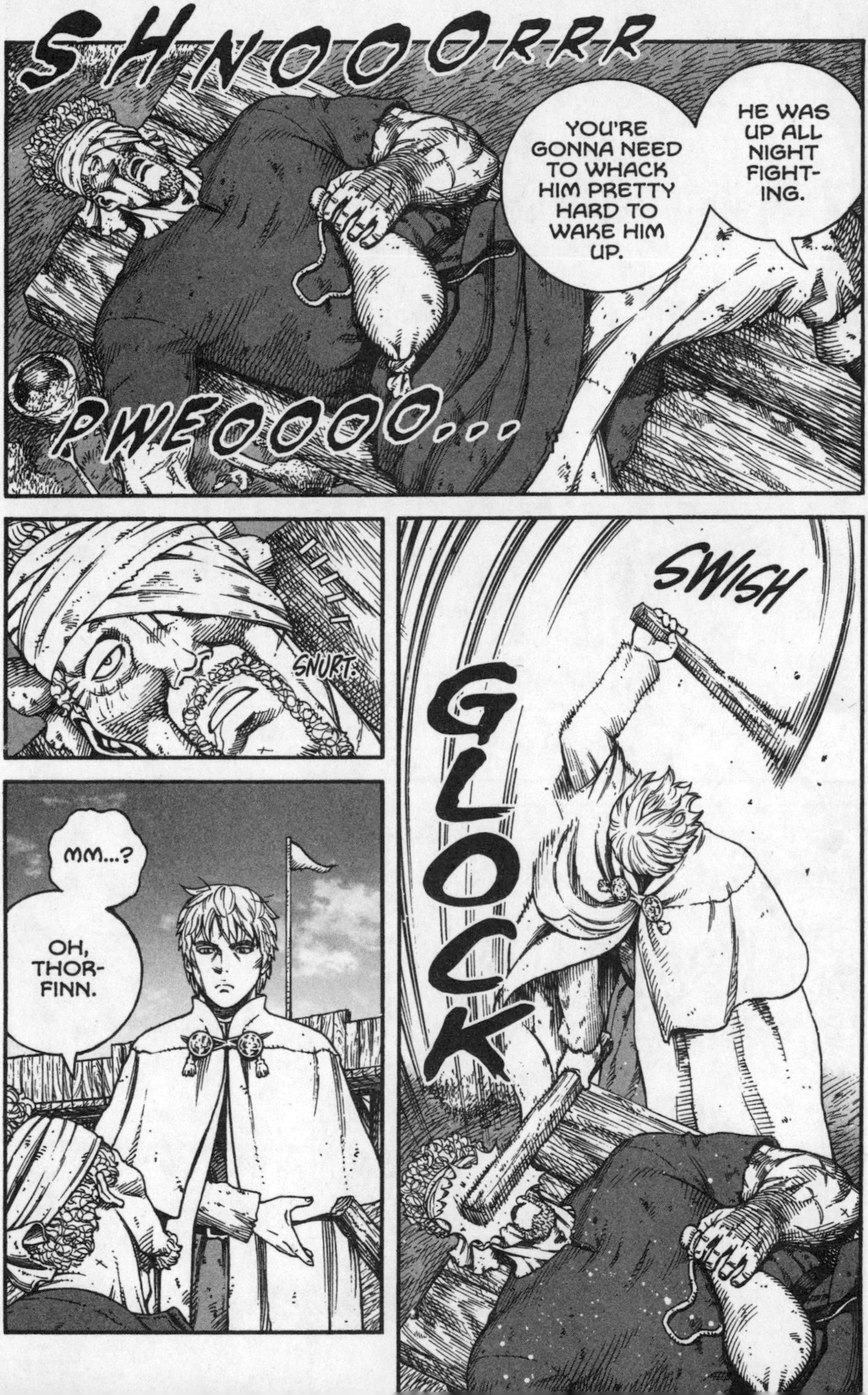
SHNOOORRR
HE WAS UP ALL NIGHT FIGHT-ING.
YOU'RE GONNA NEED TO WHACK HIM PRETTY HARD TO WAKE HIM UP.
PWEOOOO...
SWISH
GLOCK
SNURT.
MM...?
OH, THOR-FINN.

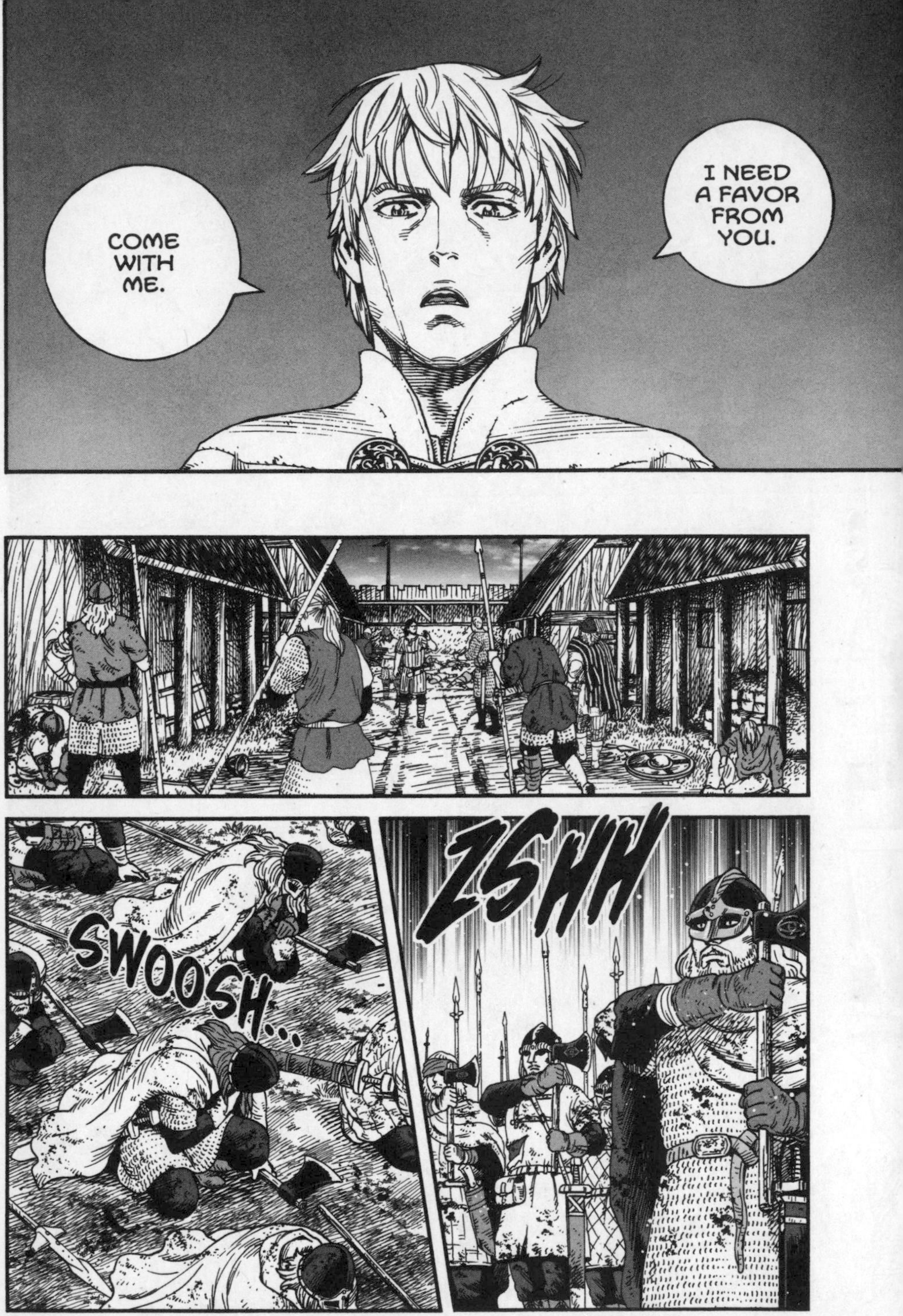
I NEED A FAVOR FROM YOU.
COME WITH ME.
ZSHH
SWOOSH...

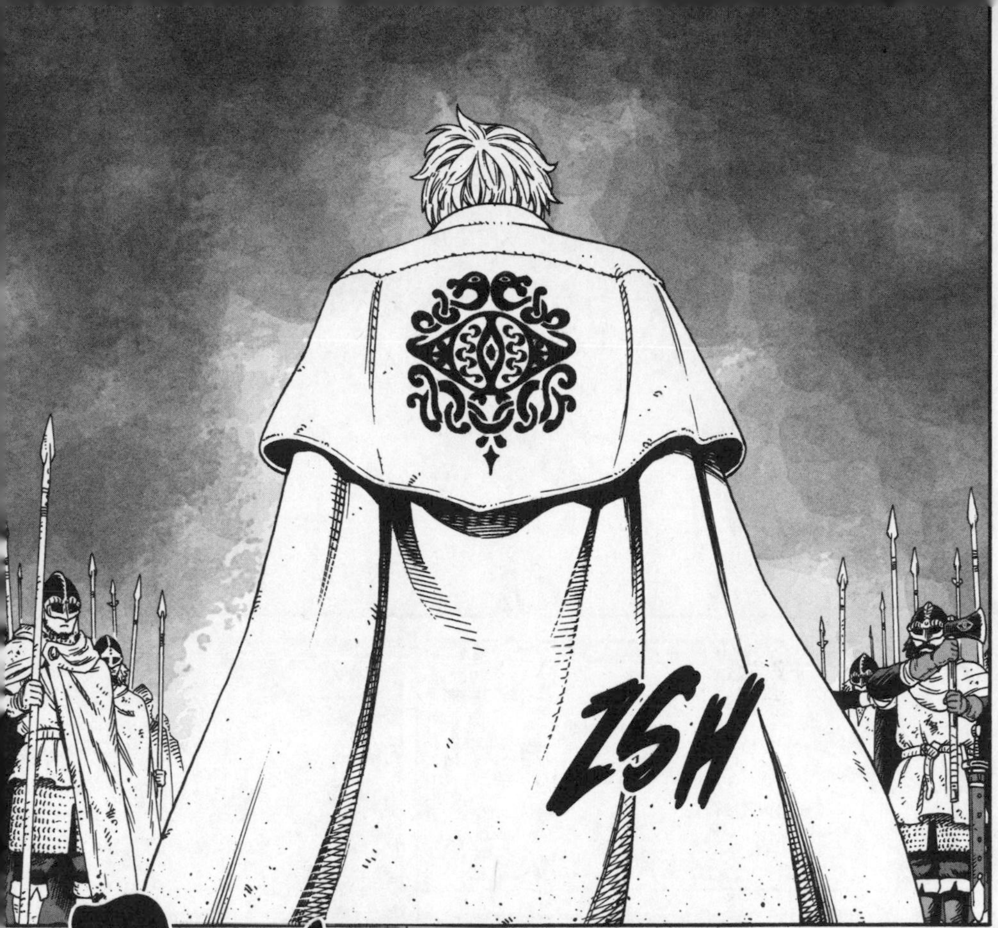
ZSH
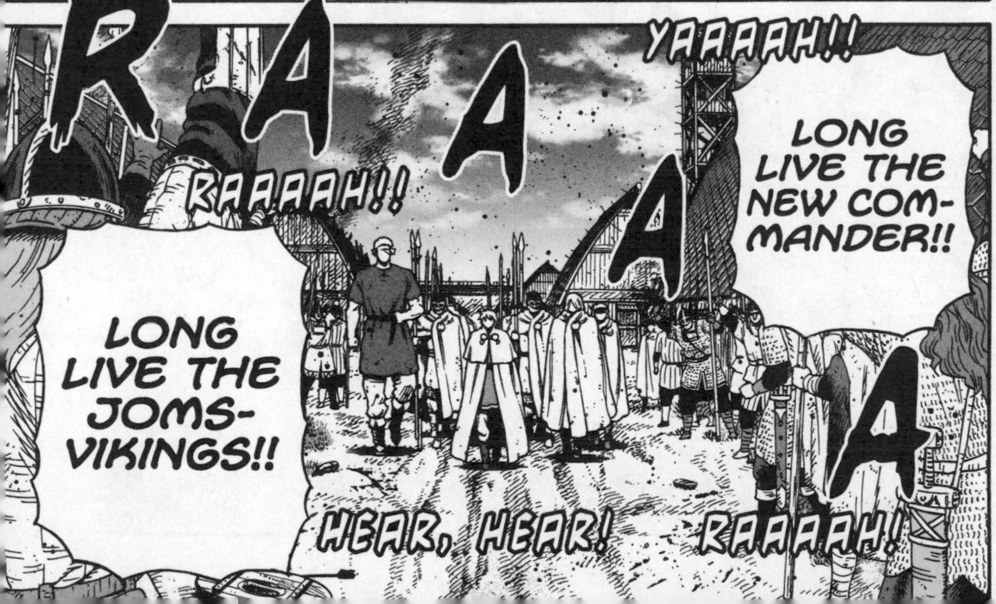
YAAAAH!!
LONG LIVE THE NEW COMMANDER!!
RAAAA
RAAAAAH!!
LONG LIVE THE JOMS-VIKINGS!!
RAAAAAH!
HEAR, HEAR!

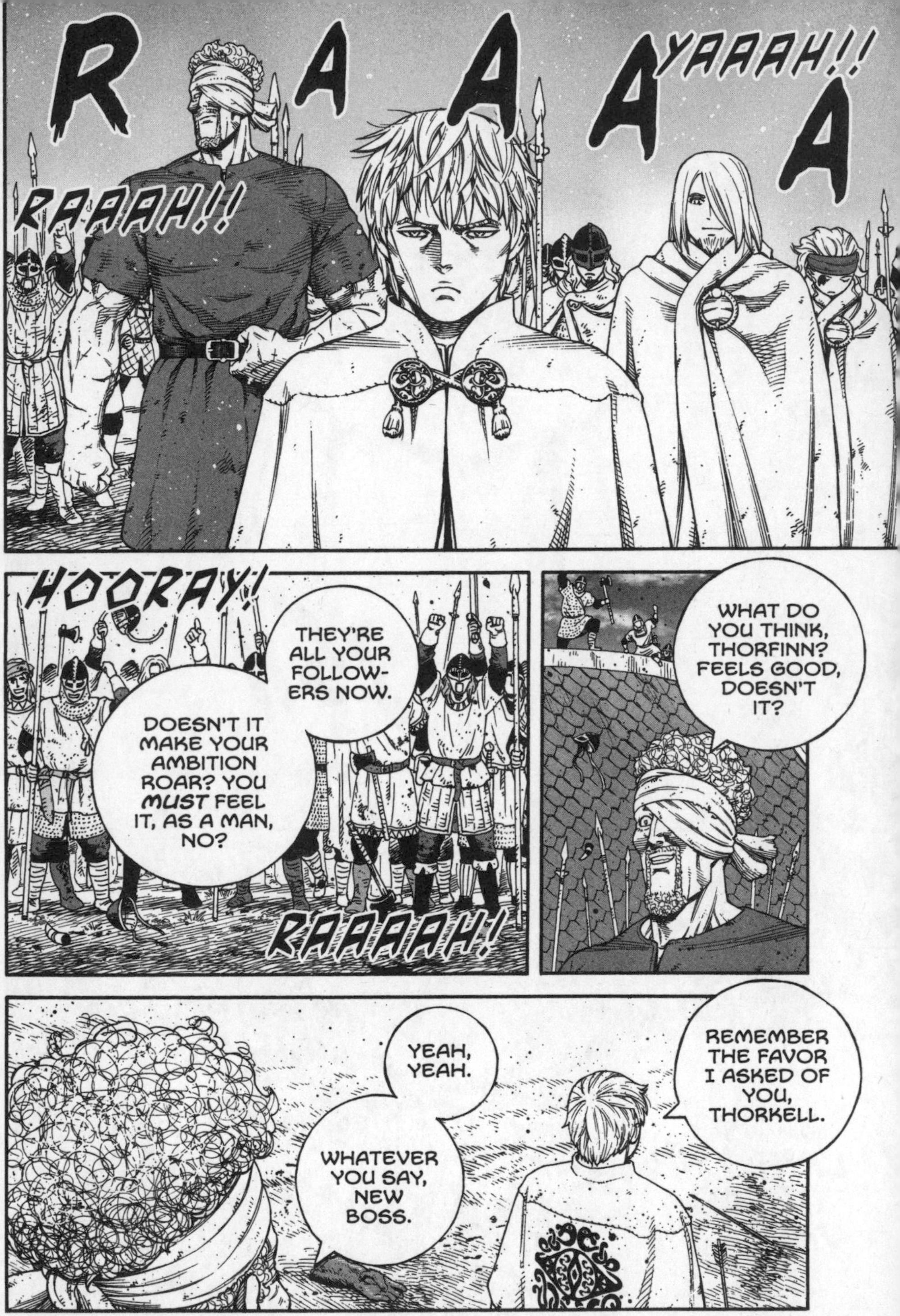
RAAAAA
YAAAAH!!
RAAAH!!
WHAT DO YOU THINK, THORFINN? FEELS GOOD, DOESN'T IT?
HOORAY!
THEY'RE ALL YOUR FOLLOW-ERS NOW.
DOESN'T IT MAKE YOUR AMBITION ROAR? YOU *MUST* FEEL IT, AS A MAN, NO?
RAAAAAH!
REMEMBER THE FAVOR I ASKED OF YOU, THORKELL.
YEAH, YEAH.
WHATEVER YOU SAY, NEW BOSS.

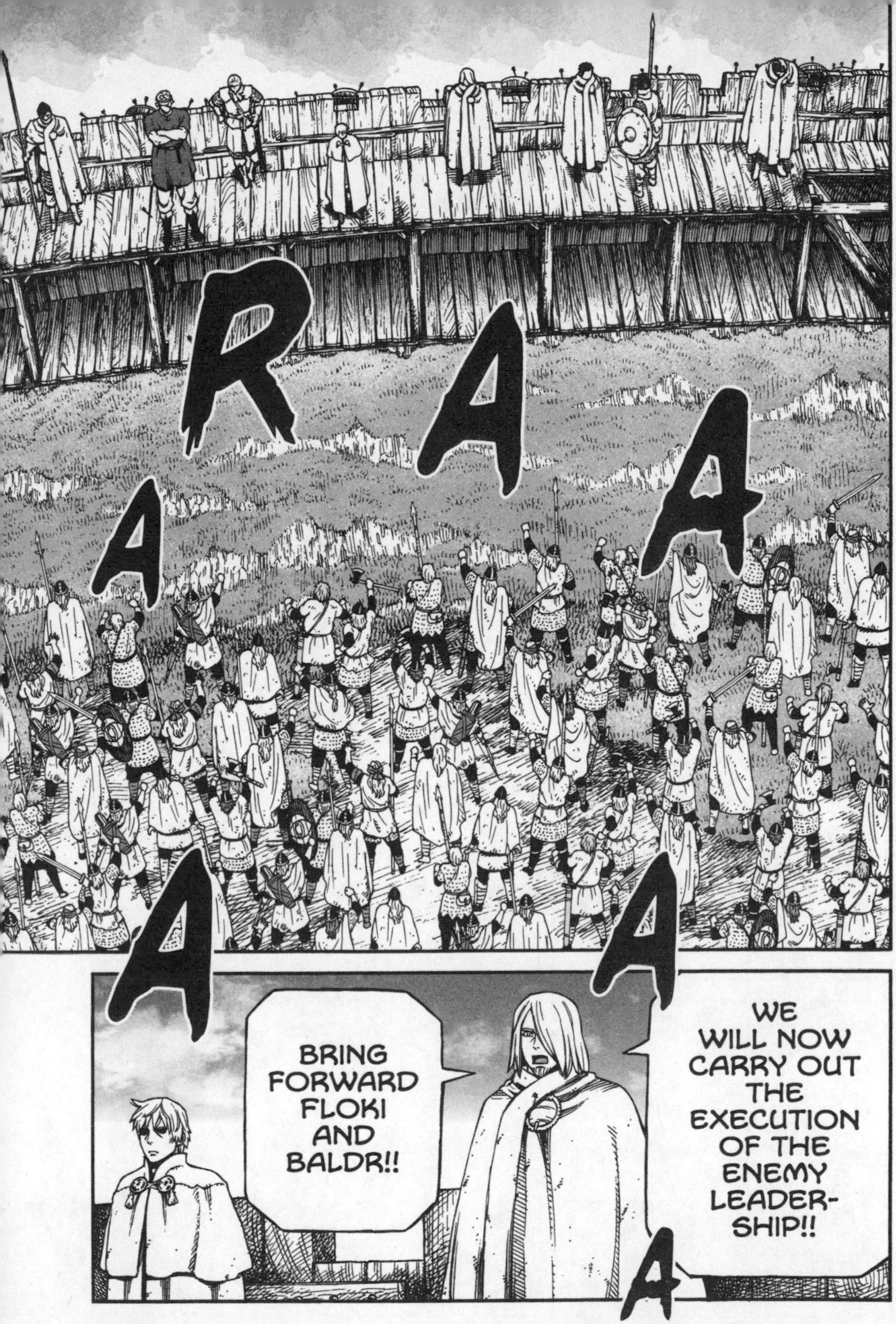
RAAAAAAA
WE WILL NOW CARRY OUT THE EXECUTION OF THE ENEMY LEADERSHIP!!
BRING FORWARD FLOKI AND BALDR!!

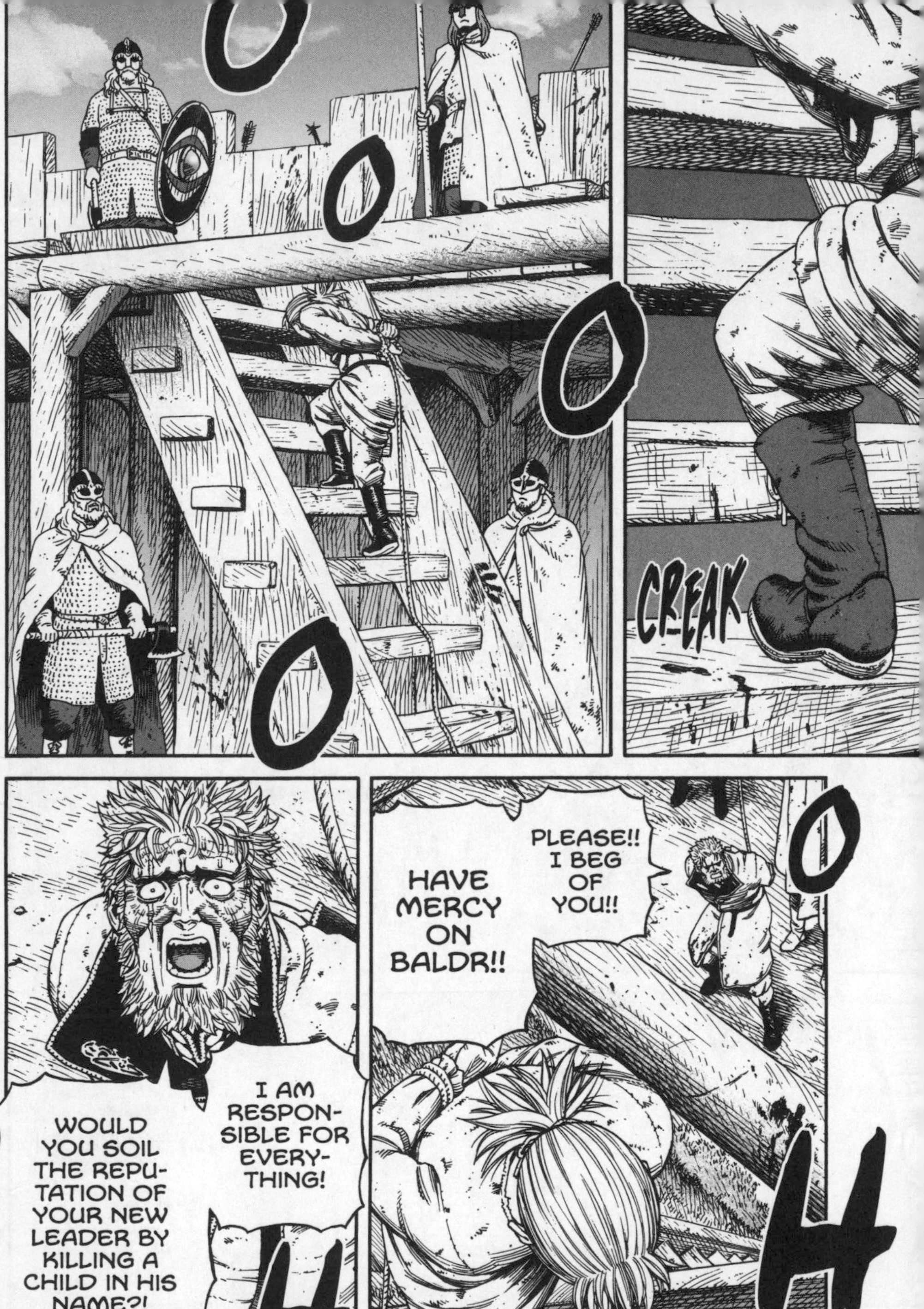
CREAK
O
O
O
O
O
PLEASE!! I BEG OF YOU!!
HAVE MERCY ON BALDR!!
H
I AM RESPONSIBLE FOR EVERYTHING!
WOULD YOU SOIL THE REPUTATION OF YOUR NEW LEADER BY KILLING A CHILD IN HIS NAME?!
H

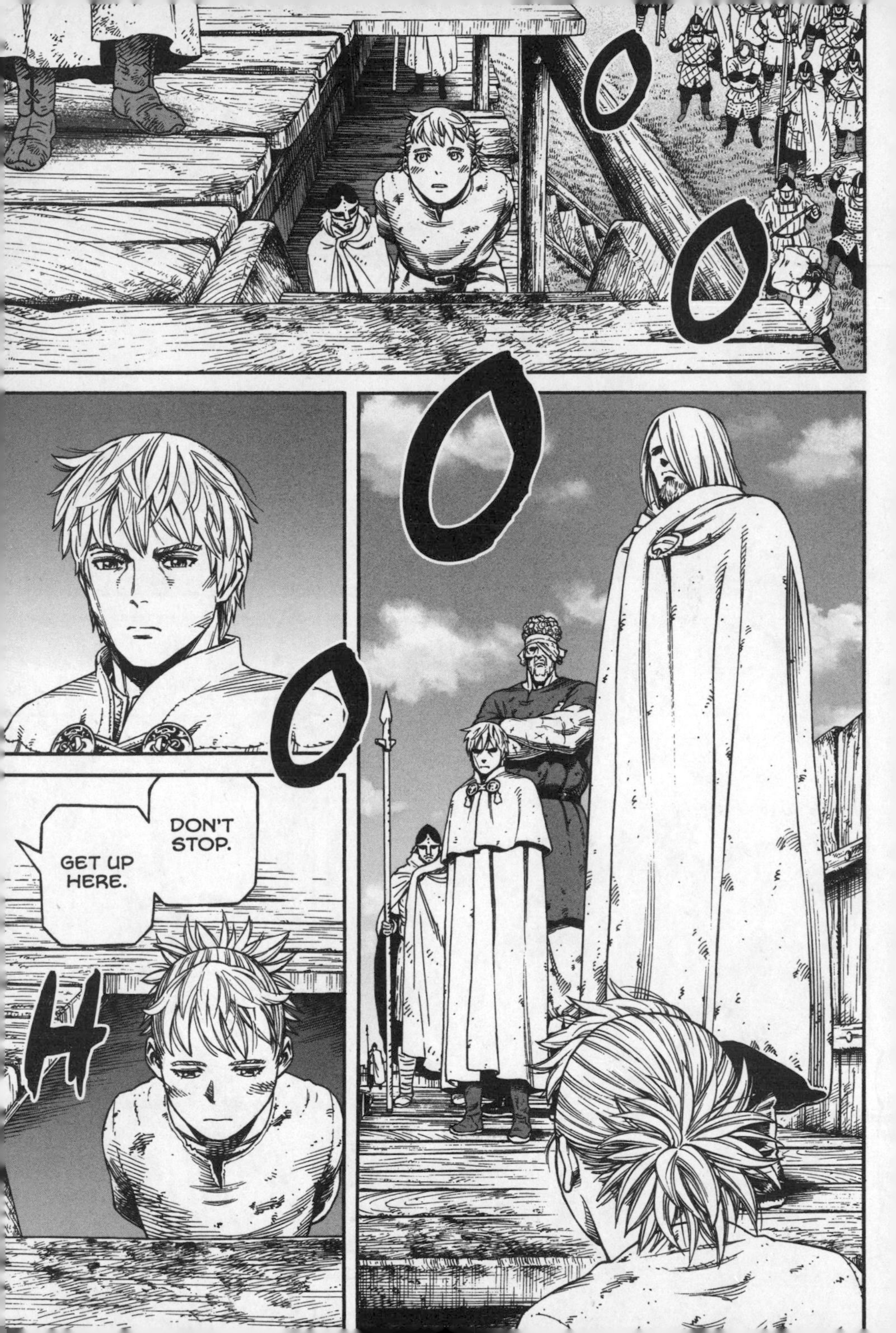
DON'T STOP.
GET UP HERE.

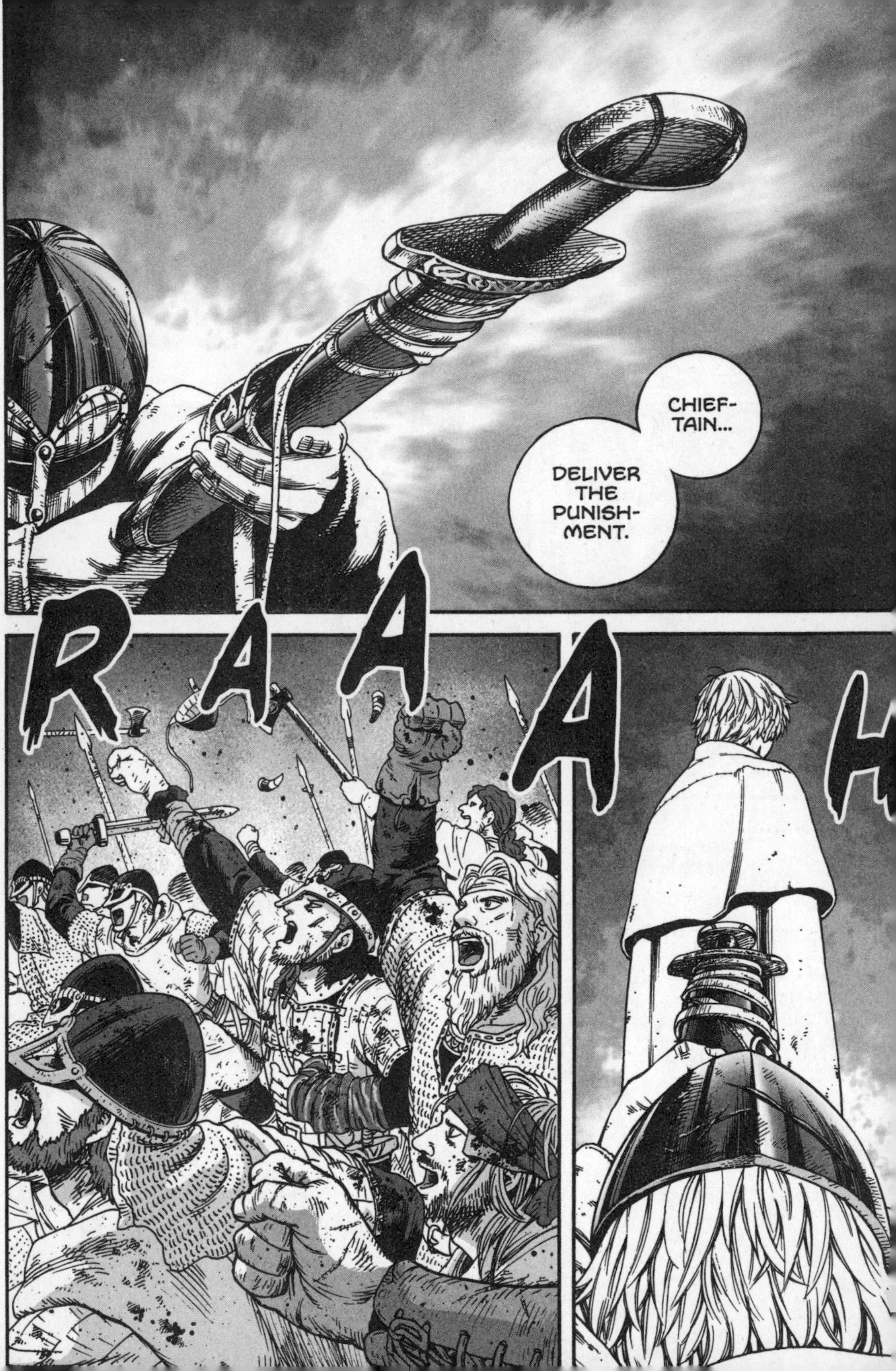
CHIEF-TAIN...
DELIVER THE PUNISH-MENT.
RAAAAH

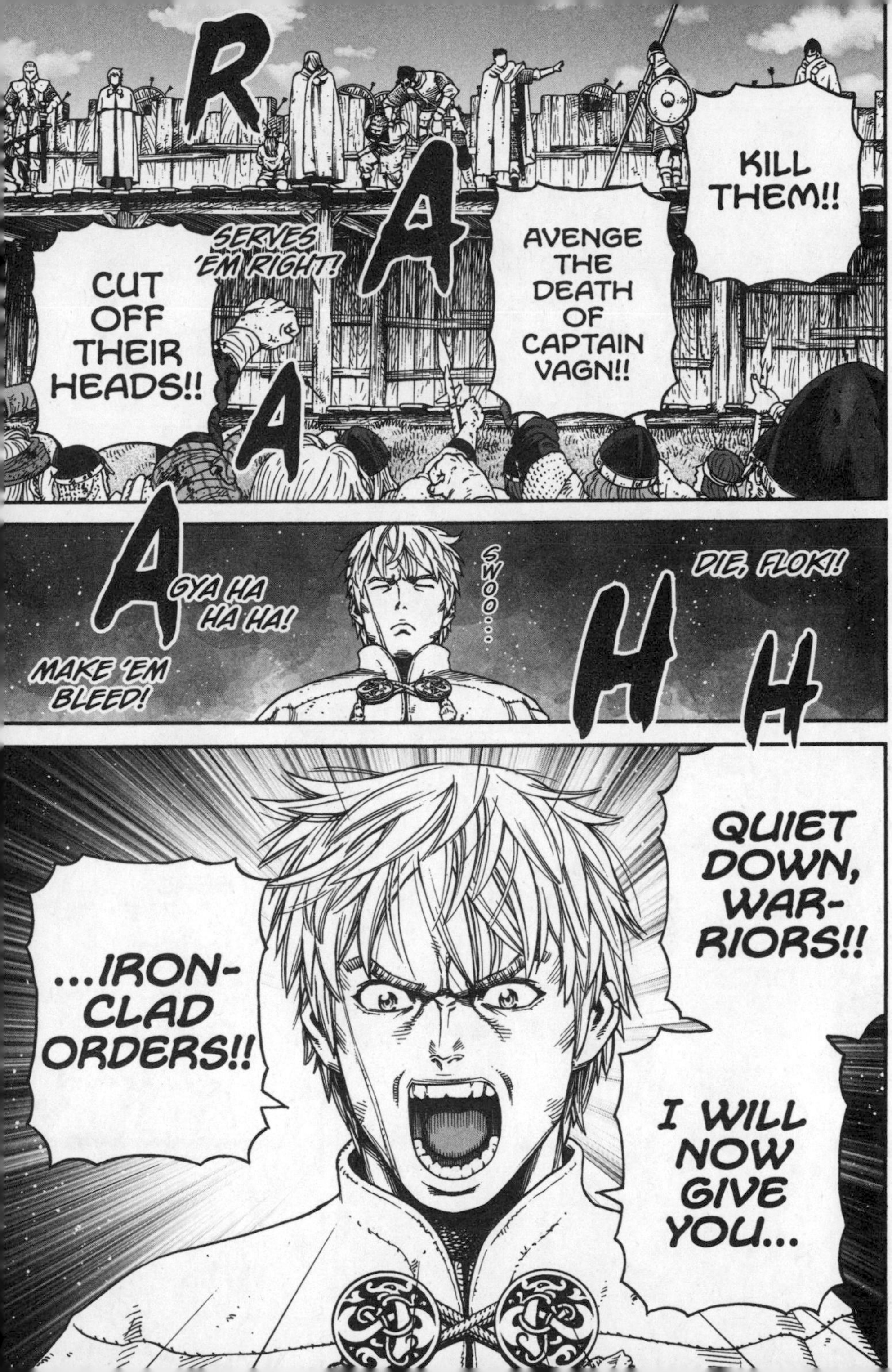

RAAAAHH
KILL THEM!!
AVENGE THE DEATH OF CAPTAIN VAGN!!
SERVES 'EM RIGHT!
CUT OFF THEIR HEADS!!
DIE, FLOKI!
SWOO...
GYA HA HA HA!
MAKE 'EM BLEED!
QUIET DOWN, WAR-RIORS!!
I WILL NOW GIVE YOU...
...IRON-CLAD ORDERS!!

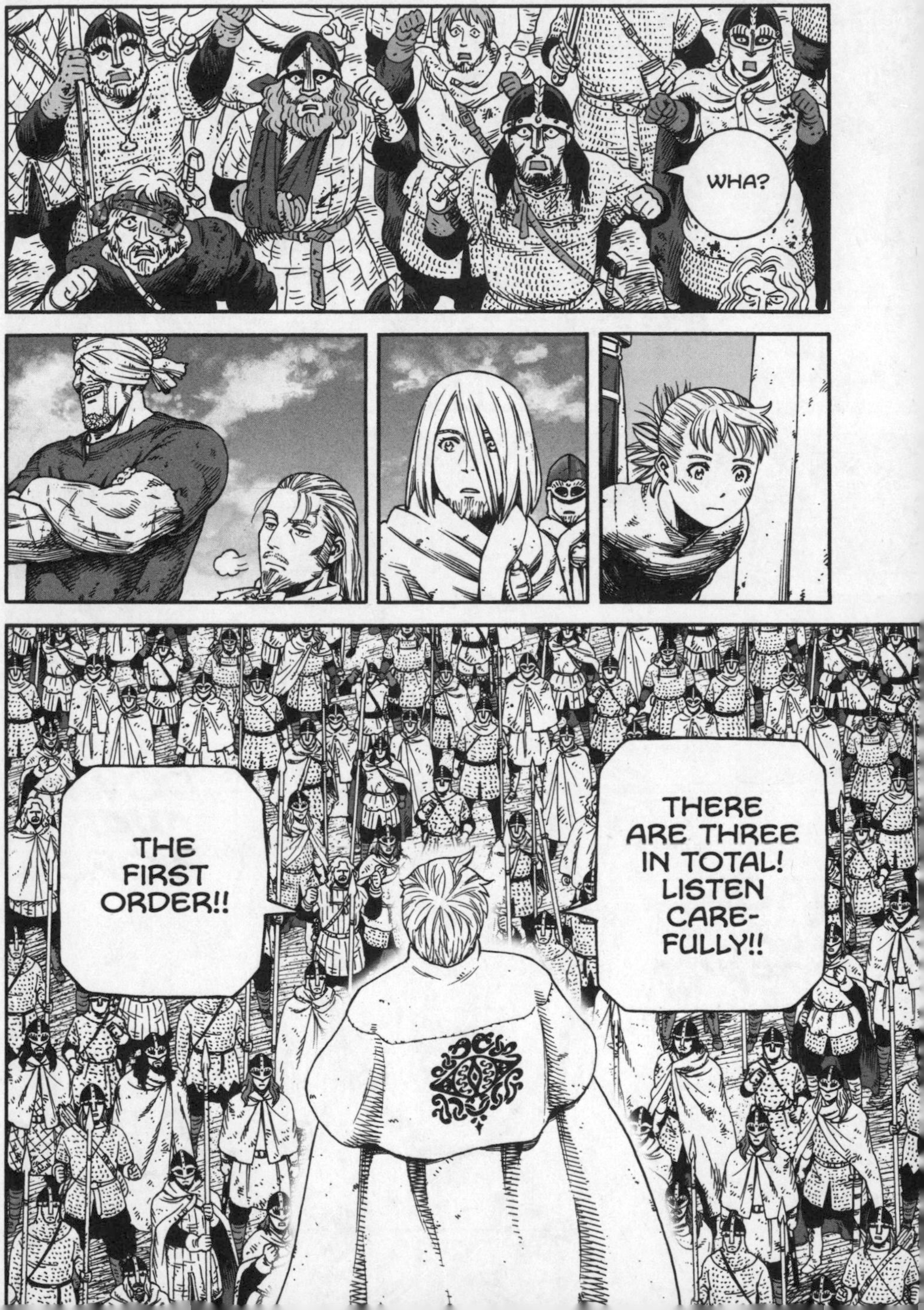
WHA?
THERE ARE THREE IN TOTAL! LISTEN CARE-FULLY!!
THE FIRST ORDER!!

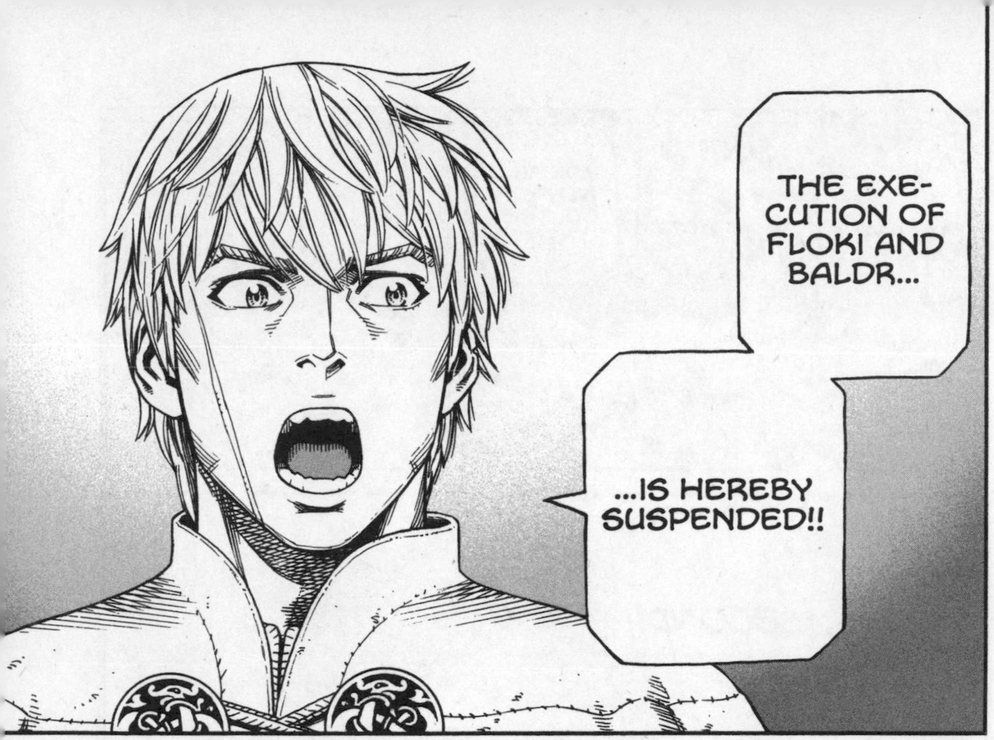
THE EXECUTION OF FLOKI AND BALDR...
...IS HEREBY SUSPENDED!!
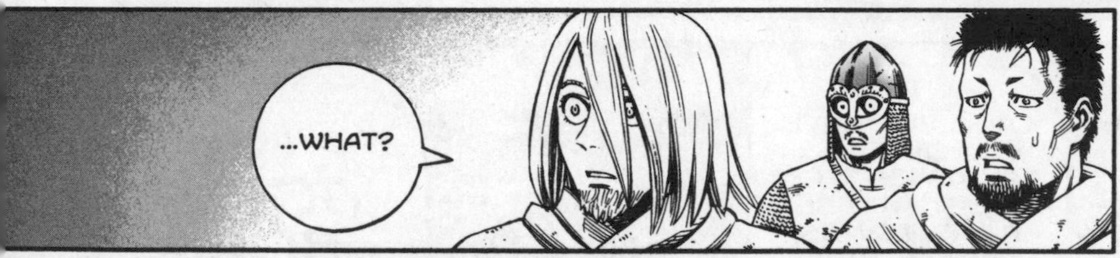
...WHAT?
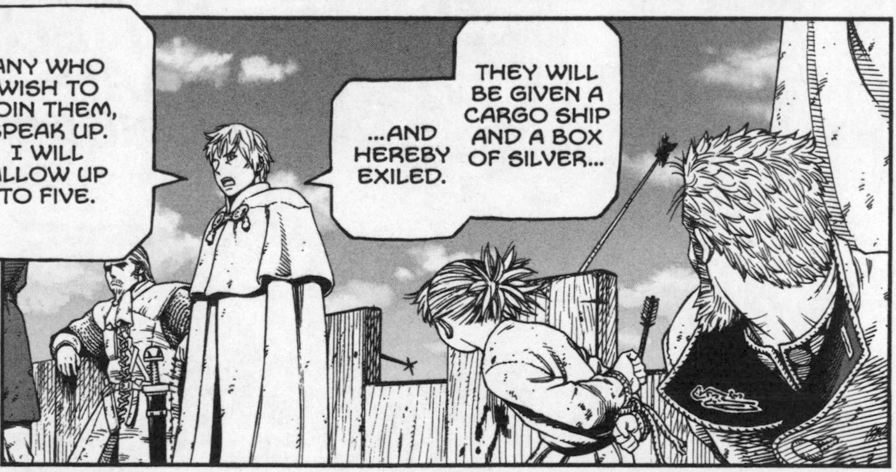
THEY WILL BE GIVEN A CARGO SHIP AND A BOX OF SILVER...
...AND HEREBY EXILED.
ANY WHO WISH TO JOIN THEM, SPEAK UP. I WILL ALLOW UP TO FIVE.

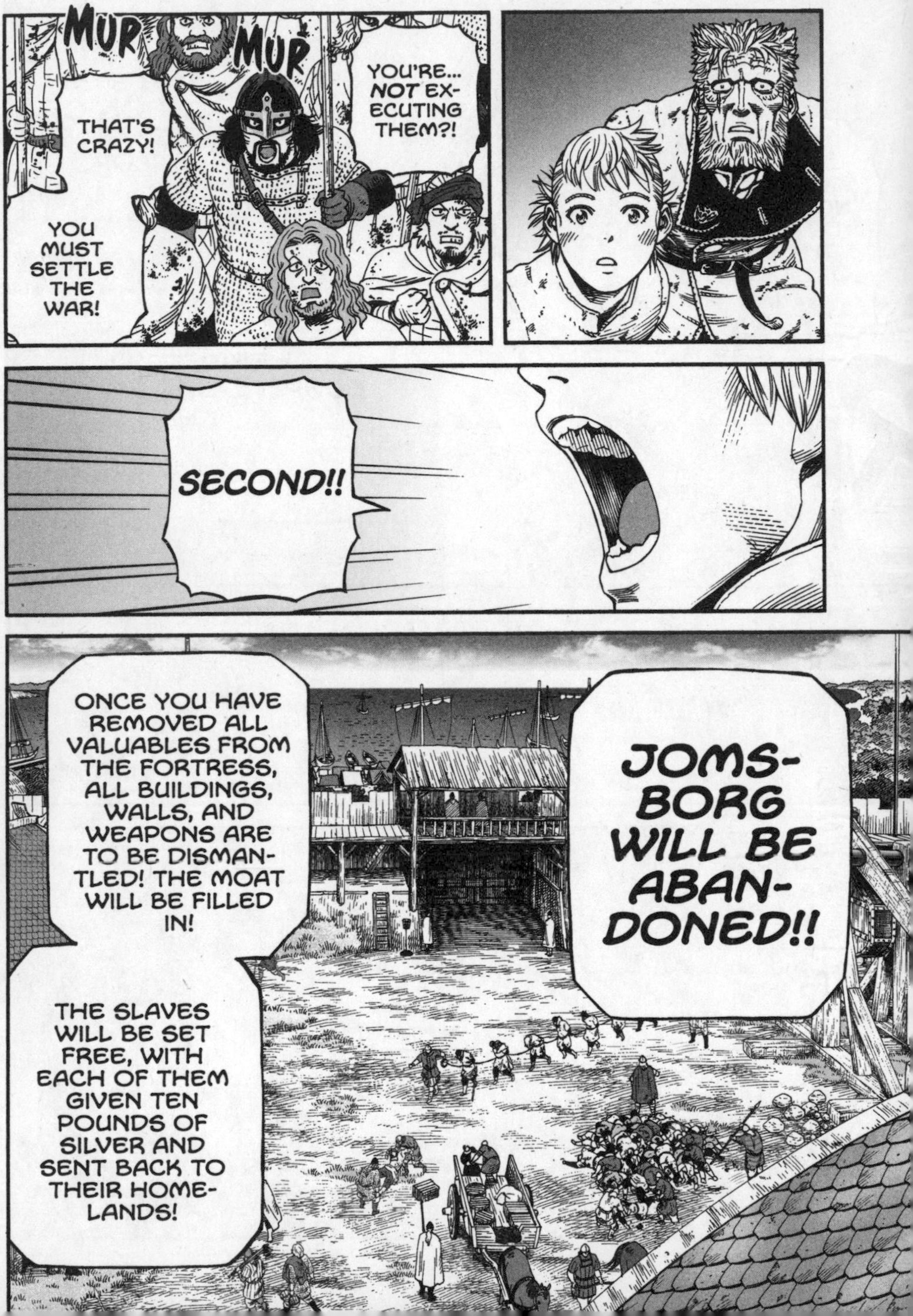
MUR
MUR
YOU'RE... NOT EXECUTING THEM?!
THAT'S CRAZY!
YOU MUST SETTLE THE WAR!
SECOND!!
JOMSBORG WILL BE ABANDONED!!
ONCE YOU HAVE REMOVED ALL VALUABLES FROM THE FORTRESS, ALL BUILDINGS, WALLS, AND WEAPONS ARE TO BE DISMANTLED! THE MOAT WILL BE FILLED IN!
THE SLAVES WILL BE SET FREE, WITH EACH OF THEM GIVEN TEN POUNDS OF SILVER AND SENT BACK TO THEIR HOMELANDS!

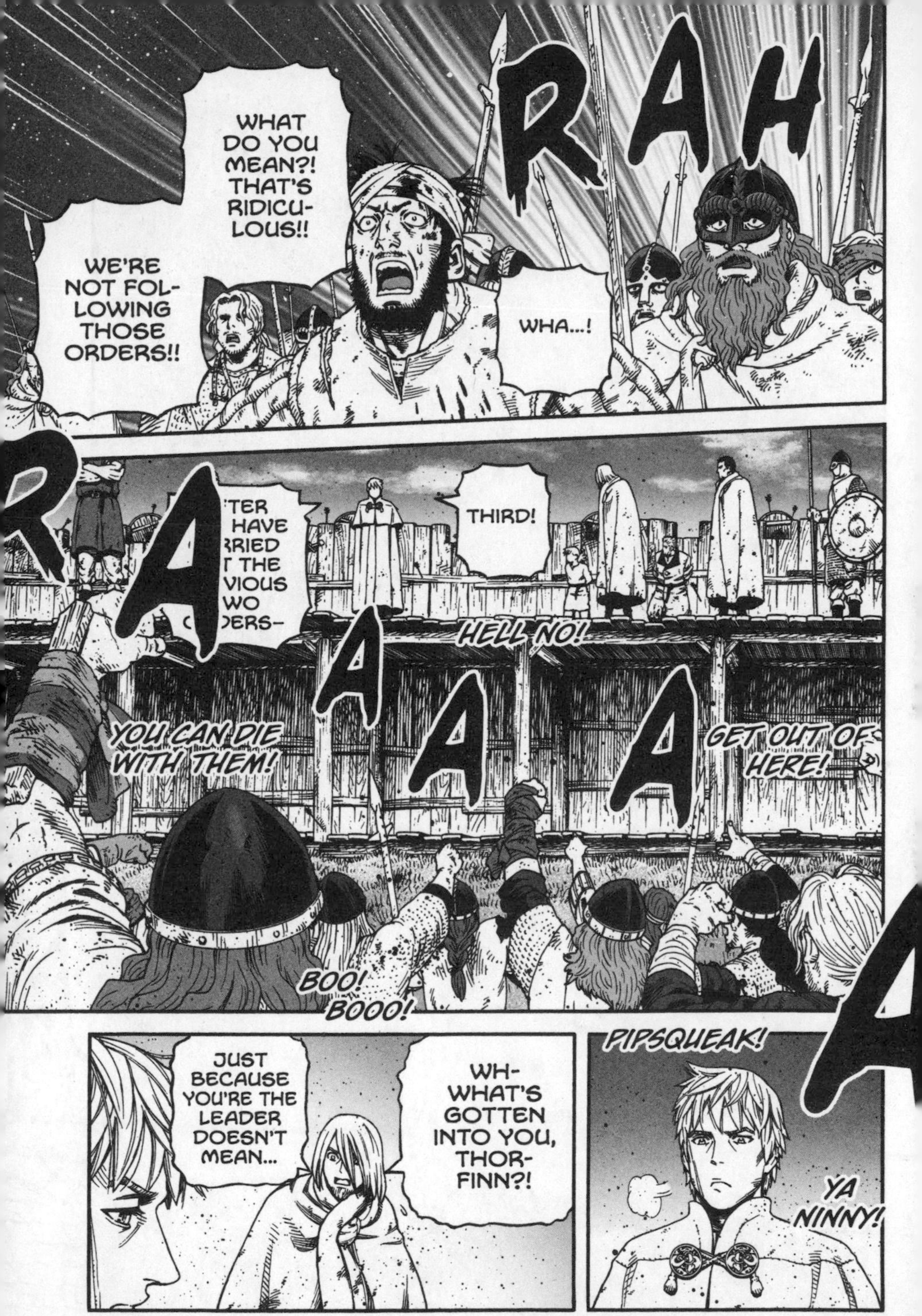
RAH
WHA...!
WHAT DO YOU MEAN?! THAT'S RIDICULOUS!!
WE'RE NOT FOLLOWING THOSE ORDERS!!
RAAAAA
THIRD!
HELL NO!
GET OUT OF HERE!
YOU CAN DIE WITH THEM!
BOO! BOOO!
PIPSQUEAK!
YA NINNY!
WH- WHAT'S GOTTEN INTO YOU, THORFINN?!
JUST BECAUSE YOU'RE THE LEADER DOESN'T MEAN...

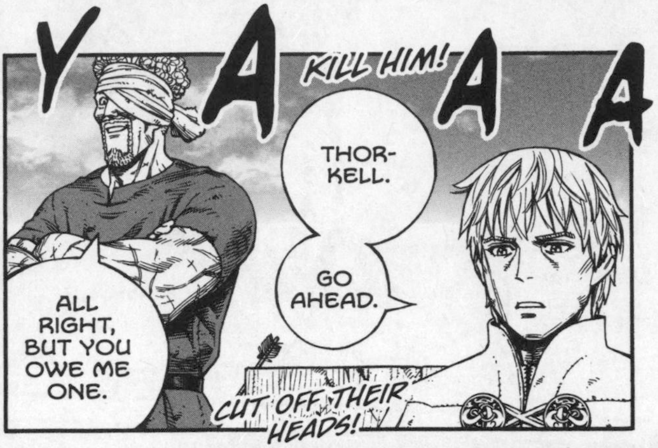
Y A A A A
KILL HIM!
THOR-KELL.
GO AHEAD.
ALL RIGHT, BUT YOU OWE ME ONE.
CUT OFF THEIR HEADS!
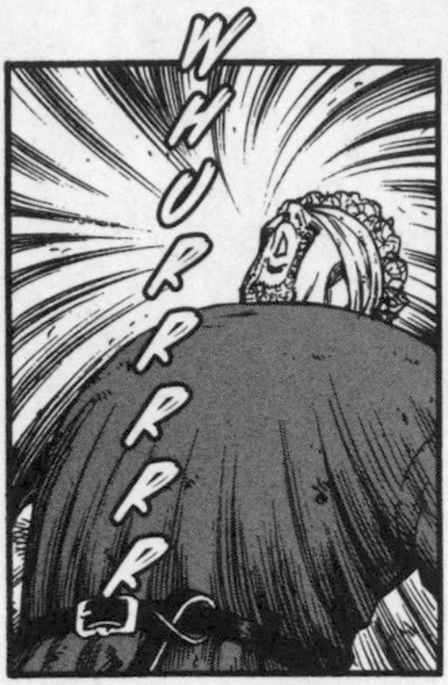
WHURRRRRR
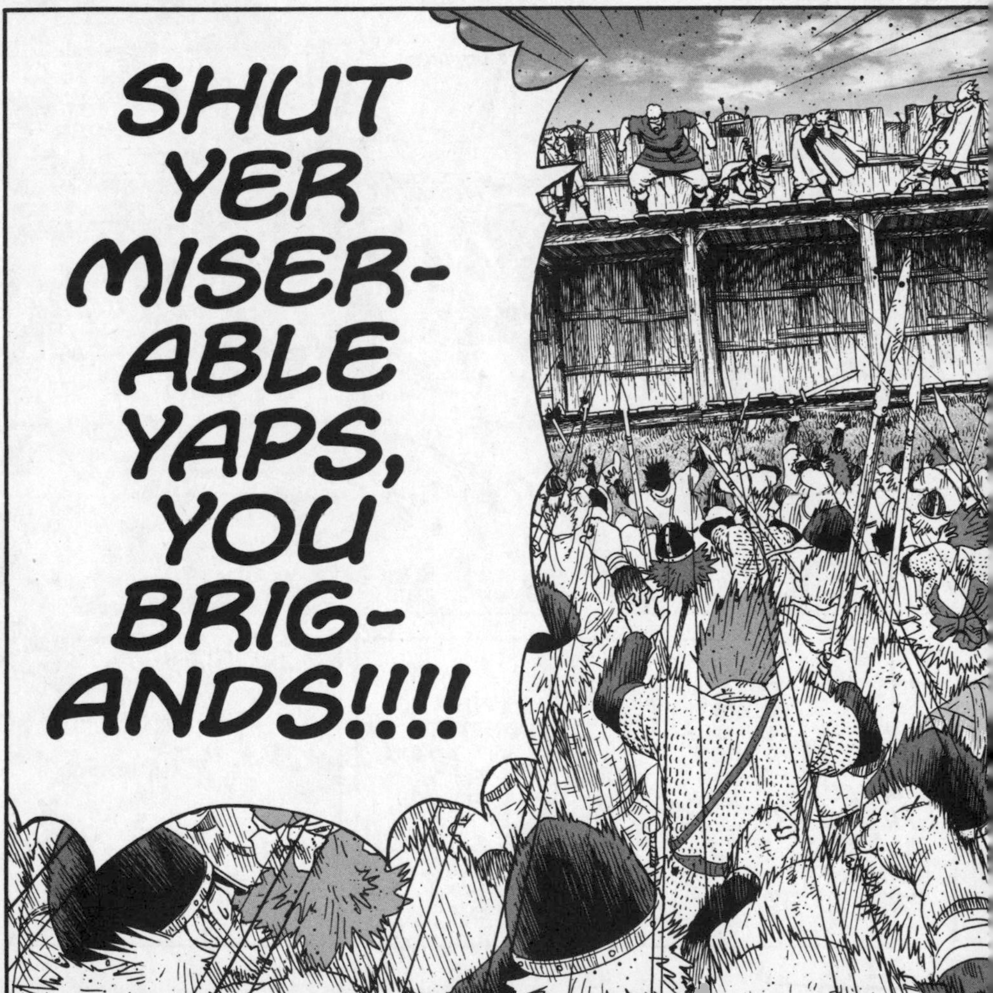
SHUT YER MISER-ABLE YAPS, YOU BRIG-ANDS!!!!

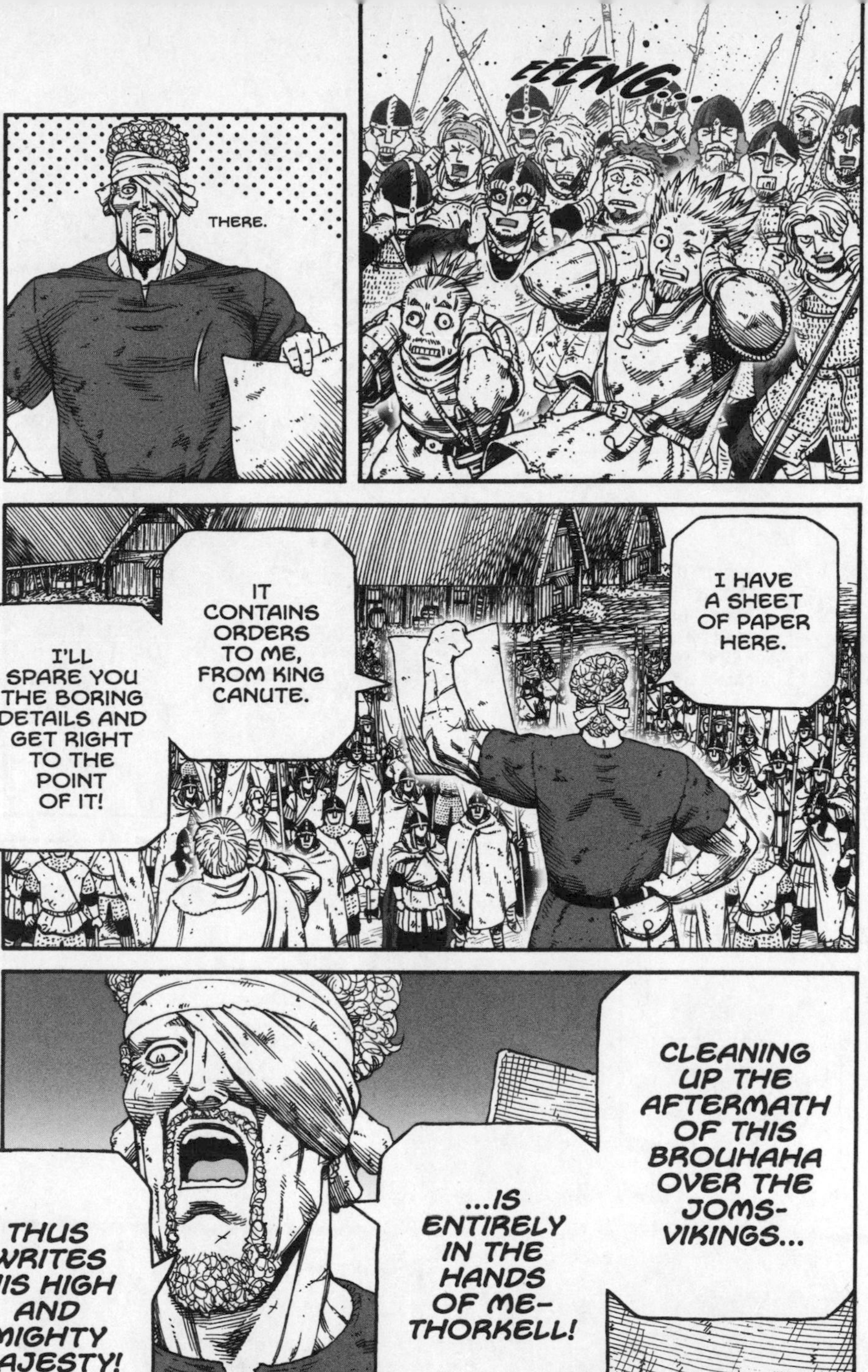
EEENG...
THERE.
I HAVE A SHEET OF PAPER HERE.
IT CONTAINS ORDERS TO ME, FROM KING CANUTE.
I'LL SPARE YOU THE BORING DETAILS AND GET RIGHT TO THE POINT OF IT!
CLEANING UP THE AFTERMATH OF THIS BROUHAHA OVER THE JOMS-VIKINGS...
...IS ENTIRELY IN THE HANDS OF ME-THORKELL!
THUS WRITES HIS HIGH AND MIGHTY MAJESTY!

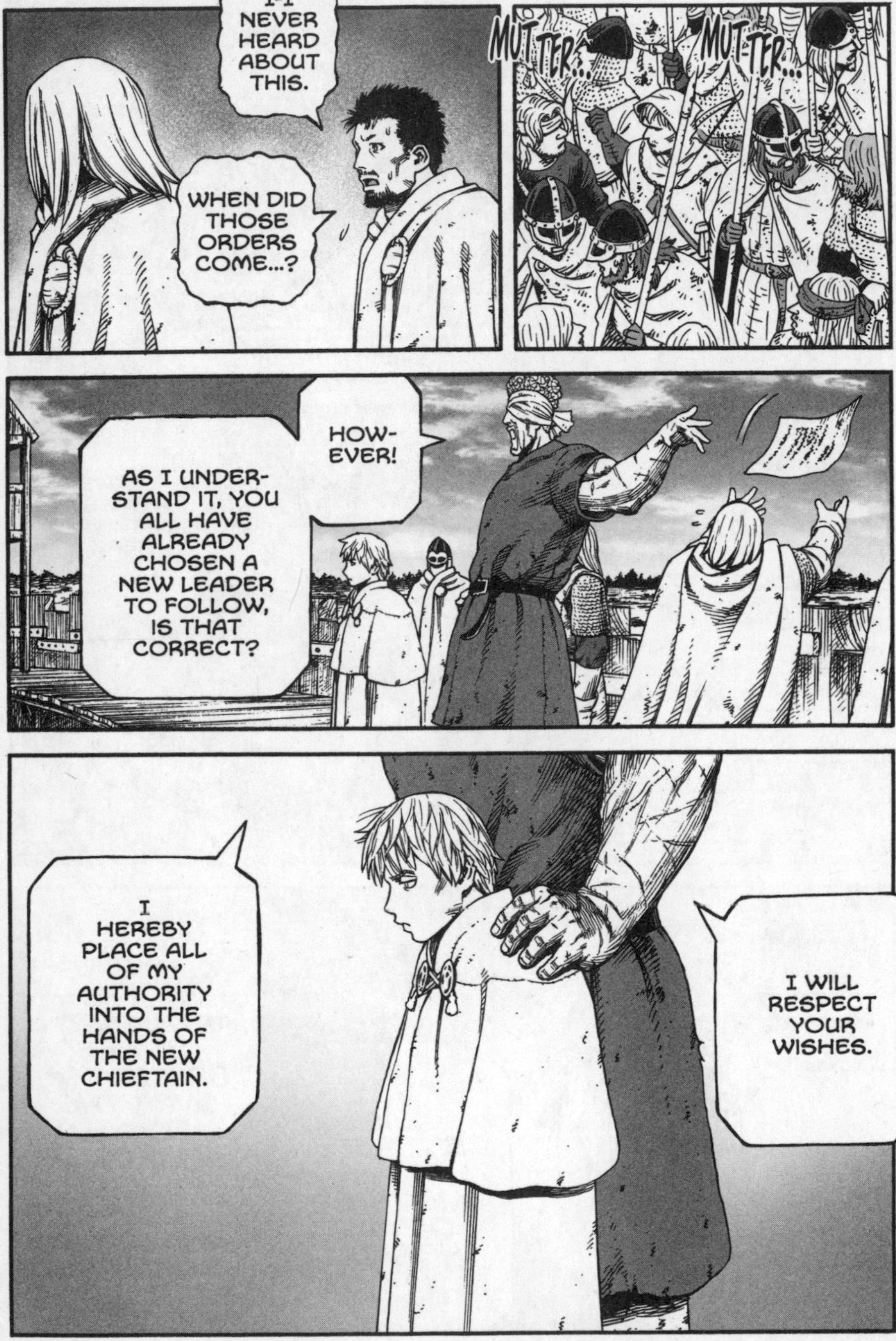
MUTTER...
MUTTER...
I-I NEVER HEARD ABOUT THIS.
WHEN DID THOSE ORDERS COME...?
HOWEVER!
AS I UNDERSTAND IT, YOU ALL HAVE ALREADY CHOSEN A NEW LEADER TO FOLLOW, IS THAT CORRECT?
I WILL RESPECT YOUR WISHES.
I HEREBY PLACE ALL OF MY AUTHORITY INTO THE HANDS OF THE NEW CHIEFTAIN.

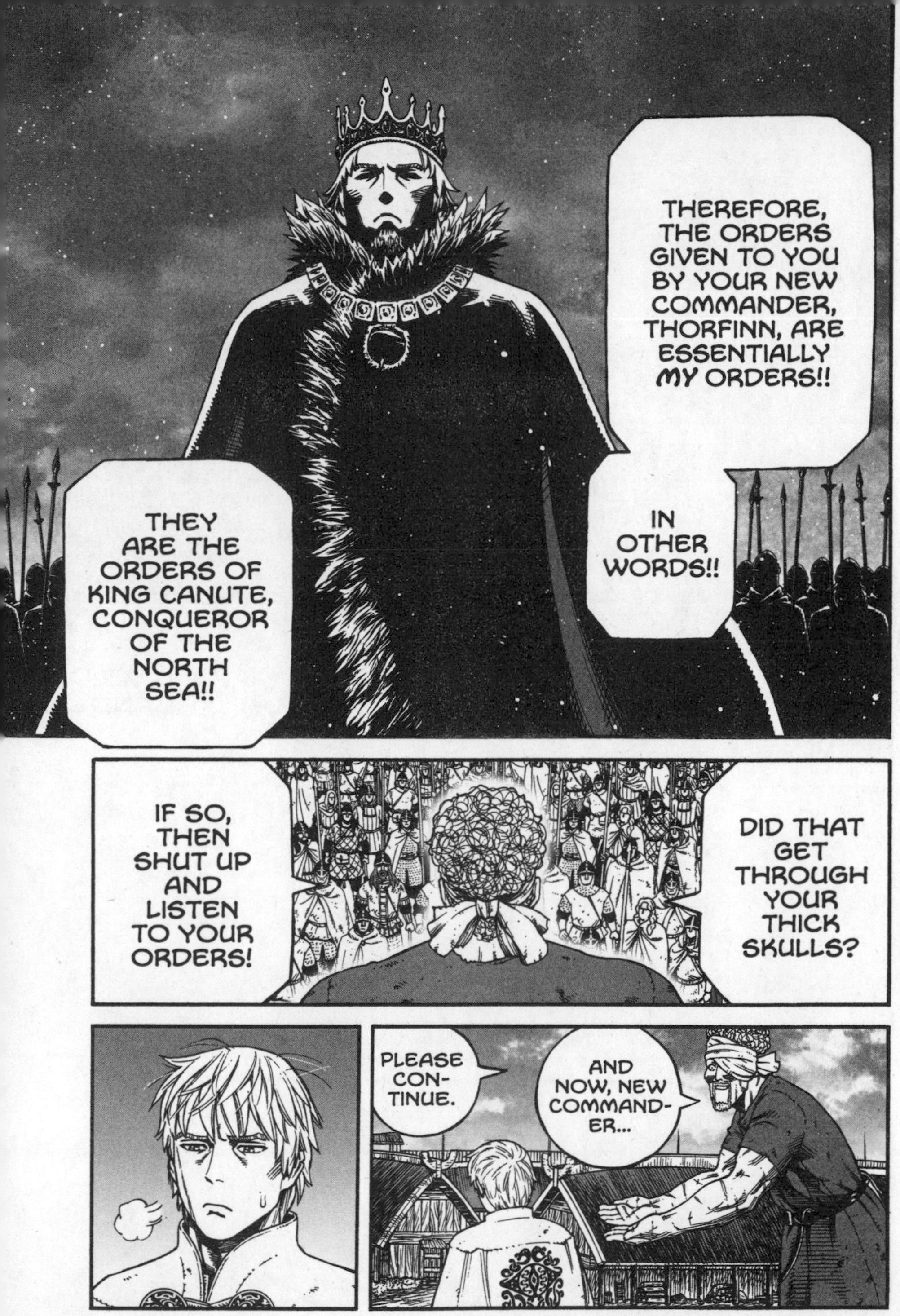
THEREFORE, THE ORDERS GIVEN TO YOU BY YOUR NEW COMMANDER, THORFINN, ARE ESSENTIALLY MY ORDERS!!
IN OTHER WORDS!!
THEY ARE THE ORDERS OF KING CANUTE, CONQUEROR OF THE NORTH SEA!!
DID THAT GET THROUGH YOUR THICK SKULLS?
IF SO, THEN SHUT UP AND LISTEN TO YOUR ORDERS!
AND NOW, NEW COMMANDER...
PLEASE CON-TINUE.

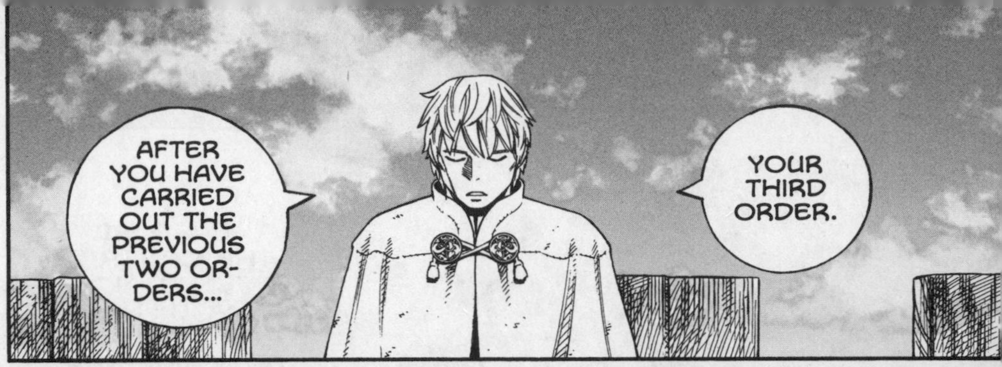
YOUR THIRD ORDER.
AFTER YOU HAVE CARRIED OUT THE PREVIOUS TWO OR- DERS...
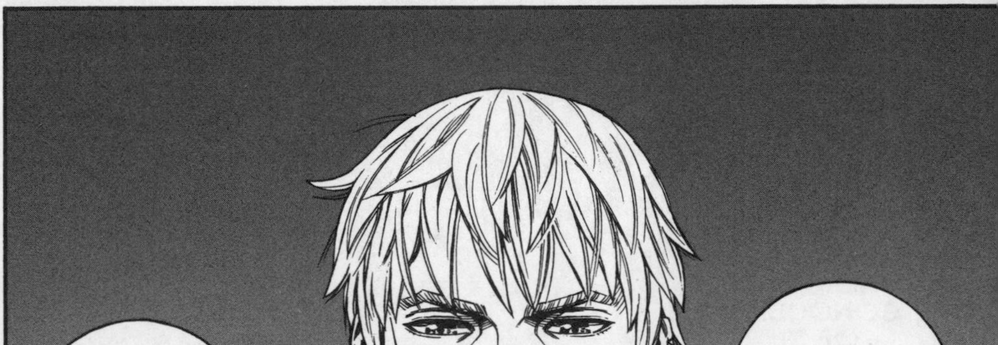
YOU WILL DISBAND...
...THE JOMS- VIKINGS.
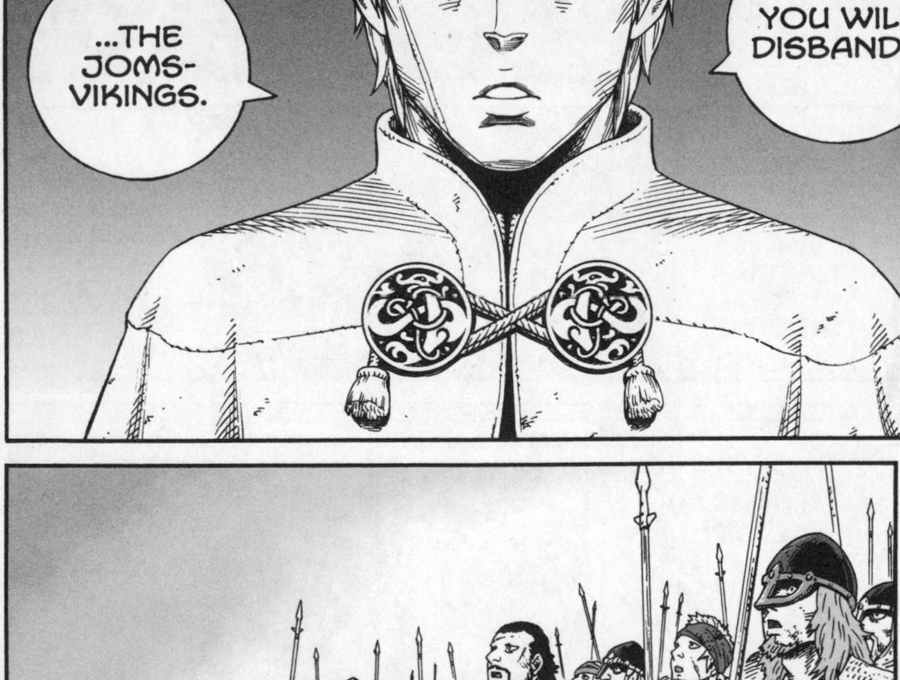

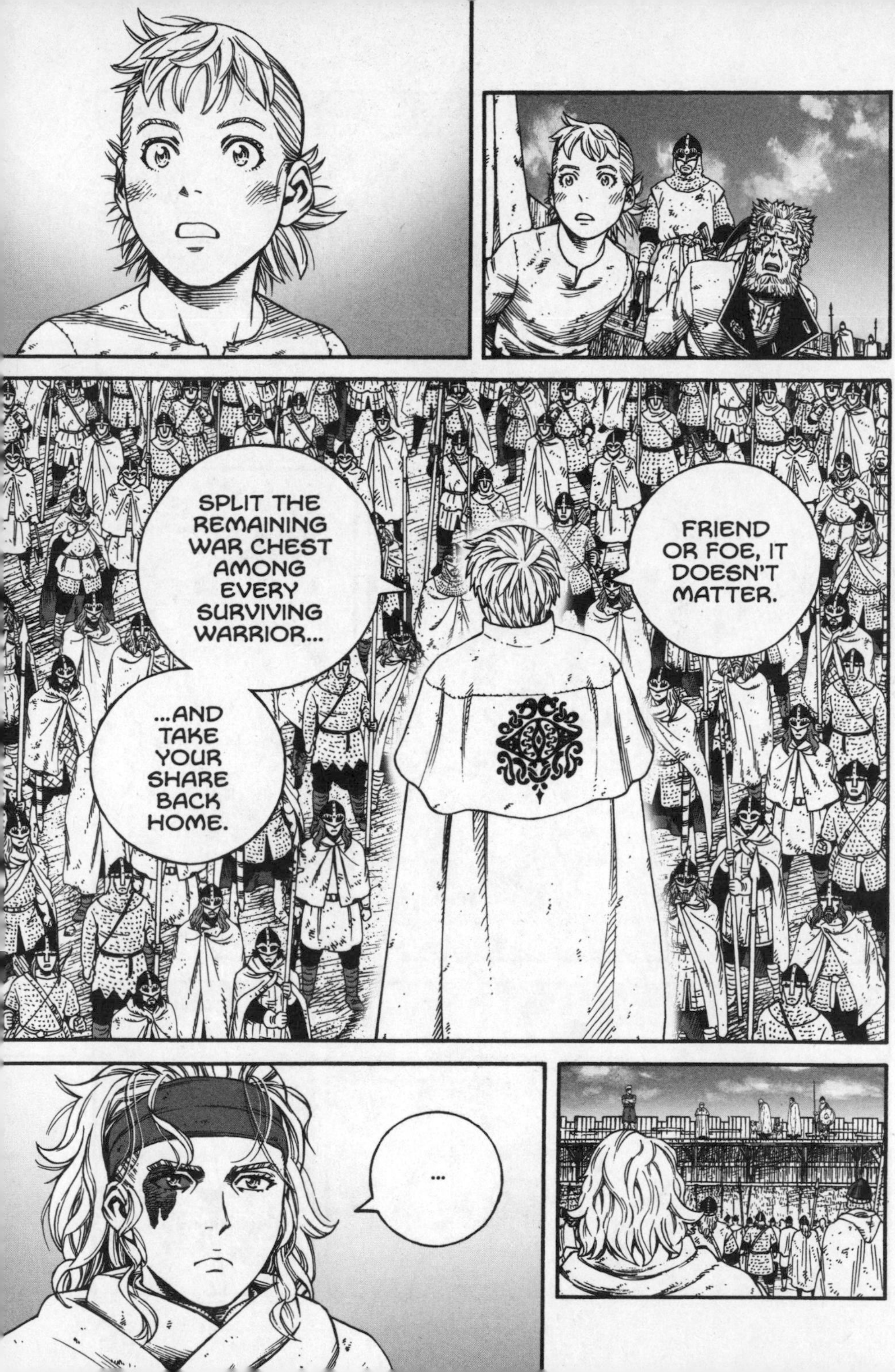
FRIEND OR FOE, IT DOESN'T MATTER.
SPLIT THE REMAINING WAR CHEST AMONG EVERY SURVIVING WARRIOR...
...AND TAKE YOUR SHARE BACK HOME.
...

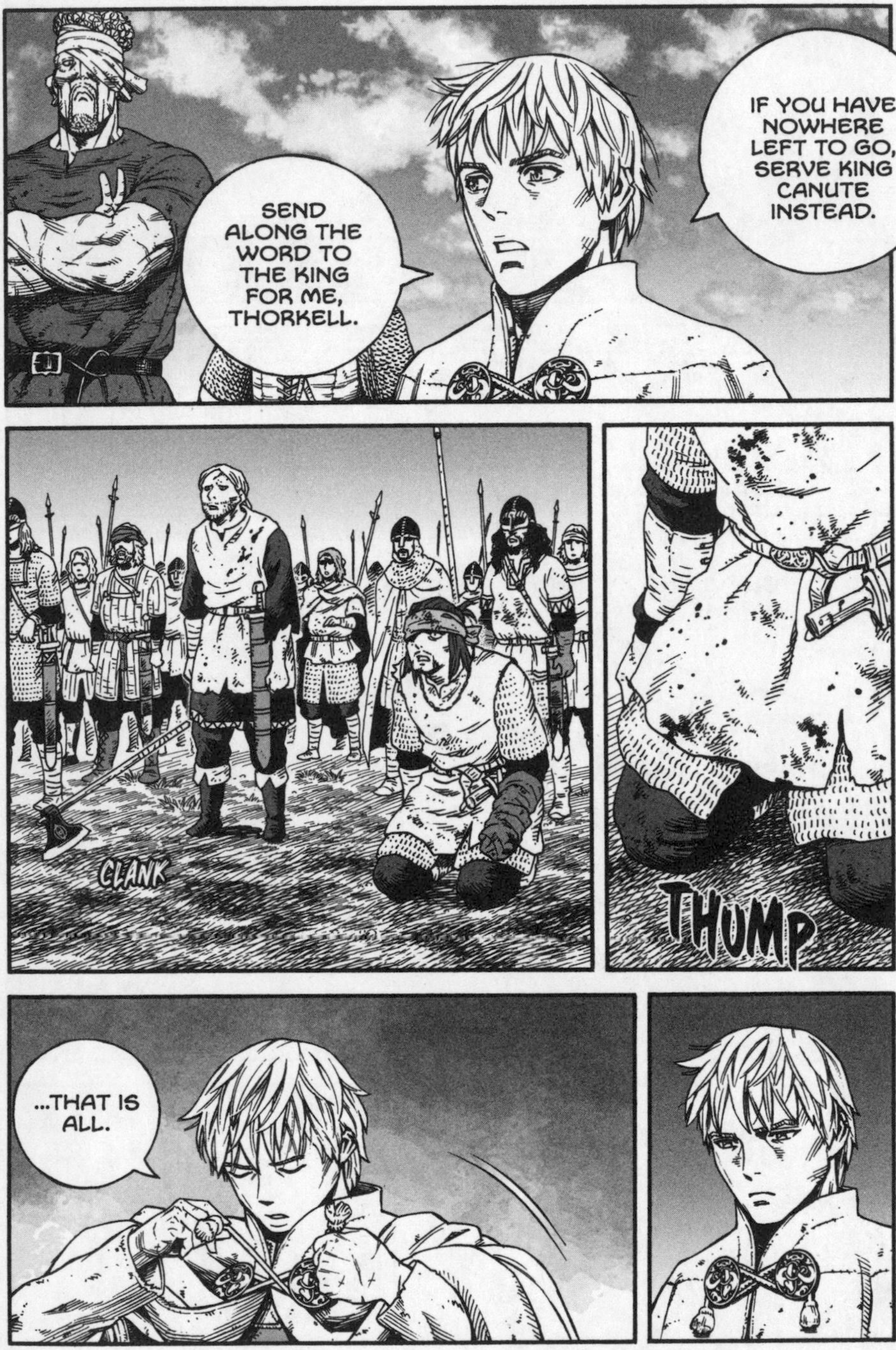
IF YOU HAVE NOWHERE LEFT TO GO, SERVE KING CANUTE INSTEAD.
SEND ALONG THE WORD TO THE KING FOR ME, THORKELL.
THUMP
CLANK
...THAT IS ALL.

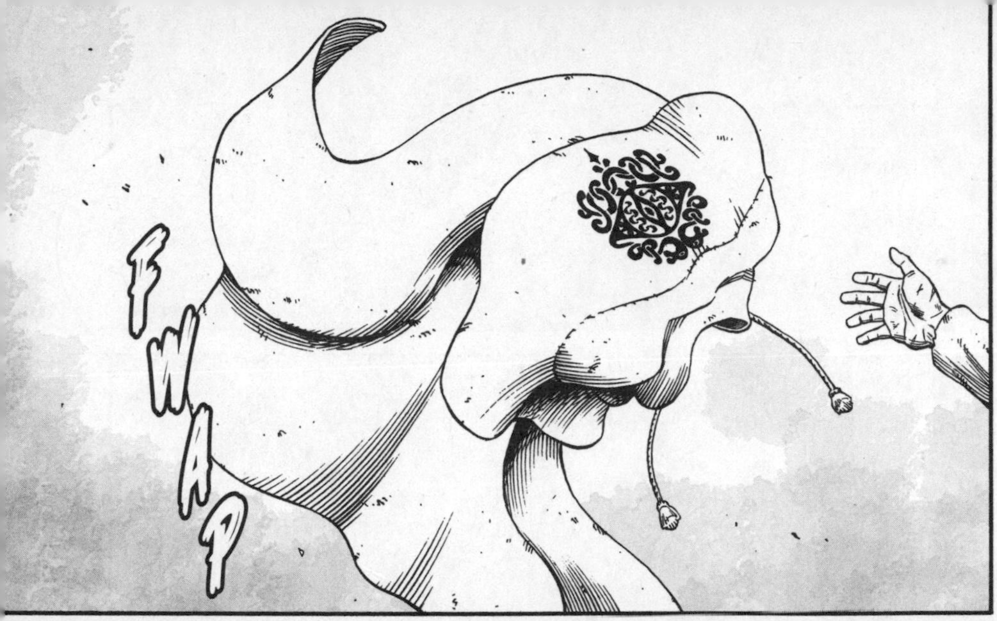
FWAP

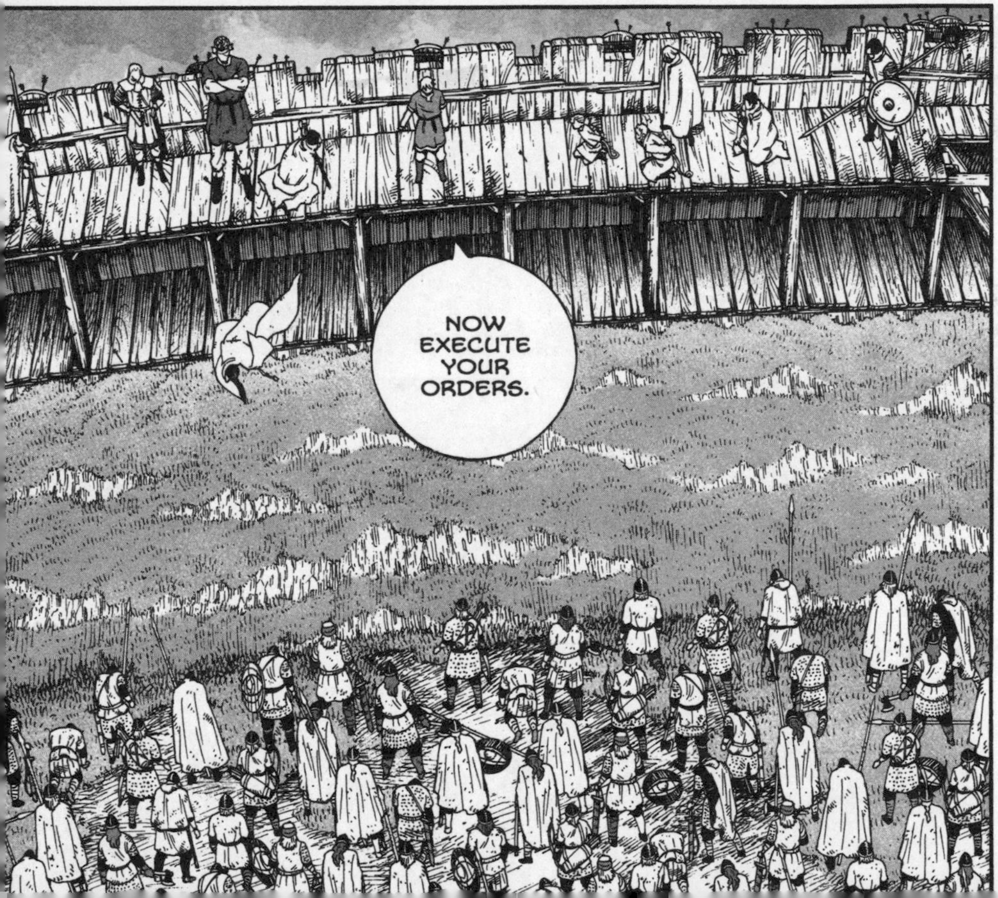
NOW EXECUTE YOUR ORDERS.

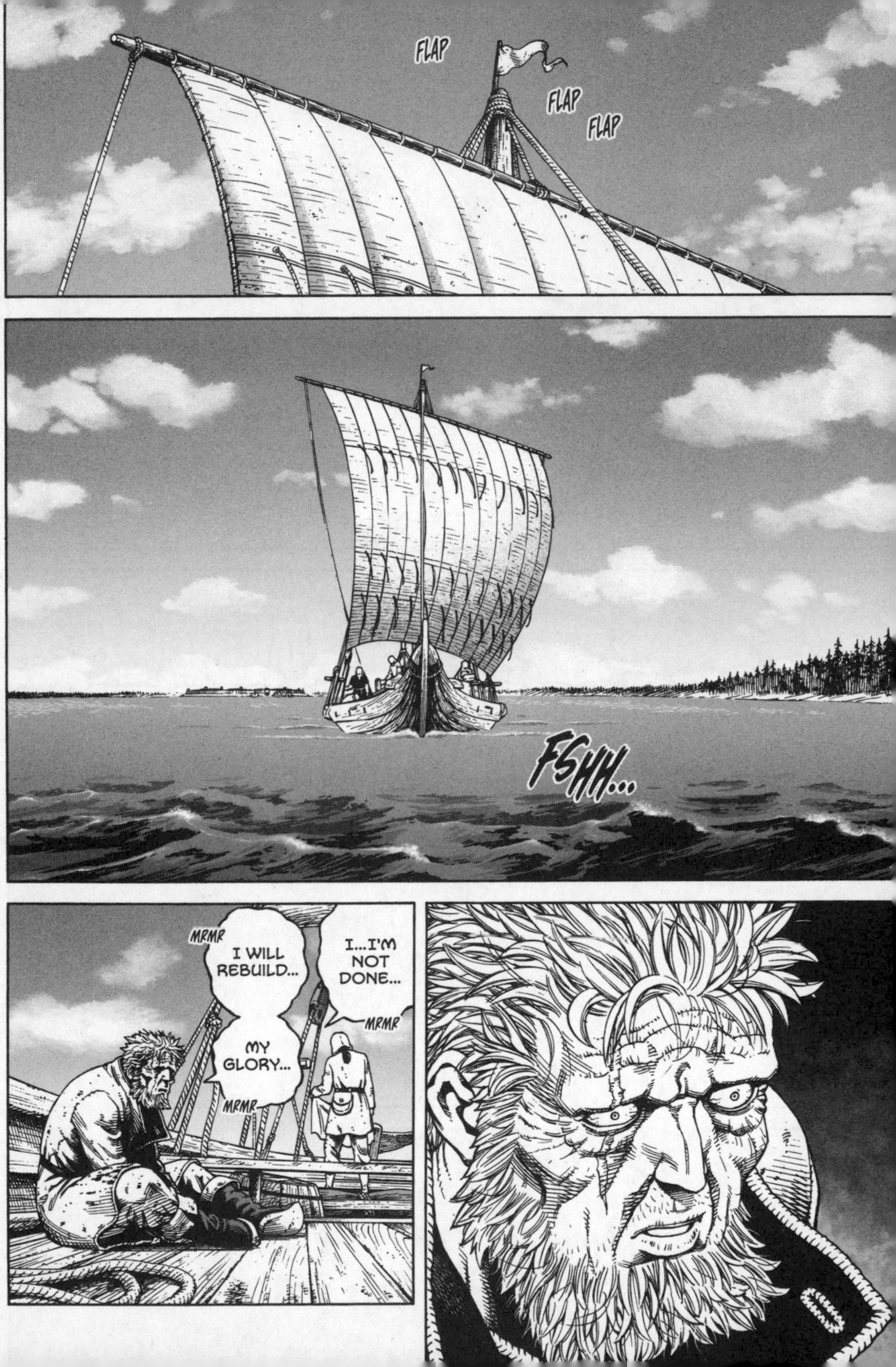
FLAP
FLAP
FLAP
FSHH...
I...I'M NOT DONE...
MRMR
MRMR
I WILL REBUILD...
MY GLORY...
MRMR

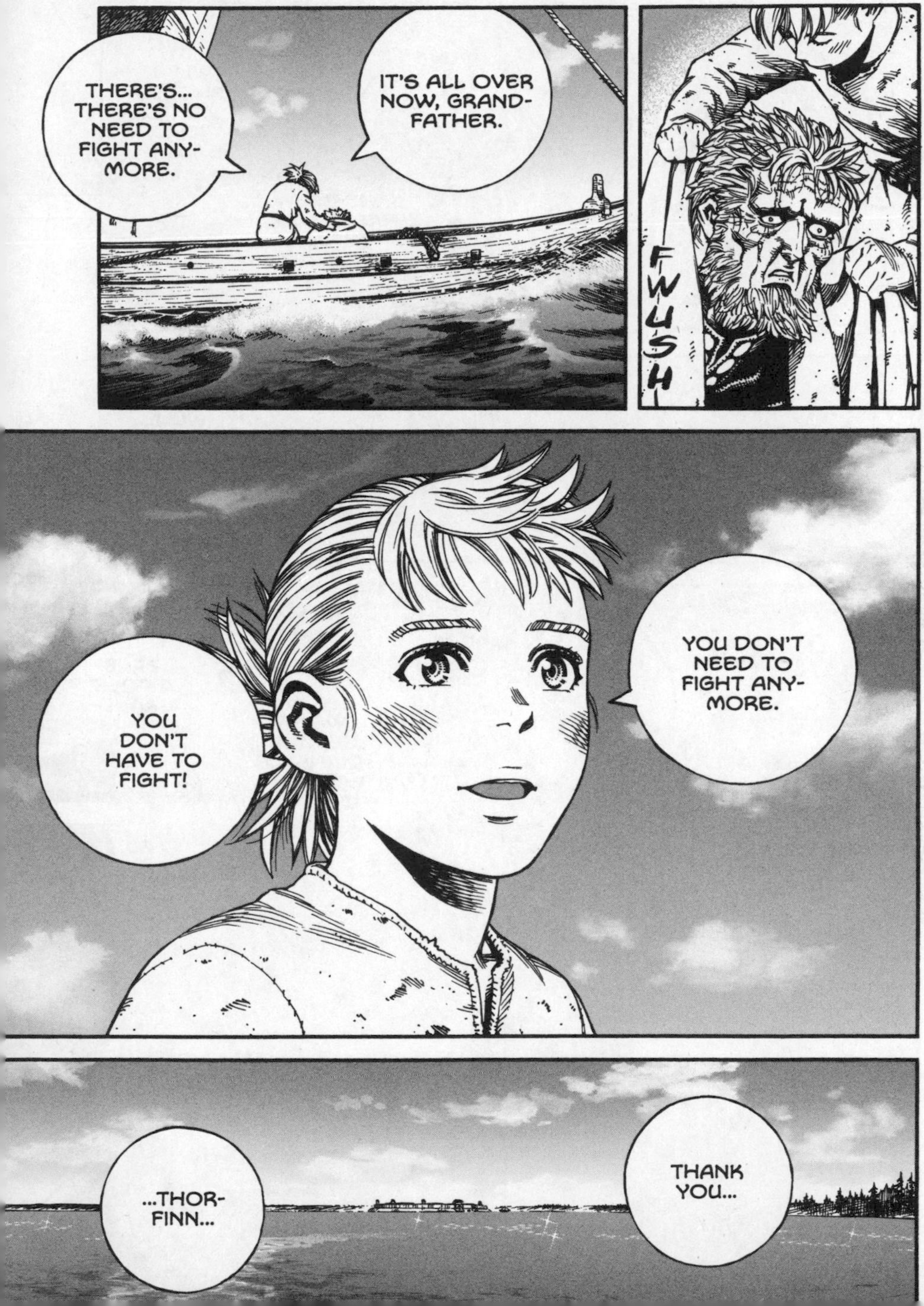
FWUSH
IT'S ALL OVER NOW, GRAND-FATHER.
THERE'S... THERE'S NO NEED TO FIGHT ANY-MORE.
YOU DON'T NEED TO FIGHT ANY-MORE.
YOU DON'T HAVE TO FIGHT!
THANK YOU...
...THOR-FINN...

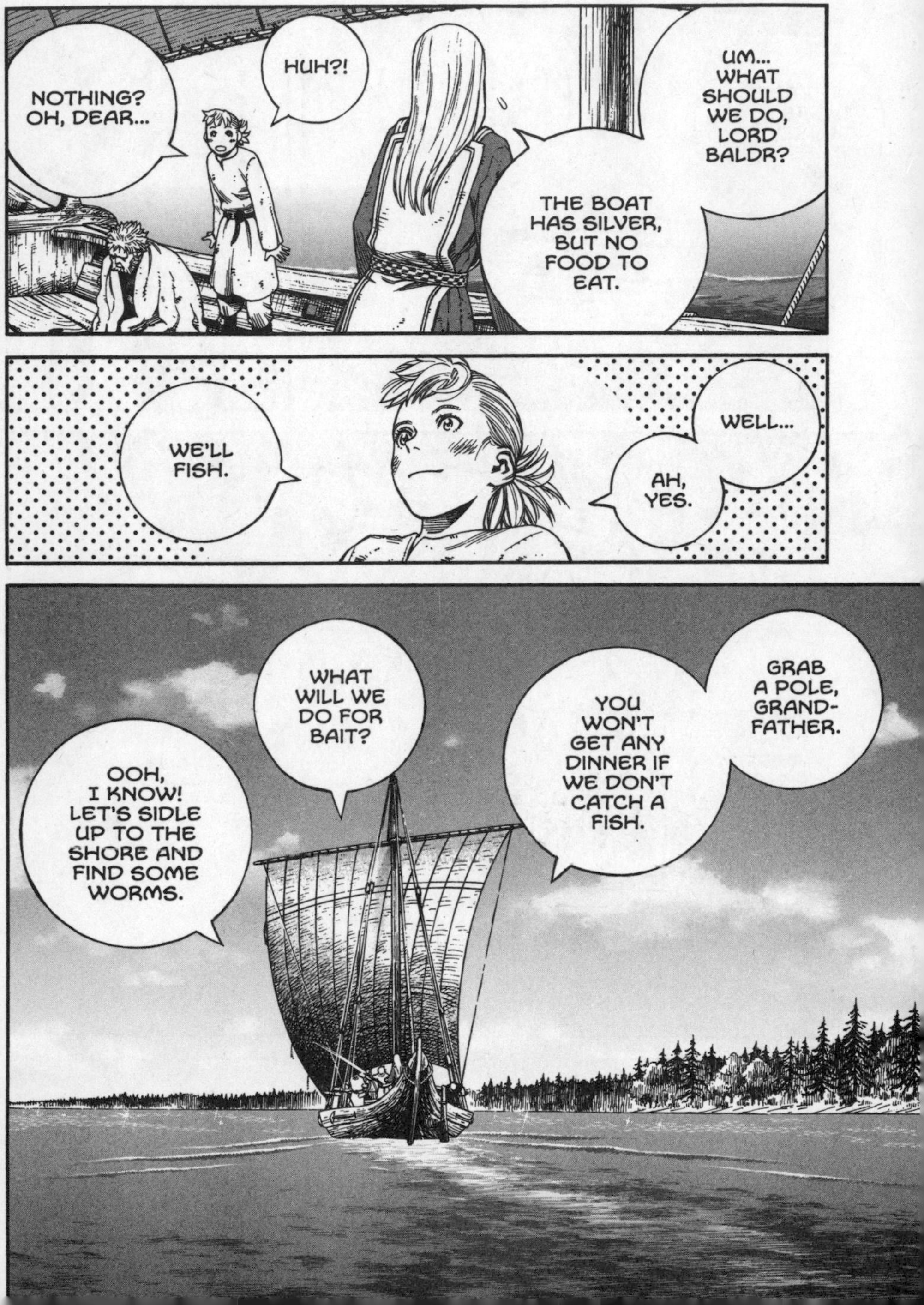
UM... WHAT SHOULD WE DO, LORD BALDR?
THE BOAT HAS SILVER, BUT NO FOOD TO EAT.
HUH?!
NOTHING? OH, DEAR...
WELL...
AH, YES.
WE'LL FISH.
GRAB A POLE, GRANDFATHER.
YOU WON'T GET ANY DINNER IF WE DON'T CATCH A FISH.
WHAT WILL WE DO FOR BAIT?
OOH, I KNOW! LET'S SIDLE UP TO THE SHORE AND FIND SOME WORMS.

CHAPTER 159 - END

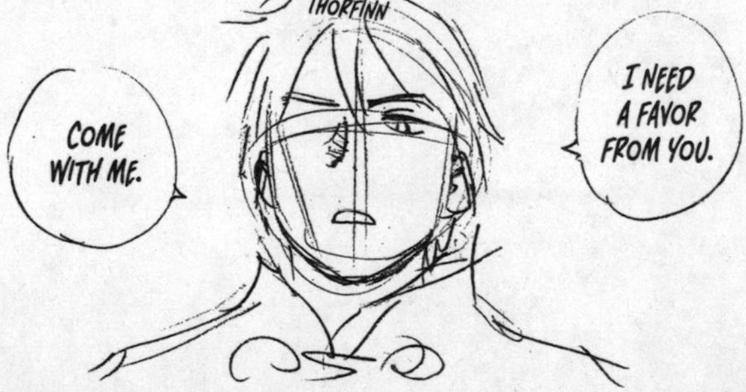
THORFINN
I NEED A FAVOR FROM YOU.
COME WITH ME.

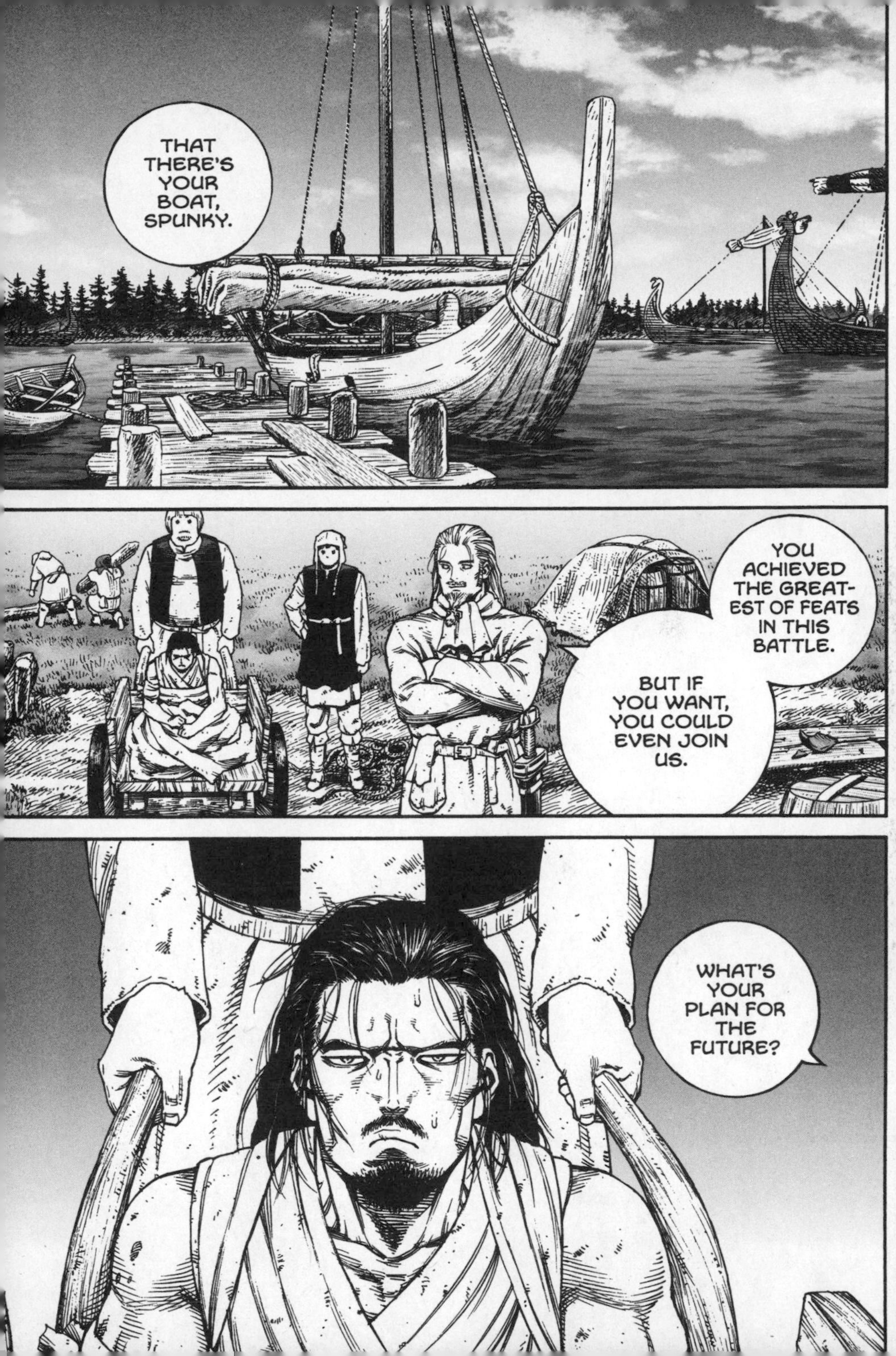
THAT THERE'S YOUR BOAT, SPUNKY.
YOU ACHIEVED THE GREATEST OF FEATS IN THIS BATTLE.
BUT IF YOU WANT, YOU COULD EVEN JOIN US.
WHAT'S YOUR PLAN FOR THE FUTURE?

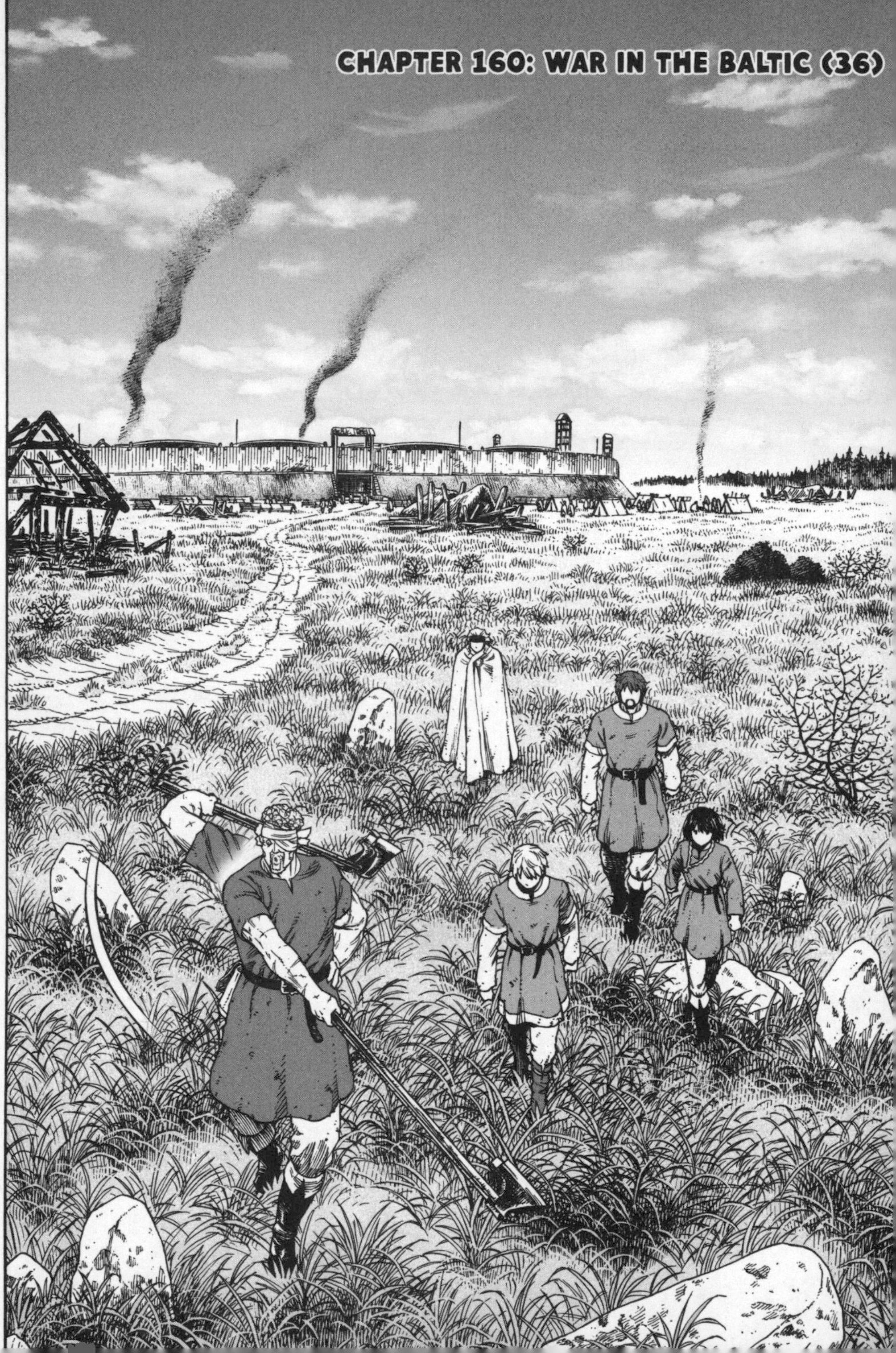
CHAPTER 160: WAR IN THE BALTIC (36)

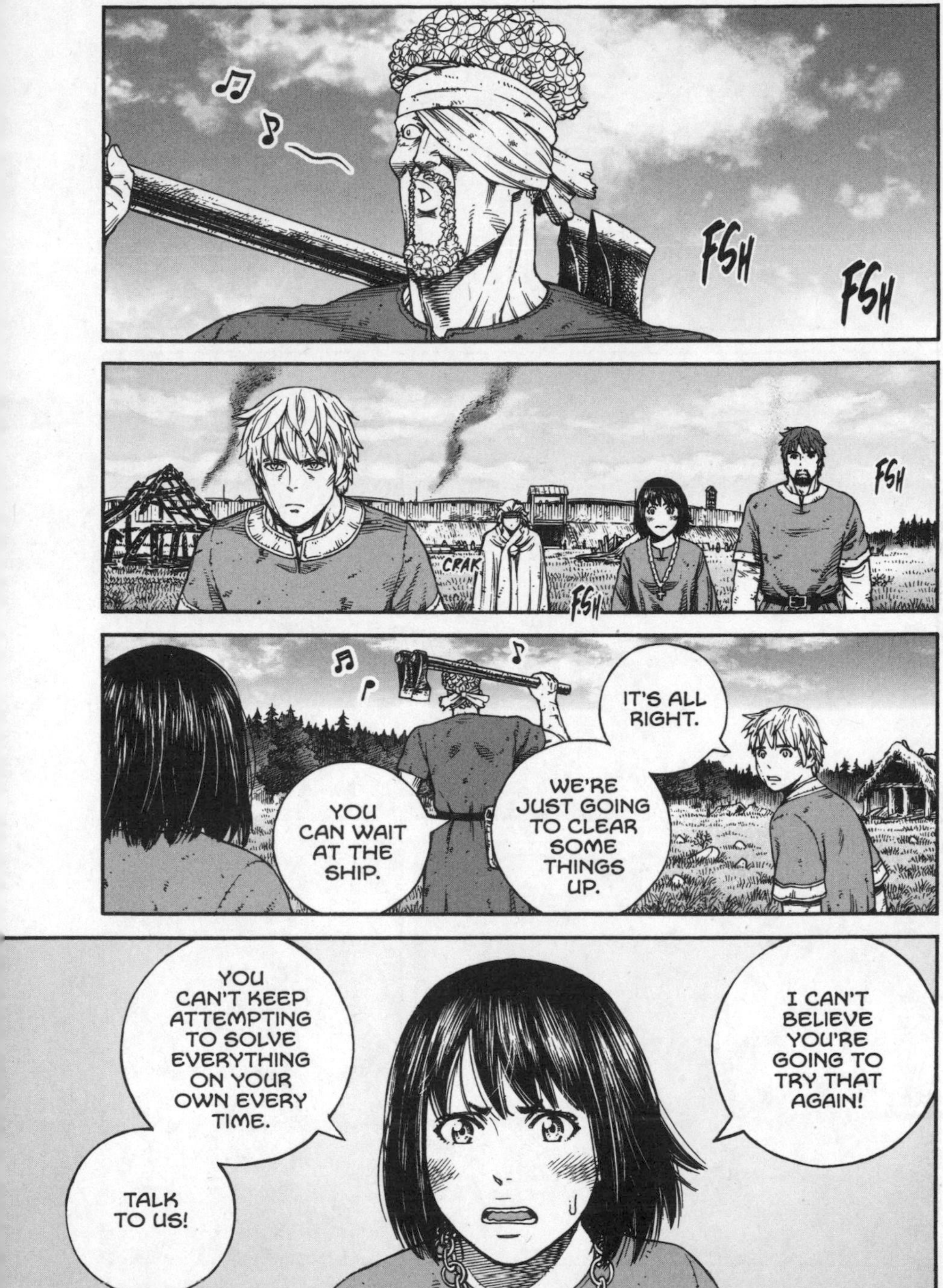
FSH
FSH
FSH
CRAK
FSH
IT'S ALL RIGHT.
WE'RE JUST GOING TO CLEAR SOME THINGS UP.
YOU CAN WAIT AT THE SHIP.
I CAN'T BELIEVE YOU'RE GOING TO TRY THAT AGAIN!
YOU CAN'T KEEP ATTEMPTING TO SOLVE EVERYTHING ON YOUR OWN EVERY TIME.
TALK TO US!

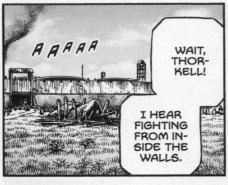

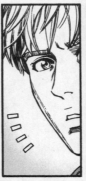

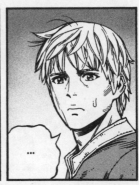

...
A A A A A
WAIT, THORKELL!
I HEAR FIGHTING FROM INSIDE THE WALLS.
YES. BECAUSE THEY'RE FIGHTING.
OF COURSE THEY ARE. YOU KNOW THEY'RE NOT THE TYPE TO OBEY ORDERS LIKE THOSE.
THEY'VE GOT TO GET IT OUT OF THEIR SYSTEM.
BUT THEY'RE ALL EXHAUSTED FROM THE BATTLE BEFORE THIS.
A FEW OF THEM DIE, AND THEY'LL GIVE UP SOON ENOUGH.

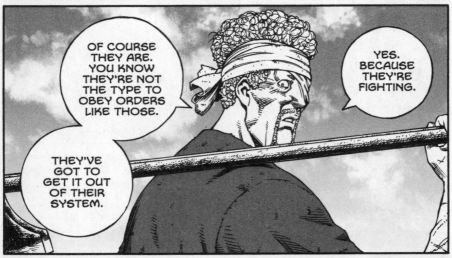

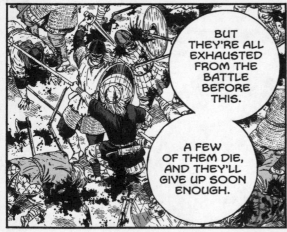

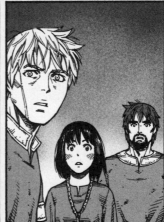

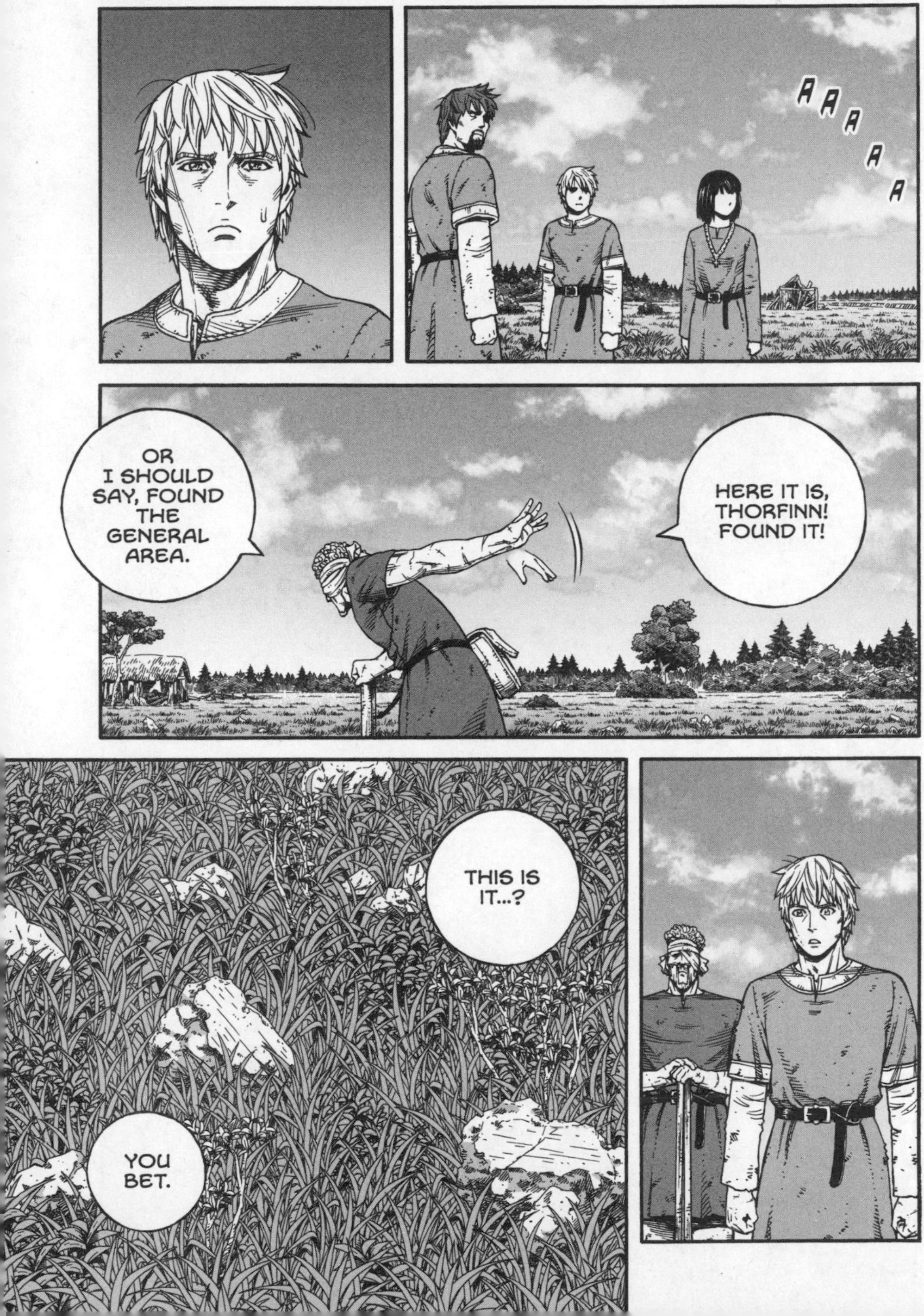
AAAAA
HERE IT IS, THORFINN! FOUND IT!
OR I SHOULD SAY, FOUND THE GENERAL AREA.
THIS IS IT...?
YOU BET.

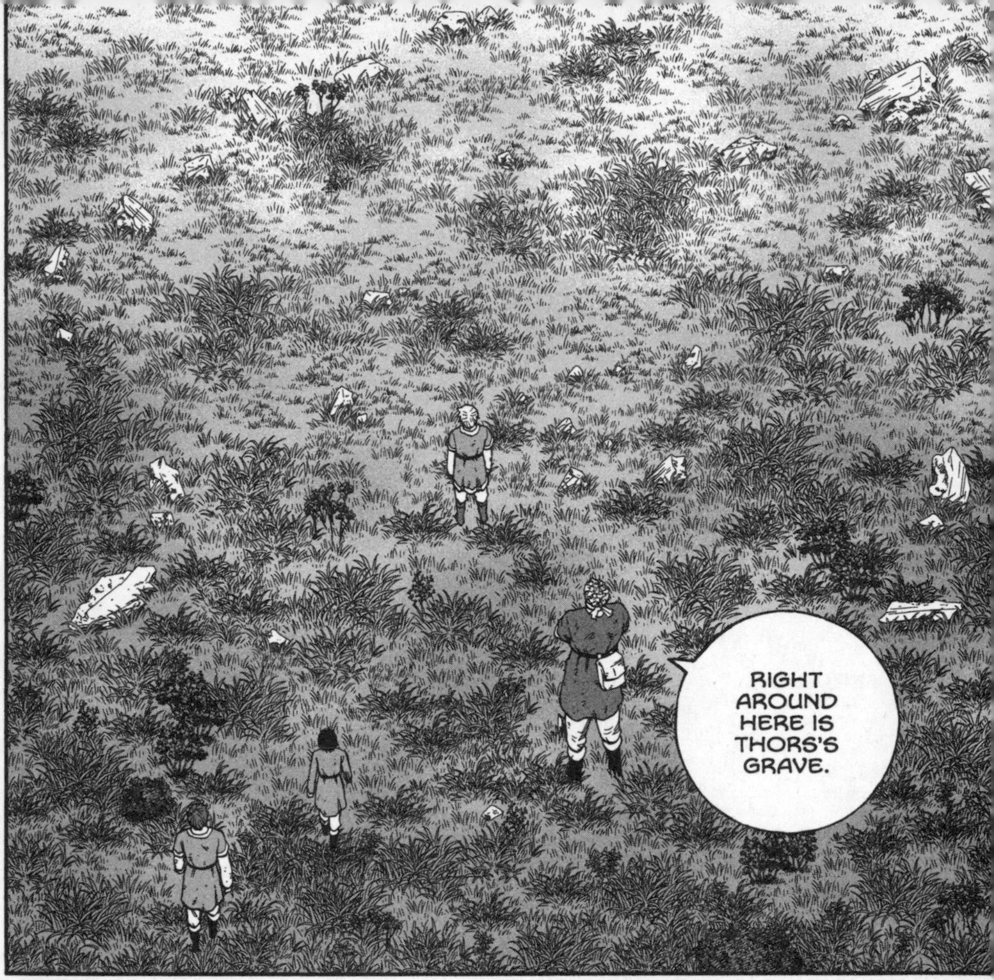
RIGHT AROUND HERE IS THORS'S GRAVE.
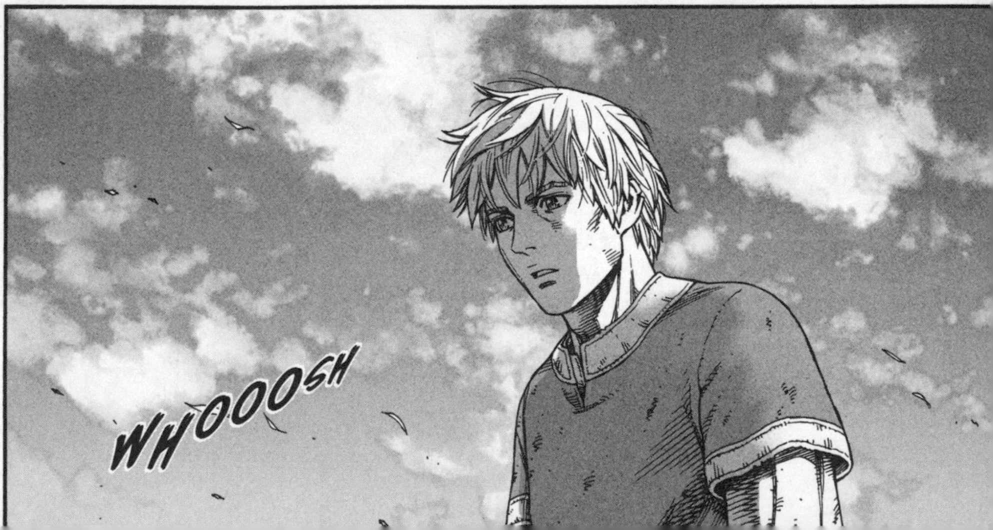
WHOOOSH

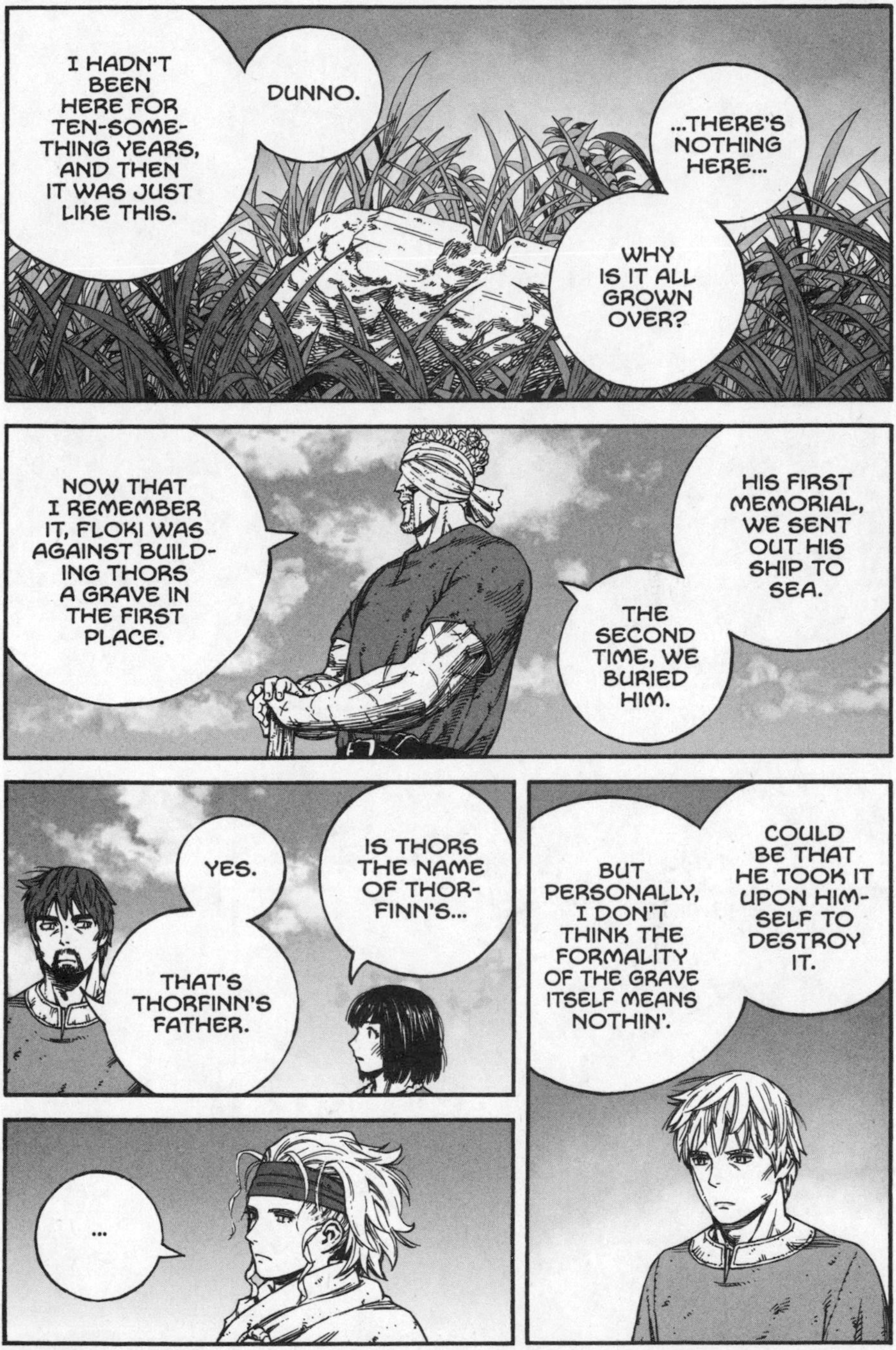
...THERE'S NOTHING HERE...
WHY IS IT ALL GROWN OVER?
DUNNO.
I HADN'T BEEN HERE FOR TEN-SOMETHING YEARS, AND THEN IT WAS JUST LIKE THIS.
HIS FIRST MEMORIAL, WE SENT OUT HIS SHIP TO SEA.
THE SECOND TIME, WE BURIED HIM.
NOW THAT I REMEMBER IT, FLOKI WAS AGAINST BUILDING THORS A GRAVE IN THE FIRST PLACE.
COULD BE THAT HE TOOK IT UPON HIMSELF TO DESTROY IT.
BUT PERSONALLY, I DON'T THINK THE FORMALITY OF THE GRAVE ITSELF MEANS NOTHIN'.
IS THORS THE NAME OF THORFINN'S...
YES.
THAT'S THORFINN'S FATHER.
...

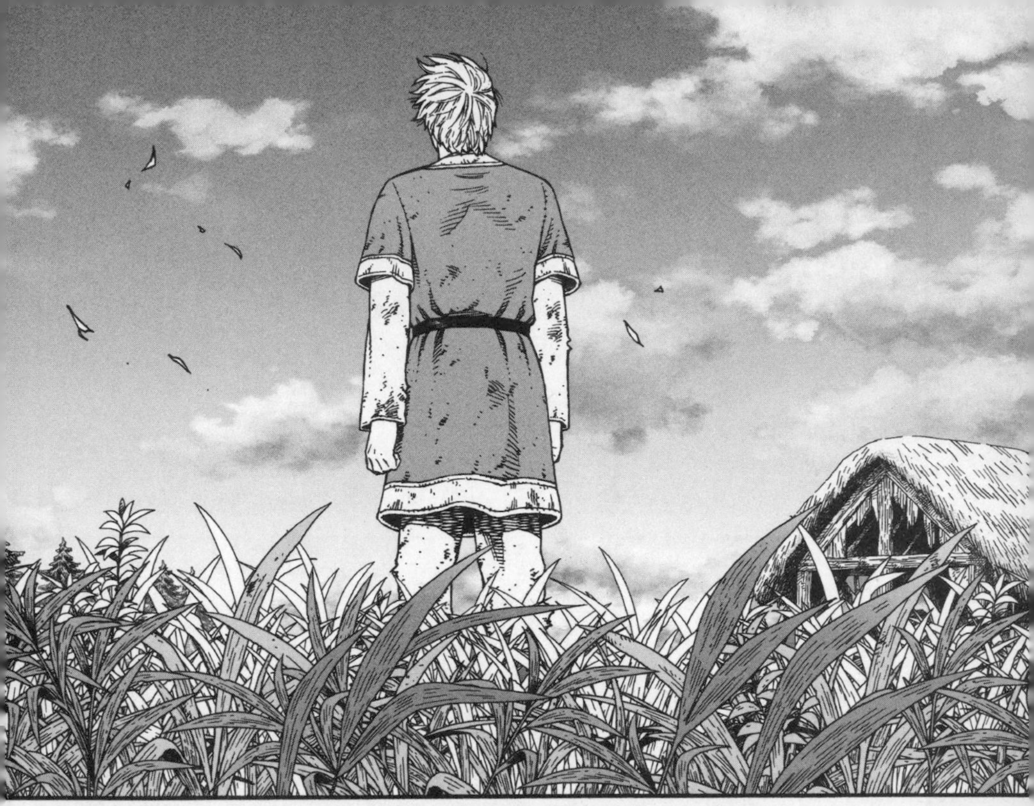

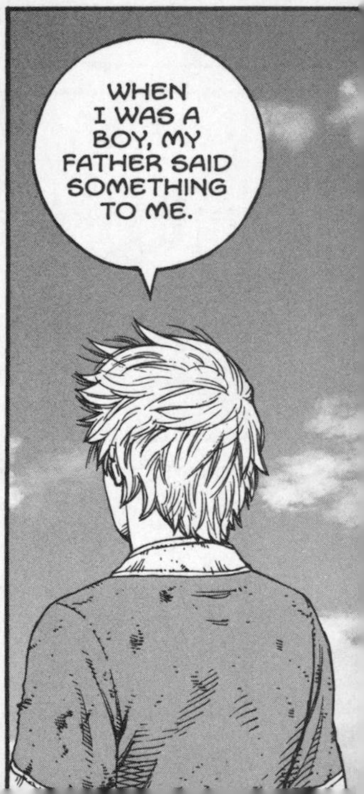

WHEN I WAS A BOY, MY FATHER SAID SOMETHING TO ME.

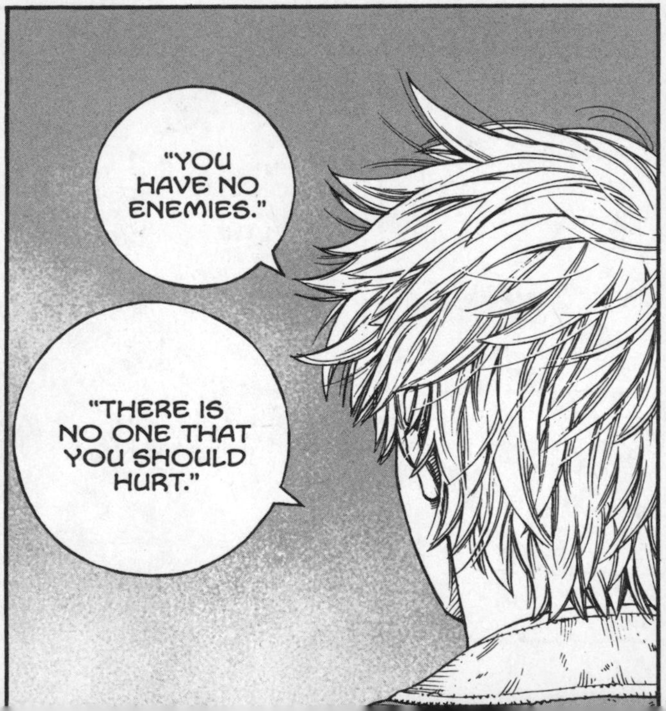

"YOU HAVE NO ENEMIES."
"THERE IS NO ONE THAT YOU SHOULD HURT."

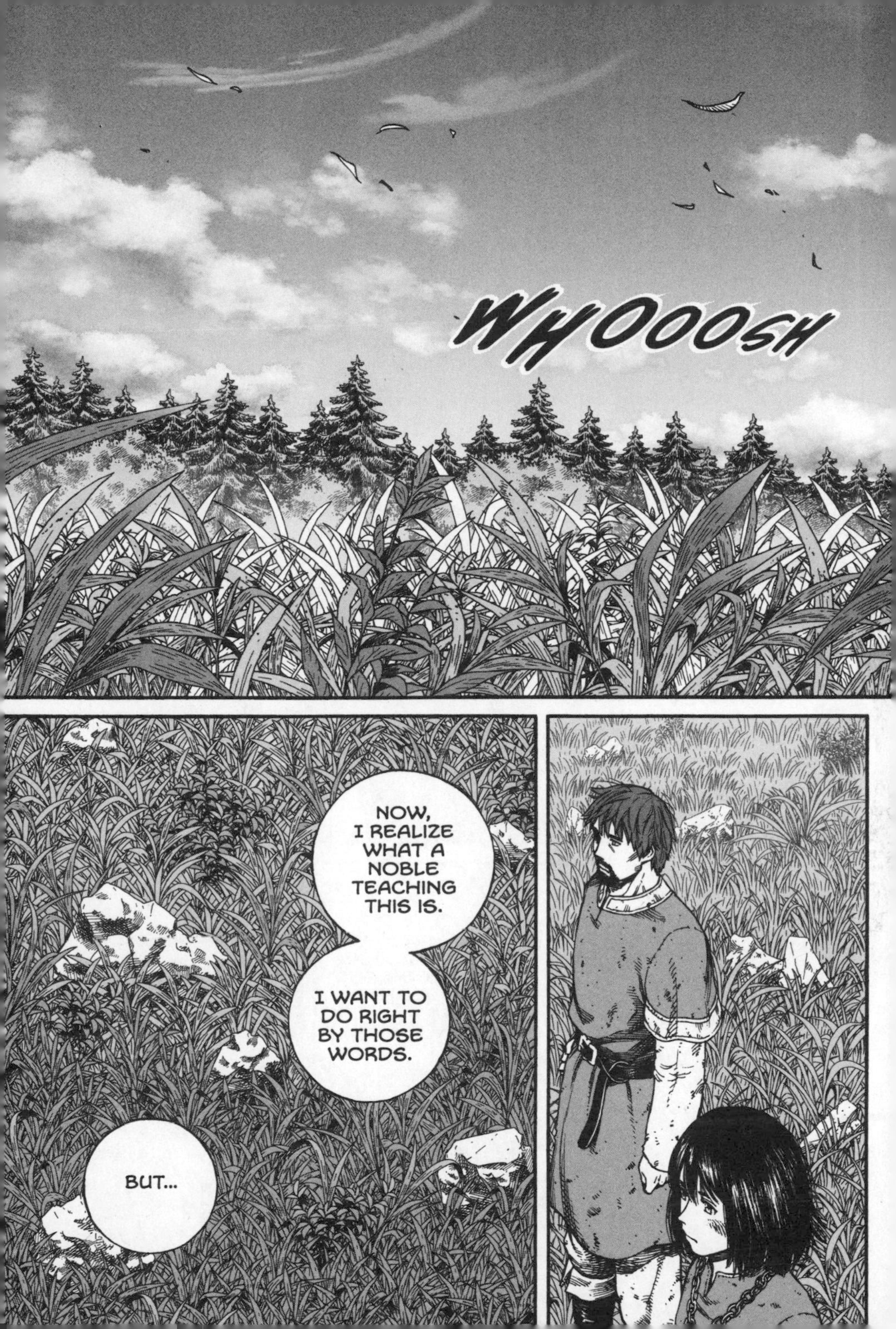
WHOOOSH
NOW, I REALIZE WHAT A NOBLE TEACHING THIS IS.
I WANT TO DO RIGHT BY THOSE WORDS.
BUT...

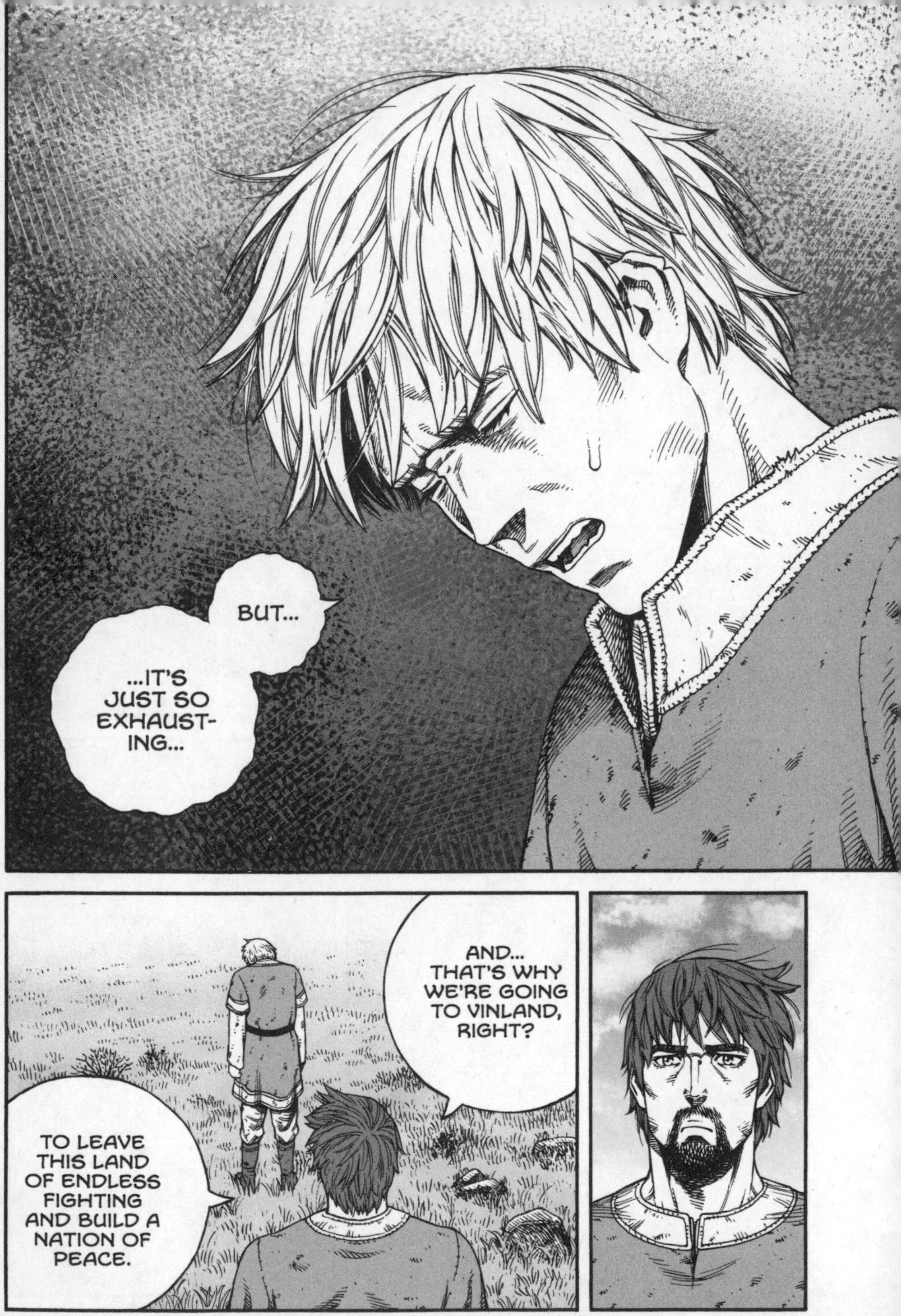
BUT...
...IT'S JUST SO EXHAUSTING...
AND... THAT'S WHY WE'RE GOING TO VINLAND, RIGHT?
TO LEAVE THIS LAND OF ENDLESS FIGHTING AND BUILD A NATION OF PEACE.

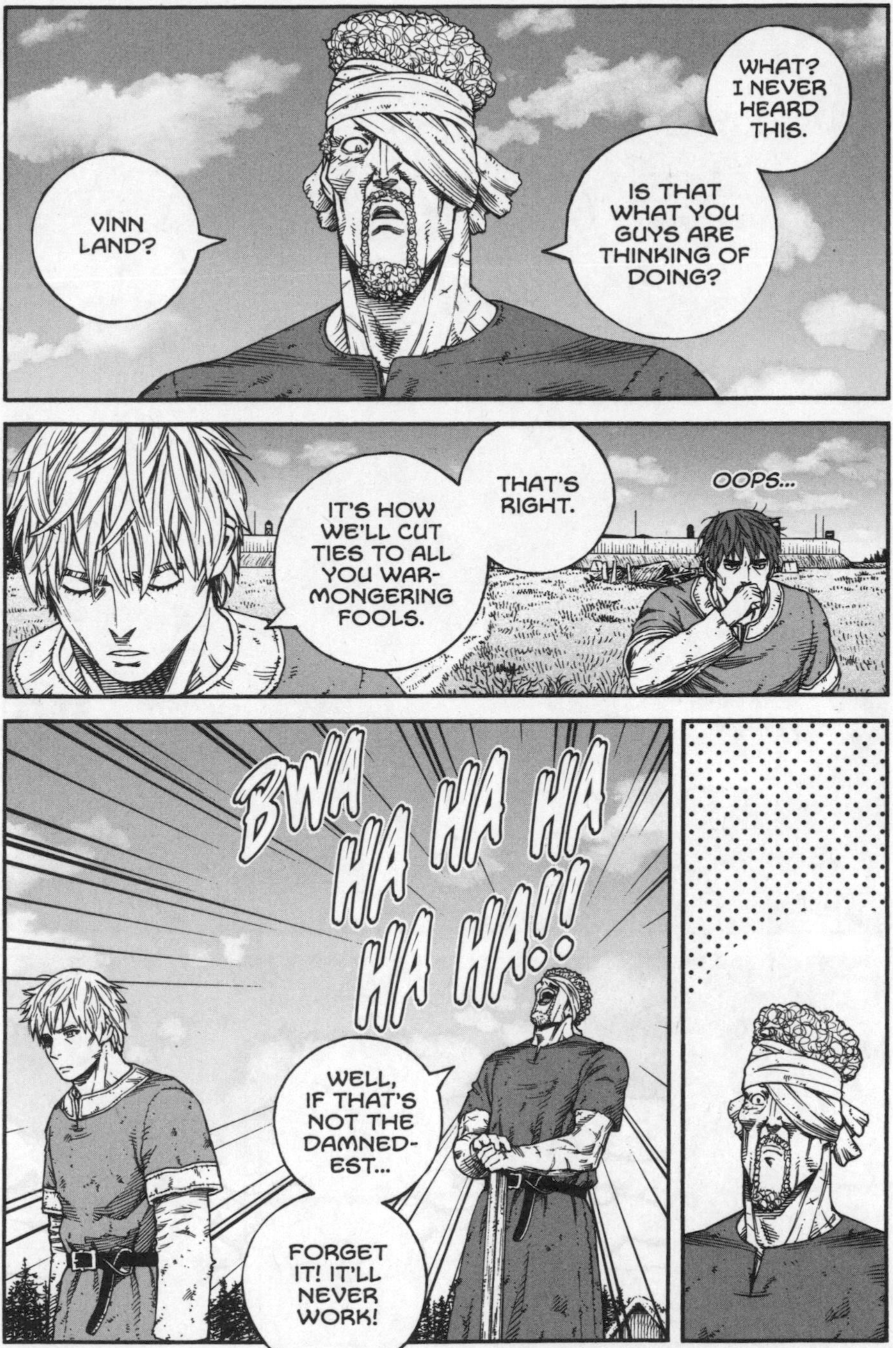
VINN LAND?
WHAT? I NEVER HEARD THIS.
IS THAT WHAT YOU GUYS ARE THINKING OF DOING?
THAT'S RIGHT.
IT'S HOW WE'LL CUT TIES TO ALL YOU WAR-MONGERING FOOLS.
OOPS...
BWA HA HA HA HA HA!!
WELL, IF THAT'S NOT THE DAMNED-EST...
FORGET IT! IT'LL NEVER WORK!

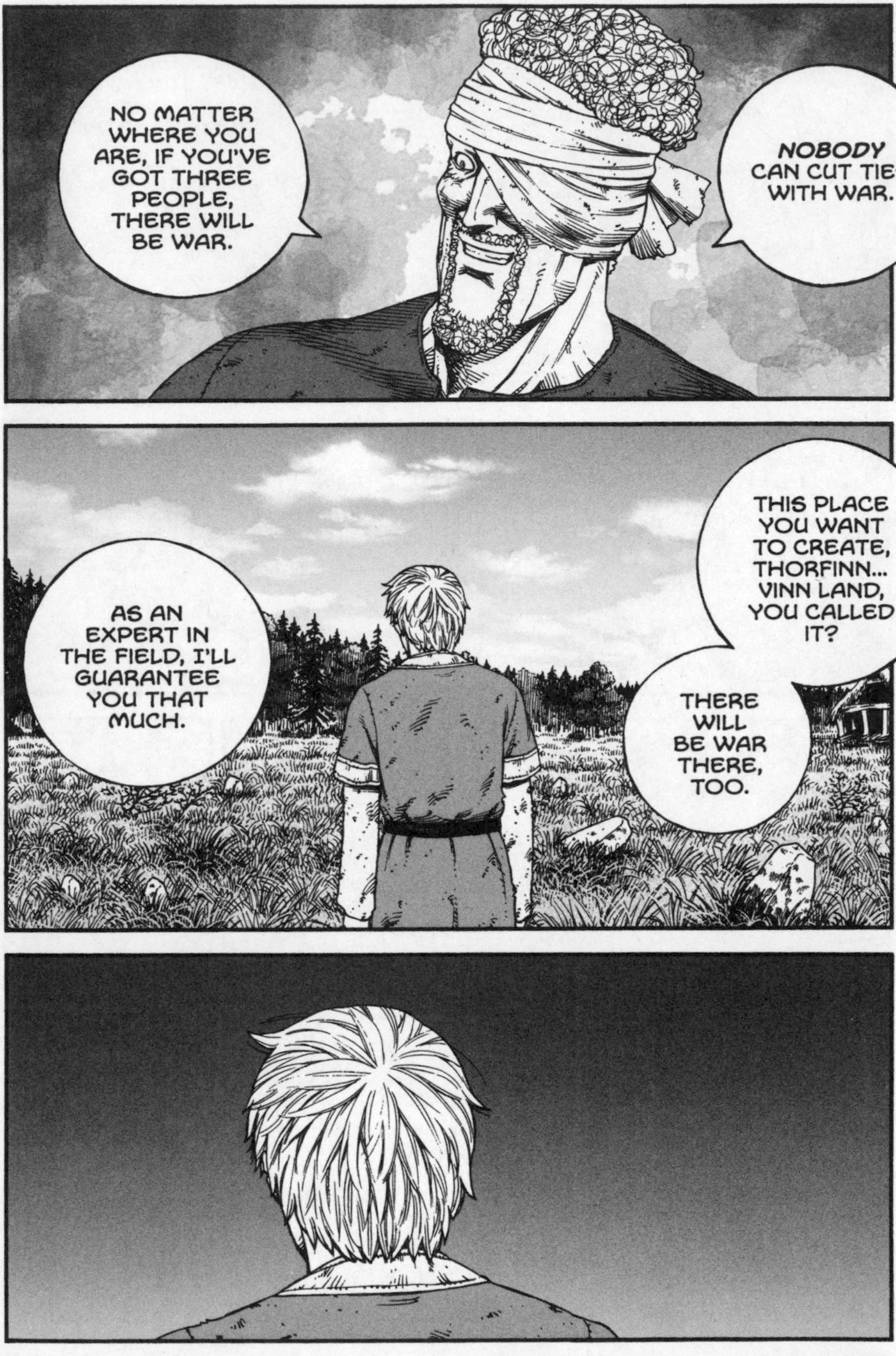
NOBODY CAN CUT TIES WITH WAR.
NO MATTER WHERE YOU ARE, IF YOU'VE GOT THREE PEOPLE, THERE WILL BE WAR.
THIS PLACE YOU WANT TO CREATE, THORFINN... VINN LAND, YOU CALLED IT?
THERE WILL BE WAR THERE, TOO.
AS AN EXPERT IN THE FIELD, I'LL GUARANTEE YOU THAT MUCH.

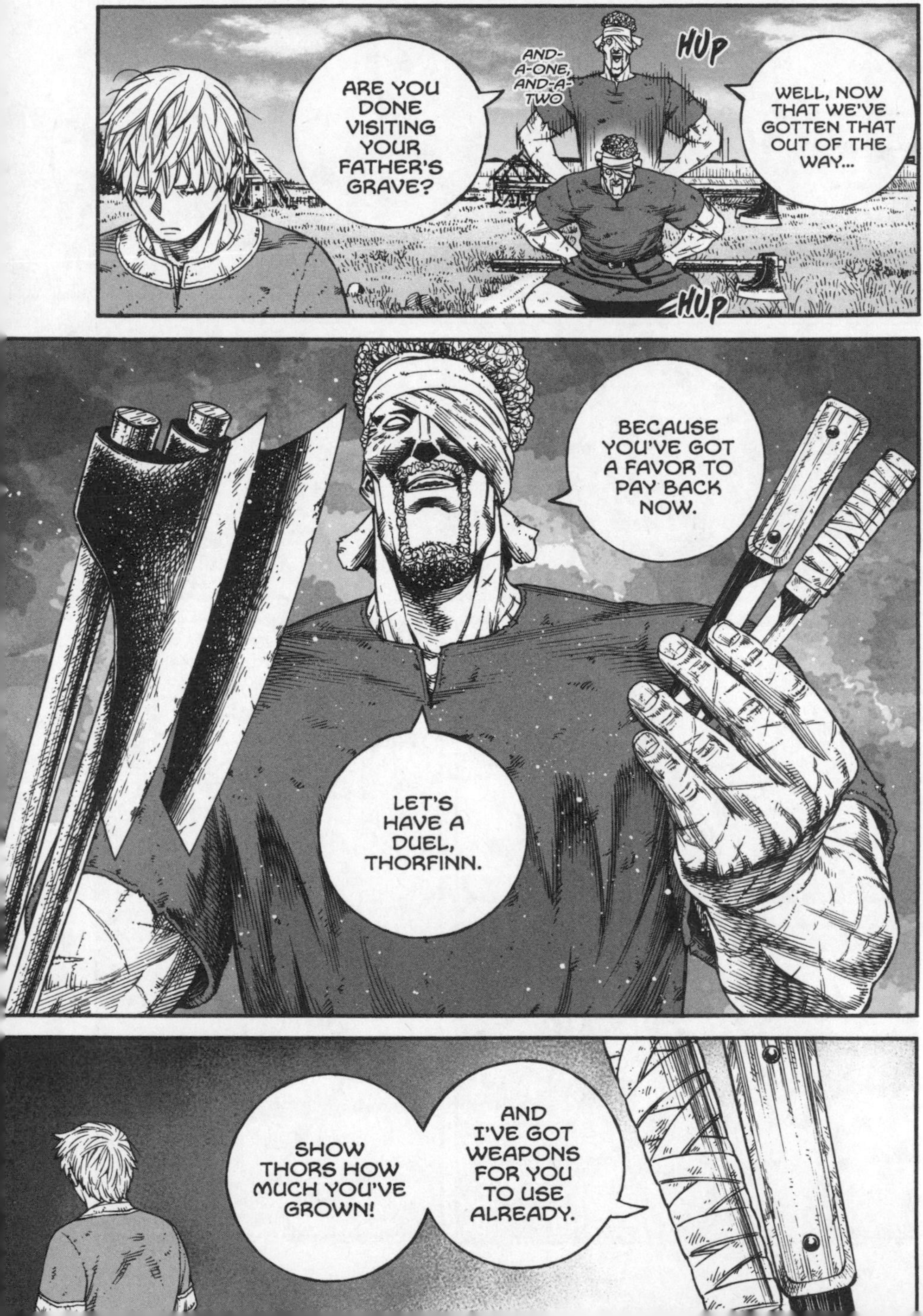
ARE YOU DONE VISITING YOUR FATHER'S GRAVE?
AND-A-ONE, AND-A-TWO
HUP
HUP
WELL, NOW THAT WE'VE GOTTEN THAT OUT OF THE WAY...
BECAUSE YOU'VE GOT A FAVOR TO PAY BACK NOW.
LET'S HAVE A DUEL, THORFINN.
SHOW THORS HOW MUCH YOU'VE GROWN!
AND I'VE GOT WEAPONS FOR YOU TO USE ALREADY.

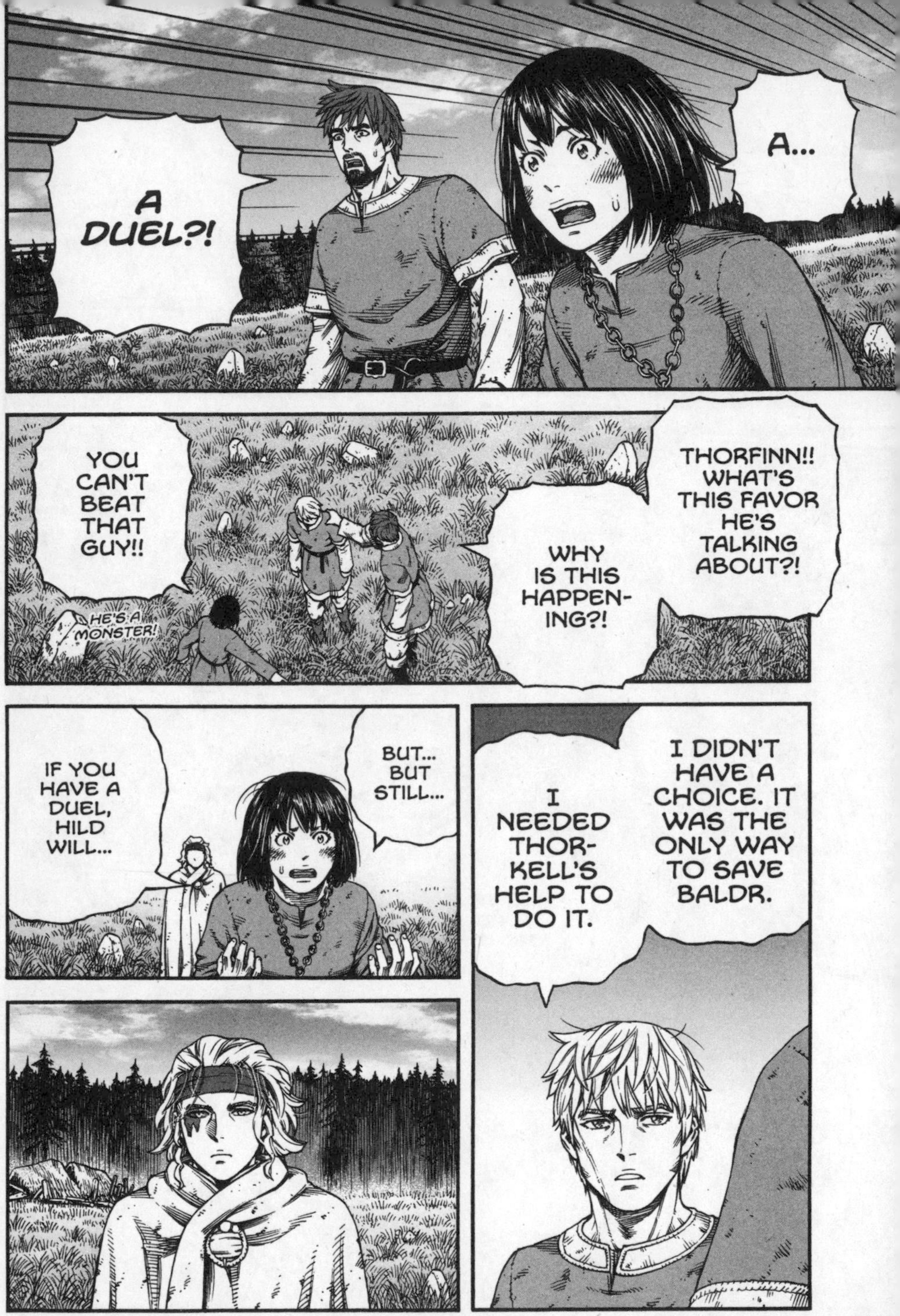
A...
A DUEL?!
THORFINN!! WHAT'S THIS FAVOR HE'S TALKING ABOUT?!
WHY IS THIS HAPPENING?!
YOU CAN'T BEAT THAT GUY!!
HE'S A MONSTER!
I DIDN'T HAVE A CHOICE. IT WAS THE ONLY WAY TO SAVE BALDR.
I NEEDED THORKELL'S HELP TO DO IT.
BUT... BUT STILL...
IF YOU HAVE A DUEL, HILD WILL...

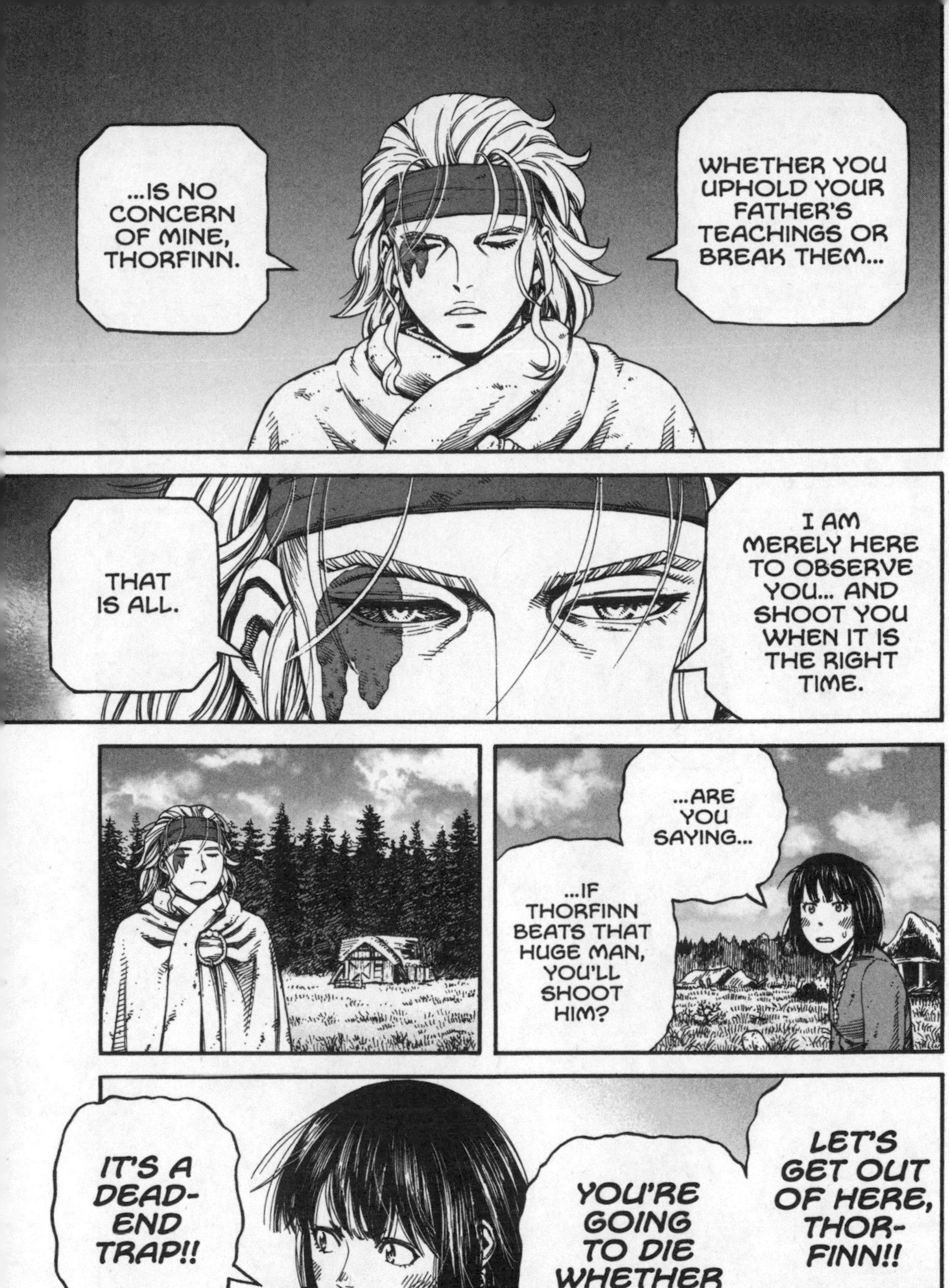
WHETHER YOU UPHOLD YOUR FATHER'S TEACHINGS OR BREAK THEM...
...IS NO CONCERN OF MINE, THORFINN.
I AM MERELY HERE TO OBSERVE YOU... AND SHOOT YOU WHEN IT IS THE RIGHT TIME.
THAT IS ALL.
...ARE YOU SAYING...
...IF THORFINN BEATS THAT HUGE MAN, YOU'LL SHOOT HIM?
LET'S GET OUT OF HERE, THOR-FINN!!
YOU'RE GOING TO DIE WHETHER YOU WIN OR LOSE!!
IT'S A DEAD-END TRAP!!

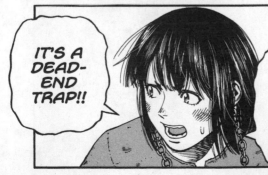

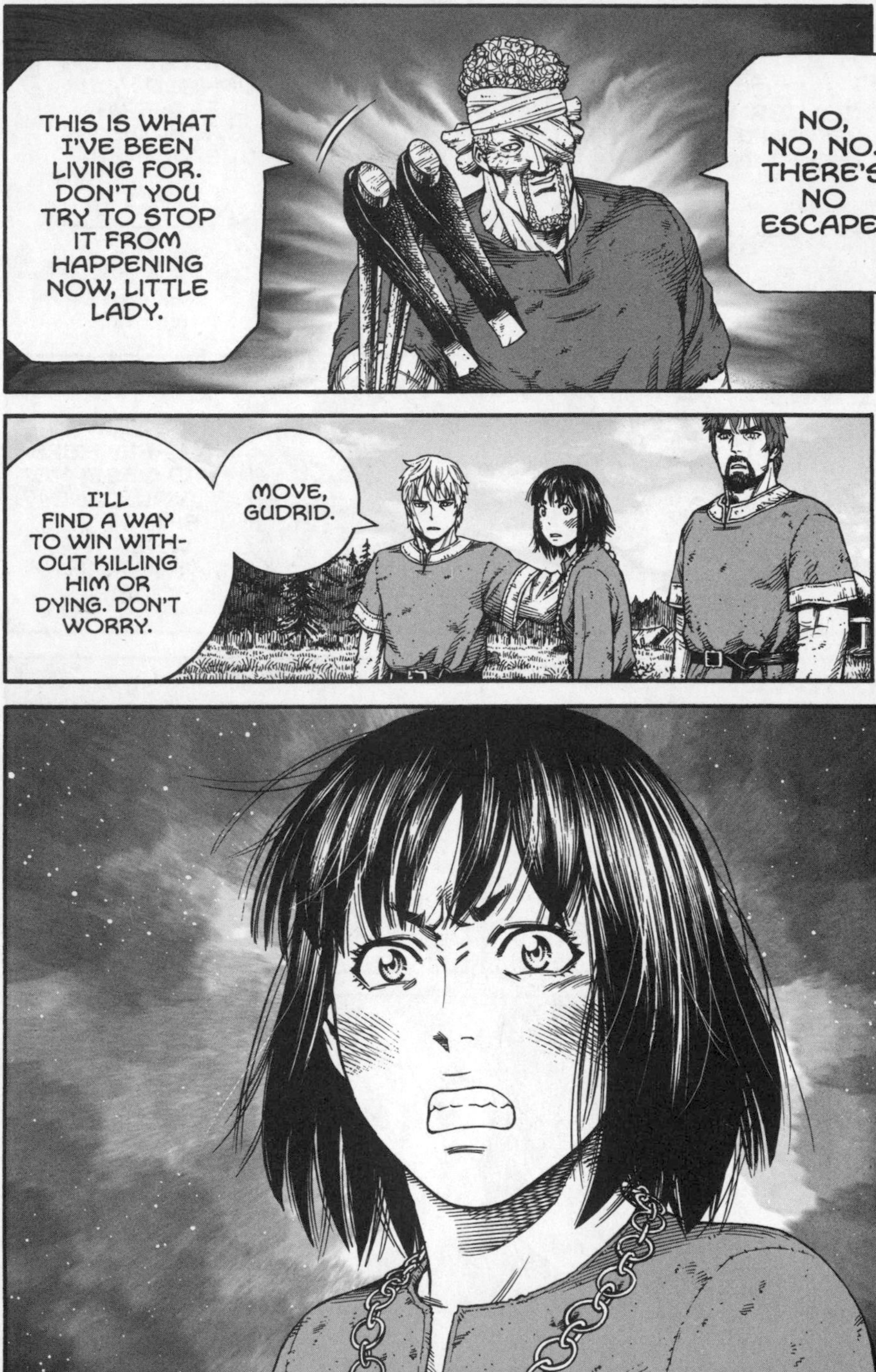
NO, NO, NO. THERE'S NO ESCAPE.
THIS IS WHAT I'VE BEEN LIVING FOR. DON'T YOU TRY TO STOP IT FROM HAPPENING NOW, LITTLE LADY.
MOVE, GUDRID.
I'LL FIND A WAY TO WIN WITH-OUT KILLING HIM OR DYING. DON'T WORRY.

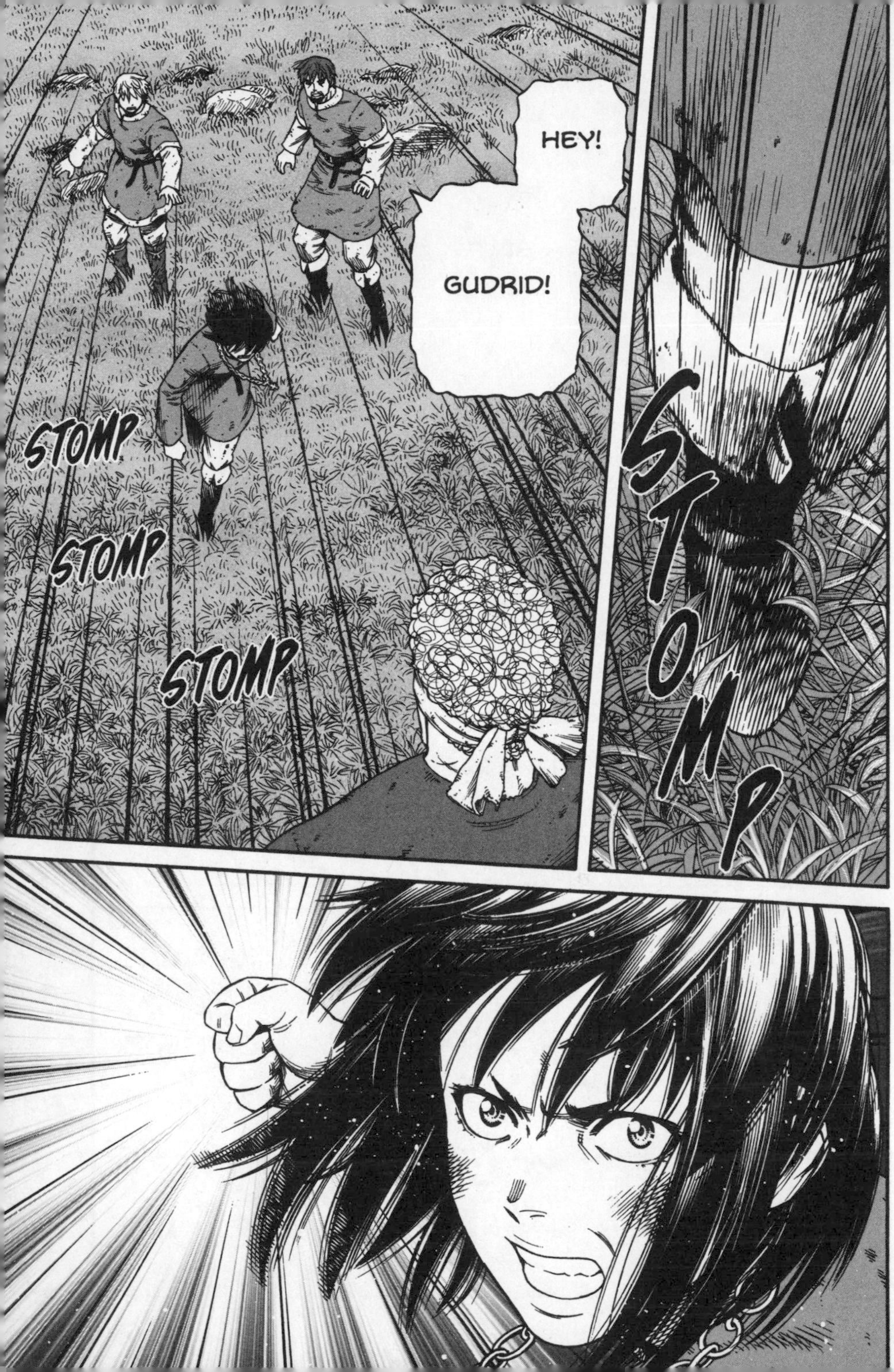
STOMP
HEY!
GUDRID!
STOMP
STOMP
STOMP

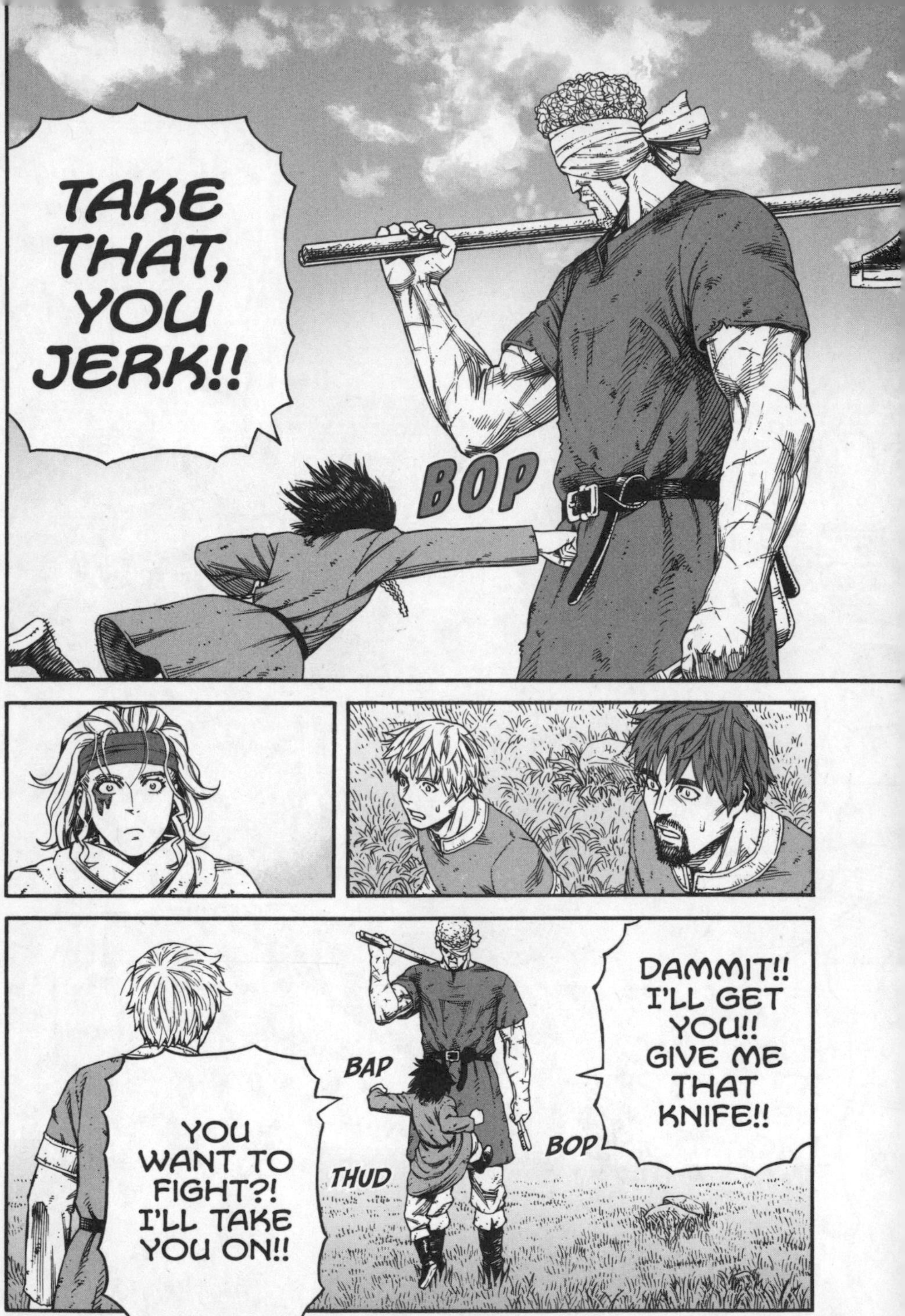
TAKE THAT, YOU JERK!!
BOP
DAMMIT!! I'LL GET YOU!! GIVE ME THAT KNIFE!!
BAP
BOP
THUD
YOU WANT TO FIGHT?! I'LL TAKE YOU ON!!

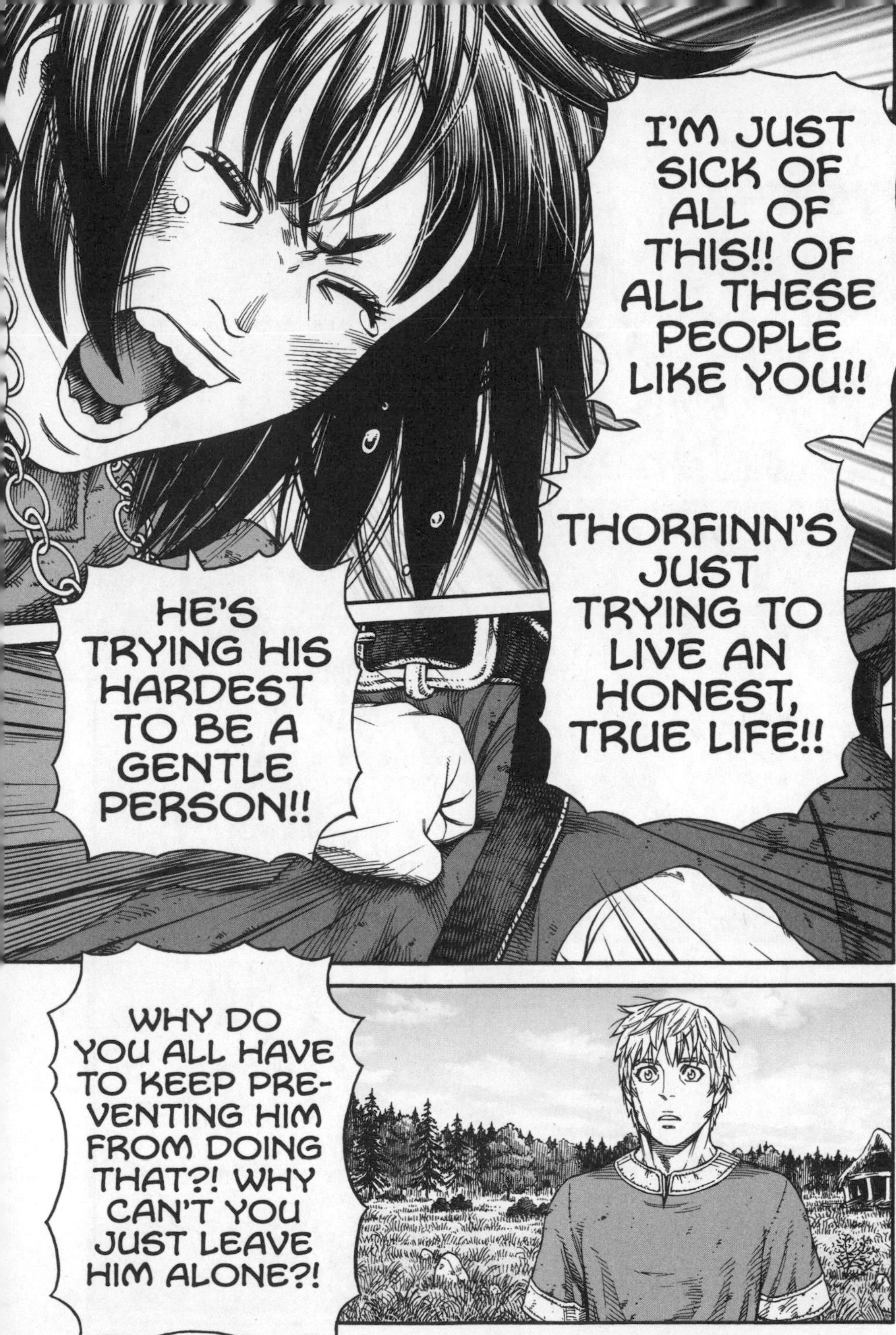
I'M JUST SICK OF ALL OF THIS!! OF ALL THESE PEOPLE LIKE YOU!!
THORFINN'S JUST TRYING TO LIVE AN HONEST, TRUE LIFE!!
HE'S TRYING HIS HARDEST TO BE A GENTLE PERSON!!
WHY DO YOU ALL HAVE TO KEEP PRE-VENTING HIM FROM DOING THAT?! WHY CAN'T YOU JUST LEAVE HIM ALONE?!

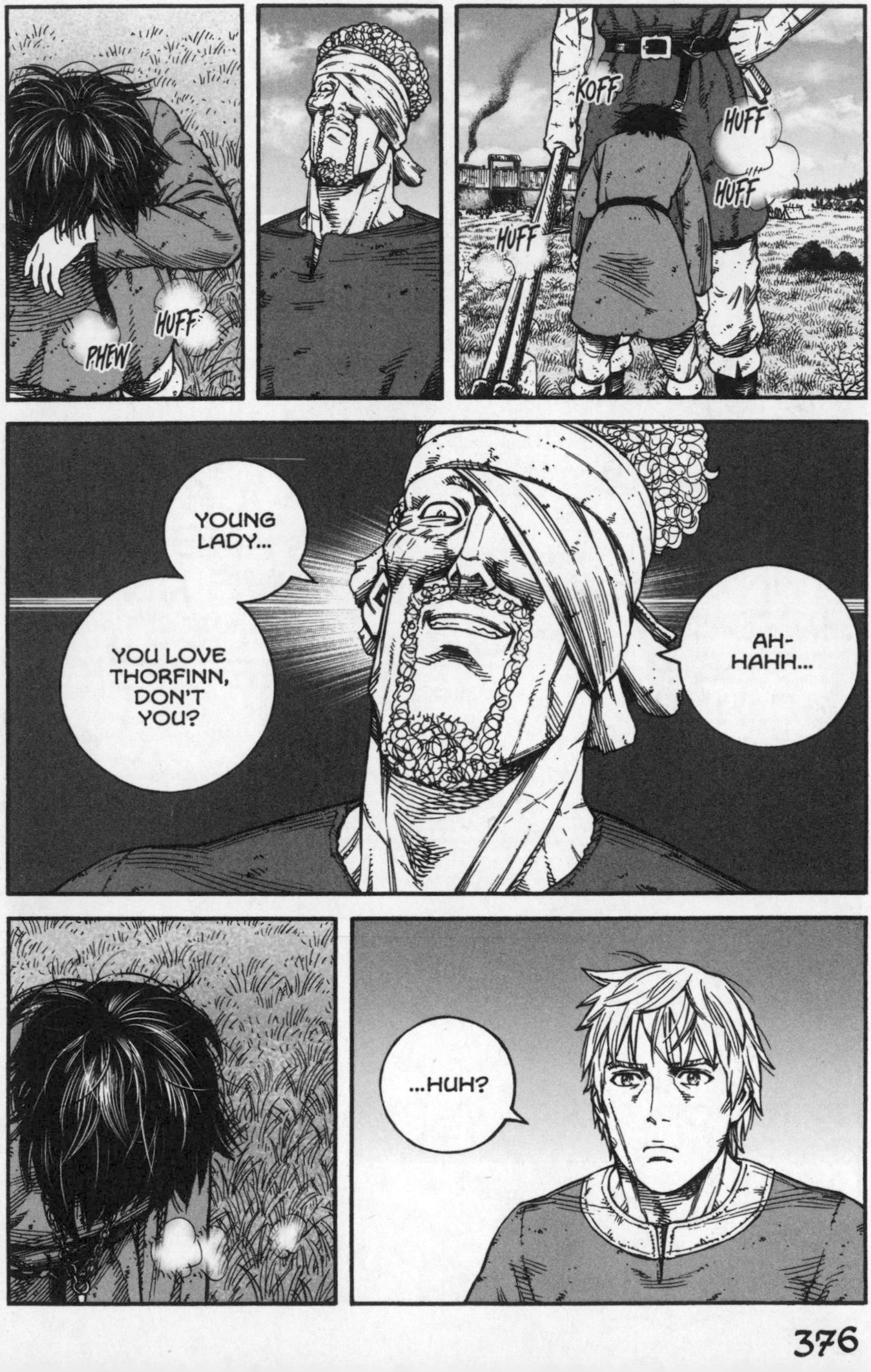
KOFF
HUFF
HUFF
HUFF
HUFF
PHEW
AH-HAHH...
YOUNG LADY...
YOU LOVE THORFINN, DON'T YOU?
...HUH?

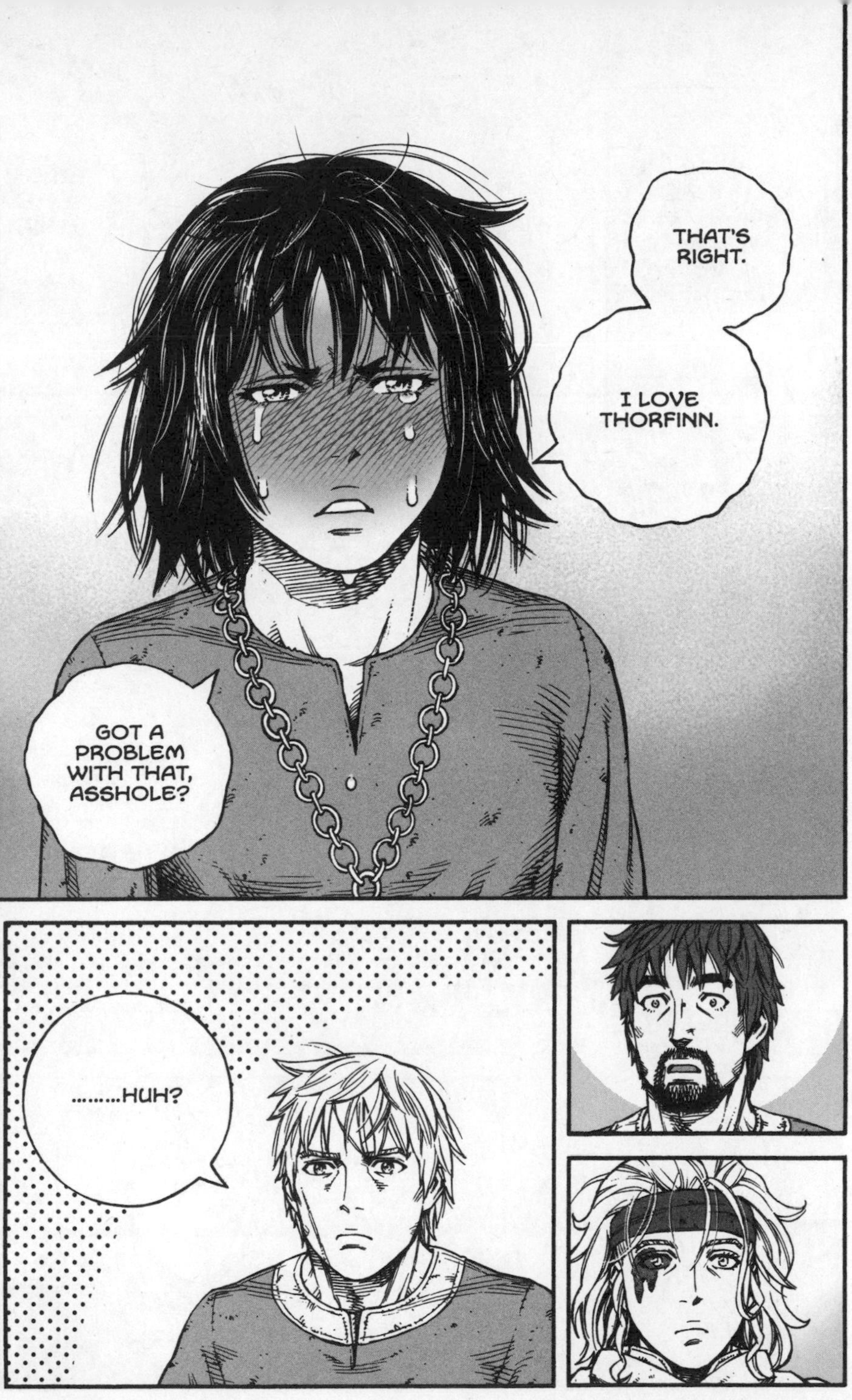
THAT'S RIGHT.
I LOVE THORFINN.
GOT A PROBLEM WITH THAT, ASSHOLE?
.........HUH?

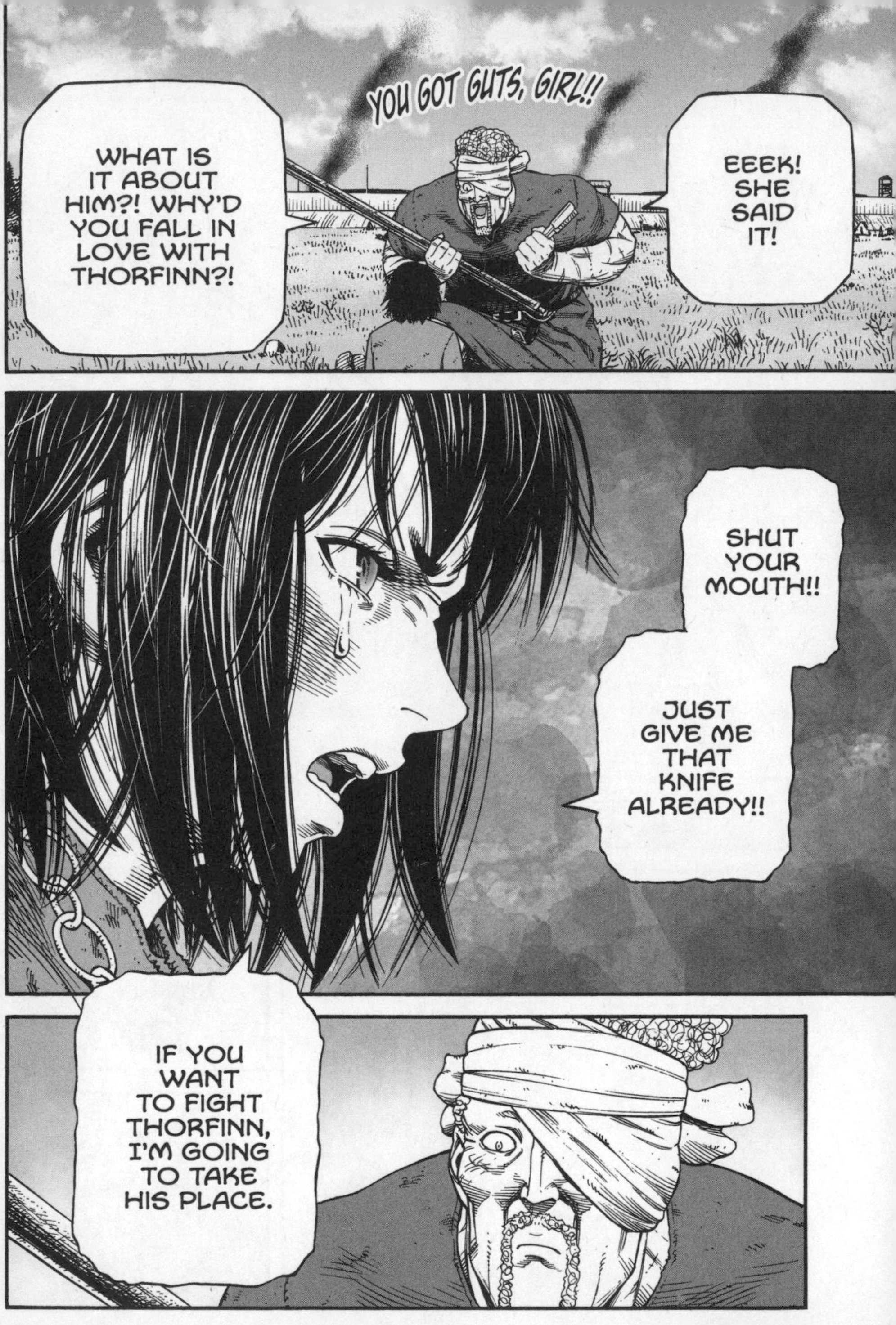
EEEK! SHE SAID IT!
YOU GOT GUTS, GIRL!!
WHAT IS IT ABOUT HIM?! WHY'D YOU FALL IN LOVE WITH THORFINN?!
SHUT YOUR MOUTH!!
JUST GIVE ME THAT KNIFE ALREADY!!
IF YOU WANT TO FIGHT THORFINN, I'M GOING TO TAKE HIS PLACE.

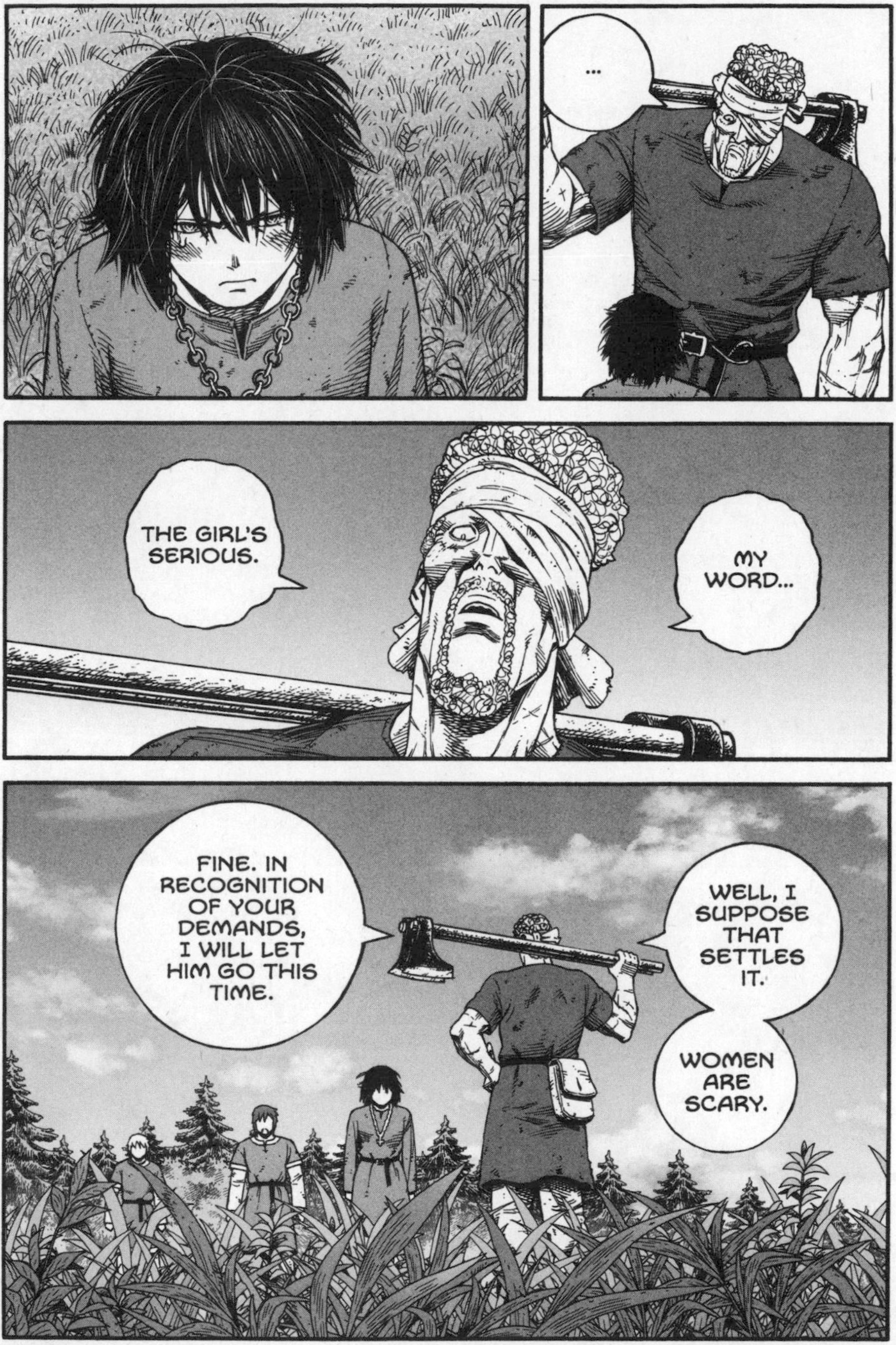
...
MY WORD...
THE GIRL'S SERIOUS.
WELL, I SUPPOSE THAT SETTLES IT.
WOMEN ARE SCARY.
FINE. IN RECOGNITION OF YOUR DEMANDS, I WILL LET HIM GO THIS TIME.

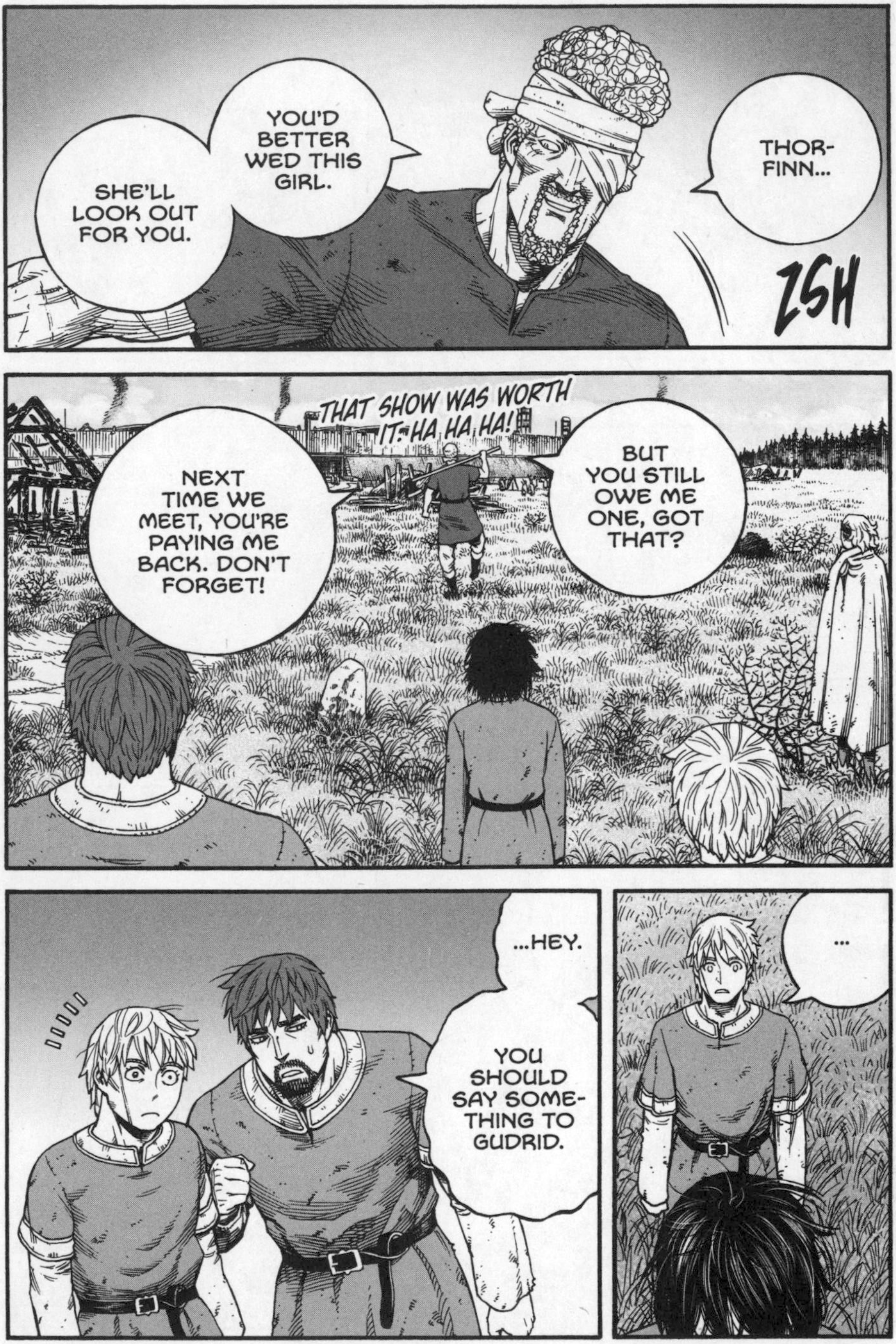
THOR-FINN...
YOU'D BETTER WED THIS GIRL.
SHE'LL LOOK OUT FOR YOU.
ZSH
THAT SHOW WAS WORTH IT. HA HA HA!
BUT YOU STILL OWE ME ONE, GOT THAT?
NEXT TIME WE MEET, YOU'RE PAYING ME BACK. DON'T FORGET!
...
...HEY.
YOU SHOULD SAY SOME-THING TO GUDRID.

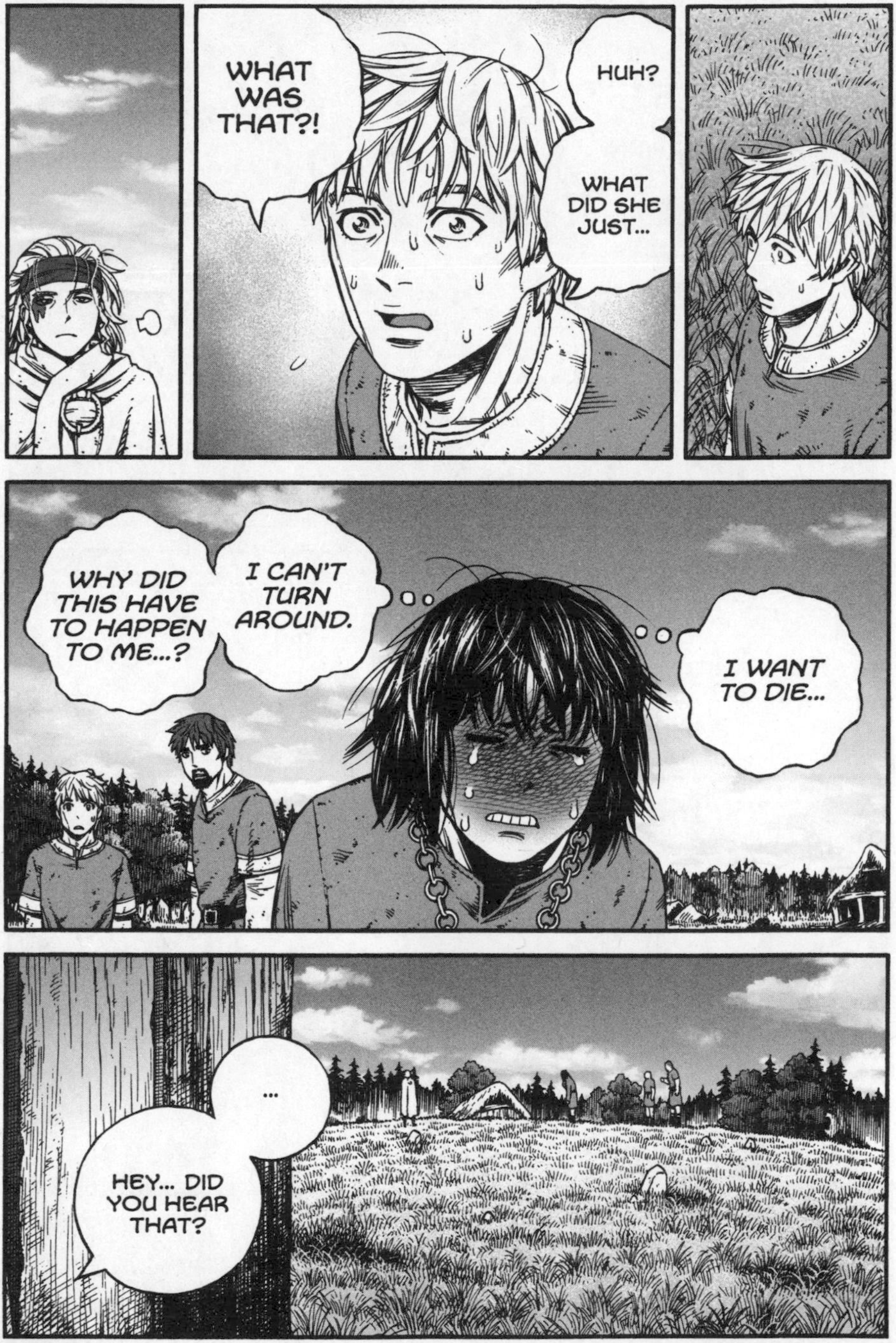
HUH?
WHAT DID SHE JUST...
WHAT WAS THAT?!
I WANT TO DIE...
I CAN'T TURN AROUND.
WHY DID THIS HAVE TO HAPPEN TO ME...?
...
HEY... DID YOU HEAR THAT?

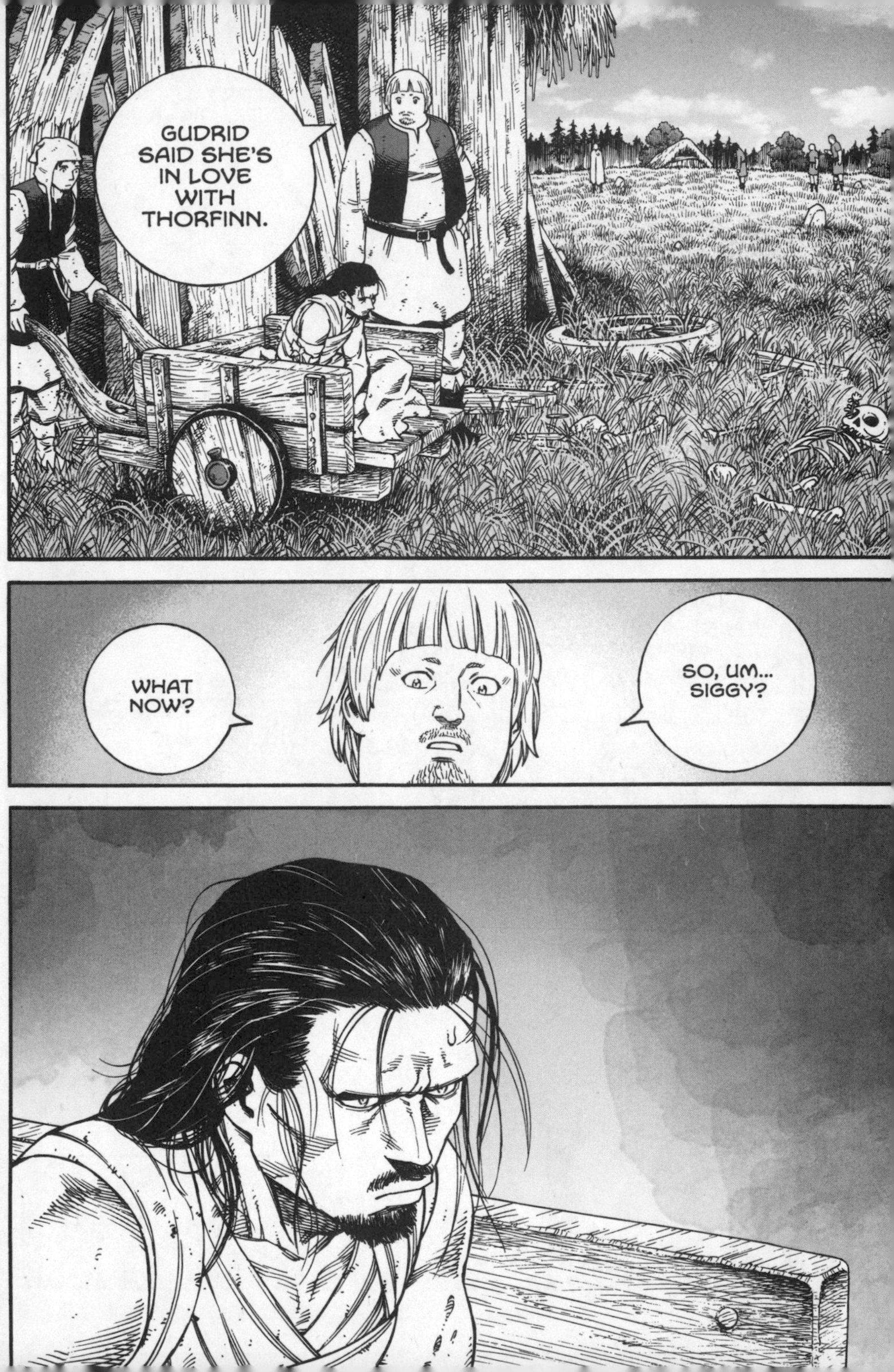
GUDRID SAID SHE'S IN LOVE WITH THORFINN.
SO, UM... SIGGY?
WHAT NOW?

CHAPTER 160 - END

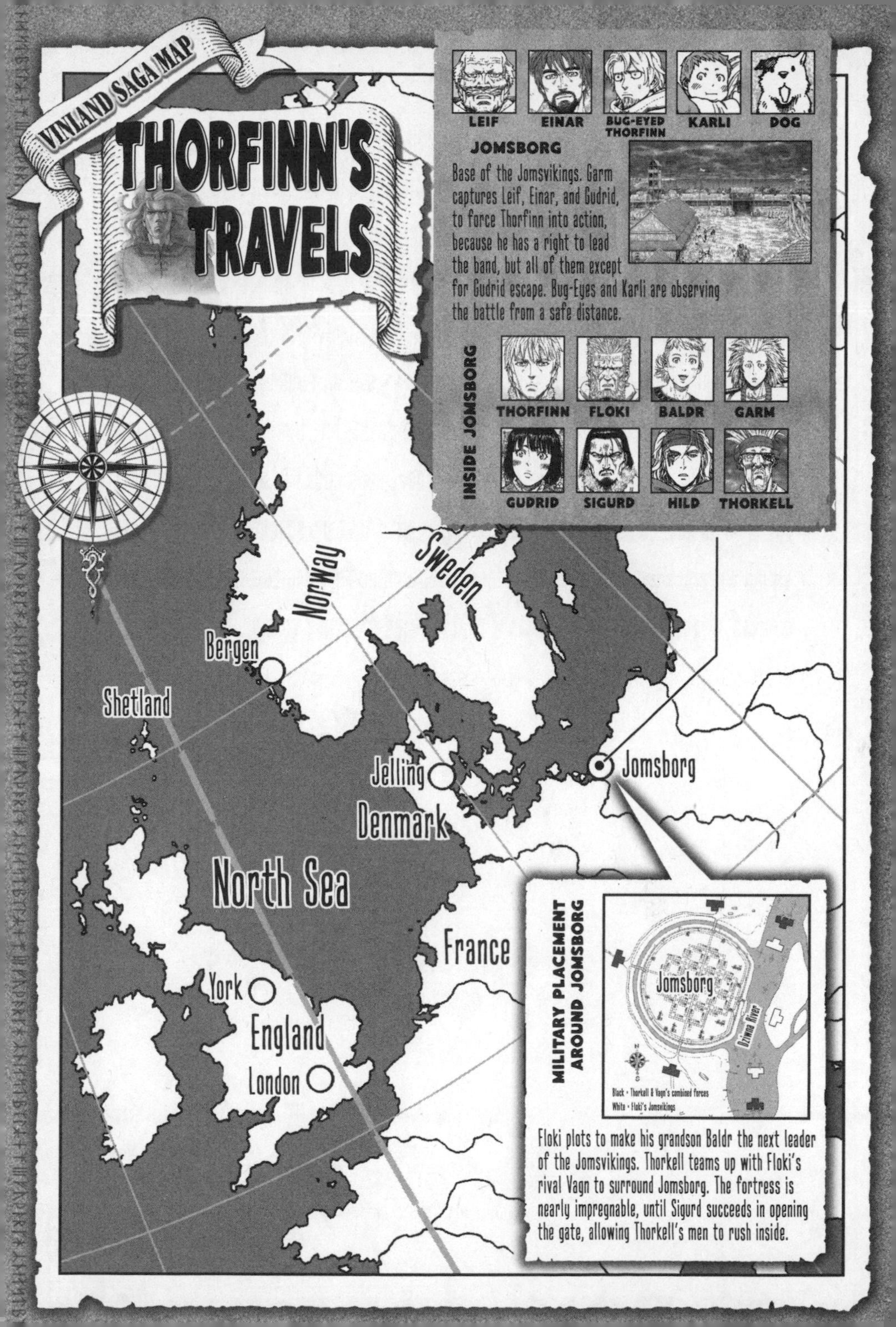
VINLAND SAGA MAP
THORFINN'S TRAVELS
LEIF
EINAR
BUG-EYED THORFINN
KARLI
DOG
JOMSBORG
Base of the Jomsvikings. Garm captures Leif, Einar, and Gudrid, to force Thorfinn into action, because he has a right to lead the band, but all of them except for Gudrid escape. Bug-Eyes and Karli are observing the battle from a safe distance.
INSIDE JOMSBORG
THORFINN
FLOKI
BALDR
GARM
GUDRID
SIGURD
HILD
THORKELL
Norway
Sweden
Bergen
Shetland
Jelling
Denmark
Jomsborg
North Sea
France
York
England
London
MILITARY PLACEMENT AROUND JOMSBORG
Jomsborg
Dziwna River
Black = Thorkell & Vagn's combined forces
White = Floki's Jomsvikings
Floki plots to make his grandson Baldr the next leader of the Jomsvikings. Thorkell teams up with Floki's rival Vagn to surround Jomsborg. The fortress is nearly impregnable, until Sigurd succeeds in opening the gate, allowing Thorkell's men to rush inside.

It's my own choice of depiction that at the point of this volume, Thorkell is in his mid-fifties in age. Despite his liveliness, in Middle Ages Northern Europe, he's an old grampaw-man. Conditions were harsh back then, and it's estimated that the average lifespan was under 50 years old. Even that young an age was difficult to reach, and over half of the people didn't survive childhood. Adults were more valuable than they are today, and it was rare to see an elderly person over 50. And that rare, precious fellow in this story is a great, big, lumbering oaf (ha-ha). For Europeans in the Middle Ages, life was short, and ended in a blink. Too short for dreams and ideals to come to fruition. So with that perspective, the way that Viking warriors lived in the ephemeral spirit, looking forward to the next life and numbed to their own death, makes a certain kind of sense to me.

MAKOTO YUKIMURA

VINLAND SAGA

Translation Notes

Garm, page 266

In Norse mythology, Garm is a hound or wolf who serves Hel, a daughter of Loki and guardian of a realm of the same name (a cognate of "Hell") that contains the dead. As a fearsome beast, Garm being freed from his chains is said to be one of the key events of Ragnarok, the final battle of gods that spells the end of the world.

HE'S GARM, THE HELL-HOUND.

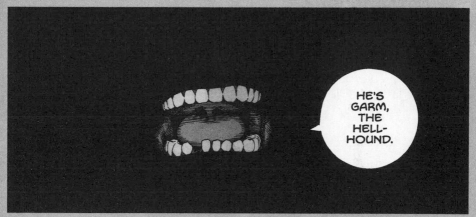

Ymir, page 291

The original giant in Norse mythology. Ymir is described as a kind of primordial being that emerges from the void and births the race of giants.

THERE YOU ARE, YOU MONSTER!!
COME, YMIR!!

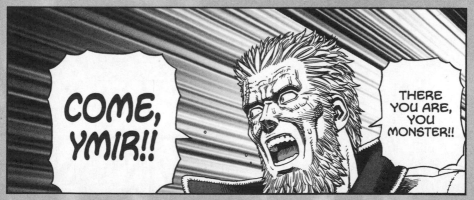

Hi, Makoto Yukimura here. *Vinland Saga*'s got an anime! When the editor-in-chief of Afternoon Magazine told me "It's getting an anime!" I responded, "What is? Are they making an anime about you?" After some discussion, the editor name-dropped the famous WIT STUDIO. Back then, I was worried about whether the editor was of a sound mind, but the time for the official announcement is here... The editor-in-chief didn't just dream it up, and it wasn't me hallucinating... Hrmmmmmghh YAHOO!! What a thing to be grateful for! And in the hands of the people at WIT STUDIO who worked on *Attack on Titan* and *Kabaneri of the Iron Fortress*? I don't have a single thing to worry about. Now I just need to make sure I don't get in the way of the anime staff! I'll be waiting quietly as an audience member. In fact, that's the best way to enjoy this— I want to sit back and relish in the *Vinland Saga* anime more than anyone else in the world! I'm happy to be a guest, rather than staff! I won't even budge from my seat in front of the TV! Now everyone, get cozy and grab a seat. Let's wait for this godly anime together. Hoo, I'm so excited...!

MAKOTO YUKIMURA

Editor's Note:
We are pleased to present you with key visuals from the *Vinland Saga* anime. The following images appeared in Afternoon Magazine's August 2019 issue.

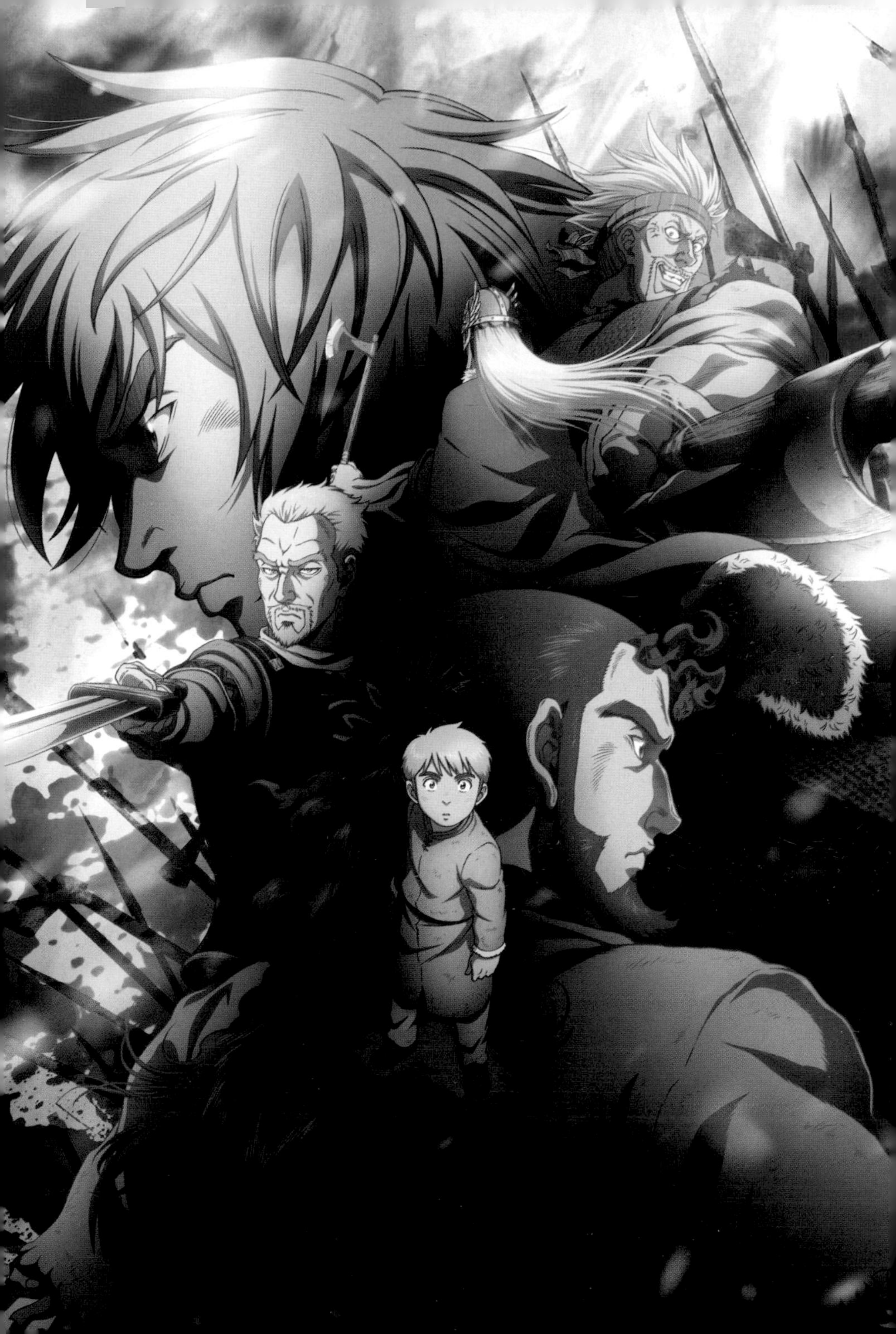

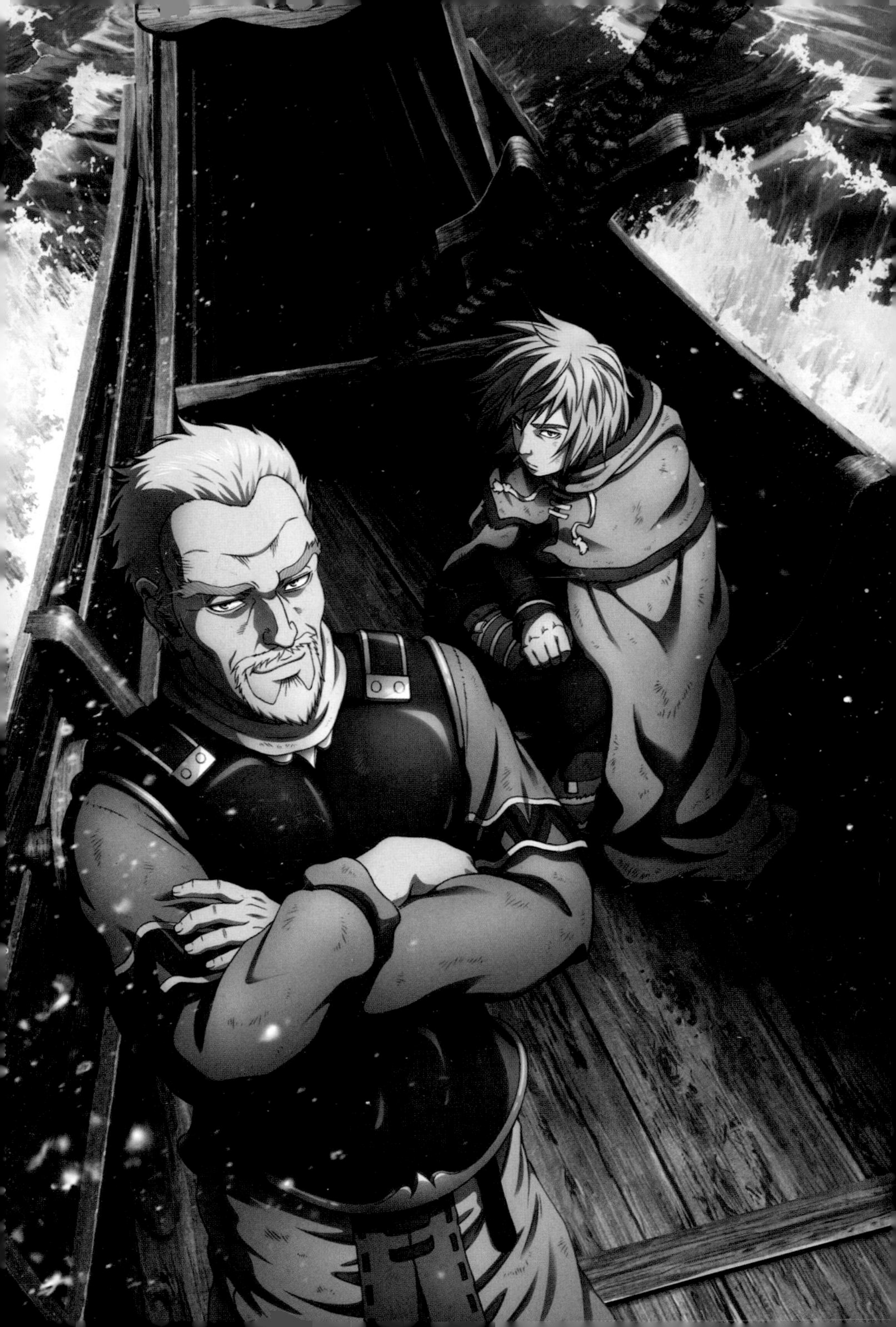

Vinland Saga 11 copyright © 2018, 2019 Makoto Yukimura
English translation copyright © 2019 Makoto Yukimura

All rights reserved.

Published in the United States by Kodansha Comics, an imprint of Kodansha USA Publishing, LLC, New York.

Publication rights for this English edition arranged through Kodansha Ltd., Tokyo.

First published in Japan in 2018, 2019 by Kodansha Ltd. Tokyo as *Vinland Saga*, volumes 21 and 22.

ISBN 978-1-63236-803-4

Printed in the United States of America.

www.kodanshacomics.com

9 8 7 6 5
Translation: Stephen Paul
Lettering: Scott O. Brown
Editing: Haruko Hashimoto
Kodansha Comics edition cover design by Phil Balsman

Publisher: Kiichiro Sugawara
Managing editor: Maya Rosewood
Vice president of marketing & publicity: Naho Yamada

Director of publishing services: Ben Applegate
Associate director of operations: Stephen Pakula
Publishing services managing editor: Noelle Webster
Assistant production manager: Emi Lotto